MANAGERIAL PSYCHOLOGY

HF5548.8
A545

MANAGERIAL

PSYCHOLOGY

By

LOYCE ADAMS, M.B.A., Ph.D.

Professor of Business Administration
Sam Houston State College

THE CHRISTOPHER PUBLISHING HOUSE
BOSTON, U. S. A.

NOV 3 1972

171969

COPYRIGHT © 1965

BY THE CHRISTOPHER PUBLISHING HOUSE

Library of Congress Catalog Card Number 65-16474

PRINTED IN THE UNITED STATES OF AMERICA

To

My Students

and

Andrea, Marky, Dick, and Elise

FOREWORD

Many people today believe that college graduates who go forth with degrees in specialized areas often lack general education background. During the twenty-two years the author has taught at Sam Houston State College the business department of that school has required its students to take a survey course in adjustment and business psychology that would in some measure add to their general education and be of value to them in their adjustment to life and work. Out of the experience of teaching this course came the desire to compile a comprehensive textbook that would cover most of the areas that have proved to be beneficial to the students who have taken it.

The writer wishes to express appreciation to those former students who, in continuing to pursue excellence, have achieved success in government, business, and education. She is grateful also to those firms, people, publishers, and periodicals that have permitted the use of material in this volume, as well as to the thousands of others whose works were used and read in preparation for writing it. She is especially grateful to: the many teachers who contributed to her background of information in the fields of management, marketing, business education, economics, and general education; her immediate superiors whose interest in her teaching and professional activities has been an inspiration; the members of her family for their everlasting encouragement.

Loyce Adams
Sam Houston State College
Huntsville, Texas

January 21, 1965

PUBLISHER'S PREFACE

The comprehensive scope of this book and its clarity of example make it, in our opinion, an outstanding text on managerial psychology. It is an able and penetrating analysis of human behavior in business and industry, and incorporates the author's many years of teaching courses in business psychology. Those in industry will find its study as rewarding as the student.

With today's increased emphasis on human relationships in business and industry, plus the interwoven complexity of society, it is not at all surprising that this book fills a definite need. Under one cover it presents an all inclusive course in managerial psychology with introductory surveys of general psychology, personality, and human behavior. It will be of special significance to the academic and business worlds for in it are found the keys to many unsolved problems that daily perplex students and businessmen alike.

Thomas A. Christopher

TABLE OF CONTENTS

SECTION I — WHAT IS PSYCHOLOGY?

SECTION II — PERSONAL EFFICIENCY

SECTION IV — INDUSTRIAL RELATIONS

SECTION V — DISTRIBUTION

SECTION VI — PSYCHOLOGICAL INFLUENCES IN ECONOMICS

MANAGERIAL PSYCHOLOGY

Managerial Psychology

CHAPTER I

WHAT IS PSYCHOLOGY?

What Is Psychology? — Psychology studies human behavior and attempts to discover laws that explain that behavior. It tries to find out how people act in given situations, to analyze feelings and emotions, to determine how people think and how their beliefs and customs become established.

The methods of getting information on human behavior are: observation, experimentation, and surveys. Each of these methods requires skill in the use of statistics and experimental and control groups.

Some of the sources of inaccuracies in psychological experimentation are: lack of trained observers; the fact that people do not see the same things when they observe, i.e., observations are themselves inaccurate; human activity is itself so complex that it is difficult to observe. For these reasons experiments must be repeated to verify their findings. If a psychological experiment is carried on by an observer studying himself, this is known as *introspection*. When the observer observes another, this is *objective observation*. Conditions under which observations are made are difficult to control. If the environment is controlled it may be detrimental to the person or persons being observed. The *genetic* method is thus used to observe and record events as they are taking place. Conditions in this method are not so rigidly controlled. In some cases neither the *experimental* nor the *genetic* method is feasible and in such cases *clinical* or *case-history* methods may be used. If the case history method is used by supplementing with the control group, it is a very valuable method.[1]

Psychological research attempts to be scientific, to use only those tools that can give accurate pictures of human behavior in its many phases. Actually, the word *psychology* stems from two Greek words which together mean "science of the soul." Before the word psychology came into our language, however, we had philosophy which, as well as being love of wisdom and mental serenity, is the science which investigates the facts and principles of reality and of human nature and conduct, logic, ethics,

1

aesthetics, and metaphysics. Thought and personal observation of the philosophers and poets gave them their answers to human behavior. They often guessed the very answers that techniques of psychological research, using scientific methods, substantiated.[2]

Psychology grew out of philosophy and medical research. From the area of medicine developed the modern day concepts of psychoanalysis and psychiatry. Psychology has come to be used in many other areas: social research of all types; marketing, advertising, and consumer research; industrial research; employment and employee research. Its tools have expanded to include, in addition to observation and experimentation, testing of all types, rating forms, and questionnaires to be used by mail, interview, or telephone.

The Quest for Truth — Dr. Irwin Edman in *Philosopher's Quest* says that the quest after knowledge and truth goes on. We may only quest; we may not arrive at definite conclusions; yet the quest goes on in every generation "and will . . . as long as the human race endures on earth." [3]

The introduction to an old geography text carries in italics:

> *The reward is in the doing,*
> *And the rapture of pursuing*
> *Is the prize.*[4]

On the same page with this quotation is found, "Hope went before them and the world was wide." [5] So men go on questing after truth; some findings about man's behavior can be determined and stated factually. Averages can be found and as averages they are truths; yet as individuals people all deviate from the so-called average that is the "normal" person.

Alfred North Whitehead said that "All western philosophy since Plato is a series of footnotes to Plato's writings. Out of Plato [who goes back to 427 B.C.] come all things that are still written and debated among men of thought." [6] Plato touched upon practically all subjects of human interest in his lifelong quest for the principles of justice. He wanted happiness for all, and he believed that by creating a thing of beauty in living offspring, in works of art, or in noble deeds, we could conquer death.[7]

In Aristotle's philosophy there was necessity for the ruling class to be concerned with both practical and ideal education of the young. Above all, however, Aristotle believed that rulers must aim "at the contentment of the ruled." To his way of thinking, contentment was to be reached through justice. He believed that happiness consisted in doing good deeds. Virtue, health, wealth, and friendship were further requisites for happiness.[8] The man of virtue acts "at the right time, with reference to the right objects, towards the right people, with the right motive and in the right way." [9]

Spinoza believed that "citizens should be governed and led, not so as to become slaves, but so that they may freely do whatsoever things are best." [10] According to Spinoza's doctrine, humanity is one body and one soul. One could not hurt others without hurting himself. Spinoza believed that there is not absolute or free will:

> ... men are mistaken in thinking themselves free; their opinion is made up of consciousness of their own reactions, and ignorance of the causes by which they are conditioned. Their idea of freedom, therefore, is simply their ignorance of any cause for their actions.[11]

Spinoza further says:

> In the mind there is no absolute or free will; but the mind is determined to wish this or that by a cause, which has also been determined by another cause, and this last by another cause, and so on to infinity.
>
> The mind is a fixed and definite mode of thought, therefore it cannot be the free cause of its actions; in other words it cannot have an absolute faculty of positive or negative volition; but it must be determined by a cause, which has also been determined by another cause, which has also been determined by another cause, and this last by another, etc.[12]

Numerous references could be given to lend evidence to the belief that all philosophy and modern science since Spinoza has been permeated with his thought.[13]

A. A. Brill, a noted lecturer and student of the father of psychoanalysis, Sigmund Freud, some three hundred years after Spinoza said in a lecture to medical doctors, "According to science . . . there is no free will . . . those who think we have perfect control of our actions see only a very small part of the whole — not more than perhaps a drop of the ocean." [14] In an earlier lecture to the same doctors, he discussed the two systems which are, according to Bleuler, found in our psyche: (1) The system of our past experiences which determines our reason and thought, and (2) the system of ergies which refers to instincts, emotions, strivings, feelings, impulses, and so forth. The ergies began before reason and intellect. "The ergies represent the dynamics of thought." [15]

Motivation, such an important aspect of the problem of managing men, was identified by Spinoza with the problem of the emotions. Man experiences joy in moving toward a chosen goal, but when he is blocked from reaching that goal he is sad.[16]

This brief resume has referred at random to a few of the philosophers and their teachings; yet it is perhaps adequate to show that a study of philosophy can help those who manage men to understand them and their motives much better. It has been said that only by comprehending the spiritual and psychological as well as the physical aspects of science can man be saved from social catastrophe.[17] Today the cross-fertilization that is taking place in the fields of science and social science is leading to simultaneous consideration of technological and social development.[18]

Psychology's Fringe Areas — Psychologists in the United States generally do not accept the techniques of research of the graphologists, phrenologists, and those who delve into the various areas of ESP (extra-sensory-perception), such as mental telepathy and clairvoyance. Yet in some countries graphologists (who determine character, aptitudes, and nervous diseases from handwriting) are employed to aid business and industry select and eliminate persons who apply for jobs. The phrenologist estimates mental abilities by studying the conformation of the skull. Researchers in England and at Duke University in this country have published works that indicate there may be a basis for believing in mental telepathy (transferring of thought from one mind to another without benefit of written and oral devices of communication) and clairvoyance (ability to discern things not present or observed).

The Fields of Psychology — Although there are approximately forty schools of psychology, it is proposed to briefly review only three of these schools here: gestalt, behaviorism, and psychoanalysis. It is out of these main fields that present-day functional psychology has grown.

BEHAVIOR PSYCHOLOGY — The behaviorist psychology, based on Watsonian, Hullian, and other theories, assumes that when a stimulus is given the response can be predicted. There are variables which act to increase or decrease response tendency. The positive components of the excitatory potential are *habit, drive,* and *incentive.* Variables which oppose excitatory potential are *conditioned inhibition* and *work inhibition.* When these are subtracted algebraically from the excitatory potential the remainder is effective excitatory potential and is the maximum response at "given levels of training, motivation, and reinforcement." [19]

The behaviorist psychology is concerned with measuring environmental conditions, but preceding the immediate environment are motivating influences, usually considered internal conditions that influence behavior. These may be *instincts, wishes, impulses, needs, urges.* Through interviewing a subject, motives can be determined prior to occurring of behavior that is predicted on the basis of the motives.

Alderson gives Hull's four elements in learning as being: *drive, cue, response,* and *reward, "cue"* being the *stimulus.* Drive, he says, is "characterized as a state of readiness of pent up energy which is released into action by the cue. The reward is the gratification arising from success in whatever is attempted." [20]

There are two effects of rewarded performance: the more performances with reward, the more complete is the learning; the negative effect, however, is that reinforcement may reduce drive and thus reduce tendency to perform.[21]

In terms of the group, there are many uses of behaviorist concepts. The idea of status is all-important in analyzing group behavior; individuals are linked to systems and sub-systems. The term "ecological" was once generally used to indicate behavior systems of societies and groups.[22]

Veblen, the "last man who knew everything," contributed theories of individual and group behavior long before the present-day mad scramble to discover motives of people. His writings touched on many concepts: conspicuous consumption, keeping up with the Joneses, the instinct of workmanship, and others.[23] He diagnosed social ills but did not offer remedies. His works were largely based on his own observations of life about him. He lacked today's techniques of market research to locate his conspicuous consumers.

The technique of direct observation can detect the stimulus and response, but there are intervening factors between the stimulus and the response, including attitudes, values, and relationships. These can be guessed at but they cannot be definitely known much less controlled by the researchers.

The behaviorist psychology, championed by Watson, was the first to influence advertising. It was assumed that if buying habits could be implanted, then advertising to stimulate the exercise of these habits would bring the desired results. Habit does influence consumer purchases. Alderson states that the fallacy of depending entirely on determining a pattern of buying habits and acting thereon lies in the "underlying assumption that because much behavior is routine no other kind is possible."[24]

GESTALT PSYCHOLOGY — Gestalt psychology is "holistic" as contrasted with the "atomistic" psychology against which it arose in protest.

Max Wertheimer is given credit for introducing gestalt psychology. His main finding was that "an object *seems* to move from one position to another when it is merely presented twice in two different places with an appropriate short time interval between both exposures. . . ." His wholly new interpretation of the phenomenon gave his work significance. His explanation is built on the hypothesis that there are "diagonal functions" or "between-processes" in the brain.[25] One of the early writers on gestalt psychology puts it like this:

. . . Whenever a central locus in the brain is excited a concentric neural spread of a certain magnitude occurs around it. If two such spots are aroused, two excitation rings are formed which predispose the areas they embrace to further excitation. If now, point *a* is stimulated, and shortly thereafter an adjoining point *b*, some kind of 'short-circuit' occurs between *a* and *b*, and a specific excitation occurs over the intervening distance. If the concentric overflow from *a* is at its maximum and similar excitation rings now come from *b*, the direction of the neural process is determined by the fact that *a* was first there. The nearer the two points *a* and *b*, the more favorable are the conditions for the arousal of the phi-process, which in itself is an extensive specific whole.[26]

Wertheimer's proposition amounts to saying that "wherever two identical phenomena are found, it is necessary to assume that the corresponding brain-processes are identical." [27] The component parts of the whole are interdependent, each being what it is because of its part in the whole.

Lewin maintains that the effectiveness of the permanent urges (drives) is dependent on the "presence of acute states of tension, to explain which notion of 'need' is more serviceable." [28] A study of a panel of food buyers supported Lewin's concept of the psychic conflict as basic in buying behavior.[29]

Wertheimer's definition of gestalt is: "A Gestalt is a whole whose characteristics are determined, not by the characteristics of its individual elements, but by the internal nature of the whole." [30]

Thesis, antithesis, and synthesis form the triple rhythm of the advance of scientific knowledge according to Hegel. Gestalt psychology rose in reaction to atomistic psychology. Katz asks whether or not gestalt psychology will arrive at a synthesis with the doctrine it attacks. In the natural sciences the atomistic view has predominated. The world of the Greek materialists consisted of indivisible, minute elements. These were endowed with specific energies. Atomistic psychology obtained its approach from this kind of thinking and depended on concepts relative to reflexes a great deal. The study of sensations that grew out of the atomistic approach might seem to justify this approach.

Atomistic psychology might say: Vanilla Ice Cream = Cold + Sweet + Vanilla Aroma + Softness + Yellow. Without making an important change in the equation it is possible to begin or end with a different element. Gestalt psychology maintains the whole "is more than the sum of its separates and not, in the positivistic sense, the sum alone." [31]

Gestalt psychologists, like the behaviorists, recognized the need to seek the causes of behavior, and they agreed that these were needs, drives, and instincts. They did not deny the influence of experience, but they believed that purely instinctive behavior occurs only in animals.[32] They believed with the behaviorists that psychology "should develop as an experimental science." As opposed to the behaviorists, however, they "emphasized the role of rational insight and conscious thought." [33]

Gestalt psychology resembles psychoanalysis in that it places emphasis on "purpose, goals, and motives rather than mechanical responses to stimuli." Both fields "accept conscious mind as a central fact, in contrast with the schools of psychology derived from Locke." Schools which followed Locke were known as the "stimulus-response behaviorism." The entire process of mental development was explained by some American behaviorists by relating this "associationism" to the neurological system. Gestalt psychology is representative of the schools which followed Leibnitz. These schools hold "the mind does not merely record experiences but accepts or rejects stimuli from the environment and organizes them into patterns determined by its own needs." Current trends are away from the Locke schools of thought to the Leibnitz. [34]

Alderson says:

> Throughout the social sciences . . . [gestalt psychology] has exerted a healthy corrective influence for the tendency to discount the role of rationality and to magnify the irrational and nonrational aspects of behavior. To the extent that rational decision-making is a major interest in marketing and economics, gestalt may be recommended as the most inviting approach to an understanding of how it functions. [35]

PSYCHOANALYSIS — Freud in the 1890's in Vienna used the method of psychoanalysis to aid the mentally ill. Clinical methods and the use of case studies had been applied before Freud (Kraft-Ebbing, u.s.w). Not until 1909 were the methods of Freud introduced into the United States; Freud in that year delivered a series of lectures at Clarke University. [36] Freud's process developed procedures of going from the abnormal back to the normal, working "into a cohesive system of thought." [37]

The psychiatrist "is first a physician, a medical graduate who has had at least one year's experience as an intern in a general hospital." Psychotherapy is probably the most important technique the psychiatrist learns to use. In this he uses multiple interviews to elicit facts relating to the patient's experiences, facts which have left conflict rather than harmony behind them. [38]

Freud and the other pioneers in psychoanalysis from their clinical experiences developed a theory of motivation. They explain neurotic breakdowns on the basis of conflicts of motives based on instinctive drives. Freud's earlier works explained the central conflict as being between the instincts of self-preservation and reproduction, a struggle of ego and sexual libido. The individual drove back into his unconscious the impulses his ego wouldn't consciously recognize. The suppressed desires had to be brought into the open in order that the motivations of the individual could be reorganized. Freud later emphasized the life and death instincts.[39]

Jung is chiefly known for his concepts of the introvert and extrovert personalities. Adler's basic instinctive drive is the will to power and in some this becomes a compensation for inferiority.[40]

Fromm and Horney place emphasis on anxieties created by loneliness and isolation as sources of maladjustments. A useful set of concepts has to do with wasted energy: ". . . general indecisiveness in either large or trivial affairs . . . ineffectual or half-hearted application of effort . . . inertia resulting from the lack of clearly defined objectives." [41]

Out of gestalt psychology and psychoanalysis has come a concept of the individual as having one all-powerful drive, that of "maintaining and enhancing a favorable self-image in the midst of the stream of experience." Some even say that "all of the vital energies are directed toward the survival of the phenomenal self rather than the physical self." [42]

Three alternatives available to the individual for dealing with his experiences are: (1) The experiences favorable to the self-image may be organized into a pattern to enhance self; (2) experiences which do not fit the self-image may be rejected or repressed; (3) experiences not related to self may be ignored. Freud believed the individual relegated his unpleasant experiences to his unconscious mind.[43]

Psychoanalysis offers generalizations about motives of individuals. It can thus offer hypotheses about behavior of consumers, but these hypotheses must be followed up by further research to determine their validity.

FUNCTIONALISM — Market researchers must take account of the rational and adaptive as well as the irrational behavior. Alderson offers the functionalist approach to motivation. This approach draws on all the fields of psychology for its methods and concepts. It is an instrumental or problem-solving approach which may be analyzed in terms of means and ends. In addition to the instrumental behavior, it recognizes congenial and symptomatic behavior. Alderson quotes Robert Sessions Woodworth's definition: ". . . functionalist psychology starts from the question of what men do and then goes on to the question of how they do it and why they do it." [44] It is a concept which has to do with ends-means relationships. Alderson says that "Both instinctive behavior and conditioned behavior are usually functional or adaptive in the sense of contributing to the survival of the individual or the group." Yet he points out that a group of psychologists calling themselves ethologists now recognize that behavior can be nonadaptive. What Freud called symptomatic behavior they call "displacement behavior." Another of the concepts of ethology is "that of levels of motivation and the threshold of response in the presence of various sign stimuli." [45] Other writers have mentioned the work of the ethologists. This group publishes a journal called *Behavior, An International Journal of Comparative Ethology*. Edited by a staff of outstanding psychologists from numerous countries, this journal is published by E. J. Brill, Publishers, Leiden, Holland, and is primarily devoted to the study of animal behavior. Human ethology, however, has been defined as a study of the "way in which human society adjusts to its environment and strives to achieve its ends." [46]

Each of the leading schools of psychology had its beginning in revolt against a previous school. The various schools, however, passed from their divergent viewpoints to the present-day state of potential convergence. The functionalism that is at present developing drew from the three main fields (gestalt, behaviorism, and psychoanalysis) out of which the other schools have grown. Actually there are only two essentially different viewpoints: the behaviorist school, which followed Locke, and the gestalt school which followed Leibnitz and emphasizes the "active and organizing aspect of mind." [47]

The Status of Psychology in the United States Today — Today many firms are engaged in psychological research of various kinds, both in this country and throughout the world. Marketing and advertising research organizations will be named and described in later chapters.

The American Psychological Association, founded in 1892, has a large membership divided among its numerous divisions which include various phases of educational psychology, general psychology, counseling, testing, geriatrics, social, industrial and business, and experimental. The Psychological Corporation, founded in 1921, is the world's largest such organization offering to business, industry, and education services in testing and research.

The first psychological laboratory in the United States was opened at Johns Hopkins University in 1883. Harvard University's William James was given the first title of "Professor of Psychology" in 1889.[48] Today most colleges and universities have courses in psychology, if not departments of psychology. Research is constantly being conducted, both in the colleges and research organizations, in all of the areas that psychology embraces; the results of this research can be found in textbooks, journals, and even the general magazines and newspapers.

A great many American college students study psychology today; few of these will, of course, become psychologists. They are studying psychology in order to better understand themselves and others, to better live and work with their fellowmen. Those who criticize today's college curriculums in business emphasize the need for more behavioral sciences.

They are not always certain what this term includes; they are fairly certain it does include psychology.

Today when even high school sophomores are writing term papers on topics once talked about only in medical schools (this writer recently read an erudite sophomore's paper on "Schizophrenia, Its Causes, Preventatives, and Cures"), it is realized that we must keep informed on the various aspects of psychology in order that these may be applied in our everyday living, both at home and at work. We must adjust, not only in human relations but to the technological changes that are taking place daily.

PROJECTS

1. As a term project, read and report on two books from two separate fields selected from the following: autobiography or biography, philosophy, and general psychology. Write a five-page typed report on each of the two books. These reports should be double spaced, but each direct quotation should be single spaced and indented five spaces on each side. Have only a few such direct quotations, if any. The left margin of each page should be one and one-half inches and the right margin should be one inch. Each page should have a bottom margin of one inch. There should be no page numbers on the first page of each of the book reports. Each page after the first page should be numbered by placing the number one inch down from the top and one inch over from the right edge of the paper. The first line on each page after the first page should be nine spaces from the top edge of the paper.

Type on the first page, two inches down from the top, the complete reference for the book, i.e., as follows:

Martineau, Pierre, *Motivation in Advertising,* McGraw-Hill Book Company, Inc., New York, 1957, 206 pages.

Your report should comment on the book read in each instance. Tell what you liked about the book. Tell what you learned from it. Briefly tell what the book was all about.

2. Write a research paper on one of the fields of psychology. Use footnotes and present a bibliography. Follow the instructions for typing the paper as given in Project 1 above.

3. Select a current issue of a news or general magazine. Make a list of the topics and stories included in the magazine that are in some way related to the subject of psychology.

ACKNOWLEDGMENTS AND REFERENCES

1 Bernhardt, Karl S., *Practical Psychology,* McGraw-Hill Book Company, Inc., New York, 1945, pp. 9–14.

2 Brill, A. A., *Lectures on Psychoanalytic Psychiatry,* Alfred A. Knopf, New York, 1947, p. 36.
3 Edman, Irwin, *Philosopher's Quest,* The Viking Press, New York, 1947, p. 275.
4 Synge, M. B., *A Book of Discovery,* T. C. and E. C. Jack, Ltd., Edinburgh, no date of publication, p. v.
5 *Ibid.*
6 Brinton, Crane, *Ideas and Men, The Story of Western Thought,* Prentice-Hall, Inc., Englewood Cliffs, New Jersey, 1950, p. 43.
7 Thomas, Henry, and Thomas, Dana Lee, *Living Biographies of Great Philosophers,* Garden City Publishing Co., Inc., Garden City, New York, 1941, pp. 11–17. (Or see Plato's works.)
8 *Ibid.,* pp. 29–30.
9 *Ibid.,* p. 31.
10 Elwes, R. H. M., *Philosophy of Benedict de Spinoza,* a translation, Tudor Publishing Co., New York, no date of publication, p. 125.
11 *Ibid.,* p. 106.
12 *Ibid.,* p. 118.
13 Will Durant, Belfort Bax, Joseph Ratner, and so forth.
14 Brill, *op. cit.,* p. 115ff.
15 *Ibid.,* pp. 32–33.
16 Weinland, James D., *General Psychology for Students of Business,* F. S. Crofts and Co., New York, 1941, p. 9.
17 Halliday, James L., *Psychosocial Medicine,* W. W. Norton & Co., Inc., New York, 1948, p. 223.
18 Menninger, William C., *Social Changes and Scientific Progress,* Fifth Annual Arthur Dehon Little Memorial Lecture at the Massachusetts Institute of Technology, Cambridge, Mass., May 1, 1951, p. 7.
19 Logan, Frank A., and others, *Behavior Theory and Social Science,* Yale University Press, New Haven, 1955, p. 63.
20 Alderson, Wroe, "Psychology for Marketing and Economics," *The Journal of Marketing,* Vol. XVII, No. 2, October, 1952, pp. 119–135.
21 Logan, *op. cit.,* p. 115.
22 Alderson, Wroe, *Marketing Behavior and Executive Action,* Richard D. Irwin, Inc., Homewood, Illinois, 1957, p. 29ff.
23 ———, "Veblen," *Fortune,* Vol. XXXVI, No. 6, December, 1947, p. 133ff.
24 Alderson, "Psychology of Marketing and Economics," *op. cit.,* pp. 119–35.
25 Hartman, George W., *Gestalt Psychology,* The Ronald Press Company, New York, 1935, p. 3.
26 *Ibid.,* p. 6.
27 *Ibid.,* p. 7.
28 *Ibid.,* pp. 208–9.
29 Bilkey, Warren J., "Psychic Tensions and Purchasing Behavior," *Journal of Social Psychology,* Vol. 41, 1955, pp. 247–57.
30 Katz, David, *Gestalt Psychology* (translated by Robert Tyson), The Ronald Press Company, New York, 1950, p. 91.
31 *Ibid.,* pp. 3–6.
32 *Ibid.,* pp. 142, 151, 164.
33 Alderson, "Psychology of Marketing and Economics," *op. cit.,* p. 128.
34 Alderson, *Marketing Behavior and Executive Action, op. cit.,* pp. 189–90.
35 Alderson, "Psychology for Marketing and Economics," *op. cit.,* p. 129.
36 Berrien, F. K., *Practical Psychology,* The Macmillan Company, New York, 1952, p. 30.
37 Brill, *op. cit.,* p. 36.
38 Lemkau, Paul V., *Mental Hygiene in Public Health,* The Blakiston Division, McGraw-Hill Book Company, Inc., New York, 1955, p. 39.
39 Alderson, "Psychology for Marketing and Economics," *op. cit.,* pp. 130–31.

40   *Ibid.*, p. 131.
41   *Ibid.*, p. 132.
42   Alderson, *Marketing Behavior and Executive Action, op. cit.*, p. 191.
43   *Ibid.*, pp. 191–2.
44   Woodworth, Robert S., *Contemporary Schools of Psychology,* Revised Edition, The Ronald Press Company, New York, 1948, p. 11.
45   Alderson, Wroe, "Major Issues in Motivation Research," *Marketing's Role in Scientific Management* (edited by Robert L. Clewett), American Marketing Association, 1957, pp. 271–81.
46   Russell, Clair, and Russell, W. M. S., "An Approach to Human Ethology," *Behavioral Science,* July, 1957, pp. 169–200.
47   Alderson, *Marketing Behavior and Executive Action, op. cit.*, pp. 189–90.
48   Hepner, Harry Walker, *Psychology Applied to Life and Work,* Prentice-Hall, Inc., Englewood Cliffs, New Jersey, 1957, pp. 11–12.

SECTION II — PERSONAL EFFICIENCY

CHAPTER II

MENTAL EFFICIENCY: HOW TO STUDY

In the last ten years a great deal has been written about the age of "goof-off" and Johnny's ability to read and write. Teachers have been accused of wanting a single salary scale in order that achievement not be taken into account in determining pay; "students" have been accused of taking "snap courses" in order that they might avoid necessity for working, thinking, and winning scholastic honors. Workers have been accused in books and articles of evading work, gold-bricking, and goofing-off. It does not matter that people generally realize that America became great on the hard work and conscientious application of teachers, students, and workers. If these people are not achieving today, there may be trouble ahead tomorrow.

Young people who have reached the level of college should know how to study. They should know that intellectual achievement is its own reward, that there is pride and great feeling of accomplishment when one has conquered a subject-matter area or solved a difficult problem. There should be pride in achievement of goals, of aims, of a job well done whether it be at the school and training level or at the place of work. Deep study may actually be something of a painful process at the time that it is being done. It is like a great many of life's prizes, however, its reward is the exhilaration that one feels when he has mastered the subject-matter, conquered the problem, turned out the excellent piece of work.

Today there is even inclination on the part of students to ostracize the people who make "A's." They are often treated much as the "rate-busters" (See Chapter XIX for definition) of industry are treated. The people who excel on examinations, because they are the reason for all others being pushed down to the lower grade levels, are looked upon as "book worms, longhairs, squares, crates, or eggheads." Not wishing to be shunned, most persons will simply aim at getting the average grade. These observations do not apply to *all* college and university students. The standards of some institutions are quite high and the students must work to pass. Further, some young people still have that goal of excellence before them. They work to make the top grades. Frequently, however, possessors of the best brains from some of the best middle- and upper-income families do not achieve. They have grown up in the relaxed atmosphere of the afternoon and evening cocktail party; they are the "party" boys and girls who know all they need to know because they know how to drink and play. Some of those in this category can be stunned into realizing not only their lack of worthwhile goals but the satisfactions that setting and achieving goals can bring. If they cannot be, some of the predictions about the future of the human race made by Ernest Hooten of Harvard some twenty years ago in his best-selling volume *Apes, Men and Morons* may prove to be correct.

Students in European universities work very hard; they generally are truly educated when they are awarded diplomas. This is not so in all of the American colleges and universities. Yet the United States system provides for out-of-class activities that develop interests, hobbies, and personality. It is generally believed that some degree of these extra activities is good provided they do not interfere with academic achievement.

At the public school level it has been estimated that Russian students learn more in three years than Americans do in four. Heavier homework assignments may be the reason.[1]

In the last several years, the writer has had foreign students who have excelled despite their language handicaps in competition with young people from some of the better public schools in the United States. There are many reasons, among them the fact that perhaps these young foreigners were outstanding among their own people. It is believed that there is another factor: they know the importance of work because they know that back at home there are many underprivileged people and that without education they, too, would be among them. The full implications of this problem are left for others to explore.

It is hoped that you college students reading this chapter do wish to make good grades and that you are willing to take from an old hand in the studying game some gentle hints. There is no royal or easy path to study; there are ways of studying that bring results. With crowded conditions in the colleges of today, it is the student who has intelligence and uses it who will first of all get into college and second will succeed after he gets there. Certainly more of the higher institutions are selecting enrollees on the basis of examinations and high-school grades.

Definition of Intelligence — There is not a unique definition of intelligence. Nevertheless, the intelligent person is considered to have certain characteristics not found in the person lacking intelligence. For one thing, he is able to adjust to change with a minimum of effort because he can call upon past experience for solving present problems as well as anticipating future ones and their solutions. He can endure delay in attainment of objectives without losing orientation to problems involved, and he can think abstractly. He is critical of himself.

Can IQ Be Changed? — Although it is considered that intelligence is an inherited factor, the computed intelligence quotient (See Chapter IX) has been found to be affected by such things as diet, environment, and training. Further, there is some question as to whether or not the measured IQ (intelligence quotient) adequately reflects ability. The Ford Foundation recently granted Williams College $125,000 for a ten-year study of students who do not make outstanding grades but who have promising qualities that cannot be scientifically measured. Dr. E. Paul Torrance, University of Minnesota, has said that seventy per cent of the most gifted children would be eliminated from consideration if the gifted persons were to be identified on the basis of intelligence as reflected in tests.

Dr. Ionel Rapaport of the University of Wisconsin is of the opinion that IQ tests measure only one kind of intelligence but that there are several kinds. There is the type of genius that understands machines, and there are musicians and artists that do not or may not possess the kind of intelligence that would be reflected in a high IQ score. Some who possess a degree of artistic ability could not, however, profit by the usual type of education.[2]

Under a grant from the United States Office of Education, Professors Jacob W. Getzels and Philip W. Jackson of the University of Chicago studied the relationships between creativity and intelligence. The creative young people were found to have a high degree of humor, to be imaginative, and to possess a high degree of curiosity. They aim toward the "offbeat" occupations and do not mind the impression they make on other people. The relationship between creativity and intelligence as measured by grades and tests was found to be low. Teachers generally like the persons of high IQ, but they find the creative young people to be bothersome. Creativeness is frequently lost because the creative young person is subdued into conforming both by parents and teachers. It is not known how to educate for creativity. An attempt is being made to discover methods of training that will encourage the imaginative and creative persons by the Creative Education Foundation of Buffalo, which is headed by Alex F. Osborn.[3]

The problems of study as presented in this chapter may be more applicable to the conformers than to the creative persons who tend to deviate from customary ways of doing things. Nevertheless, even the creative person must use some of the disciplines presented here if he is to attain success and produce beneficially with his creative efforts. Horace Mann once wrote that "A human being is not, in any proper sense, a human being till he is educated." Presumably the marks of an educated man are the ability to use his intelligence and his creative abilities, and to exercise judgment in dealing with other persons and the problems of life. The level of education one is capable of attaining is regulated to a degree by the level of intelligence.

An IQ score of 85 or lower would be a handicap to anyone seeking higher education.

Problems Involved in Study — Attitude of mind is all-important in studying. If one cannot literally pull his mind to the problem or the written word, he cannot study. Some people do not already have the desire to acquire knowledge and to solve difficult problems. On the other hand, some seem to have always had an insatiable curiosity to learn. This desire must be acquired forcefully if it is not already there. "Study" to many young people means looking over the main topics just before an examination. If they see something that looks involved or difficult, they skip this. Charts, graphs, and problems are for the ostracized "eggheads." Discipline must be exercised and the difficult idea or problem must be waded through step by step until it is seen and conquered. The good grades go to the students who know all of the subject matter under consideration, not just a few answers they have learned shortly before an examination because the "students in the know" suggested that these questions would surely be called for on the examination.

A person who studies before attending lectures, takes notes during lectures, organizes these after the lectures, reviews carefully as many times as needed for learning and/or over-learning in the problematical areas, studies the day before an examination, and then relaxes the night before taking the examination will make good grades. This is provided, of course, that he has the ability to learn.

PREPARATION FOR STUDYING: SETTING AND SCHEDULING — Preparing the mind is really the first step in studying. One cannot study if he is thinking about things that have happened in the past or things that will happen in the future. Habit is a factor here. If the studying is done in a setting that is suitable for it, the mind is more likely to fall in line. A good light, a desk, and a comfortable straight-backed chair are needed. The only time studying should be done reclining (in bed) is when a novel or a short story must be read, or if a type of studying is being done that does not require extreme concentration.

It is essential that a proper time be set aside for studying. A lot of people do all the other things first. They see the movies they want to see, date the young women (young men) they want to date, play bridge at the student union building, go to the "jive" joints and then if there is time left they study. Some research has shown that the students who live at home make the best grades; those who live at boarding houses, in dormitories, and in sorority and fraternity houses follow in that order. Some studies have also shown that the students who work to pay a part or all of their expenses while striving toward their diplomas make better grades, despite the fact that they may not have any more ability, than those who do not earn expenses. The element that makes for the difference here is probably scheduling of the time that is available for study. This does not mean that one must make out a written schedule; it means that certain hours are set aside for study and nothing else is permitted to interfere. If study is done in noisy conditions (with student "bull sessions" going, or with radio, record-player, or television blaring), study will be difficult. It takes much more energy on the part of the student to learn under such conditions.

HOW TO TAKE NOTES — Some students have a separate notebook for each course; others have one notebook with separate sections for each course. If the teacher lectures from the textbook, notes may be made in the margins of the book, and important statements may be underscored. If additional material is placed on the chalkboard, this should be written in the notebook or at the proper places in the textbook provided there is room and the student owns the book. One should react to what is read if he expects to recall the information for later use. Therefore, he should make marginal notes in the textbook and underscore significant statements. Books are like friends with whom you converse. You can talk back to them by marginal notes that agree, disagree, emphasize, and possibly even declare "I never knew that before!"

In graduate courses, especially in economics, management, and marketing, the writer has actually taken the entire semester's lectures verbatim. These lectures were transcribed as soon after they had been delivered as possible. One lecture usually averaged around twelve typed pages for each fifty-minute lecture. Later the notes were used to write answers to possible examination questions. In theory courses, when enough "big questions" had been satisfactorily answered through organizing and condensing the answers were tape recorded and could be played back during a period of calm and relaxation. Later the material was written from memory. By this time the ideas were ingrained and could be reproduced in many forms. Since the method outlined here aided the writer in acquiring over 260 semester hours of college and university credit, 120 of which are graduate hours with grades of "A" in most instances, it should be agreed by *you,* the student, that you are being told how to study by one who knows.

HOW TO WRITE PAPERS, INCLUDING HOW TO USE THE LIBRARY — Two kinds of papers are assigned to college students: the creative paper (story, essay, poem, personality sketch, or creative interview) and the research paper. The research paper may be based on primary research (done by observation, experimentation, or survey through use of personal or telephone interview or questionnaires), or, which is more likely, on secondary research which usually means library research.

Library research is best done in the following manner. Analyze the problem on which you are writing. Select the main topics. Go to the library and look up these topics in the subject catalogue. [There is usually also an author catalogue, and in technical libraries there may be a classified catalogue.] Find the books available on the main topics. If a period of time is involved, this will determine the years to be covered in looking up the topics in the various indexes that are available. For research papers in various business areas, the *Industrial Arts Index* is the best source of articles. In 1961 this index was divided and is now available in two parts, one of which covers the business field only. Other indexes that may be used include:

Agricultural Index
Annual Magazine Subject Index
Art Index
Book Review Digest
Dramatic Index
Education Index
Engineering Index
International Index to Periodicals
Monthly Catalog, U. S. Public Documents
The New York Times Index
Public Affairs Information Service
The Reader's Guide to Periodical Literature

Assume that you are to write a paper on "Motivation Research" for a course in advertising. You may decide that the main topics under which you might find helpful articles are: *"Advertising, Psychology, Motivation Research,* and *Market Research."* You would begin by looking up these headings for a certain period of time, and since motivation research is relatively new you might decide to begin with articles written in 1950. You would write at the tops of index cards 5½″ x 8″ the names of authors, names of the articles, names of the magazines or journals containing the articles, issues, and page numbers. The main headings might lead you to other headings. When you finished taking the names of the articles that seemed to be most interesting and informative, you would shuffle the cards so that all articles in *Printer's Ink* would be stacked chronologically together. Those in *Fortune, Business Week, Editor and Publisher, Industrial Marketing, Sales Management, Advertising Agency Magazine, The Journal of Marketing, Practical Psychology, Journal of Social Psychology, Journal of Applied Psychology,* and so on would likewise be stacked by magazine and date.

Your next step (if you are permitted stack privileges) would be to go to the floor in the library where the business magazines are to be found. You can take notes in your own words on the cards on which you have already written the complete references. If you wish to quote directly, copy verbatim and indicate you have done so by quotation marks. In this way you do not have to move from one magazine to another, but you can wade through all the issues of one magazine at one sitting. It may be that in large universities you will have to go to several libraries on the campus to find all of the magazines involved, as: journalism, pharmacy, engineering, education, and so on.

When notes have been taken on all of the references, you may shuffle the cards into an outline that must have been taking shape as you did your research. You may have to rearrange several times as you read, but the data obtained can be easily moved from one topic to another because of the fact that you used cards. Information from books will be handled in the same manner as that taken from magazine references. If more than one card (front and back) was needed for an article or book topic, the cards should have been stapled together. Writing the paper is a very simple task once the information has been properly obtained; if you type, the writing is that much easier. You will compose the rough draft at the typewriter, inserting references at the points they are used. In retyping, you will sometimes rewrite, and footnotes will be moved to the bottom of the page or to a single list to be used in lieu of a bibliography. When the references are placed at the bottom of the page where they are used, a separate bibliography, in alphabetical order by authors, is prepared. This may be separated by books and periodicals. To prepare this bibliography it is easy enough to rearrange your cards again in alphabetical order by authors.

Students learn to write by writing, criticizing their work, and then rewriting. They cannot begin to learn to write, however, before they have learned to read. Ideas acquired through reading, observation, and experience must come first; then write.

HOW TO IMPROVE CONCENTRATION — In all probability, the inability to concentrate (or failure to do so) is the main reason for failure in attempts to study. If interest is lacking, concentration is difficult. Thus it becomes necessary to develop interest. If one is curious about a subject, interest exists; if that curiosity is lacking, it may be necessary for the student to force interest through looking forward to rewards that will be received as a result of the acquiring of knowledge involved in the particular subject-matter area; sometimes knowledge of punishment that might result (low grades, failure, reprimand) may also stimulate forced interest. Frequently, through forcing oneself to study interest in the subject develops. The more areas of subject matter in which one becomes interested, the more likely he will be to be able to develop interest in increasingly larger numbers of areas of learning. Some students become interested in acquiring more information in order that they may be able to talk in class. Some merely want to talk because it is their nature to want to stand out; others want to ask questions because it makes them feel that they are participating; some want to argue and can't do so unless they have facts upon which to base their arguments.

HOW TO IMPROVE MEMORY — Memory is probably the chief tool used in acquiring a college diploma. Memory is essential to reflective thinking, analyzing, and reasoning (all of which are based on facts retained by memory). Even for the person who is chiefly gifted in mechanical ability, memory is extremely important. The creative person does not pluck his ideas from the air; he, too, uses memory to put things long known together in unique fashion. Memory is chiefly useful as it is applied in the various areas of problem solving.

In acquiring certain skills (shorthand, typewriting, all mechanical skills, and foreign language), memory is absolutely essential. Electric and mechanical devices have been invented to aid in teaching; these devices are helpful in strengthening memory, and they have been found useful in all subject-matter areas. They are, however, particularly valuable in teaching skills and languages. A young New Yorker named Lewis Robins a few years ago developed a system called "Reinforced Learning." In teaching foreign language, the recorded lesson teaches and then requires the student to translate (response). If he translates wrong, the machine gives him the right answer (reinforcement). The wrong answers tend to be forgotten because they are not reinforced.[4] Today there are some 4,000 language laboratories using electronic devices for teaching.

In the 1920's, Dr. Pressey, Ohio State University, developed the first "teaching machine." The machine was not sufficiently used to discover its values. From 1954-1958, Professor B. F. Skinner of Harvard University did research with machine (programmed) teaching that had positive results. In preparing programs for machine teaching material is sifted to obtain the subject matter considered essential. Frames are prepared with statements and responses. The device itself is useful only as a tool to present the subject matter which informs and teaches the student. Students have been found to learn faster, retain more, and they can proceed at the speed their own abilities dictate. International Business Machines, Inc., Eastman Kodak, Schering Corporation, and du Pont are some of the industrial firms that have successfully used programed training.[5]

In ordinary study, however, much depends upon the ability of the student to develop his own powers of memorizing. It is usually necessary to intend to remember if one is to do so. Memory can be improved through use. The following tips for improving were adapted from *Thirty Days to a Higher I.Q. for Your Child,* published by Crown Publishers, Inc.:

1. Read about ten lines of the material two or three times.
2. Cover the material and attempt to repeat it out loud. If you are interested only in the general idea, simply recite that in your own words. If you memorize exactly, as in the case of a poem, try to recite all that you can now recall.
3. If you are not completely successful, read the lines again.
4. Test your memory again. Continue in this manner until you have memorized the material.
5. Finally, write it down to help fix it in your memory.[6]

Every time that one uses an idea acquired, ability to remember it at a future date is strengthened. One must overlearn to remember for a long time, and one cannot be said to have learned a thing unless it has been stored in the memory. In most cases, it is better to study in several brief periods than to use the same amount of time at one study period.

When a thing is stored in the memory it may be for a temporary period only or permanently. For remembering something for a short period, it is necessary that there be expenditure of energy. To retain something for longer than a few hours it apparently requires little or no energy but involves minute structural changes in or near brain cells. The thing remembered is in effect implanted or imprinted on the brain. The cortical regions of each side of the brain near the ears (temporal lobes) contain neuron circuits where the long-term memories are stored. Since the brain has billions of cells, it does not run out of places to store up memories. With increasing years, however, one does have so much to remember it is necessary that he have an organized system for recalling things to be remembered. The best system is to associate these things with other ideas. Dr. James E. Birren of the National Institute of Mental Health (Bethesda, Maryland) advises people to put as many hooks as possible on the thing to be remembered. When one has trouble recalling something, he should not continue pulling on one hook. He should go back and recall the situation surrounding the acquiring of the information he wants to recall. Pull on another hook and bring up the idea. Simple recall of something recently seen is not as important as ability to organize information into over-all patterns.[7]

A useful way of remembering lists, events, dates (reasoning and association are necessary in applying these memorized facts elsewhere), known as a *mnemonic* system or device for improving the efficiency of the memory, is to find a scheme of listing by words the first letters of which spell a word or a sentence. It may be that all the words begin with the same sound, as in listing the *ways to meet situations or problems:* *f*acing, *f*leeing (taking *f*light), *f*ighting, resorting to *f*antasy (phantasy), *feinting,* or *fainting.* In recalling the indices to good company morale one might use *lic dips,* which in no way makes sense but as a device does enable the recalling of the seven characteristics of a group of people exhibiting good morale: *loyalty* to the organization, *interest* in the company and what they are doing, *cooperation,* good *discipline, initiative, pride* in the organization, and organization *stamina* (ability to adjust to changes in personnel).

HOW TO IMPROVE READING ABILITY — People who read slowly tend to read by words and phrases and to go back over the material read (make regressions). Good readers read rapidly, generally, but they vary their rate of reading to fit the subject matter. They understand what they are reading, regress rarely, think as they read, comprehend an entire line with few eye movements, underscore and make marginal notes when these are appropriate, recite to themselves, and remember what they have read. Today there are electronic devices for helping people to develop speed in reading. The Skill-Builder Controlled Reader is a 35mm filmstrip projector that may be used to present material at speeds from twelve to one hundred eight typing words per minute. The machine was developed from the Controlled Reader which in turn was developed out of the tachistoscope. These machines are used not only for improving speed in reading but for training for fast observation of planes and ships, to enrich vocabulary, to teach spelling and mathematics, to teach typewriting and shorthand, and in other ways. In training persons to read more rapidly, material is presented at varying speeds until very high speeds are reached; the students are asked to recall what they have read. The Educational Development Laboratories, Huntington, New York, have done work on materials for teaching reading.

Students should increase their vocabularies in order to read faster and with greater comprehension. Further, a large vocabulary is associated with success in business. *A knowledge of words more than any other factor correlates with outstanding success in the United States,* according to research done by the Human Engineering Laboratories.[8] Students have not believed vocabularies to be so important until recruiters on college campuses have given five-minute vocabularly tests that were the major determining factor in whether or not these students were accepted for executive training.

While skill in reading has been considered the primary medium of learning, listening is also a very important means of acquiring information. Yet, according to Nichols and Stevens, learning by listening is an area of neglect. There seems to be increasing lack of attentiveness on the part of students as they progress upward through the school years. Despite the fact that skillful listening is important in school work and in the family circle in the earlier years and in executive work, salesmanship, and conferences when they have reached the business world, people apparently do not develop their powers of listening accordingly. Nichols and Stevens call notetaking "pen and paper listening." [9]

HOW TO READ RESEARCH REPORTS — Harry W. Hepner in his *Psychology Applied to Life and Work* has devoted an entire chapter to this topic. For a fuller discussion than is presented here, the reader is referred to Hepner.[10]

A research report should be analyzed to determine whether or not factors that have been studied and/or compared have been wisely chosen. Units of measurement used should be sound. There is no way for the reader to determine whether or not there was absolute accuracy in tabulating data presented in a research report, but the person or persons doing the research should have built up a reputation for reliability. The sample used in the study should be adequate and there should be information as to the percentage of error involved in the data itself. If correlation is shown, it should be possible to estimate the error in any prediction based upon such correlation. It should be determined whether or not the data obtained for a given group of persons have been checked against data obtained on a control group. Data not checked against control groups may be discounted. Further, the conclusions of a research study should not be given much weight if they go counter to the dictates of experience and judgment. Enough studies could, however, prove that prior experience and past judgment had apparently been wrong.

HOW TO DEVELOP CREATIVE ABILITY — The writer has taken numbers of courses in creative writing. What does one do in a creative writing course? Frequently, the best work is done when the teacher inspires students to want to accomplish and then lets them follow the dictates of their own imaginations in coming up with essays, stories, and poems. Motivation may be accomplished through exchange of ideas, through letting students read their creations to members of their class, through providing a way of publishing the best of the writings produced in a class. Encouragement of the creative worker is the best motivation device; criticism of what has been created even though it may be negative is better than no reaction. Positive criticism is reward in itself while negative criticism gives a reason for thinking again and in a different way in order to create anew.

Alex F. Osborn [referred to above], vice chairman of the board, Batten, Barton, Durstine & Osborn, Inc., advertising agency, has written much on creative thinking and is credited with fathering brainstorming, a "creative-thinking" process used by groups and discussed in Chapter XIV as a means of training supervisors. In one of his early writings on creative thinking he said that if there could be a technique of creative thinking it might go something like this:

1. *Aim:* Pick out a single target. [He did this himself in sketching a mechanical invention while waiting in a railroad station and sold the idea for $300.]

2. *Fire:* You shouldn't be afraid to try out your ideas despite the fact that they might seem silly.

3. *Review:* Pick the best ideas from your list.

4. *Relax:* Let the idea simmer while you do other things. It might work itself out while you are listening to music or even a sermon. [Some call this the period of "incubation" just before "illumination" or the answer to the problem arrives.]

5. *Confer:* If the idea doesn't work out, talk it over with some-one. You might see the answer as you talk.

6. *Reload:* If you still fail, start over. Try again. Such persistence will pay off. [There must be a period of testing to see if a thing works; if it doesn't, you do have to keep trying until it does — unless, of course, you do give up.][11]

In a later work, Osborn declared that "careers depend largely upon creativity." Imagination is not only all-important in getting the job and developing on the job, it is important in marital relations, in the home, in parenthood, and getting along with one's self. Osborn sees the judicial mind as one that analyzes and weighs facts and finally forms a conclusion. The creative mind works much as the judicial mind does, but instead of reaching a verdict it comes up with an idea. Emotion may be a strong motivating force in stimulating creativity, but emotions are difficult to control and in the long run it is best to depend upon reasoning, or, as Osborn puts it, "to harness our wills." [12]

As Brewster Ghiselin has pointed out, the interest in creativity is not new considering the fact that Plato and Aristotle wrote about the creative process and writers ever since have done so.[13] Today, however, it does seem that more than usual is being written about "creativity" and the "creative process," and yet, perhaps, there are not as many truly "creative works" being produced. It is almost as if we grasped at bringing back creative writing, creative inventions, creative art, and so on by writing about how to develop creative ability and how to create. Industry, as is education, is interested in the creative process and creative persons. Ideas not only keep an individual young, they keep an industry young also.

The AC Sparkplug Division of General Motors in 1953 began a program to find out whether a person's creative ability could be predicted and, if so, what to do about it. They developed the AC Test of Creative Ability designed to test persons in or entering supervision and other persons who evidenced signs of creative ability. Through training, the program was designed to stimulate creativity. Motivating factors associated with creativeness were studied. Four approaches were used in developing imagination:

1. The check list approach. A person begins the imaginative process by attempting to find a relationship between his problem and items on a check list. Possibilities are developed.

2. The brainstorming technique. (See Chapter XIV)

3. Problem analysis. The problem is defined, data are gathered, the data are analyzed; solutions are developed and tested.

4. Technique of hypothetical situations. People are asked to solve problems within conditions and limitations of a particular setting. This is something like role-playing. (See Chapter XIV)[14]

Guilford has said that although there are some forty-seven known factors of intellect these may be grouped into three categories "according to the kind of material or content of thought." The *first* classification is: *Figural* (materials that consist of objects that may be seen and have distinguishable properties, sounds, tactual and kinesthetic materials — these constitute concrete intelligence); *conceptual* or *semantic* (verbalized meanings); and *symbolic* (code materials such as numbers, syllables, and word structures). Abilities in symbolic and semantic materials qualify as abstract intelligence. The *second* way of classifying is according to how the material of thought is dealt with: *recognizing, discovering, comprehending, remembering, convergent thinking, divergent thinking,* and *evaluating.* The *third* way of classifying ability has to do with the product or unit of thought (*figure, symbolic structure, concept*). It may be a *class of units* or a *relation between units*, a *pattern*, a *system*, a *gestalt*, or an *implication.*[15]

Creative aptitudes are reflected in the *divergent-thinking* abilities. In *convergent-thinking* the answers are restricted. They are exact and already formulated, as, the opposite of day is night. Divergent thinking searches and produces answers that are not predetermined. The result is innovation, creative thinking, and new arrangements of old ideas.

As long ago as 1908 Joseph A. Schumpeter was writing that there are not profits or rewards in industry except to the innovators, to the people who put in new businesses, who change conditions, who develop new processes, who use new channels of distribution, who create new products and services.[16] Whether Schumpeter was right or not, it must be agreed that the creative process is all important in industry in product innovation, in engineering, in advertising, in selling, and, in fact, in every business or industrial function.

For manufacturers the launching of a new product on the market is an all-important creative process that follows steps similar to those found in any other creative endeavor. Generally, getting a new product on the market involves passing through six stages: (1) the first period is one of *exploration*; it is a period of searching for ideas for the new product which must meet company objectives. (2) The ideas are analyzed and expanded into concepts of full products, a process known as *screening*. (3) A program is developed and *specifications for producing* and *marketing* the product are made. (4) The product is produced and released for testing in the *development* period. (5) Theory is tested by *testing* the product through use, and final decisions are made as to the product and its design. (6) The product is placed on the market in the stage of *commercialization*. Results are checked and improvements made. Through following these six steps, companies assure the elimination of non-profitable products in the early stages. If the product fails in the commercialization stage, such failure can probably be traced to failure in the earlier stages.[17]

MOTIVATION AND DRIVE — It is generally conceded that inner drive is the element chiefly responsible for success. Given the same intellect as another person, the person with twice the drive of that other person will accomplish twice as much provided the two are directing their energies in the same direction. If a person does not have inner drive, how does he get it? For some persons motivation is apparently inherent along with inner drive. Motivation may, however, be applied from an external force to encourage the development of drive. As in the case of *intelligence,* the terms *drive* and *motive* probably cannot be exactly defined. Drive is something that exists within an organism that causes it to strive toward obtaining goals and satisfactions of needs. Motives are the forces which instil in the organism the felt need for striving toward a goal. Motives give impetus to or arouse drive.

Two of the most important motivational antecedents are *need states* and *rewards*.[18] The basic needs such as hunger, thirst, clothing, shelter, rest, sleep, changing environment, elimination of waste, and sexual expression are easily recognizable as needs. Emotions also motivate. Fear, anger, sentiments, moods, all influence a person to act as he does. Actions, experiences, feelings are all evaluated as being pleasant or unpleasant. That which is pleasant one tends to prolong; people withdraw from the unpleasant. Organic needs, emotions, and feelings do not, however, completely explain man. He is a social being and has a tendency (inborn or trained into him) to try to win in competition with others. This may be called self-assertion. But also, man has a tendency to subordinate himself to others. This is self-submission, or self-negation. People also desire approval of others. They want to belong, to be at home. Habits once established also become motives. Activities once started carry motivation to carry them on toward completion. If an activity is interrupted, strain is produced and the individual tends to return to complete the activity when there is opportunity.[19]

When a particular emotional stage is associated with some particular object, this is a sentiment. Love and hate are the most prominent sentiments. Religion, social, and aesthetic sentiments are complex sentiments directed toward certain objects. There are many kinds of thinking (see above). Thinking, emotional states, sentiments, and the basic needs of man motivate him toward goals. Recent brain research is locating the emotional centers deep in the mid-brain, the hypothalamus. Through electrical stimulation, use of drugs, and surgery it may eventually be possible to exercise control over the basic drives in humans and to correct emotional imbalances leading to mental and psychosomatic illnesses. There may also be implications here for some degree of control of motivation.

For some persons the need to excell in given areas in order to compensate for inadequacies or failures in other areas may be a lifelong motivational force propelling them to heights of success in the areas turned to for compensation. (Chapter VI) People generally are motivated toward success by desire for: *power, wealth (security), fame (recognition), response (sex), adventure (new experience, fighting),* and *love* (although some authorities would not add this to their list, the need for tenderness, affection, and a feeling of belonging must be admitted). [The reader is referred to a very useful classification of driving forces or urges prepared by Stacey and DeMartino.][20]

How is one to use his knowledge of the factors of motivation and drive to improve his ability to study and achieve? Perhaps the first step would be to analyze himself, to determine if possible the factors that have motivated him thus far in life. In the process, it is possible that he would gain the insight that would enable him to change his approaches to problem solving if these have not proved successful in the past. Generally people will attempt to avoid disappointments and failures. They turn from failures to activities that result in success and a feeling of achievement. If a person has the intelligence to succeed in any given area of study, he should be able to succeed to a comparable degree in any other area of study. People sometimes feel that they cannot learn certain things, cannot acquire certain skills, or cannot succeed in certain types of endeavor. It becomes necessary in such cases for their attitudes to be changed. If one could be satisfied at first with small successes in these areas, the reward of success might lead to larger achievements. The more one has learned and the more ideas he has acquired the easier it becomes to learn by association; there are old hooks upon which to hang the new ideas.

The Influence of Avocational Skills, Hobbies, and Interests on Mental Outlook — If a person can develop an all-engrossing skill or hobby, the effect upon mental outlook will be good. Not only will the individual be a happier person, the hobby will probably be a stimulation to study. The reward of being able to indulge in the favorite hobby after obligations such as study or work have been met is the incentive for doing the study or work first and for doing it well in order that there may not be any nagging reminders to interfere with enjoyment of the hobby. Some people work in an opposite manner. They enjoy the hobby first and then attempt the study or work; often this leads to procrastination and this is especially true if the study or work are regarded as unpleasant. What was meant to be only temporary postponement in such cases may lead to continued avoidance.

In pursuing a hobby, it is necessary that it not become so fascinating that it prevent the attainment of success in one's study, vocation, or home life. One or more hobbies, however, according to the interests and capabilities of the pursuers, can add zest and interest to living and stimulate effort in the main areas of life, as well as be conducive to mental good health.

There are thousands of hobbies and they have been classified in many ways. Many years ago the writer started two lists, one was headed: "Things I Can Do or Have Done." The other was headed: "Things I Would Like To Do or Be Able To Do." These lists, while they were kept up only a short while as written copies, actually grew greatly during the years. Generally, there are *passive* hobbies and *creative and active hobbies. Passive* hobbies add interest to life, but they are not as satisfying as the creative ones. Outstanding among the passive hobbies are: *traveling, collecting* (coins, stamps, music boxes, beersteins, tile, bottle stoppers, dolls, salt shakers, ash trays, china, spoons, fans, paintings, etchings, photographs, figurines, records, books, furniture, and countless other items), *spectator* (movies, dramas, television, sports, ice shows, concerts), and *reading.* In a sense there is perhaps an element of the active in all of the so-called passive hobbies. Certainly in reading even for pleasure the imagination must provide its own scenes and interpretations. Further, if the reading is study the participation is very great. If collecting results in study of specialized areas it becomes active. One's study might lead to expert knowledge in such fields as history, economics, geography, politics, art, history or any one of hundreds of others. The *active* hobbies include *participation* in clubs, sports, games, music (with groups and individually), drama, problem solving, and skill building in any area. *Creative* hobbies probably bring the deepest satisfaction. They include: painting, drawing, sculpturing, designing, arranging and/or growing flowers, writing, composing, organizing, building, and even thinking. If your favorites have been left out, just insert them. These lists do not purport to be complete.

Some writers call hobbies "personal interests" and classify them as PPI (primary personal interests). One listing includes the following headings as being PPI: adventure seeking, aesthetic appreciation, conforming, diversions, wishful thinking, desire for attention, resisting restrictions, outdoor working, physical push, aggression. PPI considered to be less general than the ones just listed include: realistic thinking, cultural interest, orderliness, sociability, physical fitness, precision, wanting variety, wanting sympathetic environment, ambition, and social initiative.[21] It will be observed that some of these interests could not properly be called hobbies, as, for instance, "conforming," but tendencies toward these might determine the kinds of hobbies a person would choose. Personal interests and hobbies of applicants for jobs are considered by employment interviews right along with applicants' PVI (primary vocational interests).

In your search for interests, please keep in mind that some persons believe that "one person with a belief is equal to a force of 99 who only have interests!"

Conclusions — The person who wishes to improve study habits can do so. At first there may be an element of unpleasantness, and, in fact, deep, hard study may always have an element of pain in it, but this is certainly compensated for even at the moment of pain by anticipation of the rewards of achievement. The rewards themselves probably bring less pleasure than the anticipation of them.

The wider one's experiences in various areas of learning, the easier it is for him to grasp related areas, or even "new" areas. For if one searches deeply enough he can usually find elements of relationship exist between those with which he has developed acquaintanceship and those he presumed to be new to him. It is not believed that any given subject-matter area can be considered as being "disciplinary" in the sense that it disciplines the mind for attainment in other areas. However, it is practically impossible to find an area of learning that is not in some way related to other areas. Skills and knowledges acquired in one area may thus be an aid to acquiring skills and knowledges in other areas. There often will be transfer of knowledge from hobbies and interests to areas of vocational training and learning.

PROJECTS

1. Read and write a short report on the educational system of an European country.

2. Read from some current source on "creative thinking" or the "creative mind" and be prepared to report orally on what you have read.

3. Make a list of things you can do or have done; make, also, a list of things you would like to be able to do before you die or are too old.

4. Check out *The Techniques of Creative Thinking* by Robert P. Crawford (Hawthorn Books, Inc., New York, 1954). Read and write a critical report on the chapter that appeals the most to you.

ACKNOWLEDGMENTS AND REFERENCES

1 ———, "Education — Why Ivan Can't Play," *Newsweek*, April 30, 1962, pp. 58–59.

2 ———, "Medicine — The Mind," *Newsweek*, November 21, 1960, p. 64.

3 Fine, Benjamin, "You May Be Shortchanging Your Creative Youngster," *Houston Chronicle*, April 10, 1962, p. 4, s. 3.

4 Williams, Augustus, "Instant Education," *The American Weekly*, November 8, 1959.

5 Day, Elmore M., Jr., "Implications for the Teaching of Business by Programmed Learning," *American Business Education*, A Joint Publication of the Eastern Business Teachers Association and the National Business Teachers Association, May, 1962, p. 221ff.

6 Rosenfeld, Sam, "Memory Is Improved Through Use," *Houston Chronicle*, January 12, 1962, p. 4, s. 4.

7 Cassels, Louis, "How To Keep Your Memory Sharp," *The Reader's Digest*, August, 1962, pp. 46–49.

8 Aurner, Robert R., *Effective Communication in Business*, South-Western Publishing Company, Cincinnati, 1958, p. 151.

9 Nichols, Ralph G., and Stevens, Leonard A., *Are You Listening?*, McGraw-Hill Book Company, Inc., New York, 1957.

10 Hepner, Harry Walker, *Psychology Applied to Life and Work*, Prentice-Hall, Inc., Englewood Cliffs, New Jersey, 1957, pp. 599–607.

11 Osborn, Alex, *How To Think Up*, McGraw-Hill Book Company, Inc., New York, 1942, pp. 34–35.

12 Osborn, Alex F., *Applied Imagination, Principles and Procedures of Creative Thinking*, Charles Scribner's Sons, New York, 1953.

13 Ghiselin, Brewster, *The Creative Process*, University of California Press, Berkeley and Los Angeles, 1954, p. 1.

14 Friess, Walter J., "A Case History on Creativity in Industry," *Creativity, An Examination of the Creative Process*, edited by Paul Smith, Communication Arts Books, Hastings House Publishers, New York, 1959.

15 Guilford, J. P., "Traits of Creativity," *Creativity and Its Cultivation*, edited by Harold H. Anderson, Harper & Brothers Publishers, New York, 1959, pp. 153-155.

16 Schumpeter, Joseph A., *The Theory of Economic Development* (translated from the German by Redvers Opie), Harvard University Press, Cambridge, Massachusetts, 1934.

17 Randle, C. Wilson, "Putting New-Product Ideas Through Their Paces," *The Management Review*, American Management Association, Inc., 1515 Broadway, Times Square, New York 36, N. Y., Vol. XLVI, No. 10, October, 1957, pp. 34–35.

18 Hall, John F., *Psychology of Motivation*, J. B. Lippincott Company, Chicago, 1961, p. 283.

19 Bernhardt, Karl S., *Practical Psychology*, McGraw-Hill Book Company, Inc., New York, 1945, pp. 43–57.

20 Stacey, Chalmers L., and DeMartino, Manfred F., *Understanding Human Motivation*, Howard Allen, Inc., Publishers, Cleveland, 1958, p. 21.

21 Laird, Donald A., and Laird, Eleanor, *Practical Business Psychology*, Gregg Publishing Division, McGraw-Hill Book Company, Inc., New York, 1961, pp. 145–151.

CHAPTER III

MAINTAINING PERSONAL PHYSICAL EFFICIENCY

The Soul-Body-Mind Concept — Plato was the first to distinguish clearly between soul and body. He considered the soul to consist of three parts: (1) Instincts or drives that lead man to seek bodily satisfactions and possessions he considered to be on the lowest level of the soul; this element man shares with the animals and its seat in man is his stomach. (2) The courage or the spirit was the next highest soul element. Its seat was considered to be the heart, and it, too, was shared with the animals, but more particularly with the higher animals. The souls of appetite and courage are born of the body and they live and die with it. (3) Reason was the highest level of soul; it was not of the body but survives it.[1]

To Plato there was no more need for physical sickness than for moral sickness; both were due to ignorance and each could be eliminated by education. Should there, however, be persons unfortunate enough to be incurably sick they should be allowed to die for quick death was much better than illness that would linger on.[2]

Regardless of the part played by the desires, the heart, and the mind and aside from any religious implications involved when one is considering the soul (immortality), most of those who work with mental illnesses believe that the human being functions as a unit, mind and body. Some few still believe that the mind and the body function separately.

It is generally recognized that man has needs to develop his mind (mental stimulation, intellectual growth), to develop his body (physical exercise, rest and sleep, food), and to provide for soul satisfaction (religion, love). This chapter purports to deal with factors affecting physical efficiency, but physical and mental efficiency are considered to be very closely related. Religion will not be dealt with, but the powers of religion are admittedly great and the student is admonished not to neglect development of this area of need in his life.

The Effects of Exercise — Beardsley Ruml, known as the father of the withholding tax, is known also as a disbeliever in exercise. There are others who believe "that the case for exercise has not been finally proved." [3] Nevertheless, there is constantly accumulating evidence that physical and mental activity contribute to prolonged life, and in particular delay the on-slaught of the symptoms of age. Numbers of studies have found that per-sons who follow vocations that keep them physically active, provided the physical exertion needed for the job is not so severe as to break down the body, live longer than do persons whose work is sedentary. One study found that hard labor (indoors or out) up to the age of forty years has no effect on life expectancy. After forty, such hard labor shortens life.[4] Per-sons who keep mentally active prolong mental deterioration. Study and developing of interests (Chapter II) are the exercises of the mind.

A study of persons admitted during a given period to the Mayo Clinic revealed that one-fourth of all the adult patients entering during this period had a neurosis of some kind. When the occupations of these persons were checked, it was found that only four per cent of the railroad engineers ad-mitted during this period (100) had a purely functional disease (neu-rosis), and only nine per cent of the farmers (145) had a purely functional disease. Teachers (mostly female) had the highest incidence of neurosis (25 per cent of the 16 male teachers and 34 per cent of the 106 female teachers). Other groups revealing high percentages of neurosis were housewives, clergymen, and dentists. The conductors of this study con-cluded that persons who work manually are less likely to develop neuroses than those who do less physical work.[5]

Exercise is a chief tool of the physiotherapist. Exercises are carefully se-lected to fit the needs of patients. These are usually first used in individual treatment, although too much attention to an individual by a physio-therapist may slow down progress toward rehabilitation. Group exercise usually follows the individual therapy. Through group exercise, patients learn to take responsibility for their own exercise; they learn to work with others; they gain confidence in the treatment itself and in their ability to keep up with the group; mild forms of competition in group exercise are stimulating; they forget their disabilities in group exercise, particularly if these exercises take on the nature of game-like activities.[6]

Persons forced to exercise as a rehabilitation measure may continue their exercises (usually must) when they are returned to homes and fami-lies. Well persons should view exercise as a preventative measure. It is good for the minds and bodies of the young. It is an incentive to the busi-nessman and to those in the professions; it is diversion, adventure, and an alternate course of action. The person who was an athlete in college must, however, beware of extending his strenuous participation into later years. At mid years one usually gives up the strenuous calisthenics, tennis, foot-ball, basketball, and track for milder exercises, walking, swimming, and golf. Persons who have recovered from coronary thrombosis attacks are usually advised to walk for exercise. They still mow their lawns, paint their houses, go swimming, and play golf provided they "quit before they have to." Needless to say, these people must also, usually, "push back [from the table] before they have had enough." Even for the healthy person, extreme exercise in a short period of time (the week end) will do more harm than good.

Persons whose occupations require physical exertion should seek only milder forms of exercise away from work, if, indeed, they seek any. Some of these people find their exercise (interest) in camping; some join "trailer clubs" and tour their state and nation. In addition to the interests and exercises away from work, workers should exercise their eyes occasionally by looking away from their work, out of a window or across the room. To close the eyes for a short time and feel the relaxation this gives is a kind of exercise. People can in some measure also exercise their bodies in various ways at the work place. For instance, moving the head around in circular fashion and letting it drop forward for a few seconds is good exercise.

The Effects of Sleep — Some persons believe sleep to be the most important of the necessities for health and efficiency.[7] Persons do differ, however, in the amount of sleep they require for efficiency. Some people need fully eight hours of sleep a night; others can do on fewer hours. Too much sleep could possibly lead to retreat from obligations and the competition provided by life's pursuits.

Many studies have been done to determine the effects of sleep on physical dexterity and mental activity. One such study was done by A. S. Edwards who kept seventeen persons awake for a hundred hours. Some dozen tests in the areas of reaction time, dexterity, perception, and intelligence were given to these people each morning. Little difference was revealed as between persons who had normal sleep and those who went sleepless in such areas as hand grip and hand steadiness. Increased sleeplessness did bring on greater amount of sway and greatly reduced scores on intelligence tests. Persons in the 60th percentile before losing sleep were in the 40th and 34th percentiles after seventy-two and ninety-six hours without sleep. After they had caught up on their sleep these persons averaged at the 76th percentile. Ability to remember nonsense syllables fell and greatly so toward the end of the experimental period. The digit-memory test gave about the same results before and after the loss of sleep. Concentration became more difficult as the experiment progressed and the frustrations of the subjects led to irritability and inattentiveness. It was necessary for them to expend added effort to keep their scores from dropping even more drastically.[8]

An earlier study was made by E. B. Newman of the effect of sleep on ability to retain conceptual materials as opposed to ability to retain memorized symbols or words when study was done at different times during the day or just before going to bed. Subjects were found to retain about the same amount of essential information (theories, principles) after eight hours of sleep as after eight hours of being awake. Their ability to retain non-essentials after sleeping was greater (47 per cent) than their ability to remember the same kind of information after an interval of being awake (23 per cent). This would imply that study of rote memory material done just before sleeping will give the best results.[9]

How To Relax — Dr. Edmund Jacobson has provided the classic volume on relaxation. In this he tells of his laboratory experiments in getting patients to rest through "progressive relaxation." There are implications in this method for all persons, not just those who have arrived at need for medical care because of breakdowns and illnesses. According to Dr. Jacobson, persons can be taught to relax much as they can be taught to play golf, to skate, to play the piano, and to drive an automobile. Persons already familiar with muscular tension and relaxation (dancers, skaters, singers, athletes) may be more easily taught how to relax than others. People generally prefer activity to rest and are most unwilling to give up activities when relaxation is most needed, i.e., when they are fretful and distressed. In the case of patients, the physician must overcome unwillingness by argument, persuasion or any other means he can. As a person relaxes, the unwillingness is replaced by desire for rest. The restless and emotional patients are not the only ones in need of rest. Relaxation may be a preventative as well as a cure.

Sedatives, trips, entertainments, and suggestive procedures have been used by some for obtaining rest and relaxation. Progressive relaxation is a much more complicated and longer process involving reeducation. Dr. Jacobson's laboratory evidence showed the importance of sensations from muscular contractions in the individual's "stream of consciousness." As these sensations are reduced during relaxation (not just of a moment but over a period of time), the kinesthetic, visual, and auditory images are reduced. Complete relaxation comes when mental activity is stopped.

In effect, Dr. Jacobson's method caused the individual to begin relaxation from the extremities, fingers, toes, up through the arms and legs until the activity of muscle groups had been contracted in these *local* areas. There are sixty major muscle groups. Eventually, the relaxation extended to the entire body, reclining, and the condition of relaxation at this point he called *general*. Practice over a period of time is necessary before one can acquire the ability to relax. Relaxation may then proceed almost automatically.[10]

In a day when so many drive themselves relentlessly, it would be well for all to acquire the ability to relax and to sleep at appropriate periods. The person who can relax for a few minutes after meals and who can relax and sleep when bedtime arrives, stores up the energy required to drive through to accomplishments. Further, rest and relaxation are the only effective measures when persons are objectively fatigued (Chapter XVIII), and they are the chief remedies in all of the so-called tension diseases.

The Effects of Food — This is a day of the "diet faddists." High protein diets, high carbohydrate diets, unsaturated-fat diets (calories don't count!) specially prepared diet foods (liquid and solid), all have had and are having their day. Articles and books indict the "fat American" and tell him what to do about his condition. In the calorie count, we have almost forgotten the vitamin.

The area of nutrition (diet) is a whole field of study in itself. Food is not only an important element in determining the physical make-up of individuals; it affects mental health as well. Further, obesity is perhaps one of the most frequent causes of skin disorders. The excessive perspiration and chafing that results from heavy fat deposits can cause dermatoses. The exact causes of some skin diseases, as acne vulgaris, are not known, but most doctors place acne patients on diets considered to be well-balanced and if the patients are overweight the calories permitted are restricted.

Conditions where tissue repair is needed are treated with protein. Cutaneous symptoms often develop when there is insufficient amino acids in the food; some thirty amino acids have been isolated from proteins. Vitamin A, B complex vitamins, vitamin C, and vitamin K have been used for cutaneous lesions, but the value of vitamins beyond those supplied in a balanced diet is not definitely known. Toxic conditions can result from excessive use of vitamins A, D, and K. Nevertheless, in treating many illnesses and skin diseases, the value of adequate vitamins is recognized.[11]

Nutrition is a chief concern in the treatment of many illnesses. Of chief value to the average person, however, is the fact that nutrition is a main factor in keeping him well. Today so many teen-agers (college students are not exempt) develop poor eating habits that this has become a matter of nation-wide concern. Parents, particularly mothers, are indicted by the American Dietetic Association for failing to encourage their children to develop good eating habits. Percentage-wise, however, there are probably just as many parents who do not eat wisely as there are teen-agers. The older teen-agers are considered to have poorer eating habits than the younger ones because they are left more to their own choosing. Some of the shortages in their diets include inadequate consumption of vitamin C (found in oranges, lemons, limes, berries, greens, cabbage, bell peppers), vitamin A (found in yellow vegetables and fish), thiamine (found in beans, fruits, cereals, pork, liver, spinach), riboflavin (found in liver,

TABLE III-I

Like	Dislike	Trait Indicated
Carrots		Lustfulness. Male is affectionate and sociable but not well liked; he is easy-going and easily cheated. Female is energetic, good natured, and nosey.
Sweet Potatoes		Woman is optimistic, amiable, loved, and makes a wonderful wife.
	Sweet Potatoes	Woman is peevish, unlucky, unsociable, frigid, and may die suddenly. Man is irritable, lacks vitality, may die soon.
Tea		Refined, religious, graceful; not healthy, but live long.
Apples		Male is refined, cautious in love, has good luck, is helped by friends. Female is composed and a good wife.
Bananas		Man is tolerant, sensitive, energetic, passionate. Woman is sensitive, a good wife, but childless; she loses herself once she loves a man.
Spinach		Man lives to 60 or 70 and is reasonable in love. Woman is obedient but gets into trouble in love.
Peanuts		Man will be successful and salaried, but blind in love. Woman also will be unlucky in love, but calm.
Eggs		Man has good luck in early years, bad luck later; he is conceited but energetic. Woman is jealous, fastidious, goes to extremes in love, and is unlucky in later life.

poultry, milk, fish, cottage cheese, cereal, cake mixes, flour), iron (which is considered particularly necessary during menstrual periods and is found in liver, dark green leafy vegetables, chicken, eggs). Here is a small part of the evidence that teen-agers cheat themselves or are cheated in diet:

Six out of ten girls and four out of ten boys have inadequate diets according to the National Research Council.

Seventy-two per cent of about 7,400 Chicago children were found to have inadequate diets regardless of incomes of their families.

Fifty per cent of a large group of teenagers in New York were found by Cornell University researchers to be malnourished.

A Nebraska study found that the worst dietary offenders were thirteen-fifteen year-old girls.

The Pennsylvania Department of Health found that sixty-five per cent of children in 6,000 families were deficient in at least one essential nutrient.[12]

Aside from the fact that food is extremely important to mental and physical health, certain interesting studies have been made of traits revealed by tendencies to eat or avoid certain foods. One of these was made by Dr. Kiichi Kuriyama, head of the Kuriyama Food Research Institute in Japan. His findings are offered here merely as a matter of interest and not as being scientific findings, although Dr. Kuriyama has studied the effect of food on humans for fifty years. It is not clear whether he believes that the avoidance of a food (or desire for it) is determined by the trait or whether the trait develops because of the food eaten. The latter is implied. He says that if both partners in marriage are fastidious about food the marriage will end. If they are not fussy about food, they will live normally, happily and have gentle children.[13] For a list of foods and traits they indicate, see Table III-1.

The Effects of Nicotine — Today's student is familiar with the many published reports of the effect of smoking on physical health. One of the latest studies (reported on in countless magazines and newspapers) was made by the Royal College of Physicians in England. Lois Mattox Miller has written numbers of articles on the effect of cigarette smoking for which she received in 1957, along with James Monahan, the Albert Lasker Medical Journalism Award for "Reporting on Medical Research and Public Health." [It is perhaps somewhat ironical that Albert Lasker should so have rewarded those who have written of the evils of smoking when he himself sold so many cigarettes with the slogan "Reach for a Lucky instead of a sweet."] The following findings of the Royal College are reported in *Smoking and Health*:

Cigarette smoking is a cause of lung cancer and bronchitis, and probably contributes to the development of coronary heart disease and various less common diseases.

Cigarette smokers have the greatest risk of dying from these diseases, and the risk is greater for the heavier smokers.

The many deaths from these diseases present a challenge to medicine; insofar as they are due to smoking they should be preventable.

The harmful effects of cigarette smoking might be reduced by efficient filters, by leaving longer cigarette stubbs, or by changing from cigarette to pipe or cigar smoking.[14]

The Royal College report stated further that since 1953 at least twenty-three investigations made in nine different countries have indicated that "death rates from lung cancer increase steeply with increasing consumption of cigarettes."[15] Specific recommendations made in *Smoking and Health* include: (1) restrictions on selling tobacco to children, (2) tax increases on cigarettes but lowered taxes on pipe tobacco and cigars as the risks are considerably less for smokers of these (cigar smokers may run no more risk than non-smokers), (3) test filters for efficiency, (4) educate the public in the hazards of smoking. Findings similar to those of the Royal College have resulted from studies in the United States.[16]

The effect of smoking upon mental abilities has been studied by various researchers. Nicotine has been found to diminish the ability of a person to visualize and do creative thinking. A study made by Dr. Donald K. Pumroy of the University of Maryland reported that students who smoke do less well academically on the average than nonsmokers. Further, the study showed that the more a student smokes the lower his grades are likely to be. Smoking itself may not, of course, be responsible for these results. As Dr. Pumroy suggested, the reasons students smoke may be related to the reasons they avoid studying. He used 204 freshmen men selected at random in his study. The 119 nonsmokers had a gradepoint average of 1.98 (2.00 equaled C). The young men who smoked half a pack of cigarettes a day averaged 1.92; those who smoked one half to a full pack a day averaged 1.61; those who smoked more than a pack a day averaged 1.38. This study also showed that more smokers drop out of college than do nonsmokers. Other surveys made since 1909 (approximately ten) have produced similar results.[17]

A study made by Pechstein and Reynolds of the effect of tobacco smoke on rats resulted in their concluding that a small amount of tobacco smoke stimulates and improves learning, but smoking in excess reduces the capacity to learn to the extent of inability by the fourth generation.[18]

Findings of a study by the United States Public Health Service indicated that infants born to cigarette-smoking mothers are more likely to be born prematurely and to be smaller than the babies born to nonsmoking mothers. Smoking may be only a contributing factor and not the direct cause of the premature births. However, the study seems to indicate that without question the woman who smokes is more likely to have a small, unhealthy baby than is the one who does not smoke. The Surgeon General's report which came out in early 1964 indicated that cigarette smoking is hazardous to health. The FTC in 1964 advocated full disclosure on every pack of cigarettes, and the American Medical Association adopted the statement that "cigarette smoking is a serious health hazard."[19]

We might summarize by saying that even moderate smokers probably don't live as long as nonsmokers. Further, their mental faculties are probably depleted to some extent at least by heavy smoking.

The Effects of Narcotics — Under law a narcotics addict is considered to be more sick than criminal. The United States Narcotics Bureau may obtain convictions of addicts only if the addicts are caught with the narcotics in their possession. Likewise, dealers must be caught at the time a transaction is being completed for them to be convicted. Addicts are sent to one of the narcotic farms of the Public Health Service (Lexington, Kentucky; Forth Worth, Texas). Harry Jacob Anslinger headed the Narcotics Bureau from 1930–1962, fighting the producing, selling, and using of drugs around the world.

Narcotics are taken to create a sort of timeless forgetfulness; the pleasure is short lived and the long-run results are destruction. There are two classes of narcotics: the opium family (sedatives) and cocaine and marihuana (stimulants). A person who turns to the dream world produced by an opiate becomes dependent on the drug even to feel normal and must steadily increase his intake for satisfaction. When his needs are not satisfied by the opiate, narcotics withdrawal results. He has nausea, sweats, is chilled, has diarrhea and goes from physical pain to death. Cocaine and marihuana produce a state similar to heavy alcoholic intoxication. Today a third type of drug (LSD-25) has joined the black market ranks. It may result in suicide or psychotic reactions. This drug has been successfully used in treating mental illnesses, but it should be administered by a doctor (Chapter VII).

Under the League of Nations procedure after World War I the international drug conventions of 1925 and 1931 were drawn up. All nations were given set quotas of drug imports and exports under a system of licensing. Nevertheless, illicit trade goes on in these drugs and persons who seek escape from reality (generally because of defective personalities) turn to them, particularly to morphine.

It is probable that narcotics addicts who have survived the withdrawal period may feel the physical effects of narcotics long afterward. This may account for the fact that many so-called "cured" patients tend to revert to addiction. One of the most deplorable results of narcotics addiction is to be found in the "withdrawal babies" who have become addicts in their mothers' wombs. These babies writhe painfully, are intensely irritable, have lost appetites, and develop nausea. These are all symptoms found in the adult addict. When the babies are born their supply of heroin (morphine) is cut off and they go into withdrawal. Before doctors were aware of the cause of the illnesses of these babies, ninety per cent of the children died in states of convulsion. Chlorpromazine (trade name Thorazine), a tranquilizer (Chapter VII), is today used for a period of several months to get the babies through the withdrawal period. Although adults usually get through the withdrawal period in a few days, it has been found that the babies revert to withdrawal symptoms if the tranquilizer is discontinued in less than three months. A question as yet unanswered is "Does addiction in the womb make a child more vulnerable to the habit when he grows up?"[20]

The Effects of Caffeine — The writer once turned over her coffee cup when the waitress came around with the coffeepot at a formal dinner. A medical doctor sitting to her right said, "Aren't you having coffee?" "No, it keeps me awake," she replied. "If you had had ten or twelve cups as I have had today, it would come nearer to putting you to sleep." Caffeine does act as a stimulant when used in small quantities (one to three grains); used excessively it acts as a depressant (four to six grains).

The coffee break is an American institution and the uplift of a cup of coffee is sought by millions every day. The long-run effect of moderate use of coffee is probably negligible.

The Effects of Alcohol — Alcoholism frequently develops as a means of solving problems of adjustment. It is reverted to by persons whose "unconscious struggles are particularly painful."[21] Characteristically, alcoholics are immature persons who turn to liquor to satisfy an inadequacy. Alcoholic wives may be compensating for their inability to compete with strong successful husbands. Alcoholic husbands may have given way to weaknesses in preference to continued competition in the world of men; they may choose to be dependent on strong wives.

Mark Keller, managing editor of the *Quarterly Journal of Studies on Alcohol* and editor of the Publications Division of the Yale Center of Alcohol Studies defines alcoholism as:

> . . . a chronic behavioral disorder manifested by repeated drinking of alcoholic beverages in excess of the dietary and social uses of

the community and to an extent that interferes with the drinker's health or his social or economic functioning.[22]

There are approximately five million alcoholics in the United States, making alcoholism this country's most serious social problem today. Approximately 70,000,000 other Americans drink alcohol to a lesser degree.

Dr. Roger J. Williams, University of Texas, believes that alcoholism may develop because a congenital need for certain foods is not satisfied by diet. Most experts on the subject believe, however, that alcohol is usually an escape from mental or emotional disability. The attitudes of social groups may also have a part in setting the stage for development of alcoholism. In groups where drinking is condoned, alcoholism rates are high. Dr. Albert D. Ullman of Tufts University thinks that if persons have guilt feelings about drinking that this may lead to alcoholism. Alcoholics have often been found to be "immature, fearful, tense, anxious and keyed-up emotionally" and to have strong feelings of sin and guilt.[23]

Dr. Seldon O. Bacon, director of the Yale Center of Alcohol Studies, has outlined the ways an alcoholic may behave:

1. He begins to drink more than others at the same affair.

2. He begins to drink more frequently than others in his group, using feeble excuses.

3. He shows more of the sort of behavior that is ordinarily forbidden but is tolerated at some social drinking functions. Moreover, he is likely to invent behavior-loosening license where none exists.

4. He begins to experience frequent "blackouts" of memory.

5. He ignores the group's ordinary drinking rules and over-rationalizes his own drinking.

6. He gulps drinks rapidly, especially at the beginning of a drinking session.

7. He begins to sneak extra drinks.

8. With increasing frequency, he drinks to the point of intoxication. He loses control over the amount he drinks — and when and where.

9. He begins a series of experiments into new patterns, such as switching from bourbon, say, to vodka, drinking only at home or only after 5 p.m. He may change his drinking locale, usually finding new companions among people of inferior status. He may become a "loner."

10. He avoids all discussion of alcoholism and produces alibis and lies when forced.

11. He may begin to drink in ways unheard of to non-alcoholics — for instance, to start the day with seven or eight drinks, go on

week-long binges; skip ice, glasses, chasers and mixers; resort to canned heat, vanilla extract, etc.

12. His character and behavior, even when sober, undergo changes, and he may become quarrelsome, dishonest, self-deceiving.

13. In the final stages, there are many manifestations, such as the compulsive hiding and storing of drinks against possible future hangovers. Unless treatment is obtained, premature death may end the struggle.[24]

Alcoholics Anonymous places as first of twelve steps in a recovery program for alcoholics the admission of the individual that he was powerless over alcohol. Medical treatment and psychotherapy are required in the recovery program. In the early stages of treatment, tranquilizers and sedation will have to be used to get the patient through withdrawal symptoms and possibly delirium tremens. He must be helped through a period of dehydration and his nutritional deficiencies must be corrected. He will have to have rest until emotional and physical equilibrium can be restored. It may be necessary to treat him for the various illnesses that develop because alcoholics do not eat: cirrhosis of the liver, pellagra, and gastritis. Alcoholics Anonymous is one of the agencies in the United States that can help an alcoholic through the period of rehabilitation. Its address is: P. O. Box 459, Grand Central Station, New York 17, N. Y. There are AA chapters in local communities. Also in a position to give information and help is The National Council on Alcoholism, 2 E. 103rd Street, New York 29, N. Y.

Books that give information on combating alcoholism are:

New Primer on Alcoholism by Marty Mann, Holt, Rinehart & Winston, 232 Madison Avenue, New York 16, N. Y., 1958. $2.95.

Alcoholics Anonymous, 2nd Edition, Alcoholics Anonymous World Services, P. O. Box 459, Grand Central Station, New York 17, N. Y., 1955. $4.50.

To Know the Difference by Dr. Albert Ullman, St. Martin's Press, 175 Fifth Ave., New York 10, N. Y., 1960. $4.75.

Popular magazines today keep the public informed upon the problem that exists with alcoholism; current ones point out the fact that many of the alcoholics are women who are sheltered in home situations. It is not known that these people are alcoholics; they do not seek help and it is not sought for them because of the fear of stigma attached to the disease.

Alcohol is actually a depressant although many think it to be a stimulant because it releases their inhibitions and they think and do things that without alcohol they would avoid. Numbers of studies have shown that alcohol (even after as few as two drinks) causes increased errors in work requiring close attention (typewriting, driving an automobile). Drivers under the influence of alcohol take chances they would not otherwise take. The results are often disastrous.

Doctors at John Hopkins University have devised a set of questions that if honestly answered give an indication as to whether a person is an alcoholic or not. These are the questions:

Do you require a drink the next morning?
Do you prefer to drink alone?
Do you lose time from work due to drinking?
Is your drinking harming your family in any way?
Do you crave a drink at a definite time daily?
Do you get the inner shakes unless you continue drinking?
Does drinking make you irritable?
Does drinking make you careless of your family's welfare?
Have you thought less of your wife or husband since drinking?
Has drinking changed your personality?
Does drinking cause you bodily complaints?
Does drinking make you restless?
Does drinking cause you to have difficulty in sleeping?
Has drinking made you impulsive?
Have you less self-control since drinking?
Has your ambition decreased since drinking?
Has your initiative decreased since drinking?
Do you lack perseverence in pursuing a goal since drinking?
Do you drink to obtain social ease?
Do you drink for self-encouragement?
Do you drink to relieve feelings of inadequacy?
Has your sexual potency suffered since drinking?
Do you show marked dislikes or hatreds since drinking?
Has your jealousy increased since drinking?
Do you show marked moodiness since drinking?
Has your efficiency decreased since drinking?
Has drinking made you more sensitive?
Are you harder to get along with since drinking?
Do you turn to an inferior environment since drinking?
Is drinking endangering your health?
Is drinking affecting your peace of mind?
Is drinking making your home life unhappy?
Is drinking jeopardizing your business — your job?
Is drinking clouding your reputation?
Is drinking disturbing the harmony of your life?

If you have answered even one of the above questions with a "yes" answer, this is a warning signal that you could be an alcoholic. If you have answered "yes" to any two of the questions it is possible that you are already alcoholically ill. If you have answered "yes" to three of the questions the doctors say that you are definitely alcoholic.

Any student who has ever had a hangover knows that his ability to think, to reason, and to solve difficult problems is hindered by a hangover. The more drastic the hangover, the more severe the hindrance.

The problem of alcoholism is being met in some companies by programs designed to aid alcoholics to recovery much in the manner used by Alcoholics Anonymous. These programs are concerned first with prevention of alcoholism and second with cure and rehabilitation of those who have permitted the disease to develop.

Statistics reported in one study showed that persons who drink moderately live longer than those who do not drink at all; heavy drinkers, however, die earlier than total abstainers.[25] Although the writer has never seen an explanation as to why the moderate drinker might live longer than the total abstainer, the following is offered: Could it be that the philosophy of life, the mental outlook of the person who can once in a while take a drink (because it is the thing to do at a given time with a given group), not become a slave to drink, feel no moral qualms about the occasional drink, and then go for weeks or even months without having another drink, makes the difference? Would this type of person not be more relaxed in all of life's ventures and adventures? Would he have need to resort to liquor to solve his problem? It is likely the balance in his life would free him from the tensions of the total abstainer and at the same time from the need for drowning in alcohol to forget his mental and emotional failures.

The Effects of Humor — Dr. Ewart E. Smith, a Matrix Corporation psychologist, working under a Pentagon study contract, has scientifically established that "wit, in any given group, will alleviate tension, raise morale, and make the group more efficient." It may be that the Air Force may eventually use the detection of a sense of humor in its screening process.

Probably many a tense situation has been alleviated to some extent at the front lines of the United States Armed Forces around the world by Bob Hope and others like him. These basically sad people have a desire to make people laugh that is compulsive. Not all persons can be a Fred Allen, a Jack Benny, or a Red Skelton. For any person, however, life is made more interesting and its strains and stresses are lessened by ability to see humor even in the darkest situations. If that person can in a quip, a pun, or a turn of a phrase lighten the loads of others, he will often be the best loved person in his work group. Further, the ability to laugh, and especially at one's self, indicates good mental health and outlook. One who has this ability will find less difficulty in adjusting to the problems and situations of life.

One writer has said that jokes or humorous occurrences have three possible outcomes: (1) If the humor does not first arouse and then dispell anxiety in the hearer, possibly because of deep-seated repressions or conflict centered around the subject of the humor, then there is no reaction but only indifference to the joke. (2) If the humor does arouse anxiety in the hearer but fails to dissipate it, the hearer will react by feeling disgust, shame, embarrassment, or horror. (3) If the humor arouses anxiety and succeeds in dispelling it at once, the hearer will laugh, or chuckle and feel sudden relaxation and well being. The cause of the person's tension is often so disguised in the humor that it is not disturbing. Since laughter indicates loss of self-control to many persons, they resist responding to humorous situations. Mental patients are generally indifferent to humor or disturbed by it.[26]

Sigmund Freud wrote extensively on wit, the comic, and humor. He believed that the strongest hindrance to the comic effect of humor was the release of painful emotions. The person who cannot defend himself against the pain aroused by the humor finds no comic effect in it. If humor can enable feelings of pleasure in spite of the pain aroused by it, it becomes possible to liberate the painful emotions and at the same time suppress them. To Freud "the pleasure of wit originates from an *economy of expenditure in inhibition,* of the comic from an *economy of expenditure in thought,* and of humor from an *economy of expenditure in feeling.*" Humor, to him, is closer to the comic than wit and results when sympathy, anger, pain, compassion, or other emotions are economized in favor of response to the humorous situation. It rests in the foreconscious; wit is a compromise between the unconscious and the foreconscious. One of Freud's classic examples of wit is found in "We enjoyed the *alcoholidays.*" Humor exhibited by the responses indicating naivete, Freud places between wit and comic humor, as, the story of the little girl who "heard her parents refer to a Jewish acquaintance as a Hebrew, and on later hearing the latter's wife referred to as Mrs. X, she corrected her mother, saying, 'No, that is not her name; if her husband is a Hebrew she is a Shebrew.' " The discovery in social relations of human beings of unintentional movements, shapes, action, and characteristics produces the comic situation or result.[27]

The Effect of Dreams — Dreaming is considered to be a low grade of mental activity. In fact, the dream process is very similar to thought processes of the very young, the very old, and the very drunk. In dreaming people can make their wishes come true. Practically every person does dream and dreams about twenty to twenty-five per cent of the time asleep. The only exceptions perhaps are the very young and the very drunk. Researchers at the University of Chicago and at the State University of New York Downstate Medical Center in Brooklyn have made many discoveries about dreaming. Not a great deal is as yet known, however, about the interpretation of dreams despite the fact that much of Freud's work was in this area. One recent discovery is that the movement of the eyes while a person is dreaming reveals the visual imagery of a dream. Further, in dreams people compress and elide time much as writers do in literary works. Generally, the several dreams one has during a given night of sleep are more likely to be related than not. The lightest phase of sleep seems to come about seventy minutes after falling asleep and it is during this first light phase (which lasts only about nine minutes) that the first dream occurs. There are two other light phases; the last is usually in the seventh hour of sleep and dreams occur during these two periods also. Dreams so grip the attention of the dreamers that they lie very still while dreaming, stopping all bodily movements except for eye movements which follow the dream much as eyes follow a play.[28]

An electroencephalograph machine (EEG) and small disk electrodes attached near the eyes and the scalp of a subject are used in tracing the paths of dreams. A buzzer and tape recorder are also used. When rapid eye movements appear on the graph, a buzzer sounds. The sleeper is awakened at the moment his body begins shifting (there is a period of waiting just prior to this to let the dreamer complete his dream) and asked to dictate his dream. It is hoped through further study of the nature of dreams and their effect upon individuals to find clues to the origin of the emotions, frustrations, and forces within man that bring about many of his illnesses, not only some of those illnesses that often appear while persons are asleep, possibly brought on by dreams, such as bronchial asthma, cardiac failure, ulcer crises, and nocturnal angina, but to find clues to the origin of other illnesses as well.[29]

Freud wrote extensively of the interpretation of dreams. Dreams could enable the psychoanalyst to find the problems of the unconscious, those emotional problems that lead to neuroses and psychoses and also affect the physical effectivenes of individuals.[30]

Since Freud's death in 1939, scientists have studied the brain not only from the psychological but from the physiological viewpoint. Through using the mechanical aids available today, the dream process can be studied more carefully than it could be with the tools available to Freud.

The Effect of Positive Mental Attitude on Physical Efficiency — Lin Yutang, modern Chinese philosopher, has said that the average human mind is "charming" rather than noble, although, admittedly, there are "noble" minds as well. The Albert Einsteins of the world, however, are few in number. The English, according to Yutang, think with their "healthy skin" while the Chinese think with their "profound intestines." [31] Perhaps this is only a way of saying that "we think with our bodies." The thoughts we have must certainly influence our bodies as well.

One of the most popular volumes of the last decade in the United States is Norman Vincent Peale's *The Power of Positive Thinking*. It tells you "How To Create Your Own Happiness," and "How To Have Constant Energy," and that "A Peaceful Mind Generates Power." It advises "When Vitality Sags, Try This Health Formula." His advice aids one in overcoming the harmful emotions, and it has meant much to millions of people. It probably has aided them to achieve better mental health and, in turn, greater physical efficiency.[32]

Hippocrates held that health is a state of universal harmony. The individual is constantly striving throughout life to adjust toward attainment of that state of harmony. Many of the physical illnesses are caused by stress, frustration, or deprivation (etiological agents); the technique of treatment is to strengthen the ego defenses (inoculation). For most physical illnesses caused by germ infections, injuries, poisons in the body, and so on, there are known treatments usually because the single variable causing the disease can be isolated. A serum can be developed; action can be taken to cut off the source of the germs; a broken limb can be set. For mental illnesses, however, the problem is much greater for the single variable often cannot be found. Many preventive measures can be taken. For some doctors the prevention of mental illness is merely a part of the over-all problem of prevention of illness. Early detection of cretinism and "hunger trauma" in babies, proper emphasis on nutrition during pregnancy, prohibiting the diseases that damage brain tissue, and so on may eliminate some of the mental illnesses due to organic reasons. Nevertheless, the main contribution to development of good mental health probably rests with the study and experimentation of those who strive to understand the mind and its powers over mental and physical health.[33]

In order for one to obtain mental efficiency he must be free from worry, anxiety, jealousy, obsessions, compulsions, phobias, prejudices, hostilities, and other deep-seated emotional disturbances. Good mental health is the key to ability to adjust to the problems, situations, and barriers of life. Good mental health is a preventative measure that wards off the stress and tension diseases. Good mental health can aid in overcoming the physical and organic disabilities and illnesses when they occur. It might be said that physical and mental efficiency and health can hardly be separated.

Conclusions — The body and mind of an individual work closely together and interact upon one another. A person is influenced by many factors other than inherited ones of physical make-up and intelligence. He is influenced also by environment (Chapter IX). The effects of certain things upon his personal efficiency, over most of which he has some control, have been discussed in this chapter. Factors affecting efficiency discussed here are: exercise, sleep, relaxation, food, nicotine, narcotics, caffeine, alcohol, humor, dreams, and positive mental attitude. The influence of these factors extends beyond physical efficiency to mental efficiency and personality for all behavior may be said to be conditioned by physical health. Physical and mental health in turn influence social responses and relationships.

PROJECTS

1. Write a short research paper on any one of the topics discussed in this chapter.

2. Debate the topic "Man Is His Own Worst Enemy."

3. Read a chapter from one of the following references used in this chapter and comment in a brief report on it: No. 26, No. 31, or No. 32.

ACKNOWLEDGMENTS AND REFERENCES

1 Eby, Frederick, and Arrowood, Charles Flinn, *The History and Philosophy of Education Ancient and Medieval,* Prentice-Hall, Inc., New York, 1940, pp. 354–357.
2 Thomas, Henry and Thomas, Dana Lee, *Living Biographies of Great Philosophers,* Garden City Publishing Co., Inc., Garden City, New York, 1941, p. 16. Or see the writings of Plato.
3 Husband, Richard Wellington, *Applied Psychology,* Harper & Brothers, Publishers, New York, 1949, p. 802.
4 ———, "Smokers Less Long-Lived; Heavy Drinkers Die Earlier," *Science News Letter,* March 12, 1938.
5 Smith, Harry L., and Hightower, Nicholas C., Jr., "Incidence of Functional Disease (Neurosis) Among Patients of Various Occupations," *Occupational Medicine,* February, 1948, pp. 182–185.
6 Gardiner, M. Dena, *The Principles of Exercise Therapy,* G. Bell and Sons, Ltd., London, 1957, pp. 256–260.
7 Husband, *op. cit.,* p. 805.
8 Edwards, A. S., "Effects of Loss of One Hundred Hours of Sleep," *American Journal of Psychology,* 1941, pp. 54, 80–91.
9 Newman, E. B., "Forgetting of Meaningful Material during Sleep and Waking," *American Journal of Psychology,* 1939, pp. 52, 65–71.
10 Jacobson, Edmund, *Progressive Relaxation,* The University of Chicago Press, Chicago, Illinois, 1938, pp. 1–431.
11 Sense, Eleanora, *Clinical Studies in Nutrition,* J. B. Lippincott Company, Philadelphia, 1960, pp. 202–213.
12 Cox, Claire, *The Upbeat Generation,* Prentice-Hall, Inc., Englewood Cliffs, N. J., 1962, pp. 83–85.

13 Hansen, Leroy, "How Do You Eat?," *Houston Chronicle*, February 19, 1961, p. 2, s. 10.
14 Miller, Lois Mattox, "Lung Cancer and Cigarettes — Here Are the Latest Findings," *The Reader's Digest*, June, 1962, pp. 45–46.
15 *Ibid.*, p. 46.
16 *Ibid.*, p. 49.
17 ———, "Low School Marks Linked to Smoking," *Corpus Christi Caller-Times*, December 26, 1960, p. 10, s. 1.
18 Pechstein, L. A., Reynolds, W. R., "The Effect of Tobacco Smoke on the Growth and Learning Behavior of the Albino Rat and Its Progeny," *Journal of Comparative Psychology*, Vol. 24, 1937, pp. 459–469.
19 ———, "How Smoking Affects Expectant Mothers," *Houston Chronicle*, July 16, 1962, p. 1, s. 1.
20 ———, "Warning on Every Pack," *Business Week*, No. 1817, June 27, 1964, p. 36.
   ———, "Medicine — Sins of the Mothers," *Newsweek*, May 7, 1962, p. 84.
21 Menninger, Karl A., *The Human Mind*, Third Edition, Alfred A. Knopf, New York, 1946, p. 148.
22 ———, "Alcoholism," *Changing Times, The Kiplinger Magazine*, July, 1960, p. 33.
23 *Ibid.*, p. 34.
24 *Ibid.*, p. 35.
25 Husband, *op. cit.*, p. 816.
26 Levine, Jacob, "Responses to Humor," *Scientific American*, February, 1956, pp. 31–35.
27 Freud, Sigmund, "Wit and Its Relation to the Unconscious," *The Basic Writings of Sigmund Freud* (translated and edited by Dr. A. A. Brill), the Modern Library, New York, 1938, pp. 633–803.
28 ———, "Almost Everybody Has Dreams on Every Night," *Life*, May 5, 1958, pp. 120–128.
29 ———, "The Science of Dreams," *Newsweek*, April 6, 1959, pp. 69–72.
30 Freud, Sigmund, "The Interpretation of Dreams," *op. cit.*, pp. 181–549.
31 Yutang, Lin, *The Importance of Living*, Reynal & Hitchcock, New York, 1937, p. 62.
32 Peale, Norman Vincent, *The Power of Positive Thinking*, Prentice-Hall, Inc., New York, pp. 1–276.
33 Jahoda, Marie, *Current Concepts of Positive Mental Health*, Basic Books, Inc., Publishers, New York, pp. 1–130.

CHAPTER **IV**

PERSONALITY DEVELOPMENT: MARITAL ADJUSTMENT: CHILDREN: OLD AGE

Personality — Although many definitions have been given of personality, personality is almost as difficult to define exactly as is intelligence. Most definitions emphasize the fact that personality is reflected by a person's behavior traits, and personality has been defined briefly as being "characteristic modes of behavior." The way one behaves is determined by interaction of such influences as intelligence, experience, and physical qualities of the individual, as well as outside factors and pressures of people, events, places, and circumstances. Yet the way a person acts in a given situation, the way he characteristically adjusts, or even the influence or effect the individual has upon other people may not tell the whole story of personality. A person's personality may appear to be quite different to different persons. Some personalities cannot stand the sort of split existence they may be forced by circumstances of life to live. Others are apparently strengthened by the multiple roles they play in life. The person who is the life of a crowd and welcomed by fellow workers in their formal and informal groups because of his sense of humor, may be in his own home situation a basically sad person carrying the effects of burdens of illnesses of those nearest to him or tragedies in his own past life. The comedian may show one picture to the world; to his own family and friends, he may be either the gentlest and/or the saddest of persons, or he might be dictatorial and/or harsh in dealing with family and friends.

When people solve their problems by facing them and using direct methods of solving them, they strengthen their personalities for solving future situations and barriers. If evasive and retreat methods are used, the personality is weakened for dealing with all future problems. It is for this reason that tendency to failure becomes habitual for some people. Only great insight and strong motivation can alter the pattern.

Laird and Laird have outlined and discussed the ten stages in personality development. These have been adapted as follows:

1. Stage of dependence.
2. Stage of comfort and eating.
3. Stage of impulsiveness . . . (The toddler who acts first and thinks later.)
4. Show-off stage.
5. Stage of low boiling point. (Period of sulking when denied something or told to do something — the three-year old.)
6. Stage of stubbornness.
7. Stage of inferiority and gullibility. (Early school years.)
8. Gang stage. (Develops around end of grade-school years.)
9. Interest in the opposite sex. (Develops during high school when the gangs start breaking up.)
10. Mature independence. (Begins late in high school, or right after entering college or work.)[1]

If one is still in the "gang stage" even after entering college or work, he has failed to develop maturity. Harry A. Overstreet has written one of the most read volumes of this century pertaining to "The Mature Mind." He presents several "clarifying ideas" before telling what we can do to attain the insight necessary for maturity of mind. These are (1) We must realize that *not all adults are adult* in spite of the fact that they may appear outwardly to be grown-up. (2) *If intense emotional conflicts are left unresolved from the early years of life (fixations, arrested development) they bring on severe emotional disturbances or uneasiness in later life.* (3) *Man's nature is alterable (conditioned response).* Pavlov's experiment of ringing a bell when the dog was fed to condition the dog so that he salivated when the bell was rung even though there was no meat, along with succeeding experiments, enabled the conclusion that men as well as animals can be conditioned to alter their nature. (4) *People are characterized by individual differences.* Mature people "affirm life," that is, they throw themselves into the process of living; mature persons seek to know themselves and to perfect the powers they possess. Man, according to Overstreet, becomes himself only through linkages with the "nonself": knowledge, responsibility, communication, mature sexuality, empathy, and philosophy. This is Overstreet's *linkage theory of maturity.* When man fails to relate and habitually makes immature efforts in solving his problems, his growth is arrested and immaturity results. In certain cultural conditions, however, the immature person may effect adjustment more easily than mature persons; he is not because of his adjustment, however, a "more genuinely fulfilled person." To attain maturity of mind, the individual should have "higher expectations about individual life." One should attempt the mature response in small matters first; mature persons can distinguish between the important and the trivial and give to each its proper attention. The individual can assist himself in developing maturity by associating with groups that are engaged in mature activities. Each person should have a program for enriching and developing his mental growth; the heritage from the past is more than adequate to fill many lifetimes of seeking after only that which has been already learned, recorded, and provided, without regard to any new contributions a particular individual might make.[2]

INTROVERSION-EXTROVERSION CONCEPTS OF JUNG — Dr. Carl Gustav Jung of Switzerland, an associate of Freud's and one of the three pioneers in psychology and psychiatry (Freud, Adler, Jung), classified personalities as being generally of two types: *introvert* and *extrovert*. The extrovert characteristically seeks the company of other persons; his attention is directed outwardly toward environment. The introvert turns his attention inward upon himself and his thoughts, actions, and plans. The introvert is generally secretive; the extrovert expresses himself to others, tells them of his loves and hates, his joys and sorrows.

The person who is fairly well balanced between introversion and extroversion is an *ambivert*. Research workers, office workers, accountants, clerks, stenographers, architects, artists, designers, writers, editors, and many college teachers (most, probably) tend to be introverts. It would probably be safe to say that most straight "A" students or top-ranking students also tend to be introverts. Salesmen, most managers, lawyers, politicians, and foremen are generally extroverts. Most people probably have some of the characteristics of both the introvert and extrovert.

Introversion is identified with the schizoid type of personality and with isolationists in general (Chapters V and VI). Extroversion is identified with the cycloid or moody type of personality. The schizoid type of personality in the extreme develops schizophrenia; the extreme of the cycloid type is manic-depressive psychosis. (These terms are defined in Chapter VI.)

Numbers of writers have made up lists of introvert and extrovert characteristics and devised scales for measuring degree of introversion and extroversion. It would probably be well for persons contemplating managing others to learn to distinguish between introversion and extroversion in order to better interpret the actions of men and to better motivate them. Table IV-1, which lists some of the characteristics of introverts and extroverts, was built from many sources and experience. You should keep in mind that few if any persons would have all the characteristics of either the extrovert or the introvert.

SUGGESTIONS FOR DEVELOPING AND/OR CHANGING THE PERSONALITY — People can change their personalities if they desire strongly enough

TABLE IV-1

SOME OF THE CHARACTERISTICS OF EXTROVERTS AND INTROVERTS

Extrovert Characteristics	*Introvert Characteristics*
Decisive	Indecisive
Diplomatic	Argues
Usually carefree	Worries; moody
Rarely blushes	Blushes; self-conscious
Laughs readily	Laughs infrequently
Ready talker; fluent; at ease	Less fluent; ill at ease before a crowd
Careful of feelings of others	Outspoken; may hurt feelings
Lends money and possesions	Rarely lends possessions
Not careful of personal property	Careful of possessions
Moves rapidly	Moves more slowly
Prefers to work with others	Prefers to work alone
Makes friends easily	Makes friends seldom; shy
Boastful	Talks little about self
Conforming	More likely to be radical
Less determined	Determined and persistent
Less conscientious about work, obligations, and details	More conscientious about exactness, work, details
Less deliberative	Very deliberative
Likes group activities	Interested in ideas and books
Better loser	Poorer loser
Tells troubles to others; seeks advice	Solves problems alone
Less meticulous of appearance	Very careful of appearance
Accepts orders readily	Resists being told to act
Takes correction more readily	Does not like to be corrected

to do so. The person who is extremely introverted should occasionally get outside of his shell and become aware of other people and their interests in life. A person can retreat so far from the world of reality that the situation becomes dangerous and the way back difficult. On the other hand, the extreme extrovert has problems, too, and would do well to try to attain a better balance. Most young people think that it is much better to be extroverted than to be introverted. The best course is probably the middle road, but for certain purposes one or the other of the extremes is or may be rewarding.

Harry W. Hepner has said that we deal in three ways with annoyances: (1) We let the annoyance build up until there is so much pressure inside it may lead to a breakdown. This Hepner calls *cumulative annoyance*. (2) When ones gives up and accepts the situation in a hopeless sort of manner, he is guilty of *negative adaptation*. (3) The person who uses the *insight-meaning* approach in solving the problem, analyzes the situation and tries to understand the other people involved, to understand himself, and to find a solution to the human relations elements of the problem by *first, becoming aware of the way people adjust; second, noting what appeals to other people and leading them to ideas and subjects in which they are interested; third, responding to others in animated fashion; fourth, asking questions that permit others to present their ideas and avoiding arguments in conversation; fifth, working at a job that he likes and that enables him to use his abilities most successfully.*[3]

In studying the lives of successful people one can select the traits that have helped those persons in attaining success. Sometimes success is measured in terms of financial wealth; sometimes it is measured in terms of achievement in a given area of endeavor without regard for any financial rewards that may or may not have accompanied the achievement. Sometimes it is measured in terms of happiness and contentment. Rockefeller, Picasso, Tagore — each of these achieved in his own way and each offered something to the world. One can observe others as they solve the problems of daily life. He can choose the traits that are admirable and reject those that appear unattractive. One can strengthen his own personality by facing problems as they arise and attempting to solve them by direct methods of attack. When one must admit defeat or failure, he should turn to a positive substitute course of action and avoid evasion, withdrawal, and such other negative adjustment mechanisms as are discussed in Chapter VI.

Mental and physical health enable a person to meet life's problems directly. Man is, however, an emotional being and when his emotional life is disrupted his mental health is impaired to the extent that happiness and personality are affected. Certain emotional responses are a drain on both mental and physical health. Main among these are: hatred, jealousy, rejection, inferiority, envy, and a desire for revenge. It is essential that we control our emotions to the extent that energies that might be expended in rage and passion are turned instead to creative efforts, to love, and understanding. Since all persons feel the negative emotions as well as the positive, the struggle to maintain emotional control goes on constantly. Properly controlled, emotions are sometimes an impetus to creative effort.

Often the people who have known the greatest unhappiness and pain have left great works for the world to enjoy: Wagner, Van Gogh,

Hawthorne, Byron are only a few of the many who might be mentioned here. Happiness and success are, therefore, relative terms. For the average man these words of advice from Thomas Jefferson in his *Notes on Virginia* may suggest a course of action for his own attainment of happiness:

> Our greatest happiness . . . does not depend on the condition of life in which chance has placed us, but is always the result of a good conscience, good health, occupation, and freedom in all just pursuits.

Marital Adjustment — It is generally believed that for women home-making and child rearing are most likely to bring happiness and satisfactory adjustment. Many women do, however, carry on the vocation of homemaking along with work done outside of the home. Most men, bachelors and invalids excluded, constantly carry on two vocations simultaneously: bread-winning and marriage.

Today in the United States those willing to try "living alone and liking it" are becoming fewer in number every year. Currently, all but one man in six and all but one woman in ten are married by the time they have reached the age of thirty. Further, they marry earlier today. At the end of the last century half of all men were married by age twenty-six and half of all women by age twenty-two; now the comparable figures are twenty-three and twenty respectively. It is estimated that about ninety-eight per cent of today's teenagers will get married sooner or later, most of them sooner. At the same time, the divorce rate is up, leading to the conservative estimate that about one out of every four of the current marriages will end in divorce.

Around 400,000 divorces are granted annually in the United States; in 1861 there were only 6,500 divorces and fifty years ago there were 89,000.[4] The Public Health Service of the United States Department of Health, Education, and Welfare figures show 1,527,000 marriages for 1960 with divorces for 1959 being 395,000.[5]

Marriage is a situation in which there is continuous adjustment. When problems arise in marriage, one cannot run off and leave them or simply ignore them; it is necessary to recognize their existence and work toward their solution. Other interests constantly interfere with marriage, and a great deal of understanding is needed by each partner to live through these periods when the other interests crowd out affection, love, and marital demands.

Half a century ago women and children were valuable assets in terms of their ability to help produce on the farm and in the home, to cook, to can, to spin, to quilt, to sew, to clean, to raise chickens, and do the laundry. Today industrial products, prepared and processed foods, have eliminated the need for home production lines. Further, as far as the children are concerned, it costs around $30,000 to rear one child and send him to college. It often is more important for the wife to bring in a salary for work outside the home than it is for her to stay in the home, caring for children when the need is there or turning her efforts to community and social activities if it is not. The man of the house probably surrendered some of his other rights when he surrendered to his wife the right to aid in supporting the family. Drs. Leo W. Simmons (sociology) and Harold G. Wolff (medicine) have proposed that the high incidence of peptic ulcer in men (three times as many as for women) may have been perpetrated by man's new role in the home.

Perhaps too many people enter marriage with the belief that "Now all of my problems of life are solved; I can relax and be happy forevermore." After all, the story-book ending always has been, "And they were married and lived happily ever after." It is said today that we have the "disenchantment syndrome" among the maladies, especially do we have it among women and the upper-middle-class women in particular. This is partially due to the fact that life is too easy for them, but more perhaps to the fact that life does not deliver what the woman has been taught to expect. The job does not open up promised vistas, and then when she succumbs to orange blossoms the story-book ending eludes her. Happiness is somewhat like fame; when we pursue it too assiduously it escapes us and lights perhaps upon the shoulder of one not struggling to find it. Too often man's baser emotions lead him to seek the passing pleasures that in the long run lead to loss of happiness. Spinoza said, "To learn how to become master of one's emotions, to learn how to free oneself from their bondage, is, therefore, the primary condition of sustained and rational happiness." [6] Spinoza also said:

> . . . Again, the more the mind delights in this divine love or blessedness, the more it understands, that is to say, the greater is the power it has over its emotions and the less it suffers from emotions which are evil. Therefore, it is because the mind delights in this divine love or blessedness that it possesses the power of restraining the lusts; and because the power of man to restrain the emotions is in the intellect alone, no one, therefore, delights in blessedness because he has restrained his emotions, but, on the contrary, the power of restraining his lusts springs from blessedness itself. [7]

People must constantly adjust in life, the married ones as well as the single ones. Some married persons find deep and abiding happiness in the process of adjusting; some merely adjust to the extent that the world believes they have been successful, and they are successful in the sense that their marriages persist and their children are given the care of both parents; some fail to adjust as evidenced by the divorce rate, but many others fail to adjust in the sense that they hurt the personalities of themselves and their children.

Some writers have said that the worst time in the world for a person to marry is when he is deeply and romantically in love. The reason is probably obvious: when a person lets his emotions dominate, he forgets reason. Compatibility, age, education, environmental background, and all of the factors that are believed to be so important are forgotten when the emotions are dominating. Nevertheless, marriage without love and affection could prove to be the proverbial "hell."

One of the main criticisms of today's young people is that they frequently are trapped into early marriage by "steady dating." The advice that is being meted out by the "specialists" is "Date early, in group situations and activities; date numbers of persons, i.e., don't start early with steady dating; marry late."

STUDIES OF MARITAL FAILURES AND SUCCESSES AND CAUSES OF SAME — Numerous studies of marital success have been made. One of the first of these was made by L. M. Terman of Stanford University. Terman studied 792 couples in California during the middle 1930's. The reader is referred to *Terman's Psychological Factors in Marital Happiness* for his findings and the scale of happiness which he developed. Some of Terman's conclusions that have been confirmed by other researchers are: Longer engagements are more likely to result in good marital adjustment. His study actually showed that engagements of five years or over resulted in the greatest chance for happiness. Very close to the extremely long engagements in producing happiness, however, were engagements of one to two years and those of three to four years duration. For wives the highest happiness scores were for those who married above the age of thirty-one; for men, those who married above the age of thirty-five. There is not great difference in scores for marriages at other ages, however. Nevertheless, the lowest scores for both men and women were for those who married in the case of husbands under twenty-two years of age and for the wives under twenty years of age. Other studies have had similar results. When husband and wife have interests in common and similar backgrounds, there is greater chance for success in marriage. Happily married persons more often came from happy homes where parents were themselves happily married. When both partners in marriage were the only children of their parents the happiness scores fell ten points below the mean, but when only one partner was an only child the happiness scores were only half a point lower. Partners who had no instruction in sex prior to marriage had lower happiness scores. Income did not affect happiness scores, but the way money was managed did affect them. Children or the absence of them apparently did not affect the happiness scores. Other studies have shown, however, that children tend to keep the marriage together regardless of whether it is happy or not. Wives tended to be unhappy if their husbands were possessed of less education or mental ability than they were. Whether one had had few or many dates before marriage did not affect happiness scores. Partners whose sexual desires were about equal had higher happiness scores than those whose desires were unmatched. There was correlation between happiness and frequency of intercourse — this would not mean that a cause and effect relationship brought this about. Persons who had not experienced sex before marriage were happier than those who had.[8]

Burgess and Cottrell published the results of their study of 526 marriages in 1939. They found the poorest chance for marital happiness came for men who married under the age of twenty-two and women who married under nineteen; the most excellent chance for happiness in marriage came for men who married between the ages of twenty-eight and thirty; for women, those who married at age twenty-eight and over. Some of their other findings were:

1. American wives make the major adjustment in marriage.

2. The choice of a life partner is likely to be conditioned by the son's relationship with the mother and the daughter's relationship with the father.

3. Social adjustment of the person has a bearing upon his marital adjustment.

4. The economic factor is not significant for marital adjustment since other factors, such as cultural background, psychogenetic characteristics, social type, and response patterns, account for the economic factor. Similarity of cultural background is more important than similarity of economic background.

5. For most persons, the psychological factors (attitudes toward sex, preparation for marriage) create more problems in sexual adjustment than do biological factors.

6. Statistical and case-study methods may be used to predict marital adjustment.

7. The largest per cent of good marital adjustments was found in cases where wives were older than husbands (53.6); the second largest percentage was in cases where husbands were eight or more years older than wives (51.1). Each of these percentages was on a

limited number of cases, however. Further, the least percentage of poor adjustments was found where the partners were the same age (13.1); where husbands and wives were the same age the percentage of good adjustments was high (47.8); where the husband was one to three years older, the percentage of good adjustments was high also (47.6); where he was four to seven years older, the percentage of good adjustments dropped (38.2). The largest percentage of poor marital adjustments (35.4) also occurred when the husband was four to seven years older than the wife.

8. The husband's health is more important than the health of the wife in marital adjustment.[9]

A study published in 1948 by Landis and Landis revealed approximately fifty per cent of the marriages where the education of the two partners was the same were very happy. When the husband had four or more years more education than the wife the per cent of happy marriages for the wives was about forty-five per cent, but for the husbands was around thirty-seven per cent. When the wives had four or more years more education than the husbands, about forty-two per cent of the marriages were happy for the wives. For the husbands, however, contrary to what is popularly believed, the percentage of husbands very happily married under this condition was around fifty-eight per cent. The Landis study showed the highest percentage of happily married husbands (53 approximately) to be when the wives were three or more years older than the husbands. When there was excellent religious agreement between husband and wife, it was found that sixty-five per cent of the marriages were very happy; forty-five per cent were happily married if there was good religious agreement; only thirty-three per cent were happily married where religious agreement was fair or poor. The largest percentage of divorces (20.6) occurred when there was a Catholic father and Protestant mother. The next highest percentage was when neither partner had religious affiliation (17.9). When both partners were Catholic the percentage of divorces was very low (4.4); both Jewish (5.2); both Protestant (6.0).[10]

Hart and Shields, studying 500 marriages and using divorce as the criterion of marital failure, found the best ages for marrying were twenty-nine for men and twenty-four for women. The poorest chances for happy marriages were found to be if men entered marriage before age twenty-four and if women entered it before age twenty-one.[11]

Most studies of marital happiness have had similar findings. They tend to show that the reasons for happiness or the lack of it in marriage are dependent not upon the external factors, such as money, possessions, friends, and relatives, but are faults of the mate that are annoying; many of these faults indicate unhappiness or emotional instability in the partner with whom the fault is being found.

It is estimated that around fifteen million Americans have been divorced. Divorced persons, however, hasten to remarry. Data show that 82 out of 100 of the single men probably will marry; 95 out of 100 widowers will do so; 99 out of 100 divorced men remarry. Out of 100 single women, 70 will marry; out of 100 widows, 81 will remarry; 98 out of 100 divorced women remarry.[12]

Divorces and separations are caused by many reasons; some of the reasons have been implied in the findings of studies cited above. Often the difficulties have grown out of trivial happenings. More severe cases include: alcohol, adultery, lack of responsibility, and incompatibility. Sometimes divorce occurs when the children are grown and a man and woman left alone find that they had had nothing in common for all those years except the children. Too often, perhaps, a mate enters marriage expecting to "reform" the partner; if any reforming is necessary for a compatible marriage, it should be done before and not after the event has taken place. Sometimes the divorces of later years occur when one or the other of the partners grasps at the straws of a lost and fading youth, and instead of recapturing youth he or she merely loses a partner. All marriages must be considered to be in some ways imperfect. All partners must accept the defects along with the assets of their partners and their marriages. There will be disagreement. As the wife of Evangelist Billy Graham so aptly said, "When two people agree on everything, one of them is unnecessary."

CONSIDERATIONS IN THE SELECTION OF A MATE — An attractive middle-aged woman was once asked, "Why didn't you marry?" Her reply was, "Never the time and the place and the man altogether." Many persons probably marry because it is the thing to do; their friends are married. It is the time and the place and they decide that they are ready. The available partner, regardless of qualifications, is the one who is there to be taken to the altar. Marriage and vocation are the two areas to which people devote most of their lives. Most men spend their entire lives working toward success in these two areas; most women spend a lifetime working toward success in marriage and homemaking. They may also work outside the home, but for their marriages to be successful they must usually put marriage first. Therefore, some consideration should be given the factors that make for happy marriages. Some of the marriages being made today are based entirely on selections of partners through electronic brains. Dr. Eric Riss operates a Scientific Introduction Service in New York City that uses coded information on IBM cards to select persons who have interests, backgrounds, attitudes, and motives in common. A popular television program has used the electronic brain to introduce persons who apparently have the qualifications for succeeding at marriage together. They may then marry or not as they decide upon acquaintance with each other. Many counseling services are available today to advise couples before and after marriage. The best advice that can be given, however, is: Refrain from marrying until you have known the proposed partner long enough to know that you are compatible. Jealousy, flirtatiousness, over-dependability on parents, insecurity, neurotic tendencies, and other evidences of immaturity should warn one of the pitfalls ahead.

Family Life — Children — Chapter IX presents "home life" as one of the important factors considered in counseling. Home and family life are, in fact, probably the most important factors in determining the adjustment patterns of individuals. Among the relationships that exist in the home and have positive influence are: affection toward the child, accepting him as a member of the family and making him feel wanted; giving opportunity in the home for growth and development, encouraging hobbies and interests; mutual affection of the mother and father and opportunity for the children to admire and emulate their parents. When sons identify themselves with their fathers and daughters with the mothers, the outcome is generally good provided the parents have admirable qualities. Among the most negative of home influences are the effects of parental rejection, overindulgence, and overprotection. Numbers of studies have shown that a rejected child is more likely than any other to have deep emotional problems that lead to serious difficulties in adjusting. He may develop withdrawal, delinquency, and over-aggressiveness; in adulthood the *anxiety syndrome* form of neurosis may result.

Only children frequently have problems that those with brothers and sisters do not have. They may be spoiled and sometimes lonely, but they do usually have the security of parental love and attention. When a new baby comes into the family *sibling jealousy* often develops. This jealousy may be revealed by attacks on the body of the new baby (scratching, hitting, pinching, pushing), refusing to admit that the baby exists, ignoring the baby, or by personality changes on the part of the older child. Sewall found that of thirty-nine children jealous of their younger siblings, twenty-six showed their jealousy of these younger brothers or sisters by bodily attacks on them. He found also that two-thirds of those with age differences between eighteen and forty-two months were jealous; only a third of those whose age differences were more than forty-two months or less than eighteen months were jealous. Where mothers were oversolicitous of their children, four-fifths of the children were jealous; likewise, four-fifths of those subjected to inconsistent means of discipline were jealous. Only a tenth of the children in homes considered well adjusted were jealous, but sixty-three per cent of those in the poorly adjusted homes were jealous.[13] Sibling rivalry probably continues into adulthood in varying degrees.

Children who are expected to assume a part of the responsibility of home and family life (this means that they have work responsibilities and duties as well as social ones), who accept the authority of the parents, who develop interests and the desire to achieve goals, provided they do have parental guidance, acceptance, and love, are more likely to achieve satisfactory adjustment than those who lack these elements in home and family life.

Child psychology is a whole area of study in itself and cannot be dealt with at all adequately here. It does aid one in gaining insight into his own behavior if he knows the more important influences that are carried over from childhood to adulthood. One can better understand others, too, if he knows something of their early history; counselors and managers frequently must delve into childhood experiences to understand adult actions. The first few years in life are all important in their influence on the personality of the individual throughout the rest of his life.

Old Age — In an era when people live longer than ever before [estimated average length of life in the United States in 1960 for all races, both sexes: 69.7 years; males: 66.6; females: 73.1 years; life expectancy of 1961 babies under one year of age: all, 70.2 years; white males, 67.8 years; white females, 74.5 years; nonwhite males, 61.9; nonwhite females, 67.0][14] many must cope with the problem of aging parents in their homes. It is estimated that three-fourths of the aged persons reside with relatives. Industry must also frequently deal on a large scale with the many retired persons who seek part-time and menial work to supplement social security and retirement incomes. There are many hospitals, homes, and clubs for the aged.

Amalgamated Clothing Workers of America and the Philadelphia Clothing Manufacturers' Association have provided the Charles Weinstein Geriatric Center in Philadelphia for retired clothing workers and their spouses. These retired workers may pursue hobbies of their choice: play cards, chess, dominoes, pinochle, and other games; paint; garden; take lessons in pottery making and dozens of other things. The $300,000 clubhouse has workrooms, patio, garden, greenhouse, stage and auditorium, kitchen, library, and piped-in music. The center operates under the management of a board composed of thirteen union representatives and thirteen manufacturers' representatives.[15]

Many retired persons make new lives for themselves, utilizing in the process interesting hobbies that they have pursued as sidelines before retirement. Dr. Michael M. Dasco has suggested that in planning for retirement the manual workers should start learning why intellectuals think cultural matters are so important; intellectuals should learn that working with the hands brings pleasure. It is necessary, also, for the aged to become independent emotionally and in caring for themselves.[16]

"Old age" is another of the relative terms that is difficult to define. Some people are old at fifty; others are still young at eighty. It is believed that retirement frequently hastens the infirmities of old age for the majority of people. Those who can adapt because they have other interests and continue in a different or similar kind of work even after retirement from regular occupations, are an exception. Having to meet a work schedule makes people feel needed; when one no longer feels needed deterioration usually sets in.

It has been estimated that by 1970 the number of persons in the "over sixty-five group" will be approximately 22,000,000. The percentage of the total population that was sixty-five years of age in 1900 was around four per cent; the projected percentage for 1970 is around nine per cent.[17] The talents of many of these persons are being lost to the country as they do not seek employment after being retired at ages ranging from sixty-five to seventy in most cases. The United States government permits retirement with full benefits at age sixty-two if the employee has served the government for thirty years. Some states permit retirement at sixty with full benefits if the employee has served thirty years.

Many business firms are employing on a consultative or part-time basis the skilled technical people who are being retired from their regular occupations. Some of these persons have joined the faculties of small private and church educational institutions. In fact, a large number of military persons have completed higher degrees and obtained teaching positions after their military retirement. These people are not only rendering a service to their nation, they are probably prolonging their lives.

Many persons erroneously think that older people cannot learn. It is untrue, however, that "you cannot teach an old dog new tricks." Studies have shown that persons probably do make the highest intelligence test scores between the ages of twenty and thirty years and that there is a decrease after that. The decrease is not great, however, until after sixty years of age. Not all aspects of intelligence decline in later years. Scores on items not requiring speed in answering, such as vocabulary and information test questions, decrease little if any in later years (sixty-seventy). Vocabulary scores do start dropping after age seventy.

It has also been demonstrated that persons over sixty matched against younger people of equal occupational and educational status can grasp the meaning of standard test paragraphs as well as the younger persons and even excel them in the vocabulary tests. Studies have shown varying degrees of loss of motor skill with age; further, there is some memory loss for recalling simple repetitions that do not have meaning, and even greater memory loss in cases where it is necessary for reorganization of existing patterns of thinking to take place. Aging persons cannot perceive as well as they did in younger years; nor do they utilize the senses of hearing, tasting, and touching as well.

Although many of the world's most creative persons achieved their greatest accomplishments in later years, generally speaking the average person loses some of his creative powers with the onslaughts of age. Further, the majority of the world's great creative productions have been given to the world by the creators on the average before they were fifty years of age. [It must be pointed out, however, that "average" here is misleading. Thorndike's study showed the average age of consumation of achievement to be 47.4 years. This could mean that there were as many who accomplished after this average age as before it.] Women lose much of their drive during and after the menopause period of the late forties. The degree to which they succumb to the usual feelings of depression that accompany this period of life is dependent upon their ability to adjust as exhibited throughout their lives. Men, also, have a climacteric period but it comes later in life (sixties or after).[18]

We should remember that we do not have to stop living just because we reach a certain age. Many persons have remained actively engaged in vocational pursuits until death overtook them in late years. Senator Sam Rayburn, in his eighties, was still serving his country at the time of his death; Senator Theodore Francis Green was still running for Congress after he reached ninety. Dr. Oliver Wendell Holmes did not retire from the Supreme Court of the United States until he was ninety-two.

One of the big problems in public health is that of providing for medical care for the aged. The persons in the over sixty-five group require as much as three times as much medical care as the persons in the sixteen to sixty-four group. Without state or federal aid, even with retirement benefits and social security, many of the older persons cannot obtain the medical attention needed. This has posed a problem that in recent years has been widely debated with certain leaders demanding socialized medicine for the aged while other groups and leaders, and particularly medical personnel, have violently opposed this. Medicine itself has made great strides in the knowledge of how to care for older persons and help them in maintaining and prolonging physical and mental health. For instance, in one area alone, chlorpromazine, one of the tranquilizers (Chapter VII) is used to combat the ravaging effects of hardening of the arteries. Formerly, when this insidious disease attacked at a galloping pace, negative effects (suspicion, distrust, hallucination, forgetfulness, dizziness) set in at once. These progressed, usually in three to five years, to a stage of practical invalidism. Often the suspicion was directed at a member of the family, and the older person sometimes became dangerous in that he threatened this member of the family, occasionally carrying out the threats. With the use of chlorpromazine, however, the hardening of the arteries is arrested, the suspicions are abated, adjustment is made, and the older person can carry on routine activities of life. Forgetfulness is not abated, however, by the medication. On the contrary, it is generally accentuated. Nevertheless, these people can be useful in many ways.

Business and industry today are providing more of the goods and services desired and needed by older people, just as they are having to provide more for those in younger age brackets. The only age group not increasing greatly percentage-wise in the decade 1956–1966 is the twenty-five to forty-one year-old group which will decrease during this period by a small percentage. Those ten to fifteen years of age will increase during this period over fifty-five per cent, and those over sixty-five will increase by twenty-five per cent or more. Manufacturers base their budgets of the future on population and other data. They plan products on the knowledge of what will be demanded by age groups. Many of the products they are providing today aid the aged to adjust in the change from vocations to avocations and leisure time. Hair coloring, drugs, open-end insurance policies, hearing-aids, compact automobiles, cruises, mobile homes and life-leasing, are some of the "old-age" products in addition to food and clothing.[19]

Not only are goods and services being provided for the aged, much advice is being meted out to them. The Institute of Directors (London) has advised managers fifty years of age and over how to grow old gracefully (presumably American managers could also benefit from this advice). Managers are warned that eyesight, hearing, short-term memory, physical and mental stamina are less acute than in their younger years, and that their tendency to live in the past leads them to reject new persons, situations, and ideas. They are told also, however, that with the proper drive they can overcome the limitations of aging by proper mental attitude, and that, further, they generally tend to overestimate the encumbrances of aging anyway, although they must admit the strains of aging and not be ashamed of taking a nap after lunch. In the long run, their judgment, developed through long experience, more than compensates for the limitations of aging, and older people can learn new things, too, if they have reasonable freedom from petty distractions. Some of the suggestions the Institute offers to older executives are:

1. Learn to slow your work pace — don't try to keep on top of every detail nor a 'jump ahead' of everyone in the office.
2. Have a sanctuary — put yourself in quiet surroundings, away from the rushing office routine.
3. Guard against wishing for the 'good old days' — they may

not have been so good. Reserve judgment before rejecting a new proposal. Sift it.

4. Enrich life with broad interests and activities outside of the job.

5. Delegate responsibility. Define the task and let others do the rest. The non-delegator swamps himself with detail . . . and incurs ill feeling as well.

6. Avoid the frustration of worry about yourself, your status, or the threat of waning influence.

7. Take at least two holidays a year; a well-balanced routine of life prepares one to face retirement without dread.[20]

Conclusions — Throughout life man finds that he must continuously adjust to the problems that confront him. First, he must adjust during childhood to brothers, sisters, parents, playmates, and the various social events provided by his environment. There follows adjustment to school; later, perhaps, to college or university life. There is adjustment to a job. There is adjustment in courtship and marriage; adjustment when the new baby arrives. Frequently, the child drives a wedge between mother and father. Sometimes, mother and father form an alliance and the child is left out; sometimes, mother and child ally to exclude father; sometimes, father and child exclude the mother. With the advent of more children, life is so full of problems that before people know it they have reached the status of middle age. They look around at their lives and wonder what they have accomplished. The children have finished college and married. The parents must find new interests either together or apart. Finally, there is the period of retirement. A husband at home sometimes seems to the wife to always be getting under foot. If the husband does not find other activities and interests (provided he did not already have them), he is likely to become disgruntled, to think too much about the situation, to develop the ailments of age. Attitudes of one partner usually influence the other. Not always, of course, do the two survive to this stage. How well people meet the problems of the various stages of life (of which Shakespeare said in *As You Like It* that there were seven) will depend upon how well they prepare themselves in advance, which in turn depends upon their own development in terms of heredity and environment, and the mental and physical health they have maintained in spite of or because of these two factors.

PROJECTS

1. Analyze yourself to determine whether you are an introvert, an extrovert, or an ambivert.

2. Check Terman's list of things most and least serious for happiness in marriage (Terman, Lewis M., *Psychological Factors in Marital Happiness*, McGraw-Hill Book Company, Inc., 1938, p. 101ff). Were there any surprising elements in these lists?

3. Debate the question: "It Is the Responsibility of the Federal Government To Provide Medical Care for the Aged."

4. Read the first and last chapters of the following book and write a short summary of these two chapters: Overstreet, H. A., *The Mature Mind*, W. W. Norton & Company, Inc., New York, 1949.

5. Compare Shakespeare's "Seven Ages of Man" with Laird and Laird's ten stages in personality development.

ACKNOWLEDGMENTS AND REFERENCES

1 Laird, Donald A., and Laird, Eleanor, *Practical Business, Psychology*, Gregg Publishing Division, McGraw-Hill Book Company, Inc., New York, 1961, pp. 299–303.

2 Overstreet, H. A., *The Mature Mind*, W. W. Norton & Company, Inc., New York, 1949, pp. 1–292.

3 Hepner, Harry Walker, *Psychology Applied to Life and Work*, Prentice-Hall, Inc., Englewood Cliffs, New Jersey, 1957, pp. 174–177.

4 Havemann, Ernest, "Love and Marriage, Amid Profound Change and Personal Crisis," *Life*, September 8, 1961, pp. 99–119.

5 Hansen, Harry (editor), *The World Almanac*, New York World-Telegram and The Sun, New York, 1962, p. 302.

6 Spinoza, Baruch de, *The Philosophy of Spinoza*, edited by Joseph Ratner, Books, Inc., Publishers, New York, p. 34.

7 *Ibid.*, pp. 238–239.

8 Terman, L. M., *Psychological Factors in Marital Happiness*, McGraw-Hill Book Co., New York, 1938.

9 Burgess, Ernest W., and Cottrell, Leonard S., Jr., *Predicting Success or Failure in Marriage*, Prentice-Hall, Inc., New York, 1939, pp. 118, 349, 406.

10 Landis, Judson T., and Landis, Mary G., *Building a Successful Marriage*, Prentice-Hall, Inc., New York, pp. 140, 157, 160, 306.

11 ———, "Early Marriage and Happiness," *Journal of Social Hygiene*, Vol. 12, 1926, pp. 554–559.

12 Havemann, Ernest, "Love and Marriage, The Shadow of Divorce," *Life*, September 22, 1961, pp. 109–130.

13 Sewall, M., "Some Causes of Jealousy in Young Children," Part I of *Two Studies in Sibling Rivalry*, Smith College Studies in Social Work, Vol. 1, 1930, pp. 6–22.

14 Hansen, Harry (editor), *The World Almanac*, New York World-Telegram and The Sun, New York, 1964, p. 310.

15 ———, "Clubhouse Keeps Retirees Lively, Healthy," *Business Week*, October 8, 1960, pp. 114–116.

16 Dasco, Michael M., "Practical Ways To Be Old and Happy," Part III, Old Age, *Life*, July 27, 1959, pp. 76–90.

17 ———, "Old Age Gets Into Politics," *Business Week*, February 13, 1960, pp. 62–70.

18 Berrien, F. K., *Practical Psychology*, Revised Edition, The Macmillan Company, New York, 1952, pp. 117–131.

19 ———, "Marketing — How the Old Age Market Looks," *Business Week*, February 13, 1960, pp. 72–77.

20 ———, "Personal Business," *Business Week*, March 26, 1960, pp. 159–160.

SECTION III — MENTAL HYGIENE A TOOL OF INDUSTRY

CHAPTER V

MENTAL HYGIENE, ITS ORIGIN AND TECHNIQUES

Mental Hygiene, Tool of Business and Industry — Once the human material of business and industry was governed with a "take it or leave it," policy. Later "scientific methods" were used. Today it is recognized that mental hygiene can add to the numerous scientific methods of business and industry. Some of the contributions that can be made by mental hygiene are: (1) It offers understanding of people's emotional needs, their frustrations and attitudes. (2) It takes the point of view that satisfaction develops in positive environments. (3) It can be of aid in dealing with "cases of abnormal behavior." (4) Through consultation, either by a staff expert or by consultation groups from outside, management itself can be brought to harmony and put in better position to give leadership.[1]

Why Do Men Work? — Most personnel men and those who have done research in motivation say that workers want certain things above monetary rewards. One thing placed high by workers is "recognition as an individual who is accomplishing something worthwhile." Dr. Douglas McGregor has said that "All behavior of any kind is directed toward the individual's satisfaction of his needs." [2] Most people, of course, are not averse to having monetary rewards made as a means of recognizing their worthwhileness. The psychological and social factors may be placed above money, but "money is still highly important in terms of what employees do." [3]

Morale studies have indicated that employees, although quite interested in monetary rewards, cast their votes for:

1. Praise when merited.
2. Opportunities to make suggestions and express grievances.
3. Knowing how they stand with the boss.
4. Assurance that promotions go to those best qualified.
5. Being told about plans and changes.
6. Leadership.[4]

People want to be more than dots on organization charts. While job security and wages are important to them, they want even more to feel that the work they do is appreciated; they want to feel that they have a part in things. They also want help on personal problems. But perhaps more than anything they want to ". . . have a hand in saving themselves; they cannot and will not be saved from the outside." [5] Writers have given a great deal of space to the methods of preparing workers for change: (1) *accommodation*, which is accommodating them to the idea of change by telling all details of proposed changes long before the changes are made, i.e., gradually accustoming them to the fact that the change will take place; and (2) *participation*, which is letting them have a part in making decisions that will bring about changes by which they will be affected. Letting the group make decisions and/or accommodating it to the idea of change may lead the group to want to work. Conflicts may arise in the course of the "group decision" process; these may be more beneficial than harmful.

Today's industrial psychologists do not believe as did their predecessors that good "worker morale" is the inevitable key to success in getting workers to produce more and better goods in less time. High morale does not always produce greater output. It is not always the organization that provides the most comfortable working conditions, the social atmosphere most conducive to harmonious relationships between workers, and the most "understanding" bosses that reaps the highest production. In fact, opposite conditions along with conflicts and a certain amount of frustrations may be much more rewarding.

Scientific Management and Human Beings —Scientific management is a term that came into use in 1910. F. W. Taylor who originated "The Taylor System" has been called the father of scientific management in the United States.[6] Some present-day writers believe that management cannot be scientific because it involves "human relationships." These same people will concur that the management that uses research, facts, figures, past performances, and forecasting on the basis of factual data is better than the management that uses only hunches or recollection of past performance.

The scientific management of Taylor had its origin in the factory. It has made great strides and has expanded to include the solving of all types of management problems. Perhaps it does fall down in its application to men; nevertheless, psychology, as a behavioral science, has worked its way into industry, making its contribution along with sociology and anthropology to the study of group dynamics.

Satisfaction at Work — The mental-hygiene attitude has led industry to give workers better opportunities for social and recreational satisfactions. Don G. Mitchell, President, Sylvania Electric Products, Inc., has dwelt at length on the thesis that people in the smaller communities have many advantages over persons living in larger industrial centers. He gives numerous satisfactions to be derived from living in the smaller community: amusements, getting to work more easily, knowing people, keeping clean-minded in clean surroundings, taking part in government, knowing and understanding fellow workers, building citizenship, and so forth.[7] These and many other arguments could be given for decentralization in industry.

Mary Follett who spent much of her life searching for principles of organization believed:

> . . . that any enduring society, and continuously productive industrial organization, must be grounded upon a recognition of the motivating desires of the individual and of the group . . . that the democratic way of life, implemented by intelligent organization and administration of government and industry, is to work toward an honest integration of all points of view, to the end that every individual may be mobilized and made to count both as a person and as an effective part of his group and of society as a whole.[8]

Certainly in a small community one has more chance to count as an individual. In a small town there is community life and a better chance for good mental hygiene than in the cities where workers often feel that they have become cogs in the machinery of industry.

The whole idea of the mental-hygiene point of view is to provide such positive environments for workers that they are free of hatreds, jealousies, anxieties, antagonisms, and so forth, in so far as these things interfere with work.[9] It must, however, be kept in mind that it is human nature to struggle to overcome frustrations and some persons spend a lifetime achieving success by way of compensating for earlier frustrations. Nevertheless, for efficiency in the type of mass-production work being done in large industrial factories the need for a feeling of security and freedom from anxieties exists. To find the apparently desirable balance between worry-free environment and that which has sufficient frustrations to stimulate action is sometimes quite difficult.

In studying the behavior of workers and trying to relate their actions to their achievements, their social organizations, both outside and inside the economic organization, must be considered. ". . . any move on the part of the company may alter the existing social equilibrium to which the employee has grown accustomed and by means of which his status is defined."[10]

In one factory during World War II a design engineer laid out an inspection job. He set the workers in a row several feet apart; each woman faced the back of the woman ahead of her. In the beginning the engineer argued that there wouldn't be any work done if the women faced each other. They didn't perform too well under his setup and he reversed his decision. Placed facing each other they could talk, were happier, and did better work. People do manage to get a certain measure of social satisfaction on the job.[11] A number of similar cases involving men workers instead of women workers could be cited.

The technologists and specialists may devise the most logical and scientific of plans, all destined to aid the workers, yet their plans may not work out. Workers' social relationships and sentiments do not automatically adjust to changes in technical procedures.[12]

In the process of manufacturing or producing and distributing a good or service desired by society, an economic organization "has to keep individuals and groups of individuals working effectively together." [13] In the process it must use all of the tools available. Mental hygiene, many-faceted as it is, is but one of these tools.

One of the big problems in personnel management is to find ways of giving people basic satisfactions out of their jobs and to get human dignity on the job in the tremendous industrial organizations that exist today. Workers want to feel that they belong to a group; they want to know who makes policies. They do not have the opportunity to see finished products or feel that they are creating. These attitudes affect their work production.

What are some of the desires and needs "that block co-operation and inhibit the 'will to work'?" According to Alfred J. Marrow, the traditional answers were: ". . . legal, economic and ethical." He says that in social psychology new answers have been found:

1. The study of people's motivations must be in terms of their wants, desires or aims . . .This includes problems of hidden or unconscious desires as well as the overt and obvious motivations . . .

2. People work more efficiently and co-operatively when they can make an ego investment in their jobs and can participate in planning and in decision making.

3. People are effectively energized only if their jobs provide opportunities for self-expression, achievement and prestige.

. . . if their opportunities for status are broadened through participation their selfish demands will be socialized and will yield to co-operative satisfaction. . . .

The satisfactions that come from teamwork — especially from groups that have toiled and struggled and been successful together — are far superior to solitary achievement.[14]

Marrow is only one of many persons who could be cited on the point that when groups are allowed to set their own goals they are motivated to a greater extent to want to achieve them, and that motivation is more important than skill once the worker is past the learning stages. Probably hundreds of authoritative references could be quoted to the effect that in the final analysis one must usually solve his own problems. "We might provide him with the facts or the money he needs, or we might make some good suggestions. . . . But . . . the employee himself will usually have to decide whether and how to use the facts or the money or the advice." [15] Helping individuals and groups to solve their problems, to adjust, to be happy, and to achieve are aims of mental hygiene.

Elton Mayo in 1945 wrote that we find two symptoms of social disruption in the modern industrial society:

1. The number of unhappy individuals increases.
2. Various groups when formed are not eager to cooperate wholeheartedly with other groups.[16]

Mayo studied the industrial society of the years preceding and following the depression of the thirties; it is possible he would not find these symptoms of social disruption today. There could, however, be no quarrel with his statement that "Observation — skill — experiment and logic — these must be regarded as the three stages of advancement." [17]

People can be motivated to co-operate, to achieve; the devices of the mental hygienist can be employed to keep the individual and the team functioning. Achieving satisfactions is a matter of degree. Perfection cannot be the goal; improvement can.

Origin of Mental Hygiene in the United States — Coincident with Freud's lectures at Clark University (1909), a National Committee for Mental Hygiene was eventuated in the United States. Clifford Beers' book, *A Mind that Found Itself,* is given credit for having much to do with the origin of the committee.[18] From 1841 to 1881 a New England teacher crusaded for treatment of the mentally ill. This teacher, Dorothy Dix, was primarily interested in those already insane. The mental-hygiene movement as started in 1909 was interested in human adjustment in all of its aspects. The National Committee gave rise to the current National Association for Mental Health.[19] This association publishes millions of copies of mental-health pamphlets which may be obtained on request. In 1960 it published *Mental Health Education: a Critique* which contained a debate on the mental-health movement. Even those who do not believe that mental hygiene (psychologists, psychiatrists, sociologists, and so forth) will solve the problems of people, of industry, of the world, admit to the values of some of its concepts and to the thesis that life is a problem of adjustment, struggle, growth, and creative adaption.

The Mental Health Act was passed in 1946 in the United States. With this act came into being the National Institute of Mental Health. The act provided for three functions:

    1. Financing of education of psychiatrists, psychologists, psychiatric social workers, and psychiatric and mental health public health nurses.

    2. Financing of psychiatric and mental hygiene research.

    3. . . . incentive funds to the states for the establishment of mental hygiene programs. . . .[20]

The last of these provisions was merely the broadening of smaller-scale programs under other grants-in-aid provisions.

The research hospital for the National Institutes of Health was opened in 1953 with space for carrying on the research of the Institute of Mental Health. Under the National Mental Health Act training is divided into two administrative functions:

    1. The granting of stipends to trainees.

    2. The granting of funds to universities and other establishments where psychiatric personnel may be trained to make possible the enrichment and expansion of teaching programs. . . .[21]

Other countries have their own mental health associations, organizations, and institutes. The World Health Organization Mental Health Section concerns itself with services in those countries which invite it to do so. It collaborates with a voluntary mental health agency: the World Federation for Mental Health. National mental health associations exchange knowledge and attempt to stimulate action for the improvement of mental health through this somewhat loosely co-ordinated federation.[22]

Some of the Techniques of Mental Hygiene — The aim of the mental-hygiene movement is to prevent mental illness. Karl A. Menninger says that this movement has:

> . . . a definite objective for an increasingly large group of informed people — laymen and scientists. . . . It assumes that the distress of a personality struggling with an environment is simply struggle and not a matter of devils and witches, sin and 'orneriness,' or yet a matter of feeble intellect or feeble will.
>
> It further asumes that mental health is attainable, and our failure to attain it and retain it is to some extent dependent upon our ignorance of general principles. For while health has always been one of the chief concerns of mankind, health has meant by implication the health of the body. Few people give any attention to the climate of their emotions or to brushing their mental teeth or to giving their minds a bath or their memories a cathartic.[23]

Since Menninger wrote the above, he has been the subject of numerous magazine articles and the masses of people know about his work, as well as that of his brother William and their father Charles who founded the Menninger Clinic of Topeka, Kansas. As a result of the work of the Menningers and the thousands who joined in the mental-health movement, many more people are today "giving their minds a bath or their memories a cathartic."

Mental hygiene as it is done for someone else involves the changing of attitudes. In the process of changing attitudes, adjustments are made. As has been suggested previously, the individual must make his own adjustments. The mental hygienist's aid is that of helping an individual to change a point of view. What can be done in this respect for the individual can be done for the group.

When an individual's "normal flow of ongoing" is blocked, adjustment is called for. Some of the factors that block human actions are: *environmental, conflicting antagonistic interests and drives,* and *real* or *imagined personal defects.*[24]

People are the first requisite for mental hygiene — its first tool: clinics, conducted by people; diagnosticians, therapists, psychiatrists, psychoanalysts, psychologists, social workers, interviewers, counselors, administrators, supervisors, fellow workers; some of these terms perhaps need defining here although the techniques applied will be discussed later.

The psychiatrist is familiar with the techniques of *psychoanalysis* as introduced by Freud. He is also familiar with the use of modern miracle drugs that may prevent, retard, or cure mental illnesses; postpone and/or prevent senility; alleviate mental retardation to some degree. He is aware that decisions must be made not only as to the stage reached by the mental disturbance (diagnosis) but, also, as to which of the methods of treatment to use in its cure. He knows something of hospital management and realizes that nurses and their morale affect the quality of therapy rendered.

Psychoanalysis is performed by one who has gone through the process of personal analysis over a period of a year or more and who has psychoanalyzed patients under observation before being certified to practice on his own.

The training of the *clinical psychologist* is sometimes more intense than the training of psychiatrists and physicians in the personality function. However, under the position taken by the national professional association of psychologists, the psychologist must have medical supervision to do psychotherapy.

A team of three persons has formed the clinical service unit of outpatient clinics: the *psychiatrist,* the *psychologist,* and the *psychiatric social worker.* Outpatient clinics have developed over the period of the last forty years. They employ also *mental nurse consultants* who have special training in mental-hygiene techniques. Business and industry often provide *counselors* who have varying degrees of training for their work.

Some of the methods employed by these workers and by others engaged in changing for the better the mental attitudes of people are: interviewing; clinical methods of education, education, more specifically education for mental health; non-clinical methods, posters, pamphlets, magazines, newspaper articles, exposes, books, drama, radio, television, plays, motion pictures, lectures, discussions, institutes, workshops, and so forth. Some of these methods for changing attitudes are used to aid individuals as individuals; others are used to bring changing attitudes to groups of individuals.[25]

It is somewhat a debatable question as to whether mental hygiene is a science or an art. It is true that variables cannot be controlled for long periods of time when experimenters are dealing with man. There are techniques of studying man, however, even if these must be resolved to the observation and interpretation of living. Some experiments in mental hygiene are now under way in which observations are continuing for years so that children are being studied on into their adulthood. Observation, interview, and statistical records are the methods and devices used to pursue this study.

Those who study group and individual situations in business and industry must use the same methods. Roethlisberger has said that through "the interviewing method" and "the method of social observation" business can learn in the human situation:

> . . . what is important to people — their hopes and fears, what may be interfering with their work, what may be the sources of their dissatisfactions and difficulties, to what groups they belong, the extent and nature of their participation, their positions in informal groups, as well as the effect that technical changes, management logics, and methods of supervision may have on these factors.[26]

People of today have great opportunity to understand themselves and those with whom they live and work; so much is written to aid them to do so. They may not be familiar with the studies of worker motivation begun by Harvard psychologists in 1927 at Western Electric's Hawthorne plant. Nevertheless, newspaper and magazine articles constantly tell them what those studies discovered: that the *sentiments* and *attitudes* of people are all-important in human motivation and mental health. The *social situation* at the place of work and the *social condition* that exists for the individual outside of his place of work have great influence in determining the kind of work he does and his mental attitude toward that work, those with whom he works, and those with whom he lives.

One's job can make him ill. However, it is usually not the job itself that brings about the emotional disturbance that causes illness; it is the fact that people have personality problems and problems of adjustment that could often be solved if they had help in adjusting, if they could communicate with people who understand. It aids a great deal for a person to know that all people have problems of adjustment and that most people at times find job, family, and personal situations seemingly insurmountable.

It is good to know, too, that one whose mental health is "robust" will exhibit certain characteristics: He will have *"insight* into his own limitations." He will be able to *adapt* himself "to the uncontrollable changes of living with a minimum of emotional energy." He has *maturity*. He leads an *orderly* existence in the sense that the functions of living are so routinized that there is time, as well as energy, for more important things, the "constructive aspects of life." He is *not an extremist*, i.e., he isn't a miser, a glutton, a drunkard, and so forth. He has satisfactory *social adjustment*. He gets *"wholesome satisfactions from his chief occupation."* [27]

Many people, especially college students, get the idea that mental health is something that should concern only physicians and those who are mentally ill. Actually, it is something that should concern all people. Business executives because of the influence they have over those who work with and for them should perhaps be more concerned than others. Recognizing this, many of them annually attend seminars at the Menninger Foundation in Topeka.[28]

How Personalities Meet Problems — Karl A. Menninger's *The Human Mind* is devoted to the study of personalities prone to failure or likely to find difficulties in adjusting. He analyzes the symptoms and motives that lead to failures and the treatments and applications of psychiatry. The Menningers have done much for humanity in their contributions to the knowledge of the human mind and of human behavior. Many students and friends of this writer have found help in understanding themselves and in solving their problems by reading *The Human Mind*. It is a volume laymen can read and comprehend. Dr. Menninger himself said of this his most popular work, ". . . readers have said to me: 'I was afraid I would find myself in your book,' . . ." His reply to such statements always was, "I hope so." A person who could not find himself in this work would, according to the author, not be human, or else some of the pages of the book would have been torn out or missing.[29]

The adjustment effort of the personality in meeting the situation is described at length by Menninger. Three outcomes are possible: *success, failure,* or *compromise.* Some meet problems by fighting, some by taking flight from them [fainting, feinting, in fantasy, in flight], but some through constructive compromise attain success in other fields to make up for the failure to adjust to a given situation. Some of the situations which place unusual stress and strain on the personality are: going away to school for the first time, marriage, a new job, going to war, and so forth. [One could stretch these out to include: a new supervisor, or an old one for that matter; a death in the family; divorce; continuing in a job one doesn't like or for which one isn't properly prepared; or simply a series of small problems that at a given time seem insurmountable.]

If in attempting adjustment the person is successful, he goes on down the highway of life without being unduly noticed by his fellowmen. If failure is the result there are three outcomes: (1) a broken personality (breakdowns, suicides, and so forth would come under this classification); (2) a broken situation (crime, such as murder or rape); and (3) constructive compromise (writing, inventing, composing, teaching, telling others how to live "in response to the stimulus which their own failure to negotiate life has afforded them."[30]

According to Dr. Menninger, the broken situations, since they involve crime, delinquency, dependency, and so on, should be referred to the sociologists; the broken personalities to psychiatrists and in fact all physicians.[31] Later, however, he makes quite a case under "Legal Applications" for the elimination of distinction between asylums and jails. He would place the criminals under expert medical direction and a sentence would be "as unthinkable for a murderer as it is now for a melancholiac." The neurotic criminal is the concern of the doctor. He commits crime: to escape or take flight from the unpleasant situation; to compensate, achieve substitutes; to bolster up his ego; to express revenge; to gain maximum self-satisfaction; to respond to instinctual urges (exhibited in sexual misbehavior or in urges for independence); to satisfy the wish for punishment brought on by an unconscious sense of guilt.[32]

Seven Types of Personalities Prone to Having Difficulties in Adjusting or to Failure — In the next chapter mental illnesses, emotional disorders, and common adjustment mechanisms will be discussed. Because Dr. Menninger's classification of personalities prone to failure has helped so many who came after him, they are given here as a sort of preliminary to the types of breakdown that occur as well as why and how they occur. The average person will not find himself in the first two of these personality types; he will probably find that he has some of the characteristics of the last five at one time or another in his life. Here are the seven types of personalities with brief summaries of Menninger's discussion about them:

1. *The somatic type* — physical illness personalities. These may be classified under three headings: (1) persons whose personalities are impaired because of accidents, or disease, the physically crippled personality; (2) the illness-prone personalities, including the accident-prone individuals who "have been shown statistically to be the victims of ninety per cent of all accidents," [Data on accident proneness are given in a later chapter.] and the people who unconsciously wish to be sick; (3) personalities with physical diseases that at first are physical but which develop into disorders in "perception, thinking, feeling, and behaviour." Included in the last group are persons who may have glandular disorders, brain tumours, encephalitis (inflammation of the brain), general paresis (brain syphilis), congenital brain syphilis, hookwork, malaria, and so forth.[33]

2. *The hypophrenic type* — stupid personalities. This group includes those who have a deficiency in mental capacity. The idiots, with practically no brains, up through imbeciles, morons, and subnormals. These persons are frequent economic and social failures, and when they commit crimes they are more frequently caught than are others. Feeble-mindedness, at least some kinds, as opposed to insanity, may be hereditary. Persons in this class must usually be provided for by others. One should not jump to conclusions in classifying individuals in this class. Persons apparently dull may turn out to be quite the opposite in actuality.[34]

3. *The isolation type* — lonely personalities. These people would like to break the pane of glass between them and the rest of the world, but they don't know how. The rube, for instance, is an example. Some of the reasons for isolation: a pathological parent, poverty, wealth, real or fancied defects. The isolation type with a sense of inferiority is the most prevalent type. If this person can be made aware of the fact that "compared to certain other powers and persons in the world we are inferior, all of us," then adjustment may be made easier. For the sensible person knowledge of this fact gives no pain. If there is actually a defect which can be cured by medical treatment (the plastic surgeon, and so on), then this type of personality is more likely to adjust.[35]

4. *The schizoid type* — queer personalities. Woodrow Wilson was a schizoid. So were Samuel Taylor Coleridge, Napoleon Bonaparte, Sir Isaac Newton, Jeremy Bentham (an English jurist and philosopher), and Charles Julius Guiteau (who shot and killed President Garfield). To the list might be added: Calvin and Kant, Schiller and Rousseau, Erasmus and Spinoza, Whitler and Goldsmith, Wagner and Chopin, Robespierre and Adolf Hitler, Dickie Loeb and Jesse James, Van Gogh and Judas Iscariot, and thousands of patients residing in mental hospitals and other hospitals as well.

The common denominator of this group: inability to get along with others. Of course, at times this can be applied to all persons. In this group are included: the hard-boiled variety, the artistic variety (George Sand, for instance), the apparently stupid variety (often the numbness is a false front), the grouchy variety, the radical variety, and the suspicious variety. In the extreme the suspicious type develops paranoia. All persons entertain paranoid ideas at times, but not for long. Persistent paranoid ideas "are evidences of a breaking, if not a broken mind." The evidence of a healthy mind is the ability to throw off such ideas.

There is also mass paranoia. The psychosis of the German nation under Hitler is an example of this. [The idea of mass paranoia can be applied to any organization or group motivated by extreme fears, suspicions, and so forth. It is not meant to imply here that such a thing as a "group mind" exists; the individual members of the group do retain their own ways of thinking although at a given time they may be swayed to think and act with the group.]

Despite the fact that in general it is believed that insanity is not inherited, some psychiatrists are of the belief that an "inborn schizoid constitution" is inherited. Others feel that more probably the schizoid makeup is a result of attitudes and techniques of parents during the early years. Under the co-sponsorship and co-direction of the National Association for Mental Health and the Schizophrenia Research Program, Drs. Ralph D. Rabinovitch and Charles R. Shaw at the Hawthorn Center in Northville, Michigan, have long carried on research to determine the origin of mental illness. They have found that children reared in apparently healthy, normal surroundings, with healthy, normal parents, brothers, and sisters may become victims of childhood schizophrenia, which disease appears to them to be a biological phenomenon rather than the result of poor environment or unfortunate relationships in early years. According to Dr. William Malamud, research director of NAMH, in a UPI news release, July 12, 1964, long-time study has found that most of the afflicted children remain disturbed throughout their lives; over half of them require more or less permanent institutionalization and approximately seventy-five per cent are able to maintain only a marginal social adjustment.

The National Institute of Mental Health annually receives a large part of the over half-a-billion dollars appropriated each year (1964) by the federal government to do research. A finding of the NIMI is that a chemical known as serotonin, found in the human brain and in substantial quantity in the blood, may offer a clue as to the cause of mental disturbances.

The famous studies of Dr. Franz Kallmann indicated that out of one hundred children who had one parent with schizophrenia, sixteen would have the disease; sixty-eight per cent of the children where both parents have the mental illness will also have it. In general most students hold to the idea that the individual is probably the product of the interaction of environment and heredity.

In spite of schizoid traits many persons who have them do succeed. Others fail. Schizoid breaks may be caused by inability of the individuals to adapt to injuries, griefs, disappointments, physical diseases, and so on. The schizoid break, if it does occur, results in schizophrenia in some one of its varied forms. A break may not occur if the schizoid personality has the benefit of psychiatric help to ward it off.[36]

Treatments of the mentally ill are reserved for discussion in Chapter VII. It will be noted that the *isolation* and *schizoid* types have traits in common with the introvert as discussed in Chapter IV. In the extreme these types would tend toward schizophrenia (defined in Chapter VI).

5. *The cycloid type* — moody personalities. One week these personalities are on top of the world; the next they may be in the depths of despair. The ideas of these people are determined by their moods. The ego of this type person when a love object is lost becomes destitute. The melancholy persons may fail in school, in home life, in work, in middle life. Their "failure is a result of a depression rather than the cause." The symptoms of melancholia are: listlessness, undue preoccupation, worry, feelings of futility. Freud and his students attributed mania and melancholia to many causes. Dr. Menninger says, however, that ". . . extensive studies have shown definitely . . . that melancholia is an exaggerated response to a real or imaginary loss in the love life."

These persons who are deeply depressed are all potential suicides. The suicide is one who has taken revenge on the person who thwarted him, his lover, employer, doctor, relative. He strikes back in a way that his opponent can not strike back at him and thus accomplishes his intended purpose.

Moody personalities cannot be reasoned with, or jollied up. Trip and home treatments fail. Most depressions and excitements do subside when treated by those trained to give such treatment. Many must be their own physicians for they are the only ones who know of their depressed states. An aid in overcoming depression is to apply any skill one possesses: religion, beauty, nature, "devotion to a task," — these save from depressions.[37]

The cycloid type in the extreme becomes a manic-depressive patient; in the less extreme states he possesses some of the characteristics of the extrovert.

6. *The neurotic type* — frustrated personalities. Neurotics always contrive to defeat their own aims. The so-called normal person settles his conflicts one way or the other; the neurotic can't decide. Neurotics get satisfactions from their symptoms, escape conflict through them.[38]

The person who has a neurotic type personality and lets it develop in the extreme is said to have a neurosis (psychoneurosis). The neuroses are discussed more fully in Chapter VI.

7. *The antisocial type* — perverse personalities. These people are troublesome and sometimes even dangerous. Instead of obsessions, backaches, and fears of the neurotics, the perverse personalities, the personalities Dr. Menninger says were formerly labeled "psychopathic personalities" [they still are so labeled by many and are so labeled in Chapter VI] are persons who damage others without, in general, injuring themselves. Andrew Jackson, dissipating in gambling, racing, drinking, and cockfighting at the age of fifteen was a perverse personality. Casanova and Francois Villon were perverse personalities. Hundreds of persons in public jails are perverse personalities.[39]

Menninger's concept of the adjustment effort of the personality in meeting problems and his concept of personality types have been given here as a preview for Chapter VI. Chapter IX "Following the Conceptual Pattern for Counseling" considers more in detail factors to be dealt with in counseling and the ways a person may adjust to the problems of life.

Some of the Groups Engaged in Mental Health Research — Among the institutions and groups currently engaged in research relative to mental health being financed by the Ford Foundation, 477 Madison Avenue, New York 22, New York, are the following:

California Institute of Technology, Division of Chemistry and
    Chemical Engineering
University of California (Los Angeles), School of Medicine
Gaustad Mental Hospital, Oslo, Norway
Cornell University, Medical College
University of Minnesota, Medical School
University of Chicago, Orthogenic School
Austin Riggs Center, Stockbridge, Massachusetts

The Ford Foundation has spent over $6,000,000 on the following studies:

Survey of mental disorders in Aarhus County to identify cases and relate them to demographic and other factors; study of the island of Samso to determine what can be achieved by concentrated psychiatric therapy. University of Aarhus, Department of Psychiatry, Rissokov, Denmark.
Follow-up study on adults, in which personality measurements will be applied to selected persons for whom similar psychological and physiological data for earlier periods in their lives, from infancy to

adolescence, are available. University of California (Berkeley), Institute of Child Welfare.

Research program that includes both clinical and experimental studies of various psychological and psychosomatic disorders and their treatment. University of Cambridge, England.

Clinical investigation of the psychotherapeutic process in treating adult schizophrenia. Chestnut Lodge Research Institute, Rockville, Maryland.

Study of the process and the outcome of psychotherapies of different kinds, using the quantitative methods of academic psychology. University of Chicago, Counseling Center.

Expansion of its present Freudian studies of the early development of both normal and maladjusted children. Hampstead Child-Therapy Course and Clinic, London, England.

Expansion and coordination of its present work on constitutional bases of emotion, through experimental studies of both human beings and animals. Institute of Psychiatry, University of London, England.

Exploration of therapeutic effectiveness among psychiatric patients, with special attention to the use of the placebo as preliminary to psychotherapy. Johns Hopkins University, School of Medicine.

Neurochemical investigation of the metabolism of different parts of the brain and their correlation with mental functioning. Massachusetts General Hospital, McLean Hospital Research Laboratory.

Study of different kinds of treatment given a variety of patients at the Menninger hospital and clinic, with particular attention to the evaluation of outcome. Menninger Foundation, Topeka, Kansas.

Investigations in the tradition of experimental psychology of hypotheses deriving, for the most part, from dynamic or clinical psychology, dealing with human motivations, defense mechanisms, and similar matters. University of Michigan, Department of Psychology.

Effort by a team of psychologists and psychiatrists to develop better classifications of personality disturbances. University of Minnesota, Medical School.

Methodological experimentation, as well as substantive inquiry into the process of psychoanalytic therapy, under highly controlled conditions and with full recording and multiple diagnosis of the cases. Mount Sinai Hospital and Clinic (Los Angeles), Psychiatric Research Institute.

A study similar to that at Michigan, but dealing particularly with the interrelationship between emotional and cognitive processes. New York University, Research Center for Mental Health.

Support of expanded program of research in mental health and psychiatry, including research training of younger psychiatrists. University of Pennsylvania, Institute of Neurological Sciences.

Study of the metabolism of nervous tissue and the relationship of metabolic processes to certain hormones, nutrient materials, and drugs that have effects upon the brain or upon the mental state. Research Foundation for Mental Hygiene, New York State Psychiatric Institute.

Clinical studies of infantile development — physiological, psychological, and social. Research Foundation of State University of New York (Syracuse), College of Medicine.

Development of research personnel and systematic study of hospitalized medical and psychiatric patients to discover what part separation and depression play in developing the patients' illnesses. University of Rochester, Medical Center.

Combined genetic-biological and social-psychological study of "personality" development in animals. Roscoe B. Jackson Memorial Laboratory, Division of Behavior Studies, Bar Harbor, Maine.

A study similar to that at Michigan, with emphasis on developmental and psychodynamic studies. Stanford University, Department of Psychology.

Research program on the early phases of social development in children. Tavistock Institute of Human Relations, London, England.

Biochemical studies of the action of certain psychotomimetic drugs and of their relationship to clinical psychotic states. Worcester Foundation for Experimental Biology, Shrewsbury, Massachusetts.

Study of the influence of early experience upon later behavior, carried on under experimental conditions with primate animals. Yerkes Laboratories of Primate Biology, Orange Park, Florida.[40]

Conclusion — This chapter has merely made a claim for mental hygiene as a source of aid to management. Mental hygiene is a form of applied psychology and its origin may be traced back through psychology to philosophy. Its aims as well as its techniques are many and varied. Its objectives include not only the curing and prevention of mental illness but also the development of happy individuals who have integrated personalities and can get along with others. Not only is it concerned with the individual as an individual, but it is concerned with the various groups to which he belongs and his place in each of these groups. There are many specialists today who are equipped to aid others in meeting the stresses with which their lives become entangled, and even the specialists themselves are not immune to need for help. Perhaps the best guarantee an individual can have that he will be able to maintain good mental health is for him to acquire the understanding and insight necessary for exercising some measure of control over his own sentiments and attitudes.

To aid in understanding how personalities meet problems, Dr. Karl A. Menninger's concept (success, failure, compromise) was reviewed, and his seven personality types that have trouble in adjusting were defined. These included: somatic, hypophrenic, isolation, schizoid, cycloid, neurotic, and anti-social types.

PROJECTS

1. Using only references in current magazines and journals, write a five-page paper on "Mental Hygiene" or "Mental Health."

2. Select one of the Ford Foundation studies listed in this chapter and write a report based upon that study or on the topic of that study if the study itself or reports upon it are not available in your college library.

3. Write a five-page paper on "How Personalities Meet Problems of Adjustment."

4. Read from one of the references used in this chapter and comment upon anything that was *new* to you. This may be a chapter only or as much as you wish to read. Make your report from three to five pages long.

ACKNOWLEDGMENTS AND REFERENCES

1 Sutherland, Robert L., "Mental Health in Industrial Relations," *Mental Hygiene,* Vol. XXXIV, No. 2, April, 1950, pp. 192–195.

2 McGregor, Douglas, "Individual Productivity — Why Do Men Work?" *The Employee . . . an Individual,* Proceedings, Southwest Area Conference on Industrial Relations, May 2 and 3, 1947, Houston, Texas, p. 21.

3 Harrell, Thomas Willard, *Industrial Psychology,* Rinehart & Co., Inc., New York, 1949, p. 431.

4 Barrett, Claud B., "The Employee, an Individual," *The Employee . . . an Individual,* Proceedings, Southwest Area Conference on Industrial Relations, May 2 and 3, 1947, Houston, Texas, p. 7.

5 Marrow, Alfred J., "Psychology and Executive Efficiency," *Proceedings,* Twelve Conference Texas Personnel and Management Association, The University of Texas, Austin, November 2 and 3, 1950, p. 35.

6 Person, H. S., "Scientific Management," International Association for the Study and Improvement of Human Relations and Conditions in Industry, June, 1928 (Report on the Development of Fundamental Relationships Within Industry in the United States of America, International Industrial Relations Institute), p. 17.

7 Mitchell, Don G., "Human Dignity," *Employee-Employer Progress . . . How?,* Proceedings, Southwest Area Conference on Industrial Relations, Houston, Texas, 1952, pp. 6–9.

8 Metcalf, Henry C., and Urwick, L., *Dynamic Administration,* Harper & Brothers Publishers, New York, 1940, p. 9.

9 Sutherland, *op. cit.,* pp. 193–198.

10 Roethlisberger, F. J., *Management and Morale,* Harvard University Press, Cambridge, Massachusetts, 1952, p. 63.
11 McGregor, *op. cit.,* pp. 24–25.
12 Roethlisberger, F. J., and Dickson, William J., *Management and the Worker,* Harvard University Press, Cambridge, Massachusetts, 1950, pp. 545–546.
13 Roethlisberger, *op. cit.,* p. 27.
14 Marrow, *op. cit.,* p. 37ff.
15 Finlay, William W., Sartain, A. Q., Tate, Willie M., *Human Behavior in Industry,* Mc-Graw-Hill Book Company, Inc., New York, 1954, p. 169.
16 Mayo, Elton, *The Social Problems of an Industrial Civilization,* Division of Research, Graduate School of Business Administration, Harvard University, Boston, 1945, p. 7.
17 *Ibid.,* p. 19.
18 Menninger, Karl A., *The Human Mind,* Third Edition, Alfred A. Knopf, New York, 1951, p. 15.
19 Berrien, F. K., *Practical Psychology,* The Macmillian Company, New York, 1952, pp. 29–30.
20 Lemkau, Paul V., *Mental Hygiene in Public Health,* The Blakiston Division, McGraw-Hill Book Company, Inc., New York, 1955, p. 85.
21 *Ibid.*
22 *Ibid.,* p. 92ff.
23 Menninger, *op. cit.*
24 Berrien, *op. cit.,* pp. 34–37.
25 Lemkau, *op. cit.,* pp. 50–77.
26 Roethlisberger, *op. cit.,* p. 187.
27 Berrien, *op. cit.,* pp. 32–34.
28 ———, "How's Your Mental Health?" *The Rotarian,* October, 1958, p. 13.
29 Menninger, *op. cit.,* p. xii.
30 *Ibid.,* pp. 29–35.
31 *Ibid.,* p. 34.
32 *Ibid.,* pp. 443–460.
33 *Ibid.,* pp. 35–48.
34 *Ibid.,* pp. 48–64.
35 *Ibid.,* pp. 64–75.
36 *Ibid.,* pp. 75–107.
37 *Ibid.,* pp. 107–129.
38 *Ibid.,* pp. 129–150.
39 *Ibid.,* pp. 150–158.
40 ———, *Mental Health A Ford Foundation Report,* The Ford Foundation, 477 Madison Avenue, New York 22, New York, pp. 37–40.

CHAPTER VI

PERSONALITIES AND MENTAL ILLNESSES

Factors Affecting Mental Health — There is not uniformity of thinking as to what brings about mental illnesses. Some think that they are brought about by physiological diseases. Others believe that the primary cause of such illnesses is in the psychological stresses of life experience. Some who work with mental illnesses believe that mind and body are functioning separately; others, most in fact, believe that the human being functions as a unit, mind and body.

Stresses and strains of any sort may be the triggers to breakdowns in personality. Poorly integrated life experiences and weak constitutional core indicate that the personality structure is more susceptible to breakdown. The inherent strength of the personality must be greater to resist the greater stresses and strains put upon it. If stresses are too great, too concentrated, or of too long duration, the personality whose own emotional support is weak may develop successfully only if cushioned by the emotional support or skilled techniques of another individual. On the other hand, *if the "stress is too great, too concentrated, or extends over too long a time, no personality will have inherent strength enough to withstand it."* The result will be disease.[1]

Although most writers on the subject do make a good case for the effects of stress in precipitating breakdowns, some authorities profess doubt that external stresses as such cause illness, mental or otherwise. Gerald Gordon, du Pont psychiatrist, has listed as stress diseases: gastric ulcer, hypertension, coronary heart disease, and gastric and vascular disabilities. Even in these so-called stress diseases, he expresses belief that the stresses are more internal than external. Since this is a theory only there is implication of need for continued study.[2] Meanwhile this chapter discusses so-called emotional disorders as well as the neuroses which are themselves considered to be chiefly functional (without organic cause).

Berrien and many other writers break down into two groups the factors which contribute to mental health or illness: (1) the *predisposing* and (2) the *precipitating, exciting,* or *immediate.*[3] Some of the predisposing factors are: environment, physique and physical health, and heredity.

These are long-term factors. Most believe that the hereditary influences are indirect. The physical or bodily factors and general health that are inherited may affect mental health. The exciting or immediate causes, those which bring on (precipitate) the *neurotic* or *psychotic* condition, are varied and numerous, including failure, success, frustrations of all kinds, disappointments, threats, vicarious experiences that trigger the emotions. The discussion of long-term and short-term factors to be considered in counseling, Chapter IX, enlarges upon the predisposing and precipitating factors of adjustment.

Mental Illnesses — Generally mental illnesses are classified into two major groups: (1) *psychoses,* and (2) *psychoneuroses* or *neuroses.* The neuroses were formerly believed to become in exaggerated states the psychoses. This does not hold as only about ten per cent of the neurotics become psychotics. The psychotic is markedly different from the "normal." He is the *schizophrenic, manic-depressive,* or *paranoiac* patient. He is considered to be dangerous to himself and to others. On the other hand, the neurotic is merely a nuisance to himself and usually to everyone else. Fears and anxieties are the chief symptoms of the neurotic.

In addition to the two general classifications of mental illnesses, there are *emotional disorders* (sometimes discussed with the neuroses; *psychosomatic* is sometimes used; other terms also used include cardiac neurosis, organ neurosis, and gastric neurosis) and *psychopathic personalities.* In addition there are personality reactions and adjustment mechanisms common to all of us.

PSYCHOSES — The psychoses may be divided into three major clinical groups: *schizophrenia* (sometimes referred to as *dementia praecox,* literally precocious loss of mind, although this term is no longer used in view of the fact that the illness is not characteristic of any one age group), *manic-depressive psychosis,* and *paranoia.* Schizophrenia is characterized by disintegration of the personality. Generally, four types of schizophrenia are recognizable: (1) *dementia simplex,* characterized by lack of emotion; (2) *hebephrenia,* characterized by make-belief; (3) *catatonia,* characterized by withdrawal, stupor, negativism and incoherence, alternating periods of stupor and activity, or catalepsy (literally not moving a muscle); (4) *paranoia,* characterized by delusions of which there are several varieties, as, (a) *delusions of reference,* in which the patient considers everything as being related to himself (the laughter in the hallway, the joke, the newspaper story, and so on); (b) *delusions of grandeur,* in which the colored boy becomes the king of some island which is the figment of his imagination (this writer once interviewed one such at the state mental hospital in Austin, Texas); (c) *delusions of persecution,* characterized by suspicions in which somebody is trying to steal one's wife (or husband) or other possessions, or one fears being poisoned, shot, or otherwise killed or molested.

The *manic-depressive* is given to extremes of moods. He is highly emotional, quite in contrast to the schizophrenic. Some manic-depressives are more given to mania, some to depression; practically all alternate to some extent between the periods of mania and depression. In the manic state there is inclination to talk incessantly, move ceaselessly, and perhaps even to act violently.

In the period of depression gloom descends; at this stage, the mental state may result in suicidal attempts. Some two-thirds of suicides have been manic-depressives in the depression stage, or alcoholics; the ratio here, two manic-depressives to one alcoholic. Alcohol is a depressant, and the alcoholic's reaction after a severe orgy is similar to the depression period of the psychotic.

The United States stands about half way on the list of countries of the world when listed by numbers of suicides per total population; there are approximately ten suicides in 100,000. Nevada among the states leads in suicides. It has 20.7 per 100,000; San Francisco, with 24 per 100,000, leads among the cities; this is five times the rate in New York. Men commit suicide in the United States four times as often as do women; women do attempt suicide much more frequently than they succeed. Protestants commit suicide seven times as often as Roman Catholic and Jewish people.

Paranoia is characterized by a grudge against humanity. It may be dominated as with the schizophrenic variety by suspicions, but in the so-called "pure paranoia" the victim is able to keep everything organized. On the surface his illness may not be readily recognized. His suspicion is properly filed in "Drawer A" and his personality does not outwardly disintegrate. Suddenly he puts a gun to his head and blows out his brains, or he goes to the airport and kills a doctor whom he suspects of having an affair with his wife.

Many of those who are on the brink of mental breakdown seem to will accidents to happen to them; some contrive to kill themselves inch by inch. According to the *Encyclopedia Britannica* suicide accounts for twenty-five as many deaths as murder does. The National Save-A-Life League, founded in 1906 by the Reverend Harry Marsh Warren, New York Central Park Baptist Church, has saved thousands of men and women from suicide. Dr. Karl Menninger has said that "Hope is a necessity for normal life, and the major weapon against the suicide impulse." He defines hope as "a confident search for a rewarding life."[4]

NEUROSES — Of the neurotics Dr. Brill said: "Neurotics, as a rule, are at least of average mentality, and as a class, they constitute what one may call 'the salt of the earth.' "[5] Again he said, ". . . all *real* neurotics are schizoids." [6] The schizoid type personality is withdrawn; he is the introvert who gets many satisfactions working alone; in the extreme it is he who becomes one of the schizophrenic patients who along with other mental patients fill half of the nation's hospital beds. [The majority of mental patients are schizophrenics.]

For the student struggling for the first time to distinguish between the terms *neurotic* and *psychotic,* this modern-day favorite quip often helps: The neurotic builds castles in the air; the psychotic lives in them; and the psychiatrist collects the rent. The ailment of the neurotic is theoretically completely curable; actually it may be almost impossible to cure him because his "illness" is the very thing that gives him reason for being; it is the way he is solving his problems of life; it is the way he is adjusting. If you take away the neurosis, you have to give him a substitute for it; or he, in the process of bringing about his own cure through developing understanding and insight, finds his own substitutes.

Anxiety is actually the basis of all neuroses. Anxiety as used here is something different from fear. Its stimuli come from within; stimuli of fear come from without.

Anxiety develops for many reasons: inability to meet a problem, frustrations, failure of any sort, feelings of inadequacy. When the pressures and disappointments become so great that the resources of the individual arc not able to cope with them the result may be hospitalization or medical care. It would seem that three courses are possible: (1) Either the individual develops insight through his own efforts to understand the situation; or through the aid of a physician, a counselor, or loved ones step by step the strength and motivation enabling him to solve the problem return him to so-called "normalcy." (2) The pressures, problems, crises are removed and the individual continues to function in a more or less "normal" manner, but his personality is weakened for dealing with future problems. (3) The pressures become greater than the personality can stand and there is a breakdown requiring constant medical attention.

The anxiety syndrome develops in a situation of rejection and insecurity, or the victim may have been helped very little in childhood in solving his problems; the child who gets attention by developing illnesses tends to solve his problems in adulthood in the same manner. The person who regresses to a state of helplessness gets a certain amount of pleasure from being a childish, helpless, and dependent person. He is fearful when others are not there to be dependent upon. Some call this state *anxiety hysteria.* It is more of a worry than a phobia. It is something which in its less extreme state is familiar to all of us. For some, although it may not have developed in the extreme, worry is ever present. It is for them a way of life. Sometimes it is a thrill or a preparation for a thrill for those who lack creative outlets.

The term *neurasthenia* originally embraced any illness classified as a neurosis. It literally means exhaustion of the nerves. In the extreme it is a form of nervous breakdown. The basic difference between a person said to have an anxiety neurosis and one classified as being neurasthenic is that the neurasthenic has long failed to solve problems by facing up to them in a head-on or direct manner; he (she!) is weak, easily fatigued, irritable, moody, and, in fact, a hypochondriac. The neurasthenic may have been excessively protected and coddled as a child. Women are more susceptible to this form of neuroticism than are men, but men are not immune. There may be various reasons: girls may have been overly protected; women may have fewer interests in the home than men have in work. About a third of the work force is made up of women; it is not known that the women who work are less susceptible to neuroses than those who do not, but it is believed that they are.

A great many writers believe that all-engrossing work could be the solution to problems of the neurotics. Popular writers proclaim "Your Happiness Is in Your Hands," i.e., one who is working with his hands is happy. It has been said, too, that one who is writing poetry may have a neurotic personality but that this is much better than developing a neurosis. This is a great argument for developing hobbies. The participating or creative hobbies are best; TV, movies, and spectator sports do not furnish the absorbing outlet that writing, painting, or creating in any form with the hands or the mind do. Nor can they offer the satisfaction that comes from participating sports, musical groups, acting, or performance such as playing a musical instrument, twirling, or reciting. Interests furnish reason for being; they give the hope that is so necessary as incentive for people to continue the struggle of adjustment throughout life. Engaging in community projects, clubs, and church activities also give the individual a "reason for being." Certainly if home life and work are not sufficiently challenging interest, one should seek creative and rewarding outlets elsewhere.

Hysteria, characterized by *dissociative* or *conversion reactions,* comes about when anxieties are extreme, when the pressures of life are great or perhaps when one wants to forget extreme hurt or deny the existence of disappointments. Dissociative reactions include: *amnesia, fugue states, somnambulism,* and *multiple personalities.* The personality deals with conflict by walling off his mind from consciousness. The famous "Three Faces of Eve" is illustrative of the manner in which the multiple-personality type solves problems by developing the multiple personalities but forgetting in each of the states the activities engaged in while in the others. In the case of conversion reactions the inner conflict of the individual is represented by symbolic somatic disturbances. Blindness, loss of the use of a limb, deafness, and a variety of "tics" are examples of reactions that apparently are somatic; they may have their origin in psychological conflict and there may, in fact, be no organic basis for their existence. Some patients refuse to be cured.

There are hundreds of *phobia* reactions. Some of the more common ones are: *claustrophobia,* the fear of closed places; *agoraphobia,* fear of open spaces; *acrophobia,* fear of high places; *pyrophobia,* fear of fire; *aleurophobia,* fear of cats; *misophobia,* fear of dirt. Persons who have extreme phobia reactions tend to be moody with those they know best, although they can appear quite attractive with strangers. These people frequently seek protection from their loved ones, being highly demanding of them.

Many persons feel *compulsions* in mild form. Compulsions of this type are considered under the heading "Common Adjustment Mechanisms." It is the obsessive compulsive reaction, the insatiable desire, the mania, that becomes a problem. Some of the manias about which we read in the daily papers are: *kleptomania,* compulsion to steal; *pyromania,* compulsion to set fire; *dipsomania,* periodic insatiable craving for alcoholic beverages; *arithmomania,* obsession to count things; *onomatomania,* compulsion to repeat certain words over and over. Manias (compulsions, obsessions) and phobias (fears that persist without ostensible reason) are often classified as *psychasthenias,* although the term is not so often used today. The psychasthenic is aware of the fact that his problems come from within himself. The neurasthenic and the hysterical patient are positive that their problems do not come from within themselves. Since there is nothing organically wrong, they evidently do.

One type of neurotic is the perpetually unhappy person. The chonically depressive reaction of this person is similar to the depression state of manic-depressive psychosis, but it is not extreme enough to be classified as a mental illness. The symptoms are similar to those of the perpetual worrier.

EMOTIONAL DISORDERS — During any given week in the United States something over ten per cent of the population consults with physicians; the number of these persons considered to have no illness other than mental or emotional has been placed by various writers at something like fifty per cent. *Hypochondria* as an illness passed from the medical textbook around the turn of the century. It was then defined as being a symptom of anxiety about one's health. In the 1930's much came to be written about psychosomatic medicine (*psyche,* from the *Greek,* meaning soul or mind; and *soma,* meaning body). The term *psychosomatic* was first used by many to mean illness brought on by mental and emotional worries. Today psychiatrists and physicians take the point of view that the term means both body and mind as it was originally intended to do. Any symptom of illness reflects reactions of the complete individual; mind and body interact.

Allergies affect some eighteen to twenty-seven million persons in the United States. People who are allergic are sensitive in varying degrees to substances that do not bother others. Early studies of the allergic persons showed that hereditary factors were involved; a general hypersensitivity was considered to be transmitted from parents to children. Parents who worry and fret over their children may also contribute to their development of high sensitivity to certain substances. With some offspring the result is the opposite of this.

In 1958 the National Institute of Mental Health organized a new section to study the so-called "psychosomatic illnesses." A great number of magazine articles today proclaim: "New Hope for the Allergic," — "Psychosomatic Medicine," — "Some Sympathy Added to Science,"—"Mysterious Stomach — Always in Trouble," — "Hypochondriacs at Large," and so on. These popular articles and medical studies suggest that a relationship exists between the emotions and bodily changes; the problem is to find whether the physical affliction brings about personality changes or whether emotions affect the body. It is believed that emotions affect digestive ailments as much as do the purely organic factors. About one in ten Americans suffers at some time from ulcers. Something over a tenth of these ulcers occur in the stomach; most commonly ulcers occur in the duodenum, a portion of the small intestine lying just below the stomach's outlet valve. Overactivity of the stomach juices brings on ulcers. Although many reasons for this have been suggested, only one belief persists: the emotions have much to do with the existence of the ulcer. Among the many allergies and suggested "psychosomatic" illnesses and effects are: common colds; asthma; hay fever; eczema; acne; arthritis; obesity; hypertension or high-blood pressure, the cause of which is often emotions and it is characterized by inability to sleep, or to concentrate for any length of time; rheumatic disease; colitis; sinus trouble; and even heart trouble.

Many factors may bring on these illnesses. Other than hereditary implications and general environmental effects, two possible factors are: (1) loss, whether it be real or imagined, of a love object, causing one's anger to turn inward on himself and resulting in this "psychosomatic" reaction which the Army psychiatric classification process chooses to call *somatization* reaction; (2) feeling of guilt, causing one to punish himself with illness. Psychiatrists have contended that Claude R. Eatherly's [American Major who gave the order to bomb Hiroshima] confinement to a mental hospital and later continued psychiatric treatment, as well as his earlier attempts at crime, resulted from his desire to punish himself because of feelings of guilt. Possibly his action resulted from desire for acclaim or to be noticed; reportedly he was highly jealous of the officers who did the actual bombing for which he merely issued the "all clear" signal.

Some of the disorders of physical origin which produce mental or personality changes are: senility (*senile dementia* and *cerebral arteriosclerosis*), general paresis, alcoholism, epilepsy, brain injury, and stammering.

The effects of alcoholism, nicotine, caffeine, and drug addiction were discussed in Chapter III. Neurotic conflicts lead to *alcoholism*. The majority of alcoholics can be classified as "neurotics." A small percentage of them become psychotics, but probably the drinking does not lead to the psychosis; these people probably had psychotic personalities to begin with.

Persons who have become excessive users of morphine, opium, marihuana, barbiturates, and so forth, may have become excessive users through first using the drugs to alleviate physical pain. They may on the other hand have been led to *drug addiction* by resorting to sedatives, stimulants, and narcotics to carry them through emotional states.

Sexual deviation has taken many forms: *fetishism,* in which the individual gets satisfaction from loving objects instead of persons; *homosexuality,* in which satisfaction is gained from sexual relations with persons of the same sex; *sadism,* in which satisfaction is obtained by inflicting pain or seeing it inflicted on others; *masochism,* suffering pain or inflicting pain on one's self; *masturbation,* getting sexual satisfaction without a partner through exciting the genital organs; *exhibitionism,* gratifying desires by exposing the erogenous parts of the body; *voyerism,* obtaining satisfaction through seeing others perform sexual acts or from seeing the sexual organs of others.

Some doctors have said that all persons masturbate to some extent. Dr. Brill took the position that masturbation does not do organic harm. The persons who resort to this method for satisfaction are, however, getting inadequate results and they often develop conflicts that may lead to anxiety neurosis.[7]

A study that may have implications for persons who seem uninterested in or incapable of sexual expression was made of sixty macaque monkeys. The monkeys were raised by artificial mothers. When they reached adulthood it was found that they were totally ineffective sexually. Even when these laboratory-raised monkeys were placed with monkeys brought up under normal conditions (i.e., with their natural mothers) they failed to function sexually. Otherwise the monkeys who were separated from their real mothers and kept isolated from playmates were apparently healthy and "normal" adults. Dr. Harry Harlow of the University of Wisconsin who conducted this experiment said that it is possible ". . . that rejection, the denial of a mother, may be a necessary part of maturing. That the perfect mother, after all, is not perfect unless she is hostile, which in some undefined way, is a necessary part of being able to indulge in the sex act." [8]

PSYCHOPATHIC PERSONALITIES — Persons who will lie, steal, or use any means to get the things they want or those who live upon the "pleasure principle" have what is known as *antisocial reactions*. They are perverse in the sense that they go against the customs, beliefs, and laws of society. Persons whose crimes lead to their running afoul of the law are said to have *dyssocial reactions*. These people who are pathological liars, eccentrics, trouble-makers, moral defectives, and criminals who commit crime without justification are psychopaths. Although not all drug addicts would belong here, some few would; generally drug addicts are extreme liars.

Some of the forms of sexual deviation are considered psychopathic; the sexual criminal who commits rape or lures children to his abode for unnatural acts certainly is an extreme example of the psychopath. The "Peeping Tom" (voyerist) would be classified here. The degree to which the perversion is practiced and conditions under which it is practiced influencing the attitude of society toward it would determine whether or not the individual would be classified as a psychopath. Certainly if all persons (or even most or many) practice masturbation then this perversion (if indeed it could be called a perversion) would not cause one to be classified a psychopathic personality.

The line of demarcation between the insane and the criminals is sometimes faint. In many cases the persons classified as criminal have been compelled by factors both internal and external to commit actions they know are wrong and/or shameful. Many criminals are never caught or convicted; those who are caught may for some reason have been more susceptible to being caught. A sense of guilt, a lack of cleverness, a desire to be caught may lead some to be apprehended. The habitual criminal, known as a *recidivist,* has little chance of being helped to recover from criminal tendencies. First offenders given understanding treatment may be returned to useful lives outside of prison walls. It has been suggested that "beneath the hard shell of criminal activities there may exist a great yearning to be loved." [9] This suggests that a great deal of responsibility for crime or the lack of it may be traced to the home where love, security, and a sense of responsibility and respect for law and order are developed.

It is noteworthy that out of over 2,000 incarcerated criminals in the Texas Penitentiary System (Department of Corrections) in 1962 only two of these were Jews. The director of the system has expressed belief that the Jewish home life may be a factor involved here.

A small percentage of psychopaths are to be found in mental institutions (a majority of them probably should be); approximately a fifth of those confined to prison are psychopaths.

COMMON ADJUSTMENT MECHANISMS — Compensation (overcompensation) may be good or bad. Parents may insist that children be strong where they themselves have been weak. One such case resulted in the son killing his parents; he has for the last thirty years been confined to a mental institution as a result although at the time of the murder he was an advanced college student. On the other hand, when the student who has failed in one field works harder in some other field where he becomes outstanding, compensation is perhaps good. If anyone who is thwarted or frustrated in any action whatsoever turns to something he can do well such as typewriting, playing golf, or playing the piano, then compensation is good.

If a businessman does not like his work, he can turn to hobbies and interests that enable him to find satisfactions from life outside of work. Since, however, doing work that one likes to do is one of life's most rewarding activities, any person engaged in working at something he doesn't like (unless he sees that it will lead eventually to something he will like) should seek other employment. Business firms that employ people to work in routine and unrewarding tasks often provide satisfactions outside of work hours or at the workplace in order to compensate.

Daniel Starch a number of years ago studied the life histories of one hundred and fifty men. His study revealed that there are two forces of great power that bring about the all-important inner drive possessed by able and successful men. These are: (1) all-consuming purpose, i.e., determination; and (2) the anticipation of satisfaction of achievement. He concluded that the person with inner drive is the man who succeeds.[10]

People who overcompensate may accomplish seemingly impossible tasks. They may be determined to have the power, the money, the love, the adventure, the fame denied them at some other time.

A study of the life histories of persons who consulted the Family Society of Greater Boston in the thirties and early forties and reported on by Friend and Haggard showed that good early family relationships carry over into the working situation. In addition to taking the experiences of childhood into adult situations of life and work, the study concluded that *"The worker appears to compromise with life by going after the identical and specific satisfaction in work denied him years before."* [11]

Rationalization is the assigning of plausible and rational reasons to actions that have been precipitated by devious and emotional motives. John may say that he is breaking off his engagement to Mary because they are not yet ready for marriage; the real reason may be that he has discovered Jane.

Projection is ascribing to others one's own deficiencies, feelings, ideas, or motives. The person who steals but accuses others of stealing, the wife who is unfaithful but accuses others of infidelity, and the worker who accuses others of the kind of neglect of which he is guilty are examples of people who are projecting (or ascribing) to others their own faults. This type of adjustment weakens the personality for solving problems legitimately.

Scapegoating is the blaming of somebody or something for one's own shortcomings, frustrations, and mistakes. It is similar to projection but different in that one is in scapegoating finding someone to accuse of being to blame for the fault, the action, or failure to act of the accuser. A worker may blame his boss for work he has inadequately performed; he may say the boss failed to give adequate directions. He may "pass the buck" to a fellow worker for his own failure. He may blame the system of transportation used for his tardiness. He may blame a political party or the president when he has made bad judgment in purchasing stocks.

One who is guilty of *introjection* does not as does the projectionist try to mold the world to his way of thinking; instead, he may become a "yes man." He follows the path of least resistance and may just go along because that is the way the crowd is going. He sees no need to stand up for ideas of his own; it is so much easier to follow Joe, or Jim, or John. The boss is always right. Any organization made up of "yes men" is likely to fail once it loses its strong leader or leaders.

Negativism develops when one instead of saying "yes" to everything always says "no" to any suggestion. Some people are confirmed negativists. They may do nothing, or they may do the opposite of what is requested of them. One who must manage a negativist learns to use devious means of getting results. Action may be obtained by requesting the opposite of what is desired. Only if the negativist can be led to change his way of thinking will he become cooperative. Sometimes his "no" is merely a way of reaction. He says "no" but he acts "yes."

Sublimation is a substitute for behavior upon which a stigma is attached. If it were not for sublimation of desires frowned upon by society, the world would have few of its creative arts. Sublimation is perhaps one of the most positive of the substitute acts. Writing, painting, building cabinets, composing songs, and a thousand and one hobbies might be named as sublimations.

Seclusiveness, daydreaming and *retreats from conflict* are results of many past experiences that lead to retreat from the world of reality. This type of adjustment can, of course, be dangerous if it is extreme. It would finally result in mental illness, usually schizophrenia. Otherwise, in mild forms it is not bad except that persons may be kept from real accomplishment because of their fancied achievements. A form of daydreaming (fantasy) is the *conquering hero* mechanism. Somnambulism (sleepwalking) is like daydreaming a form of escape and has been listed as a dissociative reaction. The daydreamer becomes a hero who charges in on a white horse to save his loved one. His deeds are daring and they bring success that he usually is not able to accomplish in real-life activities. The *suffering hero* is one who becomes in his mind the worst bad man in order to get even with those who have frustrated him.

Identification is similar to the conquering hero and suffering hero mechanisms; it is different in that identification of one's self with positive persons and actions is strengthening to the personality. Members of successful groups identify themselves with their groups. Workers in a department or an industry identify themselves with each other and with their supervisors and even top management. Husbands and wives identify themselves with each other and their personalities are usually strengthened when they complement each other. When one reads a book or sees a movie he usually identifies himself with the hero or heroine (positive adjustment if not carried too far); if one is on the brink of emotional breakdown, he may identify himself with the negative character and the results could be immediately disastrous if the emulated person's crime triggers a similar crime on his part.

Compulsions may relieve tensions. The underlying dynamics of the compulsions felt by many people are somewhat like obsessive compulsions of the neurotics already discussed. These compulsions to knock on wood, to cross one's fingers, and so forth, may relieve tensions. In compulsion neurosis (psychasthenia) the compulsion is a harmful one; in mere compulsion, characteristic of so many who are otherwise considered quite "normal," the compulsion is frequently a triviality.

Emotional immaturity is characterized by *egocentrism*. The emotionally immature person may fly into a rage on slightest provocation. He may depend upon parents or parent substitutes for relieving tensions. This type of person is constantly doing things to get attention. He is like the advertiser who says "Even bad publicity is better than none." If he can't do positive things to get attention, he sometimes resorts to negative actions.

People who adjust to the dissatisfactions of life by trying to do good for other people (teachers, nurses, counselors, deans, personnel employees, welfare workers, and so forth) are adjusting positively. It might be said these people for the most part are satisfying the creative instinct just as much as is the man who fathers numerous children or the mother who gives them birth. In some cases their efforts may be considered sublimation; in others it may be considered the *do-good* or *Messiah complex*. In the extreme form this person may tend to become a *radical reformer* (as did a certain Texas General!).

Studies have shown that *radicals* are generally more pessimistic, less apt at social relations, more likely to feel inferior, and more likely to feel rejected by parents than are non-radicals. Another study found radicals ". . . to be brighter usually, better informed, slower in movement and decision, more introverted, self-sufficient, and dominant." [12] Radicals may be stimulating in an otherwise unprogressive firm; they are, nevertheless, usually poor team workers.

Regression is the tendency to live in a period that is past. Many people refer to the "good old days." Memory in some way paints a rosy glow that makes the past seem beautiful. Yet most people given the opportunity to relive the past would hesitate to accept. They cannot face up to the fact that it really was not "so wonderful as all the dreams they had." The person who keeps remembering college days instead of trying to succeed on a new job and the man or woman who continues to remember an old sweetheart are guilty of regression. Children also regress. When the ways of adjusting to childhood are carried over into adulthood, these persistent tendencies are called *persistent affect fixations*. It is possible for persons who have such fixations to change them. Some of these negative ways of adjusting have been discussed: seclusiveness, radical tendencies, emotional immaturity, hypochondria.

Habit spasms and *tics* develop to relieve tensions and possibly to get attention. To alleviate a habit spasm it is necessary not only to decrease the tensions that produced it but also to interrupt the established habit. If a twitching or fluttering eyelid has brought attention, it may be relinquished with reluctance.

Most people some of the time and some of the people most of the time are guilty of procrastination. In the extreme, this is known as *abulic obsession*. The student who puts off study and the worker who postpones getting started on his work are guilty. Interest and motivation are essential if one is to overcome this tendency. Having someone else to prod one also helps.

The *Oedipus complex* (attraction of the son toward the mother) and the *Electra complex* (attraction of the daughter toward the father) have furnished fiction and dramatic writers with numerous plots for their stories and plays. Eugene O'Neill's plays drew heavily upon them; D. H. Lawrence's *Sons and Lovers* poignantly revealed the effect of the Oedipus complex in his own life. Either of these complexes may lead one to marry a person old enough to be his mother or her father. This is not always a bad adjustment. As the famous Kinsey reports implied, the sexual adjustments of the older woman and the younger man (or *vice versa*) may be more alike than are those of persons the same age. But, of course, marriage implies a great deal more than sexual adjustment.

The Oedipus complex can be transferred from a mother to some other older woman in whom one confides and from whom one seeks the love and attention of "mother." A family friend or even one's secretary may be this "other woman." Such a relationship may be a stabilizing influence. It is well for those who manage people to be able to recognize these symptoms in themselves and in those they supervise or with whom they work.

Many persons adjust by building up *defense mechanisms* other than seclusiveness, projection, scapegoating, and so on, as previously discussed. Being highly sensitive to criticism, over-susceptible to flattery, "running down others," and making allowances for one's own inadequacies are examples of such defenses.

A lot of people tend to be over-anxious, to worry unduly about tests, jobs, or family. It has been shown that such *anxiety* may have motivating value. In one study it was found that a high-anxiety group of fifty students when compared with a low-anxiety group of fifty students did not do as well in a first attempt to trace a stylus through a maze while blindfolded; they did do better on repetition than the low-anxiety group. In a similar experiment with mirror tracing no difference was found between the two groups.[13] Another study has shown that intelligence and examination scores are not affected by anxiety.[14]

Persons who constantly resort to ill health as a means of getting attention or solving problems are said to have *invalidism*. Their illnesses may take the form of conversion reactions (discussed under neuroses, *hysteria*) or headaches, stomach aches, nausea, cramps or even the various ailments discussed under "emotional disorders." Students often have headaches, cramps, or other illnesses when faced with tests to take. Students who study and prepare for examinations have no need to resort to the subterfuge of imagined illnesses. Students who do solve their problems by developing ailments become employees who do likewise. One of management's big problems today is to know how to deal with the neurotic employee who is absent because he imagines he is ill, or whose emotions lead to illnesses that are reflected in organic reactions.

There is a further problem of distinguishing between the person who really believes that he is ill (the neurotic) and the person who is merely "getting out of work" (the malingerer).

Suppression of desires or ideas that might disturb one in a work or study situation is an essential and positive way of adjusting. When one suppresses a desire to slap someone else, he is aware of what he is doing and it is good that he has this adjustment mechanism to aid him. Society demands that we restrain ourselves from carrying out certain actions that impulses and desires would lead us into. We may be angry enough to shout at others, to kill someone, or to throw an object at someone or upon the floor. We restrain ourselves; we are aware of what we have done, and the moment passes. When one has recently lost a loved one he may feel like giving way to weeping just as a business conference gets under way. He may, in fact, later in privacy give way to his emotions. For the time being, however, he suppresses his desire. If, however, he *repressed* the very awareness of the loss to the extent of forgetting it, the action would be bad. In *California Street*, a popular modern novel, the leading character denies his wife's death to the extent that he actually believes he converses with her. This is repression at its worst. Ideas, thoughts, emotions long repressed build up inner tensions that may finally "blow the lid" so to speak. Emotional disturbances too long repressed could lead to breakdown.

Summary — It is very difficult to classify mental diseases, neuroses, and ways of adjusting. Even highly trained medical doctors are frequently unable to categorize mental and other illnesses. Reclassification seems to go on constantly. This chapter has perhaps used a simplified approach. In outline form, this is the classification that has been used:

I. Psychoses (schizophrenia, manic-depressive, paranoia).

II. Neuroses (anxiety; neurasthenia; hysteria, including dissociative reactions such as amnesia, fugue states, somnambulism, and multiple personalities, and conversion reactions such as paralysis of a limb, blindness, and deafness; psychasthenia, including phobias, obsessions, manias, and compulsions; depressive reaction).

III. Emotional disorders, including hypochondria, psychosomatic illnesses or somatization reactions (allergies, common colds, asthma, hay fever, eczema, acne, arthritis, obesity, hypertension, rheumatic disease, colitis, sinus trouble, and perhaps heart trouble; also, but equally capable of being included under II or IV or even I in some instances: alcoholism, drug addiction, sexual deviation).

IV. Psychopathic personalities (pathological liars, who lie for the joy of lying; sexual psychopaths; perverts; swindlers; confidence men; persons who commit crimes without extenuation).

V. Common adjustment mechanisms, some of which if carried to the extreme would lead to neuroses or emotional disorders (compensation; rationalization; projection; scapegoating; introjection; negativism; sublimation; seclusiveness, daydreaming, and retreats from conflict; identification; compulsions; emotional immaturity, egocentrism; Messiah complex; radical reformer; regression; persistent affect fixations; habit spasms, tics; abulic obsession; Oedipus and Electra complexes; defense mechanisms; anxiety; invalidism; repression; suppression).

No attempt has been made to classify these illnesses and ways of adjusting as organic or functional. Many suspect today that most illnesses if traced to the source could be shown to have their origin in some organic or chemical change in the body. Currently over half of the mentally ill are, however, classified as having functional ailments only, that is, there is no discovered organic origin. Neuroses and emotional disorders are chiefly considered functional, although the ailments listed under III above result in organic disturbances.

Conditions due to tissue damages and changes affect both body and mind (certainly mind, body and emotions must be closely linked). These are caused by infections, toxins, trauma, nutritional deprivation, senile conditions, cerebral arteriosclerosis, and other neurological diseases.

Knowing something of the ways people adjust will aid any supervisor or layman. The average person, however, should not attempt to deal with persons suspected or being on the verge of mental breakdown. Symptoms should be recognized and such people should be referred to proper medical authorities. Understanding personalities and their problems of adjustment can help one to deal more efficiently with the average person and to better control his own attitudes.

PROJECTS

1. Read and review in a five-page report any volume you find appealing on the subject of mental illnesses.
2. Write a four or five-page research paper on "Your Emotions Can Make You Ill."
3. Analyze your own methods of adjusting in a short paper. Classify these methods as "positive" or "negative" ways of adjusting.
4. Have a "Hobby Show" exhibiting hobbies of members of your class. The college library would be a suitable place.

ACKNOWLEDGMENTS AND REFERENCES

1   Menninger, William C., *Social Changes and Scientific Progress,* Fifth Annual Arthur Dehon Little Memorial Lecture at the Massachusetts Institute of Technology, Cambridge, Mass., May 1, 1951, pp. 31–32.
     Lemkau, Paul, *Mental Hygiene in Public Health,* The Blakiston Division, McGraw-Hill Book Company, Inc., New York, 1955, pp. 6–8.

2   Gordon, Gerald, "Some Aspects of Mental Health Among Supervisors and Executives," *Proceedings,* Sixteenth Conference Texas Personnel and Management Association, The University of Texas, Austin, 1954, p. 23ff.

3   Berrien, F. K., *Practical Psychology,* The Macmillan Company, New York, 1952, pp. 37–45.

4   ——, "Special Medicine Report," *Newsweek,* November 2, 1959, p. 64.

5   Brill, A. A., *Lectures on Psychoanalytic Psychiatry,* Alfred A. Knopf, New York, 1947, p. 53.

6   *Ibid.,* p. 119.

7   *Ibid.,* p. 177.

8   ——, "Science," *Newsweek,* January 16, 1961, p. 52.

9   Menninger, Karl A., *The Human Mind,* Third Edition, Alfred A. Knopf, New York, 1951, p. 459.

10   Starch, Daniel, *How to Develop Your Executive Ability,* Harper & Brothers, New York, 1943.

11   Friend, Jeannette G., and Haggard, Ernest A., "Work Adjustment in Relation to Family Background," *Applied Psychology Monographs,* No. 16, Stanford University Press, Stanford, California, 1948, pp. 137–138.

12   Hepner, Harry Walker, *Psychology Applied to Life and Work,* Prentice-Hall, Inc., Englewood Cliffs, New Jersey, 1957, p. 54.

13   Ausubel, David P., Schiff, Herberg M., and Goldman, Morton, "Qualitative Characteristics in the Learning Process Associated with Anxiety," *Journal of Abnormal and Social Psychology,* October, 1953, pp. 537–547.

14   Matarazzo, Joseph D. and others, "The Relationship between Anxiety Level and Several Measures of Intelligence," *Journal of Consulting Psychology,* June, 1954, pp. 201–205.

CHAPTER VII

PREVENTION AND TREATMENT OF MENTAL ILLNESSES AND MALADJUSTMENTS

Prevention of Mental Illnesses — In class this writer once used a story that appeared in *Life* magazine about the treatment of Gene Tierney at the Menninger Clinic. The report stated that Miss Tierney had found new pleasure in reading and had quoted to a reporter: *"When in disgrace with fortune and men's eyes, / I all alone beweep my outcast state, / and trouble deaf heaven with my bootless cries, / and look upon myself and curse my fate . . ."* At the time this was used in the class referred to, Miss Tierney had sufficiently recovered to marry a Houston businessman; after class, Glenn H. McCarthy, Jr., said, "Doc, you were talking about my aunt." The name McCarthy written in a rollbook had until that moment meant nothing to the young man's teacher. Suddenly it was realized that the young son of one who has made headlines (both in negative as well as positive situations), as are many others in the daily news who may seem separate and apart, was really after all merely human like the rest of us. Those people who make headlines need love and understanding just as the average person does, just as the criminal does, just as the mentally ill and the emotionally upset do. The word "understanding" is a golden key that unlocks the door to so many of life's situations and problems.

With the schools of today teaching more about mental hygiene, mental illnesses are being better understood and are coming to be regarded as being like other illnesses. They should not carry moral stigma or be regarded as signs of character weakness. They are not inherited in the sense that they are determined by the genes in the manner that height, color, and such characteristics are inherited. Mendel's laws of inheritance, in other words, are not considered to apply and parents who are mentally ill do not pass on this trait in the same manner that they do many characteristics. The tendency to develop some types of mental illnesses does run in families in the sense that the constitutions of these people and their central nervous systems may predispose them toward such illnesses. Such predispositions, as a matter of fact, more frequently than not fail to lead to insanity.

The establishment of mental health associations throughout the country, developments in medical science, legislation, and the resulting enlightenment of the populace are all contributing to progress in preventing and curing mental illnesses. For continued progress feelings should be made known to governing bodies through service clubs, civic groups, and the mental health associations. They should be kept informed of progress being made against mental illness and that the public does want, even at the cost of added taxes, provisions for study and cure of mental illnesses.[1]

It has been estimated that at any one time in the United States there are approximately 750,000 persons sufficiently mentally ill to be hospitalized. These people occupy something over half of the nation's hospital beds and about half of them are chronic cases. A much fewer number, approximately 115,000, are hospitalized for mental retardation. In addition, there are the short-term and long-term prisoners, alcoholics, and drug addicts that generally swell the number of persons who are at any given time known to be mentally ill or maladjusted. Considering the vast number of persons involved, it is surprising that there is not even more concern over research and money-raising for studying mental illnesses. It is much easier to get people wrought up over poliomyelitis and muscular dystrophy.

One clinic for each 50,000 to 100,000 of the general population is needed in the United States for outpatient services. Apparently in the cultures of the Western European style, one psychiatric hospital bed for each 200 of the general population is needed.[2]

Based upon past experience, about one in ten to twelve persons born in the United States has been or will be a mental patient. What with all of the wonder drugs and new attacks on mental illnesses, and with general orientation of so many people to the hazards and problems of mental illnesses, there are various estimates of the number of "cures" to be effected today. Generally, these range from sixty-five to eighty per cent of the first-time patients under sixty-five years of age. Some say the chance of the new patient returning home in the first twelve months after hospitalization is approximately fifty-fifty; after two years, the chance is approximately sixteen to one, and after five years, ninety-nine to one. So many new discoveries are being made today that these estimates cannot be accepted as final, despite the reliability of the psychiatrists and physicians who have made them.

The aim of mental hygiene programs is "to ensure that the personality structure is as sound as its genetically determined base permits."[3] Programs are designed to help people to assimilate or integrate experiences in order to be better able to withstand stress. Historically, mental hygiene has included the care of all types of mental diseases. While mental illnesses themselves are not new, they are a problem of our age. Further, while they are not confined to any one ethnic group, our group does have its share; and the aim of mental hygiene in our group remains the prevention and cure of all types of mental diseases, including the so-called stress diseases presumably perpetrated by modern industrialization and the inclination to live "fast."

In the United States currently some twenty-five million dollars is being spent annually in research on mental ill-health. The United States Public Health Service at Bethesda, Maryland, the National Institute of Health, spends more than half of the total expenditures for such research. The Ford Foundation spends the second largest sum for such research, and it spends the largest sum from a private source.[4]

Freud is quoted as having said: "Behind every psychoanalyst stands the man with the syringe." He suggested that psychoanalysis would probably be more important as a theory and science of the unconscious mind than as a means of curing mental illnesses.[5] Psychoanalysis is a field within a field. Most psychiatrists are trained to some extent in psychoanalysis. Something over ten per cent of the more than 12,000 psychiatrists in this country have specialized in psychoanalysis. Psychiatrists are medical doctors who use all known medical treatments for mental illnesses. Both the American Psychiatric Association and the American Psychoanalytic Association hold that only medically trained persons should practice psychoanalysis, but the latter organization will take members who are not trained medical doctors.

Many doctors today criticize psychoanalysis as a science of human behavior. They feel that it has not worked. Nevertheless, it must still be considered as a helpful tool. Its chief value may be similar to the value of some of the other tools used in the treatment of mental illnesses, such as hypnosis; it can give clues that enable doctors to use other treatments more effectively.

For a better understanding of the treatments offered by psychoanalysts and psychiatrists, seven basic tenets of psychiatry as offered by Dr. William C. Menninger are given by way of introduction to a specific listing of treatments for maladjustments and mental illnesses. These have been added to and edited, but they were first used by Dr. Menninger:

1. *The Concept of Personality.* The total person is considered by the psychiatrist. A person responds to stimuli according to what he is, the way he is built, his personality, his body chemistry, his mental life, and his social relations.

2. *Psychological Structure.* Instinctive energy drives of an individual originate in the *id*, a functional area of the personality considered to be the seat of the unconscious instincts. Knowledge, conscious thinking,

memory and feeling make up the *ego* which is sensitive to the rules of society. It is the intermediary between primitive desires that originate in the id and the requirements of the environment. The *superego*, third functional area, has a representation in conscious life essentially the same as conscience, but is itself largely unconscious. It is a kind of inhibitive censor that develops in the third or fourth year of life. Certain psychological aspects of life are given meaning by this theoretical concept of Freud. Conflicts between the id, the ego, and the superego, according to Freud, created the mental and emotional ills. Psychoanalysis could help the patient to understand that these internal conflicts go on; with understanding he could overcome the problems created by them and thus could strengthen his personality.

3. *Psychological Energy*. The two instinctive energy forces of the id, the hostile-destructive-aggressive drive, and the erotic-constructive drive make up psychological energy. The undesirable aspects of each drive are neutralized in the healthy adult when the ego fuses these primitive energies into actions and expressions that are socially approved. The ego represses from conscious recognition those aspects of the personality that are considered unacceptable.

4. *Psychological Development*. Infancy and childhood are the periods when personality is shaped.

5. *The Homeostasis Quality of the Personality*. The personality is everlastingly adjusting to "varying degrees of psychological pressure arising from forces within himself, and from the environment." There is a constant struggle to maintain equilibrium.

6. *The Role of Environment*. While inherited characteristics influence the personality, the environment of infancy and early childhood have most to do with shaping personality according to the psychiatrists.

7. *The Universality of the Application of Psychiatric Knowledge*. By studying patients, psychiatrists have come to understand much about how people think, about their emotions, and of how they behave. Knowledge accumulated is not only being used to prevent mental illness, it offers possibilities for assisting in the solution of social problems.[6]

Some Specific Preventives and Treatments Offered for Mental Illnesses —

1. *Rules for Preserving Mental Health* — These rules, given by Dr. Karl A. Menninger, are quoted verbatim:

> *Set up as an ideal the facing of reality as honestly and as cheerfully as possible.*
> *Cultivate social contacts and cultural developments.*

> *Recognize neurotic evasions as such and take advantage of opportunities for sublimation. (Substitute hobbies for habits.)*
> *Learn to know the evidences of mental pathology and how best to deal with them.*
> *Assume that the unhappy are always (at least partly) wrong.*[7]

There are two general areas of mental hygiene: primary and secondary. In the primary, prevention is the aim. *Prevention* would include:

Preparing people for stresses and strains of life such as training given in preparing people for marriage, for parenthood, for old age, for military service, for selection of life's work; education in all of its phases. The *secondary* area would include treatments given by psychiatry and psychoanalysis, treatment in hospitals and outpatient clinics, counseling, and case work.

Parents and teachers have a great influence in preventing mental illnesses. Parental attitudes of overprotection, rejection, and extreme methods of discipline contribute to the patterns of development of the personality. Further, children frequently adjust as did their parents. A study of California children classified according to those whose mothers worked, those with step parents or guardians, and those who lacked an adult male in the home, found that having a working mother did not cause a problem for the child, as long as there was proper love and guidance. Those who lived with step parents and guardians exhibited nervous symptoms more than did others. Those who did not have an adult male in the home lacked a sense of personal worth to a greater extent than did others.[8] Parents who are over-strict or who do not know what their children need are more likely to have problem children than are those who are less strict and more aware of their children's needs.[9]

2. *Psychotherapy: Individual and Group* — (a) Individual Psychotherapy attacks the conflicts that produce emotional disturbances. The people who give psychotherapy to others must be really interested in them; they must not ever appear to be making fun of them or to be disgusted with their problems. Whoever gives such treatment must understand that the patient is going to resist cure because his emotional problem is in some way giving him pleasure. There are, in general, two main forms the psychotherapy may take: (1) It may attempt to *draw out the problems of the patient* through numerous methods including letting the patient talk through free association and as the stream of consciousness dictates, letting him act out experiences, using hypnosis to induce the patient to talk, or using drugs to induce the patient to reveal his troubles. The patient's revelations act as a mental catharsis. (2) The psychotherapist (counselor, psychiatrist, psychoanalyst), may help the patient to

suppress whatever is troubling him through many techniques such as leading him to constructive and creative efforts, giving him medicines (placebos) to placate him and make him think he is getting proper treatment until he can throw off his conflict, using hypnotism and the power of suggestion to aid the patient in throwing off or forgetting, letting the patient project his emotional problems upon the analyst (transference), using drugs, using shock treatments, and the various other remedies discussed under separate headings. Ministers, teachers, deans, loved ones, supervisors, friends, may lend willing ears to the troubles of others; they are not, however, in any position to use the various methods of treatment available to psychiatrists and other medical doctors.

The rules for psychiatric counseling as given by Dr. Karl A. Menninger are given here in full. It will be seen if the reader will turn to the chapter on counseling (Chapter IX) that these rules are very similar to the rules evolved for interviewing for counselors of Western Electric's Hawthorne plant workers, which rules were evolved over a long period of research and development in the use of the so-called non-directive counseling technique which is now widely used in industry. Dr. Menninger's proposed techniques for counseling were in use with maladjusted patients prior to the development of the rules for interviewing industrial workers. Here they are:

First, show the patient that you are interested in him.

Second, don't lie to him, don't give him placebos or joke with him about his symptoms, and don't promise him anything.

Third, listen to what he has to say, listen a long time, and listen many times, alone and without interruption.

Fourth, listen without censoriousness in word or expression, without rebuke, ridicule, or amusement. Absurd as aspects of them may be, your patient's maladjustments are not funny to him.

Fifth, give no advice, no treatment, and no opinion until you know what the patient is really unhappy about; then tell him that such unhappiness *could be* (not *is*) the cause of such symptoms.

Sixth, gradually help the patient to see the connection between the unhappiness and his symptoms and to realize that he must assume the responsibility for such changes in his techniques or his environment as will be likely to give him greater peace. This, rather than allowing him to throw all responsibility on the doctor, is the rational and only permanently successful method of helping him.[10]

When the psychiatrist or psychoanalyst employs what has come to be called *psychoanalysis* (its techniques were used long before Freud despite the fact that he is known as the originator of the method), the free association, stream of consciousness technique is used. The patient talks about his problems, his thoughts, his feelings, his dreams. In the process he brings out his problems and disturbing conflicts. The doctor talks only enough to suggest or encourage the patient to continue talking, to reveal the forgotten things, the repressed emotions that may have caused his trouble. It is the telling of these things, the bringing of them out into the open that helps. If a patient cannot tell what is troubling him, because he actually doesn't know or has forgotten, hypnosis or drugs may be resorted to. Sometimes he is given a paint brush and a canvas, or modeling clay, and with these he tells what he could not say.

If in the process of psychoanalysis the patient becomes dependent upon the doctor, this is known as transference. Sometimes this develops into strong attachment akin to love; sometimes it becomes more of a resentment. It can lead to a hate that results in disaster. Patients have killed their doctors. In one recent tragic case, the patient killed the wife of her psychiatrist. Presumably, in this case it was because at a given moment in time she felt tragically alone, rejected, and unattractive. The victim was the person who was near to be killed. Such a result is rare. Psychiatrists are at a disadvantage. They may often suspect that a person is dangerous; until there is overt action to prove this, it is frequently impossible to do anything about the situation. Many of the most dangerous persons are those who suddenly act, often without warning.

The psychoanalyst's aim is to lead the patient to discover his own problems and solve them for himself. He learns his weaknesses and learns to forgive himself for them, but primarily he learns to become dependent upon himself as he is weaned away from the analyst.

TABLE VII-1

COMMONLY USED FREUDIAN PSYCHOANALYTIC TERMS

Ego, the conscious part of the mind which directs the traffic so to speak between the desires of the *id* and the requirements of society. The ego tries to keep people sensible and logical. A residual of the ego is presumably unconscious. Chiefly it is governed by memory, intelligence, practical judgment, a sense of right, perception.

Id, produces drive, creates interest, vitalizes, but also is the primitive unconscious, amoral basis of mental activity; it is perhaps chiefly motivated by the sex drive and the desires for pleasure.

Superego, governs the conscience in that it stifles impulses to do things it considers wrong; it is the seat of guilt and deep anxiety, although it is an unconscious part of the mind; it overrides intelligence and represses actions and painful thoughts and events. For this reason, when it is severed from the rest of the brain the mental patient is generally aided.

Conscious, is the part of the mind that provides awareness.

Subconscious, is neither conscious nor unconscious but is a seat of awareness just below the surface of the conscious.

Unconscious, is hidden, the seat of repressions and instincts which although we are not aware of them influence us. It is doubted now that there is such a thing as *the unconscious.* In the sense that the activities of the ego are chiefly conscious (partly unconscious) and those of the id are unconscious, the term is good.

Libido, is the drive that comes from sexual urges.

Sublimation, is the turning of unacceptable drives of the id to substitutes not frowned upon by society, creative outlets.

Inhibition, restrains one from doing things that he might do if the inhibition didn't exist. A chief attraction of alcohol to some people is that it releases their inhibitions, removes their scruples, and they can enjoy things they wouldn't otherwise permit.

Catharsis, in medicine is a dose of something that will cleanse out the contents of the stomach and intestinal tract; a mental catharsis cleanses out the mind, gets rid of the repressions and the troubling emotional problems; writing, talking, painting, working may all provide mental catharsis.

Complex, is a word that designates the control of emotions over actions to the extent that the fixed outcome affects life. Freud introduced the term "complex" but Adler put forth the theory of "inferiority complex" which has been used to explain all sorts of things.

Fixation, is an attitude or way of adjusting that has been carried over from childhood to adulthood. Obsession, regression, repression, suppression, and others of the ways of adjusting discussed in Chapter VI might also be included in this list.

Psychoanalysis, is the term applied to Freud's method of drawing from the patient the problems that have brought on his disturbance (see discussion in this chapter).

Resistance, develops in the course of psychoanalysis when the patient tries to hold on to the very problems that have caused his emotional upset because they in some way satisfy his needs.

Self-sabotage, is very similar to resistance. One who contrives always
to defeat his aims, to fail in certain areas instead of attempting
success in them, is guilty of self-sabotage. He defeats his own
aims because in so doing he retains other things or accomplishes other aims that are more important to him than success
in the particular area under consideration, which may be work,
home, care of children, marriage, love.

Transference, occurs when the patient transfers his love, hate, anger
to the psychoanalyst or perhaps to some other person who has
listened to him.

(b) *Group Psychotherapy* — Good results have been obtained in
groups of from ten to fifteen people when these people have been brought
together to talk about similar problems and difficulties. It has been found
that they often will talk in groups about things that they would not talk
about in individual conferences. In one type of group therapy, the thera-
pist merely tells the group how to proceed. He leads them to see the
similarities and dissimilarities of their experiences. The process is much
like "brainstorming" (see Chapter XIV) except that instead of people
being drawn to propose solutions to business problems or problems of
management and supervision they are encouraged to discover their own
personal problems and propose their own solutions to them. This type
of psychotherapy is useful with groups of people who have similar problems (as preparing for parenthood, coping with problems of teen-agers,
industrial workers). It is also useful with groups of mental patients who
are being prepared for return to families, or who have made progress
toward recovery. It is good for any group of mental patients who are
still able to relate themselves to the group.

A type of group therapy called *remotivation technique* developed by
Dorothy Hoskins Smith (teacher of English, now deceased) and widely
reported, has a five-step procedure: (1) *The climate of acceptance,* in
which people are called by name and complimentary comments are made
about them. (2) *The bridge to reality,* in which a poem is read leading
to discussion. (3) *Sharing the world we live in,* in which there is discussion on any topic of general interest. (4) *Appreciation of the work of
the world,* in which the patient is led to some type of creative work. (5)
The climate of appreciation, during which the patients plan some future
meeting they can anticipate. Apparently this process has had good results.

A Nigerian psychiatrist, Dr. Thomas A. Lambo, has used a "village
system" for mental patients; the patients are boarded in homes in the four
villages near his hospital. His theory is that violence is not inherent in

mental illness. Because patients are locked up, they sense the fear of their jailors and their violent reactions merely confirm expectations, Dr. Lambo believes. His is a kind of group therapy in the sense that those needing treatment are kept with groups of people. They are not isolated from society.

3. *Hypnosis* — Today many medical schools are offering courses in hypnosis and some of the leading universities are conducting research in the use of hypnosis. In the five-year period 1957–1961 the membership in the Society for Clinical and Experimental Hypnosis doubled.

Hypnosis is valuable in treating disturbed persons because suggestions can be used in the hypnotic state. Experiments performed in psychology classes which the writer took with Dr. William Giles Campbell (who later wrote a dissertation on hypnosis) showed that persons under hypnotic suggestions do not feel certain types of inflicted pain. Further, they can be told that when they are waked from the hypnotic state they will not feel this pain and they do not.

Freud used hypnosis first in his attempts to delve into the "unconscious" minds of patients to find the problems that were bothering them. He used suggestion to aid them in recovery. He abandoned the use of hypnosis in favor of psychoanalysis because cures effected through hypnosis did not seem to be permanent. However, physicians today are returning to the use of hypnosis to discover the hidden problems that cause various illnesses; they are using the power of suggestion upon hypnotized patients to help them alter habits and conditioned reflexes, relax and feel less pain or make progress toward recovery in such conditions as: peptic ulcer, dyspepsia, chronic gastritis, colitis, high blood pressure, rapid pulse, heart palpitations, multiple sclerosis, poor bladder control, menstrual cramps, speech disorders, asthma, eczema, acne, and hives. People have been helped to lose excess weight, to overcome sexual impotence and frigidity, to stop excess smoking or drinking, and to regain lost appetite. Perhaps, however, the greatest aid of the hypnotist is in discovering the underlying motives that helped to bring on disturbances. Hypnotherapy can give the clues that followed up by psychoanalysis may effect more lasting cures.

It is believed that persons retain the inferiority which predisposes them to certain of these ailments. Realizing the existence of this inferiority, their minds aggravate the resulting condition, or even perpetrate it. When their emotions can be diverted from the affected organ, cure may be brought about. They have to realize that as long as their interests and attention can be diverted from the problem organ they can be relieved of the disease and can build strength against its recurrence. Hypnosis can be an aid in helping them to begin this fight.

The point is that hypnosis itself should not be regarded as a cure; it does make the patient more receptive to treatment. It has been used as an aid not only in treating the emotionally disturbed but to bring relief from pain in cancer, in minor operations, in dentistry, and in obstetrics. It has also been used in a manner similar to the use of the polygraph (galvanometer) and truth serums in determining the validity of testimony in court trials. Further, it has been a very helpful research tool. Public Health Service scientists through inducing emotions by suggestion found that there were significant increases in fatty acids in various suggested emotional states such as depression, fear, and anger. Hypnosis has also been used by entertainers; its use here may have been more harmful than otherwise.

Hypnosis excessively used on weak personalities has been known to bring about further disturbances. The very young, the very old, the feeble-minded, some neurotics and many psychotics cannot be hypnotized or can be only with a great deal of effort. Doctors have the problem of determining whether the patients are "psychologically healthy" enough to stand the use of hypnosis in treatment. Since those needing such treatment are evidently to some extent weak psychologically to begin with, the expert's sixth sense is needed here.

4. *Treatment by Change of Environment* — Physicians sometimes recommend a change in environment with the hope that by changing environment the patient may be changed or will forget his problems. Experience has shown that generally the trip treatment will fail, especially for anyone whose emotional disturbance is deeper than the surface. The patients take their internal problems with them. It is possible, however, that external forces met with in travel and changed environments may have some bearing upon changing a person's attitudes.

5. *Treatment by Religion or a Cause* — Since hope and purpose play such a large part in mental health, religion must certainly be very important to the mental good health of many people. Religion offers not only hope for the present but hope for the hereafter. In some religions it offers the confession with its therapeutic value of mental catharsis; certainly the priest's ear is no less willing and understanding than that of the psychiatrist, and it is possibly much less expensive.

6. *Shock Treatments* — (a) *Insulin Shock.* The use of insulin as a means of aiding mental patients to recovery was discovered when patients were by accident thrown into states of coma by too much insulin. Upon coming out of the comas, it was discovered that many of these patients had clearer minds. They were not as hostile or suspicious as they had been. They could talk about their emotional troubles; better still, they

frequently had forgotten their more severe disturbances. As to why the insulin shock, the electro shock, or fever treatments are beneficial to mental patients is not definitely known. Metabolism of the patients is changed; they in some way seem to forget. Temporarily they forget a great deal, but memory of essential things remains with them and often the memories of the old troubles return in time. Good results have been claimed for insulin shock treatments but today's medical reports seem to indicate that they may be used only a tenth as much now as before the discovery of the tranquilizing drugs.

(b) *Electro-shock* is used more widely today than insulin shock. It was first introduced in 1938. At that time its use was considered dangerous because it sometimes led to fractured spines. Patients occasionally stopped breathing. They lost memory to such great extent that reorientation became difficult. The treatments have, however, been of much help in making patients more manageable, in dispelling the melancholy of men and women around fifty years of age. The not-too-complicated cases usually respond to treatment.[11]

7. *Drugs* — From the time that Pasteur discovered that certain bacteria cause certain diseases and found that there were vaccines for these, doctors have sought single cures for each of the many illnesses common to mankind. Many of the top killers have not one but many causes and no single cures have yet been found for them. Nevertheless great strides are being made in finding drugs that aid in treating most of these diseases. Even for the insanities drugs discovered during the last dozen years have become much used and successful in varying degrees.

For a long period of time the only drugs known for use in mental hospitals were such sedatives as phenobarbital and other barbiturates. These merely put the patient into a clouded state and reduced his pain. In this state it was quite difficult for constructive work to be done with him.[12]

Since 1950 two drugs, discovered and tested in the laboratories, have proved to be highly useful in the treatment of the mentally ill. In Houston, Texas, Dr. Vernon Kinross-Wright found *chlorpromazine* (trade name *Thorazine*), a drug conceived by French chemists and brought out by them in 1950, to be helpful not only to the less permanent cases of mental illnesses but to the severe schizophrenic patients. Of the first one hundred schizophrenic patients treated at Baylor University College of Medicine Affiliated Hospitals, forty-six per cent of the paranoid schizophrenics were apparently relieved of signs and symptoms of their illnesses. Most of these not only could return home, but they returned as well to occupations. Thirty-five per cent were improved to the extent that they could go home and live with minimum supervision. Fourteen per cent were some improved. Five per cent were unchanged, or became worse with use of the drug. Of the hebephrenic schizophrenics, twenty-five per cent were apparently completely recovered after treatment. Fifty per cent improved markedly; twenty per cent improved slightly; five per cent did not improve. Of the catatonic schizophrenics, forty per cent completely recovered, forty per cent greatly improved, and twenty per cent slightly improved. Dr. Kinross-Wright found that chlorpromazine was successful with manic patients as well as with schizophrenic patients; with depressive patients it was sometimes successful, but with these patients best results were obtained when the drug was used with electro-shock treatments.[13]

Mahatma Gandhi used extracts of Rauwolfia root as a tranquilizer. *Reserpine* (trade name *Serpasil*) is the result of work of Swiss chemists who isolated an alkaloid containing the medicinal properties of the Rauwolfia root concentrated five hundred times. This drug appeared in the United States about the same time as chlorpromazine and almost the same results are obtained by it. Chlorpromazine seems somewhat more effective than reserpine with schizophrenia; either drug works well with mania; depressions do not respond too well to chlorpromazine and reserpine may aggravate them. These drugs are not narcotics; they are not sedatives; they aren't "happiness pills." They do seem to be successful in restoring peace of mind.[14]

Although the depressive states apparently do not respond to the tranquilizing drugs they evidently do respond to other new drugs known as "psychic energizers." These drugs apparently elevate the patients' moods and increase their energy and alertness.

Sainz reports that chlorpromazine has not been successful to any great extent in producing cures of neurotics. It has had some effect in reducing and eliminating anxiety on the part of neurotics. It enables the psychotherapist to do his work more easily and in a shorter time.[15] Reserpine, too, has been of help in improving neurotic patients or in enabling the interviewers to obtain useful and pertinent information previously not available.[16]

In addition to chlorpromazine and reserpine, *azacyclonol* (trade name *Frenquel*) has proved beneficial in treating mental illnesses. The tranquilizing drugs have enabled people long hospitalized to return to homes and to fairly if not completely useful lives. The mother of a student of the writer was treated with tranquilizing drugs and returned to her family after having been hospitalized for something like twenty years. Needless to say, when patients so long hospitalized are returned to their families, a great deal of adjusting is required on the part of all persons concerned.

In 1955 Dr. Henry Brill of New York's Pilgrim State Mental Hospital,

Brentwood, Long Island, introduced mass use of tranquilizing drugs. The findings of Dr. Brill and his staff have been similar to those already reported above.

The chief value of the tranquilizers is that they do calm patients, rendering useless the strait jackets of old. The drugs keep patients from becoming dangerous to themselves and to others. In fact, the more violently disturbed the new patients are to begin with the better their chances of recovery. They do not fight and yell after they have had the new drugs. They can also be led to worthwhile activities.

Doctors who have taken the tranquilizers themselves to find their effect have said that they do not feel inclined while affected by them to take initiative, to tackle the tougher problems of life. Otherwise, they have not found bad effects. They consider the tranquilizing drugs to be much different from alcohol and opiates in their effect. They feel that like psychoanalysis and hypnosis tranquilizers are to be regarded as tools only. They may not cure the patient, but they do calm him. They evidently also do cure the severely mentally ill sometimes. They haven't been so effective on the neurotics, but they have made neurotics more susceptible to other treatments. Use of tranquilizing drugs has also drastically cut the use of insulin and electro-shock treatments.

LSD (*lysurgic-diethylamide*) is a drug that produces the effect of insanity (paranoid schizophrenia) in those to whom it is administered by hypodermic needle. Convicts at the state prison in Huntsville, Texas, have been used as volunteers for this induced insanity by Dr. Kinross-Wright and other researchers from Baylor University's Medical School. Similar experiments go on elsewhere in an attempt to discover how and why schizophrenia occurs. LSD was discovered in the late thirties in Switzerland; the formula for it was acquired by the United States. Its possibilities for chemical warfare were recognized as it would be possible to render an entire city helplessly insane for something like six hours by putting small quantities in the city's water supply. The drug acts also something like truth serum bringing back events long forgotten. The drug thus offers a possible aid to treatment similar to the tools of psychoanalysis and hypnosis. A person can bring out long repressed events and to the extent that recalling and telling acts as a catharsis of the mind the patient would be helped.

JB-329 (*Ditran*) is another insanity-producing drug that produces an eight- to twelve-hour psychosis not distinguishable from schizophrenia. Researchers at Ypsilanti State Hospital (Michigan) using this drug on volunteers found two other chemicals that apparently have counteracting effect on schizophrenia. One of these drugs is *cyclopentimine*. Of course the main object of research with the insanity-producings drugs is to find in effect a "vaccine" for mental illness.

Perhaps the main criticism of the use of tranquilizers is that they have been made available in quantities to the general public. A nation of people too comfortable and adjusted might be greatly lacking in heroes to defend it in time of crisis. It might lack, too, the aggressiveness essential to compete in business (or war) with nations of people who never took tranquilizers.

Dr. Nathan S. Kline has suggested that we might shrewdly wish the Russians success in producing their society lacking in basic competition; for only in competition and conflicts can there be growth. He further says that lack of tension and anxiety are often the very opposite of good mental health.[17]

It might be added before dismissing this subject that not only are people being tranquilized, the animal kingdom has been touched. Veterinaries and animal husbandry specialists of all kinds have turned to tranquilizers. With people eating eggs from tranquilized chickens, drinking milk from tranquilized cows, and eating meat from tranquilized animals of many varieties, could there be a tranquilizing effect upon the consumers of these tranquilized foods? Even man's best friend, the dog, is being tranquilized into cooperativeness.

Clarence Ellis Harbinson, who became the first "Dog's Freud," although he had no formal training in psychology or psychiatry, found that dogs have the same mental illnesses that humans do. They also have the same need for self-confidence that humans have. His treatment of dogs was, in fact, quite similar to the treatment of humans: discover the behavior pattern, discover if possible its causes (which in the case of the dog may be rejection of the owner, lack of love and understanding), find a new way for the dog to act, find a new way for the master to act, launch the two upon their way with new behavior patterns. Those who have followed Mr. Harbinson's techniques in dealing with neurotic dogs would probably find a much easier solution with tranquilizers.

8. *Surgery* — What has come to be called *lobotomy* has been successful in markedly improving some seventy per cent of the cases on which it has been tried. A small percentage of the patients on whom it has been used have died, and about twenty-five per cent of the patients have not been changed or have become worse after the operation.[18] The lobotomy is a last-resort method in treating insanity. It consists of cutting off the prefrontal area (where presumably the superego is located) from the rest of the brain. The superego is the seat of the conscience. Thus when the prefrontal lobes are severed the reason for conflict is gone. The operation does not affect intelligence and the judgment of the individual can control actions that would be counter to demands of society.

In 1956–1957, Dr. Walter Freeman, one of the two doctors who were pioneers in performing the frontal-lobe operation (Dr. J. W. Watts was the other) toured the United States, South America, and Europe to check on patients he and Dr. Watts had operated upon. Over 10,000 lobotomies have been performed in the United States. Dr. Freeman found that a third of the patients he had operated on by lobotomy, all of whom to begin with were considered incurable patients, were able to return to their homes. There was improvement in the other two-thirds.[19] In early lobotomy operations some two to three per cent of the patients died.[20]

Reasons Patients Fail to Recover — Dr. William Menninger has given some of the reasons patients have not recovered:

1. The patient is one of several hundred who must look to only one doctor for counsel and help.

2. Living conditions in most mental hospitals are not adequate for restoring a balanced mental outlook. [They have, of course, greatly improved in the last twenty years and especially in the last ten years.]

3. Little if anything is done to help patients keep in contact with the outside world or establish new relationships in it. Friends, visitors, and relatives must have the proper attitudes. After a patient leaves a hospital there must be continued readjustment with the aid of others.

4. About a third of mental patients are sixty years of age or over. This handicaps treatment when they are mixed with others who are seriously ill.[21]

TABLE VII — 2

SOME AIDS TO MENTAL HEALTH ON THE JOB

1. Be able to take criticism; view it as being offered with your best interests in mind. If you feel that it is given just to give somebody else a chance to "feel better," be mature enough to analyze the situation and not hold a grudge or carry a chip on your shoulder.

2. When you feel that everything is going against you, remember that everybody has bad days. There is a better one around the corner for you. You may come out of the period of discouragement feeling like a conqueror.

3. Like your job; if you don't like it, find one you do like. Have interesting hobbies and leisure time activities that will stimulate you for self-improvement on the job and also make you more interesting to other people.

4. Be thorough enough on the job to feel that you have been accurate where accuracy counts. The person who is a perfectionist in small details can sometimes be difficult to deal with; if you are such a person, learn to distinguish between the trivial and the important.

5. If you are a "boss," learn to delegate authority along with responsibility. Don't hold all the strings in your hand; you may hold up the works guided by one string while you are manipulating the many others.

6. Don't be afraid to accept authority and responsibility. Somebody has to. If you don't, you will be dissatisfied and will continue to shirk; in the long run, both you and your work will suffer. Accept as much responsibility as you have the capacity to handle; no superior should delegate more than this.

7. Let your friends and family be the ones to whom you sound off when you have to blow off steam because you don't like some action of a fellow worker or your boss. After you have exploded with people who will understand and excuse you, things will not look so bad and you will be much less likely to explode with your boss or those who wouldn't forget and wouldn't let you forget.

8. If there are people who constantly irk you, try to understand that you as well as they may be to blame. It may be that you have strengths they do not have or vice versa. They may, of course, have irritating traits for which you will just have to make allowances. There may be people making allowances for some of yours.

9. Learn to talk over problems with your boss in a calm and collected manner. If your boss is not the type who will give you an understanding ear, he shouldn't be a boss; your own ability to understand may aid him to become a better one, and if he doesn't he probably won't remain a boss very long.

10. If you work with people you suspect of needing psychiatric help, report to your immediate superior but do not say anything to the suspects. Be sympathetic of such people but do not cross them in a manner that will trigger acts of violence. If you are the boss and your firm has an industrial psychiatrist, consult him; if your firm does not have a psychiatrist, consult a reputable person trained in handling such cases.

Summary — While we read today of increased mental illnesses, we also see much hope for prevention and cure of mental illnesses through continued progress in scientific discoveries. Not only do we grow in knowledge of the behavior of the human being and of the motives and drives which propel him, we have as well the shock treatments, the new and successful drugs, and hypnosis which when used in combination with psychiatric counseling are having much success. Work is one of the best ways to bring about recovery in mental patients. The satisfaction that comes with achievement and the strengthening both of the personality and the ability of the individual to work with others are accomplished chiefly through work itself. Through open-minded outlook upon life and recognizing their own limitations and problems, "normal" people can forestall emotional disturbances, or drastically curtail them once the onslaught has begun. Whatever a person believes in will help. Simply finding a way to act is the solution; adjustment requires the changing of attitudes.

Through psychotherapy (therapeutic counseling) a person can alter his attitudes toward himself and his evaluation of his self worth. Such psychotherapy would also bring about a change in his attitudes toward others since it has been shown that the attitudes a person has toward others are significantly related to the attitudes he holds toward himself.[22]

PROJECTS

1. Write a research paper entitled "Mental Illnesses Should Be Regarded as Being No Different from Other Illnesses."

2. Write a paper outlining the extent to which your own attitude toward mental illness has been changed by study.

3. Report on an article in a current magazine relative to new treatments of the mentally ill; give complete reference.

4. Find and report on current material relative to ways of dealing with one's own maladjustments and/or ways of helping others deal with theirs.

ACKNOWLEDGMENTS AND REFERENCES

1 Cant, Gilbert, *New Medicines for the Mind — Their Meaning and Promise*, Public Affairs Pamphlet, No. 228, Public Affairs Pamphlets, 22 East 38th Street, New York 16, N. Y., 1955, pp. 23–25.

2 Lemkau, Paul V., *Mental Hygiene in Public Health*, The Blakiston Division, McGraw-Hill Book Co., Inc., New York, 1955, pp. 412–420.

3 *Ibid.*, p. 11

4 ———, *Mental Health A Ford Foundation Report*, The Ford Foundation, 477 Madison Avenue, New York 22, New York, p. 5.

5 Cant, *op. cit.*, p. 5.

6 Menninger, William C., *Social Change and Scientific Progress*, Fifth Annual Arthur Dehon Little Memorial Lecture at the Massachusetts Institute of Technology, Cambridge, Mass., May 1, 1951, pp. 16–18.

7 Menninger, Karl A., *The Human Mind*, Third Edition, Alfred A. Knopf, New York, 1951, p. 368.

8 Rouman, Jack, "School Children's Problems as Related to Parental Factors," *Understanding the Child*, April, 1955, pp. 50–55.

9 Cass, Loretta K., "Parent-Child Relationships and Delinquency," *Journal of Abnormal and Social Psychology*, January, 1952, pp. 101–104.

10 Menninger, Karl A., *op cit.*, p. 390.

11 Cant, *op. cit.*, p. 6

12 *Ibid.*, p. 7.

13 Kinross-Wright, Vernon, "Clinical Application of Chlorpromazine," *Psychopharma-cology*, Nathan S. Kline, Editor, Publication No. 42 of the American Association for the Advancement of Science, Washington, D. C., 1956, pp. 31–38.

14 Cant, *op. cit.*, pp. 10–15.

15 Sainz, Anthony A., "Clinical Applications of Chlorpromazine in Psychiatry," *Psycho-pharmacology*, Nathan S. Kline, Editor, Publication No. 42 of the American Association for the Advancement of Science, Washington, D. C., 1956, p. 57.

16 Kline, Nathan S., "Clinical Applications of Reserpine," *Psychopharmacology*, Nathan S. Kline, Editor, Publication No. 42 of the American Association for the Advancement of Science, Washington, D. C., 1956, pp. 104–106.

17 Kline, Nathan S., "Psychiatry," *The American Weekly*, May 14, 1961, p. 6.

18 Cant, *op. cit.*, p. 6.

19 ———, "Medicine," *Newsweek,* August 4, 1956, p. 48.

20 ———, "Psychosurgery," *Life*, March 3, 1947, p. 93.

21 Menninger, William C., "Mental Patients Can Be Cured," *The Reader's Digest*, August, 1956, pp. 13–16.

22 ———, "An Objective Approach to the Study of Psychotherapy," *American Scientist*, Vol. 37, No. 3, July, 1949, pp. 410–413.

     Sheerer, Elizabeth T., "The Relationship Between Acceptance of Self and Acceptance of Others," *Journal of Consulting Psychology*, American Psychological Association, Inc., Vol. 13, No. 3, June, 1949, pp. 174–175.

CHAPTER VIII

MENTAL HYGIENE IN BUSINESS AND INDUSTRY

What is Mental Hygiene in Business and Industry? — Improving the satisfaction or adjustment of the employee is the first objective of mental hygiene in industry. A great many factors are involved: morale; how workers are selected and trained; supervision; the entire organization, including top and middle management; labor relations and collective bargaining; the local community; the nation and the world communities; communication; fringe benefits and welfare plans; social security; time studies and motion studies; job evaluation; merit rating; physical working conditions; the informal social groups at the place of work; social conditioning in the home, church, school, and community as well as inherited characteristics and nationality; poverty and wealth; security or the lack of security; competition or the lack of it; frustrations or the lack of frustrations. The topics of industrial psychology and personnel management indicate areas that influence the mental and emotional climate of workers, both as groups and as individuals.

All of the activities of industrial relations and personnel departments are directed at achieving happiness and stability among workers. Yet it must ever be kept in mind that human emotions are inherent and when the human being is quite satisfied with the *status quo* he rarely achieves. When he is in a state of complete emotional stability he is very apt to be content to do little if anything. Achievements are the outcome of frustrations, of the spirit of competition, of compensation, of determination, of fear, of love, and even of anger. It is when the emotions are properly checked and guided into creative channels that the greatest accomplishments of life take place.

Organizations that have what seem to be the very best programs of industrial and human relations may often find that there is not proper motivation, that output is lower than in other plants with seemingly far less up-to-date managerial techniques. Management cannot do everything for workers and expect them to be creative and motivated to achieve. Nevertheless, there is belief that wise management can provide adequate benefits and the modern surroundings to give the workers pride in their organization and enough security to be unworried about the day-to-day provision for themselves and their families without destroying the inherent emotions that drive men on to accomplish. It is the climate of emotion and drive at the top, the middle, and supervisory levels of management that makes the difference.

The various areas of industrial and human relations activities are discussed in later chapters; this chapter proposes to review elements of a specific area of mental hygiene in industry: the roles of the industrial psychiatrist and the industrial psychologist and the implications of the mental hygiene approach for all who supervise and boss others.

Recognition of and Early Uses of Mental Hygiene in Industry — In 1915 a psychiatrist was employed at the Chaney Silk Company. Metropolitan Life Insurance Company began in 1922 to use a company psychiatrist. The R. H. Macy department store used psychiatric exit interviews and had a mental hygiene program described as "elaborate" from 1924–1929. Macy's psychiatrist estimated that a fifth of its employees were problems. They upset morale, produced poorly, possessed bad habits and attitudes, were nervous, were chronically ill, were disciplinary problems, were daydreamers, and so on. Many of these problems were eliminated after the mental hygiene approach had been used. As for accidents of drivers, these were reduced from eleven per one thousand vehicle days for a six months' period prior to the psychiatric program, to 3.4 per one thousand vehicle days during the six months after the installing of the program.[1]

One of the early works that called attention to the need of business and industry for psychiatric aid was by Ernest Elmer Southard, late professor of psychiatry at Harvard. He made a study which he reported in 1940 of why employees were discharged. The dissatisfactions of employees that led to discharge indicated that these people had needs which "should be met by a unified program participated in by psychiatrists, psychologists, and social case workers."[2]

Although the Hawthorne Experiments of Western Electric Company, 1929–1933, are reported on more fully in Chapter XIX and were referred to in Chapter V, they must be mentioned here as having made a great contribution in the application of "a human technique to a human factor." The Hawthorne investigators asked themselves two questions that took cognizance of the fact that the employee as a worker and as a person was indivisible:

1. Is some experience, which might be described as an experience of personal futility, a common incident of industrial organization for work?

2. Does life in a modern industrial city in some unrealized way predispose workers to obsessional responses? [3]

The Hawthorne Company attempted to meet the problem indicated by the first question above by improving communications, attempting to eliminate the sources of irritation, and letting employees have a greater part in deciding upon and determining working conditions.

The non-directed interview [see the next chapter] was employed to aid in dealing with the problems of obsessive thinking and with personality defects. The counseling program continues to be useful today at Hawthorne. The Hawthorne studies [which have had in Roethlisberger, Mayo, Dickson, Wright, Whitehead, Urwick, and Breck, as well as many other spokesmen, very wide publicity] were praised by psychiatrists who recommended findings of the studies as required reading for personnel managers and for members of their own profession who are employed by industries.[4] The writer was required in several graduate courses to become entirely familiar with the works of all of those who have written at length of the Hawthorne studies and findings.

Some Principles of Industrial Psychiatry — The principles of industrial psychiatry are those of psychiatry anywhere that it is used. The industrial psychiatrist in addition to understanding the basic needs of people and knowing all of their ways of adjusting as discussed in Chapter VI and all of the treatments and ways of dealing with maladjustments as discussed in Chapter VII, must also understand something of group dynamics and of the ways that groups may influence people to act. The industrial psychiatrist and management at any level should recognize the great importance of the social factor in work and the working situation. The informal work group as perhaps the most dynamic group process in industry is discussed at length in Chapter XIX.

The mental health of the worker is the primary concern of the industrial psychiatrist. Because many people who have been mentally ill are returned to work situations, and certainly must be if they are to maintain mental good health, there is need for psychiatrists in industry to evaluate the status of these people at the time of employment and periodically afterward. Psychiatrists know that in the final analysis people must work out their own salvation through disciplining their emotions; the psychiatrist's greatest aid may be that of helping the worker back to dependency upon himself. Good mental health is a matter of discipline.

Dr. Karl A. Menninger's suggestions for industrial psychiatrists are:
1. *Sudden or progressive failure in efficiency may arise from a variety of causes, revealed only by psychiatric investigation.*

2. *Some employees fail because they are in the wrong job for their personality make-up.*

3. *Some employees have a pattern of repeated failures (comparable to the life pattern of the habitual criminal).*

4. *Some employees suffer from unsuspected mental conditions dangerous to the public.*

5. *In many instances the most serious maladjustment problems are found not in the employees but in the employers and executives.*[5]

Distinguishing Between Industrial Psychiatry and Industrial Psychology — The *industrial psychologist* is concerned with finding the right person for the right job. He collects information on occupations; assists in redesigning jobs to alleviate monotony; makes jobs analyses; does job evaluation; designs programs for merit rating; keeps and uses records on employees; makes statistical analyses of records pertaining to successes and failures of employees, to accidents, to turnover, and so on; assists in locating the accident-prone persons; takes part in union-management relations; helps plan for placement of the handicapped workers; designs counseling programs, employment and termination interviews. The statistical and clinical methods of the psychologist are used. Clinical methods are implied in previous chapters and in Chapter IX. [It will be noted that this volume does not have a chapter on statistical methods; this is deliberate in that most colleges and universities require all business majors to take a course in statistics. Chapter X does discuss statistics as a tool of scientific management. The psychologist working in the areas of personnel management, industrial relations, marketing, consumer and advertising research must know how to determine and understand the significance of such statistical measures as: *mean, median, mode, standard deviation, correlation,* and *reliability of estimates.* The marketing research people need to know also a great deal about *sampling* and *multiple correlation.* Sampling and multiple correlation can be useful in analyzing personnel data. Most statistics textbooks, to be sure, concern themselves with economic factors such as: products; cyclical, seasonal, and secular trends; index numbers; but the student should not have great difficulty in transferring what he has learned of statistical methods to human problems and group action.]

The industrial psychologist studies employees as groups; he works at improving morale and productivity through improving job satisfactions. In dealing with employees as individuals (testing, interviewing, selecting, placing them according to ability in jobs for which they are qualified), he is helping to set the stage for better contented workers.[6]

The *industrial psychiatrist* is immediately concerned with problem cases whatever the causes of these may be and whether or not these causes revert directly or indirectly to persons responsible for employment and supervision, or to causes completely outside the realm of the work environment.

Some of the outstanding industrial psychiatrists of today are: Dr. Gerald Gordon of E. I. du Pont de Nemours & Co., Dr. Alan McLean of International Business Machines, and Dr. John MacIver of United States Steel. A young Dutch psychiatrist, Dr. Robert Turfboer, has done research in industrial psychiatry at Yale University Medical School in an attempt to show that industrial psychiatry is as much a responsibility of industrial management as is industrial medicine. In addition to aiding in the detection of mental and emotional problems of employees, industrial psychiatrists can (and sometimes do) develop research programs that result in data that enable employers and managers to better understand employees and motivate them to greater accomplishments that bring success not only to themselves but to their organizations.[7]

Supervision and Mental Hygiene — Supervision in most of its phases is either directly or indirectly concerned with the mental attitudes of human beings. As the one who must take responsibility for the actions of others, the supervisor not only must be concerned with the physical and mental differences of individuals as well as their differences in motor reaction and coordination, but he must also understand that emotional differences vary tremendously.[8] In employing workers, in introducing them to their jobs (induction) in teaching them how to do their jobs, in maintaining morale, in promoting cooperation, in maintaining discipline, in providing incentives, in dealing with the worker as a member of a union, there is necessity for understanding human beings as individuals and as members of groups.[9]

Although many of the needs of people are met outside of work, in the leisure hours of long vacations and long week-ends both in personal pursuits and in the institutions of society provided outside of work, it is still quite true that a great many of the worker's needs are met at the workplace itself. There is need for providing social intercourse at work, need to give the worker opportunity to be creative in his work (with so many routine jobs, it is often highly difficult to fulfill this need) and to express his viewpoints. He must feel that he is a part of the group; he wants recognition. His competitive spirit must be stimulated although not to the extent that it disrupts ongoing activities.

It has been demonstrated that the attitudes of workers affect output of work and that changed attitudes (either through changed techniques of supervision, development of effective informal leadership, or counseling) can result in increased output. The important incentives used in industry are: good supervision; pay; working conditions; competition; praise and punishment; participation; preparing workers for changes in methods, procedures, management, working conditions, and so on; profit sharing; stock ownership; suggestion systems; and various ways of assuring security. These are all means used by supervision and management to reassure the worker, to alleviate his fears, and reduce his stresses. They are means of keeping the mental outlook clear so that the worker can produce.

Managers and supervisors need to tune in on employees, listen for their sentiments, understand their social structures and adapt where possible the formal organization to the informal social organizations that exist within it. They need to understand the social structure of the community in which the organization functions. There is an attempt to show in later chapters that those who manage others must today be familiar to some extent at least with the larger social structures of state, nation, and world. They must be aware of the economic and political forces at work as well as with the technological changes taking place, and they need to understand the effects of these forces and changes upon workers and worker relationships.

Although many have used the ideas they have expressed, two writers have simplified this enormous problem of managers and supervisors by saying that they should seek to know:

1. What the individual is bringing to the work situation.
2. What the work situation is demanding of the individual.
3. What is the resulting equilibrium.[10]

They suggest that the individual may be helped to achieve equilibrium by:

1. Modifying his demands so that they can be better realized in the present job.
2. Changing the situation so as to allow for the fulfillment of the normal demands.
3. Using both measures.[11]

The interview and social observation offer clues to understanding of worker problems. These were the techniques developed and employed in the Hawthorne studies.

Despite the fact that many feel that human relations cannot keep up with scientific, engineering, and technological developments, numerous writers do point out that line and staff supervisors most certainly play a very important role in helping workers to adjust. Line supervisors perhaps have a greater responsibility for maintaining good human relations than do staff people; it is with the line supervisors that "human relations" have their beginning. The leaders of men whether they be line or staff must be close enough to them and interested enough in them to understand them. They must like people and know what to say to them as well as how to say it. The greatest medium of communicating to others is face-to-face at the place of work. Essentially, managers are thought of as being best if they are extroverts. Nevertheless, these same people must have enough of the introvert qualities to be reflective people who in moments of concentration, alone, can plan and create. But then, again, they must be able to plan with others. They must perhaps be above all else *adaptable*. They must possess not only the know-how of human relations and managerial principles but also the know-how of their particular phase of work (finance, production, marketing — the line areas; or, advertising, accounting, product and package research, marketing research, personnel, industrial relations, engineering, credit, collecting, office management — the staff or service areas).

Line and staff supervisors cannot be expected to be psychiatrists. They can be given training in mental hygiene; they can through experience in dealing with people develop the techniques and approaches that get results in handling people. They should be trained to recognize the symptoms of maladjustment. They should be given training in how to interview workers who are troubled. If they cannot deal with the problems of these people they should refer them to staff specialists in the personnel department (counselors, psychiatrists) or if these are available to private practitioners. It is in providing at the place of work the satisfactions that workers need that the supervisor helps most. People who have developed team spirit (cooperative and/or competitive) are much less likely to develop gnawing emotional problems that lead to problems both for the individuals and the groups in which they function.

A key to getting supervisors to play the human relations role is to be found in the training of supervisors (Chapter XIV).

Perhaps at this point it would be well to list some of the rules for maintaining good supervisor-employee personal relations. These have been gleaned from many sources and most of them have been specifically stated in this or previous chapters:

1. Give people credit for jobs well done.

2. Tell them how they are doing even if it is necessary to make critical suggestions.

3. Let people have a part in making decisions about things that affect them (*participation*). If this is not possible or feasible, then prepare

them for the idea of change by following Rule Number 4 (*accommodation*).

4. Tell people about changes that will affect them well in advance of bringing about these changes; don't just tell them once, tell them over and over again and perhaps ask them to comment upon the proposed changes.

5. Give people a chance to use their full abilities. Encourage creative people to carry out their ideas. This means that the comfort of following fixed business procedures and organizational lines will sometimes have to be sacrificed for both progress and worker morale. (Going around or across can, of course, create fiction and lead to poor human relations. Nevertheless, a certain amount of freedom from the chain of command is necessary to avoid stagnation and encourage employee development. People cannot be relegated to cubby holes and filing cabinets. They and their ideas and problems touch more persons than their immediate supervisors or those whom they themselves directly supervise.)

6. Recognize the informal groups that develop and as long as they are a contributing factor in maintaining a smoothly running formal organization avoid disrupting them and if possible utilize them.

7. Provide opportunity for workers to have access to the supervisor; listen to workers' problems; take action when action seems necessary, but often listening alone is sufficient. Direct the employee's emotions into productive channels if possible. An added responsibility may divert him from the problem and/or grievance.

8. If supervisors do not have time to listen, perhaps informal leaders could be given "assistant" jobs that would include the listening element.

9. From the above list and since all bosses have a part in administering welfare and fringe benefits, in providing working conditions, in dealing with unions, in the whole area of morale, and in procedures of communicating, it can readily be seen that bosses are the most important of all the factors that have an effect upon workers, their productivity and their morale.

Some Conclusions — Many of the techniques of mental hygiene are used by immediate supervisors who are in many industries the only persons to whom workers can go for guidance and counsel. "The supervisor constantly administers those little preventatives that keep both individuals and groups satisfied and productive." [12]

More willingness to accept professional specialists in dealing with human problems will come only as it is realized that constant attention to these problems is necessary. Staff services for counseling and therapy are provided in some companies. When these services can be demonstrated as necessary, on a money-making basis, more industries will provide them. Rehabilitation of workers through proper therapy must be paid for eventually by private industry, if not directly then indirectly through taxation. Many other writers have said this. Pfiffner said it in 1951.[13] It evidently is still true today.

Some industries, recognizing the problem of dealing with workers and rehabilitation of those who have been under medical care for mental disturbances, have attempted to set up psychiatric clinics for numbers of firms within a community. Some of these cooperative efforts have been successful. Some have met with resistance on the part of private practitioners who evidently felt that the clinics would be competition for their private practices, offering perhaps in fixed salaries less opportunity for financial success than private practice would.

Some consider that mental illnesses when they do develop are the concern of families of the people who get these illnesses. In some business and industrial firms, when a person becomes mentally ill he has as the saying goes "had it." Nevertheless, the writer has known a number of highly intelligent persons who did go "off the deep end" completely enough to be considered either dangerous to themselves and others or to be so unaware of the world about them that they were useless for all practical purposes of productive employment. In these cases the disabling effects were only for a time. These people after being hospitalized and treated for periods of up to a year and in the case of some for more than a year were all returned to useful working lives in which they gave of their talents to society in highly productive ways. In some cases the adjustments were painful, but they were made with understanding families, fellow workers, and supervisors. Most of these cases occurred within the last twelve years when so much progress has been made in the treatment of and attitude toward mentally ill persons. The writer also knew persons who thirty or forty years ago had similar mental illnesses, but because of lack of proper treatments and attitudes their conditions resulted in lives lost to society and lived out in mental institutions. Today management in progressive firms recognizes its responsibility for helping the persons who have been mentally ill to "find their way back."

There is little evidence that the work situation itself causes mental illness. Outside stresses wherever they originate do not of themselves cause harm. It is, as stated previously, the internal stresses that account for mental illnesses and stress disease.[14] The fact remains that workers do develop dissatisfactions, have emotional disturbances, and mental illnesses. The social sciences have not developed social skills that give exact answers to these human problems,[15] but they are certainly making progress toward finding some of the answers. The objective is to provide satisfactions in work for those workers who are still on the track moving the machinery of production, providing the goods and services needed and desired by themselves and all the rest of us, and getting those goods and services to us. When someone gets off the track, the kind of help that is needed to get him back on should be given. The attempt may fail, but it must be made. The first objective is all important for it concerns at least ninety-nine per cent of the nation's total work force (approximately 75,000,000 in 1964) which at any one time is apparently capable of manipulating on its own; some of these are, of course, unemployed at any given time (the percentage varies; currently it is around six per cent) and there are no satisfactions at the place of work for them. For the most part the unemployed are the unskilled workers. Both industry and government have some responsibility for aiding them to acquire skills.

Certainly because of the interaction between them, there is need to consider the technological and social developments of industry simultaneously.[16] Only by comprehending the spiritual and psychological as well as the physical aspects of science can man be saved from social catastrophe.[17]

Some companies provide a measure of employee satisfaction through letting employees have a share in management. McCormick & Company's "Multiple Management" program has recognized the "independence of the individual" and "dignity of man." Through association together and exchange of ideas, management in this company is better informed, happier, better able to obtain satisfactions for itself and in turn to aid employees to achieve more satisfactions on the job. Instead of having just a few executive officers, the company is managed by boards composed of many persons; members are elected on the basis of merit to serve on these boards. Since more people know what is happening in management, more workers are kept informed. Informed workers lose at least some of their fears. The work that is being done today in the area of human relations led Charles F. McCormick to say that he wondered if this was not the "greatest invention" that Thomas Alva Edison had predicted: one that would "get people to have the right point of view toward life." [18]

The various devices of "incentive management" — worker participation, and all of the numerous others previously mentioned (some of which are to be more specifically discussed later), while they help in keeping workers satisfied must constantly be supplemented by expert supervision and counseling. The attitudes of leaders constantly influence the attitudes of workers. It is true, however, that while the attitudes of leaders are all-important factors in managing people successfully, the ability of these leaders to understand, in a sense actually to feel, what others are feeling and thinking and how they are reacting, is perhaps the most important of the assets leaders must possess. This intuitive sense is called *"empathy."* [19] The characteristics of good leadership are discussed in Chapter XIX. This one characteristic is mentioned here because it is so important in aiding leaders to bring about healthier attitudes on the part of workers.

Although orthodox psychologists have chosen for the most part to ignore the discoveries of the *parapsychologists,* it is perhaps true that this extra sense of empathy may be akin to awareness claimed for such areas of ESP (extrasensory perception) as telepathy and clairvoyance. Oxford and Cambridge universities in England have granted doctorate degrees to persons who have done research in ESP and PK (influence of the mind over matter — *psychokinesis*). Such research continues. So little is really known about the human mind and the soul of man; it is infinitesimal, and any area that offers hope of contributing additional knowledge about them should be given an ear. By contrast, there is vast understanding of the elements of matter, as, for instance, the atom. The boots of physics take seven-league steps while the shoes of the social sciences, including the science of mind, struggle far behind.[20]

In a speech made at the International Congress on Mental Health, London, in 1948, Dr. William Line, Professor of Psychology, University of Toronto, said that the "increasing difficulty of communication between worker and management . . . is a symptom of pathology." He also implied that not only is the conception of social *ill-health* of medical origin, but professional medicine has a responsibility for sponsoring mental health work in industry.[21] This would not relieve management of its responsibility.

Mental health of workers can be improved by psychological and psychiatric help. Large companies should provide counselors to give the type of non-directive counseling that has proved to be an effective means of aiding emotionally troubled employees.[22] Large companies in most instances do provide human relations programs because they "have proof of results." Smaller businesses have not always been able to see such proof.[23] They could provide at least part-time counselors and psychiatric service.[24] Du Pont put an ex-alcoholic in charge of the rehabilitation program which it conducts to help alcoholics toward recovery. Du Pont's medical division has found that from eight-five to ninety per cent of those who do recover are promoted to better jobs. Over the years sixty-five to seventy per cent of the problem drinkers have been rehabilitated. Alcoholism in the selling group at du Pont is very low; problem drinkers seem to appear more often among chemists, engineers, draftsmen, and creative people.

Industry needs to be aware not only of the preventions of but the treatments for mental illnesses. Back and beyond this, it needs awareness of the uses of mental hygiene in all of its concepts. Hubert S. Coffey said at the Asilomar Conference of the Mental Health Society of Northern California: "Whether Mental Health is industry's newest gold mine I do not know. I do, however, suspect that there is gold in them thar hills!" [25]

PROJECTS

1. Obtain Charles P. McCormick's *The Power of People* (93 pages) and read any parts that you like. Write your reaction to what you read. Did you like it, disagree with it, find that it was nothing new?

2. Tell why you think psychology is applied in the area of personnel management that you find most interesting to you.

One of the most complete definitions of personnel management the writer has read — and memorized — is one from Jucius which is given here in order that you may choose one of the functions of personnel management about which to read: "Personnel management is *planning, organizing,* and *controlling* various operative functions of *procuring, developing, maintaining,* and *utilizing* a labor force, such that the —

a) Objectives for which the company is established are attained economically and effectively.

b) Objectives of all levels of personnel are served to the highest possible degree.

c) Objectives of the community are duly considered and served." [26]

Jucius was not original in this definition; its parts belong to others as it came from combining the ideas of earlier writers: L. Urwick (*Scientific Principles of Organization* and *The Elements of Administration*), Mary Follett (*Dynamic Administration*), Henri Fayol (*Industrial and General Administration*), Ralph Currier Davis (*The Fundamentals of Top Management*), and others. Most textbooks, because they must stick to the proved and approved facts and ways of thinking, lack originality; whatever originality they possess usually lies in the rearrangement of ideas and discoveries and in style of presentation. Some few have much more of the creative element than do others.

3. Report on any current article entitled "Human Relations in Industry," or on any article pertaining to a similar or related subject.

Read and report on any current article about the progress made in human relations as opposed to progress being made in technological development today.

5. Outline some of the problems that you think would be involved in reconciling the human and technological factors of a giant organization such as the National Aeronautics and Space Administration's Office of Manned Space Flight.

ACKNOWLEDGMENTS AND REFERENCES

1 Harrell, Thomas Willard, *Industrial Psychology*, Rinehart & Co., Inc., New York, 1949, pp. 360–365.
2 Menninger, Karl A., *The Human Mind*, Alfred A. Knopf, New York, 1951, pp. 433–434.
3 Rennie, Thomas A. C., and Swackhamer, Gladys, "Toward Industrial Mental Health," *Mental Hygiene*, Vol. XXXI, No. 1, January, 1947, p. 70ff.
4 *Ibid.*, p. 84.
5 Menninger, *op. cit.*, pp. 436–441.
6 Ogg, Elizabeth, *Psychologists in Action*, Public Affairs Pamphlet No. 229, Public Affairs Pamphlets, 22 East 38th Street, New York 16, N. Y., 1955, p. 17.
7 ———, "Management," *Business Week*, October 29, 1960, p. 70.
8 Spriegel, William R., and Schulz, Edward, *Elements of Supervision*, John Wiley & Sons, Inc., New York, 1942, pp. 67–69.
9 Knowles, William H., *Management a Human Relations Approach*, American Book Company, New York, 1955, pp. 1–476.
10 Rennie, *op. cit.*, p. 85.
11 *Ibid.*
12 Pfiffner, John M., *The Supervision of Personnel*, Prentice-Hall, Inc., 1951, p. 361ff.
13 *Ibid.*
14 Gordon, Gerald, "Some Aspects of Mental Health Among Supervisors and Executives," *Proceedings*, Sixteenth Conference, Texas Personnel and Management Association, The University of Texas, Austin, 1954, p. 30.
15 Knowles, *op. cit.*, p. 476ff.
16 Wilson, A. T. M., "Introduction," *The Changing Culture of a Factory* (by Elliott Jaques), The Dryden Press, Inc., New York, 1952.
17 Halliday, James L., *Psychosocial Medicine*, W. W. Norton & Co., Inc., New York, 1948, p. 223.
18 McCormick, Charles P., *The Power of People*, Harper & Brothers Publishers, New York, 1949, pp. 3ff, 92–93.
19 Newman, William H., and Sumner, Charles E., Jr., *The Process of Management*, Prentice-Hall, Inc., Englewood Cliffs, N. J., 1961, pp. 490–491.
20 Rhine, J. B., *The Reach of the Mind*, William Sloane Associates, Inc., 119 W. 57th St., New York 19, N. Y., 1947.
21 Line, William, "Mental Health in Industry," *Proceedings of the International Congress on Mental Health*, London, Vol. IV, 1948, pp. 175–182.
22 Harrell, *op. cit.*, p. 382.
23 Perry, John, *Human Relations in Small Industry*, Small Business Management Series No. 3, Small Defense Plants Administration, Washington, D. C., March, 1953, p.30.
24 *Ibid.*, p. 65.
25 Coffey, Hubert S., "Human Relations in Industry," *People at Work* (a symposium), Asilomar Conference of the Mental Health Society of Northern California, 2015 Steimer Street, San Francisco 15 (no date; fairly recent), p. 37.
26 Jucius, Michael J., *Personnel Management*, Richard D. Irwin, Inc., Homewood, Illinois, 1959, p. 25.

CHAPTER IX

COUNSELING: FACTORS THAT INFLUENCE PROBLEM CASES: COUNSELING INTERVIEW

What Is Counseling? — Counseling presupposes, ordinarily, the giving of advice to others or the mutually working out together of problems. Any counselor is expected to be trained in the areas of counseling, psychology, and sociology; a counselor in business must also be trained in business and economics. He should usually have had courses in management and labor relations. Most counselors, however, receive their practical training "on the job." Some people set up private businesses in various areas of counseling, as, vocational, marriage, and child-guidance. Even the advice of lawyers, doctors, and clinical psychologists would be considered counseling.

Counselors in business and industry are provided to give assistance to people who need help in problems of personal or vocational adjustment. Women workers use counselors more than do men workers. Interviews with the counselees take from fifteen to thirty minutes; several interviews are usually needed to take care of a given problem. Where counselors are provided, one counselor is usually maintained for three hundred employees.[1]

It is essential that any information given counselors be completely confidential; the counselor cannot function successfully if he cannot win the confidence of the counselee and if the counselee is not confident that what he says will not be made known to others.

The type of counseling talked about thus far presupposes that somebody with a problem comes to somebody else to get help in solving that problem. This is the *employee-initiated interview*. There are also *employer-initiated* interviews for employing, for induction, for training, for disciplining, for reviewing of workers' records and achievements, and at the time of workers' termination of employment with the firm.

Another kind of counseling program may begin with the counselor service of the organization in question. When this kind of counseling service is offered, it is sometimes called an *interviewing program*. In some companies it is called *personnel counseling*. Its purpose is to find out the problems of workers, what is on their minds, what motivates them. In the process such interviewing has been found to have other benefits, as: workers are helped to adjust; they feel better after they have gotten their grievances off their chests or after they have had a part in suggesting that changes be made at the work place (or even simply because they have had a chance to tell their personal problems to someone else. This type of interviewing has somewhat the same results psychiatric counseling does, especially when the *non-directive* approach is used. When the *directive approach* is used, the result is to obtain a list of things the worker thinks are his problems — they may not be. Directive and non-directive interviewing are discussed later in this chapter.

Perhaps some of the best counseling is done *without an interview*. This is usually done by the employee's line or staff boss, however, and not by a person carrying the title of "counselor." The supervisor or manager involved may pass on printed information to an employee that he believes will aid him; he may suggest a vacation early this year because the employee has been "on edge" for several days. He may say, "The next time you want to get away from it all, why don't you and the family go up to my place on the lake? Do you good to commune with nature for a week-end." He may realize that the employee has a problem, but he may just wait until it comes out with the knowledge that prodding would perhaps only irritate. The supervisor must be aware that his own actions will also influence the attitudes and actions of the employees.

The three major processes which result in human problems of administration are:

1. Adjustment of the individual to the industrial structure.
2. Communication and control.
3. Changes in the social structure.[2]

Counseling can serve to control and direct in these areas when other phases of management are inadequate. In fact, counselors may advise on many areas of personnel management such as employment and placement of workers, transferring workers, laying off or discharging workers, training, safety, and various fringe benefit programs.[3]

A counseling program enables management to keep in touch with the morale of the workers, and the material obtained from counseling is an excellent source of training material for supervisors.[4]

Some of the Long-term Factors To Be Considered in Counseling — A great many factors have an influence upon the worker, his attitudes, and his efficiency. The person who counsels should be familiar with the effects of these various factors. They include the *sentiments* of people (discussed more fully in Chapter XIX), many *long-term* (predisposing) factors such as general health and well-being, environment (home influence, economic factors, social factors, education), and inherited characteristics (physical make-up and intelligence), as well as the *short-term* (precipitating) factors, such as movies one may have attended, television or radio programs listened to and seen, books, magazines, and papers one has read, or countless immediate occurrences, emotional problems, and frustrations.

In fact, one's *frame of reference* determines how he will act in a given situation. One's frame of reference is all that he has ever experienced in a real or vicarious way which determines the limits of his world for problem solving. It is affected by all of the factors named in the preceding paragraph, and others such as personality, marital adjustment, and children (factors discussed in Chapter IV) as well as friends and all of the people with whom one has come in contact.

GENERAL HEALTH AND WELL-BEING — The *general health and well-being* of the individual are influenced greatly by exercise, sleep, relaxation, food, nicotine, narcotics, caffeine, and alcohol (Chapter III). Certainly, too, health is influenced by mental attitudes and ways of adjusting as discussed in earlier chapters. The counselor must be familiar with the implications of these various influences for applications to solutions of problems of interviewees.

ENVIRONMENT — *Environmental influences* begin with what is found in the home. They include: the parents and other children and persons in the early home; present family, if married; friends; activities engaged in; attitudes of parents toward the children and toward their friends and activities. Studies have shown that better adjustment is likely to result if people came from homes where there is affection, close family loyalty, hope on the part of the parents (regardless of economic and other factors), less sibling rivalry, and a tendency for members of the family to have responsibilities.

Home conditions are extremely important in the development of the individual. Studies by Sheldon and others have shown that parents are as much to blame for delinquency as are the delinquents;[5] conversely, they must be given credit for helping to develop in their children the characteristics that make for success.

Roul Tunley in *Kids, Crime and Chaos* (Harper and Brothers, 1962) indicates that affluence seems to stimulate delinquency despite the fact that most authorities on the subject, especially in the United States, still theorize that delinquent behavior is deterred by improved living conditions. In Japan, thirty-five per cent of juvenile crimes (excepting traffic violations) occur among young people from middle- and upper-class homes. In Sweden, delinquency is found chiefly among the middle-class people. Socially prominent young people in various sections of the United States have been guilty of car-stealing and dope addiction. Tunley offers examples to refute many of the theories that are usually accepted in this country. Delinquents from broken homes in a Philadelphia study were fewer than delinquents from unbroken homes; eighteen per cent of the boys joining a boys' organization in New York were delinquent at the time they joined; later twenty-eight per cent of the group were delinquent. Delinquency has been blamed on working mothers. It was found that fifty per cent of mothers in Vienna work outside the home. Although this is the highest percentage of working mothers anywhere in the world, Austria's delinquency rate is one of the lowest.[6] [Numbers of studies have shown that the fact the mother works may have no influence on delinquency.]

Most authorities agree that the attitudes of the parents toward religion and discipline are highly influential in the lives of the children. "Hope" and the ever-striving toward a "better life" on the part of the parents usually compensate for any lack of economic well-being.

Economic factors are, of course, important. Many a man or woman of success, power, or wealth achieved material success to compensate for the lack of that very element in his or her earlier life. It is not so much the amount of wealth that a family has that is important; it is the way a family manages the money that it has that counts. In a poor home where there is little to spend on luxuries, children may be treated as individuals, loved, and made to feel that they belong to the group. If all the parents could afford on Christmas were fruits, nuts, and candy, nevertheless the children may have been made happy because they hung their stockings, sung Christmas carols, and Santa visited them with what he had to offer.

Social factors may have influenced a person to be shy, to feel incompetent in crowds, with fellow workers. On the other hand, one brought up in an atmosphere of social contacts with groups such as boy scouts, girl scouts, campfire girls, various athletic teams, bands and musical organizations, community centers, church groups, and with adequate family, birthday and other special-occasion gatherings should feel at ease in most groups. Both the home and the school contribute much to the social development of the individual. What he does in the way of seeking companionship outside of the home and away from the direction of parents and school may have a positive or negative influence in his social development, depending on how well the so-called proper attitudes have been developed in the home.

Statistical analysis made by Hewitt of the records of five hundred children showed behavior patterns of three types of maladjustment: I, *overinhibited;* II, *unsocialized aggressive;* III, *socialized delinquents.* The overinhibited were shy and tended to retreat from others; they developed bad habits. They were from homes where the parents were cold and unsocial. The mother may have been, by protecting the child, compensating for rejection in her own earlier life. The unsocialized aggressives acted in unrestricted manner, doing things that often led to the police station. They were from homes where they had been rejected and were not given the love and understanding that are deemed essential for "normal" development. The socialized delinquents were typically loyal gang members; they could be adjusted to members of their "in group." Toward those outside of their groups they gave vent to their primitive impulses. Such delinquents were usually the products of homes where they did not have association with their fathers, although they had adequate association with their mothers.[7]

Education has been held responsible for many things, among them the state of affairs in technological progress of the United States as compared with Russia. (Sputnik brought such charges as *Educational Wastelands, Quackery in the Public Schools,* and "Are We Making a Playground Out of College?" Back in 1948 we may have read "The Educated Man — Taught by the Integrating Philosopher: He Is Overcoming His Chronic 'Specialties.' ") Education in this country was accused in 1958 of spending too much time on the teaching of "life adjustment" when it really should have been concentrating on teaching the sciences and mathematics and striving for intellectual achievement.[8] Schools have been charged with wasting the time of their ablest students, despite the fact that many schools are much tougher than they were twenty to thirty years ago.[9]

During World War II, progressive education was accused of having produced men who could not "take it" when the going became rough. As children they had been permitted to do what they wanted to; they had lacked the discipline of the pre-John Dewey days. When they had to meet the daily obligation to carry out an operation on which depended their own lives and the lives of others, they could not and broke under the strain. This, at least, was the theory of some who wrote on the subject. John Dewey has greatly influenced the educational system of the United States, but perhaps most would agree that his influence has been as much, and possibly even more, in the positive side as the negative. Some may have developed less stamina because they were permitted to make their own choices and may have always chosen the paths of least resistance; many others by the same token developed abilities to make decisions which led to success on the field of battle. The same thing can be said for men who sit at the helms of industrial concerns. Somewhere in between strong discipline and the permitting of young people to make their own choices in the learning process, in growth and development, probably lies the best course of action in producing people who can think for themselves and have the degree of self-discipline necessary to take action. John Dewey himself said that unless one's habits of thinking are formed it requires much effort to face a situation to discover the facts. The mind does not like the unpleasant, and facing up to a problem to find its solution is often unpleasant simply because it requires effort.[10]

Young people frequently have failed to choose the difficult courses in school. They have avoided mathematics and science. It was realization of this fact that caused the pendulum to swing back to placing of emphasis upon these areas of study, encouraging by all means possible the youth of today to take training in these "tougher" areas to the extent of their abilities to do so. The colleges and universities as well as the public schools have pursued this new course.

In 1959 two reports were published criticizing the undergraduate programs in business education (as well as some of the graduate work). One of these studies was made under the sponsorship of the Ford Foundation by R. A. Gordon and J. E. Howell, both of whom teach economics in schools of business administration. The other report was made by Frank C. Pierson, also an economics professor, and was sponsored by the Carnegie Corporation. Each of the reports indicted business education. Most of approximately 160 university colleges of business and around 400 departments and divisions of business were indicted for inadequate and inferior preparation for business success. The reports indicated that the business students were inferior to students in other areas (excepting agriculture and education). The chief weakness of the graduates of these schools was considered to be inadequate general education, i.e., English, mathematics, science, and history. Over-specialization in a particular area of business they also considered bad. Two institutions that operate business schools on the graduate level only did not receive criticism: Harvard University and Massachusetts Institute of Technology.

The Gordon and Howell report recommended four years in liberal arts or engineering with graduate school preparation (two years) in business for those who wish to become managers. Since most people probably couldn't take the six years of training, the next best course of action was to take general business (and especially a lot of economics!).[11]

Both of these lengthy studies (which appear not to be too clear on exactly how their data was obtained) have received wide attention; they have already had much influence on the colleges and universities that offer training in business administration. Curriculums have been revised to return to general business majors, with fewer of the specialized majors in the various areas of accounting, marketing, management, finance, business services, and so on. The current attitudes of education, however, have implied more, not less, of the need for behavioral sciences. While we need the scientists of Cape Kennedy, we also need a knowledge of how to organize and keep running a group of over 200,000 persons engaged in National Aeronautics Space Administration's Office of Manned Space Flight. Managers are being returned to colleges to learn about human relations and managing men, and today universities are hiring specialists in psychology and social communication. Collegiate schools of business hope to produce men who can think like men of action yet act like men of thought.[12]

Engineering and technical people are also being returned to college campuses to learn new mathematics and technologies. In the summer of 1962, thirty-two executives studied "modern engineering" under the direction of the University of California, Los Angeles. This was the second summer of the program. UCLA has taught similar courses for General Electric Company's Management Research & Development Institute.[13]

In addition to special institutes for workers and managers, training within companies is an ongoing activity, and training is being extended beyond the United States to other countries of the world. The International Cooperation Administration has institutes in many countries in which it uses United States Executives to train thousands of businessmen. The ICA does not recognize the difference between management and technical training; it helps in all areas from hand-loom weaving and bookkeeping to human relations and long-range planning for management.[14]

The International Center for the Advancement of Management Education at Stanford University was created in 1962 under a grant of $3.5 million from the Ford Foundation. Deans of the major business schools, among them Harvard, Chicago, MIT and UCLA have cooperated with Stanford in planning the seven-year program designed primarily for the college-level business teachers of some of the less economically advanced nations of the world. The participants in the program will have opportunity to do internship work with private industry.[15]

Counselors must deal not only with the products of the educational systems of the last half century in this country, they may even have to work with modern trainers and educators and in the process come in contact with the products of educational systems around the world. They may have some part in the training of leaders of business from foreign countries and in introducing them to some of the methods and techniques of management as practiced in the American enterprise system. Counselors must know a great deal about the educational systems that have produced the persons with whom they work: the earlier ones that may have stifled initiative but required students to sit in their seats, learn to spell, and memorize multiplication tables; later ones which in the teaching of life adjustment did not require people to pay attention to details or remain glued to their desks for formal recitations. They must understand the influence of the system of education upon its products. A great many people of today cannot spell; a large number are lacking in a sense of responsibility; some lack a sense of "humbleness" considered by many managers to be essential. When beginners go into industry and start telling the bosses right away what and how to do and how to run their departments, trouble is around the corner. Yet a school system is frequently responsible for such problems as these. When Johnny got up in school from his classroom seat to talk with Janie about the new boat his Pop just bought and that he was learning to run it, his personality was not thwarted by the teacher's telling Johnny to go back and MEMO-RIZE Lincoln's "Gettysburg Address" or learn a list of words he missed in spelling. In fact, Johnny probably even went on to tell Jane he would like to take her boating Saturday. He may have, and he probably took the teacher, too! Nevertheless, if grown-up Johnny's boss calls him on the carpet because he sent in a report to the president with the president's name misspelled, and if Johnny in turn gets despondent because it seems he is always being called down for errors, what can a counselor say? Johnny should be told that it isn't too late. He can still learn to spell. The solution to this problem, as to most others requiring counseling aid, is DISCIPLINE. In this case, the discipline of the individual by himself to avoid the discipline of the boss is indicated. For some people self discipline is very hard; yet most of life's greatest satisfactions and rewards come to those capable of exercising this quality.

INHERITED FACTORS — *Physical make-up* and *intelligence* are two of the factors that must be considered in counseling. Studies have shown that people who think they can size up a person by how he or she looks are usually wrong. If there is any correspondence between personality traits and the "cut of the face" it is not known exactly what these are. William H. Sheldon did differentiate some eighty-eight different combinations of three familiar types of temperament: *endomorph* (*vital* type, the fat man who likes the better things of life, interested in people, in saving himself effort); *mesomorph* (*motive* type, the man of bone, muscle, and square build, athletic, often with high cheekbones and prominent nose, who must be carefully led to decision-making, interested more in the qualities of a product than in its price); *ecotomorph* (*mental* type, likely to love beauty and science, idealist, inclined to be inhibited and restrained, the "egg-head," spare of build). By using numbers from 1–7 a person could be rated as to the degree he possessed the temperament of each of these types of personalities. 7–2–1 would indicate a high degree of endomorphy with very little of the mesomorph or ectomorph characteristics. A person who by heredity belongs to one of these classes may have an entirely different personality due to environmental influences.[16]

Kretschmer classified people into three body builds in a manner similar to Sheldon's. Kretschmer found that his *asthenic* person (tall, thin, long-legged, narrow-chested) was startlingly more inclined toward schizophrenia than toward manic-depressive psychosis; his *pyknic* (fat, short legs, large waist, sloping shoulders, little neck) was much more inclined toward manic-depressive psychosis. The *athletic* type (muscular, symmetrical development) seemed more inclined to schizophrenia. Other later studies have not confirmed Kretschmer's finding that certain body builds correspond to certain types of insanity. Dr. R. W. Husband attempted to find whether or not there was any relationship between the body build of "normal" persons and their personality types (introversion, extroversion). He found in studying several hundred college students that there was apparently slight relationship only.[17]

One of the interesting findings of Terman relative to relationship between intelligence and physique was that children with IQ's over 140 were on the average some two inches taller and ten pounds heavier than the ones who had only average intelligence. There is indication here that mental and physical traits are related. Terman's studies further indicated that the gifted children are more likely to have happy and successful lives than are the less gifted ones.[18]

The intelligence quotient is computed in the following manner:

$$IQ = \frac{Mental\ Age \times 100}{Chronological\ Age}$$

TABLE IX-1

IQ SCORES AND CLASSIFICATION OF GROUPS BY SCORES

Below 25	Idiot, under 2 years mental age
25–49	Imbecile, 2–7 years mental age
50–69	Moron, 7–11 years mental age
70–79	Borderline
80–89	Dull
90–109	Average
110–119	Superior
120–140	Very superior
Over 140	Genius

Most firms today have the IQ's of employees working for them in their files. If a counselor needs this information, it can be obtained. In Chapter XII the importance of looking for intelligence, personality, grades, and other factors in employment interviews is discussed. It is generally accepted that personality is the most important factor in measuring success in terms of income-earning capacity; grades are second in importance; intelligence comes after these two factors. It is true, however, that intelligence must be regarded as an important factor in personality itself. It is also reflected in grades made.

The relationship between intelligence and emotional stability must also be kept in mind in counseling. When 30,000 Canadian soldiers were examined it was found that those who were mentally retarded had a much higher incidence of emotional instability than those not retarded.

Some of the Short-term Factors To Be Considered in Counseling — Movies, television, radio, reading, and *immediate frustrations* and/or *situations* of all types may need to be considered in counseling. The exact part that movies, television, radio, and reading may play in stimulating a person to feel and act a certain way is not known and can scarcely be estimated with any degree of accuracy. As far back as the thirties, articles were being written, however, to the effect that the soap operas were perhaps having a negative effect upon the mental health of housewives. More currently, many have thought it possible that TV westerns and crime stories may have influenced persons to take negative action. Certainly many have felt that time spent in watching plays might have been more profitably spent in self-development through creative and participative programs.

Today's movies are often indicated as being for adults only. The homosexuality, misogyny, lesbianism, incest, violence, blackmail, and beatniks of the movies may also have some immediate effect upon the action of adults, assuming that the conditions preceding the seeing of such movies have conditioned them for such action.

It is the immediate frustration and/or occurrence or situation that precipitates a person to act, to talk back to his or her boss, to take out his feelings on a fellow worker or even a person he is supervising. Counselors must look for these precipitating factors.

Following a Conceptual Pattern in Counseling — The person who is counseling others should attempt to find their problems. The counselor should lead persons to see their own problems, to see the possible ways they can meet these problems, and to feel that whatever solutions evolved are their own. A person confronted with a problem may: *face the problem, take flight from it, feint, faint, live in a phantasy world,* or *fight.* Many writers have tackled this problem of how people meet their problems; they may use different words and different approaches but the results are about the same. There are positive ways of meeting problems (facing up to them, tackling them, using direct attack adjustment). There are negative ways of meeting problems. If a person uses negative adjustment methods long enough, his personality is weakened for using positive means of adjustment, that is, for tackling problems and solving them.

Ways of adjusting were discussed in Chapter VI. The counselor should be familiar with these, should recognize a counselee's attempt to use those ways that are negative.

The following outline of steps to be taken in counseling will assist the counselor in interviewing a counselee or the supervisor who is called upon to help an employee solve a problem:

1. Find the *problem,* the *situation,* the *barrier.* (The problem may be due to *abrupt changes,* to *lack of preparation for a task or event,* to *interruptions* or *constant harassment,* to *insufficient capacity* — health, physical, intellectual, social — to *too much capacity for a particular job.*) Abrupt changes might include not only changes at the work place, being promoted or demoted, but might also include such things as loss of a loved one, marriage, marital situations, and so on.

2. Find the long-term (*predisposing*) factors involved. (See discussion above.)

3. Find the short-term (*precipitating*) factors involved. (See discussion above.)

4. Find the *positive way of adjusting* (facing the problem, using *direct attack*). John Dewey suggested that instead of indulging in flights of fancy or dodging the problem, one simply should face the situation. To put this another way would be to say that one should *discipline* himself to take the course of action indicated for success. To get a trial balance, the accountant works until apparent errors are eliminated. To get the report typed, the stenographer stays at her desk until the job is done. To pass the test, the student studies and recites to himself or to others. He may write the possible questions with their answers. He prepares.

5. Discover the alternative ways of acting that may have possible positive value. These ways of acting have been called *substitute activities of possible positive value.* (The employee who does not like his job may find another one instead of forcing himself to comply with demands that he feels he is incapable of fulfilling. The person who becomes an accountant despite the fact that he inclines toward

the extrovert type personality may compensate for the routine type of work by engaging in social activities.)

6. Find and help the individual to *avoid the negative ways of adjusting*. (Embezzling money to compensate for a feeling of inadequacy is an example of extreme negative adjustment. There are many other less negative ways of adjusting. See Chapter VI.)

7. Help the individual to discover a solution to his problem, but if possible let him feel that he has discovered this solution for himself. Frequently the mere talking out of a problem with a counselor will result in the counselee's seeing what must be done. It is because of this that the interviewing programs carried on in some companies are so profitable. People discover and solve their problems while talking with sympathetic persons whom they trust.[19]

The Counseling Interview — A number of types of interviewing in business were mentioned at the beginning of this chapter. *Employment* and *induction* interviewing will be discussed in Chapter XII. It is important that there be a *termination interview* to discover, if possible, why a person is voluntarily leaving or why it was necessary to let him go if this was the case. Such interviewing aids in discovering information that helps to avoid similar problems in the future.

This discussion concerns the *directive* and *non-directive* interviews as they are used for one of two purposes: (1) to find out what is on the worker's mind (employer initiated), or (2) to help a person find a solution to a problem (employee initiated).

THE DIRECTIVE INTERVIEW — In this type of interviewing the interviewer asks questions. Usually the questions are more or less standard and they may have been evolved as being the ones that have been proven through past experience to be important. The directive interview (patterned, standardized) is the most useful type of interviewing for employment purposes (Chapter XII).

In the research conducted by the Western Electric Company, Hawthorne Works, Chicago, which was begun in 1927, it was found that this type of interviewing was unsatisfactory.[20] It was hard to frame a question without suggesting a significance of the question to the interviewee which the question actually did not have for him. Interviewers using this type of interview greatly influenced the findings. Even the skilled interviewers had certain preconceived ideas of what they expected to find and this may have influenced their findings; based upon their own prejudices, they were inclined to think some things more important than others without regard to the importance for the individual, the department, or the company.

When the Western Electric Company began its interviewing program, the method of interviewing was regarded as "rather simple and incidental to the material which it was hoped such a technique could obtain." [21] It was found that a person capable of interviewing had not been trained until some 20,000 interviews had taken place. It was felt that interviewing was valuable as an industrial research method because it could discover the emotional significance of events, objects, and people in the worker's experiences.

Many firms today do use the direct method of counseling. The counselor takes the initiative and gets the answers to questions deemed important in solving the interviewee's problem, or in solving the company's problem of finding what is on the worker's mind. These questions may delve into the worker's background in such areas as home, education, and work experience. They may revolve around the particular work situation currently involved. The directive interview may be quite useful in disciplining to determine the reason that discipline was necessary, to discover attitudes of the worker, and to establish an understanding between the worker and the interviewer. This kind of interviewing (counseling) is more generally done by one's immediate supervisor, however, than by a person employed in the capacity of counselor.

THE NON-DIRECTIVE INTERVIEW — The Western Electric Company concluded early in its use of interviewing for industrial research that an indirect type of interviewing was necessary in order to obtain the desired information about workers' convictions, feelings, and beliefs. It was realized that letting the worker talk at random would have its faults, too. It would require greater skill, both in interviewing and in interpreting the findings. In the process of developing a system of non-directive interviewing, a set of rules was evolved. Here are the "Rules of Orientation" developed at Western Electric:

I. The interviewer should treat what is said in an interview as an item in a context.

A. The interviewer should not pay exclusive attention to the manifest content of the intercourse. [He should, in other words, take everything with a grain of salt and read between the lines.]

B. The interviewer should not treat everything that is said as either fact or error.

C. The interviewer should not treat everything that is said as being at the same psychological level.

II. The interviewer should listen not only to what a person wants to say but also for what he does not want to say or cannot say without help.

III. The interviewer should treat the mental contexts described in the preceding rule as indices and seek through them the personal reference that is being revealed.

IV. The interviewer should keep the personal reference in its social context.

A. The interviewer should remember that the interview is itself a social situation and that therefore the social relation existing between the interviewer and the interviewee is in part determining what is said.

B. The interviewer should see to it that the speaker's sentiments do not act on his own.[22]

A person's overt behavior and what he says currently, plus his sentiments (beliefs, desires, interests), his past history, and his present social relationships (home, work, and others) all have a bearing upon the worker's (1) convictions, and/or (2) problem.

The Western Electric Company's rules for conducting the interview itself are very similar to the rules given in Chapter VII for interviewing maladjusted patients:

1. The interviewer should listen to the speaker in a patient and friendly, but intelligently critical, manner.

2. The interviewer should not display any kind of authority.

3. The interviewer should not give advice or moral admonition.

4. The interviewer should not argue with the speaker.

5. The interviewer should talk or ask questions only under certain conditions.

a. To help the person talk.

b. to relieve any fears or anxieties on the part of the speaker which may be affecting his relation to the interviewer.

c. To praise the interviewee for reporting his thoughts and feelings accurately.

d. To veer the discussion to some topic which has been omitted or neglected.

e. To discuss implicit assumptions, if this is advisable.[23]

Persons doing this type of interviewing must be expertly trained for it. The Western Electric Company was at first primarily interested in finding out the relationship between employees' complaints and their personal situations. Later they found they desired also the relationship of the workers' complaints to their social organization at the place of work. Some of the findings of this investigation are given in Chapter XIX.

An additional list of rules for the interviewer in non-directive interviewing is given here. It has been built up from many references and past experience.

1. The counselor must put the employee at ease. He should accept him and perhaps be empathic toward him, but he should not agree with him or sympathize with him.

2. He must win the employee's confidence that the information given will be kept confidential.

3. He must make arrangement with supervisors to see the employees at scheduled times for interviewing in order not to interrupt work schedules.

4. Some system for organizing the information obtained in an interview must be used. There should be major classifications for tabulating data.

5. Interview transcripts should be locked in the counselor's files and should be kept strictly confidential. Perhaps names should not be attached to them.

6. The counselor must not permit himself to become emotionally involved in the problems of the counselee; he must remain objective and detached from the situation.

7. The interviewer must not have preconceived ideas of what he is going to find out in the interview.

8. The interviewer must not direct the interview by questioning; yet he must keep the interview from becoming incoherent because of lack of guides.

9. The counselor must not feel that any action whatsoever is required of him. He may listen to complaints about supervisors, working conditions, pay, the company, the cafeteria food, the counselee's wife (son, daughter, or other person), a fellow worker, but he may not become involved in these complaints or verbally agree or disagree with them.

10. The counselor should not discuss an employee's problems with the line supervision. He should not give advice to supervisors and should make no recommendations to either the supervisor or the employee. He may stimulate the two to action, but he takes none. [The counselor may make general recommendations relative to groups of people, but he should not make recommendations relative to individuals.]

11. The counselor should develop a method of recording the findings of the interview. Interviews have been recorded by tape recorders, by the interviewers in their own handwriting at the time of the interview, and sometimes by stenographers. The last method is

not recommended as it brings a third party into the interview and permits distrust on the part of the interviewee. Some interviewers have trained themselves to recall the facts of an interview and record them after the employee has left the scene of the interview.

Non-directive interviewing is useful not only in finding the attitudes of workers that may have an effect upon their company's efficiency, it is helpful in all of the ways that interviewing may be used. It is useful to supervisors as well as counselors. It could be quite beneficial in grievance or discipline interviews. The reason that it is not so often used by businessmen as is the directive interview is that it is too time consuming. Counseling of the non-directive type is quite useful when innovations are to be introduced at the work place or in the work situation.

PROJECTS

1. Students may be asked to conduct non-directive interviews of fellow students in the classroom. Attempt might be made to discover a student's attitudes toward (1) the institution he is attending, (2) the department in which he is studying, or (3) the course he is taking. A student who was absent the previous class meeting might be interviewed to determine the cause of his absence.

2. A student might be asked to take the part of a supervisor who must interview a veteran employee of twenty years with the company (another student). This person has been absent several Mondays (following paydays) during the last six months. Use the directive or non-directive interview to discover the cause of such absenteeism. Assuming this is also a disciplinary interview, the student interviewer should take whatever action he deems necessary in the light of the findings of the interview.

ACKNOWLEDGMENTS AND REFERENCES

1 ———, "Counseling," *Personnel Women of Greater St. Louis*, September, 1952, pp. 12–15.
2 Roethlisberger, F. J., and Dickson, William J., *Management and the Worker*, Harvard University Press, Cambridge, Massachusetts, 1950, p. 601.
3 Yoder, Dale, *Personnel Management and Industrial Relations*, Fourth Edition, Prentice-Hall, Inc., Englewood Cliffs, N. J., 1956, p. 646.
4 Roethlisberger, *op. cit.*, p. 603.
5 Sheldon, W. H., *Varieties of Delinquent Youth*, Harper and Brothers, New York, 1949, p. 763.
6 ———, "Disease of Progress," *Newsweek*, June 11, 1962, pp. 96–98.
7 Hepner, Harry Walker, *Psychology Applied to Life and Work*, Prentice-Hall, Inc., Englewood Cliffs, New Jersey, 1957, pp. 267–270.

8 ———, "Education, Special Report," *Business Week*, April 19, 1958, p. 159.

9 ———, "Education, Special Report," *Business Week*, April 26, 1958, p. 88.

10 Dewey, John, *How We Think*, D. C. Heath and Company, New York, p. 103.

11 ———, "Management," *Business Week*, October 31, 1959, pp. 84–90.

12 ———, "Seasoning B-Schools With a Dash," *Business Week*, July 18, 1959, p. 112ff.

13 ———, "Management — Tough Cram Course for the Brass," *Business Week*, June 30, 1962, pp. 90–91.

14 ———, "Management — ICA 'Hires' Top Brass To Teach Abroad," *Business Week*, December 31, 1960, pp. 46–49.

15 ———, "Management — Newest in B-schools Spreads Gospel Abroad," *Business Week*, July 14, 1962, pp. 62–66.

16 Russell, Frederic, and Beach, Frank H., *Textbook of Salesmanship*, McGraw-Hill Book Company, Inc., 1959, pp. 200–201.

17 Husband, Richard Wellington, *Applied Psychology*, Harper & Brothers, Publishers, New York, 1949, pp. 652–653.

18 Terman, L. M., "Genetic Studies of Genius," Vol. I, *Mental and Physical Traits of a Thousand Gifted Children*, Stanford University Press, 1925.

19 See Hepner, *op. cit.*, pp. 43–45, 138, for a similar classification and lengthy list of change and capacity barriers.

20 Roethlisberger, *op. cit.*, pp. 270–291.

21 *Ibid.*, p. 270.

22 *Ibid.*, pp. 272–273.

23 *Ibid.*, p. 287.

SECTION IV — INDUSTRIAL RELATIONS

CHAPTER X

SCIENTIFIC MANAGEMENT IN INDUSTRY

What Is Scientific Management? — The functions of management are the creative planning, organizing, directing, supervising, and appraising of those activities of an organization that must be carried out in order to attain the objectives for which the organization came into being, i.e., providing goods and/or services needed and desired by people, while at the same time providing satisfactory incomes to workers and management and satisfactory profits to owners. Management which is scientific uses records and all other obtainable data in performing its various functions.[1]

So-called "scientific management" had its origin with an attempt to solve management problems of the individual plant. The system of techniques which resulted from the investigations of Frederick W. Taylor came to be known as "The Taylor System." The doctrine which followed and grew out of these techniques was later called "scientific management," the term adopted by a group of engineers in 1910.[2] Henri Fayol in France and Lyndal Urwick in England are given credit for initiating and perpetuating the scientific management movement in their countries.

Early writers believed that science could not go beyond the material element in business, that wherever the human factor existed science could not enter in. Some of today's writers on management, including Peter Drucker, have also professed belief that because management involves "human relationships" it cannot be scientific. Most of these persons would probably concur, however, that that management is probably best which uses facts, figures, past performance, and forecasting on the basis of both external and internal data in solving its problems.

Directing, supervising, and appraising the work of employees are all elements of control; control overlaps all the functions of management, however, and is exercised at all levels within an organization, but particularly at the point of operation. Its purpose is to see that everything is proceeding according to plan and to bring about alterations of plans when this is necessary.

The functions of planning and controlling can be delegated to other people by management, but the function of organizing can not be completely delegated. Organizing consists in deciding the work that must be done to accomplish objectives, finding people to do this work, delegating authority and responsibility to these people, establishing lines of accountability so that each employee will be accountable to one superior only, and co-ordinating the work of all employees in order that the group may accomplish objectives.[3]

Organization structure is made up of the relationships of the work to be done, people who do the work, and the physical factors of plant, equipment, and materials. The basic form of organization structure today is *line and staff*. Line people are those who are in production, sales (marketing), and finance, the departments or divisions that directly contribute to producing or distributing goods or services. They form the primary chains of command within which authority rests. All other departments are called staff departments and the staff people perform the services of giving advice, controlling, co-ordinating, investigating, analyzing, interpreting, reporting, recommending, inspecting, and facilitating.

Business objectives furnish the beginning of business thinking; other things in an organization, such as functions, leadership, personnel, physical factors, and procedures, are related to objectives through policies and standards.

Business policy furnishes a guide to action. Policies are generally classified as *basic company policy, divisional policy,* and *departmental policy* and the three levels of management, *top, middle,* and *supervisory,* are responsible respectively for the three classes of policy.

Boards of directors are, or should be, the top policy makers in their corporations. There are *inside boards* and *outside boards* and their philosophies vary accordingly. Outside boards accept or reject policies originated by management. In companies with inside or working boards policies are set by the boards.[4]

Policies may be *originated, appealed,* or *externally imposed.* In order to establish guiding principles for themselves and for those who work under them, managers at any level originate policies both broad and narrow. When special cases not covered by the originated policies arise, it is necessary for a manager to appeal to a person, committe, or board to make decisions for handling such cases. These decisions are usually incorporated in policies. Imposed policies come from such external forces as trade unions, trade associations, the government, creditors, suppliers, customers, and the public in general.[5]

Policies pertaining to personnel management are generally formulated within the department subject to approval and acceptance of line departments and, for basic policies, the board of directors. Human relations and personnel management of necessity, however, permeate every division, department, and level of a business and all persons in an organization influence and are influenced by personnel policies.

Tools of Scientific Management — All of the methods and devices by which management attempts to secure statistical and other data as a basis of decision making are the tools of scientific management. This chapter will consider some of these and succeeding chapters will consider additional ones; many of the tools and controls of scientific management will not be discussed in this volume as they pertain to non-human phases of management. Some of these include: controls of cost, inventory, flow of materials, tools, equipment, and other phases of production, as well as production planning, plant maintenance, and some of the procedures of work. There are, of course, many other miscellaneous control tools that apply primarily to the management of materials, machines, and products, such as, scheduling of output, routing of supplies and equipment, inspecting of jobs or products, testing products, and so on. Even in these areas, however, the human element is an ever-present influence. Management in any area cannot be completely separated from the human factor. The effect of physical working conditions upon employees is discussed in Chapter XVIII. Other chapters in this section will consider the following phases of personnel management: recruiting of employees, including selection standards; the employment interview; tests used in employing; training of workers and supervisors; merit rating and job evaluation; labor relations and unions, welfare plans; morale and motivation; communications; the effect of technological developments upon workers. This chapter will consider personnel management and two of its earliest specialized areas, time and motion studies as "tools of scientific management." The place of standards, accounting and budgeting, statistics, and research in scientific management, particularly as these relate to "human management" will also be discussed.

TIME AND MOTION STUDY — Time and motion study:

1. Finds correct methods, materials, tools and equipment for getting a job done.
2. Eliminates inefficient motions and unnecessary work and steps.
3. Arranges the necessary work in the best possible order.
4. Sees that each step that is necessary is performed in minimum time with maximum efficiency and ease.
5. Finds if this is the most efficient and easiest way of getting the

whole job done and if so sets this as the standard work method for the job.

6. Finds how long it takes to get the job completed and considers this the standard time.

7. Records the methods, motions, steps, and time information in such manner that it can be followed by workers to perform the job by the desired method as well as in the desired time.

Among the reasons that time and motion study is important is the fact that production costs in the United States have continued to rise, chiefly because of increased costs of labor. On the other hand, technological progress with its automation and mechanization has helped to reduce costs, and time and motion study is considered to have had a part in technological progress. Time and motion study aims at elimination of unnecessary work. In the process of achieving this aim, mechanical innovations frequently have had their origin. When operations are reduced to basic repetitive skills, it is much easier to convert them to mechanized operations. Workers are, of course, frequently suspicious of time and motion study because they fear that it may: (1) eliminate the need of workers because mechanical substitutes will be found, (2) reduce a time standard to the point that workers will lose jobs because fewer will be needed to get a particular piece of work done, or (3) increase the amount of output required of each worker in order that he may maintain income at its previous level.

It is necessary in time and motion study to have the cooperation of management, supervisors, and workers; information pertaining to a proposed study must be made available to the people concerned; they should be made aware also of factors involved in continuing study. Those who do time and motion study are generally industrial engineers who know and understand machines, materials, and methods of getting jobs done. They should, however, have a knowledge of human relations, also. They are representatives of management and are usually attached to the personnel department in some manner. In large factories the time study department is an entity in itself.

Time and motion study is applicable to almost any type of manual work. The more mental effort needed to do a job, however, the more difficult it is to study that job.[6] The student who would like to pursue the study of time and motion techniques is referred to: Barnes, Ralph M., *Motion and Time Study*, Fourth Edition, John Wiley & Sons, Inc., New York, 1958; or Nadler, Gerald, *Motion and Time Study*, McGraw-Hill Book Company, Inc., New York, 1955. He will discover that this is an entire field of endeavor requiring a high degree of specialization.

Management of time and motion study requires engineering and mathematical knowledge and skill as well as skill in human relations; operative time and motion study workers must be capable of much detail observation and paper work.

Time study had its origin in the work of Frederick W. Taylor after he became a consulting engineer for the Bethlehem Steel Company about 1898. Taylor had been a student of Wentworth's at the time Wentworth was writing an algebra textbook and was timing students to see how long it would take them to work the algebra problems provided in assignments. Taylor as a foreman in earlier jobs had used the old methods of "forcing" or "driving" men to get a job done in a minimum amount of time and was able to double machine production. He felt that the success he achieved was hard earned for his reward was in bitter relations with the men.[7] With Bethlehem Steel Company, Taylor was able through using proper rest periods and techniques for loading pig iron to increase production from an average of 12½ tons per man per day to 47½ tons per man per day. Workers were "under load" 43 per cent of the time and rested 57 per cent of the time. Wages to the laborer were increased 60 per cent and the company saved $36,417 during the period as a result of Taylor's work.[8]

Although Taylor employed both time and motion study, he is chiefly remembered in this particular area of management for his work in time study. His work included other areas of management, such as materials management, and staff (functional) organization at the factory level where he proposed eight foremen specialists with equal authority. His ideas made valuable contributions in many areas of management, but his idea for staff foremen with equal responsibility and authority has been replaced. Good organization procedure today prescribes one foreman in whom full responsibility rests. He has needed specialists to assist him, but they are divested of authority.

Frank B. and Lillian M. Gilbreth are considered to be the originators of motion study. The Gilbreths are well known to present-generation Americans through two books based on their lives and written by two of their even dozen children: *Cheaper By the Dozen* and *Bells on Their Toes*. Gilbreth as a young man (1885) was a bricklayer. He observed that bricklayers were not consistent in the sets of motions they used. Since he felt there was one "best way," he went to work to find it. He not only studied the motions to discover the best ones, he devised equipment that would enable the arranging of bricks in the most easily accessible manner. He was able to reduce the motions in exterior brick work from 18 to 4½, increasing production from 120 to 350 bricks per man per hour. As a result of his interest in motion study and engineering, he and Mrs. Gilbreth, who had studied psychology, became experts in motion study, turning to the use of motion pictures to record motions of operations and developing a microchronometer to record time in fractions of 1/2,000 of a minute. His technique came to be known as "micromotion study," and he presented it at a meeting of the American Society of Mechanical Engineers in 1912.[9]

The work of the Gilbreths, however, covered numerous improvements in building and construction work,[10] fatigue studies,[11] studies of monotony,[12] studies of transfer of skill, and work for the handicapped,[13] and development of process charts, and the chronocyclegraph, as well as micromotion study.

Gilbreth devised various types of charts for recording the breakdown of motion to be used on jobs, as well as the method of using films. It was the study of the motion being currently used by workers that led to discovery of simplified procedures. On repetitive and skilled short-cycle jobs (usually involving hand motion chiefly) that required complex breakdowns of motions, the type of chart used was called simo-chart, which was the shortened term for simultaneous-motion cycle chart. Detailed breakdowns necessitated the analyzing of basic motions or activities. The Gilbreths broke motions into eighteen basic categories which he called *therbligs*. (Gilbreth backwards with the last two letters transposed).[14] Additional symbols have been added to the Gilbreths' therblig chart to bring the total to twenty-two basic motions or activities. Even this list is not considered final as it might be considered advisable to have an even finer breakdown of hand and body motions needed for getting work done.[15] Therbligs are used not only in writing time studies but are also used in writing job descriptions and training material as well as in job evaluation. They furnish a kind of shorthand for method analysts and time study men.

One of the big problems in controlling standards is procedure to follow when a change in method of operation is indicated. If management makes the change, the standard can be changed to apply to new methods suggested by time and motion study. If an individual operator discovers an improved method, some policy should exist for putting this change into effect and for changing standards, as well as for rewarding the worker. Some of the ways that have been used in handling this problem are:

1. Under a suggestion system procedure a suggestion for improved method is evaluated for reward.

2. The operator who discovered the improved method is kept on his job using the improved method but under the old standard for

a given period of time; other workers work under the new rate. Unpleasant feelings might develop, but this can be used when skillfully handled. A variation of this is to leave the old standard indefinitely in effect for the operator. The time study people would thus feel the pressure for finding the best methods to begin with.

3. Publicity is given to the one devising an improved method.

4. A merit increase is given to the employee.

5. The operator is paid the amount saved by his method over a specified period of time; at the same time the standard for all workers is changed.[16]

RESEARCH AND STANDARDS — *Research* is the tool by which management attempts to find better ways of increasing efficiency in attaining objectives. Research is the basis for setting of standards in all areas; statistics is the tool that is employed in gathering and analyzing research data. Research is by no means confined to consumers, advertising, products, markets, costs (where both accounting and statistics are research tools), and distribution. Research is widely employed in the areas of personnel management where standards may be set or approximated.

A very recent device for doing multimillion-dollar research to help businesses locate and control weaknesses in their organizations is being utilized through a project called "Group Ten" sponsored by the American Management Association. Over two hundred companies employing almost two million workers have furnished data for computing averages and ratios in certain areas of organization. Some of the recent findings of the AMA research that can be useful to management are:

1. The size of the personnel staff increases in proportion to the increase in the number of more highly paid, unskilled workers.

2. The number of people in general administration increases as sales increase — most rapidly in the drug industry, most slowly in the food.

3. The number of workers for each first-line supervisor varies from 9.6 in industrial chemicals to 22.2 in electronics. The average for all industrials is close to 16.

4. The number of people in data processing does not reduce the number in accounting and finance.

5. Salesmen as a percentage of total work force vary from 31.1 in Company A to only 7.7 in Company B, with 22.3 as the industry average.

6. Company A has 5.1 per cent of its people in research and development and 3.5 per cent in production; Company B has 19 per

cent of its people in research and development and 37 per cent in production. Industry averages are 13 per cent and 22.3 per cent. [Individual firms can profit by comparing their data with company averages.] [17]

Standards may be defined as criteria that enable comparisons to be made and efficiency to be measured. Standards pertain to goods (quality, quantity, sizes, styles) and services (quality, degree) provided; to specifications for packages; to performance (time and motion for individuals; merit rating and job evaluation; absenteeism; project performance; group achievement); to systems, methods, and procedures for getting all kinds of work done; to all phases of production management; to marketing management; to financial management (costs, working capital ratio to be maintained, level of inventory, turnover of accounts receivable, turnover of accounts payable, owned capital to borrowed capital, numerous average ratios for industries, salary schedules, and so on); to office management and all other areas of service and staff activities; to organization structure (functions, people); to physical factors (buildings, equipment, materials handling); to consumer, product, market, distribution, personnel and other research; to personnel (recruiting; education, experience, testing, and other requirements of employees; training; activities; fringe benefits; relationships with unions; turnover of employees; morale maintenance). Individual companies set standards for themselves on the basis of internal (past performance and current testing) and external (economic conditions, trends, competitive situation) data. Industries may have a part in setting standards. The public influences the setting of standards, also. Governmental agencies, trade associations, and international organizations have a part in determining standards. Standards are not arrived at and then forgotten; they are constantly subject to change.

In addition to standards pertaining to elements of efficiency in terms of human and physical factors within an organization, there are also standards of moral and ethical conduct. Anyone studying a curriculum leading to specialization in any phase of management will probably be required to read in the areas of philosophy and ethics for business. [18] He will likely become aware of *realism, idealism,* and *pragmatism* as influences upon managerial philosophy. Idealism gives management faith to keep on trying; it aids them to pull through trying times and may be the "self-starter" to innovation, which quality in the long run is suspected of being the main factor in keeping both the individual business and free enterprise going. It is idealism that encourages the cooperation of management and technicians, the highly skilled and creative people in any organization. Idealism also encourages social planning. Rupert C. Lodge held that idealism in personnel relations (social planning) pertains only during periods of "good times." Since personnel departments presumably exist only if they can do personnel work more efficiently than line people can do it, we might say that personnel relations programs are based as much on realism as idealism and are appropriate for both good and bad times, except that for bad times there is an element of degree. Realism is the element which requires management to rely upon experience, research, and facts as bases for decision making. It dictates changes that must be made to weather the storms of depression and recession periods. Realism in the extreme denies that there is a place for social engineering, and, if followed, the course of realism may fail to gain cooperation of employees. Pragmatism follows the spirit of trial-and-error methods. It maintains that the action that must be taken to get the job done should be taken, even though it may be wrong; for action is capable of getting somewhere while theory may still be standing still. Routine management often follows this course. The pragmatist who possesses a touch of the realist may be successful in small-scale operations. In industrial management, both idealism and realism are needed. The innovators of big business, the engineers, designers, craftsmen, the "idea men" may be encouraged to produce by idealism. Accountants, statisticians, systems people, and process and industrial engineers are also essential in big business. These people provide the element of realism, and social cooperation among them may require only a minimum of pragmatism. Financial management, especially during crises, requires realism. Top executives should be adjustable; they must adapt to the situation. Since business and government must work cooperatively under the present-day system, management philosophy is almost forced to be balanced as between the three viewpoints: realism, idealism, and pragmatism.[19]

The old question "human relations management vs. authoritarian management is still being debated. Dr. Douglas McGregor, MIT, in *The Human Side of Enterprise,* maintains that the assumption of orthodox management that people dislike work and avoid it if possible (mass mediocrity) is erroneous. It is, therefore, according to him, not necessary to use the authoritarian method (high degree of direction and control) to get people to work hard in order that company objectives may be achieved. McGregor believes that "work is as natural as play or rest." He maintains that people are capable of directing themselves toward goals to which they are committed in order that their egos may be satisfied, and that people do not inherently lack ambition and avoid responsibility.[20]

A National Industrial Conference Board report prepared on sixty-one companies by Harold Stieglitz of the NICB division of Personnel Administration, concluded that management in the United States is still guided in "refining and revamping its organization" by "classic management principles." Some of these principles are: (1) clearly defined written objectives; (2) simple, flexible organization; (3) clear lines of authority and accountability; (4) each employee should have but one supervisor; (5) top management retains the right to make final decisions on company structure and managerial personnel; (6) perpetual review of organization structure; (7) since organization experts do not invent new organizations, they probably should be called reorganization planners; (8) organization planners should study, organize, and recommend; (9) organization planners should inventory personnel; (10) they should draw up organization charts adaptable to the long-run picture; (11) they should determine changes in the organization for the short-run, step-by-step development.[21]

The NICB report indicates that although corporate organization in the United States is changing, it is not from having adopted any "newfangled" theory advocated by behaviorists. Companies, the report concluded, are tending toward greater decentralization with authority being granted on lower levels; functional organization (staff) is being dropped in favor of divisionalization (on product or other bases) because of diversification and new technological marketing problems; headquarters staff organization is developing in what is called "recentralization"; some companies have a new type of executive responsible for more than one division (product divisions usually); there are more staff people who function with the president as personal assistants.[22] Despite the fact that the NICB current report indicates cold, hard planning without regard for the "human element," if one delved more closely into these companies it is believed that they would practically all have personnel departments and that business psychology and human relations would be at work wherever work was being done. Further, with Dr. McGregor, this writer believes that capacities of people are generally not fully utilized and may even be hampered by traditional control and development. It must be agreed that the setting of exact standards in human relations is practically impossible; but it must be possible to determine an optimum point between, on the one hand, dictation and control of human endeavor and, on the other, encouragement of imagination and creative effort; the factor of the probable error would remain. It might also be asked: Doesn't it also remain in even those cases dealing with non-human elements?

Even if some persons in management are reluctant to admit the value of the "behavioral science," with its advocacy of employee-centered leadership, its attempt to give job satisfaction to workers, and its attempt to create the sort of atmosphere conducive to better mental health on the part of workers, social research data indicate that human relations is all-important.

In the area of ethics, a human relations factor, executives are thinking and acting. Their action usually takes one or more of several forms: (1) resolutions to management; (2) requiring of signed statements from management stipulating that policies pertaining to matters involving ethics are being followed; (3) conferences; (4) detailed questionnaires requiring: the listing of stocks held in supplier or customer firms and other relationships with these firms, listing of activities in lives of the employees and relatives; directorships and jobs in other firms; consultant jobs; gifts and loans. Some of the companies that have used questionnaires are: Scott Paper, du Pont, U. S. Rubber, Pan American World Airways, Socony Mobil Oil, and Packard-Bell Electronics. Some companies have issued codes of ethics and statements of policy to guide their executives. It is believed by some, however, that the problem can be solved only by employing "honorable men" because honorable men already have a code.[23]

The so-called "honored professions" have three things at least in common: a code of ethics, a specialized body of knowledge and training, and licensing. Management is considered to be becoming more and more a field that is a "profession." With the adoption of a code of ethics, management would acquire another of the characteristics that entitle it to the name.

In November, 1961, forty-three management consultants in San Francisco signed a code of ethics called "minimum standards of conduct and competence" that closely follows the "code of ethics and recommended practices" of the Association of Consulting Management Engineers, New York, which has in its membership, because of its strict qualifications for admittance, only a small fraction of the thousands who call themselves "management consultants" in the United States.[24]

Management consultants might in a way also be considered managerial tools. Persons who have wide knowledge of principles of management and of statistical and research methods frequently set themselves up in private practice as consultants available to any who will pay their fees. Booz, Allen & Hamilton is one of the oldest and largest of the consulting firms, having been in operation since 1914. Edwin G. Booz largely dominated the firm from 1914 to the 1940's, and his efforts were largely centered upon human relations and "efficiency engineering." Today the firm has a vast staff of specialists in various areas of management, with experts in marketing, finance, manufacturing, and engineering dominating.

Its staff in personnel management is limited. Its operations blanket the United States and more than a dozen foreign countries. Even though the firm is currently not specializing in personnel management and is turning more toward computer application and educational management, its staff of specialists includes an executive recruiting specialist, a specialist in management appraisal and development, and a director of personnel administration, and it still practices merit rating of its partners and uses motivation in the form of profit sharing.[25]

In addition to the many management consultant firms, there are special research firms, popularly referred to as "think companies," engaged in research in many areas of government and business. Among the private profit-making research firms is Arthur D. Little, Inc., of Cambridge, Massachusetts, which employs over a thousand persons. This firm is but one of several hundred commercial laboratories that specialize in product research and testing. Other research firms include: Rand Corporation and National Bureau of Economic Research, as well as many university research organizations. There are, too, the many marketing and advertising research organizations to be considered in Chapter XXI. All of these research organizations have their impact upon the establishment of standards.[26] In addition to the Psychological Corporation and the American Psychological Association, there are many private organizations and universities engaged in social and human relations research. Among the universities are the Univereity of Michigan Social Research Center, the University of Minnesota Industrial Relations Center, the University of Chicago Industrial Relations and Counseling Centers, the California Institute of Technology Industrial Relations Section.

Companies doing research and development for the Defense Department or the National Aeronautics & Space Administration are themselves required to operate under a standard procedure. This is how Program Evaluation and Review Technique (PERT) came into being. PERT/ Cost has developed system concept and computer technology into a procedure for establishing realistic contract bids, scheduling manpower and other resources efficiently, indicating trouble spots in scheduling and costs, and revising of plans to meet deadlines for projects. General Electric Company, as a prime contractor on Polaris was introduced to PERT when Booz, Allen & Hamilton was asked to devise a system for planning and controlling the 70,000-plus parts of the job of making Polaris fly. Management Systems Corporation also worked on developing PERT. Remington Rand Division of Sperry Rand Corporation at the same time developed a similar planning and control system known as Critical Path Method, CPM. The two techniques were combined to mastermind moving the entire Chemicals Division of Olin Mathieson Chemical Corporation from Baltimore to New York. PERT/Cost follows these steps to find the most efficient method of managing a complicated project:

1. Identifies all jobs making up the project.
2. Relates them to each other in a logical network.
3. Estimates the amount of time each step will take.
4. Estimates the cost of each step.
5. Feeds the mass of data into a computer; the computer gives the budget and target date, with each step arranged in optimum order.
6. Uses the computer periodically to compare results with the original plan, and revises if necessary.[27]

ACCOUNTING — Accounting records are the chief basis of control in all areas of business operation. They have long been used to give the costs of products and they are becoming more successful in giving a more exact breakdown of marketing costs. They can be used, however, not only to apply to the physical and material elements of business, they can be used to determine organization and individual efficiency. In fact, good accounting records must conform to the organization structure. Poorly managed departments are revealed by accounting data and it is often possible to spot exact responsibility. Ratios computed from accounting records show the effectiveness of company, divisional, departmental, and even individual efforts. Accounting records are used, first, to appraise results of each element of an organization and, second, to reformulate standards and plan anew.

STATISTICS AND BUDGETING — Statistics enables a business to compare a current year's operation with previous years. Statistical methods are used in finding: long-term trends for the purpose of forecasting and budgeting; the influence of cyclical fluctuations; the influence of seasonal and other short-term fluctuations caused by unusual conditions such as wars, unusual competition, and upheavals of nature.

Statistics is a chief tool in personnel management. It is used in analyzing research data and in determining work-force requirements. For instance, the steps in finding how many persons will have to be employed in a large industrial organization during a given period are as follows:

1. *Forecast sales* by: using data to determine the long-term trend; or by having each salesman or local sales unit estimate his or its potential for the period, or by using estimated potential for the nation and computing the individual firm's percentage based upon past performance.

2. Use the sales forecast to make a *master production schedule* designed to meet sales needs; this may begin with *departmental schedules* based upon estimates of sales for each type of product produced.

3. Translate the production schedules into *requirements* for manpower — persons needed to turn out the required number of products in each department.

4. Make a table of *present working force.*

5. On the basis of past experience estimate the number of *employees to be separated* from the payroll during the period.

6. Deduct the number of separations from the present working force; deduct the resulting figure from the estimated manpower needs (Item 3) to find how many will have to be employed by departments.

Budgeting personnel requirements largely follows the steps in budgeting for any department: *sales* must be estimated first; *cost and expense* budgets are then made; finally, the *finance* budget is made. Budgeting uses accounting, statistical, and research data.

Statistical data are classified as *internal* and *external.* Internal data come from accounting records and other intracompany studies; external data come from government publications, trade organizations, published records of competing firms, and from research firms. Of chief value in personnel management, are published figures and accounts of: turnover in firms in the same industry as the company concerned; methods of pay, including incentives; absenteeism; benefit programs; job analyses, including descriptions and evaluation; merit rating; and employment practices and procedures, including standardization of tests and correlation between test results and success of employees secured on the basis of tests (validity and reliability of tests).

Statistics are also classified as being *primary* and *secondary.* Primary data is that secured from company records or by: observation, experiment, and survey. Surveys are conducted by using the telephone, personal interview, mailed questionnaire, and panels of persons who cooperate in various ways. Secondary data is secured from external and published records.

Conclusions — Principles of management apply in all areas of endeavor in a business or industrial firm. The tools of management (research, standards, accounting, budgeting, statistics, and personnel management itself) are used in varying degrees in all phases and at all levels. The remaining chapters in this section of your textbook concern themselves with areas of industrial relations and/or personnel management.

Personnel management is a staff function and it may be defined as creative planning, organizing, and controlling the operative activities of obtaining a work force, training and developing it, keeping it happy, satisfied and at the same time productive, so that the objectives of the organization, its owners, managers, and employees may be attained economically and effectively. In today's world, personnel management cannot forget some other groups either: consumers, the public at large, government, suppliers, and customers. Public relations departments have developed in recognition of the fact that there is more to business than obtaining employees and putting them to work producing a good or service.

Scientific management, in the factory or anywhere else in the organization, is simply using the techniques of scientific approach to obtain information on which to base its decisions. It does its planning, organizing, and controlling by using facts instead of by intuition, guesswork, the stated experiences of others, or recalling of its own past experiences. Organizations are much too large to rely on anything but recorded data.

At the national and international levels, two organizations have carried the banner of "scientific management." The International Committee for Scientific Management (CIOS), with headquarters at Geneva, Switzerland, has been a world organization of management associations since 1924. In 1933 the Council for International Progress in Management was organized in the United States. Its membership is made up of management associations in the United States. It (as well as the various other groups mentioned in Chapter IX) exports seminar teams of management experts to foreign countries to train their executives; it also brings foreign executives to the United States for guided study in companies and universities. CIOS meets at places around the world for exchange of ideas; it has worked on standardizing management terminology; it has collaborated with productivity centers set up after World War II; it has worked with the United Nations and with its Economic and Social Council and UNESCO.[28]

The early attempts of "scientific management" leaders to influence world economic planning were reflected by the World Economic Conference held in Geneva in 1927. The term "rationalization" was used at this conference to denote the application of scientific intellectual method, as introduced by F. W. Taylor in individual enterprises, to the co-ordination of the whole world economic activity in solving the problems of production, distribution, and consumption.[29] The term "rationalization" was originally used by psychologists. In the economic field it was first used by the Germans to describe the process of reorganization in German industrial life.[30] The meaning was enlarged upon to include the new attitudes toward the application of intellectual methods and standards of science to economic problems.[31] The commonly accepted definition is the one given by L. Urwick. He states that it may be defined as either an attitude or a process. "As an attitude it records *the belief that a more rational control of world economic life through the application of scientific methods is possible and desirable.* As a process it implies *the application of methods of science to all problems arising in the organization and conduct of production, distribution and consumption.*" [32]

PROJECTS

1. Debate the question "Human Relations Management Is Superior to Authoritarian Management."

2. Write a short paper on the management tool that is of most interest to you.

3. Report on the most interesting chapter in a volume on business ethics or business philosophy.

4. Write a short paper in defense of the contention "Scientific Management Is as Applicable to the Human Element as It Is to the Nonhuman Elements in Industry."

ACKNOWLEDGMENTS AND REFERENCES

1 Adams, Loyce, "An Inquiry Into the Applicability of Scientific Business Management Techniques to College Administration," a thesis, The University of Texas, Austin, August, 1935. Other material in this chapter has also been adapted from this source.
2 Person, H. S., "The Origin and Nature of Scientific Management," *Scientific Management in American Industry*, edited by H. S. Person, Harper & Brothers Publishers, New York, 1929, p. 14.
3 Adams, Loyce, "Business Organization and Management," *Secretary's Business Review*, edited by Nelda R. Lawrence, Prentice-Hall, Inc., Englewood Cliffs, N. J., 1959, p. 87.
4 Maurer, Herrymon, "Boards of Directors," *Fortune*, Vol. XLI, No. 5, May, 1950, p. 107ff.
5 Adams, Loyce, "A Study of Sales Training Programs in Eighty-eight Firms," a dissertation, The University of Texas, Austin, June, 1959, (University Microfilms Inc., 313 N. First St., Ann Arbor, Michigan), p. 23.
6 Hendry, John W., *A Manual of Time and Motion Study*, Third Edition, Sir Isaac Pitman & Sons, Ltd., London, 1950, p. 78.
7 Taylor, F. W., *The Principles of Scientific Management*, Harper & Brothers, New York, 1911, p. 52.
8 *Ibid.*, p. 60.
9 Sampter, Herbert C., *Motion Study*, Pitman Publishing Company, New York, 1941, pp. 4–5.
10 Gilbreth, F. B., *Motion Study*, D. Van Nostrand Co., New York, 1911.
11 Gilbreth, F. B., and L. M., *Fatigue Study*, Macmillan Co., New York, 1919.
12 Gilbreth, L. M., "Monotony in Repetitive Operations," *Iron Age*, Vol. 118, No. 19, November 4, 1926, p. 1344.

13   Gilbreth, F. B., and L. M., *Motion Study for the Handicapped*, George Routledge Sons, London, 1920.
14   Mundel, Marvin E., *Systematic Motion and Time Study*, Prentice-Hall, Inc., New York, 1947, pp. 101–105.
15   Nadler, Gerald, *Motion and Time Study*, McGraw-Hill Book Company, Inc., New York, 1955, pp. 140–141. (Chart of 22 therbligs also here.)
16   *Ibid.*, p. 542.
17   ——, "Management — Nose-count Analysis Spots Company Ills," *Business Week*, July 28, 1962, pp. 104–106.
18   Lodge, Rupert C., *The Philosophy of Business*, University of Chicago Press, 1945.
     Bunting, James Whitney (editor), *Ethics for Modern Business Practice*, Prentice-Hall, New York, 1953.
     Childs, Marquis, and Cater, Douglass, *Ethics in A Business Society*, The New American Library of World Literature, Inc., 501 Madison Avenue, New York 22, 1954.
19   Lodge, *op. cit.*
20   ——, "Management — Storm Over Management Doctrines," *Business Week*, January 6, 1962, pp. 72–74.
21   *Ibid.*
22   *Ibid.*
23   ——, "Management — Keeping a High Shine on Ethics," *Business Week*, March 25, 1961, pp. 81–88.
24   ——, "Coast Management Consultants Pledge Ethical Behavior," *Business Week*, November 18, 1961, p. 100.
25   ——, "Management — Management Experts Thrive on Own Advice," *Business Week*, April 23, 1960, pp. 104–118.
26   ——, "Special National Report — The Fabulous 'Think' Companies," *Newsweek*, July 19, 1959, pp. 21–23.
27   ——, "Management — Shortcut for Project Planning," *Business Week*, July 7, 1962, pp. 104–106.
28   ——, "Management — World's Management Spotlight Now Shifts to U.S.," *Business Week*, March 12, 1960, pp. 72–73.
29   Urwick, L., "Rational Organisation," *Rational Organisation and Industrial Relations*, edited by M. L. Fledderus, International Industrial Relations Institute, The Hague, 1930, p. 37.
30   Urwick, L., *The Meaning of Rationalisation*, Nisbet and Co., Ltd., London, 1929, p. 13.
31   *Ibid.*, p. 19.
32   *Ibid.*, p. 27.

CHAPTER XI

RECRUITING EMPLOYEES

Job Specifications — Manpower is the most valuable resource of any business organization. Materials, money, and machines are equally available to all businesses, but manpower and management differ for each organization. A great deal depends upon getting the right people to do the work that must be done. Proper recruitment of workers can best take place if (1) all jobs within an organization have been analyzed and (2) job and man specifications have been written.

Job Analysis involves the study of duties, operations, and relationships of a job, including lines of transfer and promotion. Job analysis is done by analysts who get information by observation, interview, questionnaire, and actually doing the job being analyzed. The analysis and the resulting *job description* enable setting up of a *job specification*. Sometimes the term job specification is used to refer to the description of duties that are required on the given job. In such a case, the term *man specification* is used to refer to the characteristics that should be possessed by a person qualified to do the job. Generally, however, the term job specification has come to mean both the job and the man requirements, including the job description as well as qualifications needed by the man to do the job, such as physical skills and abilities, mental abilities, knowledge, experience, responsibilities, working conditions under which he would have to be able to work, and emotional and social characteristics he would have to have in order to perform the job.

Frequently the description of mental abilities takes the form of specifying education and experience needed to do the job. In addition to educational requirements (or sometimes instead of), it may stipulate the types and degrees of mental characteristics that would be needed, as: intelligence; ability to plan and organize, concentrate, exercise judgment; verbal ability; arithmetic ability; engineering or scientific ability; memory for names, faces, places, abstract ideas, directions, spatial relations; ability to estimate quantities, qualities, and to handle variable factors. Physical specifications for a job would include ability to utilize hands, eyes, ears, legs, feet, and body to the degree these are needed and in the manner needed.

It should be mentioned here that job descriptions are necessary not only for the purpose of determining job and man specifications to be used in selecting the best qualified job applicants, they are needed also for the following purposes: distributing work loads equitably, making transfers and promotions, making job evaluations, developing safety programs, collective bargaining between management and labor, initiating changes in work procedures, and in preparing and maintaining training programs. Most of these areas are considered in later chapters. Job descriptions also incorporate time and motion studies where these are made.

Forecasts showing how many persons will be needed in given jobs by a given department during a given period (Chapter X) enable an employment department to find applicants who have the qualifications that match the job and man specifications for each of these jobs. In large organizations, the work of determining the number of persons to be employed and characteristics they should possess is the duty of a staff department (personnel), although line departments are responsible for keeping the staff people constantly supplied with information needed as to the kind of applicants needed. In some firms hiring requisitions are sent to the employment office by line supervisors. These requests to employ persons for specific vacancies are studied by employment interviewers who check the requests against job specifications in order to find the exact requirements to look for in an applicant. The job specifications used may be written by specialists who work within line divisions but are attached to the personnel department, or they may be written by line supervisors with the aid of one or more staff specialists. In some cases, outside specialists or staff specialists within the individual company have the responsibility of writing the job specifications. In most instances, applicants selected by employment personnel to match specifications are sent to line supervisors for final approval.

Time and motion studies (Chapter X) are an aid in writing job specifications; they are not, however, essential although some type of analysis must be made to write descriptions of jobs. Some types of jobs do not lend themselves as readily to time and motion study as do most factory and some routine office jobs. It may be said that approximately ten per cent of the larger firms that employ salesmen do have some type of time and motion study of their salesmen.[1] This is in spite of the fact that territories differ, distances covered are not the same, and every selling job must be viewed on somewhat of an individual basis. These studies form the basis for setting up standards and writing specifications for selling jobs.

Job Description[2]
for a SALESMAN of

FOOTNOTE: The duties and responsibilities of a salesman are subject to varying local conditions and may differ somewhat from this job description.

FUNCTION:

The salesman is responsible for selling the complete line of A. B. Dick duplicating equipment, supplies, and impression paper to present and potential users of office duplicating in his assigned territory.

DUTIES:

1. Make sales calls on present customers within his territory at frequent intervals.

   a. Prepares for calls by gathering information and sales tools necessary to accomplish specific objective.

   b. Presents new duplicating techniques or products to customers by means of presentation manual, product portfolios, customer samples, etc. to create interest.

   c. Surveys the customer's present methods and gathers all facts about the duplicating problem. Analyzes all facts carefully.

   d. Proposes specific duplicating methods and products outlining benefits to be gained. Prepares and submits complete written proposals.

   e. Demonstrates proposed duplicating methods and products to prove valuable benefits. Gives complete sales demonstration of the products involved.

   f. Closes the sale by obtaining customer's order for the "complete package" of equipment and supplies proposed.

   g. Instructs personnel in the proper use of duplicating equipment and supplies to maintain a high standard of copy quality.

   h. Finds new duplicating applications and sells them to his customers thereby increasing volume of supplies sold.

Job Description

(CONTINUED)

2. Obtains new customers within his territory.

  a. Converts users of competitive duplicating equipment and supplies to the use of A. B. Dick products by demonstrating the advantages of his products.

  b. Locates qualified prospects by making planned canvass calls on non-users of duplicating.

  c. Sells the need and use of copies to these prospects and helps them select the right duplicating process.

  d. Installs recommended A. B. Dick equipment and supplies. Trains all appropriate personnel including typists, operators and supervision.

  e. Follows up all sales to new customers to check copy quality and continued satisfaction with all A. B. Dick products.

3. Develops and maintains the confidence and good will of his customers.

  a. Merchandises his services (training operators, typists, and copy originators) by keeping his customers aware of the help he is giving them.

  b. Informs his customers of new techniques and products which he believes will improve their duplicating operation or office procedures.

  c. Makes an occasional "rush hour" delivery of supplies to customers who need them in a hurry.

  d. Maintains a courteous and friendly attitude in all customer relations.

  e. Assumes responsibility for the customers' duplicating problems and maintains confidence in A. B. Dick products by training his customers in their use.

4. Reports to the distributor offices at regular intervals.

  a. Submits orders for sales made while calling on his customers.

  b. Supplies credit information when available and gets approval of orders from management when necessary.

  c. May contact customers by telephone for appointments or concerning "trouble calls," supply orders, or requests for quotations and information.

  d. Submits the daily, weekly, or monthly reports of his sales activities that are required by management.

  e. Confers with management regarding progress of sales to specific customers and any other current sales problem.

  f. Plans his daily sales calls and assembles all necessary sales tools including product literature, samples, demonstration supplies, etc.

Job Description

(CONTINUED)

g. Maintains up-to-date customer record cards and an adequate prospect list.

h. Submits requests for national and local direct mail advertising to "soften up" his prospects.

i. Keeps management informed of the performance and prices of competitive duplicating products in his territory.

j. Gives sales demonstrations of equipment on the distributor demonstration floor to individuals and groups.

k. Attends all scheduled sales meetings.

RESPONSIBILITIES:

1. Must secure an adequate sales volume in relation to his territory potential by developing his present customers and obtaining new ones.

2. Must know his territory, its potential and his principal customers, and must use this knowledge to develop additional business.

3. Must know the complete A. B. Dick product line: what the products are used for and how to use them. Should practice to develop his skill in using all of these products.

4. Must know the basic principles of selling and further his knowledge through a continuing program of sales training. He must develop his selling techniques to a professional level, and learn business functions and how to achieve smooth procedural control through modern duplicating.

5. Must develop and maintain the confidence and good will of his customers toward himself, his distributor, and A. B. Dick Company.

6. Must know the application, sales features, and prices of A. B. Dick products and how to demonstrate them effectively in terms of customer benefits.

7. Must know the distributor's office procedure and cooperate with office personnel by adhering to the established paper work routine.

8. Must know the distributor's sales policies, practices, and terms, and interpret them to to his customers.

9. Must call on each customer at frequent, planned intervals as his potential warrants, according to a Call Assignment Plan.

DUTIES AND RESPONSIBILITIES OF ROUTE SUPERVISORS
SWIFT & COMPANY

I. IMPROVE MORALE OF SALESMEN
    A. Sell himself — convince salesmen that his job is to help them become *better* salesmen.
    B. Sell the cooperativeness of other people in Swift & Company to both salesmen and customers.
    C. Sell the character of Swift & Company.

II. ESTABLISH PRACTICAL TRADE COVERAGE AND DISTRIBUTION OF SWIFT & COMPANY PRODUCTS
    A. Determine total potential of each territory by individual outlets.
    B. Determine what share of this potential we should set as an objective.
    C. Determine through whom we should do this business.
        1. Break-down by sizes and types of accounts.
    D. Establish efficient route schedule.
        1. Call frequency by individual customers.
        2. Proper allocation of time with individual customers.
        3. Coordinate delivery service with solicitation.
    E. See that we obtain volume and distribution of our products with these customers determined under "C" in quantities in line with our potential.
    F. Know and keep in contact with various trade organizations — cooperative buying groups, retail dealer associations, bakery associations, etc., for the purpose of maximum promotion of our products through their individual members.

III. DEVELOP SALES PROFICIENCY BY EDUCATION AND TRAINING — ON THE JOB, GROUP MEETINGS, CORRESPONDENCE.
    A. Improve product knowledge.
    B. Practical application of the Solicitation Pattern — development of each of the five steps of the "Science Comes to Selling."
    C. Proper use of all selling tools.
        1. Product Reminder Book.
        2. Portable Showcase.
        3. Store Tested Sales Plan Bulletins.
        4. Retail Advertising Reference Book.
        5. Sales-Maker.
    D. Techniques for developing loyal dealers.
    E. Handle customer complaints.

IV. TRAIN MEN IN PROPER HANDLING OF DETAIL WORK
   A. Sell importance of this phase to overall performance.
   B. Most efficient methods of writing orders, daily sales reports, collections, claims, resales, etc.
   C. Importance of and how to analyze and record weekly volume and result report (2999 or log.)
      1. Impress salesmen with importance of being result conscious — get the high dollar.

V. PERSONNEL RESPONSIBILITIES
   A. Recruitment of salesmen.
   B. Assisting manager in evaluating and up-grading sales personnel.

VI. MANAGEMENT RESPONSIBILITIES. (May not share with salesmen.)
   A. Confidential report on salesmen and territory.
   B. Reduction or addition of sales routes.
   C. Route expenses.
   D. Vacation schedule.
   E. Routing of specialty salesmen.
   F. Determine and correct fundamental causes of losing routes, and unsatisfactory volume performance.
   G. Work hand-in-hand with sales manager to whom he is directly responsible.[3]

One of the most complete time and motion studies of salesmen was made of wholesale drug salesmen and reported on by James H. Davis, Ohio State University. Data on time spent by the ten most efficient and ten least efficient country salesmen were compared. Among the interesting facts unearthed by the study was that the efficient group spent 73.6 per cent of its call time in activities considered essential. The least efficient group spent only 50.7 per cent of its time in essential activities.

Recruiting of Employees in General — There are two sources of labor supply — *external* and *internal*. The internal source provides employees through transfer, promotion, or possibly demotion. The internal source may also include not only persons on the payroll of a parent company but those on the payroll of its subsidiaries. It may include persons who have been on leave of absence, laid off, or who left the firm voluntarily but offer themselves for rehiring. Some firms classify persons employed on the recommendation of employees as coming from internal sources. External sources include: advertising for labor and selecting from best qualified applicants; selecting from labor that comes to the employment office to seek employment; utilizing union sources of labor in skilled trades such as carpentry and bricklaying; using employment agencies (public, private, school, and college). Eventually, of course, all replacements must come from external sources. Because of the dangers of "inbreeding" (making all promotions from within the organization), some firms have a policy of obtaining a certain number of persons from outside the organization, especially for managerial positions. It is considered safe from the viewpoint of bringing in "new blood" to make approximately twenty per cent of promotions from outside.

The United States Employment Service began operating in 1918, but in its early years it was used chiefly for placing farm, migrant, and unskilled labor. In 1942, the various state employment agencies were merged with the USES. During World War II the rules under which the USES operated were established by the War Manpower Commission; since 1949 the USES has operated under the Department of Labor. State employment offices may work cooperatively with other state employment offices throughout the United States. All of these are affiliated with the USES. These offices not only bring applicants and employers together, they use batteries of tests (Chapter XIII) to determine whether or not applicants have the qualifications needed to do the work for which agencies recommend them.

Private employment agencies often specialize in placing persons in given areas, as: hotel maids and housekeepers, secretarial workers, accountants, statisticians, salesmen, engineers, managers. A given agency may handle combinations of these areas. Private agencies charge workers they place a fixed percentage of wages earned by the workers during a given period of time. In some cases agencies have been guilty of collusion with employers by placing workers, collecting their percentage, and then splitting percentage collected with the employers who in turn dismissed the workers. The workers then returned to the agency to obtain other jobs and the cycle began again. Generally, state and local governmental action, plus action on the part of reputable agencies has reduced or eliminated unscrupulous action on the part of the private employment agencies.

Schools, colleges, and universities operate employment agencies in the sense that they bring employment interviewers to their campuses in contact with students who have registered with them. Only a nominal fee is charged for the service. Managerial, technical, and skilled employees are often obtained through interviewing members of the senior class during their last semester in school. College and university service departments (there may be many of these involved on any given campus) schedule student interviews for the companies that send recruiters to the campuses.

Some firms keep records on persons according to the source of supply. Through studying ratings of employees, turnover, records of grievances, and disciplinary action taken, it is possible to evaluate the employees in terms of the sources through which they were obtained.

Recruiting of Salesmen — Sources of obtaining persons to be trained for selling vary widely, depending upon the product to be sold and the technical knowledge needed to sell it. From the moment a sales recruit is interviewed, if there is any possibility he may be employed, the struggle for his mind begins. One sales manager said that "the quest for sales recruits today is so competitive that it is a problem in itself, the solution of which only leads to a bigger problem — how to win the recruit's mind and loyalty." It is necessary to convince him of the value to him of any ideal to which he will be loyal.[4]

The Arma Division of the American Bosch Arma Corporation gives credit to its "personalized placement" procedures for keeping its technical recruits happy and its turnover low. College recruits are invited to the company for tours under the guidance of employees who are also recent graduates. Arma pays salaries commensurate with the background and experience of the new employee, converting education, military service, and experience into dollar equivalents on the basis of competitive salaries as revealed by the industry-wide survey.[5]

General Electric and Westinghouse go to college campuses for recruits. Men employed to sell for these firms must have engineering and scientific backgrounds. Each year teams of recruiters from GE alone select about one out of three of the college seniors who have technical majors at the larger educational institutions. Items considered in selecting applicants include: interests, grades (*B* or better average), plans, membership in organizations or fraternities, and work experience. Interviewees, on the other hand, are usually interested in housing and living expenses, pension plans, moving allowances for employees changing from plant to plant, and in rent costs. Some forget to inquire about the opportunities for promotion.[6]

Not all companies, however, go to colleges for sales and other recruits. One company president said that his firm would let the others employ the college man; his firm two years later would make an offer the young man could not resist.[7]

The Lily-Tulip Cup Corporation, whose products never exist by themselves but always as the solution to problems, or as better ways to do the same old thing ("You'll never catch a cold from a Lily Cup"),[8] tells in its booklet entitled, *So You Need To Find a Salesman?* how it recruits. Lily uses newspaper advertising and employment agencies. It also seeks applicants through such groups as: Sales Executives Club, Rotary Club,

Kiwanis Club, Lions Club, Masons, Knights of Columbus, Chamber of Commerce, and trade associations. Other sources of applicants are: friends, social and business, churches, persons attending courses in public speaking and salesmanship, and college placement bureaus. The Lily booklet recommends that all sources be used and records be kept to see which sources are best.[9]

The Metropolitan Life Insurance Company district managers in districts located throughout the United States and Canada recommend applicants for sales jobs. Regional Field Management Vice Presidents approve or disapprove the recommendations.[10] The Goodyear Tire and Rubber Company advises those who sell its tires to owners of trucks and fleets of trucks to look for a man already on the payroll, one who gets along with people and likes to work, but he doesn't have to be the so-called "sales type"; Goodyear believes that "it is better to take a chance with a man you know will stay with you rather than an unproved stranger."[11] Roos and Daily have also suggested that while satisfactory age, background, and experience are important factors in selecting a salesman, these cannot substitute for personal acquaintance.[12]

From a study made by the writer of eighty-eight of the outstanding firms of the United States, it was found that the most popular source of sales trainees is recruiting from other companies, with school and college recruiting being the second source. Fifty-three companies, or 60.23 per cent, use other companies as a main source of sales trainees, with twenty-eight of these using other companies as the only main source. Forty-eight companies, or 54.55 per cent use schools as a main source of sales trainees, and twenty of these companies use schools as the only main source. Twenty-three companies, or 26.14 per cent, use their own companies as one of the main sources of sales trainees, with six of these using their own companies as the only main source.[13]

Selection standards for salesmen may be based on: information revealed on the *application blank* or *personal history (weighted* or not weighted), or in the *application letter; education* and/or *special training,* and *grades; psychological* and *aptitude,* or *other tests; employment interview or interviews; references; checking of selectees' qualifications against job specifications;* and a *physical examination.*

A National Industrial Conference Board study in 1954 showed that many companies are using weighted application blanks, printed interview forms, patterned interviews, and tests tailored to the needs of the individual companies.[14]

A *weighted application blank* is one that assigns point values to the answers obtained on the blank. It is believed that more companies than this study revealed are experimenting with weighted application blanks, or weighted personal histories, in employing at all levels and for most types of workers, including salesmen. One researcher found by studying eighty-two managers that a "scoring system for personal history items" is the best single predictor of managerial success.[15]

When the weighted blanks are used, correlation procedures determine the most important factors among such items as: physical characteristics, background, experience, training for sales jobs, height, weight, age, marital status, and work experience. One study showed that salesmen who had no dependents were thirty-five per cent below the average of new salesmen in total sales. Men who were married but without children sold four per cent above the average, while married men with children sold eighteen per cent above average. Companies also attempt to determine what characteristics may be associated with failure in selling, and for different companies and different products degrees of relationship may vary, making it necessary for companies to take some measure of responsibility in building their own weighted blanks.[16]

The weighted application blank was found to be used by nineteen firms out of eighty-eight studied by the writer, or 21.59 per cent of the firms.

The Metropolitan Life Insurance Company uses a four-page application blank covering, in addition to name, social security account number, address, and other personal items, the following main headings: (1) General Background, (2) Education, (3) Marital Status and Dependents, (4) Economic Situation, (5) Social Activities, (6) Health, (7) Business Experience, (8) References.[17]

The Lily Tulip Cup Corporation emphasizes the importance of picking the right man for the job. Qualities it desires in a man are: hard worker, steady worker, good producer, happy in job, will stay with the company, will not be a problem. It uses what men have done in the past as an indication of what they will do in the future. There are ten steps in Lily's selection process: (1) a preliminary interview to spot those who might qualify; (2) a projective interview to discover attitudes; (3) an application blank for those still in the running; (4) check on references; (5) eligible candidates receive a patterned interview to explore their background, training, experience, and attitudes; (6) tests are given to discover sales aptitude, personality, ability, social intelligence, and personal adjustment; (7) a check is made of the applicant's home situation and wife; (8) a physical examination is given; (9) employment interviews; (10) outside agency makes an investigation and reports directly to the general sales manager.[18]

The Victor Adding Machine Company places a great deal of emphasis on getting a man who has the ability to work, study, keep up his enthusiasm, and "play on the team."[19]

Dozens of degrees of skill and background are required on the part of the salesman, varying according to the type of selling being done. Within certain limitations, however, it is possible to generalize on standards and procedures for selection of salesmen. Of eighty-eight firms studied by this writer, sixty-eight required high-school graduation for sales-training selectees. Thirty-four of the companies, or 38.64 per cent, require college training in addition to high school. Another eighteen companies stated that college was desired but not required. (See Table XI-1, page 196, for degree preferences.) Twelve firms, or 13.64 per cent, require special sales training prior to employment.

Forty-nine of the companies, or 55.68 per cent, said that they consider grades important; twenty-three firms, or 26.14 per cent, said they do not consider grades important. Seventeen firms stated that they take selectees who have below-average grades; forty-two companies, or 47.73 per cent, will not take applicants with below-average grades. The forty-two companies represent 71.19 per cent of the fifty-nine firms that answered the question; the twenty-nine companies that did not answer the question implied by their omission that they do not take people with below-average grades. Forty companies, 45.45 per cent of the eighty-eight, prefer top-ranking grades, but sixty-four companies, or 72.73 per cent, said that they will take applicants with average grades.[20]

Table XI-1 shows that sixty-five of the eighty-eight firms, or 73.86 per cent, use one or more tests in selecting sales trainees. Thirty-seven of the firms using tests (over half) had already *validated* the tests, that is they had accumulated enough data to have proof that the tests they use predict success in selling. *A test is valid if there is a high degree of correlation between test scores and success on the jobs for which the test was used as a selection device;* putting it another way, *a test is valid if it tests for what it purports to test.* Some of the companies were in the process of validating their tests at the time of the study. Thirty-four companies reported that they have measures of reliability of the tests they use. *Tests are considered reliable if they give approximately the same test scores when given over to the same persons within a reasonably limited time.* If a long enough period of time has elapsed, the person being tested may have acquired additional skills and knowledges that would cause a changed score on the test. Frequently, reliability of a test is checked by breaking the test into two parts. It is considered reliable if the persons tested make approximately the same scores on each part of the test. This eliminates taking up two test periods to measure the reliability of a test.

Practically all companies use the interview in employing salesmen. In addition to the individual interview, twelve companies out of eighty-

MEDICAL REPORT FORM 21

Is he physically capable of handling the job? This is a required item. In fairness to the man and to the Company, it is required that a physical examination be completed before the man is actually hired.

Arrangements for this examination should be made by you with the local physician (an M.D.) in whom you have confidence.

The attached Medical Report Form is the one which should be used in all cases.

When arranging for a physical, advise the doctor by phone or in writing that the applicant is seeking a sales position and outline for him the physical requirements of the job. Point out that there will be constant travel by car; heavy sample cases (25-35 lbs.) may have to be carried; that there will be long hours — some night work.

Request the doctor to write on the back of the form that in his professional opinion, the applicant is (or is not) physically capable of handling such a sales assignment.

SALES APPLICANT MEDICAL REPORT FORM[21]

(To be filled in by physician and mailed to:)

Name_____ Age_____

Address_____ Place of Birth_____

Married (   )   Single (   )   Widower (   )   Divorced (   )

Past History:

    Illnesses:

    Surgery: .

    Accidents:

Family History:

	Living or Deceased	Age	Cause of Death
Mother			
Father			
Brothers			
Sisters			
Siblings			

Ht._____ Wt._____ P._____

    At Rest

    After Exercise

    1 min. after Exercise

Measurements:

    Chest at rest

    Chest expanded

    Waist

MEDICAL REPORT

Head:

    Eyes

        Vision - Snelling   R.   L.

                       R.   L.

    Nose

    Throat

    Dental

Chest:

    Heart

        Enlargement

        Murmurs

        Arrhythmia

    Lungs

Abdomen:

    Muscalature

    Hernia

    Masses

    Fluid

Genito Urinary_____

Rectal_____

Extremities_____

Neuro-Muscular_____

Deformities_____

Wasserman_____

FINDINGS

1. Applicant is free of any serious limiting handicaps which would prevent carrying out of normal duties and responsibilities of the job described under "Job Description — Salesman" Lily-Tulip Cup Corporation.

_____

2. Applicant possesses following physical disabilities which are not considered serious:_____

_____

_____

3. Applicant possesses physical disabilities which would seriously impair his ability to carry out normal job duties and responsibilities:_____

_____

COMMENTS_____

_____

_____

_____

PHYSICIAN'S SIGNATURE_____

STREET ADDRESS_____

CITY & STATE_____

LILY-TULIP CUP CORPORATION [21]

APPLICATION FOR SALES POSITION

Date _____

TO THE APPLICANT:

Every person entering our employ has the opportunity to become a successful and permanent member of our organization. Our experience has shown that certain basic qualifications are essential for success in sales work. This detailed application form is intended to assist you in presenting those facts about yourself which will enable us to evaluate your possibilities as a prospective Lily-Tulip salesman. Please consider each question carefully and give us all the information requested. It will, of course, be kept completely confidential.

PERSONAL

Name _____ Age _____

Present Address _____ Telephone _____

How long have you lived at your present address? _____ Years _____ Months

Other addresses last three years _____

Date of Birth _____ Social Security No. _____ U. S. A. Citizen? _____

Are you Single,   Married,   Divorced,   Widowed,   Separated,   Remarried?   (Circle correct designation)

If married, how long? _____ Wife's First Name _____ How Many Children _____ Ages _____

Whom do you partially or entirely support in addition to your immediate family? _____

PHYSICAL

Height------ Weight--------- Date of last physical exam.----------------------------- Purpose------------------

How many days have you lost through illness during the last three years?------------------------------------

What was the cause?--- Present state of your health.-----------------

Are you willing to take the required physical examination by a designated physician at our expense?------------

Do you have any physical disabilities?---

GENERAL

Do you own a car?---------------- Year------- Make---------------------------- Model-----

Do you have full use of it for work?---

If you do not own a car are you in a position to finance the purchase of one?--------------------------------

Have you a current driver's license?---------- No------- Yes------- What state?--------------------

Has your driver's license ever been revoked?--------- No------ Yes----- If "yes," explain---------

Any auto accidents last 10 years?--------- No------- Yes-------- If yes, give details------------

Who referred you to this company (check) employment agency----------------- Lily-Tulip Employee----------

College placement bureau-------------- Newspaper advertisement------------- Lily-Tulip Wholesaler----------

Came of own accord------------ Other (comment)--------------

Do you have any friends or relatives who work for Lily-Tulip? (Name)----------------------------------

FORM #5755

YOUR EDUC

SCHOOL	NAME AND LOCATION OF SCHOOL	COURSE	YEARS
			FROM
HIGH SCHOOL			
COLLEGE			
GRADUATE SCHOOL			
BUSINESS COLLEGE OR NIGHT SCHOOL			
OTHER COURSES OR SPECIAL TRAINING			

HAVE YOU HELD ANY JOBS DURING YOUR SUMMER VACATIONS?_____WHAT KIND?_____

YOUR BUSINESS

Beginning with most recent position, list company names and addresses of all previous employment, including self employment. *Omit sales positions.*	KIND OF BUSINESS	POSITION	

YOUR SALES E

Beginning with most recent position, list company names and addresses of all previous employment. For *sales positions only.*	KIND OF BUSINESS LIST SPECIFIC PRODUCTS SOLD	TERRITORY WORKED	WHOLESALE,

NAL ASSETS

.TTENDED TO	GRADUATE?	TYPE OF DEGREE RECEIVED	SCHOLASTIC STANDING (In what quarter of the class did you stand?)	EXTRA CURRICULAR ACTIVITIES

-- . HOW MUCH DID YOU EARN?--

'ERIENCE ASSETS

*Please place a check mark to the left of the company name in those cases where you were self employed or employed in a family business.

	EMPLOYMENT DATES		MONTHLY EARNINGS		IMMEDIATE SUPERVISOR	WHY DID YOU LEAVE?
	FROM	TO	START	END		
					NAME AND TITLE	
					NAME AND TITLE	
					NAME AND TITLE	
					NAME AND TITLE	
					NAME AND TITLE	

RIENCE ASSETS

TRADE INDUSTRIAL, ETC.	EMPLOYMENT DATES		MONTHLY EARNINGS				IMMEDIATE SUPERVISOR	WHY DID YOU LEAVE?
	FROM	TO	START		END			
			SAL.	COMM.	SAL.	COMM.		
							NAME AND TITLE	
							NAME AND TITLE	
							NAME AND TITLE	
							NAME AND TITLE	

YOUR PERSONAL BALANCE SHEET

What is the approximate monthly rate of all your living expenses? ------------

Do you own your own home? ------------Monthly mortgage payments including taxes and insurance------------

If you rent, what monthly rent do you pay? ------------Do you own your own furniture?------------

If your wife works, what is her occupation?------------Full time------------Part time------------Mo. earnings------------

Do you (or your wife) have any source of income other than what you would receive from us?------------Yes------------No------------

If so, amount of such income, yearly------------

Do you board?------------live with parents?------------live with others?------------

Relationship------------Monthly cost------------

Do you carry life insurance?------------If so, how much?------------

Are you in debt currently?------------Details------------

Do you owe money on your car?------------If so, how much?------------

MILITARY SERVICE

Have you served in the Armed Forces?------------If so, branch of service------------

Duties------------

Rank and date of induction------------Rank and date of discharge------------

Type of discharge------------Present military status------------

SUPPLEMENTARY INFORMATION

Have you set a goal for yourself (kind of job at which you want to be working) in the next five years?_____

What recognition have you received as a result of participating in scholastic, business or military activities?_____

Sports and hobbies in which you participate_____

Clubs or societies to which you be ong (other than labor organizations or organizations whose names would reveal the race, creed, color, or national origin of their members)_____

Any objections to traveling?_____ To moving to another city?_____ Yes_____ No_____

Are you willing to take a sales aptitude test?_____ Yes_____

Territory preferences_____ If accepted, when can you start?_____ No_____

Do you have any objections to our checking your present employer? Yes_____

READ CAREFULLY BEFORE SIGNING

The undersigned applicant certifies that the foregoing statements are true and correct to the best of applicant's knowledge and belief and authorizes Lily-Tulip Cup Corporation to investigate any of the information given; understands that any misrepresentation of fact or failure to disclose any material fact may be sufficient cause for termination; acknowledges that employment by Lily-Tulip Cup Cor-

poration is not for any specific period of time regardless of the manner in which compensation may be stated or payable and is subject to termination by the company at any time without obligation to pay compensation except for services actually rendered prior to termination.

_____
SIGNATURE OF APPLICANT

APPLICATION FOR ENROLLMENT [22]

For

A. B. DICK BASIC SALES TRAINING ON-THE-JOB

TO:

A. B. DICK COMPANY
Sales Training and
Applications Development Dept.
5700 West Touhy Avenue
Chicago 31, Illinois

FROM:

(Distributor and City, State)

Please enroll _____ for the training indicated below.
(NAME OF MAN TO BE TRAINED)

Length of service with distributor _____. Education: High School_____yrs. College_____yrs.

Previous experience in duplicating, if any?

J — **ON THE JOB**

NEW ON-THE-JOB COURSES   (OPTIONS)
(J 1, 2, 3, and 4)   Check ➧

① The complete, 6 months **ON-THE-JOB BASIC SALES TRAINING COURSE**
   Includes all processes — for new man.   ☐

② This man has completed part of previous **ON-THE-JOB COURSES.**
   CONVERT HIM TO THE CURRENT 6 MONTHS COURSE.   ☐

③ This man has completed all the previous **ON-THE-JOB COURSES** and has received
   his Mimeograph Specialist Pin.
   Enroll him in refresher course to qualify for **DUPLICATING SPECIALIST**   ☐

④ This man will be a **MARKET SPECIALIST.**
   Enroll him in the **ON-THE-JOB COURSE** for: _____
   WRITE IN THE PROCESS

CHECK OR WRITE IN ONE

B — **BASIC TRAINING MANUAL**

THE BASIC TRAINING MANUAL (L-5693) is needed for **ALL ON-THE-JOB** Sales
Training Courses. **INDICATE YOUR REQUIREMENT BY CHECKING ONE** ➧

① Send **BASIC TRAINING MANUAL** (L-5693) with course.
   (THE MANUAL WILL BE MEMO BILLED)   ☐

② We already have **MANUAL** and will provide it for Trainee.   ☐

CHECK ONE

I understand we will be billed for the up-to-date demonstration sets provided with the Spirit
and Azograph Assignments.

I agree to supervise this man through the Training as
outlined in the Sales Manager's Guide.

Signed: _____
DISTRIBUTOR OR SALES MANAGER

ADVANCED COURSE (NILES)

A salesman who completes the course options J 1, J 2, or J 3 above is then qualified for the
TWO WEEKS' ADVANCED SELLING & DUPLICATING TECHNIQUES COURSE at Niles.
If you wish to reserve a place in this course for this man now — **CHECK HERE** ➧   ☐

READ & CHECK

APPLICATION OR ENROLLMENT

22 For

A. B. DICK SALES TRAINING AT NILES, ILLINOIS

TO:

A. B. DICK COMPANY
Sales Training and
Applications Development Dept.
5700 West Touhy Avenue
Chicago 31, Illinois

FROM:

(Distributor and City, State)

Please enroll _____ for the training indicated below.
(NAME OF MAN TO BE TRAINED)

Length of service with distributor _____. Education: High School____yrs. College____yrs.

Previous experience in duplicating if any?

N | **AT NILES - SALES TRAINING COURSES**
Schedules for specific courses will be published. **Check** ◥

NILES TRAINING

① ADVANCED SELLING and DUPLICATING TECHNIQUES — 2 weeks
   Requirement: Complete ON-THE-JOB COURSE, options J1, J2 or J3.
   DATE PREFERRED

② APPLICATIONS and SYSTEMS-ON-THE-JOB and 2 — one week semesters at Niles.
   Write for prospectus. Two qualification tests are given.
   DATE PREFERRED

③ BASIC PRODUCT and SALES TRAINING (No offset) — 3 weeks
   (In lieu of ON-THE-JOB Assignments I, II, III B and Forms Design).
   Requirements — See "B" below.
   DATE PREFERRED

④ BASIC OFFSET, PRODUCT and SALES TRAINING — 3 weeks
   (In lieu of ON-THE-JOB Assignment III and Forms Design)
   Requirements — See "B" below.
   DATE PREFERRED

⑤ OTHER — (as scheduled and announced)
   Specify _____

CHECK APPROPRIATE BOX and INDICATE PREFERRED DATE

B | **THE BASIC TRAINING MANUAL** (L-5693) is needed to complete the Special Assignment
as a pre-requisite for admission to the Basic Courses N 3 and N 4 above.
INDICATE YOUR REQUIREMENTS BY CHECKING ONE ◤

BASIC TRAINING MANUAL

① Send **BASIC TRAINING MANUAL** (L-5693) with pre-requisites for
   Basic Course (N 3 or N 4)
   (THE MANUAL WILL BE MEMO BILLED)

② We already have **MANUAL** and will provide it for Trainee.

CHECK ONE for course N3 or N4

I have read and I understand the information on
the back side of this form.

Signed: _____
DISTRIBUTOR OR SALES MANAGER

REMARKS:

eight studied use a *panel* type of interview. In a panel interview, two or more persons interview the applicant at the same time. A good many of the firms use *multiple* interviewing of sales applicants. The applicant may be selected by a recruiter from the personnel office. He may then be interviewed by a sales supervisor in a district or branch office. In some cases, even a home-office sales executive interviews before the candidate is finally hired.

Most firms prefer married men, and in most cases married men with families for selling jobs. A few do prefer single men but generally for selected assignments only. Most firms prefer men twenty-four to thirty years of age at the time of employment.

Firms generally check on references. In many instances persons employed for selling are bonded and are minutely investigated by both the bonding company and the employing company. Most companies match selectees' qualifications to job specifications.

One consulting company has requested clients not to test applicants for selling jobs if one or more of the following items is present: (1) instability of residence; (2) failure in business within two years; (3) divorce or separation within two years; (4) excessive personal indebtedness; (5) too high a previous standard of living; (6) unexplained gaps in the employment record. There is evidence to indicate that there may be value in using such "knock-out" factors if the labor market will permit this at a given time. If two or more of the factors are present it is a better indication of possible failure in selling than if only one is present.[23]

Choosing a Vocation — Vocational guidance and counseling has been defined as being the giving of aid and help to someone trying to choose a vocation. *Vocational selection* is the process used by a person to select his own vocation or by business in selecting from a field of candidates the one who seems to be best qualified for a given job. As seen from the discussion in this chapter, the process of selecting applicants may be quite involved. In the course of testing, interviewing, and checking on applicants some employment interviewers do give vocational guidance. They may tell the applicant that he is not qualified for the job for which he applied but that he apparently would do well in some other occupation.

If an applicant would study his qualifications, study the company to which he is going to apply for a given job, and study the requirements of the job, he would be much better prepared for making the application. He would also know whether or not he is qualified for the job before he applies. One source of information about occupations is the *Dictionary of Occupational Titles* (U. S. Government Printing Office). Additional library research could be done. An interview with some person doing the kind of work he wants to do, however, would be a good source for an applicant to use in obtaining information about a particular kind of work before making application for it.

A person studying his own qualifications for employment should probably seek the aid of trained persons who can give aptitude tests and help him evaluate himself in other ways. Generally the advice of friends and relatives is not considered to be adequate. Nor do people always rate themselves accurately in determining whether or not they have the traits and characteristics that would enable them to attain success in a particular vocation. Some writers have suggested that one of the best methods an intelligent person could use for selecting a vocation would be to find a problem that needs a solution and devote a lifetime to solving it. That, of course, is what the persons engaged in National Aeronautics and Space Administration activities are doing today. That is what Thomas A. Edison did in finding a way to give us the electric light and other inventions.

One should probably not only take tests to determine his aptitudes for doing a chosen vocation, he should also check into the demand for employees in this field. At the time of the preparation of the report of the Commission on Human Resources and Advanced Training there were insufficient prospective graduates from colleges and universities in the following areas: natural sciences, engineering, dentistry, medicine, nursing, and teaching in both colleges and public schools. At the Ph.D. level there were insufficient prospects in: psychology, social science, and humanities; and in applied biology in home economics.[24]

With the increasing complexity of business, larger numbers of accountants, personnel workers, market research specialists, economists, engineers, and statisticians are needed. The increasing age of the population will make it necessary for more physicians, dentists, and nurses to be trained to meet demands. More librarians, recreation leaders, radio and television technicians will be required because of increased leisure time. The shifting of population from the rural to urban areas will cause increased demand for more social workers, lawyers, and others who are engaged in handling social problems. In all of these areas, most of which can be classed as "professional," the college degree is an almost essential asset. This is one of the reasons for the intense competition for the qualified college graduate. The demand generally is for the "quality" graduate, the person who has good grades but also has developed socially to the extent that he may be considered to possess "broadened perspectives." It is estimated that at some of the large universities as many as seventy-five per cent of the graduates get jobs through the recruiters that come to the campuses.

The Strong Vocational Interest Test (Stanford University) and the Kuder Preference Test (Duke University) are two of the most used tests to determine if an individual has interests that would indicate success in a chosen field. The Strong test has five parts to determine whether a person likes, dislikes, or is indifferent to one hundred occupations, thirty-six school subjects, forty-nine amusements, forty-eight activities, and forty-seven peculiarities of people. Part VI determines preferences on certain activities, self ratings, persons one would have preferred to have been, and club offices one would prefer to hold. Separate tests for men and women have been proved to be highly reliable for persons who are of college age. Checking the results and converting the scores on several professions into standard scores, percentile ranks, or letter ratings takes a good deal of time. The Strong tests are highly valid for determining possibility of success based on interests. The tests do not show whether or not a person has mental ability and aptitude for being successful in the areas of interest indicated by the test scores in various occupations. For this reason vocational guidance counselors generally give in addition to the interest test some type of intelligence test. They may also give an aptitude test and a personality test. It is debatable as to whether an individual should be told his intelligence test score. In some cases, this might not have negative effects. Generally, the counselor simply indicates to the counselee that his test scores indicate that he would be successful in certain vocations. He may also try to dissuade a person from attempting to prepare for entering a field that demands greater mental ability than his test scores indicate he has. Personality tests are valuable as an aid in analyzing a person's emotional adjustment habits. Some temperaments are not suited to certain occupations (Chapter IV).

The Kuder test does not give scores in specific occupations or professions. Test results are shown on a profile sheet (chart) that indicates degree of interest in the following ten areas: outdoor, mechanical, computational, scientific, persuasive, artistic, literary, musical, social service, and clerical. Since Chapter XIII discusses tests used in employing, only the types of tests most valuable in giving vocational guidance are mentioned here.

Generally when a college senior contemplates finding employment he will take one of the following courses of action:

1. Go to some friend or relative who is in a position to aid him in obtaining employment. One should not, however, expect "pull" to get him by. Managers are responsible to their superiors, boards of directors, and owners. They cannot afford to keep a person on the payroll who is not paying his own way. If one should get a job with pull, he would have to keep it with ability and work.

2. Answer an advertisement by letter or at an employment office. The application letter is briefly discussed in Chapter XII.

3. Go to his college placement office, or to a private or governmental placement office. He should go prepared with credentials in hand: personal data sheet (Chapter XII), transcript of work, application photographs, and possibly letters of reference.

4. Go to an employment office and make application in person. Take all information necessary to properly complete an application blank.

5. Write a prospecting application letter to an employment office or to numbers of employment offices. It is possible that an application letter may be required in any of these five cases. If the letter is required of you, your problem is to: select facts, arrange them in order, and present them concretely.

Conclusions — A business firm recruits employees from its own ranks, from other companies, and from schools and colleges. Generally when recruiters go to college campuses to interview they are looking for managerial talent or technical specialists. Other employees are recruited through advertising, public and private employment offices, and selecting from among the applicants who come to a firm's own employment offices. An applicant's qualifications (as revealed from interviewing, tests, records, references, and the application blank) are matched against job and man specifications. Presumably the person who has the best qualifications for the job gets it. Frequently, however, it is the person who knows how to make the best presentation of his qualifications who gets the job.

PROJECTS

1. Obtain Standard Form 57, U. S. Civil Service Commission, Application for Federal Employment, from your local post office and fill this out completely (type).

2. Find an advertisement in a daily newspaper for a person to fill a position for which you are qualified. If you are not sure about requirements of the position, do some research first. Then write a "self-analysis" of yourself for this position using the following outline:

I. Your understanding of the requirements for the job: knowledge, experience, training and skills needed to do the job; an outline of what the job itself would entail.

II. How your education, training, and special skills fit the requirements.

III. How your experience fits the job requirements.

IV. Any special qualifications and items of interest about yourself that might help you get the job.

3. Read and report on a current article about recruiting of employees.

TABLE XI-1[25]

NUMBER AND PERCENTAGE OF 88 FIRMS USING METHODS, TECHNIQUES, PROCEDURES, AND SO FORTH AS INDICATED IN SELECTION OF SALES TRAINEES

Method, Technique, Procedure, Etc.	Number	Per Cent
Trainees Come Principally from Own Companies	6	6.82
Trainees Come Principally from Other Companies	28	31.82
Trainees Come Principally from Schools	20	22.73
Trainees Come Principally from Own Companies and Other Companies	3	3.41
Trainees Come Principally from Own Companies and Schools	6	6.82
Trainees Come Principally from Other Companies and Schools	14	15.91
Trainees Come from Own Companies, Other Companies, and Schools in About the Same Proportion	8	9.09
High School Graduation Required	68	77.27
College Required in Addition to High School	34	38.64
Engineering Degree	7	7.95
Liberal Arts Degree	6	6.82
Engineering and Business Degrees	1	1.14
Liberal Arts and Business Degrees	6	6.82
Liberal Arts and Engineering Degrees	1	1.14
Any of the Degrees Named Satisfactory	13	14.77
Special Sales Training	12	13.64
Grades Considered Important	49	55.68
Application Blank	86	97.73
Weighted Application Blank	19	21.59
Letter of Application	22	25.00
One or More Tests Used in Selecting Sales Trainees	65	73.86
Validity of Tests Used is Measured	37	56.92*
Reliability of Tests Used is Measured	34	52.31*
Firms Using Interview in Selecting Sales Trainees	87	98.64
Firms Using Panel or Board Type of Interview	12	13.64
Individual Interview by Sales Supervisor	82	93.18
Individual Interview by Personnel Department Interviewer	45	51.14
Firms Preferring Single Man as Sales Trainee	7	7.95
Firms Preferring Married Man as Sales Trainee	11	12.50
Firms Preferring Married Man With Family as Sales Trainee	46	52.27
Firms that Will Take Women as Sales Trainees	9	10.23
Firms Preferring Under 25 Years of Age for Sales Trainees	7	7.95
Firms Preferring 25–30 Years of Age for Sales Trainees	62	70.45
Firms Preferring Over 30 Years of Age for Sales Trainees	11	12.50
Firms that Check on References	80	90.91
Firms that Match Sales Selectees' Qualifications to Job Specifications	69	78.41
Firms that Make Time and Motion Studies of Salesmen	10	11.36

*Per cent of 65

ACKNOWLEDGMENTS AND REFERENCES

1 Adams, Loyce, "A Study of Sales Training Programs in Eighty-eight Firms," a dissertation, The University of Texas, Austin, June, 1959, (University Microfilms, Inc., 313 N. First St., Ann Arbor, Michigan), pp. 55–57. (This study was used for other material in the chapter for which footnotes have not always been used.)

2 ———, *A Career in Sales and Sales Management*, Basic Training Manual for Salesmen of A. B. Dick Products, A. B. Dick Company, Chicago 31, Illinois, 1957, pp. 29–31.

3 ———, Route Management, Swift & Company, Union Stock Yards, Chicago 9, Illinois.

4 Wade, C. Norman, "Why Today's Sales Recruits Are Different," *Sales Management*, Vol. 79, No. 8, September 20, 1957, p. 120ff.

5 Fernow, Charles S., "Personalized Placement Pays Off in College Recruitment," *Personnel*, American Management Association, 1515 Broadway, Times Square, New York 36, N. Y., Vol. 34, No. 4, January-February, 1958, pp. 77–80.

6 Klaw, Spencer, "Seniors: $750 a Head," *Fortune*, Vol. LV, No. 3, March, 1957, pp. 136–137ff.

7 Hobbe, Stephen, *Employment of the College Graduate*, Studies in Personnel Policy, No. 152, National Industrial Conference Board, Inc., 460 Park Avenue, New York 22, N. Y., 1956, pp. 3–39.

8 ———, "What's the Matter with American Salesmanship?," *Fortune*, Vol. XL, No. 2, September, 1949, p. 67ff.

9 ———, *So You Need To Find a Salesman?*, Sales Personnel Development Department, Lily-Tulip Cup Corporation, 122 East 42nd St., New York 17, N. Y., pp. 1–20.

10 Letter from Thomas M. Stokes, Metropolitan Life Insurance Company, One Madison Avenue, New York 10, N. Y., December 20, 1957.

11 ———, *Profitable Commercial Selling*, The Goodyear Tire & Rubber Company, Akron, Ohio, 1956, pp. 1–23.

12 Roos, Erik E., and Dailey, Charles A., "Ground Rules for Better Salesman Selection," *Sales Management*, August 16, 1957, p. 96.

13 Adams, *op. cit.*, pp. 251–252.

14 Umemura, George M., *Keys to Efficient Selling and Lower Marketing Costs*, Studies in Business Policy, No. 71, National Industrial Conference Board, Inc., 247 Park Avenue, New York 17, N. Y., 1954, pp. 13–15.

15 Kurtz, Albert K., "The Weighted Application Blank," *Experience with Psychology Tests*, Studies in Personnel Policy, No. 92, National Industrial Conference Board, Inc., 247 Park Avenue, New York 17, N. Y., 1948, pp. 24–26.

16 Phelps, D. M., *Sales Management*, Richard D. Irwin, Inc., Homewood, Illinois, 1953, pp. 540–599.

17 Adams, *op cit.*, pp. 79–89.

18 ———, *Field Manager's Guide*, Selection Procedure, Lily-Tulip Cup Corporation, *op. cit.*, pp. 1–71.

19 ———, *Salesmen's Basic Training Guide*, Victor Adding Machine Company, 3900 North Rockwell Street, Chicago 18, Illinois, 1953.

20 Adams, *op. cit.*, pp. 80–85ff.

21 ———, *Field Manager's Guide*, Selection Procedure, Lily-Tulip Cup Corporation, *op. cit.*

22 ———, *A Career in Sales and Sales Management*, Basic Training Manual for Salesmen of A. B. Dick Products, A. B. Dick Company, Chicago 31, Illinois, 1957.

23 Harrell, Thomas W., "The Validity of Biographical Data Items for Food Company Salesmen," *Journal of Applied Psychology*, Vol. 44, No. 1, February, 1960, pp. 31–33.

24 Wolfle, Dael, *America's Resources of Specialized Talent*, Harper & Brothers, New York, 1954, p. 77.

25 Adams, *op cit.*, pp. 117–118.

CHAPTER XII

THE EMPLOYMENT INTERVIEW
AND THE APPLICATION LETTER

The Importance of the Employment Interview — Interviewing is one of the most universally used devices in selecting from among applicants for positions those who are to be employed. The employment interviewer (or the department head who does his own interviewing) may assume that he has the ability to learn in the course of an interview about the applicant's personality, mental qualifications, physical and emotional well-being, social qualifications, education, skills, and experience. In other words, he may feel that if given the information about the requirements of a job in terms of work to be done and the qualifications of the man to do the work, he can size up an applicant in an interview and decide whether or not that applicant should get the job. Such an interviewer would have strong belief in his own system of eliciting information from an applicant and would very likely depend heavily upon his own hunches. He would probably also let his personal biases influence him greatly. Some interviewers who work like this may actually be successful. Trained interviewers generally, however, realize their inability to get a complete picture of an applicant through an interview only. It is for this reason that they employ the many other devices mentioned in the chapter on recruiting.

Numbers of studies have shown that interviewers do not generally agree on their ratings of applicants. One early study was made by Walter Dill Scott who found that in rating thirty-six sales applicants, six interviewers could not agree in the case of twenty-eight of the applicants whether they belonged in the upper half or the lower half of the applicants.[1] Another study compared the ratings of fifty-seven applicants by twelve interviewers. One applicant was variously ranked by the different interviewers: 1, 2, 6, 9, 10, 16, 20, 21, 26, 28, 53, 57. The two interviewers who rated the applicant *1* and *2* placed him at the very top of the fifty-seven candidates; but two other raters placed him at or near the bottom. These twelve interviewers widely disagreed in their rating of other applicants as well.[2] In another case where seven interviewers rated eleven applicants, one applicant was placed first by two executives and tenth by a third; another applicant was rated second by one interviewer and eleventh by another one. There was general lack of agreement in practically all of the cases.[3]

Nevertheless, the employment interview continues to serve as a means of getting information from applicants about their experience and other qualifications. It also serves as the medium through which the applicant is given facts about the company and the kind of situation in which he would be placed were he to receive the position for which he is applying. He is usually told the possibilities for growth and development of the company and his opportunities to grow and develop with it. The interview is also considered to be useful in establishing a feeling of rapport and cordial relationship between the interviewer and the applicant. To the applicant the interviewer temporarily becomes "the company." In its broadest sense employment interviewing might be considered to be that interviewing that is used not only in *selecting* an employee, but in *inducting, placing,* and *terminating* him should he leave the company for any reason. In this broader sense interviewing becomes not only one of the most used employment devices, it becomes also a highly valuable one.

Employment interviewers should be possessed of: ability to talk in many areas of knowledge; ability to win the confidence of those whom they interview; knowledge of the requirements of jobs for which they are interviewing, in terms of both job and man specifications; knowledge of how to use all other employment devices as well as interviewing; knowledge of human nature; ability to initiate conversation and to sort out, reject, and select information from what an applicant says; specialized training in employment procedures and employment psychology.

In a *preliminary* (sometimes called *rail* because applicants pass by a rail where a special interviewer asks a few appropriate questions to determine their suitability for employment) *interview,* the interviewer is interested only in obtaining enough information to enable him to decide whether the applicant has qualifications that might enable him to fill certain job openings. If he decides affirmatively, the applicant is asked to fill out an application blank and return for further questioning. He probably will also take employment tests before the next interview. The second interviewer should prepare himself for the interview by studying the job specifications. He should also study the candidate's application blank, test scores, and any other information he has on the applicant such as an application letter, a picture, reference letters, or a transcript of high school or college work.

The employment interviewer who interviews the man who gets through the "rail" interview should generally follow certain rules. From numerous sources and experience the writer has built up a list of things the interviewer should do.[4] He should:

1. Interview in a private office where there would not be interruptions.

2. Go into an interview with clearly defined purposes in mind.

3. Treat the applicant courteously, attempt to put him at ease, and win his confidence.

4. Ask general questions that lead the applicant to talk freely and listen without interrupting.

5. Ask more specific questions when the applicant fails to give needed information; prompt the applicant when he stops talking in a manner that keeps the conversation going but does not rush the applicant.

6. Delve into the applicant's background sufficiently to enable a decision as to whether the applicant would fit into the organization and do the type of work for which he has applied in a manner similar to the performance of the best of the present employees engaged in that type of work.

7. Avoid injecting his own ideas into the conversation except as they apply significantly to the particular interviewee and his problems.

8. Put himself in the place of the interviewee and attempt to see his point of view.

9. Examine himself occasionally and try to eliminate his own special prejudices.

10. Avoid putting answers into the interviewee's mouth; avoid, also, questions that can be answered with a flat "yes" or "no."

11. Avoid questions that might embarrass the applicant or appear to make sport of him.

12. Attempt to separate facts from implications.

13. Achieve a definite conclusion to the interview, as: (1) there may be nothing at all now for the applicant and probably will be nothing in the future; (2) there may be at a definite time in the future something for him; (3) the applicant may be placed on a waiting list of preferred applicants; (4) the applicant may be sent to the line or staff department where there is possibility that he will finally be employed.

14. Pave the way for the next interview (by manager or supervisor) if the applicant is considered suitable for employment and there is a place for him. This may involve giving information about the company, its policies, benefits, and expectations. This depends

upon whether it is customary for applicants to be accepted in the departments after they have passed the employment office. It depends also upon whether or not this is provided for in a subsequent employment office interview.

15. Reject applicants who do not prove to be suitable in such manner that they feel compensated for the interview and the time taken despite the fact that they were not employed.

16. Check upon himself occasionally; recordings may be used to do this; a secretary may be present and take notes. Comments made later may throw light upon the effectiveness of the interview.

17. Record ratings immediately after the termination of the interview. Many interviewers record ratings and answers to questions during the interview. Some, however, consider that this makes the free exchange of ideas much more difficult to the extent that it is distracting to the interviewee.

What the Interviewer Should Look for in the Employment Interview — There are certain objective factors which can be obtained from recorded data but are often also brought out or observed in an interview: education, skills, experience, reasons for leaving previous employment, physical condition, age, marital status, promotability, and intelligence (test results); personality (outgoing, turned inward) may be viewed objectively by the interviewer, but not all personality factors are detectable in the interview. The interviewer may note voice, attitudes, social traits, ability to talk, enthusiasm, eagerness. He may try to detect neurotic tendencies from complaints, ability to concentrate on the matter at hand, and mental alertness.

A survey made by Frank S. Endicott, Director of Placement, Northwestern University, of 225 large and medum-sized companies showed the relative weight companies gave to various factors considered in selecting employees. In all fields the factor considered most important was *personality,* including poise and appearance. Good *grades* were second in importance. In accounting and engineering, however, the scholastic record was considered especially important. Campus *activities* were much more important than high grades for those going into fields of selling.[5]

Richard W. Husband, industrial psychologist, compared the 1956 status of the members of his college class (Dartmouth) with their 1926 status. He obtained 275 answers from 368 graduates. Those graduates who had been outstanding in anything while undergraduates were the ones who replied. Husband found that thirty-one per cent of these men were earning over $20,000 annually in 1956. The men who were "barely graduated" showed much lower than average earnings in 1956. The median income of the 1.50-1.69 grade-point-average group was $10,625. Incomes progressed in direct relation to the grade-point average. Husband's study included numerous points other than grades. The picture on intelligence test scores and their correlation with 1956 income was similar to the picture on grades. The study also showed that the more activities the graduate engaged in while in college, the higher the present-day income. While high grades were revealed to correlate directly with incomes, Husband said that his findings give support to the recruiter who prefers the "B" student who took part in activities to the "A" student who did not.[6]

In the study made by the writer on eighty-eight firms (Chapter XI), it was found that the interviewers in practically every case noted the following items when interviewing prospective sales trainees: voice and appearance, past work experience, initiative, physical condition and health, attitudes, and personality. Marital status and age could presumably be determined from the application blanks, but in the case of seventy-seven out of the eighty-eight firms marital status was noted also in the interview; in eighty out of eighty-eight of the firms the age was also noted in the interview.

The Westinghouse Electric Corporation interviewers who select sales trainees look for: (1) personality, (2) scholastic standing, (3) evidence of ability to cooperate, (4) recommendations made by persons qualified to make them, and (5) promise of executive abilities capable of development.

Monsanto Chemical Company's memorandum of interview in addition to the usual basic information blanks contains blanks on hobbies and interests and the following personal characteristics: complexion, height, and weight; irritating, or likable; colorless, or animated; ill at ease, or poised; well dressed and neat, or poor taste and carelessness in dress; individualistic, or teamworker; diffident, or confident; retiring, or forceful; affected, or natural; phlegmatic, or peppy; flighty, or stable; shy, or aggressive; crude, or polite; quiet, or loud; egotistical; humorless; sluggish; jittery; griper; cocky maturity; initiative in conversation; aggressiveness. Scales are used for rating the applicant during the interview on these individual items.

Two interview sheets are used by the Monroe Calculating Machine Company, Inc. The first is used to get first-hand impressions. If the interviewee seems that he would be a suitable Monroe salesman, he is given an application blank and asked to complete it and return for a definite appointment at which he receives a second and "full" interview with the interviewer using the second interview sheet which provides for a very careful rating immediately following the interview on numbers of items under personal traits (initiative, approach, voice, and tact). Other items that may be noted in the interview and substantiated by studying references: honesty, whether he is a hard worker or not, loyalty, moral habits, ability, self-control, ability to follow instructions, poise and appearance,

INTERVIEW RATING SHEET [7]

FOR

PERSON INTERVIEWED_____

ADDRESS_____CITY_____STATE_____

VOID
SAMPLE ONLY

Monroe Calculating Machine Company, Inc., General Offices, Orange, N. J.

A   ATTITUDE

1   Attitude Toward Job

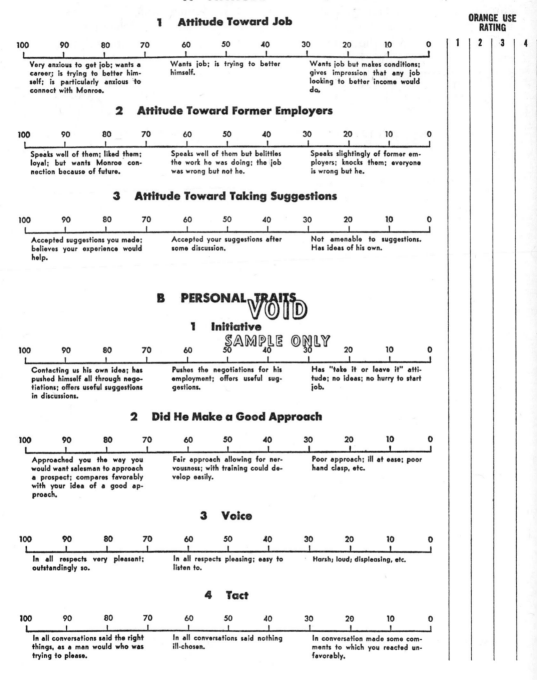

| 100 | 90 | 80 | 70 | 60 | 50 | 40 | 30 | 20 | 10 | 0 |

Very anxious to get job; wants a career; is trying to better himself; is particularly anxious to connect with Monroe.

Wants job; is trying to better himself.

Wants job but makes conditions; gives impression that any job looking to better income would do.

Rating columns: 1 | 2 | 3 | 4

2   Attitude Toward Former Employers

| 100 | 90 | 80 | 70 | 60 | 50 | 40 | 30 | 20 | 10 | 0 |

Speaks well of them; liked them; loyal; but wants Monroe connection because of future.

Speaks well of them but belittles the work he was doing; the job was wrong but not he.

Speaks slightingly of former employers; knocks them; everyone is wrong but he.

3   Attitude Toward Taking Suggestions

| 100 | 90 | 80 | 70 | 60 | 50 | 40 | 30 | 20 | 10 | 0 |

Accepted suggestions you made; believes your experience would help.

Accepted your suggestions after some discussion.

Not amenable to suggestions. Has ideas of his own.

B   PERSONAL TRAITS

VOID

1   Initiative

SAMPLE ONLY

| 100 | 90 | 80 | 70 | 60 | 50 | 40 | 30 | 20 | 10 | 0 |

Contacting us his own idea; has pushed himself all through negotiations; offers useful suggestions in discussions.

Pushes the negotiations for his employment; offers useful suggestions.

Has "take it or leave it" attitude; no ideas; no hurry to start job.

2   Did He Make a Good Approach

| 100 | 90 | 80 | 70 | 60 | 50 | 40 | 30 | 20 | 10 | 0 |

Approached you the way you would want salesman to approach a prospect; compares favorably with your idea of a good approach.

Fair approach allowing for nervousness; with training could develop easily.

Poor approach; ill at ease; poor hand clasp, etc.

3   Voice

| 100 | 90 | 80 | 70 | 60 | 50 | 40 | 30 | 20 | 10 | 0 |

In all respects very pleasant; outstandingly so.

In all respects pleasing; easy to listen to.

Harsh; loud; displeasing, etc.

4   Tact

| 100 | 90 | 80 | 70 | 60 | 50 | 40 | 30 | 20 | 10 | 0 |

In all conversations said the right things, as a man would who was trying to please.

In all conversations said nothing ill-chosen.

In conversation made some comments to which you reacted unfavorably.

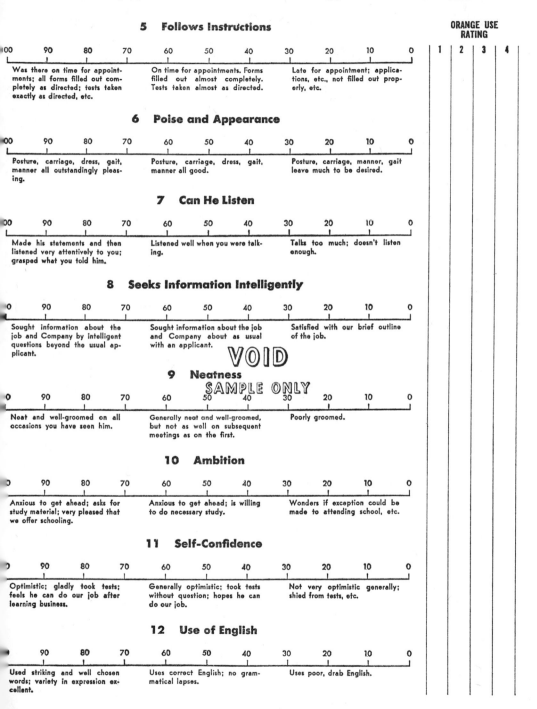

5   Follows Instructions

| 00 | 90 | 80 | 70 | 60 | 50 | 40 | 30 | 20 | 10 | 0 |

Was there on time for appointments; all forms filled out completely as directed; tests taken exactly as directed, etc.

On time for appointments. Forms filled out almost completely. Tests taken almost as directed.

Late for appointment; applications, etc., not filled out properly, etc.

6   Poise and Appearance

| 00 | 90 | 80 | 70 | 60 | 50 | 40 | 30 | 20 | 10 | 0 |

Posture, carriage, dress, gait, manner all outstandingly pleasing.

Posture, carriage, dress, gait, manner all good.

Posture, carriage, manner, gait leave much to be desired.

7   Can He Listen

| 00 | 90 | 80 | 70 | 60 | 50 | 40 | 30 | 20 | 10 | 0 |

Made his statements and then listened very attentively to you; grasped what you told him.

Listened well when you were talking.

Talks too much; doesn't listen enough.

8   Seeks Information Intelligently

| 0 | 90 | 80 | 70 | 60 | 50 | 40 | 30 | 20 | 10 | 0 |

Sought information about the job and Company by intelligent questions beyond the usual applicant.

Sought information about the job and Company about as usual with an applicant.

Satisfied with our brief outline of the job.

VOID
SAMPLE ONLY

9   Neatness

| 0 | 90 | 80 | 70 | 60 | 50 | 40 | 30 | 20 | 10 | 0 |

Neat and well-groomed on all occasions you have seen him.

Generally neat and well-groomed, but not as well on subsequent meetings as on the first.

Poorly groomed.

10   Ambition

| 0 | 90 | 80 | 70 | 60 | 50 | 40 | 30 | 20 | 10 | 0 |

Anxious to get ahead; asks for study material; very pleased that we offer schooling.

Anxious to get ahead; is willing to do necessary study.

Wonders if exception could be made to attending school, etc.

11   Self-Confidence

| 0 | 90 | 80 | 70 | 60 | 50 | 40 | 30 | 20 | 10 | 0 |

Optimistic; gladly took tests; feels he can do our job after learning business.

Generally optimistic; took tests without question; hopes he can do our job.

Not very optimistic generally; shied from tests, etc.

12   Use of English

| 90 | 80 | 70 | 60 | 50 | 40 | 30 | 20 | 10 | 0 |

Used striking and well chosen words; variety in expression excellent.

Uses correct English; no grammatical lapses.

Uses poor, drab English.

ORANGE USE RATING

1   2   3   4

The following points are rated from interviews with references.

C   RESULTS OF INVESTIGATION

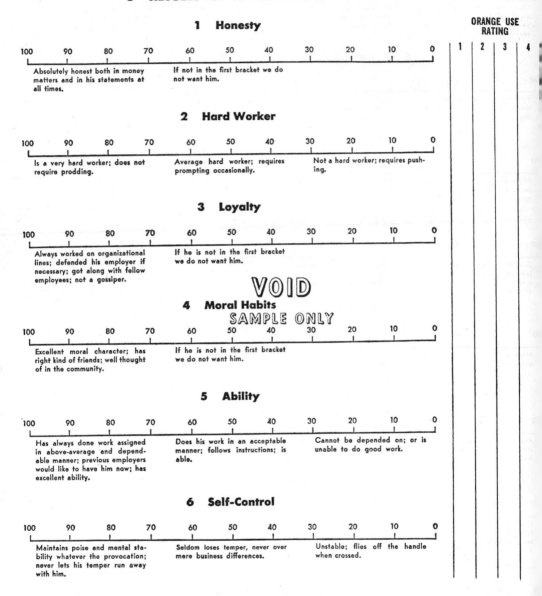

1   Honesty

ORANGE USE RATING

100   90   80   70   60   50   40   30   20   10   0   1   2   3   4

Absolutely honest both in money matters and in his statements at all times.

If not in the first bracket we do not want him.

2   Hard Worker

100   90   80   70   60   50   40   30   20   10   0

Is a very hard worker; does not require prodding.

Average hard worker; requires prompting occasionally.

Not a hard worker; requires pushing.

3   Loyalty

100   90   80   70   60   50   40   30   20   10   0

Always worked on organizational lines; defended his employer if necessary; got along with fellow employees; not a gossiper.

If he is not in the first bracket we do not want him.

VOID

4   Moral Habits

SAMPLE ONLY

100   90   80   70   60   50   40   30   20   10   0

Excellent moral character; has right kind of friends; well thought of in the community.

If he is not in the first bracket we do not want him.

5   Ability

100   90   80   70   60   50   40   30   20   10   0

Has always done work assigned in above-average and dependable manner; previous employers would like to have him now; has excellent ability.

Does his work in an acceptable manner; follows instructions; is able.

Cannot be depended on; or is unable to do good work.

6   Self-Control

100   90   80   70   60   50   40   30   20   10   0

Maintains poise and mental stability whatever the provocation; never lets his temper run away with him.

Seldom loses temper, never over mere business differences.

Unstable; flies off the handle when crossed.

INTERVIEW RATING SHEET

DIRECTIONS

When checking this Rating Sheet it is very important to fix in your mind the information you have gathered in the interviews and investigations, and then estimate each quality carefully and to the best of your ability. The following example illustrates the method of checking. In this case the person filling out the Rating Sheet has estimated that the attitude of the applicant toward securing the job is good; that he is anxious to take up the work as a permanent career; that he is doing so because he wants to better himself and feels he can gain this end through a connection with Monroe.

A   ATTITUDE

1   Attitude Toward Job

| 100 | 90 | 80 | ✓ 70 | 60 | 50 | 40 | 30 | 20 | 10 | 0 |

Very anxious to get job; wants a career; is trying to better himself; is particularly anxious to connect with Monroe.

Wants job; is trying to better himself.

Wants job but makes conditions; gives impression that any job looking to better income would do.

VOID

SAMPLE ONLY

Have you looked up references?_____   Are you satisfied that we want this man?_____

BRANCH MANAGER_____DATE_____

FIELD SALES MANAGER_____DATE_____

FOR ORANGE_____DATE_____

ability to listen, ability to seek information intelligently, neatness, ambition, self-confidence, use of English.[8]

Many studies have been made to determine what employers value most in office employees. Most of these have placed accuracy at or near the top of the list of personal and character traits. Other traits that have ranked high: dependability, responsibility, initiative, courtesy, appearance, cooperativeness, honesty, ability to follow directions, ability to communicate, punctuality, and mental alertness. Additional traits not always ranked so high: trustworthiness, judgment, loyalty, cheerfulness, voice quality, integrity, enthusiasm, interest, industry, adaptability, consideration, sincerity, decisiveness, poise, and so on. It will be noted that many of the traits valued most highly could not be adequately determined or observed through interviewing alone. Performance and other tests, transcripts of work, and references have to be used to get this information.

The Free or Uncontrolled Interview — The whims and biases of the interviewer (who generally is a person with little training for interviewing) direct the course of the uncontrolled interview. Writing a number of years ago Richard Stephen Uhrbrock stated that the typical employment interviewer in industrial firms in the United States is a person with about two years of high school training. Any special training in the techniques to use in employment he usually got from someone with as limited a background as his own. In all probability he hadn't even read books on interviewing techniques.[9] Many such interviewers depend almost solely upon their own personal prejudices and biases, and their interpretations of information received are highly subjective. For instance, they might believe that a person with previous work experience in a given occupation is to be preferred at all times over all other applicants regardless of potential of certain of the other applicants. Table manners may be the one factor that impresses them and gets the job for the applicant, regardless of his other qualifications or lack of them. For some such interviewers, personal appearance is the sole factor considered.[10] One study showed that wearing of glasses or not wearing of them might have an effect upon an interviewer. It was found that people who wear glasses tend to be rated as more intelligent and industrious generally, but they are not rated more honest.[11]

In all probability there are many more trained interviewers today than at the time Uhrbrock described the average employment interviewer. A great many more employment interviewers have had some college training and some have had specialized instruction in the art of interviewing, with emphasis upon factors to look for in the interview.

The Directed Employment Interview — The interview that is directed may be referred to as *area, patterned,* or *standardized.* There are different shades of meaning to these terms. Nevertheless, each of these three types of employment interview is organized and the interviewer goes into the interview with a fixed purpose of obtaining answers to certain specific questions. In most cases some method of recording the most important answers will be used. Uhrbrock has reported on one interviewer who looks for high degree of scholarship, interest in manufacturing, high physical energy, and an integrated personality when he interviews college men for technical jobs. Ten questions this man has found useful are:

1. What was your major course, or field of concentration while in college?
2. How many men were in your graduating class?
3. Where did you stand in scholarship in that group?
4. Did you ever fail a school course?
5. Tell me, in detail, how you spent each summer since you were graduated from high school.
6. What college subjects have you *disliked* most? Why?
7. What illnesses or operations have you had?
8. What books (not assigned as part of your regular school work) have you read, during the past year, because of your interest in the author or the subject-matter?
9. What different careers have you considered seriously?
10. How do you spend your leisure time?[12]

In some cases the area interviewer does not ask specific questions, but he asks general questions relative to education, experience, hobbies and activities, home and family background, health, and any other personal history items that are considered important. In this manner he gets the specific answers he needs.

The terms patterned and standardized are generally used synonymously although in some cases a distinction is made. The patterned interview is one that obtains answers to a list of specific questions that have been considered to be important. The standardized interview, too, obtains answers to a list of specific questions, but through a process of checking on the degree of relationship between answers to the questions and success on the job weights may be assigned the answers and the applicant may receive a general rating on the interview in terms of point values. An employment office could, of course, insist on a patterned interview without the element of standardization injected by study of employees to determine the factors most highly related to success and those related to failure and basing the questions upon these. It is the same distinction that is made between an objective test that is merely an objective test and one that is a standardized objective test.

Laurence Siegel reports on a comparison of ratings from a "patterned" interview and success on the job. It was found that out of 108 truck drivers employed regardless of the ratings they were assigned in interviews, 75 per cent of those who received outstanding ratings remained successfully on the job after eleven weeks; 38.5 per cent of those who received good ratings were successfully employed after eleven weeks; only 26.1 per cent of those rated only average and 13.3 per cent of those rated poor were still in service after eleven weeks.[13]

An earlier study made by Hovland and Wonderlic and variously reported by Berrien, Hepner, Siegel and others, showed similar results. The Diagnostic Interviewer's Guide covering *work history, family history, social history,* and *personal history* was used to rate three hundred applicants at the Household Finance Corporation. It was found in checking on those who had remained on the job, resigned, or been dismissed that the higher rating on the D.I.G. the greater the percentage of persons still on the job. Further, the lower the scores made on the D.I.G. ratings, the larger the percentages dismissed. Only a few of those with high scores had been dismissed.[14]

The standardized employment interview is generally considered to be the most valuable one to use in selecting employees. In a study made by Yonge it was found that the interview that is standardized but nevertheless permits free exchange of ideas between interviewer and interviewee is very useful in assessing the qualities of an individual for employment. Yonge concluded, in fact, that the standardized interview is the most valuable type to use.[15]

The Non-directive Interview — In Chapter IX the rules for non-directive interviewing in counseling as they were evolved at the Western Electric Company were given. These same rules apply in employment interviewing that is considered to be non-directive. If the person doing this type of interviewing is not highly trained in what to look for in the interview, the result will be similar to the result of any free or uncontrolled interview. If one is highly skilled and experienced, this type of interviewing may be greatly beneficial in selecting applicants.

One study reported the following results after the non-directive interview, supplemented by checking on references, training, and home situations (visits), had been used in employing telephone workers:

1. The percentage of turnover cases which could be ascribed in whole or in part to faulty selection, while the labor market was growing tighter, has declined steadily.

2. The department supervisors say they are getting people better fitted for the work. Follow-up studies bear this out.

3. Interviewers who have used both the questionnaire and the non-directive method say the latter enables them to make more effective appraisals.

4. Applicants frequently tell interviewers they liked the interview

because it did not seem like an interview. They had expected to be asked a lot of questions; instead, they just had a pleasant chat.

5. Other companies in the Bell System that have adopted this method report similar results.[16]

The Probing Interview — The probing type of interview is useful in two ways: (1) to find underlying drives and motives of an individual applicant; (2) to determine what the applicant would do in a given work situation.

In attempting to discover an individual's motives such questions as the following might be asked: "What person has influenced you more than any other? How? Why? What do you think about the educational system under which you have received your education and training? If you were asked to give a lecture advising parents of teen-agers on some of the pitfalls that they might avoid and how, what are some of the main ideas that you would emphasize?"

In trying to find out if an applicant for a selling job could handle certain situations, you might ask: "What would you say to a customer who is about ready to buy but suddenly says that he must go pick up his wife who is waiting for him?" If the applicant handles that one satisfactorily you might ask, "What if he still will not buy but says that he prefers to have his wife's opinion, consent, or advice before closing the deal?" The probing here would determine knowledge of how to close the sale as well as persistence of the applicant.

This type of employment interview is similar to the depth interview used by the psychiatrist to discover what is bothering a patient; it is simply not as extended and does not go as deeply into motivation. It is also similar to the type of interviewing done in motivation research. In a sense, it is similar to role-playing (Chapter XIV) in that the applicant is placed in the position of having to act out a part, and in the course of acting the part he reveals certain of his motives and/or abilities.

As with the non-directive type of interviewing, this type of interviewing requires a highly skilled interviewer. For the average large business organization with an element of centralized control of employment procedures, the standardized interview can be developed by the experienced and expert persons, and interviewers with lesser skill can still be fairly successful in getting answers to the prescribed questions. Unskilled interviewers could not, however, successfully handle non-directive and probing interviews.

For any given firm it is necessary to have numbers of standardized interview forms depending upon the nature of the jobs to be done. Interview rating forms for bench and shop workers, office workers, supervisors, technical experts, and managers should vary to fit the situation. For interviewers at the different stages of interviewing, forms used for recording information will also vary.

Panel Interviewing — The panel interview is one conducted by a committee or board consisting of two or more (usually three or more) persons. As reported in the previous chapter, this type of interview was found to be used by 13.64 per cent of the eighty-eight companies whose sales training programs were studied. It has the advantage of enabling several persons to inject their ideas of what is important for the firm to know about an applicant into the interview. Further, they can later exchange ideas about the applicant, discuss his strong and weak points, and point out factors that need additional investigation. For managerial and highly skilled occupations, this type of interviewing offers much and probably should be used even more than it is at present.

In some cases the panel interview has evolved into a type of oral examination for employment. The oral test may be designed to discover such things as initiative, perseverance, ability to meet and overcome obstacles, ability to make decisions, and ability to plan and put plans into effect. Ordway and O'Brien have discussed this type of interviewing as being a type which might be done by an individual interviewer or by a group.[17]

Psychologists from the National Institute of Industrial Psychology, London, have assisted employers in evaluating candidates through individual interviews, tests, and studying of their credentials. When the candidates were narrowed down (preferably to eight persons) they were then observed by an employer group (preferably three persons) at an informal social occasion (dinner followed by conversation). The psychologist introduced a topic of interest to the candidates and then the employer group and the psychologist let the candidates talk for about an hour, after which time questions were asked the applicants. The next morning the candidates were given a special problem to discuss and solve. The employer group and the psychologist later reviewed the candidates' qualifications. When this procedure was used twenty times in 1946 there was agreement in every case as to the candidate to whom a position should be offered.[18]

The Induction Interview — While induction is discussed in Chapter XIV as being a part of training, the induction interview is mentioned here as being one phase of employment interviewing. After an applicant has been selected for employment, he is given information considered essential for him to have in order to begin work effectively. Through interview, booklets, and films, employees are welcomed to the company. They are often told something of the history of the company. They are given explanations of fringe benefits and information about activities, pay, opportunities, and the particular job they will do. This information interview may be conducted in the personnel office as a standard procedure. If so it would be supplemented by the employee's supervisor who would give additional information pertaining specifically to the new employee's duties and particular customs of the department in which he will work.

A follow-up interview several days after employment or at the time the employee receives his first pay check may prove profitable. Information desired by the employee can be given to him. The interviewer can determine whether the employee is adjusting to his new job situation.

The Termination Interview — The termination or exit interview is not universally used. Companies that do use this type of interview generally find that the information obtained is very valuable. People who voluntarily resign are led to give reasons; this, in turn, enables the company to eliminate weaknesses that exist at the place of work. In addition to giving this type of information which is useful to both the employing department and the personnel department, the exit interview when given to persons who are discharged will aid the employment department in finding its own weaknesses in placing employees. A further advantage of exit interviewing is that it gives opportunity for creating goodwill for the company, and it sometimes dissuades persons from leaving. The Metropolitan Life Insurance Company has reported that in one group of 4,600 employees who intended leaving employment during an eleven-month period, 195, 4.2 per cent, decided because of the exit interview to stay with the company.[19]

The Letter of Application — If a letter of application is to be used in seeking employment it should be very carefully prepared. Some college students send out many prospecting letters during their senior year. If these are properly written and give the information needed by employment managers or department heads to whom they are addressed, they open up opportunities for interviews. For some types of employment they actually get the jobs. College teachers are frequently offered positions on the basis of application letters accompanied by photographs, transcripts, and letters of recommendation (or by names of references who can send their recommendations directly).

Discussion of the application letter was deliberately left until this point. By now the reader realizes that going through the hurdles of being recruited for a job may be quite involved. An attempt has been made to give some idea of what information employers look for when they contemplate placing new people in their organizations and the devices these employers use in getting this information.

You should regard your application letter as a sales letter. If a one-part letter is used, you should formulate your chief selling points in view of knowledge of job requirements, and then write a rather full letter proceeding along these lines:

1. Catch the reader's interest in the opening by referring to the advertisement being answered, the person who told you about the position, your previous contact with the reader, or your prior interest in his firm.

2. Give all the information needed about previous experience, education, and background in order to convince the employer that you are the best qualified person for the position he wants filled (or for which you are applying in the hope that he has a need for a person with your qualifications). If possible, arrange your education, training, and experience in order so that it seems that there has been constant progress toward the position you are seeking. It is usually best to avoid mentioning salary until it is brought up through interview or follow-up correspondence.

3. Such personal information as age, health, nationality, church membership, and leadership in school, civic, social, or church organizations may be important. Use judgment in determining how much of this to include in your letter.

4. Give evidence that what you have claimed in discussing your training and experience is correct. You may enclose copies of letters of recommendation or list persons who have given permission to use their names as references.

5. Write a strong conclusion asking for an interview or some other definite action. Avoid the use of such words as hoping, trusting, awaiting, and anticipating. Participial endings are not only weak, they generally result in incomplete sentences.

6. Use plain white bond 8½" x 11". Address the person to whom you are applying (employment manager, personnel manager, or department head for whom you would like to work) by name.

The two-part letter is used more than the one-part letter. When you use this, you write a shorter letter designed to make the reader interested in finding out more about you. The personal data sheet enclosed with the letter should give full information which the reader can find by turning a page. Make your letter reflect personality, character, and ability. Don't just say that you received a diploma. Say that you learned certain things in the courses you took. If you have had any type of work experience during the summer or while you have been in school, you should attempt to show that this experience has taught you the importance of cooperating with and working with and for your supervisors. It has probably taught you a good many things that would be valuable on any type of job. Even though your work may have been waiting on tables or doing janitor service on the campus, you learned to be prompt and dependable. You learned to satisfy your boss. Further, you learned to schedule your studying and social life in such manner that these did not interfere with your work assignments.

A letter of application is not given here because "copybook" letters are considered *"verboten"* by most employment managers who generally can spot such letters very readily. Your letter should reflect your personality, characteristics, and abilities. It should be *your* letter. Within the bounds of the outline given above, you should attempt to be original. You may, however, refer to the personal data sheet included in this chapter, or go to a good business writing (correspondence, communications) textbook for a similar personal data sheet form.

PERSONAL DATA SHEET

Raymond Austin
3148 Blank Street
Blankville, Texas   Telephone W-7568

EDUCATION

1948–1952 — Attended Stamford High School. Was graduated May 25, 1952.
1952–1956 — Attended Blank University. To be graduated June 1, 1956, with a major in business administration.

EXPERIENCE

1952–1953 — Worked in Magnolia Service Station, W. Swenson, Stamford, Texas. Immediate superior: S. R. Stanton.
1953–1954 — Worked as a janitor in Ferguson Hall, Blank University. Immediate superior: Mark Reeves.
1954–1955 — Worked as night watchman for the Western Compress and Storage Company, Blankville, Texas. Immediate superior: A. L. Stewart.
1955–1956 — Worked as student grader of mathematics papers. Immediate superior: J. E. Barring.

PERSONAL DETAILS

Physical characteristics:
    Health — good   Weight — 155 pounds
    Height — 5 ft., 8 in.   Age — 20 years
Church membership — First Baptist Church, Blankville, Texas.
Out-of-class activities: Business Administration Club, A Cappella

Choir, Debating Council, Pi Kappa Delta (Debating Fraternity), Social Science Club.

Special achievements: Election to Alpha Chi, scholarship fraternity made up of the upper scholastic tenth of the class.

Special skills: Can use the various business machines, such as the calculator, the ten-key adding machine, and the adding machine. Can type at the rate of 60 words a minute. Can take dictation at the rate of 100 words a minute and transcribe with accuracy.

REFERENCES

Mr. J. Carlton Smith, Professor of Business, Blankville College, Texas.

Mr. Henry J. Smith, Registrar, Blank University, Blankville, Texas.

Rev. George W. Blevins, Pastor, First Baptist Church, Blankville, Texas.

Miss Amelia Smith, Instructor of Business, Blank University, Blankville, Texas.

The Letter of Introduction — The purpose of a letter of introduction is to tell who the person being introduced is and why he is being introduced. It should aid him in establishing a business or a social contact. The introduction will sometimes request that the reader, presumably a personal acquaintance of the writer, assist the person who is introduced in finding employment, in meeting other businessmen, or in locating and compiling certain information.

Whatever the purpose of any particular letter of introduction, you should make it human and natural. In making an oral introduction you do not say, "I have been asked to introduce Mr. Blank, who hands you. . . ." You go ahead and make the introduction. When the occasion for making an introduction is simple, a card with the words, "Introducing Mr. Henry Blank," and your signature, may be used.

If you have occasion to write a letter of introduction this is a good outline to follow:

1. Introduce the person and identify him in the first sentence. "Shake hands with Henry Blank, a research chemist with the X Y Z Company, who has been assigned to check. . . ."

2. Give briefly the reason for writing the letter.

3. Supply briefly whatever information you think is needed about the person being introduced.

4. Express appreciation for any courtesies that may be rendered the person being introduced.

If you have need of a letter of introduction for yourself, obtain it from somebody who knows you, knows the person to whom you wish to be introduced, and will do a good job of writing the letter.

The Letter of Recommendation — Many people think when they have written into a letter of recommendation all the superlatives in the English language that they have a finished masterpiece. A letter of recommendation is going to have something to do with the molding of the life of the person who goes on the job, and it may affect the lives of persons with whom he is going to work. The man who receives the letter has every right to expect that it is an honest opinion of the writer and that it objectively appraises the applicant.

If a young man asks you to write and recommend him for a position which you think he is unqualified to fill, you are doing injury to yourself, the prospective employer, and the young man if you recommend him. The employer will have to have the unpleasant experience of firing the young man later; your honesty will be placed in doubt; the young man will face a problem of finding employment with the fact that he was fired working against him, although he may be qualified for some other type of work.

A letter of recommendation should tell just what is known to be the truth. Tell what the person has done and can do and let the record speak for itself. The reader may then judge as to whether or not the applicant is the person he needs. You cannot safely make a statement which says, "I know he will make good for you." You can only say what the applicant has done and, in some instances perhaps, what you believe he will do. You cannot *know* what he will do.

If you ask someone to recommend you, it should be a person who can give specific information about your background and ability, or someone who can testify as to your character traits from firsthand knowledge. Frequently employers prefer to use the telephone to obtain information about applicants. In the long run the telephone generally proves to be less expensive than sending out letters of inquiry (or reference blanks) since it saves time and response is more certain. Further, the employer is more likely to get honest appraisals since the reference will speak more frankly over the telephone than he will write.

Conclusions — The employment interview and the application blank are almost universally used selection devices wherever people are employed be it in a business, industry, government, or social organization. Interviewing has not been, nor is it, a scientifically accurate means of selecting employees. Much progress has been made in recent years, however, in developing interviewing procedures designed to pick better employees. Persons who interview applicants must have job information (usually in the form of a job specification) before they can select a given applicant for a particular job.

In employment interviewing there is often a preliminary interview (rail) to weed out unpromising candidates. Candidates are eliminated during this interview on such factors as: (1) physical disabilities; (2) inadequate education, training, or experience; (3) age; (4) inappropriate personality.[20] Those not eliminated are given a full interview. Persons selected for specific types of work are sent from this interview to departmental interviews with supervisors or managers. If finally accepted in these departments, induction interviews are generally given. If the employee leaves the firm, a termination interview may be given. Employment interviewing embraces selecting, inducting, placing, and terminating.

Employment interviewing may be done by a panel (committee or board) of persons. The employee can be tested in the areas represented by the panel members. The panel would generally be made up of persons from the line or staff department where the applicant proposes to work, from the personnel department, and from line management. The panel can give the applicant information about the company and the field of work in which he is interested; further, the several viewpoints of panel members would presumably be better than the viewpoint of one interviewer. One study, however, has found that the panel interview showed no superiority over the individual interview. Role playing was about equally successful with the interviewing procedures. A small job management problem used as a selection device in the study showed little promise for predictive effectiveness. A group discussion problem showed up in this particular study as perhaps the most promising of the selection instruments used. In this group discussion, comparable evaluation of four candidates at a time was enabled.[21]

Employment letters, i.e., application, introduction, and recommendation, have been given brief discussion in this chapter. Most students have the opportunity to study these letter forms at length in other college courses.

PROJECTS

1. If you completed the Project 2 assignment given in Chapter XI, use the information prepared in that assignment and write a two-part letter of application for the position for which you wrote your "self-analysis." If the assignment was not done, find an advertisement in the daily newspaper for a person to fill a position for which you are qualified. Write a two-part letter of application for this position. Attach the advertisement by tape at the bottom of the letter.

2. Simulate an employment interview using four characters: an interviewer, a receptionist, an applicant who does everything wrong (chews gum, is seated before being asked, interrupts, asks "What I would like to know is about the salary," is dressed wrong, and so on), an applicant who does everything as nearly correctly as possible (is dressed appropriately, is reserved, waits for questions, asks for information when given an opportunity).

ACKNOWLEDGMENTS AND REFERENCES

1 Scott, Walter Dill, "The Scientific Selection of Salesmen," *Advertising and Selling*, Vol. 25, 1915, pp. 5–6, 94ff.
2 Hollingworth, H. L., *Vocational Psychology and Character Analysis*, D. Appleton & Co., New York, 1923, pp. 115–119.
3 Uhrbrock, Richard Stephen, "The Personnel Interview," *Management of the Personnel Function*, edited by I. L. Heckmann and S. G. Huneryager, Charles E. Merrill Books, Inc., Columbus, Ohio, 1962, p. 542.
4 Jucius, Michael, *Personnel Management*, Fourth Edition, Richard D. Irwin, Inc., Homewood, Illinois, 1959, pp. 219–223.
   Uhrbrock, *op. cit.*, pp. 530–531.
   Hepner, Harry Walker, *Psychology Applied to Life and Work*, Prentice-Hall, Inc., Englewood Cliffs, New Jersey, 1957, pp. 298–301.
   Bingham, Walter Van Dyke, and Moore, Bruce Victor, *How To Interview*, Harper & Brothers, Publishers, New York, 1941.
   Fear, Richard A., *The Evaluation Interview*, McGraw-Hill Book Company, Inc., New York, 1958, p. 102ff.
5 ———, "College Graduates and Industry . . . Is the Honeymoon Over?," *The Management Review*, American Management Association, Inc., 1515 Broadway, Times Square, New York 36, N. Y., Vol. XLVII, No. 2, February, 1958, pp. 45–47.
6 Husband, Richard W., "What Do College Grades Predict?," *Fortune*, Vol. LV, No. 6, June, 1957, pp. 157–158.
7 ———, *Monroe Manual of Procedure for Employing and Training Sales Personnel*, Monroe Calculating Machine Company, Inc., General Offices, Orange, New Jersey.
8 Adams, Loyce, "A Study of Sales Training Programs in Eighty-eight Firms," a dissertation, The University of Texas, Austin, 1959, (University Microfilms, Inc., 313 N. First St., Ann Arbor, Michigan), p. 104ff.
9 Uhrbrock, *op. cit.*, p. 530.
10 Hepner, *op. cit.*, pp. 288–290.
11 Thornton, G. R., "Effects of Wearing Glasses Upon Judgments of Traits," *Journal of Applied Psychology*, American Psychological Association, Inc., Vol. 28, No. 3, June, 1944, p. 207.
12 Uhrbrock, *op. cit.*, p. 538.
13 Siegel, Laurence, *Industrial Psychology*, Richard D. Irwin, Inc., Homewood, Illinois, 1962, p. 95.
   McMurry, R. N., "Validating the Patterned Interview," *Personnel*, American Management Association, Vol. XXIII, No. 4, 1947, pp. 270–271.
14 Hovland, C. I., and Wonderlic, E. F., "Prediction of Success from a Standardized Interview," *Journal of Applied Psychology*, Volume XXXIII, 1939, pp. 537–546.
15 Yonge, K. A., "The Value of the Interview: An Orientation and a Pilot Study," *Journal of Applied Psychology*, Vol. XL, 1956, pp. 25–31.
16 Moyer, N. A., "Non-directive Employment Interviewing," *Personnel*, Vol. XXIV, No. 5, March, 1948, pp. 383–387.

17 Ordway, Samuel H., Jr., and O'Brien, James C., *An Approach to More Objective Tests*, Society for Personnel Administration, Washington, D. C., Pamphlet No. 2, June, 1939.
18 Fraser, John Munro, "New-Type Selection Boards in Industry," *Occupational Psychology*, 1947, Vol. 21, pp. 170–178.
19 ———, *The Exit Interview*, Policyholders' Service Bureau Group Insurance Division, Metropolitan Life Insurance Company, 1942, p. 18.
20 Fear, *op. cit.*, p. 17.
21 Glaser, Robert, Schwarz, Paul A., and Flanagan, John C., "The Contribution of Interview and Situational Performance Procedures to the Selection of Supervisory Personnel," *Journal of Applied Psychology*, Vol. 42, No. 2, April, 1958, pp. 69–73.

CHAPTER XIII

TESTS USED IN EMPLOYING

Extent to Which Employment Tests Are Used — The wide employment of tests by the Armed Forces in order that better use of abilities of members might be made is one of the factors that has led to increased use of tests in business and industry. In some cases, it is probable that tests may have been used too extensively. Further, too much reliance has often been placed upon them. Daniel M. Goodacre, III, Training and Personnel Research, the B. F. Goodrich Company, warns against utilizing tests in selecting employees unless there is evidence that the tests have been used successfully in selecting persons for similar work. A sales-selection test that came to a Goodrich sales training supervisor was accompanied by a manual that was filled with statistics but offered no evidence the test had been successfully used to select salesmen. Goodacre recalls a warning of the American Psychological Association made some years ago: A test should be accompanied by a manual describing how to interpret the test and indicating the relationship between test scores and job performance measures.[1]

Erik E. Roos and Charles A. Dailey also warn against putting too much faith on psychological tests. They say that such tests should be used as aids but not as substitutes for managerial decisions based on numerous factors. Instead of depending too much on tests, a prospect's work history should be studied and evaluated properly. Seeming stability may show up to be lack of initiative. Frequent job changes may on the surface seem bad; study may show there was reason behind them. Demonstrable sales enthusiasm is "a must" for salesmen. Further, men who are to sell the company, its products, policies, and practices, must not be "yes-men." They must be able to defend their convictions. An interview of a prospective salesman should find what his attitudes to previous positions are. When he gives his likes and dislikes he will reveal perhaps whether or not he has been carrying his part or has merely been a "free rider." Applicants themselves can point out their own strengths and weaknesses if given the opportunity.[2]

In spite of the fact that there are many warnings not to depend solely upon tests in selecting applicants for positions, tests are a widely employed device. Properly used they justify the costs of testing in business offices, factories, and schools. In 1956 Bernreuter's Personality Inventory was said to be selling over one million copies a year, over a thousand different tests were being published, and it was estimated that three-fourths of all business and industrial corporations were using tests in selecting and upgrading employees.[3]

In a given year the Psychological Corporation supplies 400,000 clerical job applicant tests to firms ranging from banks to laundries, and it assists from 150-200 firms in evaluating higher-level employees for promotion or transfer. Science Research Associates tests thousands of persons for its approximately 11,000 clients. The Civil Service gives around 5,000,000 tests annually; the United States Army annually tests thousands of draftees and volunteers with special proficiency tests that aim at covering each of some 800 types of jobs for enlisted men.[4] One study found that of practically all of the giant companies, over half of the large ones, and at least one out of four of the companies employing 250 or fewer persons have testing programs.[5]

Industrial Psychology, Inc., Tucson, Arizona, advertises that 3,000 companies use the Job-Tests Program to: select better employees, reduce personnel, reduce employee turnover, increase productivity and quality, rate employee performance objectively, decrease supervisory problems, make objective audits of personnel, increase employee morale, and lessen manpower requirements. The firm offers tests for various types of clerical, mechanical, sales, technical, and supervisory jobs.

Many testing firms aid business, industry, and higher educational institutions in selecting employees and students. Many of the business and industrial firms conduct their own testing programs. The Educational Testing Service of Princeton, New Jersey, which administers the Graduate Record Examinations for persons who wish to do graduate work, is the largest producer of school tests. The research division of this large testing service, supported by the Carnegie Corporation, made a recent study (1962) using fifty-three judges to grade essay examinations. The correlation between grades given was .31. There was some correlation in mechanics and wording but zero correlation in form and flavor and a minus .02 correlation to "ideas," the four categories in which grades were given. It was concluded that there is currently no satisfactory way to test either by objective or essay examination for three components of good writing: form, flavor, and ideas. One's record of achievement still stands as the best test that can be employed in writing or other creative areas.

The extensive use of testing and the great variety of tests available for testing programs are reflected in the various editions of the widely used mental measurements yearbooks. The last edition of these is: Buros, Oscar Krisen (editor), *The Fifth Mental Measurements Yearbook,* The Gryphon Press, Highland Park, New Jersey, 1959.

Kinds of Tests and Examinations Used — Traditionally, tests have been classified many ways: written vs. oral; subjective vs. objective; prognostic (testing to predict success, aptitude) vs. diagnostic (to find or analyze deficiencies or reasons for difficulties or failure); group vs. individual; informal vs. standardized; performance vs. paper-and-pencil; speed vs. power. Tests in business and industrial firms are generally classified according to purpose, as, intelligence, aptitude, interest, personality, skill, knowledge and/or achievement. These tests may be paper-and-pencil tests, oral, or performance. They may be speed or power tests. Some tests measure speed while some are designed to measure ability to cope with increasingly difficult problems; most tests, however, measure both speed and power. Most of the paper-and-pencil tests are objective, that is, they would be scored the same by any grader. The objective tests are generally made up of true-false, multiple-choice, completion, and matching questions. A variation of the true-false test is the yes-no.

A *standardized* test is one in which both the testing procedure and the content of the test have been prescribed and fixed so that persons who are tested at different places and times may be compared on the basis of test scores. Conditions for administering and scoring the test are prescribed; generally *norms* or standards of normal performance have been established in order that results of the test may be evaluated against these. A *norm* is a score that is average or typical for a given test when used with a specified population.

A person's *percentile rank* on a given test indicates the percentage of scores that lie below the score made by this person. A percentile rank of 66, for instance, means that 66 per cent fall below this score.

INTELLIGENCE TESTS — As stated in Chapter II, *intelligence* has been variously defined as being ability to adjust to the environment and as ability to learn, although there is no unique definition of the term. The first intelligence test was administered by Alfred Binet in 1905. During World War I, the United States Army used the Alpha and Beta tests for general intelligence. Out of the vast accumulation of data from testing done by the Army came the occupational hierarchy of intelligence. Accountants, writers, teachers, lawyers (professional people) headed the list on intelligence test scores; draftsmen, clerk-typists, radio repairmen (technical workers) made the next highest scores; the third group, according to test scores made, was composed of the persons whose jobs called for less skill; the common laborers were at the bottom of the scale. Each group, however, did overlap with preceding groups.

Out of the early use of intelligence tests has come the vast numbers of tests used today. Nevertheless, even the intelligence test is not as yet a perfected device. Some persons argue that since utilization of intelligence depends upon the extent to which one employs the intellectual capacity he possesses, the intelligence test should also include a test of drive, incentive, or motivation. There are others who think that while these things should not be ignored in assessing the individual's total abilities, the testing device would not be successful if it attempted to measure both the intellectual and nonintellectual traits without differentiating between the two.[6]

Thorndike divided intelligence into three types: social (ability in dealing with people); concrete (ability to deal with things such as apparatuses of trades and science); abstract (verbal and mathematical ability). Abstract intelligence is the type tested by most intelligence tests, and it is heavily weighted even on the tests especially designed to discover social and concrete intelligence.[7] Thorndike's intelligence test (CAVD test) measured four areas of abstract ability by testing for: sentence completion, arithmetical reasoning, vocabulary, and ability to follow directions. Thurstone used statistical analysis to find the following primary mental abilities or aptitudes that relate to each other: memory, number, perceptual, reasoning, spatial, verbal, and word fluency.[8] Work on identifying mental abilities continues, and it is realized that the many special aptitudes that can be isolated encompass particular mental abilities. The intelligence test must be considered a specialized form of aptitude test.

The test of abstract intelligence is probably the most widely employed of the various selection tests used by business and industry. Generally, however, this test should be supplemented by other tests. It shows a certain kind of capacity only; it does not show knowledge or skills possessed; it does not show interest in a given field of work; it does not show initiative, creative ability, or drive; it does not reveal peculiarities of personality; it does not show mechanical aptitudes. For some types of work, however, a given level of abstract intelligence is desirable, and a test of abstract intelligence enables elimination of persons who fail to possess that given level. It is also possible for persons to have too much intelligence for given types of occupations to be challenging to them. As a result they become bored, do poor work, have accidents because they are not concentrating on the job at hand, or resign making it necessary to bear the expense of recruiting again. The intelligence test can reveal persons who have too much as well as too little capacity for certain jobs. A firm that takes only those persons who possess high intelligence test scores will find that it has too many managers and too few workers.

Many firms have evolved their own mental aptitude tests. Some of the most used of the standard intelligence tests are:

Otis Self-Administering Tests of Mental Ability, Arthur S. Otis and Thomas N. Barrows, and Otis Quick-Scoring Mental Ability Tests, Arthur S. Otis, World Book Company, Yonkers-on-Hudson, New York, and Chicago, Illinois.

Wechsler-Bellevue Intelligence Scale, David Wechsler, Psychological Corporation, 522 Fifth Avenue, New York 8, N. Y.

Revised Stanford-Binet Scale, Lewis M. Terman and Maud A. Merrill, Houghton-Mifflin Co., New York.

Wonderlic Personnel Tests (Forms D and F are adaptations of the Otis test) of Mental Ability Higher Form, Wonderlic Personnel Test Company.

Thurstone Test of Mental Alertness (Revised Edition), Thelma Gwinn Thurstone and L. L. Thurstone, Science Research Associates, Chicago.

In some instances the longer intelligence tests have been shortened without much loss in effectiveness of the tests. Through a method called Manifest Structure Analysis the 75-item Otis S-A Test of Mental Ability, Higher Examination: Form B was shortened to twenty items (1958). The testing time was shortened from thirty minutes to eight minutes. Correlation between scores made on the long and short forms was .72 for the standardized sample; cross-validation (defined later) resulted in a correlation of .82 between the scores obtained on the long and short forms. Manifest Structure Analysis is based on probability of certain response patterns occurring at specified levels, ranks, or scores.[9]

The Wonderlic Personnel Test is a short group test of mental ability which was designed for industrial testing use. It is available in five alternate forms, A, B, D, E, and F. Each test has fifty test items and requires twelve minutes to take. Forms D, E, and F were developed from the Otis S-A Test. Forms A and B were developed by Wonderlic. Five-hundred-and-ninety male applicants for apprenticeship programs in a large manufacturing company were broken into five groups of 118 to a group. Each of these five groups was given one of the forms of the Wonderlic Personnel Test. This study, reported in 1959, revealed that Form B of the Personnel Test was more difficult than the other forms. Results from Forms B and F differed from each other, and the difference could not be attributed to difference in educational level by test form. The researchers recommended that Form B not be considered directly equivalent to the other four forms of the test, and further that Form D not be considered as equivalent to Form F in industrial testing situations similar to the one in their study. The findings of this research are significant since Wonderlic has suggested that Forms A and B or D and F might be the best combinations to use when two forms of the test are to be used.[10]

The various factors which introduce biases into intelligence tests have concerned psychologists for some time. One of these factors has been socioeconomic status. The Lowry Reasoning Test Combination in an effort to eliminate such bias used stimulus materials common to all status groups. The test was found by one group of researchers to be relatively free of social status bias and to measure the intellectual function. They reported that it is easy to score and administer and that it does not depend on a high level of verbal ability. It consists of two sets of twenty-five questions each.[11]

THE APTITUDE TEST — *Aptitude* has been defined as being "a condition or set of characteristics regarded as symptomatic of an individual's ability to acquire with training some (usually specified) knowledge, skill, or set of responses, such as the ability to speak a language, to produce music. . . ." This is a broad definition that does not assume aptitudes to be inherited or that people are born possessing them. Aptitudes must properly be considered, however, to be the result of "the interaction of heredity and environment." [12]

An aptitude test measures knowledge, skill, ability, or other characteristics that indicate a person can successfully (or unsuccessfully) learn or learn to do certain things. It is a prognostic test, one that can predict a given type of learning. Aptitude tests may encompass testing for aptitudes (ability to learn) physics, chemistry, engineering, foreign language, medicine, dentistry, arithmetic, law, clerical work, music, success in school or college, selling, accounting. There are also aptitude tests that test for manual dexterity and mechanical aptitudes.

In studying the relationship between ability, interest, and aptitude, one researcher concluded that aptitude is a joint function of ability and interest and that predicting success over a relatively long period of time depends much more on interest than ability; further, predicting success over a relatively short period of time depends much more on ability than on interest. If aptitude actually is a joint function of interest and ability, it must also then be a function of the time interval to be used for determining success.[13]

Jack Klein of the Klein Institute for Aptitude Testing, New York, has estimated that ninety per cent of the applicants for sales jobs are tested in some way before being hired. His firm tests, reports, and interprets the results of tests for many clients. Charges for these services may run from $20 to $150 per person selected depending upon the kind of employee being selected. The Kendall Company and Lily Tulip Cup Corporation started with Klein over twenty years ago and still use the services of the testing firm. Klein compares the factors that are important in hiring a a man to a three-legged stool: history, interview, tests. The stool needs all three legs to stand. He recommends that tests be given only to persons a firm would want to hire, that is, the firm should select the employee as if there were not to be tests. Then he is tested; the test merely confirms or refutes prior judgment. Klein believes that the future of aptitude testing will bring in more testing of creative abilities. Tests will be contrived to determine a person's ability to produce new product ideas, or show specific specialization aptitudes.[14] Testing for aptitude in life insurance selling has long been successful.

From Table XIII-1 it will be seen that in a study made by the writer it was found that the intelligence test is used more than any other in selection of salesmen. Other tests used by thirty-five to forty of the eighty-eight companies are: personality, interest, vocabulary or verbal, arithmetic or number, and emotional stability. Memory and speech were used by relatively few of the companies. Miscellaneous tests listed as being used include: mental alertness, sales senses, test by Walter V. Clark Associates (Activity Vector Analysis), field test (canvassing), practical judgment, Klein, mechanical comprehension, social intelligence, tests by Verne Steward and Associates (California). Tests are a widely used selection device but in no case in the study of eighty-eight firms were they found to

TABLE XIII-1[15]

NUMBER AND PERCENTAGE OF 65 OUT OF 88 FIRMS
USING TESTS IN SELECTING SALES TRAINEES
AND TYPES OF TESTS USED BY THESE FIRMS

Firms and Tests	Number	Per Cent of 65	Per Cent of 88
Firms Using One or More Tests	65	100.00	73.86
Personality Tests	40	61.54	45.45
Aptitude Tests	49	75.38	55.68
Interests Tests	37	56.92	42.05
Memory Tests	7	10.77	7.96
Speech Tests	5	7.69	5.68
Intelligence Tests	54	83.08	61.36
Vocabulary or Verbal Tests	36	55.38	40.91
Arithmetic or Number Tests	36	55.38	40.91
Emotional Stability Tests	35	53.85	39.77
Miscellaneous Tests	10	15.38	11.36

be depended upon solely. They are considered supplementary to the various other techniques and devices employed in selection.

Metropolitan Life Insurance Company uses the following tests: *aptitude index* (which indicates the probable success an applicant will have selling life insurance); *learning aptitude test* (which shows the applicant's learning ability); *accounting aptitude* (which tells about the applicant's potential ability in accounting). The correlation between success in selling insurance in 1954-1955 and the learning aptitude test (Kuder-Richardson Formula 21) was high. For Form A of the test it was .88, and for Form B it was .94. Other tests were not found to have such a high degree of validity, but there was positive correlation in these areas also. (See Table XIII-2.)

A number of aptitude tests have been found to be predictors of selling success or failure. One of these is the J. J. Berliner & Staff Aptitude Test

TABLE XIII-2[16]

METROPOLITAN LIFE INSURANCE COMPANY
ONE MADISON AVENUE, NEW YORK 10, N. Y.
AGENCY SELECTION TEST SCORES

————————————————————District

Re Agency Applicant————————————————————————————
　　　　　　　　　　　(Last)　　　　　　(First)　　　　　(Middle)

AGENCY SELECTION TEST SCORES—SCORES range from 9 (distinctly superior) to 1 (distinctly inferior). A score of 5 is average.

————— The Aptitude Index score indicates the probable success an applicant will have selling life insurance. The table on the back ————[next page] shows the first twelve-month production record of Agents in each score group.

—————The Metropolitan Learning Aptitude Test score shows the applicant's learning ability. The table on the back [next page] —————shows the percentage of Agents expected to be above average in Agency Training Center final examinations in each score group.

—————The Metropolitan Accounting Aptitude Test score tells about the Applicant's potential ability in accounting. The table on the —————back [next page] shows the percentage of Agents expected to be above average in accounting performance in each score group.

An Asterisk (*) in the Aptitude Index box Above indicates that we are unable to score the Aptitude Index answer sheet which the applicant failed to complete correctly. We will be able to give you an Aptitude Index score when the applicant has completed the items listed below:

Part I ————————————————— Part II —————————————————
　　　　　　　(There should be just one mark in each row and column.)
　　　　　　　Research Section Field Training Division.

TABLE XIII-2
(*Continued*)

SELLING APTITUDE

Twelve-Month Record for Agents Appointed in 1954 and 1955

Aptitude Index Score Group	Number of Agents per Group	Average Honor Club Points*	Average Ordinary Placed
9	228	1,664	$168,368
8	354	1,698	167,011
7	526	1,594	158,053
6	613	1,526	148,352
5	598	1,404	131,716
4	405	1,276	118,620
3	209	1,280	124,038
2	68	1,317	117,328
1	31	1,056	103,129

The average Ordinary Placed per man per month in 1955 was $11,728 or $140,736 on an annual basis. The average Honor Club Points in 1955 was 1,464 per Agent.

*Group and arrears points excluded.

LEARNING APTITUDE

Percentage of Agents Expected to be Above Average in Agency Training Center Final Examination for Each Score Group.

Metropolitan Learning Aptitude Score Group	Percentage
9	89
8	82
7	73
6	62
5	50
4	38
3	27
2	18
1	11

ACCOUNTING APTITUDE

Percentage of Agents Expected to be Above Average in Accounting for Each Score Group.

Metropolitan Accounting Aptitude	Percentage
9	80
8	74
7	66
6	58
5	50
4	42
3	34
2	26
1	20

for Salesmen. In one study empathy test scores for thirty-two automobile salesman were found to be significant predictors of sales records. The test scores were even more highly significant predictors of job success of sales crew members as ranked by their sales managers.[17] Any test, however, may be helpful or harmful according to whether it is properly used or not. Whether achievement, intelligence or differential aptitude tests should be used depends on the functions to be served.[18] "The Aptitude Index," issued by the Life Insurance Sales Research Bureau, Hartford, Connecticut, has been successfully used in selecting salesmen.

The use of aptitude testing for selection of executive trainees (or executives) has sometimes been questioned. In an experiment by *Fortune*, reported in 1954, fourteen company presidents and board chairmen, twelve brilliant scientists, and twenty-nine middle management people who had been selected for advanced-management training, took tests including Thurstone Temperament and the Test of Practical Judgment, and in the case of the presidents, board chairman, and scientists, the personal audit. It was found that not one corporation president came completely within the "acceptable" range. They got only half of the answers on "How Supervise" questions right, and they did poorly on the employee-relations questions. Over half of the scientists fell under the twentieth percentile for sociability. Middle management people scored badly on practical judgment, but they did well on sociability and stability. Eight of the forty-three management men were between the fortieth and sixtieth percentiles on sociability and the others were at the extremes, making a median figure somewhat meaningless. Some of the people who received high "steadiness" scores on the personal audit scored poorly on the Thurstone "stability" scale. Many of those who scored high on "contentment" also had low "tranquility" scores.[19]

This is only one of the many reports on tests that have indicated that selection of executives on the basis of tests alone may tend to eliminate the very persons who have the drive and initiative to excel in reaching managerial positions. Some of the factors needed for managerial efficiency may be detected through testing. Certainly it may hold true, as has often been said about testing in general, that while tests do not pick the man who will succeed, they do help to eliminate persons who might fail. In the case of executives, the tests evidently might also eliminate some who would succeed. In some areas such as mechanical, clerical, and selling aptitudes, excellent results have been obtained through using tests. One reason for weaknesses of tests in selecting executives is the difficulty of measuring drive, creative ability, ability to organize and initiate activities, and consideration for others. Under the discussion of personality tests the personalty test developed by Stevenson, Jordan, and Harrison for appraising management personnel and called "Employee Questionnaire" is discussed.

Tests which have been successfully used in determining motor and manual abilities encompass the following areas: manual dexterity, mechanical aptitude, auditory acuity, visual acuity, color vision, and clerical ability. Some of the tests available in these areas are:

Purdue Mechanical Performance Test

Test of Mechanical Comprehension, G. K. Bennett and others, Psychological Corporation, New York

Prognostic Test of Mechanical Abilities, California Test Bureau, Los Angeles

MacQuarrie Test for Mechanical Ability, T. W. MacQuarrie, California Test Bureau, Los Angeles

Minnesota Clerical Test

Revised Minnesota Paper Formboard, Psychological Corporation, New York

Stromberg Dexterity Test, Psychological Corporation, New York

General Clerical Test, Psychological Corporation, New York

The Psychological Corporation of New York and the Central Electronic Company of Chicago have introduced testing machines for finding computer programmers and electronic equipment trouble-shooters. The machines present a series of logical problems that become increasingly complex. A display panel with buttons and lights indicating various relationships is used. The testee's record in solving problems through pressing buttons reveals his method of investigation, ability to organize complex information, speed, and reactions to making errors. These machines may have value for testing engineers, salesmen, and executives.[20]

THE INTEREST TEST — Early interest tests attempted to find interests that were characteristic of certain groups, as: scientists, philosophers, businessmen, poets, artists, musicians, social workers, politicians, diplomats, clergymen and so on. The Allport-Vernon Scale of Values (1931) was one such test. Closely akin to the interest tests are those that measure attitudes, such as prejudice, trust, tolerance, and so on. The Kuder Preference Test and the Strong Vocational Interest Blank are the two tests discussed in Chapter XI as being most successful in aiding young people (generally high school seniors and college students) to find the fields in which they would be most likely to be successful according to interests. The nearer an individual is to employment age, the more valid are the scores on these tests for predictive purposes. Interest tests do not, however, indicate that a person possesses the aptitude (mental ability, especially) to succeed in a given field. They show that the testee likes, dislikes, and is indifferent to the same things that persons who are already successful in certain fields like, dislike, and are indifferent to.

Research done at the Industrial Relations Center of the University of Minnesota measured interests of Air Force Officers using the Strong VIB. The evidence gathered brought conclusion that measured interests should receive increased emphasis as a factor in military selection and classification procedures for Air Force officer specialists. Interest tests, supplemented by other tests, are an effective device for use in selecting employees.[21]

THE PERSONALITY TEST — As stated in Chapter IV, personality is difficult to define. It is made up of both mental and biological factors and these in turn interact with the environment. First attempts at evaluating personality were made through using rating scales that attempted to determine whether a person was ascendant or submissive, extrovert or introvert. The Allport A-S Reaction Study, G. W. and F. H. Allport, Houghton Mifflin Company, New York, was one such scale. More recently the Adjustment Inventory, Hugh M. Bell, Stanford University Press, California, has been widely used. This test checks on home, health, social, emotional, and occupational adjustment.

Other personality tests:

> Minnesota Multiphasic Personality Inventory, S. R. Hathaway and J. C. McKinley, Psychological Corporation, New York
> Guilford-Zimmerman Temperament Survey, J. P. Guilford and W. S. Zimmerman, Sheridan Supply Co., Beverly Hills, California
> Bernreuter Personality Inventory, Stanford University Press, California

The Activity Vector Analysis published by Walter V. Clarke Associates, Inc., was found in one study of 522 male agents (1958) to be valid for predicting success-failure among life insurance agents. When this measure is combined with personal history measures that have been found to be valid predictors of success-failure among life insurance agents a higher degree of success in prediction is obtained. Aggression and social confidence are characteristics needed for success in life insurance selling. Among the personal history variables, age alone could be used to predict failure; applicants below twenty-five or more than forty-five years of age are not likely to succeed in selling life insurance over a sustained period of time. A cross-validity study of 97 successful agents and 438 unsuccessful ones (1961) upheld the findings of the first study.[22] Some studies have shown that the time element, that is time spent in taking tests, may be significant for measuring personality.

The Humm-Wadsworth Temperament Scale consists of 318 items. The choice of "Yes" or "No" for 164 of these items is considered to indicate the existence of seven personality components: normal (N), hysteroid (H), manic (M), depressive (D), artistic (A), paranoid (P), and epileptoid (E). The scale was standardized by testing people already employed who had nothing to lose by the test. When it was tried on applicants it was found to bring more "No" answers than it had during the standardizing period. Despite the fact that there is provision for correction for this, the research done by Smith and Marke (who first tested 24 persons in an applicant situation and then two other groups of 33 and 35 and compared with a Swedish group of 978 job applicants) led them to conclude that even if corrected for "no-count" test profiles from the H-W test "often include too many uncertainties to be accepted as indicative of a person's temperament." Since this conclusion might also apply to the other questionnaires where persons rate themselves, the investigators suggest that more projective techniques or "more rigorous experimental procedures" should be used for personality testing.[23] Smith and Marke followed up their study of the H-W Scale to determine whether or not the lack of consistency found in their study was due to choice of subjects and found that it was not. Rather they concluded, after using the scale on 508 male applicants for industrial work, that lack of consistency was due to "vague or ambiguous definitions of the components; the clumsy manner in which several items, otherwise often acceptable, were formulated; a frequently recurring moralistic bias distorting the neutral, exploratory aim of the inventory; and, last of all, the uncritical empiricism which guided the choice of items for the scale and allowed no further revisions." [24]

Projective testing techniques have been successful in testing personality. The term *projection* means unconsciously attributing ideas, wishes, attitudes, feelings, or characteristics to other persons or objects. One's own needs or faults may be attributed to others. (See definition in Chapter VI.) In a projective test a person reveals his own motives and personality through projecting upon the test situation, without being aware that he is doing so, his own needs, values, perceptions, and feelings. The Rorschach Ink Blot Test is thought to reveal motives, abilities, and personality. This and other projective tests are used in the specialized field of marketing and advertising research known as "motivation research." As techniques of motivation research, these tests are discussed in Chapter XXII. The techniques of using and interpreting the tests are different as between personality and motivation research testing; nevertheless, the character of the testing is essentially the same. For employment testing purposes, the projective tests are probably chiefly valuable for giving clues to be followed up in the interview.

One projective-type test recently devised for personality testing employs a picture that is exposed by steps. Subjects make sketchy drawings of what they have seen and write short comments. The test has enabled discovery of repression, isolation, denial, reaction-formation, identification with the aggressor, and turning against the self. It is called "Defense Mechanism Test" and is administered to groups.[25]

Meyer and others have made extensive studies of management personnel to determine personality characteristics and how these are related to success in the management hierarchy, to education, and to age. Meyer and Pressel made the first study on 459 cases (1949-1952); the second study was made by Meyer and Fredian on 678 cases (1955-1957).

The Employee Questionnaire, a personality test developed and used by Stevenson, Jordan & Harrison in personnel appraisals was used for these studies (EQ-B for the first; EQ-C for the second). Seven scales of the EQ-B were: objectivity, social dominance, social extroversion, drive, detail, emotionality, and adjustment (poor). EQ-C was made up of these seven plus nine others: social consideration, judgment and decision, adjustment somatic, psychopathic tendencies, drive persistence, recognition anxiety, personal achievement motivation, compensatory achievement motivation, and independent achievement motivation. "Drive" was modified to "drive irritability."

A study of Table XIII-3 will show that independent achievement was most marked in the upward hierarchy trend of the EQ-C scales (with no reversals at any of the six hierarchy levels), and it was significant at the .001 level. Detail (downward trend) and social dominance (upward trend) were the second and third most marked scale trends. Other management hierarchy studies also show ascending social dominance and descending detail scores. Judgment and decision (upward), recognition anxiety (downward), and drive irritability (downward) were fourth, fifth, and sixth most marked trend scales. Other scales presented in Table XIII-3 had slight hierarchy trends.

Only four of the scales used on the EQ-C test did not have observable trends: objectivity, social extroversion, drive persistence, and compensatory achievement motivation. The greatest difference in hierarchy trend findings between the original study (data for which are not presented here) and the second study was in the failure of the top hierarchy group to follow the hierarchy trends. In all twelve hierarchy trend scales, excepting independent achievement motivation, the Level I average was a reversal of the trends established at the other levels. There were no such reversals for Level I in the first study.

Education trends in the second study were more marked than in the first study, probably because graduate training and grade school and two years of high school were added in the second study. Excepting detail and the scales that did not have trends for age, the trends for education were opposite those for age. The researchers offer as a possible reason for the hierarchy reversals at Level I the fact that on the average people in Level I have somewhat less education that those in Level II, but they have a higher age; thus the reversal of the actual education trend and the continuation of the actual age trend might account for the reversals in hierarchy trends at Level I.[26]

THE ACHIEVEMENT TEST — Achievement tests attempt to find out how much knowledge has been acquired in a given area, or to what degree certain skills and techniques have been acquired. For educational purposes tests are given to determine achievement ages at various grade levels. The EQ (education quotient) or AQ (achievement quotient) may be obtained by testing to determine the educational or achievement age, and then EA or AA is divided by CA (chronological age) and multiplied by 100. EQ or AQ would normally be 100.

Achievement tests are available to test knowledge and/or skills acquired in vocabulary, spelling, reading, arithmetic, algebra, plane geometry, foreign languages, accounting, bookkeeping, shorthand, typewriting, adding machines, calculators, and in other areas. Two of the educational achievement tests are:

> Stanford Achievement Tests, T. L. Kelley, R. Madden, E. F. Gardner, L. M. Terman, and G. M. Ruch, World Book Company, Yonkers, N. Y.
>
> California Achievement Tests, E. W. Tiegs and W. W. Clark, California Test Bureau, Los Angeles.

Among the skill tests is the Seashore-Bennett Stenographic Proficiency Test consisting of letters to be taken from dictation and transcribed. Most firms, however, have made their own proficiency tests for selecting typists, stenographers, and secretaries. There is also the annual examination given by the Institute for Certifying Secretaries, a department of the National Secretaries Association. Secretaries who pass this examination, which covers achievement not only in specific shorthand and typewriting skills but in human relations, business, economics, accounting, and law receive the Certified Professional Secretary award. The CPA indicates degree of achievement in accounting and auditing; the CLU indicates achievement in insurance; there are many other such titles awarded on the basis of examination and indicating high degree of achievement in given areas of learning. Persons applying for jobs offer these titles and the certificates testifying to them as evidence of knowledge and skills acquired. Where no such titles are possessed, proficiency tests are frequently administered. In the field of selling, for instance, the performance test is used. In some cases the test is a trial period on the job.

TABLE XIII-3[27]

EQ-C TEST SCALE MEANS AND SIGMAS ACCORDING TO HIERARCHY LEVEL

	Hierarchy Level											
	I N=30		II N=44		III N=144		IV N=253		V N=78		VI N=129	
EQ-C Scale	M	SD	M	SD	M	SD	M	SD	M	SD	M	SD
Independent Achievement***	7.2	1.7	6.5	2.3	6.3	1.9	6.1	1.8	5.7	1.9	5.7	1.8
Detail***	5.1	1.2	4.6	1.2	4.9	1.6	5.5	1.6	5.8	1.2	5.9	1.5
Social Dominance***	6.5	2.1	6.5	1.9	6.5	1.9	6.2	1.9	5.6	2.1	5.5	1.9
Judgment and Decision**	6.0	1.6	6.9	1.5	6.7	1.6	6.4	1.7	6.3	1.6	6.0	1.7
Recognition Anxiety***	4.3	1.3	3.6	1.3	3.6	1.3	4.1	1.6	4.3	1.5	4.5	1.7
Drive Irritability**	4.7	1.4	3.7	1.8	4.1	1.6	4.3	1.5	4.5	1.4	4.5	1.5
Adjustment Psychological*	2.8	1.7	2.6	1.6	2.9	1.5	3.0	1.8	3.3	1.6	3.4	1.7
Social Extroversion**	7.5	2.0	7.4	2.1	7.7	2.2	8.0	1.9	7.1	2.3	7.4	2.0
Objectivity	5.7	2.1	6.1	2.7	6.3	1.9	6.0	2.4	5.9	2.3	5.7	2.1

*, **, and *** indicate, respectively, significance at the .05, .01, and .001 levels for a single classification F test.

TABLE XIII-4[28]

EQ-C TEST SCALE MEANS AND SIGMAS ACCORDING TO EDUCATION LEVEL

EQ-C Scale	Education Level											
	Graduate N=60		4 Years College N=189		2 Years College N=117		4 Years High School N=246		2 Years High School N=29		Grade School N=34	
	M	SD	M	SD	M	SD	M	SD	M	SD	M	SD
Independent Achievement	6.9	1.9	6.2	1.8	6.4	1.6	5.7	1.7	6.0	2.0	5.4	2.4
Detail	4.4	1.6	5.0	1.6	5.4	1.4	5.8	1.3	5.9	1.2	6.1	1.6
Social Dominance	6.9	1.9	6.6	1.4	6.4	1.7	5.6	2.0	6.2	1.9	5.0	1.7
Judgment and Decision	6.8	1.4	6.8	1.4	6.5	1.8	6.1	1.6	5.6	1.6	5.0	1.8
Recognition Anxiety	3.2	1.2	3.7	1.5	3.9	1.5	4.4	1.4	4.6	1.5	5.2	1.9
Drive Irritability	3.7	1.8	4.1	1.4	4.3	1.6	4.5	1.5	4.5	1.7	4.7	1.6
Adjustment Psychological	2.4	1.4	2.7	1.5	2.9	1.6	3.3	1.7	3.6	1.4	4.3	1.9
Social Extroversion	8.2	1.9	7.9	2.2	7.9	2.0	7.8	2.1	7.3	1.9	6.5	2.4
Objectivity	6.4	2.4	6.2	2.3	6.0	2.1	5.8	2.2	5.8	2.2	5.6	2.0

TABLE XIII-5[29]

EQ-C TEST SCALE MEANS ACCORDING TO AGE LEVEL

EQ-C Scale	Years 20–30 N=126 M	Years 30–40 N=318 M	Years 40–50 N=173 M	Years 50+ N=57 M
Independent Achievement	5.9	6.2	5.9	5.7
Details	5.7	5.3	5.1	5.7
Social Dominance	6.1	6.2	6.1	5.7
Judgment and Decision	6.5	6.4	6.3	6.1
Recognition Anxiety	4.1	3.9	4.1	4.4
Drive Irritability	4.3	4.3	4.3	4.3
Adjustment Psychological	2.8	3.0	3.1	3.4
Social Extroversion	7.7	7.8	7.6	7.1
Objectivity	5.8	6.1	6.1	5.3

THE MEDICAL EXAMINATION — Some companies maintain their own medical staffs for administering medical examinations at the time of employment. Such departments also examine employees who are returning from sick leaves or long vacations, and they check all employees periodically. In some instances, psychiatrists are maintained to check applicants. Companies that do not have their own medical staffs may send applicants to private practitioners. Types of examinations that may be required before employment include: (1) general physical and medical examination; (2) visual, auditory, and dental examinations; (3) examinations for communicable diseases; (4) psychiatric examinations; (5) and visits to the homes of applicants.

The Battery of Tests — As has been implied in the discussions of various types of tests used in employment, not just one test but several tests should be used in most cases. When several tests are used to get a more complete picture of an applicant's qualifications, these are called a *battery of tests*. A battery of tests given for supervisors, for instance, included the following:

1. Strong Vocational Interest Blank for Men
2. Kuder-Preference Record
3. Wonderlic Personnel Test
4. Classification Test for Industrial and Office Personnel
5. How Supervise
6. General Clerical Test
7. Test of Mechanical Comprehension
8. Guilford-Zimmerman Temperament Survey[30]

One recent study attempted to find the best tests for predicting success in supervisory training programs. Of the tests used the How Supervise? Scale (File & Remmers) predicted success best on total criteria used in the supervisory training program (r = .69). Multiple correlation between the three psychological tests and the total criteria was .77. The other two tests: Wonderlic and F Scale, a measure of authoritarian personality (Adorno, Frenkel-Brunswick, Levinson, and Sanford).[31]

In June, 1916, work on testing in the selection of salesmen was begun by psychologists on the staff of the Bureau of Salesmanship Research. One early battery of selection tests, first used primarily in insurance, but also used in other fields, is included in the Steward Personnel Appraisal System. This is made up of four tests (mental ability, personality, interest, traits). It includes also: a personal inventory of background factors which is really an application blank; a four-page folder containing hundreds of items in twelve categories, called "guide to appraisal decision"; a twelve-page manual containing instructions for the candidate to use in the completing of the tests and blanks; and a thirty-two-page manual designed to aid employers of sales people to make the best use of the completed tests and blanks.[32]

Two tests found to have value for differentiating levels of success among life insurance agents (study made in 1959) are: Sales Comprehension Test and Sales Motivation Inventory published by Martin M. Bruce in 1953.[33]

At a 1950 conference of the Texas Personnel and Management Association, Robert C. Behn of the Texas State Commission said that through studying extremely successful people in jobs his group had attempted to find test relationships to job success through eight steps: (1) job analysis, (2) selection of criteria, (3) selection of tests, (4) selection of sample and administration of tests to the sample, (5) statistical and analytical treatment of data, (6) establishment of test norms, (7) check studies at different points, (8) follow-up studies of both the individual on the job and his employer. Through these steps fifteen tests, eleven paper and pencil and four apparatus, had been built to test basic aptitudes including intelligence, verbal ability, numerical ability, space perception, form perception, clerical perception, aiming ability or eye-hand coordination, motor speed, manual dexterity, and finger dexterity. Behn stated that personality tests were not used in his work because they had not been shown to predict job success.[34] The United States Employment Service (USES) today uses a General Aptitude Test Battery (GATB) (Dvorak, 1956) which yields scores in the following nine areas: Intelligence (G), Verbal Aptitude (V), Numerical Aptitude (N), Spatial Aptitude (S), Form Perception (P), Clerical Perception (Q), Motor Coordination

(K), Finger Dexterity (F), Manual Dexterity (M). Goodacre of the B. F. Goodrich Company has highly recommended the General Aptitude Test Battery developed by the United States Employment Service as being "one of the most thorough aptitude test batteries available." Studies made by Goodrich show that valid psychological tests may be more easily developed for skilled workers than for managerial and supervisory personnel. For store managers, Goodrich tried the Wonderlic, PRI Classification, Allport-Vernon, Kuder, Strong, Guilford-Zimmerman, and Aptitude Associates Sales Aptitude tests. Goodacre reported that Goodrich met with little success in validating this battery. About all the store manager battery revealed was that the interests of store managers and undertakers are similar! The type of test in which applicants are subjected to situations similar to job requirements is suggested by Goodacre; he feels that situational testing might give results in selecting sales, supervisory, and managerial personnel.[35]

A test battery to determine potential ability to operate the IBM proof machine has been devised. High abstract numerical ability, numerical intelligence, and perceptual skill enable an operator to attain speed and accuracy in listing and to minimize lost time in solving problems related to the work. All three of the abilities assure a good operator; two of the abilities indicate that good performance can probably be counted on. The following test battery is recommended to have a very good selective efficiency and to increase production by about thirteen per cent (the only one of these tests that did not correlate significantly with the criterion was the vocabulary test):

The Short Employment Tests (SET)
Clerical Aptitude (CA-1)
Vocabulary (V-1)
Arithmetic (N-1), Psychological Corporation, New York
Hay Number Perception Test (Form A)
Hay Number Series Completion Test (Form B), Aptitude Test Service, Swarthmore, Pennsylvania[36]

Numbers of test batteries are available to determine manual dexterity. With so many industrial operations involving fine manipulative work, such as that on transistors, it is often necessary to distinguish ability to use the hands and make fine visual discriminations. Some tests have been especially designed to distinguish finger dexterity; one recent study, however, failed to separate the finger dexterity factor although it used tests that had previously been considered successful in this area.[37]

Science Research Associates of Chicago markets a battery of tests that attempt to determine the creative ability in scientists and engineers. It goes into background and working environment and includes a searching psychological examination. This set of tests requires sixteen hours to administer by a skilled person. It is highly expensive and relatively new.[38]

The Test Profile — Test results must be recorded in some form. The test profile is a graphic method of indicating test scores so that they can be interpreted quickly. Using the areas of testing covered by the USES Test Battery, the hypothetical profile for John Doe given here was constructed. It was assumed that test scores had been converted into percentile ranks. John Doe would probably not be employed for jobs requiring high degree of verbal and mathematical skill; he would probably do well on jobs requiring manual and finger dexterity and motor coordination, but this would depend upon the degree of ability required for a given job.

Factors in Selecting Tests — A test should be capable of being administered objectively, and it should not require so long to take that subjects would become bored and lose interest. The *population* on which the test was standardized should be stated in the manual provided with the test. The manual should state *norms* for the test in terms of percentile

ILLUSTRATION XIII-1

TEST PROFILE OF JOHN DOE

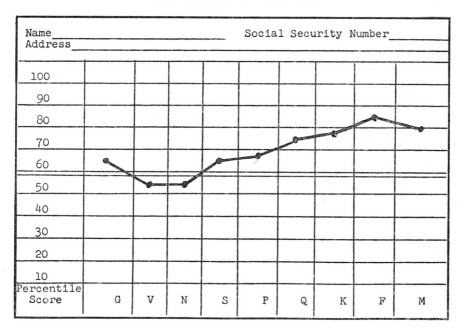

rank or standard score. For tests used in education the norms might be in terms of age or grade. As pointed out earlier in the chapter, the norm must be in terms of the typical score made by a given population on the test in question. *Percentile rank* has also been defined. *Decile rank* is sometimes used; it indicates the one-tenth part in which a tested person's score places him, as the top tenth, the bottom tenth, and so on. The *standard score* indicates the distance a particular score is from the mean in terms of standard deviation.

A test's *reliability* can be determined before it is used by a given firm in employment testing (reliability and validity were defined in Chapter XI). The *validity* of a test may be established before it is used in employing certain types of workers, as for instance certain manual dexterity tests may have proved valid in selecting workers for certain types of manual jobs. They would be valid for selecting a given firm's manual workers provided the same type of work is involved. Most firms check on the validity of tests by using them over a period of time and keeping data to show how successful they have been. One of the best ways of validating a test is to employ all applicants regardless of the scores they make on the test. The scores should be kept on record until a later date at which time some criterion of worker efficiency (merit rating, still on the job, output, and so on) should be correlated with the test scores. Validity of a battery of tests is determined by multiple correlation.

Tests are not of much value if they have a coefficient of validity that is less than .50, as the forecasting efficiency in such a case is only 13.4 per cent.[39]

The critical score is the point at which it would be better not to employ an applicant since persons making that score are more likely to fail than succeed on the job. This is obviously not an inflexible score as it might be raised or lowered depending upon the applicants available to fill vacancies and the abilities of those applicants as revealed by their test scores.

Cross-validation is concerned with finding out how good the best choice out of a number of possibilities really is. After statistical methods have been used to find the best tests to use in a battery of tests, cross validation on a new group of subjects should show how good the choice is. Just because a certain relationship held true for a given group, it should not be assumed that it would hold true for the next group. The second group should be a relevant sample of different people and the combination of tests and the scoring system used in experiments on the first group should be used unchanged on the second group.[40]

It is necessary also to watch the *weights* assigned to each part of the total on a single test or to each of several tests used. One way of determining the contributions made by the parts is to compare the correlations of the parts with the whole. If vocabulary, arithmetic, and checking on a clerical test give standard deviations of 8.0, 4.4, and 13.9 respectively and if a total score is used, checking has the greatest weight in the score. The simple total may give greater weight than should be given to a given part. It is possible to weight tests equally in a total by transforming raw scores on individual tests so that their standard deviations will be the same. At any rate, data should be examined to see that some parts of a test have not been over or under weighted.[41]

The Advantages of Using Tests — Perhaps the advantages of using tests have been implied throughout this chapter. Two tables are given here to show the results of a seven-year follow-up study made on persons who took the Differential Aptitude Tests in 1947. The areas tested were: Verbal Reasoning, Numerical Ability, Abstract Reasoning, Space Relations, Mechanical Reasoning, Clerical Speed and Accuracy, Spelling, and Grammar (Sentences). A study of Tables XIII-6 and XIII-7 will show how persons in various occupations ranked on the tests as compared to persons in other occupations. The reader can form his own conclusions as to the predictive value of various tests for different occupational fields.

Properly used, tests can predict success or failure in a given vocation. They can also be used to upgrade employees although it is estimated that only about ten per cent of the companies do use tests for upgrading.[42]

A Self-Development Activity program has been put into effect in a number of companies. It begins with a battery of standard tests and a twenty-page workbook of questions on relations between superiors and subordinates. A person who takes the test gets an analysis of himself. He can then take courses to increase abilities or attempt to make changes in his personality according to his desires. The Herrold organization prepares the tests and analyzes the results.[43]

Summary — Tests are widely used as a selection device in the giant and large companies. Smaller companies cannot always afford their own testing programs but are using testing centers that give certain standardized tests that have been validated for occupations of a general nature. Single tests are sometimes used; test batteries designed for specific occupations are more generally used. Tests are of little value unless reliability and validity have been established and unless some type of norm for a given population has been established. Types of tests used in employment are: intelligence (specialized intellectual aptitudes), aptitude, interest, personality, and achievement. Medical examinations are generally also given. Results of testing are recorded numerically, verbally, or graphically in what is called a test profile.

TABLE XIII-6[44]

PERCENTILE EQUIVALENTS OF AVERAGE SCORES OF STUDENTS TESTED
IN 1947 IN RELATION TO OCCUPATIONAL FIELD IN 1955

GROUP	N	PERCENTILES							
		VR	NA	AR	SR	MR	CSA	Spell.	Sent.
MEN									
Engineers	22	84	89	86	81	86	74	79	81
Draftsmen	21	47	47	50	67	53	61	44	51
Technicians	49	42	45	45	48	53	51	37	34
Businessmen	21	57	58	54	36	45	64	58	55
Salesmen	39	56	49	58	50	52	55	55	49
Clerks	46	39	41	46	50	43	45	47	46
Supervisors-Foremen	21	43	44	43	52	46	69	48	35
Factory Workers	37	43	27	34	52	54	28	29	32
Building Tradesmen	21	32	33	45	50	38	43	35	27
Laborers	24	38	21	28	29	35	32	36	25
Students (Current)	107	76	74	72	62	63	68	72	76
Military Personnel	132	67	67	63	64	64	58	64	66
WOMEN									
Teachers	49	81	84	81	74	71	73	72	82
Nurses	28	78	75	73	77	64	58	70	66
Stenographers	126	58	56	54	52	52	61	67	56
Clerks	198	46	45	48	48	49	52	46	40
Housewives	277	57	50	55	59	58	52	54	42

TABLE XIII-7[45]

PERCENTILE EQUIVALENTS OF AVERAGE SCORES OF STUDENTS TESTED
IN 1947 IN RELATION TO EDUCATIONAL ATTAINMENT BY 1955

GROUP	N	PERCENTILES							
		VR	NA	AR	SR	MR	CSA	Spell.	Sent.
MEN									
Advanced Degree	41	86	84	76	61	66	75	82	87
College Graduate*	214	79	79	73	67	68	71	74	78
Some College	179	61	57	60	57	56	58	60	57
Special School**	97	40	31	46	46	49	49	33	31
No Further Education	178	34	30	36	42	43	38	35	32
WOMEN									
College Graduate	122	84	84	78	70	70	67	76	82
Some College	128	70	66	68	64	64	57	63	64
Special School**	120	55	49	54	54	49	49	46	45
No Further Education	399	42	40	43	49	50	51	49	40

* Includes those with advanced degrees.
** Non-degree-granting institutions. Most of the men attended business, technical,
   or fine arts schools; the majority of women went to secretarial, nursing, or fine
   arts schools.

Tests should be used with discrimination by persons trained in their administration, use, and interpretation. They should be used in conjunction with other selection devices. The degree to which test results can be utilized in employing will, however, depend upon the number of applicants available and their qualifications as revealed by various selection devices.

A brief resume of the selection program of one giant company (over $28 billion in assets) is given in conclusion: The American Telephone and Telegraph Company, which employs approximately 750,000 persons was selected by a panel of nearly 300 presidents and chairmen of companies as being one of the ten best managed companies out of the thousands of companies in the United States. The study was made by *Dun's Review* Presidents' Panel. AT&T was selected as one of the ten best managed companies on the basis of its corporate vitality. This company employs some 2,500 college graduates annually in anticipation of training them for district-level management jobs that will open up in the company. Since it had long ago found that college graduation alone did not guarantee aptitude, it made two major studies to improve its employment techniques. First it studied 425 management men who were either recently hired college graduates or young non-college men just entering management. Second, the records of approximately 17,000 college men who had been with the Bell System for ten years or more were surveyed to find the relationship between performance in college and later success. Good scholars in general were found to have progressed further in the business than poor ones. Leadership in extra-curricular activity was an additional useful guide in predicting success, although not as accurate a guide as scholastic standing. Having worked one's way through college was not a significant factor. The result of the surveys is that Bell's 800 part-time recruiters that go to some 500 colleges to find recruits seek for talent in the top half of each school's graduating class. Applicants are tested by use of the Educational Testing Service's School and College Ability Test (SCAT). Only ten per cent of new employees fall into the lowest SCAT score quarter (1963) as opposed to twenty-five per cent when this type of testing was started in 1958. AT&T itself does not do direct college recruiting since its own executive staff is recruited from its associated companies.[46]

PROJECTS

1. Have the Kuder Preference Record Vocational Form CM, published by Science Research Associates, 57 West Grand Avenue, Chicago 10, Illinois, administered to the class by the school testing center or the class

teacher. Have profiles prepared from the results and presented to each student.

2. Read and report on the use of tests in selecting persons for the particular occupation you desire to enter upon completion of your school program.

ACKNOWLEDGMENTS AND REFERENCES

1 Goodacre, Daniel M., III, "Pitfalls in the Use of Psychological Tests," *Personnel*, American Management Association, Inc., 1515 Broadway, Times Square, New York 36, N. Y., Vol. 34, No. 5, March-April, 1958, pp. 41–45.

2 Roos, Erik E., and Dailey, Charles A., "Ground Rules for Better Salesman Selection," *The Management Review*, American Management Association, Inc., 1515 Broadway, Times Square, New York 36, N. Y., Vol. XLVI, No. 11, November, 1957, pp. 52–54.

3 Humm, Doncaster G., "An Appraisal of Personnel Testing," *Advanced Management*, Vol. 21, No. 2, February, 1956, pp. 16–19.

4 ———, "Testing: Can Everyone Be Pigeonholed?," *Newsweek*, July 20, 1959, pp. 91–93.

5 Habbe, Stephen, "Developments in Psychological Testing," *Management of the Personnel Function*, edited by I. L. Heckmann and S. G. Huneryager, Charles E. Merrill Books, Inc., Columbus, Ohio, 1962, pp. 556–557.

6 Freeman, Frank S., *Theory and Practice of Psychological Testing*, Henry Holt and Company, New York, 1955, p. 63.

7 *Ibid.*, pp. 69–72.

8 Thurstone, L. L., *Primary Mental Abilities*, University of Chicago Press, Chicago, Illinois, 1938.

9 du Mas, Frank M., "A Manifest Structure Analysis of the Otis S-A Test of Mental Ability, Higher Examination: Form B," *Journal of Applied Psychology*, Vol. 42, No. 4, April, 1958, pp. 269–272.

10 Kazmier, Leonard J., and Browne, C. G., "Comparability of Wonderlic Test Forms in Industrial Testing," *Journal of Applied Psychology*, Vol. 43, No. 2, April, 1959, pp. 129–132.

11 Lebo, Deall, Andrews, Robert S., and Lucier, Omer, "The Lowry Test: A Simple Status-Free Measure of Intellectual Ability," *Journal of Applied Psychology*, Vol. 43, No. 6, December, 1959, pp. 411–412.

12 ———, *Test Service Bulletin*, The Psychological Corporation, 522 Fifth Avenue, New York 18, N. Y., p. 2.

13 Ferguson, Leonard W., "Ability, Interest, and Aptitude," *Journal of Applied Psychology*, Vol. 44, No. 2, April, 1960, pp. 126–131.

14 ———, "What's the Status of Sales Aptitude Tests Today?" *Sales Management*, March 18, 1960, p. 102ff.

15 Adams, Loyce, "A Study of Sales-training Programs in Eighty-eight Firms," a dissertation, The University of Texas, Austin, 1959, (University Microfilms, Inc., 313 N. First St., Ann Arbor, Michigan), p. 95.

16 ———, From a two-page printed form 10180 (5–57), Metropolitan Life Insurance Company, One Madison Avenue, New York 10, New York.

17 Tobolski, Francis P., and Kerr, Willard A., "Predictive Value of the Empathy Test in Automobile Salesmanship," *Journal of Applied Psychology*, Vol. 36, 1952, pp. 310–311.

18 ———, *Test Service Bulletin*, The Psychological Corporation, No. 51, December, 1956, p. 3.

19 Whyte, William H., Jr., "The Fallacies of 'Personality Testing'," *Fortune*, Vol. L, No. 3, September, 1954, p. 117ff.

20 ———, "In Management," *Business Week*, November 28, 1959, p. 166.
21 England, George W., and Paterson, Donald G., "Relationship Between Measured Interest Patterns and Satisfactory Vocational Adjustment in Air Force Officers in the Comptroller and Personnel Fields," *Journal of Applied Psychology*, Vol. 42, No. 2, April, 1958, pp. 85–88.
22 Merenda, Peter F., and Clarke, Walter V., "The Predictive Efficiency of Temperament Characteristics and Personal History Variables in Determining Success of Life Insurance Agents," *Journal of Applied Psychology*, Vol. 43, No. 6, December, 1959, pp. 360–366.
   Merenda, Peter F., and others, "Cross-Validity of Procedures for Selecting Life Insurance Salesmen," *Journal of Applied Psychology*, Vol. 45, No. 6, December, 1961, pp. 376–380.
23 Smith, Gudmund, and Marke, Sven, "The Influence on the Results of a Conventional Personality Inventory by Changes in the Testing Situation: A Study on the Humm-Wadsworth Temperament Scale," *Journal of Applied Psychology*, Vol. 42, No. 4, August, 1958, pp. 227–233.
24 Smith, Gudmund, and Marke, Sven, "The Internal Consistency of the Humm-Wadsworth Temperament Scale," *Journal of Applied Psychology*, Vol. 42, No. 4, August, 1958, pp. 234–240.
25 Kragh, Ulf, "The Defense Mechanism Test: A New Method for Diagnosis and Personnel Selection," *Journal of Applied Psychology*, Vol. 44, No. 5, October, 1960, pp. 303–309.
26 Meyer, Henry D., and Fredian, Alan J., "Personality Test Scores in the Management Hierarchy," *Journal of Applied Psychology*, Vol. 43, No. 3, June, 1959, pp. 212–220.
27 *Ibid.*, p. 214.
28 *Ibid.*, p. 215.
29 *Ibid.*
30 Clay, Hubert, "Experiences in Testing Foremen," *Personnel*, Vol. XXVIII, No. 6, pp. 466–470.
31 Neel, Robert G., and Dunn, Robert E., "Predicting Success in Supervisory Training Programs by the Use of Psychological Tests," *Journal of Applied Psychology*, Vol. 44, No. 5, October, 1960, pp. 358–360.
32 Halsey, George D., *Selecting and Inducting Employees*, Harper & Brothers, New York, 1951, pp. 174–176.
33 Murray, Lester E., and Bruce, Martin M., "A Study of the Validity of the Sales Comprehension Test and Sales Motivation Inventory in Differentiating High and Low Production in Life Insurance Selling," *Journal of Applied Psychology*, Vol. 43, No. 4, August, 1959, pp. 246–248.
34 Behn, Robert C., "A Case History in the Use of Tests in Selection, Transfer, and Promotion," *Proceedings Twelfth Conference*, Texas Personnel and Management Association, November 2 and 3, 1950, The University of Texas, Austin, pp. 92–96.
35 Goodacre, *op. cit.*
36 Harker, John B., "Cross-Validation of an IBM Proof Machine Test Battery, *Journal of Applied Psychology*, Vol. 44, No. 4, August, 1960, pp. 237–243.
37 Bourassa, G. Lee, and Guion, Robert M., "A Factorial Study of Dexterity Tests," *Journal of Applied Psychology*, Vol. 43, No. 3, June, 1959, pp. 199–204.
38 ———, "Testing: Can Everyone Be Pigeonholed?," *Newsweek*, July 20, 1959, pp. 91–93.
39 Guilford, J. P., *Psychometric Methods*, McGraw-Hill Book Co., New York, 1936, p. 364.
40 ———, "Methods of Expressing Test Scores," *Test Service Bulletin*, The Psychological Corporation, No. 48, January, 1955, p. 5ff.
41 ———, "Watch Your Weights," *Test Service Bulletin*, The Psychological Corporation, No. 52, December, 1957.

42 ——, "What's the Status of Sales Aptitude Tests Today?" *Sales Management*, March 18, 1960, p. 102ff.

43 ——, "Management: Testing Managers Without Heat," *Business Week*, September 19, 1959, pp. 76–81.

44 ——, "The D.A.T. — A Seven-Year Follow-Up," *Test Service Bulletin*, The Psychological Corporation, No. 49, November, 1955, p. 3.

45 *Ibid.*, p. 2.

46 Brooks, Thomas R., "People Vitality — and AT&T," *Dun's Review*, April, 1963, p. 53ff.

CHAPTER XIV

TRAINING

Extent of Training — An American Management Association study made of several thousand companies in the period 1952-1954 by Lyndall F. Urwick and others [reported on in four parts] found that fifteen per cent of corporations with 250 or more employees had programs for developing management personnel; about ten per cent of the corporations with fewer than 250 employees had such programs. Some of the eighteen or more methods of executive development reported in the AMA study were: (1) opportunity to act for a superior while the superior is temporarily absent, (2) opportunity to carry out a special assignment, (3) working on committees, (4) job rotation, (5) transfer. Various methods used were to improve: (1) knowledge, (2) communication ability, (3) social sensitivity and feelings of responsibility for company and community activities. Most firms had some type of training for operative employees. Training of employees was found to be chiefly designed for the following purposes: (1) to keep employees informed concerning economic education (a large segment of management apparently thinks only in terms of economic education; another feels that this type of education is not within the realm of management's responsibilities and that employees may look upon it as propaganda); (2) to give socio-political education; (3) to give general education; (4) to keep employees informed concerning the company, (5) to give vocational training. The researchers recommended that management should do more research to find the results of training and to discover the techniques of training that are most effective.[1]

Sales Training — As early as 1887 the National Cash Register Company attempted to standardize sales talks; in 1893 that company held its first sales-training class. Westinghouse Electric Corporation has also been in the business of conducting sales courses since the turn of the century. The period of rapid growth of sales training, however, has been within the last twenty years.

In the study conducted in 1957 by this writer it was found that eighty-two out of eighty-eight of the outstanding companies studied had training programs for salesmen that involved formal classes of some type; the other six firms had on-the-job training. Types of courses given to sales trainees are indicated in Table XIV-1.

Many companies consider *induction* (the period of introducing, orienting, and indoctrinating employees) to be a part of training. The basic objectives of induction are similar for most companies. The trainee is prepared for training by being made to feel that he belongs and by imparting to him a favorable attitude. Proper techniques in induction are

TABLE XIV-1[2]

NUMBER AND PERCENTAGE OF 86 OUT OF 88 FIRMS THAT USE
COMBINATIONS OF METHODS AND PROCEDURES AS INDICATED IN INDUCTION,
ORIENTATION, AND INDOCTRINATION OF SALES TRAINEES

Combinations of Methods	Number	Per Cent of 86	Per Cent of 88
A, C, D, E,	1	1.16	1.14
A, C, D, E, F, G, H,	11	12.79	12.50
A, C, D, E, F, G, H, I	15	17.44	17.05
A, C, D, E,　G, H,	3	3.49	3.41
A, C, D, E,　G, H, I	1	1.16	1.14
A, C,　E, F, G, H,	1	1.16	1.14
A,　D, E, F, G,	1	1.16	1.14
A,　D, E, F, G, H,	9	10.47	10.23
A,　D, E, F, G, H, I	7	8.14	7.95
A,　D, E, F, G,　I	1	1.16	1.14
A,　D, E,　G, H,	3	3.49	3.41
A,　D, E,　G, H, I	5	5.81	5.68
A,　D,　F, G, H, I	1	1.16	1.14
A,　E,　G, H,	1	1.16	1.14
C, D, E, F, G, H,	3	3.49	3.41
C, D, E, F, G, H, I	6	6.98	6.82
C, D, E,　G, H, I	1	1.16	1.14
D, E, F, G, H,	7	8.14	7.95
D, E, F, G, H, I	4	4.65	4.55
D, E,　G,	1	1.16	1.14
D, E,　G, H,	1	1.16	1.14
D, E,　G,　I	1	1.16	1.14
E,　G, H,	1	1.16	1.14
E,　G, H, I	1	1.16	1.14
No Answer	2	——	2.27
Totals	88	100.00	100.00

Key: A. Employee Handbook
C. Film About Company
D. History of Company
E. Product Information
F. Company Earnings and Profits Discussed

G. Explanation of Pay Deductions
H. Rules and Regulations for Employees Given
I. Visits to Company Divisions

considered to reduce employee turnover. They reduce grievances; they save time and trouble. Eighty-five of the eighty-eight companies referred to above gave *product information* to sales-trainee inductees; eight-five companies explained *pay, deductions,* and such other items as *fringe benefits* to their trainees. Other methods and devices used by half or more of the companies answering the questionnaire were: *employee handbook, film about the company, history of the company, discussion of company earnings and profits, rules and regulations* for employees, and *visits to other company divisions.* Various trade associations give aid in induction through publications furnished their members. Letters to the inductees are also a much-used device in attitude creation.

The induction period varies greatly from company to company due to products involved, channels of trade used, and the degree of knowledge and skill needed by a company's salesmen. Those firms having short induction periods are generally producers of soft goods, or are merchandising or insurance firms; firms having longer induction periods are producers of technical equipment requiring complicated product knowledge to sell. In such firms, induction is, of course, overlapping with training.

Most firms indoctrinate sales inductees with their sales and training policies; more than four-fifths of the companies have written sales and

TABLE XIV-2[3]

NUMBER AND PERCENTAGE OF 88 FIRMS GIVING FORMAL CLASS TRAINING TO SALES TRAINEES IN COURSES AS INDICATED

Courses	Number	Per Cent of 82	Per Cent of 88
Organization and Management	50	60.98	56.82
Sales Management	39	47.56	44.32
Policy	59	71.95	67.05
Speech	37	45.12	42.05
Business Letters	22	26.83	25.00
Report Writing	34	41.46	38.64
Human Relations	47	57.32	53.41
Credit Department Functions	52	63.41	59.09
Business Law	12	14.63	13.64
Vocabulary Building	18	21.95	20.45
Company Records and Reports	61	74.39	69.32
Advertising	56	68.29	63.64
Market Research	41	50.00	46.59
Marketing Channels	53	64.63	60.23
Salesmanship	80	97.56	90.91
Product Conferences	76	92.68	86.36
Manufacture of Product	66	80.49	75.00
Use of Product	65	79.27	73.86

personnel policies; better than two-thirds have written sales-training policies.

The following brief statements of topics covered in subject-matter areas listed in Table XIV-2 are adapted from "A Study of Sales-training Programs in Eighty-eight Firms." [4]

Organization charts, company policies, managerial principles, and establishment of lines of responsibility and authority are some of the topics studied in courses pertaining to *organization and management*. Some companies offer courses related to organization and management which are variously entitled business management, service training and management, and supervisory development.

Sales management relates to those activities concerned with planning, organizing, and controlling of operations designed to get a product or service to the consuming public. The topics studied in sales management vary widely. They include: product development and testing, packaging and labeling, brands and trademarks, forecasting of sales and setting of sales quotas, pricing, sales programs and campaigns, and various phases of managing sales personnel.

A course in *policy* usually covers general company policies, division policies, and specific policies relating to a certain product, or to certain products. For each company these vary, making it necessary for companies to develop their own courses and sales-training manuals.

Speech is emphasized in many phases of sales training. In salesmanship courses it is stressed in sales talks or in role playing. One sales-training manual that gives lessons in speech stresses the necessity of talking clearly, conversationally, earnestly, and animatedly, and of making pauses punctuate. The speaking rate recommended is approximately 105 words a minute. Another training booklet gives advice on effective speaking and discusses appearance, mannerisms, notes, memory, striving for perfection, using the library, and how to organize a speech.

The Goodyear Tire and Rubber Company established a Better Letter Department over forty years ago which wrote and conducted courses in letter writing. The firm still issues a letter-writing manual. Among readings this manual recommends for letter writers are "Lincoln's Gettysburg Address," Franklin's *Autobiography*, the *Sermon on the Mount*, Charles Lamb's *Essays*, Joseph Addison's *Sir Roger de Coverly Papers*, and George Bernard Shaw's writings. Goodyear still provides numerous pamphlets on letter writing for private study. See Chapters XIX and XX for other types of *communication* in which some training may be given.

Companies have their own forms and procedures for *report writing* and must develop their own training guides and aids. Sometimes only one course covering the two areas of letter and report writing is given.

Most companies stress the need for better *human relations* even when they do not give formal training in this area. One training manual covers such topics as: industry, confidence, enthusiasm, tact, courage, appearance, speech, manner, study, and health, all of which contribute directly or indirectly to human relations training. One writer has said that the first step in human relations training is recognition of need for change on the part of the trainee. In addition to self-appraisal, the trainee should have experience on the job in applying the skills learned in formal classes.[5]

Salesmen must know that sales are being made to firms whose credit rating is good. Salesmen learn to use the services of their own company credit men and those of credit agencies. They are taught company policies relating to *credit*. Formal training in *business law* as it is applicable to certain types of business and industrial operations is provided by relatively few firms.

Although only a fifth of the companies in this study give a vocabulary-building course, most companies emphasize the need for *vocabulary* development and two-fifths of the firms use a vocabulary test in selecting sales trainees.

Whether formal training in *keeping records* is given or not, salesman do have to keep records. Three-fourths of the companies apparently give formal training in record keeping. The National Cash Register salesmen are required to keep records as follows: (1) daily plan card, (2) record of calls made, (3) weekly summary, (4) monthly summary, (5) prospect file. Reports must be made promptly; the job is too sizable if postponed and results are inaccurate.[6] Sales management respects accounting as an aid. The accounting department is often permitted a hand in training salesmen; it frequently prepares materials used in instructing in record keeping.[7]

A large number of sales trainees learn how to utilize the *advertising* phase of promotion in the personal selling phase; as indicated by this study fifty per cent of the eighty-two companies that give formal training to sales trainees include special training in *market research*. Many companies have only recently established market research departments. Of 195 companies taking part in a survey made by Richard D. Crisp and Associates, forty per cent established their market research departments after 1952. Market research has given increased attention to these areas: profitability of different markets, development of standards for performance of salesmen, advertising effectiveness, evaluation of sales methods, and competitors' activities.[8] McKann-Erickson's marketing services vice president, H. I. Gafer, has said that market analysis ranks first among the components of the marketing operation. A study of the market must precede all other decisions in the development of an over-all marketing policy or program.[9] In some companies the salesmen do most of the market research; they must, therefore, be trained to know what information is desired and how to obtain it; market research supplies the sales trainer with information on customer buying motives; it discovers new uses for products; it provides knowledge of profitability of the various products.

The nature of the product being sold, and the steps in the process of getting the product from the manufacturer or processor to the consumer, industrial or otherwise, determine the amount of attention that must be given in developing concepts of the *channels* of distribution. A firm that sells to many types of buyers, large and small, wholesalers, retailers, or company dealers, or direct to industrial consumers, must give training that will enable visualizing the entire set-up for marketing its product.

Salesmanship courses as such usually cover such topics as history of the industry and the company, knowing the merchandise or product, knowing the customer, knowing the market, knowing the competition, and knowing oneself. The basic elements of salesmanship are usually taught. (See Chapter XXIII) *Product conferences* on both the manufacture and use of products are widely used in sales training.

In addition to the subjects named above, some companies provide formal training in the following areas: field application; competitor's products, or competition; who uses products and how; systems training; laboratory work on use of product; taxes; how to dress (Schering Corporation); estate planning; controls of business; observations and practice in production departments, metallurgy, machine shop; data processing, procedure study, form design, organization simplification; territory management; packaging art and design; packaging engineering; product development. One company commented that judgment and human relations are emphasized in all courses; another underscored marketing clinics at headquarters to give new men an over-all picture of company executives of all departments appearing on programs to sell functions and future of the departments.

Methods used in teaching sales trainees are summarized in Table XIV-3. Adapted from "A Study of Sales-training Programs in Eighty-eight Firms." is the following statement about these methods: [10]

Lectures should usually be supplemented by use of the blackboard (chalkboard) or other means of supplementing the spoken word. Body and facial movements, animated voice, concrete illustrations, and apparent interest in what he is saying aid a lecturer in putting over ideas. Planned questions usually form the basis of the *guided discussion*; new questions arise, however, and the discussion leader must be adaptable.

Some writers say that the type of *panel* in which short talks are first made by participants, followed by questions and answers, is usually not successful. It is possible that such panels (sometimes called forums) fail because of lack of skill on the part of of their members or chairmen. Competent panel members may conduct an effective session by making short talks followed by questions and answers back and forth among the panel members. This requires a leader capable of keeping one or two persons from dominating.

TABLE XIV-3[11]

NUMBER AND PERCENTAGE OF 80 OUT OF 88 FIRMS USING METHODS INDICATED IN FORMAL CLASSES FOR SALES TRAINEES

Methods of Teaching	Number	Per Cent of 80	Per Cent of 88
Lectures	72	88.89	81.82
Guided Discussions	72	88.89	81.82
Panel Discussions	48	60.00	54.55
Demonstrations	76	95.00	86.36
Questions	77	96.25	87.50
Narrating Examples	69	86.25	78.41
Cases	65	81.25	73.86
Brainstorming Sessions	32	40.00	36.36
Role Playing by Trainees	70	87.50	79.55
Individual Reports by Trainees	56	70.00	63.64
Committee Reports by Trainees	19	23.75	21.59
No Method Named	2	——	2.27
On-the-job Training Only	6	——	6.82

Demonstration is interspersed with other methods and devices in teaching. This is shown by the following review of two lessons from Swift & Company's *Introduction to Salesmanship*: In Lesson XXIX the student is assigned a product on which to give a three-minute sales talk. The talk is graded on effective use of the persuasion pattern and his portable showcase. Lesson XXX presents sales technique through use of a turnover chart, a film entitled "Science Comes to Selling," and Swift products and props for sampling. The student sees the film which emphasizes that advertising, salesmanship, and samples are the three most effective ways to move merchandise. The art of sampling is then demonstrated.

Questioning may be of the question-and-answer type where questions are designed to find out how much the student knows, or to get information from him. They may be placed to stimulate discussion and thought. The entire group or an individual may be questioned; in either case, the question is put to the group first so that all will listen. There is inevitably an overlapping of this method with other methods.

In *narrating examples,* salesmen may be asked to give examples of how they have made sales, or of techniques they have used in any one of the steps used in selling. Sales trainers or sales executives may relate their experiences in selling or even tell about the experiences of others. The *case method* of teaching is similar to narration of examples. Properly used it requires study of case material, determining the problem involved, and the offering of solutions to the problem. The case approach may thus become the basis for class discussion, or even a brainstorming session.

Alex Osborn [see Chapter II] is credited with fathering the creative-thinking process known as *brainstorming*. The best brainstormers easily recognize a problem. They quickly visualize numbers of solutions, new relationships, and a variety of approaches. William J. Tobin in *Sales Management* says that the best brainstorming period is from forty minutes to an hour with a coffee break. He divides brainstorming into three phases: (1) idea getting (group suggestions); (2) idea evaluation (by the total group or a sub-committee — ideas on 3" x 5" cards can be rapidly shuffled for evaluation); (3) assignment of ideas (field testing with reports on results of putting the ideas into practice).[12]

A study made by Donald W. Taylor, Yale University psychology professor, found that brainstorming inhibits rather than stimulates creative thinking. Professor Taylor used ninety-six Yale students in his study. Forty-eight of the students worked individually on three problems suitable for brainstorming sessions. The other forty-eight students formed twelve four-member randomly selected groups. Records showed that the individuals produced fewer ideas on the average than the groups. Quantity did not reveal quality, however; nor did results show whether or not the larger number of ideas produced by groups resulted from group interaction. The responses of the forty-eight individual participants were tabulated as if the forty-eight were members of twelve groups, four to the group. Performance of the nominal groups was compared with performance of the real groups. The twelve real groups were inferior to the nominal in "average number of ideas produced, the average number of unique ideas, and the quality of the ideas generally." Taylor suggests that *group performance might be inferior because group members fear criticism, or persons in a group might tend to follow the first trend of thought offered instead of pursuing a variety of approaches.*[13]

[There are four groups of relevant studies pertaining to creative thinking: "(1) those attempting to differentiate the creative from the non-creative persons by various measures such as tests, personality, and biographical data (Creative Education Foundation, 1958); (2) those attempting to find effects of factors that might inhibit productive thinking; (3) those attempting to employ individual and group problem solving procedures; (4) those attempting to evaluate lectures and workshops in creative thinking." At the University of Buffalo, Meadow and Parnes attempted "to evaluate the effects of a creative problem-solving course on creative abilities and selected personality variables." Osborn's method was used to test three hypotheses: that the method used in the course would produce a significant increment (a) in quantity of ideas, (b) in quality of ideas, and (c) in three personality variables — need achievement, dominance, and self-control. The experimental group, as compared with the control group, attained significant increments on the two measures of quantity of ideas; they also attained significant increments on three out of five measures of quality of ideas; they showed a significant increment on the California Psychological Inventory Dominance scale. *This study implies that a creative problem-solving course (brainstorming) can increase practical creativity and influence personality.*][14]

A later experiment conducted by Meadow, Parnes, and Reese found that one group of students produced more good solutions to problems from the AC Test of Creative Ability when working under brainstorming conditions than did another group of students working under non-brainstorming instructions.

It may be concluded that brainstorming is useful with small groups in discussing problems; a great deal depends upon the persons using the process and upon the leaders. Some firms have, however, discontinued using it because they felt it did not get results, that is, it failed to result in creative ideas.

In *role playing* students act out parts. In some cases prepared scripts are used; in other cases a problem situation is given and students act out the parts of salesmen and customers. In the later case, each student must act in terms of what the other one says. Discussion should follow role playing; this is as important in the teaching process as the skit itself. The demonstration differs from role playing in that it usually involves a definitely set pattern with specific props. Role playing requires on-the-spot creative action when no skit is used. When a prepared script is used, the role playing usually turns into acting. The person who plays the part of the salesman in a role-playing situation should leave the training room while the trainer tells the other trainees the objections to be raised, and obtains suggestions from them as to how the objections should be met. The person who plays the part of the salesman studies the problem while waiting to be called back into the room to enact his part.

Written *reports* on personal experiences of salesmen may be used in training; salesmen, as discussed under "narrating examples," may report orally on their experiences. In addition, written research reports may be prepared by trainees and used as the basis of oral discussion. *Committee reports* are thought by some who write on methods of teaching to stimulate students to perform at a higher level than they would if they worked alone. It would seem that sales trainees would be no exception to this rule, and that profitable use could be made of committee work and committee reports in such training. Salesmen, of course, often work alone or in pairs. If the selling of the company's product requires assistance of numerous persons, from engineers to production and sales managers, these people must learn to work with others. Committee work for them is invaluable in training.

TABLE XIV-4[15]

NUMBER AND PERCENTAGE OF 82 OUT OF 88 FIRMS USING VISUAL AND AUDIO-VISUAL AIDS AS INDICATED IN SALES TRAINING

Visual and Audio-visual Aids Used	Number	Per Cent of 82	Per Cent of 88
Models	52	63.41	59.09
Displays	66	80.49	75.00
Motion Pictures	68	82.93	77.27
Slides	61	74.39	69.32
Slidefilms	61	74.39	69.32
Opaque Projectors	37	45.12	42.05
Flip Charts	64	78.05	72.73
Flannel Boards	47	57.32	53.41
Blackboards (Chalkboards)	75	91.46	85.23
Playlets	24	29.27	27.27
Manuals	71	86.59	80.68
Maps	37	45.12	42.05
Bulletin Boards	31	37.80	35.23
Posters	37	45.12	42.05
Pictures, Diagrams, Blueprints, Cartoons	60	73.14	68.18
Company Forms	70	85.37	79.55
Public-address System	28	34.15	31.82
Stage with Curtain Effects	17	20.73	19.32
Luncheons, Dinners, and Formal Programs	56	68.29	63.64
Textbooks	55	67.07	62.50
Study Guides	56	68.29	63.64
Television	2	2.44	2.27
Disc Records	25	30.49	28.43
Wire Recorders	11	13.41	12.50
Tape Recorders	58	70.73	65.91
Phonograph Records	35	42.68	39.77
No Visual or Audio-visual Aids Reported	6	——	6.82

Visual and audio-visual aids used in teaching sales trainees are summarized in Table XIV-4. Adapted from "A Study of Sales-training Programs in Eighty-eight Firms," is the following statement about these aids:[16]

Models show products or objects in reduced or enlarged size according to practicability. Types of models frequently used are: (1) those that reveal features of design and are externally correct, or block models; and (2) those which are transparent and show the inside working parts. Full-size demonstration stores, or miniature replicas, are used in teaching store layout for dealers. Goodyear Tire and Rubber Company has a store planning and merchandising laboratory at Akron, Ohio, where it gives dealers who come to Akron a chance to see efficient merchandising. There are three fully equipped full-size stores with exterior identification available for inspection. The laboratory gives: (1) dealer consultation service, (2) development service, (3) customer planning service, and (4) field merchandising service.[17]

Displays show the product in a setting or in use. Food manufacturers or processors often provide company-trained persons to assist food brokers and wholesalers with display problems. "Tension-producing design factors," as used by Ernest Dichter, motivation researcher, to apply to packages may also be applied to display at the dealer or store level. The product reaches out to the customer and permits rehearsal of its use.[18] Products attract attention to themselves in display in the store, in the office, or at any point where a salesman shows what he has for sale. Where display of a product is not practicable, suitable *models, pictures, diagrams,* and *blueprints* are used.

Over 3,500 companies and trade associations are estimated to be currently sponsoring one or more 16mm movies. These films are probably being seen by some 20,000,000 persons each week.[19] Most of these films are for institutional advertising, but they are often also used in sales training; other films relate directly to training. Many companies list training films in their sales-training manuals. The Lily-Tulip Cup Corporation, in addition to using Dartnell-produced films on general selling techniques, has the following films pertaining to specific products.[20]

"Paper, Guardian of Health," described as the "Story of Paper-making with Color Trailer of Lily Products and Markets."
"The Lid Is On for Keeps," a color movie on packaging of ice cream, showing the product in use.

A few sources of motion pictures and others films are:[21]

Blue Book of 16mm Films
Education Screen Inc.
64 E. Lake Street
Chicago, Illinois

The Index of Training Films
Business Screen Magazine
812 N. Dearborn Street
Chicago, Illinois

Directory of Film Sources
Victor Animatograph Company
Davenport, Iowa

Modern Talking Pictures
Service Inc.
45 Rockefeller Plaza
New York 20, N. Y.

Film Council of America
600 Davis Street
Evanston, Illinois

Slides and *slidefilms* are widely used in training. The National Food Brokers Association provides slidefilms and phonograph records to accompany them. The National Association of Retail Grocers also has numerous color-sound-slide films on food-store selling. NARGUS films on selection and training may be rented for ten dollars each or bought for thirty-five dollars each; booklets reproducing the films are twenty-five cents each.[22] Most automobile manufacturers provide dealers with slidefilms and accompanying recordings to use in training salesmen in prospecting, making the customer contact, demonstrating, and closing the sale. *Opaque projectors* are especially helpful in showing pictures, forms for reporting, letters, and advertisements.

Flip charts are sometimes called "turnover charts,"' or "easel pads." An easel-type stand supports the charts, each of which may be turned over after being used. It has become difficult to just make a talk; speakers, teachers, trainers, put on a "presentation." The flip chart is just a part of the show. It is an especially valuable device for giving statistical data or summarizing key ideas.

When the trainer wishes to effectively build a sequence as he talks, *flannel boards* are useful; otherwise a prepared bulletin board could be employed. Another advantage of the flannel board is that each display can be quickly put up and taken down, so that several displays can be built during one training period.

Blackboards (*chalkboards*) are good not only for material and ideas prepared in advance, but they are good for that which arises out of the situation. They can be used for the unexpected problem and the list developed by trainees. The blackboard is the most popular visual aid used by companies that participated in this study.

The *short skit* (*playlet*), such as is used by the Elmer Wheeler Training Institute, has been found particularly effective in teaching sales techniques. Company writers, either from sales training or advertising, usually write the plays and skits used. Plays must fit the type of product and the customer's situation.

Sales-training manuals outline and discuss the steps to be taken and the materials to be covered in training. Next to blackboards, manuals are the most popular type of visual aid used by companies participating in this study.

Maps are used in teaching salesmen how to map territories, or in showing them how to plan the methods and means of travel on their routes; *bulletin boards* are used in training rooms for display purposes, and to make announcements to trainees when they live in dormitory-type residences during training; *posters* are used to emphasize training ideas. Some firms sell items that require salesmen to read *blueprints*; *pictures* and *diagrams* are used when the products themselves cannot be conveniently used; *cartoons* are used for relaxation and to bring in the light touch.

Company forms of many kinds are used in appraising the work of salesmen and by the salesmen themselves in reporting on and analyzing their own sales.

The *public-address system* is useful in teaching public speaking, and it is very valuable for use by the trainer in all methods of teaching. When the sales-training department can have its own training room, the ideal situation is to have this furnished with all of the training aids and facilities for using them. The *platform*, or *stage with curtains*, is of great help in putting on plays, skits, or in role playing.

At the opening of a training session, the trainee can be made to feel welcome at a *dinner, luncheon,* or *formal program*. These devices are also sometimes used at the conclusion of a training period. In some cases the formal program held at the conclusion of a training period becomes, in effect, a "graduation exercise."

The majority of companies prepare their own textbooks and/or sales-training materials, but these are supplemented in most instances by numerous recommended readings that include not only the more recent textbooks on salesmanship but also the popular-type books on selling. *Study guides* are outlines, summaries, or tests. Tests are usually objective, employing true false, multiple choice, and completion forms for stating questions. *Television* was reported as being used in sales training by only two firms; *wire recordings, tape recorders,* and *phonograph records* are widely used. Tape recorders enable sales trainees to hear their own voices.

On-the-job training of salesmen (only type of training used by six of the eighty-eight firms) is given by supervisors and senior salesmen. Home-office formal class training without field formal training was given in the case of thirty-five out of eighty-eight of the firms; thirty-one of the firms had formal training both at the home office and at the branch or field offices; field or branch formal class training only was provided by sixteen of the firms. The period of training ranged from one to two days to one to two years, with six months being the most popular training period. Thirteen of the eighty-eight firms also use college and university classes for advanced sales training. Sixty-one of the eighty-eight firms will pay a part or all of the expenses if salesmen want to take beneficial professional courses, providing the salesmen pass these courses.

Eighty-six of the eighty-eight firms provide one or more of the following types of continuing training: sales meetings, conferences, correspondence courses, guided reading, and planned travel. Fifty-four of the sixty-one firms that sell to distributors furnish materials and props to distributors for training; forty-five firms furnish trainers to distributors; forty-two firms train persons who later train distributor salesmen; only seven firms do not give help to distributors in sales training.[23]

Eighty-four of the eighty-eight firms use one or more of the following ways of following up on effectiveness of sales training: quizzes and tests, trainee reports, inspection of supervisors, customer rating reports, employee rating reports, lower turnover due to training, higher morale due to training, sales records are compared to potentials or quotas, and computation of profits from each salesman's sales.[24]

A few recommendations for sales training not implied in the above findings are summarized here:

For sales training to be successful some one person should be in charge of it and responsible for its results. For uniformity this person should be called "Manager of Sales Training." In most instances those persons who attain supervisory or managerial rank in the selling division should have had actual selling experience in addition to having the other qualifications considered necessary in supervisors and managers.

There must be careful selection for a sales-training program to succeed. The high cost of preparing a man for his job of selling, sometimes $10,000, can be offset only if he is the right man for the job and if he stays with the company long enough to pay for his training. The company that gets, trains, and keeps the college recruit eliminates the high cost of salesman turnover. The colleges should try to do a better job of giving practical training to those who plan careers in selling.

Once selection has been accomplished, much can be done during the induction period to "sell" the prospective salesman on his company. Companies apparently do a good job of imparting company, product, and other information to the inductee. Beyond this, however, lies an area that is quite difficult to measure. The sales trainee can be made to feel that he belongs to a group, that he has been accepted, and that his company is his new home. Too often, however, the inductee goes away from a lecture on company history feeling not a part of but apart from *the* (not *his*) company. Good or bad human relations permeate all phases of induction and training. Obtaining information on the status of the human relations element in sales training can be done, however, only through participation in a company's training program, or, perhaps, through conferring with the trainees themselves. In either case information is usually distorted by subjective evaluation. Many firms do offer human relations courses to trainees. These courses by no means assure that the firms themselves have good human relations in their own induction and training programs.

Sales training should be continuing. Just as products and distribution channels are subject to change, the job of the salesman in the economy of the United States is an ever-changing one. Only through continuing training can he be kept abreast of changes. The salesman's reports and sales results offer the best clues to the success or failure of the training he has been given or is being given. The job of checking on these two sources is also never-ending. Continuing improvement of sales training on the part of business and industry is merely a part of a larger continuing program: the improvement of products and services offered to consumers.[25]

Training of Industrial Workers — General Electric Company has adopted what has been called the Kelly Plan [developed by Walter Sherman, Chief of Civilian Training at Kelly Air Force Base, San Antonio, Texas, where the civilian employees vary from five to thirty thousand and are engaged in practically all activities to be found in industrial plants] to discover the training needs of an individual. Training, in this case, is for persons already employed. Three raters evaluate an individual's performance, one of these being his immediate superior. Responsibilities of the person are outlined, and he is rated on each responsibility by the appraisal group. The worker's boss then calls him in for an interview during which he does not tell the worker wherein he is weak. He asks the subordinate to rate himself on each of his responsibilities. Generally, the worker points out the very weaknesses that the other raters have discovered. This is the beginning point in finding the training needs of the worker. Specialized training or conferences may be the answer to helping him to improve. One of the main advantages of the interview, however, is that it aids the worker to gain the insight needed by him before he can begin to improve or will want to take the steps necessary to profit by his awareness of new values.

At Kelly, this procedure was first used for workers; GE took the technique and improved upon it to develop its own plan of training supervisors.[26] Generally the beginning point in any training program is to find the areas of training need. In many instances the matter of training is simply to give a new worker the needed skill to perform his job; in many cases, it is a matter of teaching the old employee a new and better way of getting the work done.

Some of the methods of training operative employees are: *on-the-job training, vestibule training, apprenticeship training, learner training, internship training,* and *outside courses.*

On-the-job training is used to some extent with every new employee, and it may be used in teaching workers change-over methods. Some worker who is himself a skilled operator teaches the new employee, or the supervisor may be the one who teaches him. In some instances an instructor is provided to teach all new employees how to perform right on the job. If an instructor is used, he should be qualified and well trained, and should have job descriptions and possibly time and motion studies to aid him in training workers. Further, there should be some method of checking up on the results of training.

Vestibule training is that given when the workers are placed in working conditions similar to those at the actual work place. The name for this type of training was taken because a vestibule is the entrance-way through which one must pass before he goes into the main room. A large group of people can be trained using this method without upsetting the flow of work at the factory or in the office. Equipment similar to that at the workplace must be provided; the out-of-date cash register cannot be used to teach an operator how to use a new one.

Apprenticeship training is used in training persons for certain skilled trades, crafts, and technical skills. Some of the types of workers who are generally trained by the apprenticeship system are: bricklayers, carpenters, draftsmen, electricians, engravers, lathe and milling workers, painters, plumbers, printers, stone masons, and toolmakers. In apprenticeship a trainee works with a skilled worker for a period of anywhere from two to six years, depending upon the nature of the work. Upon completion of the training period, the worker is eligible for membership in the trade union for his particular type of work, as, for instance, the Typographer's Union, oldest in continued existence in the United States. Unions can restrict entry into given trades by curtailing apprenticeship programs. The federal government established an apprenticeship training service in 1937 that gives aid and assistance with the training of apprentices.

Learner training is given workers when the employers feel that public or privately operated schools can provide training in areas in which the workers are weak, as, for instance, in arithmetic, reading, or operating certain shop machines. *Internship training* is similar to learner training, but it is different in that the schools or colleges provide subject-matter curricula for students who are then permitted for a certain period of time, possibly a full semester of eighteen weeks, to work in business or industry to strengthen their knowledge in the given area of study by practical experience. Training in distributive occupations is frequently given in this manner. The program requires close cooperation between the educational institution and the company doing the employing; conferences are generally held about the employee and reports on his work experience are required.

Similar also to learner and internship training, but again different from them, are the various *vocational, trade, correspondence* and *other outside courses* taken by workers of their own volition to improve their skills and knowledges.

Persons responsible for training should be well trained in the principles of learning, methods of instruction, and the types of visual and audio aids available to use in instructing. The supervisors are themselves constantly involved in training in one way or another. It is thus quite important that supervisors have adequate training.

Training programs are generally considered successful only if they result in increased output, decreased costs, and better satisfied workers.

Training Supervisors — According to one extensive study, the morale of supervisors is generally higher than the morale of employees, but "the morale of employees is related to that of supervisors: the higher the morale of supervisors, the higher the morale of their employees." [27]

The Institute for Social Research, University of Michigan, studying workers in many types of organizations, has found that (1) there is a very close relationship between the kind of supervision given an employee and the satisfaction he gets from his work; (2) supervision that is too close is more likely to be associated with lower productivity while more general supervision is associated with higher productivity; (3) employee-centered supervisors train their subordinates for promotion; (4) worker morale is dependent upon the extent to which employees think their superior wants to discuss their work problems with them; (5) work groups are more productive when there is high group pride and loyalty; (6) workers aid one another in high productivity groups; (7) greater group pride and loyalty result when the supervisor treats his subordinates as human beings; (8) good supervisors can identify with their employees and understand them and their needs; (9) better supervisors use the principles of accommodation (preparing workers for change) and group participation in making changes or decisions that affect the group.[28]

Since supervisors are such an important factor in determining worker morale, it is essential that they be well trained. Perhaps the most essential need of supervisors is in the area of human relations: they need to be understanding, to be sensitive to the needs, ideas, and feelings of others. They need ability to feel empathy (see Chapter VIII for discussion of the supervisor's role in keeping workers happy).

The Training Within Industry section of the War Manpower Commission stated that the supervisor needs: (1) knowledge of the work; (2) knowledge of responsibilities; (3) skill in instructing; (4) skill in improving methods; (5) skill in leading. TWI provided four ten-hour programs and over 23,000 TWI trainees instructed 1,750,650 in these: job instruction, job methods, job relations, and program development training:

   I. Job instruction training:
      A. How to get ready to instruct;
         1. Have a time table.
         2. Break down the job.
         3. Have everything ready.
         4. Have the work place properly arranged.
      B. How to instruct:
         1. Prepare the worker.
         2. Present the operation.
         3. Try out performance.
         4. Follow-up.
  II. Job methods training:
      A. Break down the job.
      B. Question every detail.
      C. Develop the new method.
      D. Apply the new method.
 III. Job relations training:
      A. Get the facts.
      B. Weigh and decide.
      C. Take action.
      D. Check results.[29]

The four-step method of TWI was as follows:

   I. PREPARATION: Prepare the listener to receive new experience:
      A. Put learner at ease.
      B. Tell him the title of the job.
      C. Explain the purpose of the job.
      D. Explain why he has been selected to learn.
      E. Help him relate his past experience to the job.

II. PRESENTATION: Set the pattern in his mind.
   A. Introduce him to tools, materials, equipment and trade terms.
   B. Demonstrate the job, explaining each step slowly and clearly.
   C. Review with him what he should know up to this point: title of job, purpose of job, steps to be taken.
III. APPLICATION: Help him form habit.
   A. Supervise his doing the job.
   B. Question him on weak and key points.
   C. Have him repeat until he has developed the manual skill and/or habits of thought.
IV. TEST: Check the success of your instruction.
   A. Have him do the job alone.
   B. Inspect job against standards of performance.
   C. Discuss with him where he goes from here, whether to production work or new learning experience.[30]

While supervisors are trained in most of the ways that workers are and most of the methods used in training salesmen are used in training supervisors, probably the most common ways of training supervisors are by the *conference method*, through *role playing*, and in *brainstorming sessions*.

There are many types of *conferences*. What some have called the *pure conference* is a problem-solving or creative-thinking type of conference. In this type of conference the brainstorming methods previously discussed may be used. The group seeks in the conference to find solutions of problems which are posed by the leader or possibly by the group itself.

The *controlled conference* is one in which the supervisors are taught various things and the leaders impose their opinions, ideas, and information upon the group. The leaders do most of the work and there may even be drill of the supervisors; nevertheless, trainees are permitted to participate, to comment, and to ask questions.

The *directed conference* is similar to the controlled one; the leader knows the solution but he desires that the group follow a certain course in arriving at this answer and his control is directed to this goal. A work simplification conference might be conducted in this manner; the idea would be to develop creativity but also to teach a method.

In the JRT program under TWI the conference is one that is led in the sense that there is movement from one major step to the next, constantly following a given sequence. This might be called the *led con-ference*. There is also the *guided conference* which is largely free and is used when the case method is used; only enough guidance is given to keep the participants on the subject. The one hundred per cent *free conference* is very likely to lead to chaos. The method used in conduct-ing the conference should be determined by the objective to be accom-plished and the nature of the group involved.[31]

Various studies have indicated that group discussions and nondirec-tive procedures are effective in promoting attitude change and in im-proving emotional adjustment. A study by Di Vesta (1954) found that both directive (lecture) and nondirective approaches in teaching a human relations course for military hospital administrators produced similar positive effects. A study by Miner (1960) found that a course in psychology for seventy-two supervisors in the research and develop-ment department of a large corporation resulted in inducing a more favorable attitude toward supervisory work, although the course placed emphasis on lecture method and research findings.[32] Presumably, one should not rule out even the lecture method in training supervisors; this again depends on the nature of material being covered, the kind of super-visors being trained, and the trainers.

One study found that programmed textbooks used in a sixteen week course for trainees in a 7070 Data Processing System servicing course resulted in significant gains in achievement and reduction of training time for the course in the six experimental classes as compared to two control groups in which the lecture-discussion method was used.[33]

One research at the Fels Group Dynamics Center, University of Delaware, found that feedback within a group of fifty-four male and forty-nine female first level supervisors (foremen) resulted in increased group productivity and problem solving efficiency, as well as increased self-insight. Feedback in this case consisted of discussion and/or in-formation coming out of the meetings of feedback subgroups. In the control group there was no subgrouping for feedback purposes.[34]

Executive Development — Self-development on the job is probably the way the majority of managers and executives receive training. For most companies the first big problem is to discover persons who have leadership (management, executive) potential. College graduates are recruited with this in mind. Integrity, emotional stability, managerial ability, and leadership in human relations, as well as a certain degree of technical ability in a given area of management are the general re-quirements for success in managerial training or development.

In addition to *on-the-job* training, the following general methods of training executives are being used: *understudy plans, rotation plans, multiple management plans, conferences, role playing,* and *formal classes* of all types.

Understudy plans bring trainees into positions as assistants to persons whose responsibilities they begin to assume in a gradual manner. They are trained by the man "ahead" to take over his duties. There are a number of reasons why this type of plan sometimes meets with difficulties. An executive may be very reluctant to give somebody the secrets which he feels that he has paid the price of years to attain. He may also want to hold on to the reins as long as possible and in time the understudy may lose hope of ever being promoted. Some studies have shown that the closer a person is in earning power to the man just ahead of him, the lower his morale is likely to be.[35] There is a third type of problem that may result when understudy plans are used: the other persons in a department or division who may have held hope for promotion to higher levels lose hope. They feel that the understudy has the "inside track" and there is no reason for them to continue to work hard for promotion that obviously is going to some other person.

Multiple management was given brief discussion in Chapter VIII. *Rotation plans* are chiefly used in training supervisors and middle management people. Generally, a plan of rotation is worked out to give training in various areas of a particular department so that the trainee can become familar with all phases of work. He will then be better prepared when the time comes for promotion. This type of training is often used in department stores. The college recruit may work out of general sales on his first assignment after training. Later, after working in many sales departments, he may work in various administrative offices; eventually, he is made head of stock in one or more departments for a period of time. Finally, he is made assistant buyer for a department. Then his training will usually be received in a particular department where he is permitted to specialize, and his promotions will be up the ladder to head buyer for a division (manager). A variation of job rotation is known as the *flying squadron* method of training. The trainee is sent to a different duty every time an emergency arises and there is need in a given department for a replacement. These people who are capable of being shifted from one assignment to another receive valuable experience in training for executive duties, and at the same time the work they do permits the various departments to continue operating uninterruptedly.

One of the new methods of giving management training is known as the *"business or management game."* For businessmen it is considered to be like a good game of bridge; for students it is more like the real thing.[36] IBM equipment, the Ramac 650 computer, is fed data simulating the economy of a given industry by mathematicians, and given the results of company operations over a hypothetical period of time. Teams of managers (or students) make decisions every thirty minutes for several hours and receive quarterly reports from the Ramac. The problems on which players must make decisions may run the gamut of line and staff activities. The effectiveness of this method of teaching depends upon the effectiveness of the programs fed the machines and upon the follow-up procedures for evaluating players' decisions.

Earl Planty has stated that executive development in Johnson & Johnson is a "continuous process which is accomplished most fully through each executive's day-to-day work with his subordinates, supplemented by other developmental activities." Dr. Planty listed these other activities as follows in a speech made at a Texas Personnel and Management Association Conference (adaptations have been made):

Multiple Management: In three of the Johnson & Johnson companies there is an Auxiliary Board somewhat like that of McCormick and Company, Inc. In one company, four members of the board of directors were promoted to their positions from the Auxiliary Board.

Role playing: a role playing program has been given for plant superintendents in Johnson & Johnson, for the board of directors of one subsidiary, and for executives of another.

Case studies: Case studies have been offered major executives in sessions led by professors from leading universities; middle management, divisional sales managers, and the engineering division have had case studies.

Evening dinner meetings: Board members, directors, vice-presidents, and the echelon just under the vice-presidents have approximately half a dozen meetings each year with lecturers of national reputation.

Specialized conferences: These conferences last several days and are held each year for personnel directors, controllers, material handling specialists, production and sales specialists, and other professional or technical men from subsidiaries.

Harvard, Columbia, Northwestern, M.I.T., University of Western Ontario, and other Advanced management courses: Board members, works managers, and other major executives have taken these courses.

Wharton School of Finance: Seasoned executives have taken the course in executive management given during summers at this school.

Review of Economic Conditions: General economic trends and special trends of interest to the company are reviewed bi-monthly by the Econometrics Institute for board members and those who report to them.

Reading: This is a seventeen-hour course in improvement of reading that relies upon the Science Research Associates Reading Accelerator and the Harvard Reading Films and Teaching Aids; it has almost doubled reading speed with no loss of comprehension.

Conference leadership: Executives take a ten-hour course in conference leadership.

Public speaking: Professors of speech from metropolitan universities and businessmen teach this sixty-hour course to executives.

In-plant-conferences: These conferences are designed to improve communications; major executives have also taken a twenty-hour course in interviewing techniques; conferences have also been held on ways of raising money, issuing stock, and, also, on individual financial guidance.

Psychiatric group study: Executives in production were given a course in human motivation in which they tried to better understand themselves and others.

Out-of-town conferences: These conferences have been held for sales trainees, merchandising executives, production people, and others.

Short courses, seminars, school and college programs: In addition to attending special seminars and institutes, some executives take night courses. In one year executives completed 280 courses at Rutgers University alone. There is also active participation in American Management Association development programs and in National Industrial Conference Board programs.

Job rotation: This has been tried for managers in office and production work and found to be broadening and strengthening.

Counseling: Much executive development comes through individual counseling on personal problems.

Staff meetings: Weekly or fortnightly staff meetings develop those who are in charge of the meetings; chairmanship is sometimes rotated.

Professional, public, and community service: In these positions authority, power, and prestige of position do not help one; he must sell himself and his ideas. This is good for one in an authoritarian hierarchy.

Carefully planned executive audits: The basis for participation in the above activities is in the personal audit of an executive's needs and the resulting program of development for him. There is not a company-wide required program in keeping with the company's practice of decentralization. Subsidiaries are encouraged to participate in activities established by the parent company and to undertake other development work as it is considered needed.[37]

Not only are executives being trained, in many cases training is being provided for their wives. Companies often provide special programs for wives at conferences for executives. In 1962 Radcliffe College inaugurated a twelve-week course of sixty hours for thirty management wives who were given training in the highlights of regular Harvard Business School courses in management, finance, and marketing. This pilot program was designed to give them a better understanding of management and was described by the program director as being an experiment to provide management wives "with an overview of business." [38] This new development in management training is in keeping with the fact that many firms interview the wife before they employ her husband for an executive position.

Summary — Formal training programs have had rapid growth during the last twenty years. These programs are highly expensive, however, and they cannot be provided unless the results they produce make up for the cost. A National Industrial Conference Board survey in 1961 showed that college placement directors are divided as to whether they believe the college recruit should be trained on the job or in formal classes. They believe that formal training should be made shorter, cheaper, and more concrete. College recruits themselves prefer formal training. About thirty-five per cent of the 1960 college graduates went into formal training programs designed to prepare them for specific jobs; another twenty-five per cent received the same type of orientation given all new employees; the rest received on-the-job training.[39]

Some business and industrial firms are using "programmed instruction" in their training departments. Factual and routine material can be taught in this manner. In programmed training, information is given in sentences or short paragraphs that are arranged in logical order in "frames" that are presented with each frame building upon the material that preceded it. In this manner material may be presented from easy to difficult.[40] This type of training was referred to in Chapter II. It has been used to improve memory and reading ability.

Since 1949 the Institute for Humanistic Studies in Aspen, Colorado, has attempted to bring cultural enrichment to executives. Most of those who participate (some 1,600 by the 1964 session) in the seminars are sent by company presidents who believe that the executives can profit from acquaintance with the ideas of "thinkers from Socrates to Taft, and Machiavelli to Marx." [41]

PROJECTS

1. Outline a training (induction) program for new stenographers who are to work in a stenographic pool.

2. Use the following case for role playing involving a supervisor and worker: A janitor who has been employed by your company for twenty years has often been absent from work or tardy on Monday following pay day during the last several months. As supervisor of the maintenance crew you have previously tried to find out the cause of this and have warned him that he would have to improve his attendance record. Now you have an interview scheduled with him. Assume that this is a training period for supervisors and act out the interview.

ACKNOWLEDGMENTS AND REFERENCES

1 Urwick, Lyndall F., "Management Education in American Business, General Summary," *Management Education for Itself and Its Employees*, Part I, American Management Association, 330 West 42nd Street, New York 36, N. Y., 1954.
2 Adams, Loyce, "A Study of Sales-training Programs in Eighty-eight Firms," a dissertation, The University of Texas, Austin, 1959, (University Microfilms, Inc., 313 N. First St., Ann Arbor, Michigan), p. 128.
3 *Ibid.*, p. 148.
4 *Ibid.*, pp. 147–170.
5 Lunken, H. E., "How Do You Train a Person," *Advanced Management*, The Society for Advancement of Management, Inc., 74 Fifth Avenue, New York 11, N. Y., Vol. 22, No. 11, November, 1957, p. 4.
6 Wilson, John M., *Open the Mind and Close the Sale*, McGraw-Hill Book Company, Inc., New York, 1953, pp. 222–230.
7 Davis, James H., *Handbook of Sales Training*, Second Edition, Prentice-Hall, Inc., New York, 1954, p. 294.
8 Merrill, Harwood F., "The Listening Post," *Management News*, American Management Association, 1515 Broadway, Times Square, New York 36, N. Y., Vol. 31, No. 4, April, 1958, p. 6.
9 Gardner, Burleigh, "How the Social Sciences Are Used in Advertising," *Printers' Ink*, December 11, 1953, p. 50ff.
10 Adams, *op cit.*, pp. 171–182.
11 *Ibid.*, p. 172.
12 Tobin, William J., "Why Your Competitors Brainstorm," *Sales Management*, Vol. 77, No. 7, September 21, 1956, p. 82ff.
13 ————, "Brainstorming — A Bar to Creativity?," *Personnel*, American Management Association, Inc., 1515 Broadway, Times Square, New York 36, N. Y., Vol. 34, No. 5, March-April, 1958, pp. 5–6.
14 Meadow, Arnold, and Parnes, Sidney J., "Evaluation of Training in Creative Problem Solving," *Journal of Applied Psychology*, Vol. 43, No. 3, 1959, pp. 189–194.
Meadow, Arnold, Parnes, Sidney J., and Reese, Hayne, "Influence of Brainstorming Instructions and Problem Sequence on a Creative Problem Solving Test," *Journal of Applied Psychology*, Vol. 43, No. 6, December, 1959, pp. 413–416.

15 Adams, *op cit.*, p. 183.

16 *Ibid.*, pp. 179–195.

17 Umemura, George M., *Keys to Efficient Selling and Lower Marketing Costs*, Studies in Business Policy, No. 71, National Industrial Conference Board, Inc., 247 Park Avenue, New York 17, N. Y., 1954, pp. 15–16.

18 Dichter, Ernest, "How Good a Salesman Is Your Package?," *The Management Review*, American Management Association, Inc., 1515 Broadway, Times Square, New York 36, N. Y., Vol. XLVII, No. 1, January, 1958, pp. 34–35.

19 Spielvogel, Carl, "The Growing Audience for Business Films," *The Management Review*, American Management Association, Inc., 1515 Broadway, Times Square, New York 36, N. Y., Vol. XLVII, No. 4, April, 1958, pp. 74–75.

20 ————, *Field Training Handbook*, The Sales Personnel Development Department, Lily-Tulip Cup Corporation, 122 East 42nd Street, New York 17, N. Y., p. 30.

21 Guiher, J. L., *An Eye Opener*, Program Development Department, The Training Division, The Goodyear Tire and Rubber Company, Akron 16, Ohio, pp. 1–30.

22 ————, *Manual on Procedure for Recruiting, Selecting, Interviewing, and Guiding New Staff Members*, National Association of Retail Grocers, 360 North Michigan Avenue, Chicago 1, Illinois, pp. 1–18.

23 Adams, *op cit.*, pp. 201–237.

24 *Ibid.*, pp. 238–248.

25 *Ibid.*, pp. 249–266.

26 McCarthy, John J., "Controversial Issues in Training," *Proceedings of the Sixteenth Conference*, Texas Personnel and Management Association, The University of Texas, Austin, October 28–29, 1954, pp. 67–80.

27 ————, *Annual Report 1953–1954*, Industrial Relations Section, California Institute of Technology, Project 5, Surveys of Employee Opinion.

28 Likert, Rensis, "Motivation: The Core of Management," *Personnel Series*, No. 155, American Management Association, Inc., 1953, pp. 3–7.

29 ————, *The Training within Industry Report*, War Manpower Commission, Washington, D. C., 1945.

30 Cort, Robert P., "How to Get an Idea Across," *Personnel*, American Management Association, July, 1951, pp. 46–51.

31 McCarthy, *op. cit.*

32 Miner, John B., "The Effect of a Course in Psychology on the Attitudes of Research and Development Supervisors," *Journal of Applied Psychology*, Vol. 44, No. 3, June, 1960, pp. 224–232.

33 Hughes, J. L., and McNamara, W. J., "A Comparative Study of Programed and Conventional Instruction in Industry," *Journal of Applied Psychology*, Vol. 45, No. 4, August, 1961, p. 231.

34 Smith, Ewart E., and Kight, Stanford S., "Effects of Feedback on Insight and Problem Solving Efficiency in Training Groups," *Journal of Applied Psychology*, Vol. 43, No. 3, June, 1959, pp. 209–211.

35 Hepner, Harry Walker, *Psychology Applied to Life and Work*, Prentice-Hall, Inc., Englewood Cliffs, New Jersey, 1957, p. 453.

36 ————, "Management — Intercollegiate Business Games," *Business Week*, November 28, 1959, pp. 177–178.

37 Planty, Earl G., "Developing Management Ability," *Proceedings of Seventeenth Conference*, Texas Personnel and Management Association, October 20–21, 1955, pp. 35–42.

38 ————, "Management — Wives Learn Executive Worries," *Business Week*, January 13, 1962, pp. 46–48.

39 ————, "Management — College Recruits Want More Formal Training Programs," *Business Week*, March 11, 1961, p. 139.

40 Leonard, George B., "Programmed Instruction," *Reader's Digest*, September, 1962, pp. 205–212.

41 ————, "Education — Sunshine Seminars . . . ," *Newsweek*, July 27, 1964, pp. 48–49.

CHAPTER XV

MERIT RATING AND JOB EVALUATION

Distinguishing Between Merit Rating and Job Evaluation — Merit rating rates the man; job evaluation rates the value of the job to the company. Merit rating indicates degree of efficiency of employees on specified jobs within given classifications; it appraises the characteristics and performance of employees. Job evaluation does not measure men at all; it measures jobs. Merit rating is sometimes called by other names such as "service rating, development rating, or progress rating." In merit rating some type of rating scale is usually used for evaluating the performance of the employee and/or estimating his character and personality traits. Merit rating is done for a number of purposes: (1) It serves as a basis of counseling with employees relative to their strengths and weaknesses, why they are being promoted or why they are not. (2) It forms a basis of making transfers and promotions, giving pay increases, and demoting. (3) It helps to discover persons who are qualified for managerial positions, especially in the large companies where qualified people could be overlooked. (4) It keeps executives from passing superficial judgment on their employees. Forced to make objective ratings, they discover strong points in persons they had looked upon as perhaps being average in all respects. This obviously works in the reverse also. (5) Superiors will tend to be more observant of their employees when they know that they have to fill out rating forms periodically. (6) If fellow workers are permitted to rate each other in cases where ratings are by a superior, a fellow worker, and a subordinate worker, the workers become better judges of others and themselves and have a better basis for self improvement. (7) Employees probably work harder and strive for improvement when they know somebody is going to rate them, and that something will be put down in black and white relative to their performance and attitudes. (8) The raters become better judges of human nature and of people because they must temper their own judgments to those of others, for rating systems do, in general, require that there be more than one rating. Whether raters talk over their ratings with one another or not, a rater probably refrains from going to extremes or letting his personal prejudices influence him too much when he knows that his own attitudes would by contrast stand out when his ratings are compared with those of other raters. Sometimes raters are required to talk over their evaluations and arrive at a consensus rating. Generally, however, separate ratings are recorded and used in interviewing the employee.

There are many difficulties in using a merit rating system. Frequently the work of each individual in a department is so much a part of the work of all individuals in the department that ratings on individual performance cannot be given. In such cases the ratings must be of the employee characteristics that bring about efficiency in production. When the employee has been rated on these characteristics, his contributions are implied. These might include: dependability, cooperation, loyalty, honesty, perseverance, initiative, industriousness, leadership, mental alertness, thoroughness, ability to get along with others, and so on. In general, characteristics and contributions should not be included on the same rating scale, or if they are on the same scale there should be a division between the two types of ratings. The ratings of all persons in a department on the characteristics that are important for their work may reveal the reason for a given department's excellence or lack of excellence.

Kinds of Merit Rating Scales — There are many kinds of rating scales. A given firm may have all of these in use as each department tends to work out the scale that seems best for it.

The general types of rating scales are as follows:

RANKING: This type of rating requires that raters rank the workers in a department from "best" to "worst." In its simplest form this would not require a scale. Each man would simply receive a rank. If there are twenty persons in the department, *No. 1* would be considered the most efficient and *No. 20* would be considered the least efficient. If the workers are to be ranked in comparison with each other on given traits, then rating forms would have to be used. One man might be rated *No. 1* on dependability and *No. 20* on appearance. If as many as five traits are used, each man would have five separate ratings which would result in a composite score. The worker with the smallest score would be considered the most efficient; the worker with the largest score would be considered the least efficient. This method of rating is not often used. It is difficult to rank persons when so many of them may be about average.

MAN-TO-MAN COMPARISON, OR PAIRED COMPARISON: This type of rating was used during World War I by the United States Army. It is impractical because it takes too much time and requires too many fine decisions. It would certainly not be feasible in rating persons in a large department. To rate even ten persons by this method would require forty-five ratings. To illustrate:

Man Number	Rated Against Man Number
1	2, 3, 4, 5, 6, 7, 8, 9, 10
2	3, 4, 5, 6, 7, 8, 9, 10
3	4. 5, 6, 7, 8, 9, 10
4	5, 6, 7, 8, 9, 10
5	6, 7, 8, 9, 10
6	7, 8, 9, 10
7	8, 9, 10
8	9, 10
9	10
10	0

Letting X = Number of Persons to be Rated, the equation for computing number of sets of judgments that would be required when paired comparison is used is:

$$\frac{X\ (X-1)}{2}$$

If the number of persons to be rated is twenty, the number of sets of judgments (the judgments would depend on characteristics or traits being rated) would be computed as follows:

$$\frac{20\ (20-1)}{2} = \frac{380}{2} = 190$$

The total impossibility of this method is seen when you consider that if even five traits are to be rated this would require 950 judgments.

GRAPHIC RATING SCALE: This type of scale is probably used more than any other. Some writers have suggested that not over nine to twelve traits should be rated. These should be common specific traits, and they should be capable of being understood in the same manner by all persons. The following are samples from a graphic rating scale that provides for rating on characteristics and performance:

A. CHARACTERISTICS

Attitude	Interested in work; seeks ideas	Likes to try out new ideas	Doesn't like to accept suggestions	Slow to accept better methods
Relation-ships	Good team worker	Cooperates to the degree essential	Works just fairly well with others	Difficult to get along with

B. PERFORMANCE

Quality of work	Excellent performance	Usually good job; few errors	Work passable	Careless; many errors
Quantity of work	Rapid worker; high output	Meets average production	Has difficulty meeting average	Slow; very low production

The following short sample is taken from a rating scale prepared by the Ford Motor Company Training Department; it was used by supervisors to rate themselves:

A GOOD SUPERVISOR IS —

FAIR — He gives the same consideration to all of his men. He enforces discipline equally and has no favorites. He gives all men an equal opportunity. He gives praise or criticism where it is due without partiality. He accepts responsibility for his own mistakes and never passes the buck.

1   2   3   4   5

OBJECTIVE — He does not act on impressions, guesses, or hearsay. He does not jump to conclusions. He is not swayed by his personal likes, but judges men by their merits on the job. He weighs all the facts carefully and considers the effects of his actions, before he comes to a decision.

1   2   3   4   5

The other items covered in the scale: RESOURCEFUL, DEPENDABLE, LOYAL, ENTHUSIASTIC, ALERT, DIPLOMATIC, EXPRESSIVE, RESPONSIBLE, SELF STARTING, HONEST, INSPIRING, PROUD. The score is found by adding the ratings; the lower the score the higher the rating. A rating of *14* would be the highest that could be received and would mean TRULY OUTSTANDING; a rating of *70* would mean IN NEED OF CONSIDERABLE IMPROVEMENT and would be the lowest rating possible. A former student of the writer rated himself at "*32*" in 1952 when he was a supervisor for Ford; in 1962 he was general manager of one division of a competing automobile company.

Another form provided by a former student of the writer is called "Progress Report." It was designed to rate employees in an oil company and covers the following areas: SKILL, INDUSTRY, ATTITUDE, LEADERSHIP, DEPENDABILITY, and CAPACITY TO DEVELOP. The rater is asked to state whether or not he thinks the worker is capable of filling a better position and, if so, what position. Provision is made on the form for eight degrees of rating, as follows:

1. SKILL

| Indifferent work | Satisfactory work | Good work | Excellent work |

See Illustration XV-1 for a complete rating form used by the USAF.

Because raters often tend to go down the line checking all factors in the same column as they did the first factor, it has been suggested that the graphic rating form could be improved upon by using scales of varying length and by avoiding the numbering of scales from low to high or high to low as is usually done. This would avoid what is known as the "halo" error or the reverse of the "halo" error. Raters generally think of a person as being "totally high" or "totally low" and if they are forced to stop and consider each element being rated they may discover that the person thought to be "totally high" may be not quite so high in some traits; likewise, the person thought to be "totally low" may have a few redeeming features. Another way to avoid the "halo" error is for raters to rate each employee on only one characteristic at a time.

FORCED-CHOICE RATING SCALE: This type of rating was developed in order to improve accuracy and to further reduce the possibilities of biases and "halo" errors. It is, however, not as practical a device as the graphic rating scale because it is difficult to use in counseling. It is, also, very difficult to construct a scale of this type as it requires the use of statements that are of neutral value in evaluating a person as well as statements that are discriminatory. The rater must select from a number of statements the one that is *most* descriptive of the worker (or supervisor) and the one that is *least* descriptive of him, as:

Most	Least	
A	A	Avoids responsibility
B	B	Inspires pride in the organization
C	C	Lacks a sense of humor
D	D	Offers suggestions[1]

The rater is not quite sure which of the statements counts favorably and which counts unfavorably for the ratee. Most raters therefore oppose this form of rating.

BEHAVIOR CHECK LIST: Many forms of behavior check lists are used. In developing one Army rating scale a list of 900 statements pertaining to behavior was first drawn up. Later these were reduced to 300 when all statements of traits considered not to be *universal* and *observable* and *distinguishable* were thrown out.[2]

As was pointed out in earlier chapters, tests to determine creative ability have not been perfected; nor have behavior check lists to evaluate creative performance. Nevertheless, considerable work has been done in recent years to determine items considered valid for purposes of determining creativity.

In one study, twenty male research supervisors of a major oil company were asked in an interview to describe the most creative and least creative man they supervised. No definition of creativity was given them. From some 900 statements collected in the interviews, 143 were selected as being non-redundant and were used in a check list with values ranging from five (describes the man exactly) to one (does not describe the man at all) on each item. Seventy-eight research persons were rated by their supervisors, after which the director of research, the assistant director of research, and the assistant manager of the research center evaluated all seventy-eight research personnel under the assumption that they were selecting the men who would make the most *significant, original,* and *lasting* contributions to research in a new research organization to be headed by the rater in each instance. Each rater selected the fifteen persons he considered to be most creative in the light of the criteria; then the next sixteen most creative were selected. This procedure was continued until all persons were included in one of five groups, A-E. Through statistical methods an average interrater reliability coefficient of .73 was obtained. An IBM 705 computer calculated validities for the 143 check list items from which a submatrix was developed. The results of this study are shown in Table XV-1. Validity is indicated by r_v and the highest correlation of that item with some other item in the type is indicated by r_{ic}. The last column indicates the number of the item with which the item

I. IDENTIFICATION DATA

1. LAST NAME—FIRST NAME—MIDDLE INITIAL	2. GRADE	3. PERMANENT AF GRADE	4. AFSN
5. AERONAUTICAL RATING	6. PAFSC	7. PERIOD OF REPORT — FROM / TO	
8. ORGANIZATION	9. PERIOD OF SUPERVISION	10. REASON FOR REPORT	

II. DUTIES

III. PERFORMANCE FACTORS (Compare this officer ONLY with officers of the same grade)

1. JOB KNOWLEDGE

| NOT OBSERVED | SERIOUS GAPS IN HIS KNOWLEDGE OF FUNDAMENTALS OF HIS JOB. | HAS A SATISFACTORY KNOWLEDGE OF ROUTINE PHASES OF HIS JOB. | IS WELL INFORMED ON MOST PHASES OF HIS JOB. | HAS EXCELLENT KNOWLEDGE OF ALL PHASES OF HIS JOB. | HAS EXCEPTIONAL UNDERSTANDING OF HIS JOB. EXTREMELY WELL INFORMED ON ALL PHASES. |

2. COOPERATION

| NOT OBSERVED | INCLINED TO CREATE FRICTION. DOES NOT GET ALONG WELL WITH OTHERS. | SOMETIMES INDIFFERENT TO OTHERS. COOPERATES TO A FAIR DEGREE. | GETS ALONG WELL WITH MOST PEOPLE. | WORKS IN HARMONY WITH OTHERS. A VERY GOOD TEAM WORKER. | EXTREMELY SUCCESSFUL IN WORKING WITH OTHERS. ACTIVELY PROMOTES HARMONY. |

3. JUDGMENT

| NOT OBSERVED | HIS DECISIONS OR RECOMMENDATIONS ARE WRONG MORE OFTEN THAN RIGHT. | IS PRONE TO NEGLECT OR MISINTERPRET FACTS. COMMITS OCCASIONAL ERRORS IN JUDGMENT | JUDGMENT IS USUALLY SOUND AND REASONABLE. | HIS JUDGMENT CONSISTENTLY RESULTS FROM SOUND EVALUATION OF ALL THE FACTORS INVOLVED. | OUTSTANDINGLY SOUND AND LOGICAL THINKER WITH AN EXCEPTIONAL GRASP OF THE SITUATION INVOLVED. |

4. MANAGEMENT QUALITIES

| NOT OBSERVED | INEFFECTIVE IN THE CONSERVATION OF MATERIEL OR ECONOMICAL USE OF MAN POWER. | UTILIZES MEN, MONEY, AND MATERIALS IN A BARELY SATISFACTORY MANNER. | CONSERVES MEN, MONEY, AND MATERIALS BY IMPLEMENTING AND MAINTAINING ROUTINE MANAGEMENT PROCEDURES. | IS EFFECTIVE IN ACCOMPLISHING SAVINGS IN MEN, MONEY, AND MATERIALS BY DEVELOPING IMPROVED MANAGEMENT PROCEDURES. | EXCEPTIONALLY EFFECTIVE IN THE UTILIZATION OF MEN, MONEY, AND MATERIALS. |

5. LEADERSHIP

| NOT OBSERVED | FAILS TO COMMAND. UNABLE TO EXERT CONTROL. | MANAGES IN SOME INSTANCES TO OBTAIN EFFECTIVE COOPERATION. | DEVELOPS ADEQUATE COOPERATION AND TEAMWORK UNDER NORMAL CIRCUMSTANCES. | COMMANDS RESPECT OF HIS SUBORDINATES. IS EFFECTIVE EVEN UNDER DIFFICULT CIRCUMSTANCES. | OUTSTANDING SKILL IN DIRECTING OTHERS. INSPIRES CONFIDENCE EVEN UNDER VERY DIFFICULT CIRCUMSTANCES. |

6. COMMUNICATION FACILITY

| NOT OBSERVED | UNABLE TO EXPRESS THOUGHTS CLEARLY. LACKS ORGANIZATION. | EXPRESSES THOUGHTS SATISFACTORILY ON ROUTINE MATTERS. | ORGANIZES AND EXPRESSES THOUGHTS CLEARLY AND CONCISELY ON ROUTINE MATTERS. | EXCELLENT COMMAND OF WRITTEN AND ORAL EXPRESSION. CONSISTENTLY ABLE TO EXPRESS IDEAS CLEARLY. | OUTSTANDING ABILITY TO COMMUNICATE IDEAS TO OTHERS THROUGH WRITTEN AND ORAL EXPRESSION. |

7. PROMOTION POTENTIAL

| NOT OBSERVED | DEFINITELY LIMITED. PRESENT JOB IS TAXING HIS CAPABILITIES. | PRESENT GRADE IS COMMENSURATE WITH ABILITY. | HAS THE CAPACITY FOR FURTHER GROWTH AT NORMAL RATE. | VERY PROMISING PROMOTIONAL MATERIAL. CAPABLE OF INCREASED RESPONSIBILITY AND ADVANCEMENT. | ONE OF THE FEW EXCEPTIONAL OFFICERS. SHOULD BE CONSIDERED FOR MORE RAPID PROMOTION THAN HIS CONTEMPORARIES. |

8. ADDITIONAL FACTORS

FACTORS	INADEQUATE	SATISFACTORY	COMPETENT AND EFFICIENT	EXCELLENT	OUTSTANDING
a.					
b.					
c.					

AF FORM 77 SEP 58   JUN 58 EDITION OF THIS FORM MAY BE USED.   **USAF OFFICER EFFECTIVENESS REPORT**

IV. OVER-ALL EVALUATION (Compare this officer ONLY with officers of the same grade)						
UNSATISFACTORY	MARGINAL	AN ACCEPTABLE OFFICER		A DEPENDABLE AND TYPICALLY EFFECTIVE OFFICER	A VERY FINE OFFICER OF GREAT VALUE TO THE SERVICE	ONE OF THE VERY FEW OUT-STANDING OFFICERS I KNOW.

V. COMMENTS OF REPORTING OFFICIAL (Be factual and specific. Add comments which increase the objectivity of the rating.)

VI. AUTHENTICATION BY REPORTING OFFICIAL

NAME, GRADE, AFSN, AND ORGANIZATION	DUTY TITLE	SIGNATURE
		DATE

VII. REVIEW BY INDORSING OFFICIAL

NAME, GRADE, AFSN AND ORGANIZATION	DUTY TITLE	SIGNATURE
		DATE

. U. S. GOVERNMENT PRINTING OFFICE : 1956 OF—482971

under consideration has the highest correlation. In each type, inspection shows that two items have their highest correlations with each other; the fact that several items may have their highest correlation with the same item suggests that subtypes exist.[3]

The researchers in the study just summarized do not claim that their list of items for assessing creativity are valid discriminators between the creative and non-creative persons; they do suggest that the items may be discriminators and point out that research is being conducted to determine the validity of the items when they are used in forced-choice form.

Cautions in Using Merit Rating Scales — The following are a few of the factors to be considered in installing and enforcing a merit-rating system:

TABLE XV-1[4]

TYPAL STRUCTURE OF ITEMS VALID FOR THE ASSESSMENT OF INDIVIDUAL CREATIVITY

Number	Item	r_v	r_{ic}	Item Number
	TYPE A			
1.	Is conversant on the latest technical developments in his field	.62	.77	7
2.	Looks for new ways of doing things	.58	.73	7
3.	Stimulates the creativity in his associates	.56	.68	5
4.	Has represented his superiors in other departments of the research center	.55	.59	3
5.	Has expressed a desire to work on highly complex problems	.55	.69	14
6.	Has expressed a desire to be eminent in his field	.53	.57	3
7.	Uses the latest techniques to solve problems assigned to him	.51	.77	1
8.	Has tackled problems others avoided	.44	.67	7
9.	Participates in the activities of the professional societies of his chosen field	.41	.45	1
10.	Has supervised the work of others in his area of specialization	.41	.44	4
11.	Puts diverse pieces of information together to arrive at a valid conclusion	.38	.53	13
12.	Has proposed entirely new approaches to a problem	.38	.70	2
13.	Develops hypotheses	.37	.70	7
14.	Seeks knowledge for its own sake	.36	.69	2
15.	Relates his own past work to his present problem	.36	.53	4

16. Has improved upon the recommendations of his superiors	.32	.53	2
17. Follows instructions	−.26	.29	19
18. His approach to every problem is unique	.24	.56	8
19. Enthusiastic about all problems on which he works	.24	.48	16
20. Questions generalized statements for specifics behind them	.24	.54	14

TYPE B

21. Has overlooked significant implications of his work	−.53	.85	23
22. Uses procedures which are outmoded	−.49	.73	21
23. Has neglected significant facts arising from his work	−.48	.85	21
24. Approaches a problem in trial and error fashion	−.44	.63	21
25. His personal problems have adversely affected his work	−.43	.53	23
26. Has ignored details which would invalidate his work	−.37	.79	23
27. Fails to sell his ideas	−.35	.73	26
28. Fails to follow through on his own best ideas	−.35	.71	23
29. Has reached conclusions unwarranted by the available information	−.34	.78	23
30. Admits to his technical shortcomings	−.31	.31	21
31. Is disdainful of nontechnical personnel	.28	.38	34
32. His written reports include irrelevant information	−.28	.76	29
33. Watches the clock	−.27	.43	29
34. His biases influence the objectivity of his interpretations	−.25	.61	29
35. His writing style confounds the problem he is reporting upon	−.24	.73	32
36. Is preoccupied with his pet projects	.23	.44	34
37. Has underestimated the time necessary to complete a project	.23	.32	36

TYPE C

38. Can transform theory into practical application	.53	.78	42
39. Has called attention to significant side results in the work of others	.53	.62	38
40. Has grasped technical relationships which have stymied others	.44	.74	38
41. Is energetic	.43	.54	44
42. Presents convincing technical arguments in support of his point of view	.42	.78	38
43. Has expressed a desire to become a member of management	.39	.47	44

44. Comprehends a problem upon its first presentation	.37	.68	38
45. Works overtime	.33	.46	41
46. Identifies the logical steps in his work before he begins	.29	.70	42
47. Has developed short-cut methods	.28	.49	39

TYPE D

48. Asks for the reasons behind management's procedural changes	.32	.50	49
49. Has questioned the orders of his superiors	.32	.50	48
50. Openly seeks recognition for his accomplishments	.26	.35	49

TYPE E

51. Fails to recognize unworkable techniques	−.30	.58	52
52. Has chosen to use a method which has already been proven to be unproductive	−.28	.60	53
53. Has proposed ideas which are contrary to known facts	−.24	.60	52

TYPE F

54. Is a technical perfectionist	.35	.62	55
55. His literature searches are exhaustive	.28	.62	54

TYPE G

56. Interrupting his work disorganizes him	−.37	.63	57
57. Has expressed a desire to work on only one problem at a time	−.35	.63	56

TYPE H

58. Has expressed a desire to remain at his present level of responsibility	−.32	.67	59
59. Has requested routine jobs	−.24	.67	58

Note — Coefficients greater than .38 are significant at the .001 level of confidence. Coefficients greater than .31 are significant at the .01 level of confidence. All other coefficients are significant at the .05 level of confidence.

1. Merit rating is (or should be) an objective method of obtaining systematic information about the workers' characteristics and performance in addition to whatever other information is available from production records (which would be highly objective when piece-rate or incentive methods of pay are used).

2. Employees should be permitted a part in planning the rating system.

3. Care should be taken to perfect the system and the scale used;

ambiguity should be eliminated if possible, and the traits should be objective.

4. The employee should be rated upon *what he is* and *what he has accomplished;* he should not be rated upon what he could do if he would, although in some instances a rater is asked to evaluate a worker's potential for advancement.

5. More than one person (generally two or three) should rate an employee. In some cases the immediate supervisor and his supervisor rate a worker. In some instances this is not practical if the second supervisor does not know the workers rated. In some companies a fellow-worker is one of the raters; in some instances workers are asked to rate their supervisors. It is useless to have a rating by a person who docs not know the ratee.

6. Not all people are capable of making accurate judgments of others. The characteristics that seem to be related to a person's ability to judge others are: intelligence, emotional adjustment, understanding of oneself, social orientation, and social skill. The person who is rating others also needs to have a background similar to that of those he is rating, or some other appropriate norm.[5]

7. After a merit-rating system is installed, it should not be permitted to develop into a record-keeping system only; the ratings must be used in interviews with the persons who were rated. The ratings must mean something in terms of promotion in salary or rank, and sometimes in terms of transfer and demotion. Chiefly, however, they are valuable to let people know how they are doing and wherein they need to improve. Presumably the best result is for an employee to gain the insight needed for appropriately appraising himself, and for developing new goals and working toward them.

8. Counseling with employees on the basis of merit ratings requires skill and understanding. All of the rules of counseling (Chapter IX) should be recalled.

Basic Systems of Job Evaluation — Job evaluation generally begins with job analysis, which means a full study of the job from which a job specification can be written. In some instances this requires time and motion study. (Chapter X defines these terms.) This job specification gives a basis for employing applicants qualified to do the job, but in the course of studying the job in all of its aspects it can at the same time be evaluated, that is, its worth to the organization can be measured. This requires that job analysts first have some basis for evaluating the functions of each job. These analysts may be from the industrial engineering section, or they may be from the personnel department. Sometimes job evaluation is done by committees composed of persons from these departments and the operating departments involved in the evaluations. The evaluation may be done by specialists from outside the company who are brought in just for job-study purposes, but these people would need much help from company employees, supervisors, and management. In companies where unions are active, job evaluation is influenced by the union's collective bargaining and any evaluation program must be a cooperative effort of the analysts, the labor union, the personnel department, and all the departments whose jobs are involved in the evaluations. Executive, professional, and certain technical jobs are generally not evaluated.

Job evaluation was pioneered by the Chicago Civil Service Commission in 1909 but grew very slowly before World War I.[6] Some industries have attempted to set up job evaluation factors and procedures on an industry-wide basis. The California aircraft industry did set up such a program. In some cases such a procedure is thought by employers to play into the hands of the unions and their industry-wide collective bargaining. This in turn, these employers believe, would lead to more government control.[7] Nevertheless, it is thought by many that employers should work toward standardization of job classification and evaluation.

Jobs in the metal trades have been more or less standardized by work of the National Metal Trades Association; the National Electrical Manufacturers' Association has also contributed to standardization of job classification and evaluation methods for electrical workers. The National Office Managers Association has done much work toward achieving a standardized plan of evaluating office jobs. Tables XV-2 and XV-3 show the NOMA plan.

Job evaluation begins with the obtaining of complete information about the job (see discussion of the job description in Chapter X). In addition, some system for evaluating and classifying each job must be selected and used. The first step is to determine the factors that are considered important in getting the job done; the second step is to decide on the approach to be used.

Generally the functions employed in evaluating jobs encompass the following: (1) education or knowledge required to do the job; (2) experience required to do the job; (3) difficulty of the job (in terms of physical demands, effort, and skill required); (4) physical working or job conditions (including hazards); (5) personal and social conditions of the job; (6) responsibility required by the job; (7) supervision given by holder of the job; (8) supervision received by holder of the job.

There are four main ways of approaching the evaluation of a job. Two of these may be called *qualitative* methods and two may be designated as being *quantitative* methods.

QUALITATIVE METHODS:

1. *Ranking method*
2. *Classification method*

QUANTITATIVE METHODS:

3. *Point method*
4. *Factor comparison method*

The net result of each of these methods of evaluating jobs is generally about the same: jobs are classified, usually by being placed within job or grade levels. Wage rates are then established according to these job or grade levels; rates for one level usually overlap with the next higher level in order that seniority and merit may be considered in making promotions within a given level. Within an educational institution, for instance, the following classification is ordinarily used for the teaching staff, and the salary scale (nine-month basis) is purely fictional:

> Professors — $9,000-$12,500
> Associate Professors — $7,500-$10,500
> Assistant Professors — $6,000-$8,500
> Instructors — $4,200-$6,500
> Assistants (usually graduate student instructors)—
> $900 per course taught

Requirements for promotion within a rank or from one rank to another would probably be determined on a basis of merit and seniority. For instance, to be promoted to an assistant professor from instructor would perhaps require a master's degree or a specified number of hours beyond the master's degree. To be promoted to the level of associate professor might require three years of successful service for the given institution and sixty hours beyond the master's degree; to be promoted to the level of professor might require four years of successful service and the Ph.D. Promotions in salary within a rank might be on the basis of semester hours of work completed, as, for every six hours completed a raise of $150 in the nine-month scale might be received.

1. *Ranking method:* In using this method, the jobs in an organization are ranked according to their value to the organization. Jobs within a given department are related to each other by simply ranking them from highest to lowest in value to the particular organization. In the industrial organization the supervisor of a department is of invaluable aid in assisting the job analysts to rank jobs in his department. Then, with the aid of middle and top executives, these jobs are related to other jobs in the

organization by the analysts. The job descriptions (or specifications) are used as the beginning point in attempting to determine which jobs require the most work, the higher degree of education, and the highest degree of all the other factors mentioned above (or whatever specific factors the analysts have decided to use).

When the jobs have been ranked they are usually arbitrarily placed in classes. Twenty ranks might thus be reduced to ten classes and the wage scale for a class enables wage promotion within the class itself.

The ranking method of evaluation is used if a more complete plan has not been installed; in effect, even when no plan at all is presumed to be used this one is in some measure being followed. The administration has simply not taken the time to formalize its method of determining its wage and salary scale. Certainly, however, the factors considered in evaluating jobs by formal methods are also considered to some extent by management even when no formal system is available. As a matter of fact, many companies do not have definite programs for wage and salary administration.[8] The result is that different rates may be paid for the same kind of work due to lack of standardization in job titles and lack of adequate job studies, although each manager may conscientiously attempt to evaluate jobs within his department on some basis of comparison.

A study made in 1947 covering 3,498 companies with some six and a half million employees showed that 69.4 per cent of those companies with over 5,000 employees had some type of job evaluation plan for hourly workers while there were formal plans for evaluating salaried jobs in 57.8 per cent of these companies. Fifty-seven per cent of all the companies responding in the study had job evaluation plans of some type.[9]

For smaller companies, the classification method (without formal quantitative measures in point values) is the type that is recommended, provided the jobs are not too complex or numerous. The ranking system should be used only when a better method cannot be provided, and probably, also, only in the smaller companies.

2. *Classification method:* When the classification method is used the job classes (job or grade levels) are established first. The jobs are then studied using the same approach that is used in the ranking method, that is, the job descriptions are analyzed to determine the degree of difficulty, education, training, experience, hazards of work, responsibilities, and so on required by the job. The job is then automatically assigned by the raters to a particular job class. Civil Service jobs in the United States are assigned grade levels, as, for instance, persons who teach in the Dependent School Detachment of the United States Army in Europe (or other overseas stations) are assigned the rating GS-7.

The GS stands for "General Schedule" and 7 is the classification given the job of teaching. The first year of service is at the minimum wage for any job in Grade 7 (GS-7). Each year thereafter, on the basis of seniority and satisfactory service rendered, there is a stipulated increment in pay. The longevity rates for one grade level overlap to a very high degree with the rates paid in the next grade level due to the fact that provision is made for a person to receive pay increases for doing the same job well for a long period of time.

3. *Point method:* The point method is the most widely used method of job evaluation. The first step in using this system is to definitely determine the factors to be used, factors that are common to all of the jobs involved in the evaluation. The next step is to decide upon the values to be assigned to each of these factors. After this it is necessary to study each job to determine the degree to which it possesses each of the factors being used. If, for instance, education is given a total weight (maximum point value) of 200 and for a particular job education is considered to be only half as important as it is for the top job being rated, then education would receive 100 points. Each factor would be considered in like manner and the job would receive a total point value. Jobs would be ranked according to their total point values. Finally, the wage scale would be determined by converting point values to dollar values.

Table XV-2 shows the plan of the National Office Management Association. The factor "Elemental," has been given one-fourth of the total possible point values. This factor is used to serve as a "leveling device" so that inequalities may be eliminated. NOMA uses the following illustration to explain how this works:

> . . . assuming that all jobs in an office had been evaluated through the use of this plan, each job would have been credited with 250 points for the 'elemental' factor. Next, assume we compared total points credited to all jobs and found the high job to be 'general clerk A' with 850 points, and the low job 'messenger' with 320 points — the ratio is 2.66 to 1. If we eliminate the 'elemental' factor from our evaluation, 'general clerk A' would be credited with 600 points and the 'messenger' with 70 points. This would change the ratio to 8.57 to 1. Which ratio is nearest to being correct? Is the job of 'general clerk A' worth 2.66 times that of 'messenger,' or is it worth 8.75 times as much?
>
> Further, to illustrate, let us suppose that with this plan in effect, point values in relation to going rates, were determined to be 30 cents per point per month. The rate for 'general clerk A' would be $255 and the rate for 'messenger' would be $96. Is the differential

reasonable? If it is, the question of need for using an 'elemental' factor is answered. The remaining question is, 'Should the "elemental" factor be fixed, and should it be 25 per cent of the total?' The answer is: What is submitted herewith is but a plan to be used as a guide; it does not necessarily follow that users must adhere to the point values which have been allocated to individual factors.[10]

The steps recommended by NOMA in using its plan of job evaluation for office workers are:

1. Obtain complete description of each job to be evaluated.
2. Review each job description carefully and indicate thereon any item needing special consideration.
3. Have available a supply of Job Analysis Sheets.[11]

TABLE XV-2[12]

CLERICAL JOB EVALUATION—NATIONAL OFFICE MANAGEMENT ASSOCIATION

Factors	Maximum Point	Value	Percentage to Total
1. ELEMENTAL		250	25%
2. SKILL			
(a) General or special education	160		16
(b) Training time on job	40		4
(c) Memory	40		4
(d) Analytical	95		9.5
(e) Personal contact	35		3.5
(f) Dexterity	80		8
(g) Accuracy	50		5
Total		500	50%
3. RESPONSIBILITY			
(a) For company property	25		2.5
(b) For procedure	125		12.5
(c) Supervision	50		5
Total		200	20%
4. EFFORT			
(a) Place of work	5		.5
(b) Cleanliness of work	5		.5
(c) Position	10		1
(d) Continuity of work	15		1.5
(e) Physical or mental strain	15		1.5
Total		50	5%
Grand Total		1000	100%

* Used by permission of the National Office Management Association, 1927 Old York Road, Willow Grove, Pa.

Job evaluation committees are warned by NOMA that they should not concern themselves with the salary to be paid, only with the rating of the job itself in terms of point values. Salary is determined later on the basis of point values assigned to jobs, incentives, and merit rating. Further, it is emphasized that raters must be thoroughly familiar with definitions of the evaluation factors. The plan is intended to be used only in evaluating clerical jobs below the rank of administrative, executive, or professional employees, as defined by the Fair Labor Standards Act.[13]

The following definitions are only slightly condensed from the full definitions used by NOMA:[14]

1. ELEMENTAL — 250 points: This covers characteristics such as honesty, appearance, deportment, physical fitness, etc.

2. SKILL — 500 points:

    a. General or Special Education — 160 points: This covers the minimum basic knowledge an employee should have to dispose of the duties of a job properly. This may include previous experience.

(1) Grammar School or its equivalent	$4 \times 10 = 40$
(2) High School or its equivalent	$4 \times 13 = 52$
(3) College or its equivalent	$4 \times 17 = \underline{68}$
	160

    b. Training Time on Job — 40 points: This represents the experience an employee must have on the job being evaluated before he can be considered fully competent to handle it.

(1) 1 to 6 days =	0
(2) 2 to 4 weeks =	1–8
(3) 2 to 6 months =	9–20
(4) 6 months to maximum =	21–40

    c. Memory — 40 points: This represents the demand that is made on an employee for memorizing certain functions of his work.

(1) Routine job — minimum memory required =	0
(2) Memory would be desirable =	1–4
(3) Requires certain items =	5–8
(4) Requires memory of many items =	9–20
(5) Complex items occasionally =	21–40

    d. Analytical — 95 points: This represents the complexity of the job to be evaluated and is a measure of the demands made on an employee's judgment and ingenuity properly to do the assigned work. Included therein should be the credit allowed for the number and importance of decisions an employee must make of his own accord without recourse to supervision.

    (1) Routine job   =   0

    (2) Requires some judgment, ingenuity, and initiative   =   1–20

    (3) Requires considerable judgment, ingenuity, and initiative   =   21–45

    (4) Jobs entirely analytical; no routine; jobs varied   =   46–95

e. Personal Contact — 35 points:

    (1) Normal employee relationship   =   0

    (2) Within own department   =   1–5

    (3) Elsewhere within the company   =   1–10

    (4) Contacts with the public   =   1–20

f. Dexterity — 80 points: This factor represents credit allowed for the demands of a natural or acquired physical ability that is necessary to perform all manual duties of the job.

    (1) None   =   0

    (2) Low   =   1–20

    (3) Medium   =   21–50

    (4) High   =   51–80

g. Accuracy — 50 points:

    (1) Work verified — not serious in case of error =   0–10

    (2) Work not verified — not serious in case of error   =   11–20

    (3) Work verified — serious in case of error =   21–30

    (4) Not verified — serious in case of error =   31–50

3. RESPONSIBILITY — 200 points:

a. For Company Property — 25 points:

    (1) Not responsible for more than desks and related equipment   =   0

    (2) Responsible for typewriters, adding machines and/or similar equipment   =   1–10

    (3) Responsible for cash funds or valuable papers   =   11–25

b. For Procedure — 125 points: This factor gives credit for the degree of responsibility placed on a position for performance of duties in accordance with policies or procedures set by the company. The responsibility may pertain to the drafting of contracts, orders, etc.; handling items of a confidential nature, or passing out information where divergence from set procedures may result in a loss of money, time or would adversely affect operations in own department, operations in other departments, or relations with customers or the public.

	Confi-dential	Loss of Money	Opera-tions in Depart-ment	Opera-tions in other Depart-ments	Rela-tions with Public
(1) None	0	0	0	0	0
(2) Low	1– 5	1– 5	1– 5	1– 5	1– 5
(3) Medium	6–10	6–10	6–10	6–10	6–10
(4) High	11–20	11–20	11–20	11–20	11–20

Compensating factor values applicable to any
unusual conditions in any bracket   1–25
Maximum applicable to any combination   125

c. Supervision — 50 points: This factor is used to evaluate supervision exercised over others, such as that of a group leader, who, in addition to doing essentially the same type of work, is responsible for the flow of work within the group and, in some degree, for the correctness of the work performed by the group. The number of persons supervised should be considered.
  (1) None   =   0
  (2) Low   =   1–10
  (3) Medium   =   11–25
  (4) High   =   25–50

4. EFFORT — Physical Factors — 50 points:
  a. Place of Work — 5 points: This allows for credit due the job because of physical surroundings and environment, such as noise, heat, light, atmosphere, hazards, etc.
    (1) Good   =   0
    (2) Fair   =   1–2
    (3) Poor   =   3–5
  b. Cleanliness of Work — 5 points: This gives credit for working conditions relative to the immediate position. Immediate surroundings may be ideal, but the nature of the job may be mussy; viz., mimeograph, ditto or carbon paper, etc.
    (1) Clean   =   0
    (2) Moderately dirty =   1–2
    (3) Very dirty   =   3–5

   c. Position — 10 points: This covers demands made on a person
to dispose the task properly . . . it is normal to have positions
such as sitting for a while, then walking, then stooping. If
these are not distributed in a normal manner, credit should
be allowed.

    (1) Normal   =   0

    (2) Tiring   =   1–4

    (3) Very tiring   =   5–10

   d. Continuity of Work — 15 points: This refers to the continuous performance on a job. It may vary from duties that
may be normal in nature, where an employee may momentarily change or stop work, to a type of job that requires
continued concentration and attention for a definite period
of time.

    (1) Intermittent   =   0

    (2) Fairly continuous   =   1– 4

    (3) Constant   =   5– 9

    (4) Monotonous   =   10–15

   e. Physical or Mental Strain — 15 points: This refers to mental
eye or nervous strain. It would be enhanced by constant interruptions, close concentration or figure work.

    (1) Normal   =   0

    (2) Low   =   1– 4

    (3) Medium   =   5– 9

    (4) High   =   10–15

NOMA has also prepared job descriptions of typical office positions.
Using these descriptions and close study of all jobs the "Job Analysis
Summary" of Table XV-3 was obtained.

4. *Factor Comparison Method:* This system is the second most popular method of evaluating jobs. In using this system all jobs are related
by means of factorial comparison to certain key jobs in the organization.
It involves the following steps:

1. Study of the job descriptions for each job.

2. Compare these jobs using key factors such as the ones used
by NOMA in Table XV-2 or the following factors which have been
frequently used: MENTAL REQUIREMENTS, SKILL RE-
QUIREMENTS, PHYSICAL REQUIREMENTS, RESPONSI-
BILITIES, WORKING CONDITIONS.

3. Select key jobs, usually not over twenty, and arrange them
in order from high to low using mental requirements as the basis of
ranking.

4. Rank each job on each of the other factors used.

5. Allocate base pay for each of the key jobs on the basis of the amount of pay for each of the factors involved.

6. Relate all jobs to the key jobs giving them factor values equivalent to the factor values assigned to the jobs to which they are most similar. A job might have the same mental requirements as the key job rated highest; its physical requirements might be the same as for the job rated third, and so on.

7. Assign base pay for these jobs on the basis of rates previously assigned the rankings of the various factors on the key jobs.

Using Job Evaluation in Setting Wages — When the point or factor comparison methods of job evaluation are used, it is relatively easy to convert the ranks to monetary units. Key jobs in a given study might be assigned values as shown below and a job related to these and other key jobs would receive an evaluation on the basis of the job it was most like on each of the factors used. In this case, this job was like Jobs 2 and 3 on all factors excepting working conditions and on that factor it was similar to another key job.

	Key Job 2		Key Job 3		Job Related to Key Jobs	
	Rank	Rate	Rank	Rate	Rank	Rate
Mental requirements ..	1	$ .75	2	$ .70	1	$ .75
Skill requirements	5	.30	4	.35	4	.35
Responsibility	2	.40	2	.40	2	.40
Physical requirements ..	8	.15	7	.20	8	.15
Working conditions	6	.20	6	.20	5	.25
		$1.80		$1.85		$1.90

In the case of the point system, point ranges are usually assigned fixed salary range, as, 950–1000 points, $450–$500; 900–949 points, $425–$475 (using a fixed range of $50, overlapping). This would be the same result as using a salary base of $500 for 950–1000 points and $450 for 900–949 points, with a fixed range of $50. For the first job, the range would be $475–$525 and for the second it would be $425–$475. If a percentage range of ten per cent were used, the salary range for the first job would still be $475–$525; for the second job it would be $427.50–$472.50.

In some instances the points assigned to a job may be multiplied by a fixed sum as was suggested in the NOMA study reported on above.

TABLE XV-3

JOB ANALYSES SUMMARY

JOBS	ELEMENTAL	SKILL — GENERAL OR SPECIAL EDUCATION	SKILL — TRAINING ON JOB	SKILL — MEMORY	SKILL — ANALYTICAL	SKILL — PERSONAL CONTACT	SKILL — DEXTERITY	SKILL — ACCURACY	RESP. — COMPANY PROPERTY	RESP. — PROCEDURES	RESP. — SUPERVISION	EFFORT — PLACE OF WORK	EFFORT — CLEANLINESS	EFFORT — POSITION	EFFORT — CONTINUITY	EFFORT — PHYSICAL STRAIN	TOTAL POINTS
TOTAL POINTS	250	160	40	40	95	85	80	50	25	125	50	5	5	10	15	15	1000
Accountant - Cost	250	130	40	25	60	20	30	35	15	50	15	0	0	0	10	10	690
Accountant - Division	250	140	40	30	75	25	30	40	20	100	40	0	0	0	10	12	812
Adjuster	250	126	40	40	45	35	50	50	10	125	0	0	0	0	4	4	779
Approver	250	143	40	40	40	30	10	45	0	125	0	0	0	0	4	2	729
Approver - Claim	250	143	40	40	30	30	10	35	0	125	10	0	0	0	4	2	719
Bookkeeper	250	92	20	40	20	15	80	25	25	70	0	0	0	0	9	9	655
Bookkeeper A	250	160	40	40	70	15	20	50	25	100	0	0	0	0	4	9	783
Bookkeeper A	250	100	20	25	20	10	50	15	10	70	0	0	0	0	0	0	570
Bookkeeper B	250	120	40	40	50	15	20	25	10	70	10	0	0	0	0	0	650
Bookkeeping Mchn. Oper.	250	100	20	10	40	5	50	15	10	70	0	0	0	0	0	0	570
Bookkeeping Mchn. Oper.	250	50	20	0	20	0	50	15	10	10	0	0	0	0	10	10	445
Calculator Operator	250	66	10	4	0	0	80	50	5	0	0	0	0	6	15	15	501
Calculator Operator	250	70	20	0	0	0	50	15	10	10	0	0	0	0	10	10	445
Cashier	250	100	40	20	40	20	30	35	15	40	10	0	0	0	10	5	615
Clerk II	250	109	25	8	20	5	0	25	0	70	0	0	0	0	0	4	516
Clerk - Accounting	250	109	25	12	20	5	0	25	0	70	0	0	0	0	0	4	520
Clerk - Accounting	250	160	35	35	40	15	0	35	0	100	10	0	0	0	0	15	695
Clerk - Audit	250	120	20	20	50	10	10	50	25	70	0	0	0	0	5	0	630
Clerk - Balance	250	126	40	40	45	15	80	25	10	70	25	0	0	0	9	9	744
Clerk - Collection	250	92	20	40	20	35	50	25	0	70	0	0	0	0	4	9	615
Clerk - Cost	250	90	40	10	10	10	30	30	15	25	5	0	0	0	5	5	525
Clerk - Cost	250	160	35	35	40	15	0	35	0	100	10	5	5	0	0	15	705
Clerk - Cost	250	100	40	20	45	15	50	25	10	70	0	0	0	0	10	10	645
Clerk - Coupon	250	92	8	8	0	5	30	25	0	25	0	0	0	0	4	4	451
Clerk - Customer	250	126	40	40	45	35	50	25	0	125	25	0	0	0	0	4	765
Clerk - Disbursement	250	100	20	20	30	15	50	25	0	70	0	0	0	0	10	10	620
Clerk - Filing	250	40	4	8	0	0	35	40	0	25	0	0	2	4	4	15	427
Clerk - Filing	250	92	20	20	20	15	30	40	24	40	0	0	0	2	4	4	562
Clerk - Filing	250	40	8	0	0	0	5	20	0	0	0	0	0	3	12	0	338
Clerk I - Filing	250	92	15	4	0	15	20	15	0	25	0	0	0	0	5	4	445
Clerk - General A	250	140	40	40	80	35	20	35	25	100	25	0	0	0	4	9	803
Clerk - General A	250	160	40	40	95	35	20	50	25	100	25	0	0	0	0	9	849
Clerk - General A	250	120	20	20	20	15	45	25	10	70	25	0	0	0	0	0	615
Clerk - Information	250	92	8	20	0	15	30	10	0	25	0	0	0	0	4	4	458
Clerk - Junior	250	40	8	2	0	10	10	0	0	10	0	0	0	4	4	2	340
Clerk - Mail	250	92	8	8	0	15	0	10	25	25	0	2	5	10	0	0	450
Clerk - Payroll	250	92	12	40	20	15	50	50	10	125	0	0	0	0	0	9	673
Clerk - Payroll	250	105	35	40	10	10	35	10	10	97	0	2	0	0	9	9	622
Clerk - Photo	250	65	8	5	0	5	80	10	10	25	0	0	0	0	0	0	458
Clerk - Railway	250	92	20	40	20	0	80	50	10	70	0	0	0	0	9	9	650
Clerk - Senior	250	130	40	30	45	15	80	50	20	100	40	0	2	3	4	5	814
Clerk - Stock	250	40	8	4	5	0	10	20	10	0	0	0	0	3	3	0	353
Clerk - Tabulating	250	66	8	4	0	0	20	50	0	0	0	2	0	4	9	0	413
Clerk - Time	250	50	40	15	0	15	30	30	15	25	0	0	0	0	5	5	480
Correspondent - Sr.	250	126	20	40	20	25	20	15	5	97	0	0	0	0	4	2	624
Dividend Enterer	250	65	8	8	0	0	15	5	0	25	0	0	0	0	0	0	376
Duplicating Mchn. Oper.	250	40	4	0	0	0	20	0	10	0	0	0	2	4	4	0	334
Duplicating Mchn. Oper.	250	70	8	4	0	0	60	10	10	10	0	0	0	10	15	0	452
Filing Writer	250	110	20	30	35	5	50	25	10	70	0	0	0	0	0	0	605
Key Punch Operator	250	53	12	0	0	0	80	0	0	0	0	2	0	6	15	15	433
Key Punch Operator	250	43	35	20	0	0	50	0	10	70	0	5	0	0	12	12	507
Key Punch Operator	250	109	20	4	0	5	80	10	10	25	0	0	0	0	15	15	543
Messenger	250	40	0	8	5	5	0	5	0	0	0	0	0	4	4	0	321
Paymaster - Assistant	250	160	40	40	85	15	0	50	25	125	50	0	0	0	10	15	865
Purchasing Assistant	250	160	40	40	30	30	0	35	0	100	10	0	0	0	0	9	704
Purchasing Assistant	250	160	40	40	85	35	0	50	0	125	10	0	0	0	10	15	820
Receptionist	250	92	12	40	20	35	20	45	5	70	0	0	0	2	0	0	591
Receptionist	250	100	20	30	20	35	20	25	0	70	0	0	0	0	0	10	580
Secretary	250	110	20	30	30	20	40	25	20	125	0	0	0	0	2	0	672
Secretary - Executive	250	125	20	30	45	35	50	50	10	100	0	0	0	0	10	15	730
Stenographer	250	50	10	10	0	5	30	30	15	20	0	0	0	0	5	0	425
Stenographer	250	115	40	20	20	15	40	25	15	50	10	0	0	0	4	9	613
Stenographer	250	110	12	20	25	5	40	20	10	20	0	0	0	0	2	0	514
Stenographer	250	105	20	4	0	10	50	0	10	10	0	0	0	0	4	0	463
Switchboard Operator	250	53	4	20	0	35	20	20	5	70	0	0	0	6	0	4	487
Switchboard Operator	250	105	20	30	5	30	35	10	10	70	0	0	0	0	9	12	586
Transcribing Mchn. Oper.	250	92	12	4	0	15	80	0	10	25	0	0	0	0	15	15	518
Transcribing Mchn. Oper.	250	110	12	8	10	10	40	10	12	20	0	0	0	0	5	0	487
Transcribing Mchn. Oper.	250	100	40	30	25	5	80	20	10	40	0	0	0	0	0	0	600
Typist	250	92	8	8	0	0	30	25	10	25	0	0	0	0	4	0	452
Typist	250	92	8	4	0	5	30	10	10	10	0	0	0	0	15	4	438
Typist	250	120	12	8	20	10	45	10	10	20	0	0	0	2	5	0	512
Typist	250	90	8	4	0	0	45	5	5	0	0	0	0	0	0	0	407
Typist	250	73	14	14	0	0	50	5	10	70	0	0	0	0	4	4	494
Typist	250	92	15	0	0	5	40	10	10	20	0	0	0	4	9	4	459
Typist	250	70	10	0	0	0	50	0	10	0	0	0	0	0	5	0	395
Typist - Tabular	250	100	20	15	20	5	80	15	10	0	0	0	0	0	0	0	515

*Used by permission of NOMA, 1927 Old York Road, Willow Grove, Pa.

This is generally considered undesirable. The point-value ranges give a basis for grade levels (job classes) and a fixed salary range for each grade level permits leeway for promoting within a given grade on the basis of seniority and merit rating.

Ways of Paying Salesmen and Sales Trainees — Since factors used for other salaried positions cannot be successfully used in most sales jobs, methods of adjusting must be employed. These include the evaluation of special factors that pertain to selling only in the over-all rating of the selling job.[16]

Factors used by Pitney-Bowes in evaluating selling jobs are: (1) complexity and judgment, (2) education and training, (3) experience and skill, (4) initiative, (5) accuracy, (6) contacts with others, (7) physical demands, (8) working conditions, (9) supervisory responsibility.[17]

Salary, commission, and bonus are the basic ways of paying salesmen. A company's plan may use one, two, or all of these. Prior to 1930 salesmen were often paid on straight salary, or straight commission. Economic and social measures of the 1930's and 1940's gave new emphasis to security. The performance bonuses of World War II days entered into sales compensation plans. The growth of the 1940's made it necessary that plans for paying salesmen be attractive as well as competitive. Today's trend is to have a base salary for security and an incentive compensation for attaining certain specified objectives.[18]

In 1947 the National Industrial Conference Board reported that in 1937, 37.8 per cent and in 1947, 47.2 per cent of the companies used salary plus incentive.[19] A study of 1,200 sales forces made by Professor Tosdal of Harvard in the early 1950's found the following practices:

20 per cent, straight salary.
23 per cent, commission, or commission and bonus (without fixed salary).
57 per cent, combination of salary and commission.[20]

More recent studies by the Sales Executives Club of New York, the American Management Association, and the Dartnell Corporation show:

About 15 per cent, straight salary.
About 20-25 per cent, on performance without fixed salary.
About 60-65 per cent, combination of salary and commission or bonus.[21]

Drawing accounts when provided rarely reach the level of commissions it is expected the salesmen will earn. Commissions range widely — from one per cent on generating equipment, for instance, to twenty-five per cent on machine tool components and parts. The commissions may be paid on total sales, sales over quota, or sales over a previous year. A commission on anything other than total sales may actually be an incentive bonus for performance exceeding a standard. Bonuses may be: (1) arrived at through statistical measures of sales volume, profit, or other factors; (2) based on general performance of sales duties, personal development, or other factors that require evaluation made by judgments. Bonus plans may give salesmen bonuses on the profit contribution of their territories (gross profit less expenses for which they are directly chargeable and which they can control).[22]

Sales trainees are generally paid on a salary basis; a small percentage of them are paid salary plus commission and/or bonus. During the training period (or a part of it) some trainees receive room and board.

Approaches to Making Changes in Work or Pay Scales — It has been pointed out in earlier chapters that people tend to resist change of any kind. Two of the best ways to avoid disruption of on-going activities by interposing a change in procedure are: (1) constantly tell the workers that the change is to be put into effect, and let them see the preparation for bringing about the change; (2) let the workers themselves have a part in planning for the change. In the case of both merit rating and job evaluation the workers should have full information as to what is being done. They should be on the committees that plan the merit-rating system; they should know what is being done when their jobs are studied (job analysis) and descriptions are written of them. Both they and their supervisors should approve a job specification once it has been written, and sometimes they do and should have a part in writing the specification.

There are numerous piece-rate systems, some of which are very difficult to understand. It is unwise to use any system that workers find too hard for them to use in computing their own pay rates. They may trust the clerks and machines that make up the payroll, but they usually also like to be able to check the figures themselves. The same may be said for any system of job evaluation: the workers like to know what is going on. They want a system they can understand. People not only tend to fear change, they generally tend to fear anything they don't or can't comprehend. Piece-rate systems are set up on the basis of standards established for jobs after these have been studied and the average output determined, sometimes on the basis of time and motion study. Care must be taken to set the standards correctly; if all workers can attain a standard with ease, it was set too low to begin with. Changing a standard after it has been set is quite difficult. (See Chapter XIX-Group Self Disciplining and Group Pressures.)

Summary — There are five general methods of merit rating (rating a worker on performance and/or personal and work characteristics): ranking; man-to-man comparison, or paired comparison; graphic rating scale; forced-choice rating scale; behavior check list. Four types of job evaluation (determining of the value of a job to an organization, measuring the job) predominate: qualitative methods: ranking and classification; quantitative methods (most often used): point and factor comparison.

Managerial jobs are quite difficult to evaluate. Because a given individual frequently is worth a great deal more in a given managerial job than another person would be, job evaluation at the managerial level usually evolves into evaluation of the performance of the man in the position. Texas Instruments, Inc., uses the following factors in evaluating managerial performance (they can be used only in terms of performance on the job): education, intelligence, experience, drive and initiative, ability to work with people, ability to lead and inspire men, creativeness, problem-solving ability, judgment, ability to handle authority, willingness to take responsibility, willingness and ability to work hard for long hours.[23]

After studying ten representative management evaluation plans, Sibson classified the factors used into three categories: (1) KNOW-HOW (requirements of duties, knowledge, planning required, mental application, understanding required, administration, original thinking, creative ability, managerial techniques); (2) RESPONSIBILITIES (initiative, accountability, effect on profits, responsibility for personnel relations, responsibility for policy making, responsibility for policy interpretation); (3) RELATIONSHIPS (supervision exercised, demand for leadership, influence on policy making, influence on methods).[24]

Researchers at the University of Chicago concluded from an extensive study of merit ratings by peers and observers, reported in 1960, that "individual differences in rater frames of reference contribute to the differences between the ratings a man receives in different groups." It was found, also, that peer ratings were systematically more positive than the ratings made by observers (See Table XV-4).[25]

A number of studies dealing with factor analyses of job evaluation have concluded that instead of the ten or more factors usually used, only three or four factors are needed in order to produce the same results. Basic factors according to these studies are those concerned with skill demands, responsibilities, working conditions, and job hazards. Various studies have also attempted to measure the reliability of evaluations by correlating ratings made by different raters at different times. Most of these have shown that trained analysts do consistently produce

TABLE XV-4[26]

MEDIAN CORRELATIONS BETWEEN PEER AND OBSERVER RATINGS FOR
SEPARATE SESSIONS*

Trait	Physical	Verbal	All
Liking	.40	.46	.44
Maturity	.54	.55	.54
Breadth of interests	.57	.53	.54
Leadership potential	.67	.72	.70
Number of useful ideas	.75	.70	.73
Considerateness	.40	.59	.49
Assertiveness	.83	.86	.84

* The medians are based on rank correlations for each of 192
sessions, half of each kind (i.e., peer and observer). For each
session, N = 6.

TABLE XV-5[27]

ESTIMATES OF RELIABILITY BASED ON INTERCORRELATIONS AND
COMPONENTS OF VARIANCE (WRIGHT AIR DEVELOPMENT DIVISION,
UNITED STATES AIR FORCE)

Factor	Single Rater		Average of 5 Raters	
	Inter-correlation	Component of Variance	Inter-correlation	Component of Variance
1. Knowledge	.775	.157	.945	.480
2. Physical Skills	.572	.294	.869	.675
3. Adaptability and Resourcefulness	.608	.172	.885	.509
4. Responsibility for Money and Materials	.587	.254	.876	.629
5. Responsibility for Safety of Others	.757	.406	.939	.787
6. Responsibility for Directing Others	.562	.024	.865	.129
7. Physical Effort	.693	.451	.918	.804
8. Attention	.665	.196	.908	.549
9. Job Conditions	.798	.523	.951	.845
10. Military and Combat	.692	.220	.918	.585
Total Score	.790	.185	.949	.521

the same results. A study by Harding made of certain aspects of the job evaluation system of the United States Air Force found that a simple averaging of independent ratings very closely approximated consensus ratings derived from discussions between two judges. Contrary to other studies, however, this one concluded that it may not always be advisable to reduce the number of factors in job evaluation. This conclusion was reached because only a small amount of variance in each of the factors could be predicted from the other factors (See Table XV-5).[28]

A study made by Lyman W. Porter of the University of California, Berkeley, found that there is little difference between bottom and middle managers in how they ranked thirteen common personality traits in terms of perceived importance for success in their respective jobs. Traits indicating cooperativeness were ranked high by both groups although there was a moderate trend for these traits to be rated as more important for bottom management jobs than for middle management (See Table XV-6).[29] It will be noted that these personality traits may be used in merit rating, that is, in rating the man. Factors used in Table XV-5 are used in evaluating or measuring the job.

TABLE XV-6[30]

MEAN SCORES AND RANKS FOR TRAITS BY MANAGEMENT LEVELS

Trait	Bottom Management (N = 64)		Middle Management (N = 76)	
	Mean Score	Rank	Mean Score	Rank
Aggressive	6.17	8	6.34	7
Conforming	4.73	11	3.21	11
Cooperative	9.78	1	9.13	1
Dominant	1.72	13	1.42	13
Energetic	7.25	3	7.45	4
Flexible	6.59	5	7.08	5
Independent	2.16	12	2.53	12
Intelligent	8.89	2	9.08	2
Original	5.27	10	6.04	9
Persevering	6.31	7	6.47	6
Poised	5.44	9	5.46	10
Self-Controlled	7.17	4	7.68	3
Sociable	6.52	6	6.11	8

PROJECTS

1. Using the information in Table XV-2 and information concerning NOMA definitions of the factors used in that table, evaluate any office job that you may have held during summers or while in school. If you have held no job, evaluate a job held by some person you know.

2. Using the information contained in Table XV-1, make a rough estimation of your own creative ability.

ACKNOWLEDGMENTS AND REFERENCES

1   Bittner, Reign, "Developing an Employee Merit Rating Procedure," *Personnel,* American Management Association, January, 1949, p. 290.
2   *Ibid.,* p. 281.
3   Buel, William D., "The Validity of Behavioral Rating Scale Items for the Assessment of Individual Creativity," *Journal of Applied Psychology,* Vol. 44, No. 6, December, 1960, pp. 407–412.
4   *Ibid.*
5   Taft, Ronald, "The Ability to Judge People," *Psychological Bulletin,* January, 1955, pp. 1–21.
6   Milkey, Robert F., "Job Evaluation After 50 Years," *Management of the Personnel Function,* edited by I. L. Heckmann and S. G. Huneryager, Charles E. Merrill Books, Inc., Columbus, Ohio, p. 518.
7   Aspley, John Cameron, and Whitmore, Eugene (editors), "Job Analysis and Evaluation," *The Handbook of Industrial Relations,* The Dartnell Corporation, Publishers, Chicago, 1948, pp. 541–542.
8   Wallace, R. F., "Job Analysis, Description, and Classification," *Management of the Personnel Function,* edited by I. L. Heckmann and S. G. Huneryager, Charles E. Merrill Books, Inc., Columbus, Ohio, p. 488.
9   Milkey, *op. cit.,* p. 519.
10   ———, "Clerical Job Evaluation. . . ," *Office Executive,* December, 1959, p. 16.
11   *Ibid.,* p. 14.
12   *Ibid.*
13   *Ibid.,* pp. 12–24.
14   *Ibid.,* pp. 16–17.
15   *Ibid.,* p. 20.
16   Earl, Elmer W., *Determining Salesmen's Base Pay a Role of Job Evaluation,* Studies in Personnel Policy, No. 98, National Industrial Conference Board, Inc., 247 Park Avenue, New York 17, New York, 1948, pp. 1–36.
17   ———, *You and Your Job at Pitney-Bowes,* Pitney-Bowes, Inc., Stamford, Connecticut, April 1, 1957, p. 7.
18   Wilson, Charles J., "Common Characteristics of Compensation Plans for Industrial Salesmen," *Marketing's Role in Scientific Management,* edited by Robert L. Clewett American Marketing Association, 27 East Monroe St., Chicago 3, Illinois, 1957, pp. 161–171.
19   Earl, Elmer W., Jr., *Salesmen's Compensation Plans,* Studies in Personnel Policy, No. 81, National Industrial Conference Board, Inc., 247 Park Avenue, New York 17, New York, 1947, pp. 13–22.
20   Wilson, *op. cit.,* p. 163.
21   *Ibid.,* pp. 163–164.
22   *Ibid.,* p. 166.
23   Haggerty, Patrick E., "Executive Development at Texas Instruments, Inc.," *Proceed-*

ings, Twentieth Conference, Texas Personnel and Management Association, The University of Texas, Austin, October 30–31, 1958, p. 23.

24 Sibson, Robert E., "Plan for Management Salary Administration," *Harvard Business Review,* November-December, 1956, pp. 104–5.

25 Fiske, Donald W., "The Consistency of Rating by Peers," *Journal of Applied Psychology,* Vol. 44, No. 1, February, 1960, pp. 11–17.

26 *Ibid.*

27 *Ibid.*

28 Harding, Francis D., Madden, Joseph M., and Colson, Kenneth, "Analysis of a Job Evaluation System," *Journal of Applied Psychology*, Vol. 44, No. 5, October, 1960, p. 356.

29 Porter, Lyman W., "Perceived Trait Requirements in Bottom and Middle Management Jobs," *Journal of Applied Psychology,* Vol. 45, No. 4, August, 1961, p. 235.

30 *Ibid.,* p. 233.

SUPPLEMENTARY READING LIST

Johnson, Forrest Hayden, Boise, Robert W., Jr., and Pratt, Dudley, *Job Evaluation*, John Wiley & Sons, Inc., New York, 1946.

Jucius, Michael J., *Personnel Management,* Fourth Edition, Richard D. Irwin, Inc., Homewood, Illinois, 1959.

Lytle, Charles Walter, *Job Evaluation Methods,* Second Edition, The Ronald Press Company, New York, 1954.

Patton, John A., and Littlefield, C. L., *Job Evaluation,* Richard D. Irwin, Inc., Homewood, Illinois, 1957.

CHAPTER XVI

LABOR RELATIONS AND UNIONS

What Is Meant by Industrial Relations? — Today in the United States we have on the one side collectivism in industry, on the other side collectivism in labor. It is not inconceivable that the leaders in these two ostensibly opposing forces should be led eventually to collaborate despite the fact that Elton Mayo said, "While material efficiency has been increasing for two hundred years, the human capacity for working together has in the same period continually diminished." [1] Mayo also stated that "collaboration in an industrial society cannot be left to chance." [2] Government has been constrained to intervene when labor has been most oppressed, but the pendulum swings and when labor has been too much imbued with power government has also taken action.

There must be some degree of cooperation between management and labor. The firm's industrial relations department or division (or the labor relations section of the personnel department) is the first place that representatives of management and the union get together for resolving conflicts, arriving at agreements, and writing labor contracts. All departments are responsible for labor relations, but the industrial relations department is engaged in working directly with union and labor problems and in promoting the various benefit programs for labor.

Americans sometimes lack belief in either side of industrial leadership. The business leader was in the "doghouse" after the crash of 1929 and until the late thirties. Around 1940 the labor leader took his place. The power and strength of labor organizations has since that time even more than before it influenced wages, hours, working conditions, politics, and through politics labor legislation. In the late 1940's, however, the tendency was to return some of its lost power to management. Certain subtle but persistent forces, nevertheless, seem to indicate that management and labor are actually not too far apart in their objectives. Any management conference usually reveals that those who are in charge of industrial relations policy are to some degree sympathetic with labor's problems. These managers, however, must usually take the side of owners in wage negotiations despite the fact that they themselves often have only small incentive ownership if any at all. They, as a result, sometimes find that they participate in negotiating for men classified as "laborers" hourly wages which are comparable to, or possibly in some cases exceed, their own white collar salaries. In spite of the fact, too, that they are willing to concede that the man in the boiler room is due his share in the price of the commodity produced for society, labor negotiations are generally painful to the men who sit around bargaining tables and negotiate wage contracts.

The term *industrial relations* has evolved as the term that encompasses the over-all administrative function of directing the total personnel and labor relations program. It is responsible for personnel policies, programs, and organization (including recruiting, placing, training, promotion, transfer, termination of employment, merit rating systems, job analysis, job and man specifications, and job evaluation). It is also responsible for negotiating labor contracts (collective bargaining in all of its aspects), handling grievances, employee services and benefit programs, counseling (or other help such as legal aid), communications, wage and salary administration, records and reports on employees, and personnel research. It is responsible through its legal section for interpreting and enforcing laws relating to labor and labor relations.

Other chapters have concerned themselves with the functions of counseling, employing, training, merit rating, job evaluation, communicating, and so on. This chapter will deal specifically with collective bargaining, grievances, labor unions, and labor laws. Anyone planning a career in industrial relations would need to take special courses in labor history, labor problems, and labor law, in addition to the usual courses in personnel management, human relations, and, possibly, collective bargaining.

Collective Bargaining — Workers have traditionally been interested in *pay* and *hours of work*. Labor negotiations concern not only these factors but many others such as: working conditions; senority rules for promotion, transfer, and layoff; other promotion, transfer, and layoff conditions; replacements, retirement and pension plans; sickness, accident, hospitalization, and death benefits. Some of the topics under wage agreements alone are: merit increases; voluntary wage-benefit plans; telephone expenses of employees required to maintain telephone services in their homes; pay for emergency work; shifted tour pay (pay for being required to work more than two short shifts — changes — a week); pay for less than twenty-four hours' notice of new starting time; pay for being given less than twenty-four hours' notice of new starting time; pay for being less than eight hours off between old schedule and beginning of new; vehicle mileage allowance; moving expenses; meals and mealtime pay; subsistence pay; call-in pay (pay for being called in when there is no work); sick leave pay; severance pay; vacation pay; holiday pay; premium pay for Sunday work; overtime pay; night premium pay; shift premium pay; travel pay; premium pay for dirty work; call-back pay; guaranteed annual wage; supplementary unemployment benefits; profit sharing; stock ownership.

Collective bargaining is that bargaining that takes place between management and labor and in particular that involved in arriving at agreement upon what should go into the labor contract. It is the method by which agreement between the representatives of management and labor is reached. Labor is given the right under law to organize for the purpose of bargaining collectively through its duly appointed representatives. Management is compelled by law to bargain with labor and in doing so it must observe the regulations of federal and state law. Labor must also observe these laws. Some of the laws regulate labor unions, workers, and employers in their relationships with each other; other laws pertain to hours and wages, social security, safety, and health of employees.

Collective bargaining grew out of the fact that the individual worker was not in position to bargain alone with powerful business and industrial organizations. Earlier organizations of craftsmen (guilds) had both employees and employers in their memberships. When journeymen (apprentices) found that the master craftsmen were making the entering of their crafts or trades more difficult, these journeymen sometimes formed groups to deal with the master craftsmen. In the United States the first union was probably that of cordwainers in 1792 in Philadelphia. Some of the early unions in this country were: typographers, 1850; stone-cutters, 1853; hat-finishers, 1854. It is said that 32 such unions existed by the end of the Civil War.[3]

Collective bargaining was a chief purpose of early labor unions; it has remained a chief purpose of unions today. Most of the early labor groups included in their statements of aims the aim to combat the combinations of owners. T. V. Powderly, who guided the destiny of the Knights of Labor through that organization's most productive years, wrote in 1889:

The year 1859 came upon the people of the United States, and found them suffering and in distress. Beggars and tramps began to ask for bread. . . . The panic of 1857 had reduced many to beggary. . . . With the erection of the factory commenced the combination of capital and capitalists.

Every two, three, ten or fifty men, who united their wealth for the purpose of instituting a manufacturing establishment, formed a combination of employers, and to that extent were members of a union whose object was to make profit from the sale of their product, and to secure from other men as much labor as possible, at the lowest rate of compensation.

For one workingman to attempt to successfully compete with a union of that kind was sheerest nonsense; such a thing was, and is an impossibility. . . .

After the formation of unions of capitalists, began the formation of labor unions, and away back in the early days of the republic we can trace the organization of crafts here and there for their own advancement and protection. Step by step the organization of labor unions can be traced, until the year 1859 found men of all callings looking about them for a relief from idleness and want.[4]

Grievances — When employees have dissatisfactions or complaints that they believe have not received consideration, these become grievances. Three types of complaints leading to grievances were uncovered by the Hawthorne studies. The first of these, relatively few in number, had to do with tangible objects that could be seen and touched and had some part in the physical operations of a department or plant, as, "This machine won't work." The second type had to do with sensory experiences (other than seeing and touching), but for which there were no agreed upon definitions in terms of operations. They were based on subjective reactions, as, "The working conditions are terrible in this department," or "The work is too hard." They involved reactions to heat, cold, pain, nausea, thirst, hunger, and tension brought on by fatigue. The third type of complaints involved the sentiments of workers, their hopes and fears, dreams, and fantasies, as, "The boss isn't fair," "The company isn't what it used to be." Attitudes influence workers to bring about complaints of this type. Such complaints cannot, therefore, be judged apart from the situations of the persons who make them.[5]

It is necessary to know why and how often complaints are being expressed in order to handle these complaints and prevent occurrence of grievances. Many complaints never reach management; when the complaint does reach management, however, the complaining employee should feel that he can express his opinion to his supervisor (or perhaps to a counselor or someone making a morale survey) without fear of reprisal against him. If the complaint is expressed to a counselor or surveyor it is not settled at this point, but enough complaints of the same type should receive action based upon tabulations of results of counseling or surveying. If a complaint expressed to a supervisor is not settled, it becomes a grievance and there should be some formal procedure for handling it. Generally, it should be put into writing (after all facts pertaining to it have been gathered) and passed on up to the next level of management. In unionized firms the business agent or shop committee might become involved. If a grievance reaches top level management, or the international representative of the union, and if the grievance is not settled, it may be necessary for an arbitrator to come into the picture. When a solution has been applied to a grievance, it should be followed up to see that problems were worked out satisfactorily and that the trouble that existed was eliminated.

The best way to handle grievances, of course, is to prevent their occurring. It is not possible to know how successful a manager is in preventing grievances except by the smooth functioning of his organization. Attitudes, willingness to listen and help, skill in interviewing and counseling, all play a part in preventing grievances and in settling them once they have been permitted to develop.

If a grievance is permitted to become a large problem between management and the union, mediation, conciliation, and arbitration are methods provided for settling the difficulty — otherwise strikes and court action may result. The Erdman Act (1898) provided for mediation and conciliation between parties when they requested it (the act also prohibited railroads from discharging employees because they belonged to labor unions). The Railway Labor Act (1926) was the first federal act to recognize labor's right to organize without interference.

The National Labor Board established by the National Recovery Act, 1933, was set up to help settle labor disputes. When the NIRA was declared unconstitutional in 1935, a new act (National Labor Relations Act) was immediately passed establishing the National Labor Relations Board, which arranges for orderly collective bargaining and settles labor disputes. Labor may file charges with the NLRB if a firm will not bargain in good faith. Unfair labor practice charges are prosecuted upon the decision of a General Counsel appointed by the President with the consent of the Senate.

The following brief statement summarizes the procedures for settling labor disputes:

The Federal Mediation and Conciliation Service helps in settling disputes of labor and management. This service, provided since 1913 by the Department of Labor, was made an individual agency for the Labor Management Relations Act (Taft-Hartley) in 1947. Mediation, conciliation, fact-finding, and compulsory arbitration are four means of settling disputes which may involve government-agency action. Voluntary arbitration, a fifth method of settling difficulties, is by mutual agreement of the labor-management groups and is administered by the parties, by the American

Arbitration Association, or by some other agency selected by the parties. In conciliation, the go-between tries to get the two groups together so that each may see the other's viewpoint. The mediator goes even further in trying to get the two groups to see eye to eye. Arbitration, however, requires that a third party hand down a decision in the dispute. A sixth procedure for settling disputes, litigation, results when the disputes cannot be settled otherwise. One party summons the other to appear in court, and the court's decision, presumably, settles that particular dispute.[6]

Implications of Labor Unions — KINDS OF UNIONS — On March 3, 1859, machinists and blacksmiths met in Philadelphia to organize the first national union of these trades. No previous very successful effort to form a national union of any one trade had been made. It is true, however, that the typographers who unionized in 1850 did develop into a national union and it is today considered the oldest union in continued existence in this country. The National Labor Union (1866), the Industrial Brotherhood (1874), and the Knights of Labor (1869), were the three national unions that dominated from 1866–1889. The Knights of Labor evolved as the most powerful and long-lived of these. Much secrecy was employed in the early years of the Knights of Labor because it was felt that otherwise its members might be exposed to the scrutiny and wrath of their employers.[7]

Most of the early labor unions wrote long lists of aims and purposes. These usually included the aim to educate. They also opposed the bringing of a "servile race" into the country to tamper with the labor of the American workingman. In the case of the NLU the statement was made that:

> . . . women are entitled to equal pay for equal services with men; that the practice of working women and children ten to fifteen hours per day, at starvation prices, is brutal in the extreme, and subversive of the health, intelligence, and morality of the nation, and demands the interposition of law.[8]

One of the chief stated aims of the Knights of Labor was "to organize the masses into an association where they can be educated." [9] For different people the Knights of Labor was different things: (1) political, (2) cooperative, (3) the boycott, strikes, and so on. Its most marked characteristic has been said to be "reformism" which the Knights themselves continued to call "education." [10]

From the time of the Haymarket bomb, May 4, 1886, the Knights of

Labor began to lose ground. In December, 1886, the American Federation of Labor was formally organized at Columbus, Ohio. It grew out of the Federation of Trades of which Samuel Gompers had been president in 1885. It is for this reason that 1881 is sometimes given as the date of origin of the AFL. This group and all others grew out of long movements, smaller groups, and the combining of those groups.[11] Gompers remained a moving spirit of the AFL for many years. This union became known as a craft union. The Committee for Industrial Organization in 1935 offered industrial unions a central group with which to affiliate. The name of this group was changed in 1938 to CIO. The AFL and CIO began operating in 1955 as the AFL-CIO with a top governing body made up of officers and members (originally three from each of the former groups). A number of independent and company unions continue to function outside the AFL-CIO. Total union membership in the United States has been variously estimated. It is currently thought that there may be approximately 20,000,000 union members in all groups with the majority being in the AFL-CIO.

There are four main discernible strands in the American labor movement: *fraternalism, collective bargaining, cooperation,* and *politics.*[12] An extensive study of labor history is necessary to untangle these strands. In early unions the attempt to secure better wages was sometimes not a concerted demand made upon an employer, but an agreement made between the workers themselves that each of them would refuse to work for less than a stipulated minimum wage.[13]

Today collective bargaining is a main function of unions, although remnants of the other strands referred to above are still to be detected. Through collective bargaining, unions have gained better wages, improved working conditions, reduced hours, and fixed the type of work to be done by certain groups of workers. Through the right given it by members, the union executes contracts covering the terms and conditions under which workers perform. Work stoppages (strikes) continue to be the most effective weapon of the unions in enforcing their demands. Some types of strikes are illegal under the Labor Management Relations Act. The jurisdictional strike to require employers to permit only certain union or craft members to do certain types of work is one of these; other types of strikes generally considered illegal are: sit-down, slow-down, and sympathy strikes. Primary boycotts are legal means of enforcing union demands but secondary boycotts are not. When employees refuse to buy the product of their employers, this is primary boycotting. When they refuse to buy from a firm that purchases from their employers, a secondary boycott exists. When workers refuse to buy products made by a firm whose workers are striking, or whose workers have refused to unionize, this is also considered secondary boycotting. Picketing is another of the methods used by unions to enforce demands; mass picketing, however, is not legal under the LMRA.

WHY WORKERS PARTICIPATE IN UNIONS — Employers sometimes feel that when their employees turn to a union they are disloyal to the company. They should realize that employees generally do not join unions because they are dissatisfied with their company or their employer. *Human dignity,* a right to have a say in what is taking place, the right to be heard on grievances, and the desire to belong to the worker group are among the reasons workers join unions.[14] In the early days of labor unions, the union was frequently a substitute for all that the worker had left behind (family, friends, community, state, church) in the "Old Country."

Workers who join unions may be quite loyal (probably usually are) to their companies as well. A study by Purcell of a unionized Swift plant (1949–1952), showed that seventy-three per cent of the workers were positively favorable to both the company and the union; eighty-eight per cent of the stewards held dual allegiance.[15]

While workers want the security of belonging to a union and the feeling of dignity that this gives, and while they are loyal to the union in strikes, they often do not participate in union meetings and they do not like to accept union offices. They do not hesitate, however, to criticize those persons who do accept the union's offices. The union is a "way of life" for only a small group of today's workers; it is a very important method of representation for the majority.[16]

WHY WORKERS STRIKE — When workers strike they usually do so on some basis pertaining to salary or wage rates. Generally, this is because uniting workers around any other grounds for striking would be quite difficult. The average worker does not realize that it is a rare case when anybody "wins" in the prolonged strike. Workers generally in such a case cannot ever get back in dollars of pay the sum lost during the period of strike; owners, of course, suffer; consumers, too, suffer because the added costs of the owners and the losses of the strike period are passed on to the consumers.

Back of the monetary reasons for striking, there are usually fears or frustrations that enable leaders to win the favor of workers for striking. Airline pilots may, for instance, be led to strike for higher pay now, although their deep-seated reason for striking may be fear of earlier retirement or new planes requiring a different type of training from that they possess. Any group of persons under prolonged stress may be led to fight back in one way or another. A study made by Alexander H. Leighton during World War II of the prisoners in the Colorado River

Relocation Center, Poston, Arizona, found that the following kinds of stress are disturbing to the emotions and thoughts of individuals:

1. Threats to life and health.
2. Discomfort from pain, heat, cold, dampness, fatigue, and poor food.
3. Loss of means of subsistence (money, jobs, business, property).
4. Deprivation of sexual satisfaction.
5. Enforced idleness.
6. Restriction of movement.
7. Isolation.
8. Threats to children, family members, and friends.
9. Rejection, dislike, and ridicule from other people.
10. Capricious and unpredictable behavior on the part of those in authority upon whom one's welfare depends.[17]

Three ways that individuals universally react to authority when they are subjected to stress that is disturbing to their emotions are: *cooperation, withdrawal,* and *aggressiveness.* Communities may often be divided into three groups according to these three types of reactions. The aggressive people are the ones who are getting results, but their aggression may be of two types: (1) that that will free them from the authority causing the disturbance to their emotions and thoughts, and (2) that that will lead to violent, confused action.

Leighton's study found that the following factors helped to bring on aggressive acts and expressions among those whom he studied: (1) "A reduction in fear of the Administration and a realization that the aggressive individual could hide in the mass of people who made up the Center." (2) ". . . continuation without relief of most forms of stress, with an increase in some of them." (3) ". . . the fact that because of frustrations and uncertainties, attempts at cooperation continued to be more immediately punishing than rewarding." Although coercion might have prevented aggressive acts, it would have retarded cooperation; aggressiveness was controlled and directed in such manner that it often proved useful both in altering conditions that aroused the feelings and in alleviating the feelings themselves.[18]

Major W. E. Mayer of the United States Army along with others assigned to the Special Medical Intelligence project on Korean prisoners of war interviewed the men returned from Korean prisons. These prisoners were under stress for a considerable period of time and would be expected to act in one of the three ways stipulated above: cooperation, withdrawal, or aggressiveness. These men, however, were subjected to "brainwashing" and the result was that although they were in community camps where they were as lightly guarded as with a ratio of one armed guard to a hundred soldiers, without machine gun towers, searchlights, or electrical or barbed wire fences, no American ever escaped. There was never any organized resistance of any kind. Thirty-eight per cent of the men died in spite of the fact that conditions appeared to have been much better than those in Japanese P.O.W. camps in World War II and better than most of the German P.O.W. camps. There is a great implication here for keeping some degree of aggressiveness alive in any group; it may be the spark that helps to keep the group itself alive. The men in these camps did react by cooperation and withdrawal. In general, four techniques were used in the "brainwashing" process: (1) The men were given lengthy lectures about the decadent condition of the capitalist system and about their own weaknesses. The lecturers were generally apparently well educated. The captives were forced to stand for long periods listening to the prepared lectures; they heard the same things over and over. This phase of the "brainwashing" was a process of indoctrination. (2) The prisoners were not delivered any good news letters, just the letters that carried bad news. (3) The prisoners were encouraged to cooperate. They were told that if they cooperated there would be "no slave camps, no work gangs, no road crews, no coal mines." The persons who might have been effective leaders were segregated (colored troops were also put in separate camps). Only one in twenty was segregated "in order to deprive the other ninety-five per cent of any form of effective leadership." The prisoners were encouraged to inform and were rewarded for doing so; the persons upon whom they informed, however, were not punished, but the "instructor" had a heart-to-heart talk with these people. In these talks the culprits were asked to see the error of their ways, confess, and say they wouldn't repeat their anti-social behavior. Because nobody was punished, it didn't seem bad to inform. Apparently, by the end of the first year of the Korean war there was one reliable informer in every group of about ten American prisoners. More than this collaborated to some extent. The soldiers got to the place that they couldn't be sure about anybody. (4) The prisoners were brought together in small groups to confess their shortcomings, failures, and poor attitudes. At first these sessions seemed harmless; men felt better for having "expiated" their guilt. Then, however, they got to feeling they had gone too far; they had exposed too much of themselves. They set about listening to the others, collecting information on them; but they withdrew from conversing in the normal manner and avoided their fellow confessors; they just "couldn't be sure with these people."

As a result of the findings of those who interviewed American soldiers who were Korean prisoners, a 247-word "Code of Conduct" was written, and among other things that the American soldier endorses in this code are these two statements: "I will continue to resist if I am captured. . . . If I'm ever captured by an enemy I will not accept favors from him. I will not make any promises to him." [19] The implications here for anyone dealing with people under stress are that to kill their initiative through cultivating total compliance and dependence and/or extreme withdrawal is to kill their aggressive tendencies, and when the aggressive tendencies are killed they frequently lose hope entirely and are of no use to themselves or others; they may, in fact, simply die. There should not be attempt to stamp out aggression if the group is to be kept useful; but aggression should be channeled into creative outlets.

Principal Labor Laws and Their Implications — The Clayton Act of 1914 exempted labor unions from the provisions of the Sherman Act of 1890 which prohibited conspiracy to combine in restraint of trade. The Sherman Act made it illegal to obtain a monopoly on a commodity in trade. The labor of human beings was declared by the 1914 act not to be a commodity in trade. Prior to 1932 contracts could be enforced to require workers to promise not to join unions. These were known as "yellow-dog" contracts. The Norris-LaGuardia Act, 1932, outlawed such contracts and restricted the use of court injunctions to limit activities of unions. The act also gave workers the right to organize and bargain collectively. It also recognized the worker's right to refuse to associate with his fellow workers. The act did not, however, contain penalties that could be used in enforcing it. The National Labor Relations Act of 1935 (also known as the Wagner Act) not only gave labor the right to organize but it required employers to bargain collectively with representatives of labor if the employees desired this.

The Labor Management Relations Act of 1947 (also known as the Taft-Hartley Act), amended the NLRA. The Conciliation Service under the LMRA was organized as an independent agency known as the Federal Mediation and Conciliation Service. The agency may offer its services on its own motion or the request of any party to an industrial dispute.[20]

The LMRA makes provisions for the rights of employers and employees, while at the same time keeping the right of the union to organize and bargain collectively. The act outlaws the closed shop (one that requires workers to be union members at the time of employment); it requires that the majority of workers vote to have a union shop before one may exist (in a union shop workers must join a union after they are hired); it requires that the authorization to deduct dues from an employee's paycheck be in writing; it requires that financial reports be made annually by the unions to their members.

In addition to the controls on picketing, boycotting, and sympathy strikes mentioned earlier in the chapter, the LMRA placed certain other controls on the unions: They must bargain in good faith with the employers; they may have to wait for a 60-day cooling-off period before they can strike legally when a contract is about to terminate; they may not require pay for employees who have not worked (requiring pay for work not done is known as "feather-bedding").

Employers in addition to having to bargain collectively may not restrict employees from organizing or interfere in the administration of their organizations; they may not fire or refuse to hire persons because they are union members; they may not discriminate against employees because they belong to a union, have filed charges, or have given testimony under the LMRA.

There are many state laws that deal with pay, hours, and union activities, such as the right to strike, picket, boycott, and so on. Anyone working in industrial relations should become familiar with the laws that pertain to his particular phase of work. Those who deal with wage administration, payrolls, unemployment compensation, and retirement benefits should study pertinent state laws and be familiar with the provisions of the Fair Labor Standards Act (1938) and the Social Security Act (1935), as well as the numerous amendments to these acts.

For those who wish to specialize in laws pertaining to wages and hours, the history of acts passed and cases based upon them will prove to be interesting reading. Only two acts passed prior to the FLSA will be mentioned here, however: the Bacon-Davis Act, 1931, required that prevailing wages be paid for public construction; the Walsh-Healey Act, 1936, required that firms contracting to do work for the government not only pay the prevailing community rate but pay time and a half for overtime after eight hours of work in a given day.

The 1961 amendment to the FLSA required that firms engaged in interstate commerce today pay a minimum wage of $1.25 an hour (the first minimum pay was twenty-five cents an hour). For all hours worked over forty hours a week, the individual worker in these firms must be paid time and a half. Firms that do only intrastate business are exempt; further, if employees who work on interstate business can be segregated, the others may be legally excluded from the provisions of the law. Administrative and professional employees are exempt. Numbers of types of firms are exempt, as, retail firms that do seventy-five per cent retail or service business and fifty per cent intrastate business, and those engaged in agriculture, fishing, and transportation. Firms that process agricultural and other seasonal products are partially exempt. Amendments have continued to make provisions for exemptions, as, newspapers, sawmill and logging operations, Western Union agencies, taxicab companies, and telephone exchanges. The FLSA prohibits the employment of children sixteen to eighteen years of age in hazardous occupations, even when their parents are the employers; it also contains by reenactment other provisions of the 1916 Child Labor Law which was declared unconstitutional.

It is generally thought that the FLSA raised the wage level for unskilled workers, but that it did not bring about a comparable raise for skilled workers. The minimum wage of the FLSA is not to be considered a standard; union contracts may set wages for each type of job, or they may leave wage setting to job analysts and job evaluation so long as FLSA minimums are met, and, in general, wages are higher than the FLSA minimum.

The Social Security Act has been amended many times since it was first passed in 1935. It provides for old-age, survivors, and disability insurance (OASDI). The OASDI and the various state laws that provide for payment of benefits to unemployed workers give workers a type of security unknown to them before the 1930's. Benefits under OASDI will be paid only upon the filing of a claim; retired workers who fail to file claims will receive payment for a period of twelve months preceding the filing of the claim, but payment will not be made for more than twelve months if they have neglected to file for a period longer than this. Since the Social Security Act is so often amended, the reader is referred for the provisions of the act and its amendments to a pamphlet that may be obtained from his local post office.

Unemployment compensation benefits are regulated by state laws which vary in the amounts that may be paid and the period of time payments may be received. Supplementary unemployment benefits (SUB) and unemployment compensation have led business to try to find ways of stabilizing employment.[21]

Conclusions — This chapter has only attempted to "skim" the subject of labor unions and labor laws. Each of these topics is far too extensive to try to do more than touch upon it in a book of this type. It is believed, however, that anyone who is to work with employees in any capacity, and particularly in a managerial capacity, would have a large gap in his background if he didn't have some knowledge of labor unions and labor laws and how these came about. To many persons labor history is a fascinating field of study with certain implications for those who study business psychology. We could not go far into the subject here for to do so would have been to bog down. Nevertheless, the student should realize the long chain of events that led through history to a kind of enterprise system that recognizes the worth and dignity of workers as reflected in the rights given them to organize and bargain collectively.

The student should realize that a firm's welfare plans cannot be understood and operated apart from its union relationships (provided the firm is unionized) or apart from legal action such as the Social Security Act. If the firm is not unionized, knowledge of why unions exist and recognition of the rights of workers to unionize if they so desire should certainly prove beneficial in dealing with the workers. Union leaders are themselves receiving further education (through the National Institute of Labor Education) designed to prepare them for better leadership and to give the academic objectivity it is felt they need to remove personal biases.[22] Owners, management, and labor function together and each group is dependent upon the others. Where collective bargaining is involved, all three groups are affected and participate in such bargaining through their representatives. When bargaining fails, government is the chief referee. The techniques for collective bargaining cannot be formalized.

Any number of illustrations of collective bargaining at work might have been used here: newspapers, airlines, automobiles, railroads. Recent steel industry bargaining is briefly reported on. From 1940 through 1958 six industry-wide steel strikes with numerous government interventions resulted in an eight per cent average annual increase in employment cost per man-hour. Billions of dollars were invested to improve steelmaking facilities and improve operations efficiency during this period with an average annual increase in steel shipments per man-hour in the industry of less than two per cent per year, compounded annually. Steel settlements since 1960 have been different in that both the 1962 and 1963 agreements were effected without the use of economic force or the threat of it. Both the union and the steel industry reflected their desire to eliminate need for periodic inventory buildup and liquidations formerly caused by fixed-term agreements, crises, deadline bargaining, and strikes. The agreement effected in 1963 provided that it would continue in force until either party on or after January 1, 1965, should give 120 days' notice of termination. This was to permit any company that needed no more strike-hedge inventory than it could build up in 120 days to forego such buildup until reopening notice might be served by the union or the industry.[23]

PROJECTS

1. Obtain a pamphlet from your local post office on the Social Security Act and its amendments. Be prepared to report orally on the act's provisions.

2. Find your own state laws relative to unemployment compensation. Be prepared to report orally on these.

3. Look up and report in writing on your state's special laws (if any) relative to labor unions and their activities.

4. Write a short paper on "Why a Student of Business Psychology Should Know Something of Labor History, Labor Unions, and Labor Law."

ACKNOWLEDGMENTS AND REFERENCES

1 ———, "Labor," *Fortune*, October, 1949, p. 200.
2 Mayo, Elton, *The Social Problems of an Industrial Civilization,* Harvard University, Cambridge, Mass., 1945.
3 Yoder, Dale, *Personnel Management and Industrial Relations,* Fourth Edition, Prentice-Hall, Inc., Englewood Cliffs, New Jersey, 1956, p. 358.
4 Powderly, T. V., *Thirty Years of Labor, 1859 to 1889,* Excelsior Publishing House, Columbus, Ohio, 1889.
5 Roethlisberger, F. J., and Dickson, W. J., *Management and the Worker,* Harvard University Press, Cambridge, Mass., 1950, pp. 255–269.
6 Adams, Loyce, "Business Organization and Management," *Secretary's Business Review,* Prentice-Hall, Inc., Englewood Cliffs, New Jersey, 1959, p. 101.
7 Powderly, *op. cit.,* pp. 33, 137, 147.
8 *Ibid.,* p. 104.
9 *Ibid.,* p. 280.
10 Ware, Norman J., *The Labor Movement in the United States,* 1860–1895, A Study in Democracy, Appleton & Co., N. Y., 1929, p. xiii.
11 *Ibid.,* p. 256.
12 *Ibid.,* p. 320ff.
13 Commons, John R., and Associates, *History of Labour in the United States,* Vol. 1, The Macmillan Co., New York, 1921, p. 133.
14 Eby, Herbert O., "Labor Relations and Collective Bargaining," *Management of the Personnel Function,* edited by I. L. Heckmann and S. G. Huneryager, Charles E. Merrill Books, Inc., Columbus, Ohio, p. 449.
15 Stagner, Ross, "Dual Allegiance as a Problem in Modern Society," *Personnel Psychology,* Spring, 1954.
16 Sayles, Leonard R., and Strauss, George, "What the Worker Really Thinks of His Union," *Harvard Business Review,* May-June, 1953.
17 Leighton, Alexander H., *The Governing of Man,* Princeton University Press, Princeton, New Jersey, 1945.
   Hepner, Harry Walker, *Psychology Applied to Life and Work,* Prentice-Hall, Inc., Englewood Cliffs, New Jersey, 1957, p. 501.
18 *Ibid.*
19 Mayer, W. E., "Brainwashing," a lecture delivered at the Conference of Professors of Air Science, Maxwell Air Force Base, November 27, 1956.
20 Taft, Philip, *Economics and Problems of Labor,* Stackpole and Heck, Inc., New York, 1948, p. 540.
21 Adams, *op. cit.,* pp. 111–115.
22 ———, "Labor-Union Leaders Go Back for Liberal Education," *Business Week,* August 25, 1962, pp. 68–69.
23 Cooper, R. Conrad, "Of People, Power, and Principles," *Proceedings,* 25th Conference Texas Personnel and Management Association, The University of Texas, Austin, Texas, October 24 and 25, 1963, p. 40ff.

CHAPTER XVII

LABOR RELATIONS: WELFARE PLANS

Formal Plans — Merlyn S. Pitzele, former Labor Editor of *Business Week* and member of the New York State Board of Mediation, has said that ". . . labor will never stop. It will not be content with Hillquitt's Socialism or Stalin's Communism. . . . It will still want to go on from there to the ever-beckoning, never attainable 'More, always more!' " It is this which Mr. Pitzele said gives labor its long-run affinity with American management.

> . . . Because this is precisely the quest of American business. It wants dynamic, expanding enterprises in a dynamic, expanding economy. It wants to make more, sell more, do more. No government bureaucrat, no brain truster, no commissar can help that American worker and his family who Sam Gompers talked about to an ever-improving life. Only the intelligence, the skill, and the genius of American management can do that — and wants to, indeed, has vital interests of its own in doing it.
>
> Thus the long-run interests in American labor and American business are the same. The way will be cleared for them to cooperate in achieving their common end when each has achieved understanding of the other's needs and problems. . . .[1]

Management philosophy wherever it exists does so and is important only "as it helps human beings achieve their goals — both individual and group goals."[2] In its search for effective ways of "releasing and directing the productive energies of individuals and groups,"[3] management has tried many formal programs and incentive systems, other than an effective wage administration plan and forms of incentive pay. These various plans are generally designed to give the worker some of the specific wants considered to be the three basic aspirations of all human beings: (1) *security* (job permanence, ability to pay the bills, confidence that comes from knowing that one's job has been well done); (2) *opportunity* (people may not want to pay the price for advancement, but they want to know that they have the chance); (3) *recognition* (that comes from feeling their work is important; being recognized by their bosses; knowing the part their jobs play in the company's over-all program and being told how they are doing in their jobs; being kept informed about the company's plans and their effects upon the workers). A study by Elmo Roper found that these three "wants" are common; he, however, broke the third one into: *desire to be treated like human beings* and *a sense of human dignity*.[4]

To satisfy these wants of people, companies have instituted a great many formal systems: all of those involving pay, promotion, vacations, disability, unemployment benefits, wage supplements, pension plans, and so on as covered in union contracts; rest periods; orientation programs; suggestion systems; counseling; company publications; community relations programs; employee homes; insurance; medical services; stock ownership; profit sharing. It is not, however, always the company that has the most or the best formal system that has the best industrial relations. Practically all studies have shown that it is the quality of the supervision given and the relationship that exists between men and their superiors and among the men themselves that bring about good or bad relations within a department or a firm. Nevertheless, benefit programs and benefits continue to increase, largely because people believe that the free enterprise system should furnish them certain satisfactions, security, and protection.

Profit Sharing — Someone has suggested that this should be renamed "profit and loss sharing." If workers are to have a part in the success of their enterprise, it is argued they should not quit when the team is losing.[5] Sharing of profit with workers is based upon the recognition that capital and labor provide the means of producing goods. When capital has received its interest (for borrowed capital) and dividends (for owned capital) and labor has been paid for its services, profit sharing would be a way of sharing between labor and capital (the two contributors to making the profits possible) any available excess. Such a system should encourage cooperative effort throughout an enterprise. Some profit-sharing plans have been successful in developing team spirit; others have failed. In most cases it is thought that a firm that can succeed with profit sharing could succeed without it.

Profit sharing was used in England as early as 1870 and in France as early as 1842. The first record of a plan in the United States is the plan in effect at the glassworks plant of Albert Gallatin, New Geneva, Pennsylvania, in 1794. There were thirty-two profit-sharing plans on record in the United States in 1889.[6] Three of the companies that have had successful plans are Procter & Gamble, Hormel, and Nunn Bush Shoe Co., the Procter & Gamble plan having been begun in 1887.

Among the reasons that profit sharing has not been as successful as some have thought it would be are the following: (1) Payment of profit to the employee does not coincide with his effort; he would rather have a fixed wage right now. (2) The worker may work hard to help increase the firm's profits and he may look about him and see others who were doing only a minimum of work are collecting the same amount of profit that he is getting. (3) When there are no profits "to share" the worker loses faith in the company and may even begin to doubt the honesty of its executives. When he sees that a company executive was awarded a bonus of $175,000 over and above his $240,000 salary, he begins to figure how much profit that would be to distribute to workers; generally, of course, it would be infinitesimal in the giant corporation that would pay such a salary bonus. (4) Workers sometimes have not been stimulated to produce more by the profit-sharing plan because the better workers have brought their production down to the level of the poorer ones since all the workers share alike in the profits (usually on some basis of relationship to salary).

Over a third of 167 companies reporting in a study by the National Industrial Conference Board reported they were dissatisfied in some manner with their profit-sharing plans.[7] A study of more than 300 profit-sharing plans covering 750,000 workers revealed that the large companies considered their plans successful more often than small companies did; financial and professional firms rated their plans successful more often than did manufacturing and mercantile enterprises; non-union companies rated their plans higher than did unionized companies.[8]

Firms which have had success with profit sharing have reported variously that their plans have resulted in: fewer grievances, better cooperation and team spirit, reduced turnover of labor, more harmony and pleasure during working hours, reduced numbers of rejections of work output, and increased output. In reporting in 1948 on the profit-sharing plan that had developed over a period of twenty-seven years in his company, F. W. Willey, President, Willey-Wray Electric Company, Cincinnati, Ohio, said:

Let it be understood that even after these many years, perfection is still ahead. Even with only 30 people, it is difficult to bring every one up to a full understanding and 100 per cent cooperation. For many years and from many sources workers have been told that management is too smart and tricky and must never be trusted. Many of our current laws were written on such premises. The development of confidence is a long uphill pull and requires untold patience and simon-pure motives. There is great satisfaction when some such plan produces a sort of human fellowship while some managements are still saying "damn the help." [9]

The director of personnel with the Sunnen Products Company of St. Louis, stated in a speech made in 1948 that the fine spirit existing in his company had grown out of the company's profit-sharing plan; the company had never had a union.[10]

For profit sharing to work effectively, it would seem that both employees and management should want it. Furthermore, there should be continued educating of all employees with regard to the advantages of profit sharing and how it works in the particular company concerned. Employees should feel that they are treated the same, i.e., that each person receives profit in proportion to his contribution to the firm as revealed by his salary which should be evidence of his worth in comparison to others. This presupposes sound policies with regard to wage and salary structure.

In general it might be concluded that profit-sharing plans have flourished during periods when the economy was on the upswing. They have floundered and died during periods of recession and depression. The most usual plans for supplementing take-home pay today are *pension plans* and *deferred profit sharing*. The World War II years and the postwar years added thousands of such plans approved by the Internal Revenue Service. The deferred profit-sharing plan has been particularly attractive to small companies. In such companies it is a substitute for the pension fund; in the large companies it supplements the basic pension plan.[11]

Stock-purchase Plans — It is the belief of some that stock-purchase plans should furnish more incentive to the worker than profit-sharing schemes since the ownership of stock brings a sense of owning something about which decisions may be made as most of the stock issued under stock-purchase plans carries voting privileges. Only a small percentage of workers participate in stock-purchase plans, however, and in many instances these do not stay with their plans. In fact, the worker who buys stock may find that he is forced to sell it at the very time that it has dropped in price, i.e., during a period of recession or depression. In some instances the need to sell might come during a strike period when company stock prices have declined. Workers who do buy stock and have paper profits suddenly erased feel resentment toward their companies. If the workers are adequately compensated and purchase stock with the intention of holding it for investment purposes in order that it may contribute to their retirement income, then the stock-purchase plan should contribute to improving morale providing enough workers participate.

Some firms have stock bonus plans as a means of providing deferred compensation. The benefits of these plans are similar to those of profit sharing except that they are not dependent on profit. Generally these are for executive and management people only.

Fringe Benefits — Studies in Milwaukee, Cleveland, and other industrial areas have shown that fringe benefits make up as much as twenty to twenty-five per cent of gross payroll. These fringe benefits include the employer's share of legally required payments such as social security, workmen's compensation, and unemployment compensation which items make up some two to six per cent of gross payroll; voluntary and agreed-upon benefits bring the percentage up to the higher figure. A large part of what is included in fringe benefits is not taxable.

Many persons believe fringe benefits to be powerful morale-building devices. Nevertheless, it can be argued that initiative is often destroyed when too much security is given an individual and employee initiative is certainly considered one of the indices of good morale. The average applicant for a position is, however, usually as much interested in the fringe benefits as in the salary he will receive. He may even take the job offer that pays less if the benefit picture is more favorable.

Company-owned automobiles and residences are sometimes provided by companies at little or no rental cost to the employees. To many people this seems merely a way of getting and keeping the workers, of making them feel compelled to remain with the firm out of a sense of obligation or for security's sake. It also relieves the employee of considerable responsibility for personal business dealings such as would be involved in contracting and paying for these items. Among some of the more common fringe benefits not discussed at length here are: employee insurance, health and accident insurance, unemployment benefits, company publications, and community programs and/or centers provided for entertainment, self-betterment, and recreation.

Suggestion Systems — Prior to World War II only a few suggestion systems had been formally installed, although some plans had been in effect since the twenties. Today such plans seem to be fairly widespread. Current information can be obtained about them from the National Association of Suggestion Systems.

Suggestions may concern safety; increased efficiency in various service, staff and line operations, including improvement in production; economy; and conservation.

Suggestion systems are generally originated and governed by joint committees made up of management and labor. They operate under many different plans designed to win the confidence of the employees and to encourage them to respond. Some firms use suggestion boxes into which the employee suggestions may be dropped; others use a more formal route through the passing of suggestions up the line with immediate superiors having the right to approve or reject further consideration by designated suggestion committees.

The most common practice in making rewards for suggestions is to relate the rewards to the savings made by them. If this cannot be easily done, as in the case of safety awards, then some standard sum or range may be set, as *$5*, or *from $5–$10*. Total rewards paid out by some companies run into the millions of dollars. To succeed the plans should have active participation of the administration, and employees should be completely informed as to the types of suggestions desired and the possible rewards for them.

It has been the practice of small concerns to conduct contests for suggestions; larger firms usually conduct extended campaigns. Definite rewards are announced for the suggestions made in contests; those who make suggestions in campaigns are usually rewarded when the suggestions are put into effect, or, in some cases, prizes are awarded periodically.

Firms that use a net-saving formula receive more than double the number of suggestions received by those that use a gross-saving formula.[12]

Summary — Formal welfare plans and the many fringe benefits provided for employees today are so numerous that these have only been briefly reviewed in this chapter. The various plans are highly expensive to employers. At the same time, they must bring benefits to the employers or they cannot be substantiated for tax deduction purposes. In some instances the benefits are taxable to the employees themselves.

Employers should be able to expect reduced turnover of employees, better morale, greater production efficiency, and better employees because of these plans. As a matter of fact, such improvements have not always resulted. Where it has been believed that some improvements have been made, the exact extent of these has often not been measurable. Practically all studies have shown that the immediate supervisor is the one factor most responsible for morale and/or output. Having the plans will not assure a firm that its industrial relations will be the best or even good; not having the plans marks a firm as nonprogressive with competing firms and with prospective employees.

The benefits to the employer may be quite indirect and not measurable, yet they are assumed in most cases to exist. Where there are benefit programs it is generally the leadership back of them that counts most heavily in their success or failure.

To indicate the great variety of wage supplements that may be found in various companies, the following enumeration is taken from a study by Charles W. Sargent:

A. Pay for time not worked
  1. Vacations
  2. Holidays
  3. Lunch periods
  4. Sick and maternity leaves
  5. Medical care time (at the plant)
  6. Personal excused-absence time
     a. Death in family
     b. Shopping time
     c. Medical and dental care time (away from plant)
  7. Jury duty time
  8. Voting time
  9. Wet-time (time lost due to inclement weather)
  10. Witness time
B. Monetary awards and prizes for special activities and performance
  1. Anniversary awards
  2. Attendance bonus
  3. Plant neatness bonus
  4. Service bonuses and awards
  5. Quality bonus
  6. Prize awards in employee contests relating to safety, waste reduction, morale, and other subjects
  7. Suggestion plan awards
  8. Other nonproduction bonuses or awards requiring some special employee activity or service
C. Bonuses, contributions, and profit sharing, for which the employee renders no direct regular or special service
  1. Current profit-sharing payments (not related to provision of retirement income)
  2. Savings (thrift) plan contributions
  3. Stock purchase plan contributions
  4. Sale of company stock at less than current value
  5. Christmas or year-end bonus
  6. Separation allowance (dismissal, severance, or terminal pay)
  7. Lay-off pay or allowance
  8. Military induction bonus
  9. Military service allowance
  10. Supplements to unemployment or workmen's compensation
  11. Family allowance

    12. Educational subsidies or tuition or expense payments (when not related directly to the employee's job)

    13. College scholarship awards to employees' sons and daughters

D. Payments to provide employee security and financial protection against various hazards and contingencies

    1. Legally required payments

       a. Old-age and survivors' insurance

       b. Unemployment insurance

       c. Workmen's compensation

       d. State disability insurance

    2. Other payments to provide protection (by insurance or otherwise) against

       a. Death

       b. Non-occupational accident, sickness, and dismemberment

       c. Hospitalization expense

       d. Medical expense

       e. Surgical expense

       f. Retirement (pension and, in some cases, deferred profit-sharing plans)

    3. Employee welfare fund contributions

    4. Administrative costs of employee benefit programs

E. Practices and services that benefit employees primarily

    1. Credit union facilities

    2. Food service costs or losses

    3. Employee discounts

    4. Music lessons, golf instruction, and other services rendered at reduced cost or at no cost to employees and dependents

    5. Garden plots

    6. Vacation, health, and hospital facilities provided at low cost

    7. House financing[13]

PROJECT

Read and write a short report on at least one welfare plan currently in operation at an industrial firm.

ACKNOWLEDGMENTS AND REFERENCES

1 Pitzele, Merlyn S., "Organized Labor—Its Motives and Objectives," *Proceedings,* Southwest Area Conference on Industrial Relations, 1949, p. 37.

2 Richardson, Howard L., "A Present-day Philosophy for Management," *Proceed-*

ings, Seventeenth Conference, Texas Personnel and Management Association, Austin, October 20-21, 1955, p. 55.

3 Worthy, James C., "Democratic Principles in Business Management," *Advanced Management,* March, 1949.

4 Nicholson, David H., "Incentive Management," *Texas Personnel Review,* Tenth Texas Personnel Conference, November 4-5, 1948, Vol. 7, No. 1, April, 1949, p. 102.

Beaver, Thomas A., "The Personnel Background and Policies of The Ford Motor Company," *Proceedings,* Sixteenth Conference, Texas Personnel and Management Association, October 28-29, 1954, p. 34.

5 Willey, F. W., "Profit Sharing as an Incentive," *Texas Personnel Review,* Tenth Texas Personnel Conference, November 3-5, 1948, Vol. 7, No. 1, April, 1948, p. 24.

6 Hepner, Harry Walker, *Psychology Applied to Life and Work,* Prentice-Hall, Inc., Englewood Cliffs, New Jersey, 1957, p. 482.

7 —————————, *Profit Sharing for Workers,* Studies in Personnel Policy, No. 97, National Industrial Conference Board, 1948, p. 247.

8 Hepner, *op. cit.,* p. 484.

9 Willey, *op. cit.,* p. 29.

10 Nicholson, *op. cit.,* p. 103.

11 Meyer, Mitchell, and Fox, Harland, "Profit Sharing for Retirement Income," *A Management Sourcebook,* edited by Franklin G. Moore, Harper and Row, Publishers, New York, 1964, pp. 466-474.

12 Hepner, *op. cit.,* p. 491.

13 Sargent, Charles W., " 'Fringe' Benefits: Do We Know Enough About Them?," *Personnel,* Vol. 30, No. 6, May, 1954, pp. 462-472. Also in *Management of Human Resources,* edited by Paul Pigors, Charles A. Myers, and F. T. Malm, McGraw-Hill Book Company, New York, 1964, pp. 406-7.

CHAPTER XVIII

EFFECT OF WORKING CONDITIONS ON EMPLOYEES

Working Conditions vs. Human Relations as Morale Builders — The Hawthorne studies and other studies in the area of motivation have indicated that supervision, human relations, and the attitudes and sentiments of people have more to do with both productivity and job satisfaction than do the physical factors of the environment. General Motors once studied seventy-nine of its own plants and found that there was no difference in output as between the modern up-to-date factories and the older, less modern ones. Human relationships and camaraderie among the given group seemed to be the determining factor.[1]

Nevertheless there is agreement (at least among architects and space designers) that many physical aspects of modern offices and plants do have some effect upon efficiency. In offices the three aspects of physical conditions of work that receive top priority attention today are: *noise control, good lighting* designed for facilitating the performance of certain jobs, and *air conditioning*. A good *communication system* is also considered vital.[2]

In plants, the layout of work, conveyor systems, attractiveness, and such facilities as cafeterias, lockers, washrooms, and parking lots are very important in attracting workers and in bargaining with unions. Music in factories and offices, rest periods, and certain other related factors are given brief discussion in this chapter.

Effect of Noise on Workers — The extent to which noise affects a worker is dependent upon a number of factors including the type of work that he is doing. The Industrial Health Research Board, Great Britain, found that noise does not greatly impair the efficiency of workers engaged in simple motor tasks, but noise does affect efficiency to an extent. Persons engaged in certain kinds of mental work are more affected by noise than are those engaged in mechanical work, presumably because motor tasks are more readily automatized.[3] Some people are considered to be noise prone and noise is particularly offensive to them. *In general, research in the area of the effect of noise upon workers has concluded that when workers are really distracted by noise one of two things will occur:* (1) *they will increase their expenditure of energy, or* (2) *decrease their output.*

Three fourths of 1,974 companies surveyed by the National Office Management Association in 1960 were found to have some degree of sound conditioning in their offices. The companies reported the following advantages: improvement in morale (43%); improvement in accuracy (29%); improvement in quantity of work done (16%); less lost time (4%); less turnover of employees (4%).

Aetna Life Insurance Company recently installed noise smothering acoustical materials throughout its New York headquarters building. Engineers measured noise levels both before and after the installations were made and found that noise had been reduced by 14.5 per cent. A follow-up study by the industrial relations staff revealed that errors of typists were reduced by 29 per cent; employee turnover was reduced by 47 per cent; absenteeism fell by 37.5 per cent.[4]

Noise is not only a problem in factories and offices, it is a problem in transportation facilities and terminals, and in whole communities where industrial noises, jet airplanes, automotive vehicles, and other noise makers abound. Noise is defined as being "unwanted sound" and such unwanted sound is a problem because it may interfere with oral communication on the job or during leisure hours. It may affect behavior; it may produce either temporary or permanent hearing loss. It is of concern to many persons including: acoustical engineers, physicists, electrical engineers, designers of military equipment, aeronautical engineers, mechanical engineers, ventilation engineers, builders, architects, city planners, public health officials, industrial hygienists, otologists, physiologists, psychologists, transportation authorities, industrial designers, business executives, lawyers, and compensation experts.[5] The student is referred for an exhaustive look at noise from the engineering viewpoint to Cyril M. Harris' *Handbook of Noise Control,* McGraw-Hill Book Company.

Because continued noise may result in permanent loss of hearing, legislation has sometimes included deafness as an occupational hazard. The oldest workmen's compensation law in the United States is The Federal Employees' Compensation Act enacted in 1908. It covers civil employees of the Federal government. Under this act an employee may receive as much as $6,300 for total loss of hearing in one ear and as much as $24,200 for total loss of hearing in both ears. The Harbor Workers' Compensation Act (1927) allows for payment to maritime workers of up to $1,820 for total loss in one ear and up to $7,000 for loss in both ears. Railroad workers are given special treatment under the Federal Employees' Liability Act and seamen are given special treatment under the Jones Act (Merchant Marine Act). The remedies of these workers are founded on negligence; reductions are made where comparative contributory negligence can be shown. State laws generally provide schedules of fixed benefits that control payments for permanent loss of hearing. These laws cover accidental injuries, but in some states where there are separate laws for occupational disease the loss of hearing due to prolonged noise may be covered.[6]

In early 1963 the California legislature voted to adopt an industrial safety measure under which companies are required to (1) make rigid surveys of noise hazards, and (2) provide effective equipment and training for the protection of workers in areas where high noise prevails. It is believed that this will bring about action against the hazards of industrial noise in other states. The most often used danger level of constant noise throughout a complete workshift is eighty-five decibels. [A *decibel* is a measure of sound and sound is measured by *sound-level meters*.] The amount of harm that noise does to the hearing cannot, however, be measured in terms of decibels only. High frequencies are usually more damaging than lower frequencies in the 20-cycle-to-20,000 cycle-per-second speech range. A survey made a few years ago by the American Industrial Hygiene Association resulted in the conclusion that: (1) fifty per cent of American industrial machines produced ninety to one hundred decibels of noise, and (2) fifty per cent of all plant areas had levels of between eighty-five and ninety-five decibels. Because of the prevalence of dangerous noises in industry, it has been urged that audiometer hearing tests should be given as a part of physical examinations. Since hearing losses uncovered by such tests are usually permanent, the only action that could be taken would be to attempt to prevent further damage through ear protectors such as muffs or plugs. A recent survey of 1,148 plants revealed that fewer than a fourth of the employees exposed to noises great enough to warrant wearing of protective devices were actually wearing them. Excessive noises can frequently be cut down drastically by use of simple measures such as mufflers and sound equipment.[7]

More than ten years ago courts ruled that employees could not collect for hearing damages that had resulted from ordinary industrial noise. Fifteen states still held to this view in 1963. In New York, Wisconsin, and California employees can collect even though they may not have missed a single day's pay because of hearing losses. Successful claims in the past have been for cases where the employees failed to hear the speech range of sound in tests given at 500, 1,000, and 2,000 cycles per second. California's recent legislation provides for a test of 4,000 cycles per second. The Noise Research Center has estimated that 4.5 million people work in areas where there is intense noise; if only ten per cent of these people should file claims the total would be approximately $250 million, making the potential cost of hearing loss due to the noise factor greater than that of any other occupational disease. The Noise Research Center's studies indicate that industry usually is the cause of the hearing losses attributed to it and not just a scapegoat for natural losses in hearing. The average man in his fifties who has not been exposed to industrial noises has a four per cent chance of needing a hearing aid to hear normal speech; the industrial worker from a high-noise work area has a twenty-six per cent chance of needing the hearing aid.[8]

ILLUSTRATION XVIII-1[9]

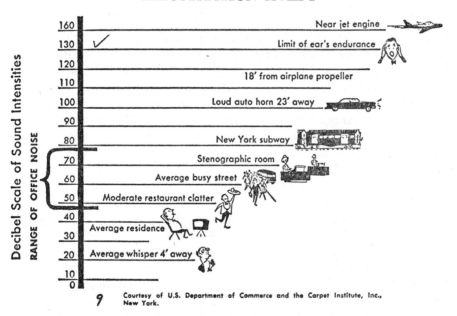

9   Courtesy of U.S. Department of Commerce and the Carpet Institute, Inc., New York.

The Effect of Music on Workers — The 1960 survey made by NOMA found that eighteen per cent of 1,974 companies had music systems in offices. The companies reported that providing for music on the job reduced fatigue and monotony in some types of office work. In factories it has been found that music tends to reduce the strain of noises. Sound engineers have reported that people become accustomed to noise by developing a psychological deafness to it. These people are, therefore, able to hear other sounds, such as music, above the din and clatter of regular factory noises. People who plan music programs for industry suggest music of progressive stimulation for periods of fatigue. They claim that by beginning with moderate stimulation and gradually increasing the pace to the end of the period there is a carry-over effect of an hour or more. Some authorities, however, work on the theory that there should be a gradual decrease in stimulation from the beginning of the day to the end.[10]

In general, research on the use of music in industry has concluded that music should be provided: (1) when work is routine, manual, and monotonous, and (2) when the workers want music.

Effect of Lighting on Workers — Many persons do not have 20/20 vision [ability to read at 20 feet characters ⅓ inch in diameter; the acuity of an eye that can distinguish at 20 feet only characters of twice this size is designated as 20/40, and so on]. One study found that some forty-five per cent of 200,000 workers in diversified industries did not have 20/20 vision. Since twenty-five per cent of the 200,000 not only had poor eyesight but had not obtained glasses to correct this defect,[11] it can be concluded that management should be concerned with this factor. Thirty per cent of workers in a given department of Motorola, Inc., were found not to be able to see well enough to do effective work; sixty-three per cent of those with poor vision were rated by their supervisors to be below average workers. Motorola's records indicated that there was a relationship between below-average eyesight and above-average absenteeism. Absences dropped when eyesight was corrected; complaints with regard to product defects fell eight per cent below the previous year's complaints, and employee turnover fell by ten per cent although many additional workers had been employed.[12]

Better Vision Institute studies indicate that one out of every three workers in the United States needs glasses. Forty per cent of all workers are visually unqualified for their work. Fifty per cent of office and textile workers and seventy-five per cent of garment workers have defective vision. Defective eyesight is found in different age groups as follows: fifteen-year-old, twenty-three per cent; fifty-year-old, seventy-one per cent; over-sixty-year-old, ninety-five per cent plus. While advancing age is a contributing factor, improper color and lighting have also taken their toll of eyesight.[13]

In considering the effect of illumination three aspects of lighting should receive attention: (1) *brightness or intensity,* (2) *quality or color,* and (3) *diffusion or distribution.*[14]

The *foot-candle* is the measure of *light intensity,* which measure may be taken by *light meters* or *visibility meters.* Today's standards call for a minimum of one hundred foot-candles of light for reading; older offices have provided the average worker with about thirty-five foot-candles. One study indicated that the increase of light from thirty-five foot-candles to one hundred resulted in improvements in a number of ways, including improvement in typewriting through the elimination of errors.[15]

With regard to the *color quality* of light, red rays come to a focus at a greater distance from the lens than do blue rays. Color quality, in general, however, has little effect upon functions performed in industry. Under sodium-vapor lamps, often used for highway lighting, visual acuity is improved when discriminations of size and shape are required near the threshold. Near the threshold speed of seeing has been found to be twenty-eight per cent faster under sodium-vapor lighting. Speed of seeing objects considerably above the threshold was found to be only 0.003 seconds faster with sodium light than with tungsten.[16]

One of the most common errors in lighting is *unevenness in distribution*. Glare should be eliminated from shiny surfaces; fluorescent lamps, shielded with glass or plastic units to reduce glare and permit an evenly diffused light are ordinarily preferred. The NOMA survey made in 1960, previously referred to, indicated that fluorescent lighting had replaced incandescent lighting in eighty-three per cent of the offices surveyed. Lighting engineers now sometimes throw light upward to bounce off of the ceiling; sometimes they send it directly downward but with the glare eliminated. Glare not only reduces efficiency of the worker it also brings about feelings of fatigue.

Three sources of reflected light which affect the eyes are: (1) *the ceiling and walls;* (2) *the eye-level area,* including the machines, equipment, tables, or benches being used; (3) *the floor.* Glare from any of these sources or violent contrasts in brightness as between the areas may bring about headaches or fatigue. Colors that reflect light should not be used except on ceilings or areas high enough above the line of vision not to contrast greatly with product, machine, or work level colors. Floor paints with as much as forty per cent light reflectance of walls within the worker's level of vision. The area where the worker's eyes rest and the area he sees when he looks from the work level should represent near-identical reflectance values, i.e., should be complementary colors. Lighting and color must work together.[17]

Color in the Office and Factory — Color affects people and their output practically anywhere they may work. Color and form create illusions. Lighter colored objects look smaller than darker ones. A vertical column broken by a different color at the base will look less tall than the column that is the same color right down through the base. Color has many and varied psychological results.

The following stories are related to indicate some effects of color upon workers: (1) Women engaged in high-precision welding used gas jets placed in a circle. When the work benches were painted sky blue (a cool color), the machines were painted light orange to contrast with the dark gas jets, and dark blue was placed under the machines to heighten the visibility of machine parts, operators in all sections asked for color plans. The plant became cleaner as the workers reacted favorably to the brightening up of their work place; there was a marked decrease in rejects and breakages. Within a week, for instance, rejects on one item decreased by two-thirds. (2) At Jones and Laughlin Steel Corporation a color-engineering project in the Wire and Rope Division resulted in a drop in accidents of thirty-eight per cent within a six-month period; absenteeism was reduced from about five per cent to less than two per cent; labor turnover was reduced greatly; the efficiency of operators on complicated wire-twisting equipment rose from the start of the color project to the time of its completion by eighty-five to ninety per cent. (3) At the Rod and Wire Division of the Detroit Steel Company at Portsmouth, Ohio, the accident-frequency rate was reduced by seventy-five per cent after a functional color plan had been adopted; severity of the accidents fell from .90 to .37. Quality and quantity of production were improved. (4) Absenteeism in a New York precision-tool plant was reduced by sixty per cent, and rejects by forty per cent when color had been properly co-ordinated on machinery and walls. Production went up fifteen per cent. (5) Accident rate fell in a Brockton, Massachusetts, shoe factory when light green, blue, orange, and cream paint brought light freshness to the work of people who had formerly worked with black machines, black thread, and black shoes. Attention-compelling background colors helped direct attention to moving parts. Less eyestrain and nervous fatigue were reported by workers.[18]

Painting telephone booth interiors red has been used to stimulate people to speed up their telephone calls; restaurants have turned from gray-green to red-and-yellow combinations to speed up patrons who had previously cut down patronage turnover because they were inclined to linger too long. Color affects insects as well as people. Flies appear to find blue repugnant while mosquitoes seem to like blue. Most animals, however, are color blind.[19]

Warm colors properly used not only create a pleasant environment, they stimulate and promote efficiency. Warm colors can also make a work place seem too warm, or they can make a work place that seemed too cool appear to be warm enough. Cool colors can make a warm work place seem cooler.[20]

For technical discussions of color engineering and color planning the student is referred to: *Color in Business, Science, and Industry,* by Deane B. Judd, John Wiley & Sons, Inc., New York; *Color Planning for Business and Industry,* by Howard Ketcham, Harper & Brothers, Publishers, New York.

Effect of Air Conditioning on Workers — Seventy-two per cent of the offices surveyed by NOMA in 1960 were found to have air conditioning. Air conditioning reportedly increased both morale and productivity. Draftsmen at Detroit Edison Company increased output by fifty-one per cent during the summer after installation of air conditioning.[21] A study made by General Services Administration found that air conditioning increased production, reduced errors, improved morale, and cut down on absenteeism. During the past twenty years, however, only ten per cent of the plants built have been air conditioned. Air conditioning was thought of as a fringe benefit that should be negotiated. If the union could get it, it was provided. One air-conditioning company vice-president has estimated that a billion dollars will be spent during the last part of the 1960's in the air-conditioning of plants.

In certain types of plants air conditioning is essential. In electronic plants even small particles of dust cannot be tolerated. In automated plants changes in temperature and humidity can cause costly delays. The story is told of a tape-controlled machine that between two and three o'clock every day started spitting out blanks. Experts worked on it for a month before someone noticed that a shaft of sunlight struck the machine during that hour. Normal production was resumed as soon as the window blind was lowered.[22]

Plants producing electronic equipment or parts have to have especially efficient janitorial service in addition to air conditioning [Chapter XX].

Mechanical Safety Devices — Most large industrial firms today provide some type of safety education and plan for proper safety equipment. Safety masks, safety shoes, safety suits, safety helmets, and safety gloves are examples of safety equipment that may be issued to or required of workers in hazardous occupations, particularly those such as welding and those that require the handling of hot metals. Color is used to paint danger zones and to indicate that smoking is not permitted in given areas. Electronic devices are used to stop machines when hands or arms come within areas of danger. Today's plants are designed for moving materials and equipment with the greatest degree of dispatch and efficiency and with safety for workers.

It is estimated that $1 out of every $10 industry spends today goes for conveyors, lift trucks, overhead cranes and assorted devices for moving goods in and out of factories. Materials handling [where the opportunity for accident could be great with less efficient methods and equipment] accounts for up to eighty per cent of all indirect labor costs in plants and almost half of the total cost of manufacturing.[23]

Accident Proneness — Safety devices, proper tools, and equipment can help to reduce accidents. In most work groups, however, it has been found that the majority of accidents occur to the same people who are referred to as being "accident prone." Studies in different plants have revealed that anywhere from eighty to ninety per cent of the accidents occur to the same people. Careful selection of workers may help to reduce accidents by eliminating people who might be accident prone. Psychological tests pertaining to emotional stability and physical fitness, plus careful interviewing and checking of work histories has enabled some companies to reduce preventable accidents. Safety training and careful supervision may be the most beneficial approach to reducing accident rates.

Fatigue — The conditions of tension and fatigue are not identical. When people who have not done hard work complain that they are fatigued, they are probably just bored; their condition is psychological and is due to lack of exercise rather than to too much muscular activity. This type of fatigue is generally referred to as being *subjective fatigue*. *Tension* is also generally considered to be a psychological state, but it usually is associated with mental overwork and worry, pain, a nervous constitution, lack of sleep, or stress, particularly if it has become chronic. When fatigue develops as a result of overwork, muscles have functioned so long that there is depletion of the available glycogen precursor, or there is need for oxygen to reconvert by-products of muscular activity into precursors. This condition may lead to what is called *objective fatigue*. When fatigue or chronic tension are due to psychological reasons, physical exercises and psychotherapy may be used in treatment. Noise control and changes in lighting, color, or other physical factors of work may have the effect of reducing subjective fatigue. Acute objective fatigue cannot be alleviated by physical exercise; rest and relaxation are necessary.[24]

What has been called objective fatigue here has sometimes been called *cumulative fatigue*. Those using the term have said that it is caused by overwork or lack of rest. Subjective fatigue has been called *monotony*. Both types of fatigue generally produce discontent and may in the long run contribute to industrial unrest. Regularly provided rest periods tend to reduce the degree of monotony and fatigue.[25]

Rest Periods — *Work rules* generally cover minimum standards of conduct and performance on jobs, including hours of work and rest periods. For certain types of workers some of these rules do not apply, or even if they do apply they sometimes are not observed. According to one fairly recent survey it was found that three-fourths of the companies provided two paid rest periods of ten to fifteen minutes each per day. In half of the firms that did not have authorized rest periods the employees took them anyway.[26] A survey made in 1955 indicated that ten per cent of the companies that had rest periods granted twenty minutes for them. This survey indicated that 128 of 170 companies had formal policies pertaining to rest periods; another 23 of the companies granted time off but did not have work rules or policies regulating such time off. Only 19 of the 170 companies did not allow rest periods. Practically all companies do have rest periods today. In some instances time is taken off at the desk or the work place for refreshment. Mutual Life Insurance Company of New York estimated that it saved $130,000 annually by having coffee delivered to workers at their desks.[27]

One of Great Britain's largest refineries, the Fawley plant of Standard Oil (New Jersey), streamlined its work rules for employees and added forty per cent to plant capacity without increasing the work force (1962). Workers were receiving more take home pay for a forty-hour work week than they received for a fifty-hour work week under the old plan. Three changes were made to bring about this new system: (1) the practice of using three helpers for five craftsmen was abandoned (the helpers or "mates" had aided on heavy jobs and brewed tea); (2) tea breaks and clean-up time were reduced; (3) rigid lines of job demarcation were eased. Changing the work rules was a long and difficult task. The Emerson Consultants, Inc., assisted in bringing about the changes which included consolidating some of the supervisory levels. The first step in effecting work rule changes after the management itself had been reorganized was to mentally prepare the union and the workers for change; it required three months to get union permission to talk with the workers. Eighty-five work rule changes were presented to the union after eighteen months of talking with workers; three months of bargaining followed. Most of the changes were accepted and for eighteen additional months the changes were slowly effected; 400 mates were retrained for other jobs. A senior lecturer in industrial relations at Oxford University, Alan Flanders, writing about the new plan was of the opinion that eliminating overtime and archaic work rules enabled this plant to rid itself of a problem symptomatic of failures of British industry. Workers in the plant still have their tea, but it is taken during natural breaks in the work flow; tea-brewing time was eliminated by issuing thermos jugs.[28]

Communication Systems — Some of the principles of communication are discussed in Chapter XIX and cybernation, which includes the element of feedback in automation, is discussed in Chapter XX. At this point it is merely being suggested that a good system of communications is very important. An agriculture products company based in Minneapolis designed its offices around communication equipment. To allow managers to keep in touch with market conditions while at the same time issuing, buying, and selling instructions to traders, a closed-circuit television system was installed to keep an electronic eye on trading boards at the Minneapolis Grain Exchange. To keep the company's 150 scattered offices, including one in Switzerland, apprised of current prices and buying needs, a teletype network was set up. In addition, each of the 600 employees was provided a private telephone number through a Centrex dialing system. The floors occupied by the company had special mail chutes connecting them with a mail room in the basement located next to a substation of the United States Post Office.[29]

Design and Sites for Future Plants — According to Arthur D. Little, three social factors will determine the environment in which future plants will operate: *urbanization, population explosion,* and the *automobile.* At present eighty-five per cent of the population is in the metropolitan areas. The number of automobiles that will be congesting the highways in the future may make Frank Lloyd Wright's mile-high building a necessity. American business was spending at the rate of $13 billion annually in 1964 for new plant construction. Enterprise does not reach the moment when everything is exactly right for its continuing, or if it does that moment is the beginning of its decline. The economy of the United States is based on the production of items that are constantly changing. Half of the new products that go on the market, according to a recent Booz Allen study, are commercial failures, and the average life of the successful products is only two years.[30]

New buildings are putting in ceilings twenty feet high to take care of unforeseen purposes (formerly twelve- or fourteen-foot ceilings were thought adequate) such as installing overhead conveyors. Working floor space is made more flexible by installing water, gas, power, and other utilities overhead. More land than is needed for a plant site is acquired in order to be prepared for future exigencies. Walls are put in in such manner that they are removable, and they may even be constructed so that they will work right into other buildings not yet on the drawing board. Plants are designed with the view of enabling productivity to be increased. They are also, however, designed for attractiveness.[31]

Parking lots are important in employer-employee relations. Workers are as likely to strike over not having parking space as over failure to get increased pay. The designer of a factory must:

> . . . coordinate and deal with broad areas of engineering, economics, social science, behavioral science, physical science and architectural design. Above all he must be a businessman who is knowledgeable in the functional, financial and corporate requirements and objectives of modern management.[32]

Schenley Vice President Theodore C. Wiehe has said: "The effect of pleasant surroundings, although immeasurable by any known yardstick, has helped increase employee efficiency and morale." [33]

There are a great many important factors to be considered about a given area before a plant is located there. Some of these factors are: *freight costs, taxes, wage data, availability of labor, availability of markets,* and *climate.* The Municipal Service Department of Dun and Bradstreet furnishes such information as the following for use by a firm considering locating in a given area:

Changes in Population During a Given Period of Time
Population Per Square Mile
Characteristics of the Population (Urban, Non-Farm, Farm)
Educational Attainments of the Population
Personal Income Per Capita
Average Weekly Earnings
Average Hourly Earnings
Average Weekly Hours
Major Industries
Total Work Force in each of the Major Industries
Population by Age Groups[34]

In considering a store location site it is necessary also to determine the traffic at the point of the proposed location and to anticipate the possibility of shifts in traffic due to highway or other proposed or anticipated changes. The population growth rate in the area and the competitive facilities available should be determined.

Sears, Roebuck and Company, picked by the *Dun's Review* Presidents' Panel for its planning ability as one of the country's ten best-managed companies, has been particularly successful in using scientific study plus experience and imagination in reaching decisions and making plans for the future. In the area of store location alone the company makes exhaustive investigations into the many factors that will determine success or failure of the operation once the store has been built.[35]

General Food Corporation's effort to consolidate its Jell-O operations illustrates the problem of picking plant sites. A consulting firm recommended that the company should locate in the East on or near the seaboard because the raw materials such as cocoa beans, coconuts, and tapioca used in making the product were delivered by ship. The company's figures on freight cost of inbound and outbound shipments made the Middle Atlantic region seem the most attractive site. This region was also near the company's eastern sales and distribution centers. It was necessary to locate near a sugar refinery since sugar was a raw material needed in great quantities. The company considered locating dockside in a port city. The cost of building, maintaining, and operating a dockside location was found through study to more than offset the savings of such a location. Study, however, confirmed that there was need to settle near a general cargo port. The search narrowed to three cities from which final selection was made of Dover, Delaware. Dover had inadequate power, waste disposal, and zoning protection; the city, however, took steps to accommodate GF on all three of these points.[36]

Conclusions — Many of the factors discussed in Chapter XX have implications for the subject-matter of this chapter as well. The people who manage or supervise others generally must be concerned to some extent with the physical factors as well as the human factors of work. Many specialists in various phases of engineering advise and aid company officials in planning for locating, building, designing, and equipping business and industrial buildings. Lighting, noise control, color, communciations, rest pauses, layout of work, company cafeterias and/or other means of feeding, and numerous work rules involving both physical and human factors of work require managerial planning. A line or staff manager is generally primarily concerned with getting out the work of his particular specialization, but he cannot escape in the modern organization some element of responsibility for the conditions under which that work is performed.

PROJECT

Read and be prepared to discuss orally a recent article on one of the following: noise control, lighting, color, air conditioning, rest periods, fatigue, or factory design.

ACKNOWLEDGMENTS AND REFERENCES

1 Stessin, Lawrence, "Good Feeling Is Key to Productivity, Survey Suggests," *Forbes Magazine,* October 1, 1952.
2 —————, "The Walls Come Tumbling Down," *Dun's Review,* September, 1963, p. 123ff.
3 Pollack, K. G., Bartlett, F. C., Weston, H. C., and Adams, S., *Two Studies in the Psychological Effects of Noise,* Industrial Health Research Board, Great Britain, Report No. 65, 1932.
4 —————, "The Walls Come Tumbling Down," *op. cit.*
5 Harris, Cyril M. (editor), *Handbook of Noise Control,* McGraw-Hill Book Company, Inc., New York, 1957, p. v.
6 *Ibid.,* p. 38-35 and 38-36.
7 —————, "The Growing Industrial Battle Against Dangerous Decibels," *Dun's Review,* June, 1963, p. 45ff.
8. *Ibid.*

9 Hepner, Harry W., *Psychology Applied to Life and Work,* Prentice-Hall, Inc., Englewood Cliffs, New Jersey, 1957, p. 375.
10 ——————, "Your Plant Doesn't Have To Be So Noisy," *Industrial Relations,* January, 1948, p. 23.
   McDaniel, R., "How Music Increases Office Production," *American Business,* Vol. 15, April, 1945, pp. 22ff.
11 Luckiesh, Matthew, "Foot-candle Levels Threshold, Ideal, Optimum, and Recommended," paper presented at the National Technical Conference of the Illuminating Engineering Society, New Orleans, September 15-19, 1947, General Electric Company, Cleveland, Ohio.
   Hepner, *op. cit.,* p. 365.
12 Piper, Kenneth, "Motorola's Vision Program Pays Off," *Advanced Management,* September, 1951, pp. 24-25.
   Hepner, *op. cit.*
13 Ketcham, Howard, *Color Planning,* Harper & Brothers, Publishers, New York, 1958, p. 104.
14 Berrien, F. K., *Practical Psychology,* The Macmillan Company, New York, 1952, p. 279.
   Hepner, *op. cit.,* p. 366.
15 ——————, "The Walls Come Tumbling Down," *op. cit.*
16 Berrien, *op. cit.,* pp. 282-283.
17 Ketcham, *op. cit.,* pp. 104-106.
18 *Ibid.,* pp. 90-92.
19 Stouffer, Lloyd, *Popular Science,* June, 1947, pp. 124-126.
   ——————, "Color Punches the Time Clock," *The Management Review,* American Management Association, September, 1947, p. 452.
   Hepner, *op. cit.,* p. 372.
20 Seghers, C. E., Office Management Association of Chicago Monthly Bulletin, April, 1948.
   ——————, "Color in the Office," *The Management Review,* American Management Association, September, 1947, p. 452.
   Hepner, *op. cit.,* p. 372.
21 ——————, "The Walls Come Tumbling Down," *op. cit.*
22 ——————, "Dividends from Design," *Dun's Review,* March, 1964, p. 116ff.
23 ——————, "Material Handling's New Sophistication," *Dun's Review,* March, 1963, p. 107ff.
24 Rathbone, Josephine Langworthy, *Corrective Physical Education,* Sixth Edition, W. B. Saunders Company, Philadelphia and London, 1959, pp. 127-152.
25 Scott, Walter Dill, Clothier, Robert C., and Spriegel, William R., *Personnel Management,* McGraw-Hill Book Co., New York, 1961, pp. 452-453.
26 French, Wendell, *The Personnel Management Process: Human Resources Administration,* Houghton Mifflin Company, Boston, 1964, p. 102.
27 Hepner, *op. cit.,* pp. 390-392.
28 ——————, "Management—How to Change Work Rules," *Business Week,* March 31, 1962, pp. 50-52.
29 ——————, "The Walls Come Tumbling Down," *op. cit.*
30 ——————, "Dividends from Design," *op. cit.*
31 *Ibid.*
32 *Ibid.*
33 ——————, "The Walls Come Tumbling Down," *op. cit.*
34 ——————, "Plant Location: Where the People Are," *Dun's Review,* March, 1964, p. 106ff.
35 Buckley, Noel, "How Sears, Roebuck Plans for the Future," *Dun's Review,* October, 1963, p. 44ff.
36 ——————, "The Rough-and-Tumble of Site Location," *Dun's Review,* March, 1963, p. 97ff.

CHAPTER XIX

MORALE, MOTIVATION, AND COMMUNICATION

Characteristics of Leaders — Any person who is going to manage other people must be able to perform the functions of management: *planning, organizing,* and *controlling.* The characteristics of leaders have been named by many writers. Koontz and O'Donnell have given the qualifications and characteristics of leaders as being: *intelligence; leadership, ability to communicate; facility in scientific methodology and analytical ability; breadth of interests; moral values; judgment, including mental and emotional maturity; initiative; powerful inner drive and intense desire to manage; personality; and ability to cooperate.*[1] To this list others have added: *empathy and understanding; knowledge of social and economic conditions* (implied in breadth of interests); *freedom from narrow technical specialization; adequate education to assure that one will be accepted by those with whom he works; and organizing ability* (implied in leadership ability). Newman and Summer in a chapter on "leading" concluded that leadership must serve to broaden purposes if management is to be effective: "(1) guiding and motivating subordinates and (2) understanding their feelings and operating problems."[2]

Studies made by the Personnel Research Board, Ohio State University, in cooperation with International Harvester Company, found two leadership qualities to be *consideration* (friendliness, respect, mutual trust) and *initiating structure* (organizing procedures, communication channels). Foremen who worked under management possessing these qualities possessed them to a higher degree, indicating that "leadership behavior is not a thing apart but is imbedded in a social setting."[3]

Morale, motivation, and communication cannot be separated one from the other. Any manager who is effective is aware of this. Not only must company and departmental policies be known to supervisors and workers, but management's philosophy must be known to them if these people are to understand why executive thinking is what it is. They must not only know what the philosophy is; they must accept it. Morale building is a matter of integrating the interests of workers and management.

Davis has said that great leaders have always recognized the importance of morale by whatever name they called it. Social problems of laborers began with the technological developments of the Industrial Revolution (last decades of the eighteenth century in England). Labor made attempts from the first to improve its condition, as did some leaders who recognized that it was socially, economically, and politically desirable to link employee welfare to industrial development. Specialization, mechanization, and large organization led to the loss of the identity of the individual.[4] Labor, as pointed out in previous chapters, turned to unionization for protection and identity. Management came to clearly realize the importance of morale; it did not, however, see as clearly exactly what morale is or how to develop and maintain it. It knew, of course, that morale meant attitudes and that the attitudes of workers could determine the success or failure of their companies, just as the attitudes of the industrial organizations within an industrial society can bring about the overthrow of that society.

Indices of Good Morale — Davis has indicated the indices of good morale in an organization are: (1) the willing *cooperation* of its workers; (2) their *loyalty* not only to the organization itself but to its leaders; (3) evidences of *good discipline;* (4) evidences of *organizational stamina* or the ability of the organization to adjust to adversity; (5) workers' *interest* in their work as evidenced by their contributions and efforts to overcome obstacles; (6) *initiative* as revealed by creative effort and decision-making in emergencies providing the authority of others has not been usurped; and (7) *organizational pride,* as revealed by the belief of workers that their organization is superior.[5] The basic test of morale as stated by Davis is "the extent to which the individuals and groups composing the organization will voluntarily subordinate, in a reasonable degree, their personal objectives to the organization's service objectives." [6] For Davis (as for many others) the service objectives are those concerned with providing the legitimate good or service (economic value) desired or needed by society, society being any given group.[7]

It will be noted that Davis' *indices of morale* are abstractions. They would generally be accepted by those who have studied factors of morale and motivation. The problems of morale and motivation, however, have brought on much research and the findings of such research have not been uniform. Western Electric in 1924, believing that administration needed a scientific approach to problems of employment effectiveness, began a study to find the effects of illumination on workers' output. For three years the effects of illumination on output were studied. When illumination was increased for the experimental group the workers' production rose; so did the production of the control group, although illumination for that group had not been increased. When the illumination for the experimental group was then reduced to the level of moonlight the production of both groups continued to rise. The confusion brought on by this experiment led to the famous Hawthorne studies that began in 1927 with the cooperation of psychologists from Harvard. Personnel people in industry are expected to be familiar with these studies (reported on in dozens of volumes and referred to in countless others) in spite of the fact that some studies made since have resulted in findings that have been in disagreement, partially at least, with the Hawthorne findings. In fact, the findings of the Hawthorne Studies were not always clear-cut and uniform.

The Hawthorne Studies — The Hawthorne Studies that began at the Western Electric Company's Hawthorne plant at Cicero, Illinois, in 1927 lasted for five years. W. J. Dickson and Harold A. Wright of the Western Electric Company, and Harvard professors F. J. Roethlisberger, Elton Mayo, L. J. Henderson, and others planned and conducted the Hawthorne experiments. The tons of data that resulted from studying two groups of workers (one of women assemblers and one of men wirers, solderers, and inspectors) and interviewing thousands of employees was sifted through to produce: *Management and the Worker* by Roethlisberger, Dickson, and Wright; *Management and Morale* by Roethlisberger; *Social Problems of an Industrial Civilization* by Mayo, and many other volumes. Students have been required in personnel management courses to memorize the intricate details of these studies which furnished a basis for evaluating the significance of human relations within the work group (the *social situation*), *social conditioning,* and *communications.*

Since the Western Electric research is classic in the area of human relations, some of the results of that research are reviewed here. This brief review is being given despite the fact that the writer, having spent several full semesters of graduate work in courses devoted to these studies, knows so well the dangers involved in trying to summarize their findings.

In a chapter entitled "The Road Back to Sanity," Roethlisberger in *Management and Morale* emphasized the thought that *"A human problem to be brought to a human solution requires human data and human tools."* [8] The stated aim as the study began with five girl assemblers and one layout girl in April, 1927, was to find "the relation between conditions of work and the incidence of fatigue and monotony among employees." [9] Temperature and humidity were measured hourly and the output of each girl was constantly recorded by an automatic recording device. The hours of sleep each girl slept each night and the kind of food each girl ate for each meal daily were recorded. Quality records were kept. The girls were given physical examinations periodically. After five years of studying these girls, expert statisticians tried to relate their variations in output with changes in physical circumstances of the girls. There were no significant correlations. The investigators had, however, discovered after only two years of record keeping that they had been upon the wrong track. There had been changes in hours of work, introduction of rest periods, rest periods in the morning with lunch, and other changes. Production continued to climb. Then someone suggested going back to the original conditions of work. They did but output remained high.

The experimenters felt they had been robbed of their experimental tools, i.e., measurement of physical conditions of work and effects of shorter hours, rest periods, and so forth. They now began a period of interviewing workers to find what they liked and/or disliked about their work environment. This was an entirely new idea at the time and the early failure of formal methods of interviewing led to the development of non-directive interviewing which has since been used by many other interviewers and counselors (See Chapters IX and XII). The researchers concluded that "the behavior of workers could not be understood apart from their feelings or sentiments." Sentiments as used by those who wrote up the studies referred not just to feelings and emotions but to such phenomena as loyalty, integrity, solidarity, social organization, beliefs, courage, devotion, honesty, truth, goodness, fear, anger, jealousy, envy, and other pathological behavior patterns. They found also that "sentiments are easily disguised, and hence are difficult to recognize and to study," and that "manifestations of sentiment could not be understood as things in and by themselves, but only in terms of the total situation of the persons." [10]

The social relationships of the girls in the relay assembly room influenced their output; this has led to a great many further studies with regard to informal social groups in industry. Roethlisberger saw every item and event in the industrial environment as an object of a system of sentiments, with jobs socially ordered to the extent that *"the social structure of any particular company determines the kind of collaboration, the kind of people who will stay in the company, and the kind of people who will reach the top."* [11] The *social conditioning* outside the place of work was also important, however, and it interacted with the *social situation* that existed at the place of work, that is with the formal and informal social groups and their motives, particularly the motives of the informal groups.

The discovery of informal groups as a strong motivating force in industry led to further study of formal organization structure and to investigation of the social groups themselves. It was found that there are five social groups in industry: (1) *management;* (2) *supervisors,* through whom control is partially exercised; (3) *technical specialists,* through whom control is also partially exercised; (4) *office workers and clerical assistants;* (5) *shop, bench, and machine workers.* It was not enough, however, to know the relationships existing between these various groups; within each group of workers at any given place of work there were informal groups that influenced morale and output.[12] The researchers concluded that the social organization of industry cannot be "treated independently from the technical problems of economic organization. . . ." A company might through any move alter "the existing social equilibrium to which the employee has grown accustomed and by means of which his status is defined."[13] Communication is interfered with when management fails to understand its social structure.

A group of fourteen men and their supervisor were also studied at the Hawthorne plant for several years beginning in November, 1931. The purpose of the study was to determine the degree to which worker output was a form of social behavior and the degree to which informal groups did establish norms and control output. The men's group was composed of: nine wiremen, formally organized in three groups with three men to the group; three soldermen, one for each group of wirers; two inspectors; one supervisor. Although the formal organization gave official status to the supervisor, inspectors, wiremen, and solderers in that order, there were informal cliques that cut across the formal groups. Four basic sentiments were found to be operating within the men's work group in the Bank Wiring Observation Room: (1) workers should not turn out too much work or they would be known as "rate busters," although a given worker might be permitted to exceed standard output for a time and other workers might even help him after they had completed their quotas in order that he might pay hospital bills for a member of his family — once the bills were paid, however, restrictions were again in order; (2) workers should not turn out too little work or they would be known as "chislers"; (3) workers should not report to the supervisor anything that might work to the detriment of a fellow worker or they would be known as "squealers"; (4) workers should not be "too officious," that is, inspectors even though they were inspectors should not act like inspectors. The men wished to protect their group from interference by management and, in particular, against what they considered to be the ignorance of management; they resisted threats from the outside that might alter the character of their work group.[14]

The group of women workers at Western Electric's Hawthorne plant came to the point of disciplining themselves; they developed common loyalties and if a girl wanted to take off from work she didn't ask the supervisor, she asked the other girls. Their sentiments became closely integrated with the desires of management. The men workers, on the other hand, restricted output at levels they considered adequate by contriving breakdowns and wasting time. The researchers argued to begin with that the workers were afraid that if output went too high the rate might be lowered, there might be layoffs, the hours of work might be changed, or supervisors might reprimand them. Since none of the men had ever experienced any of the things they were apparently guarding against, their actions were not based on logic. They had merely assumed that a fixed, unchanging piece rate was economically desirable and that they could control management's actions by acting in a certain way. There wasn't, however, anything in the behavior of the men to show conscious planning of opposition to management. They simply acted to maintain their own social organization.[15]

The informal organization in the relay room was quite different to that in the other room. It might be argued from the relay assembly test room experiment that the "company can do almost anything it wants in the nature of technical changes without any perceptible effect on the output of the workers." It might be argued just as effectively from the bank wiring observation room experiment that the "company can introduce hardly any changes without meeting a pronounced opposition to them from the workers."[16]

The following quotation sums up the relay test room findings but does not explain the variation in findings between the two experiments:

> . . . The Relay Assembly Test Room experiment showed that when innovations are introduced carefully and with regard to the actual sentiments of the workers, the workers are likely to develop a spontaneous type of informal organization which will not only express more adequately their own values and significances but also is more likely to be in harmony with the aims of management.[17]

The differences in the two groups can be explained only by comparing the functions of the two groups: The women's early fears of change had been abrogated and they had formed a new social group that allowed development of their own objectives; the men never got beyond fearing what change might do to them as a group.

The chief contribution of the Hawthorne studies is probably to be found in the degree to which the attention of management and researchers as well has been brought to the importance of social groups and informal organizations that exist not only among work groups but among management groups as well.

Pareto's General Sociology — Eleven years before the Hawthorne studies, in 1916, Pareto's writing on sentiments was published, and four centuries before Pareto, Machiavelli wrote of the influence of sentiments on the actions of men at a time when sentiments influenced countries through their rulers. Both Elton Mayo and L. J. Henderson were quick to point out that physical sciences have a system which scientists can agree upon; social sciences involve sentiments and these cannot be agreed upon. Nevertheless, the social sciences continue to make progress and Pareto is considered to have made a major contribution. According to Pareto:

1. *A Residue Is a Manifestation of a Sentiment.*
2. *A Derivation Is a Nonlogical Argument, Explanation, Assertion, Appeal to Authority or Association of Ideas or Sentiments in Words.* It is determined by the residues.[18]

An example of a residue: Christian practice of Baptism, which is illustrative of the sentiment of the integrity of the individual. A derivation is an explanation of the ritual. Residues are more important than derivations; residues of religion precede the derivations of theology. These are Pareto's six classes of residues (the first two are most important):

1. *Instinct of Combination:* Sentiments that mark men who like novelty, adventure, and find new ways of doing things, cutting loose from the old, the tried. Men who are not easily shocked, who hate discipline: ATHENIANS, FOXES. Change and new combinations are implied.

2. *Persistence of Aggregates:* The residues that do not change or if they do they change slowly, such as customs and religions. Sentiments of men who like regular ways; solid discipline, tradition and habit. SPARTANS, LIONS.

3. *Need for Manifesting Sentiments By External Actions:* Religious rituals, for instance.

4. *Residues Related to Sociability:* Persistent.

5. *The Integrity of the Individual and What He Considers Dependent on Him:* Persistent: family, religion.

6. *The Sexual Residue.*

Derivations:

    1. *Affirmation:* introduction of an unfounded assertion into an argument which benefits the proposition being defended.
    2. *Authority.*
    3. *Accord with Sentiments.*
    4. *Verbal Proofs.*

Pareto's concept of equilibrium: If a small modification of the state or the system is imposed upon it, a reaction will take place and this will tend to restore the original state, very slightly modified by the experience. The individual, according to Pareto, has a *direct utility,* and an *indirect utility.* As a member of a collectivity his utility is indirect. The utility of the collectivity (group) is direct, considered apart from other groups (protection from outside interference), and indirect (obtained by influence of other groups). The group has values for itself; it is prior to the individual. A large population might have a great advantage for protection from outside but a disadvantage within the group. The residues of persistent aggregates of sociability and of integrity are the most important; morals and religion may be seen to be essential to the survival of society. Pareto is far from clear on how a conservative society with the residues of persistent aggregates changes into another kind of society. He did have the Yen and Yang concept of the pendulum swing.

Productivity of Congenial Work Groups and the Supervisor's Part — The Hawthorne experiments, having revealed that the work group is stronger and more powerful than the wishes of management, led to other studies in the functioning and motivation of work groups. The so-called *sociometric technique* was developed by J. L. Moreno; this technique attempted to find the cliques, acceptances, rejections, and dominant personalities within a group. In many variations the method has been used by numbers of researchers. One method of using the technique is to let workers choose one or more workers with whom they would most like to work and at the same time one or more workers with whom they would least like to work. The results are indicated in the following sociogram which shows that "A," "R," and "Q," are isolates since no one selected them. "K" is indicated as the natural leader with "H" running a close second.

By using the sociometric technique Van Zelst found that experimental groups of carpenters and bricklayers who had been permitted to select the people with whom they would work not only saved material and labor cost (as compared to the results obtained from similar control groups where the foreman, as was normally done, assigned the men

ILLUSTRATION XIX — 1 [19]

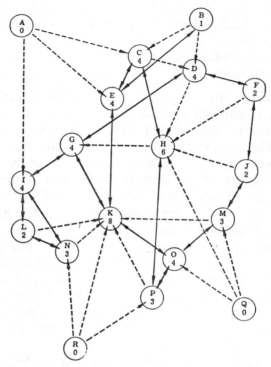

Raymond H. Van Zelst's Sociogram. Each member of a work group of eighteen carpenters was asked to nominate the three men with whom he would most like to work. Votes received by each individual are indicated in the circles.

arbitrarily to work crews) but attained greater satisfaction as workers.[19] The Institute for Social Research of the University of Michigan has done research to find "the principles of organizational structure and the principles and practices of leadership that are responsible for high productivity and high job satisfaction." Findings of the Michigan research that pertained specifically to the relationship between supervisors and workers were used in Chapter XIV. The research results published first in the AMA Personnel Series No. 155 indicated the great part played by the supervisor. A consistent finding of the research which has been carried on in a variety of organizations has been *"that there is a marked relationship between the kind of supervision an employee receives and both his productivity and the satisfactions which he derives from his work."* (Italics inserted.) This study used two major criteria to evaluate the effectiveness of administration: (1) man-hour productivity or a similar measure of achieving productivity goals; (2)

job and other satisfactions derived by employees or members of the group.

Some additional findings selected from Likert's report are: (1) little relationship exists between employees' attitudes toward the company and their productivity; (2) in some situations less productive sections participate in recreational activities more often than do those sections that are more productive; (3) an over-all favorable attitude toward an employee's company results in less absenteeism (and it is suspected that it also results in less turnover and the attracting of a better labor force during a tight labor market); (4) employee-centered supervisors not only train employees to do the present job well but they tend to train the employees for the next higher job; (5) low productivity sometimes leads to closer supervision but closer supervision may be the cause of low productivity; (6) when general supervision is given as opposed to close supervision it is necessary to keep the workers well-informed; (7) the greater a supervisor's skill in using group methods of supervision, the greater are productivity and job satisfaction of the workers; (8) in instances high morale and high productivity are found to exist together, while in other situations low morale may be found with high productivity or high morale with low productivity (the reasons are related to the kind of supervision that exists but the significant finding is that the kind of supervision that results in the highest productivity also results in the highest morale); (9) for both the blue collar and the white collar workers, there is a marked relationship between worker morale and how much employees feel that their boss is interested in discussing work problems with the work group; (10) high-production work groups perform well more often than do low-production groups in the absence of their supervisors and this is probably one of the reasons for the greater productivity of high-production groups; (11) work groups with high group pride and loyalty are more productive because of the fact that they cooperate more, of their own initiative and help one another get the work done, and they show more teamwork; group willingness to help one another seems to come from a better team spirit and better interpersonal relationships that the foreman has developed in the group through group methods of supervision and assigning work tasks as a whole to the group while low group loyalty seems to occur in cases where the foreman deals with workers individually and makes individual work assignments; (12) when a superior treats subordinates as human beings, greater group loyalty and pride result; (13) good supervisors are able to identify with their employees and keep psychologically close to them; it is important for supervisors to accept the goals of the over-all organization and to have a clear understanding of the role and function of their work groups in achieving the over-all goals; (14) group participation and involvement are beneficial at all levels in an organization. Likert in his summation of findings says that the results suggest as do results of other research that "every human being earnestly seeks a secure, friendly, and supportive relationship and one that gives him a sense of personal worth in the face-to-face groups most important to him . . . his immediate family group and his work group." He develops other informal groups if his formal work group is hostile. He is not seeking to be coddled in wanting friendly supportive relationships; he is seeking a sense of importance by doing difficult but important tasks which help to implement the goals he is seeking.[20]

Likert has reported also on the application of the findings of the Institute for Social Research of the University of Michigan through tests involving hundreds of employees in widely different kinds of industries. Chart 2 shows the results of one of these tests. It is based on an experiment by Coch and French who employed the participation approach in designing changes to be made in jobs.

ILLUSTRATION XIX-2 [21]

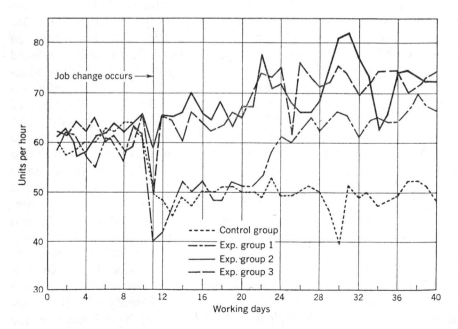

The effect of participation on production.

[The student is referred to the original study for complete details; only a summary of the findings is given here.] The control group in the Coch and French study went through the usual factory routine. Selected group members from the experimental *group one* participated to the extent of approving the change after being given full information as to need for it; these people selected operators to be specially trained, and a meeting with these operators resulted in interest and cooperation throughout the change; these operators also trained the others. This approach is perhaps partially participation and partially what has been called accommodation, i.e., accustoming the workers to the idea of change. Experimental *groups two and three* were smaller. They went through much the same kind of meetings to plan for the change; all the operators in these two groups participated directly (participated fully) in the designing of the new jobs and they made many suggestions but, as with group one, no formal group decision was reached. This study implies the need for personnel departments to make line people (supervisors) aware of the results of human relations research and to aid them in applying it. Need for education of foremen is indicated in the fact that seventy-eight per cent of the foremen in one well-managed company indicated that the most important thing they do is production while only seven per cent indicated human relations and fifteen per cent indicated both production and human relations.[21] The secret to production may lie in human relations skills and the application of human relations research findings.

Later research by the Institute for Social Research, University of Michigan, involving data from a nationally operated company, comprising thirty-two geographically separated units varying in size from about fifteen to over fifty employees, resulted in the following as reported by Likert:

> [Managers who] have a *favorable attitude toward men score* achieve significantly higher performance than those who have an unfavorable score. Managers who have a supportive attitude toward their men and endeavor to build them into well knit teams obtain appreciably higher productivity than managers who have a threatening attitude and rely more on man-to-man patterns of supervision. (The correlation coefficient is 0.64.)[22]

The findings of some studies have seemed to indicate that satisfied workers are more productive than dissatisfied ones. The Michigan research just reported on found conflicting patterns of relationship between morale and productivity. A survey of attitude studies by Brayfield and Crockett reached the conclusion that they found very little evidence to indicate that employee attitudes of "the type usually measured in morale studies" bear any appreciable relationships to job performance.[23] Productivity is dependent upon many things including motivation (*and certainly dissatisfied persons often accomplish much more than satisfied ones*), the kind of supervision that is given, the ability of the executives, the ability of the supervisors, the ability of the employees, and the tendency of members of work groups to produce at the same level as the group. Robert Kahn of the Institute for Social Research of the University of Michigan found a "characteristic of the cohesive work group is that the individual workers in it will tend to produce at the same level." [24]

The fact that low-production workers may report a high degree of satisfaction with their work situations has led some writers to dismiss the "human-relations approach" as a manner of solving some of the problems of management. James Menzies Black has accused the human relations people of exhibiting "a management philosophy that emphasized a buttery kind of human relations . . . spreading cheer throughout industry." He advises managers not to rely too heavily on "data produced by other companies or by universities" in making their plans for management-development. He says that generalities should be used as "a background against which specifics become meaningful" and that "education is attained by hard mental discipline." His interesting discussion concludes by hailing "farewell to the happiness boys" and proclaiming the finish of "interwoven togetherness." Management, under the philosophy that he extols would "no longer shoulder all the responsibility for the company's success, while employees are protected from the consequence of low-quality work, inefficiency, and indifference because they have somehow confused the 'right to work' with the 'right to draw a paycheck.' " [25] Despite such criticism, however, it is not likely that the whole field of human relations will collapse at one fell swoop; failure in communication, lack of understanding, and attitudes are the guilty factors in bringing about opposing points of view with regard to human relations, and the existence of opposing viewpoints is perhaps healthy. As Donald R. Schoen has pointed out, the term "human relations" means "so many different things to so many different people." To the Hawthorne researchers human relations was conceived of as "a field of research, teaching, and practice, just as is the field of medicine." Human relations under this concept is "not concerned with making everyone happy or sugar-coating harsh reality" and it "is *not* and should not be equated in toto with the job of management or executive leadership." [26]

A leading advocate of the use of "participation" to release energy and intelligence among the masses of workers, Joseph N. Scanlon, has a broad background including experience as a cost accountant, industrial engineer, steelworker, president of a local union, Director of Research and Engineering for the United States Steelworkers of America (CIO), and staff member of MIT's Industrial Relations Section. Scanlon's early work in participation was with a committee of steelworkers whose ideas were used in a program of action that resulted in "reduced costs, improved quality of the production, and a solvent company." There are no formal rules and regulations in the "Scanlon Plan." Success of the plan in a given firm is dependent upon the willingness of management at all levels to accept criticism from employee and management ranks within the organization itself. Two of the most troublesome obstacles to effective use of the idea of participation of workers is to be found in "(1) the initial loss of prestige and consequent opposition of middle and lower management people and (2) the inability of the organization to make important decisions on an explicit basis." Enthusiasm of workers who enjoy their work and take pride in their accomplishments are the results of a successful program of participation.[27]

A paragraph is borrowed from Fred Witney to further argue for continued research in human relations and labor-management relations in industry and the application of the findings of such research:

> The dedicated scholar has no ax to grind. His only objective is to broaden the frontiers of knowledge for the benefit of society; research in the field of labor relations is motivated chiefly by the desire to help in the establishment of a sound labor relations program. Today our free institutions are being challenged by foreign doctrines. Therefore it is more important than ever before to demonstrate that the employer-employee relationship, conducted within a free enterprise system, can function for the benefit of all concerned. Above all, the production and dissemination of knowledge is a prerequisite for this goal. It is at this level that the university has played, and will continue to play, an indispensable role.[28]

Robert N. Anthony, author of *Management Accounting*, stated in this textbook that "New control concepts are likely to originate primarily from discoveries in the field of social psychology." He has implied that the problem of control is more likely to be found in *human relations research*, the *factors that motivate* people, *leadership characteristics, organization principles*, and effective *communication* than in that other useful tool of management, accounting.[29]

What Is Communication? — Some persons view communication as the foremost problem of management. Others have said that all the talk about communication, the prescriptions, the gimmicks, and the activity have failed. Frank E. Fischer has stated that if communication has failed it is because: (1) too much attention has been paid to its media and devices and not enough to its content and purpose; (2) executives have thought communication was simple and have relied upon publications for employees, personnel counseling, reading racks, and economic indoctrination; (3) they have spent too much time talking when they should have spent some of it listening.[30]

Communication implies a two-way exchange of information and/or feelings between two or more persons. The person initiating the communication process must first know exactly what he wishes to communicate and must have the words, the understanding, the empathy, and, if necessary, the facial expressions and gestures to convey his meaning exactly. The majority of communication at the work level is done orally. The manager or supervisor who communicates to a worker must see that he has been understood. He must often "play back the record" in order to get the worker's interpretation of what has been communicated. There must be a form of feedback from individuals and groups in order to know that the message that was intended was interpreted according to plan. If it was not, a new way must be found to put the message over. This may involve educating workers and even certain segments of management to change their attitudes. Research has shown that people are influenced by their beliefs, knowledge, and ways of thinking to put their own interpretations upon what they hear, read, or observe.

The average college business major takes at least one course in "business writing, business communication, or business and/or economics research writing." It is not the intent here to teach either speech or writing. If one has reached the college level without having acquired the basic elements of communication, then he does not belong in college. What are the basic elements? Vocabulary, grammar, information, ideas, and understanding appear to be essential, yet ideas and information may be conveyed through other media than words. These other media include: charts, graphs, diagrams, figures, tables, symbols, pictures, models, actions, musical notes, electronic devices, and so forth. Thought is essential to communication; beyond thought, the only essential is a medium for conveying it. While communicating may be done without words, words are the chief medium used by the communicator. They furnish the power by which a manager or leader gets work done through others.

To write or speak well one should know human nature and the motives of people even better than he knows his subject. He must have the background for thinking for the thought behind the words is basic. The communicator must be able to put himself in the place of the reader or hearer; each person and each group of persons may require not only a different approach but a different set of words or even a different medium. Most communication does begin with what is said or written; it cannot be done in many cases without words.

A study made by the Human Engineering Laboratories concluded that an executive's vocabulary correlates with his salary and that "An extensive knowledge of the exact meanings of English words accompanies outstanding success in this country more often than any other single characteristic which the Human Engineering Laboratories have been able to isolate and measure." [31] Despite the fact that managers should be familiar with technical words, in communicating with others it is frequently necessary for them to translate these into simple language. General Electric called on many scientists and engineers and asked them "What level of reading difficulty should we expect our technical readers to tolerate?" The answer that came from one of the company's top industrial engineers was: "The General Electric *Review* should give complete coverage of the company's most significant technical advances, and should be written in a language so easy to comprehend that a bright high school senior could read and understand every word." A GE manager said, "Our business world needs young people whose minds are packed with facts, but with the boldness of imagination to release them in a form that is easy and pleasant to take." [32] An essay entitled "Why Study English?" written by a GE public relations man was reproduced in enough youth magazines to reach an audience of six million teen-agers. In reprint form it was distributed to over half of the nation's public schools and to some of its colleges. The theme of this article was a statement by Peter Drucker to the effect that "ability to express ideas in writing and in speaking heads the list of requirements for success." [33] A Harvard University president, Charles W. Eliot, said some years before Drucker wrote: "The chief test of a sound education is the ability to speak and write one's language well."

Lines of Communication — Communication in business is usually done for the purpose of informing, instructing, or requesting information. It is often used also to persuade and win belief; it is sometimes used to entertain or to impress. Not only are problems solved by communicating, they are averted by clear instructions and the proper passing of information to employees, stockholders, suppliers, dealers and other middlemen, consumers, financial institutions, and governmental agencies. Within the business organization communication is thought of as being: (1) *down-line,* (2) *up-line,* and (3) *cross-line.* Down-line and up-line are also referred to as *vertical* communication; cross-line has also been called *horizontal* communication. *Down-line communication* includes:

1. Information about jobs — pay, profit-sharing, wage incentives, pensions, hours, overtime, other employee benefits and programs, duties, and responsibilities.

2. Information that will help an individual co-ordinate his work with the work of others — vacations, standards of conduct, plans, objectives, and policies.

3. Information about the company — expansion plans, profits, advertising, sales, research, new products, markets, and so forth.[34]

It has been said that nine-tenths of industrial communication takes place orally, face-to-face.[35] Nevertheless, business uses many devices and techniques other than the non-verbal ones referred to above to communicate downward within a given division, department, or section. Some of these are: bulletin boards; house organs; employee handbooks, other booklets, and safety manuals; letters; minutes of meetings; staff meetings; mass meetings of all types, including union meetings; intercommunication systems; luncheons, dinners, and other formal programs; training groups and committees; all types of committees; conferences; payroll inserts; reports; conducted tours; demonstrations; advertising; telephone, telegraph, cablegram, posters; written business procedures and systems; reading racks with company information and reports, safety and health information, general inspirational material, home and family material, technical information, economic and social material. Some of these devices are also used for up-line communication. Companies often use the community resources such as schools, public meetings, and civic clubs to communicate to their employees.

A national survey of 519 companies indicated that 98.5 per cent of the companies used bulletin boards to communicate to hourly workers; only two other media were used by over half of the companies: letters or bulletins (64.5 per cent); payroll inserts (59.9 per cent).[36] One survey made by the Opinion Research Corporation revealed that employees felt management couldn't be counted on to look out for the best interests of employees except in the case of safety in which area "management has done the most consistent and dramatic job of purposeful communication." [37]

The majority of large companies today publish newspapers and magazines for employees (house organs). These may carry success stories and news items about employees, educational articles, humor, and company information. Some companies publish an educational type magazine designed to inform employees about the products and technical progress made by their companies and a news type paper or magazine to pass on stories of the individual accomplishments of members of the personnel. The latter type of publication lends itself to being published by separate divisions or departments in order that the stories may be designed for a particular audience.

It is generally best in passing on financial information to employees to use brief versions of annual reports rather than complicated statistical details.[38]

Up-line communication includes the formal reporting upward within the lines of organization; it includes, also, the results of morale surveys, and the grievances and desires of workers as expressed to their superiors in the ordinary course of business. Use of the participation idea is dependent upon "listening" to up-line communication. Detecting and using the informal groups that develop in all formal organizations results in up-line communication also. This may be accomplished by immediate superiors in the formal organization or by use of counselors (Chapter IX) and immediate superiors.

Employee attitudes and morale are not capable of being easily or exactly measured. Some abstract ways of judging the morale of employees were listed in the introduction to this chapter. *Morale or attitude surveys* to find out what employees are thinking may be conducted through interviewing or written questionnaires. If they are made as a part of a continuing counseling and interviewing program, it is likely they will result in more accurate and useful information than they would if a surveying group from outside came into a given company to get the information in a brief period of time. Studies have shown that morale improves when a continuing counseling program is used to find out the problems and interests of workers, providing management uses this information to eliminate the sources of irritations and grievances and strengthen the sources of pride, interest, initiative, cooperation, and loyalty. In some cases *employee committees* may be used to find the state of morale in a given department or group. *Employee* and *production records* are also a source of information on morale: *employee turnover,* in terms of both *accession rate* (number of employees hired during a given period divided by the average number of employees as obtained by averaging beginning and ending total employees) and *separation rate* (number of employees separated during a given period divided by the average number of employees as obtained by averaging beginning and ending total employees); *absences and tardiness; sick leaves; long rest periods or lunch hours; early quitting; number of suggestions submitted where formal suggestion system is used; number and types of grievances submitted; disciplinary action taken; merit rating; amount of output; quality of output.* High morale is the result of integrating interests and good communication, but records such as those just mentioned can indicate employee attitudes. High absenteeism, for instance, may be the symptom of low morale. Outside factors, however, may have caused the absenteeism, so if records are used they may have to be supplemented by observation and/or surveys or other research. Absenteeism in some companies has been found to be greatest just before and after holidays and on the first days of important events such as the hunting season. In such cases, morale might be very high although absenteeism is also high. Some companies provide for shutdowns when they anticipate a high degree of absenteeism.

Cross-line communication implies cutting across the formal lines of organization, as when an advertising employee goes to the production department to get information relative to a product to be advertised. If the advertising employee is not acting under the instruction of his superior (who either has the authority or has requested it for the special case) this would not be following organization channels; following channels presupposes going up one chain of command high enough in the chain to a manager with enough authority to consult with a person of equal or perhaps less authority in another chain of command. Some employees, however, are capable of "cutting red tape" and crossing lines without antagonizing their superiors; others do not have this gift. The gift is perhaps a touch of daring together with knowing the right people and being able to communicate with them precisely. Where authority is distributed or divided among several managers in order that they may work together on a given project, this is known as *shared authority;* there may also be shared authority in the handling of certain grievances through formal procedures. If two or more persons pool their delegated authority to make a decision affecting the department of each of them, *splintered authority* is said to exist. This type of action is frequently taken in order to eliminate the referring upward of problems requiring decisions. It is people who know how to use their shared and/or splintered authority and who possess the ability to communicate who get work done and open up or preclude from formation the bottlenecks that slow down operations.

The *grapevine* is also a means of communication and although it is chiefly used perhaps for up-line and cross-line communication it can be used for down-line communication also. Workers get much of their information from other workers. The Industrial Relations Section of the California Institute of Technology, in surveying over 50,000 employees of eighteen different companies, found that from ten to forty per cent of employees said they got most of the information they received about their companies from fellow employees. Employees, however, prefer to get information from their superiors in conversation or group meetings; they will accept the information through bulletin boards, plant papers, bulletins, or letters. They prefer not to depend on the grapevine.[39] Nevertheless, the locker room, the lunch counter, and the water fountain continue to be centers at which grapevine information is passed on, and according to some estimates information passed from worker to worker is accurate about ninety per cent of the time.

Management has employed various plans for using the grapevine to get information to employees. Among these are: (1) asking small groups of employees what rumors they have heard and attempting to supplement their knowledge if the rumors are true, or to allay them if they are false (*rumor clinics*); (2) placing *rumor boards* at strategic locations on which employees may write the rumors they would like to know about; (3) holding meetings with the *natural* leaders to inform them in order that they may pass on more accurate information.[40]

Management Attitude Toward Communication and Morale Surveys — According to a survey made by the Industrial Communication Research Staff of Purdue University of the presidents of one hundred leading corporations (although only seventy-three responded), there is a definite relationship between communication and employee productivity; over ninety per cent of the respondents (seventy-three, of whom all but twenty were presidents) believed that there is a relationship between breakdowns in communication and labor disputes. Most of the respondents believed management effectiveness to be dependent upon ability in oral communication, although only twelve out of fifty-one thought that most top managers possess ability to communicate effectively. They felt that natural talent is a factor in communicative ability, although not the only factor, and that such ability is improved by training and experience.[41]

Management realizes that there are many pitfalls in conducting morale surveys. In the first place, such surveys require a great deal of careful preparation by persons with adequate training and knowledge of the techniques of framing questions that will reveal the desired attitudes and not just those things that employees think management wants to hear or that they are able to or wish to reveal. If surveys are made, the results should be made known not only to management but to employees as well, and within a reasonable length of time in order to capitalize on current interest.

A survey made by the National Industrial Conference Board of the production employees of two companies indicated the close relationship that seems to exist between morale and freedom to communicate. The two groups of employees were matched with the exception that those in one plant (Plant B) had participated in an active program of communication for some years. The findings of the survey are abbreviated as follows:[42]

		PLANT A	PLANT B
1. Does your company do a good job of telling you what is going on and what's being planned?			
ANSWER:	Very good job	18%	55%
	Doesn't do much	22%	14%
2. Does your foreman ask your advice before deciding things that affect you?			
ANSWER:	Hardly ever	65%	40%
	Almost always	11%	26%
3. Can you talk things over with your foreman when you want to?			
ANSWER:	Yes, I always can	34%	56%
	Hardly ever	5%	0%
4. Do you feel a part of your company?			
ANSWER:	I feel I really belong	29%	62%
	I feel I just work here	42%	14%
5. How does your company compare as a company to work for with other companies?			
ANSWER:	Worse than average	4%	3%
	Just average	35%	19%
	One of the very best	20%	45%

Administering Change — In summary the findings of a famous case study of human relations in a factory are given here. It was found that relations have:

1. *Dominant assumptions,* i.e., expectations the individual has about himself in relation to another that he brings to any contact with another person.

2. *Overt behavior,* i.e., the interaction of two people and common activity in which they engage.

3. *The individual's own feeling about this overt behavior.*

4. *The individual's evaluation of his relationship that he carries into the future.* An evaluation arrived at during one interaction becomes the assumption for the next.[43]

Five generalizations about technological change and communication could be made as a result of the study:

1. Each person brought a frame of reference to the situation.
2. Communication was impaired when people brought together frames of reference which were incompatible.
3. Communication was facilitated when people had complementary frames of reference.
4. Communication was facilitated when someone was able to recognize and accept a frame of reference different from his own.
5. Communication was facilitated when there was in the situation someone who had some insight into his own frame of reference: who realized he had to be perceived as a source of help before he could be helpful.

It was found that: (1) individuals with roughly the same training and experience, occupying equal positions at the same pay are not necessarily interchangeable parts, (2) technological change brings change in interpersonal relations. It was recommended that the administrator think in a way that will allow him to take account of these changes; *he should conceive of the organization as a social system.*

How to Achieve Clarity in Communications — Shortly before his death James Thurber, noted American humorist, was quoted as having said that English is a living language and therefore change is inevitable, but that care should be taken in order that the language not "crack like a dry stick in the process, leaving us all miserably muddling in a monstrous miasma of mindless and meaningless mumbling." [44] One might say that Thurber in this instance admirably administered a simile and an alliterative alarm! Thurber's alarm was over the infiltration of our language by countless coined words and phrases. Although clarity in communication may be achieved through concreteness, concreteness is not necessarily achieved when one has coined verbs from nouns or introduced Beatnik terminology into written or oral communications.

Numerous writers have emphasized the need for written or oral communication to have *clearness, completeness, consideration* of the other person, *concreteness, correctness, courtesy,* and *conciseness.* Aurner called these qualities "The Positive C-Qualities." [45] Some people achieve these qualities with seeming effortlessness; their almost intuitive minds and picture words make others *see, hear, smell, taste, feel,* and *compre-*

hend. Persons who resort to the abstract jargon of their particular fields of work or areas of specialization frequently are as difficult to understand as are those who use coined expressions and Beatnik phrases to achieve their particular brand of specificness. Short and simple English words arranged in the order of straightforward thought are the safest to use if one wants exact comprehension.

Two examples of "obfuscation" and "jargon" within a given branch of knowledge are given here. They caused Lawrence R. Klein, after fifteen years as editor of the Labor Department's monthly review, to take a year off to see if he could discover why government bureaucrats write so badly.

> In the current stages of the ongoing postattack productivity study, the identification of the enervating effects of a decreased caloric diet upon physical productivity indicates the need to plan, pre-attack, for adequate caloric food stockpiles.
>
> The psycholathic deviate scale indicated that business agents as a group tended to be personable but to have little emotional depth and to have not internalized the societal norms.[46]

The first quotation means "that soldiers should have a square meal ready for them after fighting," and the second one means that "business agents usually are *nice guys but bums*."

Many companies give training in communication to management people at all levels. Some have used as authority for emphasis upon plain writing and speaking the writings of Flesch and Gunning.[47] Gunning developed *The Fog Index* for measuring readability. This index employs two factors: *short words* and *short sentences*. The Flesch method of computing readability scores considers *syllables per word, sentence length, personal words*, and *personal sentences*. There are other factors that must be considered, however; even nonsense sentences and clauses could be rated upon these factors. *Thought is still the main element of a sentence*. If the thought is clearly expressed in a short sentence containing short words and some personal words, the idea obviously should be easily comprehended.

Clarity in writing and speaking is often obtained through the use of figures of speech (Chapter XXIII). Perhaps it takes both practice and artistry to use figures of speech successfully, but when they are used by an artist figures of speech can clarify. Clarity may be obtained also by charts, graphs, tables, and other means of visual presentation. The basic secret to "clarity" in writing and speaking, however, must lie not so much in the words or methods one chooses but in the clarification and unification of ideas before one begins. Fischer's *ten commandments of good communication* begin with this thought. Here they are:

1. *Seek to clarify your ideas before communicating.*
2. *Examine the true purpose of each communication.*
3. *Consider the total physical and human setting whenever you communicate.*
4. *Consult with others, where appropriate, in planning communications.*
5. *Be mindful, while you communicate, of the overtones as well as the basic content of your message.*
6. *Take the opportunity, when it arises, to convey something of help or value to the receiver.*
7. *Follow up your communication.*
8. *Communicate for tomorrow as well as today.*
9. *Be sure your actions support your communications.*
10. *Last, but by no means least: Seek not only to be understood — be a good listener.*[48]

Effective Listening, Reading, and Silence — A programmed course in "effective listening," designed for Charles Pfizer & Co., Inc., and used by over fifty other companies combines pencil and paper exercises with tapes and frames to teach students how to listen. Programmed instruction in other areas of human relations has been used by the Human Development Institute, Inc. (Atlanta), in training employees of many firms and particularly in "changing their attitudes." Basic Systems, Inc. (New York), also has programmed instruction (defined in Chapter XIV) designed to influence employee behavior.[49]

Ability to read is often as important as ability to listen. Students and employees can be taught to read more effectively; programmed instruction can also be used for this (Chapter II). Four groups of officer candidates at Maxwell Air Base took a special speed-reading course which enabled them to increase their reading speeds (with markedly improved comprehension at the faster speeds) by the following percentages: 52 (Group A); 48 (Group B); 86 (Group C); 75 (Group D).

Knowing when not to communicate is important. Simply by saying nothing, managers can bring the motivating power of anxiety into play. Because of this, silence itself can make a contribution to the manager-subordinate relationship and promote communication. One consulting psychologist has suggested that silence may be used to encourage subordinates to think through a problem before giving the answer; if the manager is silent, the subordinate under the stress of silence will attempt to do his best to bring a good solution to the problem. Managers also can use their own silence to encourage subordinates to submit ideas; this, in the long run, gives them greater personal satisfaction. A manager's silence may also lead to the uncovering of emotionally charged information. Resentments and grievances are brought into the open.[50] When this technique of "silence" is used by a manager, he is really using the counseling technique of the "non-directive" interview. The same rules of interviewing apply. There is, perhaps, a little more need for the employee to feel that he is in a situation where there is an exchange instead of a monologue. There is need even in the non-directive interview for the superior to take some initiative for keeping the subordinate talking.

The Texas Medical Center, Houston, has seen fit to build research centers to study in the areas of audiology, speech pathology, experimental phonetics, information theory, reading disabilities, speech, and hearing. Findings of such research centers will undoubtedly be beneficial to those who work with communications in business, industry and education.

Conclusions — Mary Parker Follett said that every social process has three aspects: *interacting, unifying,* and *emerging.* To her the fundamental principle underlying every field of human activity is *organization, relatedness.*[51] Interacting, unifying, emerging, organization, and relatedness all imply *communication.* Roethlisberger said that:

> . . . differences in modes of thought and ways of viewing things may make communication in some instances almost impossible. . . . If there is to be successful communication between the top and bottom of an industrial organization, these differences in modes of thought must be more clearly recognized. . . . The failure on the part of management to understand explicitly its social structure means that it often mistakes logical coordination for social integration. This confusion interferes with successful communication up and down the line as well as between different groups within the industry.[52]

Rogers and Roethlisberger wrote that real communication occurs when people listen with understanding. When it is apparently impossible for different parties to communicate because of lack of understanding, it is necessary to create a situation "in which each of the different parties come to understand the other from the *other's* point of view."

> . . . This has been achieved, in practice, even when feelings run high, by the influence of a person who is willing to understand each point of view empathically, and who thus acts as a catalyst to

precipitate further understanding. . . . Mutual communication tends to be pointed toward solving a problem rather than toward attacking a person or group.[53]

The reader may recall the function of the President of the United States in 1964 in bringing together the officials of the railroads and the officials of the railroad unions in settling a dispute of several years' duration between these two groups. At a time when released frustrations of the groups might have resulted in national crisis, the "catalyst" producing understanding was a man able to appeal to each group to make sacrifices and back down from the hard and fast positions it had previously taken.

The student will find that much has been written on the use of committees and decentralization as a means of integrating and/or using the ideas of people who do the operative work in industry: salesmen, production foremen, project engineers, and cost analysts. When authority is delegated to lower echelons, however, up-line, down-line, and cross-line communications must continue more than ever to be strong.[54] Industry must continue its research into motivation; the results should be used not only in industry but in education as well. General Electric Company's Management Research and Development Institute, first staff college ever created by a company for the higher education of its own executives, centers its curriculum around GE's "four basic criteria for the manager who develops himself in the process of developing others":

1. He should be a balanced 'generalist' rather than only a functional 'specialist.' He should be able to plan, organize, integrate, and to measure as his way of getting results mainly through the work of others, and to do all this in terms of department and company objectives as against any excursions for the sake of his own ego enhancement.

2. He should serve the concept of the best balance of interest among customers, employees, shareowners, vendors, dealers, government and the community.

3. He should lead by persuasion rather than command, by example of integrity and largeness of view, earning the respect of associates by encouraging participation in contrast to the order-flinging martinet who invokes table pounding to mask immaturity, both administrative and emotional.

4. He should recognize human limitations as well as potentialities for growth; that while everyone has an improvement stretch, it remains impossible to turn a mediocrity into a first-rate executive.[55]

Good communications are the result of good management. Good management uses whatever means it must to obtain good communications: formal channels, informal groups, grapevine methods, decentralization, continued feedback of information through informal and formal means, committees, morale surveys, education, training, and the many devices for imparting and receiving instructions, information, and feelings. When it is necessary to indoctrinate employees in order to bring their attitudes into line with management goals, this is done. Techniques such as group participation and accommodation are used for overcoming resistance of employees to change. It is inherent for people to want to hold on to the *status quo,* managers simply because habits have been formed and it is the path of least resistance not to change, workers for the same reason plus the fact that they fear change may result in lowered wages, increased work assignments, or both, or possibly they may even fear the losing of their jobs. Good management accomplishes change with the least amount of friction and loss in output of work, but good management is aware that the people who accomplish the most may not be those who are the most content. On the contrary, they may be persons who are consciously competing for recognition and achievement, or they may be persons striving for success in terms of any number of outcomes such as financial reward, power, or approval in order to compensate for not having had these in some earlier time. The competitive quality may be turned to useful purposes by management; within the ranks of management itself some of the best work is done in departments where managers themselves are competing.

Inventors of the past have given us the devices of communication from shorthand and the typewriter to Telstar and digital computers; leaders who would employ these devices must have the ideas to communicate and the intuition and judgment to know how best to communicate them. Research must go on, too. As far back as 1918 when Standard Oil of New Jersey began its "Representative Plan" companies were trying to find out what their workers were really thinking. Psychologists and other social scientists in that company, as well as in many other companies, have worked ever since to find out what stimulates people to work best and how best to identify people of promise early in their careers.[56]

PROJECTS

1. Read and write a brief report on a current article pertaining to business communication.

2. Write four questions that could be used to find the "morale" of the members of your class as a group.

3. What do you believe to be the chief factors that motivate you to achieve?

ACKNOWLEDGMENTS AND REFERENCES

1   Koontz, Harold and O'Donnell, Cyril, *Principles of Management,* Second Edition, McGraw-Hill Book Company, Inc., New York, 1959, pp. 312-16, 339-40.

2   Newman, William H., and Summer, Charles E., Jr., *The Process of Management,* Prentice-Hall, Inc., Englewood Cliffs, New Jersey, 1961, p. 493.

3   Fleishman, Edwin A., Harris, Edwin F., and Burtt, Harold E., *Leadership and Supervision in Industry,* Ohio State University Studies, No. 33, 1955.

4   Davis, Ralph Currier, *The Fundamentals of Top Management,* Harper & Brothers, Publishers, New York, 1951, Chapters 15-16.

5   *Ibid.,* pp. 552-557.

6   *Ibid.,* p. 546.

7   *Ibid.,* pp. 97-102.

8   Roethlisberger, F. J., *Management and Morale,* Harvard University Press, Cambridge, Massachusetts, 1952, p. 9.

9   Roethlisberger, F. J., Dickson, W. J., and Wright, Harold A., *Management and the Worker,* Harvard University Press, Cambridge, Massachusetts, 1950, p. 3.

10 Roethlisberger, *Management and Morale, op. cit.,* pp. 19-21.

11 *Ibid.,* p. 45.

12 *Ibid.,* Chapter III, and other writings on the Hawthorne Studies.

13 *Ibid.,* pp. 59-62, Chapter IV.

14 *Ibid.,* Chapter II, and other general readings.

15 Roethlisberger, Dickson, and Wright, *op. cit.,* Chapter XXIII.

16 *Ibid.,* Chapter XXIV.

17 *Ibid.,* pp. 561-562.

18 Henderson, Lawrence J., *Pareto's General Sociology,* Harvard Press, Cambridge, Massachusetts, 1947.

19 Van Zelst, Raymond, H., "An Interpersonal Relations Technique for Industry," *Personnel,* American Management Association, July, 1952, pp. 68-77. Also: Van Zelst, Raymond H., "Sociometrically Selected Work Teams Increase Production," *Personnel Psychology,* 1952, pp. 175-186.

20 Likert, Rensis, "Motivation: The Core of Management," American Management Association, Personnel Series, No. 155, New York, 1953, pp. 3-21. Also in: *Management: A Book of Readings,* edited by Harold Koontz and Cyril O'Donnell, McGraw-Hill Book Company, New York, 1964, pp. 355-366; Likert, Rensis, *New Patterns of Management,* McGraw-Hill Book Company, New York, 1961.

21 *Ibid.* See p. 40 of last-named reference. Original copyright: Coch, Lester, and French, John R. P., Jr., "Overcoming Resistance to Change," *Human Relations,* Vol. 1, No. 4, 1948, pp. 512-532.

22 Likert, Rensis, "Measuring Organizational Performance," *Harvard Business Review,* March-April, 1958, Vol. 36, No. 2, pp. 41-52.

23 Brayfield, Arthur H., and Crockett, Walter H., "Employee Attitudes and Employee Performance," *Psychological Bulletin,* September, 1955.

24 Hepner, Harry W., *Psychology Applied to Life and Work,* Third Edition, Prentice-Hall, Inc., Englewood Cliffs, New Jersey, 1957, p. 409.

25 Black, James Menzies, "Farewell to the Happiness Boys," *Management Review,* May, 1961, pp. 38-47.

26 Schoen, Donald R., "Human Relations: Boon or Bogle?," *Harvard Business Review,* November-December, 1957, pp. 41-47.

27 Shultz, George P., "Worker Participation on Production Problems: A Discussion of Experience with the 'Scanlon Plan'," *Personnel,* November, 1951, Vol. 28, No. 3, pp. 201-210.

28 Witney, Fred, "The Era of Sophisticated Labor Relations," *Business Horizons,* Spring, 1962, pp. 83-90, and reproduced in *Issues in Business and Society,* edited by William T. Greenwood, Houghton Mifflin Co., Boston, 1964, pp. 248-256.

29 Anthony, Robert N., *Management Accounting,* Revised Edition, Richard D. Irwin, Inc., Homewood, Illinois, 1960, p. 594.

30 Fischer, Frank E., "A New Look at Management Communication," *Personnel,* May, 1955, Vol. 31, No. 6, pp. 487-495.

31 Aurner, Robert R., *Effective Communication in Business,* Fourth Edition, South-Western Publishing Company, Cincinnati 27, 1958, p. 151.

32 Pingree, George, "Communications Ability Industry Demands of the Business Graduate," a speech delivered at the ABWA Convention, Baker Hotel, Dallas, April 8, 1955.

33 Drucker, Peter, "How To Be an Employee," *Fortune,* May, 1952.

34 Adams, Loyce, "Principles of Organization in Business," *Secretary's Business Review,* edited by Nelda R. Lawrence, Prentice-Hall, Inc., Englewood Cliffs, New Jersey, 1959, p. 80.

35 Hepner, *op. cit.,* p. 476.

36 —————, "Personnel Practices in Factory and Office," Fifth Edition, *Studies in Personnel Policy,* No. 145, National Industrial Conference Board, Inc., New York, p. 54.

37 Wolff, Tom, "Are You Getting Across to Your Workers?" *Personnel,* American Management Association, September, 1955.

38 —————, *The Management Review,* American Management Association, August, 1948, p. 427.

39 —————, *Annual Report 1953-1954,* Industrial Relations Section, California Institute of Technology; Project 5, "Surveys of Employee Opinion."

40 Kleiler, Frank M., *The Management Review,* American Management Association, April, 1955, pp. 265-266.

41 Lull, Paul E., Funk, Frank E., and Pierson, Darrell T., *Business and Industrial Communication,* Purdue University, June, 1954; *Advanced Management,* March, 1955; *The Management Review,* American Management Association, May, 1955, pp. 289-291.

42 Fischer, Frank E., *op. cit.*

43 Ronken, Harriet O., and Lawrence, Paul R., *Administering Change—A Case Study of Human Relations in a Factory,* Harvard Press, Cambridge, Massachusetts, 1952.

44 —————, "The English How She Is Spoke," *Newsweek,* February 13, 1961, pp. 87-88.

45 Aurner, *op. cit.,* p. 53ff.

46 Haswell, James M., "Editor Puzzled—Checks Propensity for Obfuscation," *The Houston Chronicle,* July 19, 1962, p. 4, s. 3.

47 Gunning, Robert, *The Technique of Clear Writing,* McGraw-Hill, Book Co., Inc., New York, 1952.
Flesch, Rudolf, *The Art of Plain Talk,* Harper & Brothers, New York, 1946; *The Art of Readable Writing,* Harper & Brothers, 1949, and *How to Test Readability,* Harper & Brothers, 1951.

48 Fischer, *op. cit.*

49 —————, "Programming Harmony," *Business Week,* April 18, 1964, pp. 142-144.

50 Farr, J. N., "How to Communicate with Silence," *Nation's Business,* June, 1962, p. 96.

51 Follett, Mary Parker, *Dynamic Administration,* edited by Henry C. Metcalf and L. Urwick, Harper & Brothers, Publishers, New York, 1940, pp. 198-202.

52 Roethlisberger, *Management and Morale, op. cit.,* pp. 63-66.

53 Rogers, Carl R., and Roethlisberger, F. J., *Harvard Business Review,* July-August, 1952, Vol. 30, No. 4, pp. 46-52.

54 ——————, "Managing Your People," brochure compiled by editors of *Nation's Business,* 1615 H. St., N. W., Washington 6, D. C., p. 43.

55 *Ibid.,* p. 22.

56 ——————, "Within the Family," *The Lamp,* Standard Oil Company (New Jersey), 30 Rockefeller Plaza, New York 20, N. Y., 1957.

CHAPTER XX

OF PEOPLE AND TECHNOLOGY

Fluidity of the class structure of the United States has been one of the outstanding characteristics of the nation's life. Even the recognition of the laborer as a class came late. It was only when laborers ceased to look on land as a means to implement change in working conditions that they became labor conscious, i.e., that they realized they must operate from the job to better conditions of work. This was a rejection of agrarianism, but it came slowly. Very few citizens of the country ever accepted their economic status as being permanent or even temporarily permanent. The way to improve a man's condition was always open and the able and ambitious could take that way. The individual could always find an individual solution, or if he failed to do so he recognized this failure and was prone to accept the condemnation of it. The belief was strong that the immigrant who accepted starvation wages and lived in crowded slums could get out of them if he had it in him. It was for this reason that there was scarcely any humanitarian literature in this country during the nineteenth century as there was in England. People did rise, and the smart ones got rich; the literature of the country reflects this thesis. Novels dealing with social problems found this solution. The girl who was thrown out into the streets (over whom Thomas Hood wept tears in England) in this country married the employer's son.

Periodically, however, the *great depression* came and swept back to their original states many who had risen to great wealth through their own distinct brands of individuality. The great depression of the 1930's arrived and the government stepped in with its many social measures of the period.

There has been a clear distinction between the development of life in the *rural* and *urban* areas. With mechanization of the farms fewer people were needed to work them, and with the growth of industrial giants more and more people were required in the factories and offices of the country; a nation that had been largely agrarian became largely industrial. Technological changes had made wage earners of everyone.

Throughout the developments that took place in this country, the *frontier* and the *frontier legend* played their parts. In the frontier there was pressure for conformity. To achieve goals for which they were striving it was necessary for people to conform. The frontier is considered by some to have been a safety valve where the dissatisfied of society could go. They thus relieved the organized societies they left behind them of their dissatisfactions. Some people, however, have questioned the "safety valve" theory. Generally, frontiers did offer opportunity for growth and development and would be conceded by most to have been economic safety valves if not social ones.

Frontier *labor relations* from the 1870's on were often marked by violence. The people who went West were generally people who were rising. They bettered their conditions by their moves; revolutions generally come from people who are rising. Although vested wealth stayed in the East, mobility was for average people a feature of life. This prevented people from having the feeling or sense of belonging. Labor organizations helped to give this feeling to some. The first labor group to operate successfully was the printers; tramp printers always had a job for they had a craft they could carry on anywhere.

Another feature emphasizing the individualism of this country was its *protestantism*. The protestant tradition denies authority. Its members make decisions without relation to others. Much of the migration after 1890 was Catholic, however, and this brought about a division between the old group and the new. Since the Second World War and possibly since the first, too, there has been a change from inner-directed individuals to other-directed individuals.

Along with the *dignity of the individual,* the *sanctity of private property* has been traditional. Life, liberty, and property were things to be protected by law and the courts. Many people, of course, had no property so the courts made everybody a property owner by saying that a "man's labor is his property and subject to all the laws of property." The acceptance of this was necessarily limited, but it is nonetheless significant.

The nation has been influenced by continuous groups of *reformers.* From slavery reformism, middle-class reformism, labor reformism, to social reformism, there have been many reform movements. Today it is practically an impossibility to tie together the threads that have been woven into the pattern of the past that has evolved into our present day with its giant economy, its bureaucrats in government, and its high standard of living despite its poverty stricken and unemployed minorities.

In Russia the United States is held up as a *rival nation* to be exceeded if possible. The Russian people are urged to make personal sacrifices to surpass the United States in both industrial and military accomplishments. Almost since the end of World War II we have been in a cold war with this country which strives to surpass us. During this period, however, the progress made by the United States in the area of technology alone has been phenomenal. Two strong powers in the world each striving to excel the other often operate much as competitive managers within a business firm frequently do. Each may spur the other on to ever higher attainments.

It is realized that to attempt to discuss the technological revolution and its influence on the lives of the people is to undertake a pretentious task. It is realized also that in the process of abstracting many factors that led to established results have been excluded from consideration. This may lead in many cases if not to direct error on the part of the writer to misconception on the part of the reader. Nevertheless, it is felt that one cannot discuss human relations, communication, or for that matter any other factor of management today without giving some consideration to technological developments during the past decade.

It is hoped that the student will gain the impression while reading this and succeeding chapters that from the time of the first steam engines to this day when engineers already have the know-how for building a human heart it has been the innovation, the new product, change, and development that have kept the industrial enterprise system moving forward in health and achievement. *Harvard University in 1964 is beginning a ten-year study financed by International Business Machines Corporation to discover how technology is changing the world.*[1] The student cannot wait until 1974 to begin to know the answer to this question; he will be living the answer. The changes may have taken place and another cycle brought on by other great discoveries and/or innovations will have begun before the Harvard study has ended.

It is true that no study to date has satisfactorily answered the question as to how fast industry is automating or the extent to which automation has created jobs as opposed to displacing workers. Nor do we know whether the jobs that will result because of automation will be more satisfying than were the jobs destroyed by it. According to IBM's president, however, there is a business consciousness today on the part of the individual firm that is looking outward to discover the effects of the firm's actions upon the rest of the economy. IBM's action in financing the Harvard ten-year study is merely a reflection of that company's concern as to its own influence.

Despite the dearth of scientific research on the effects of technological development upon workers and society today, the literature and such data as were available have been used as a basis for the last part of this chapter. First, however, here is a summary of observations made by Elton Mayo in *The Social Problems of an Industrial Civilization* which in some measure called upon earlier research done by Harvard University for data. Published in 1945, the book reflected the thinking of many regarding our industrial society of that day. Mayo's materials and observations came out of a period when both depression and war had disrupted world society. Nevertheless, the student will find that there are applications for Mayo's theses in today's industrial civilization which though probably not threatened by automation does face change because of it.

The Social Problems of an Industrial Civilization[2] — H. G. Wells in *New Machiavelli* wrote of the village of Bromstead, a pleasant country village that had been replaced by slums. LePlay in 1829 doubted that rapid technical and industrial development was beneficial to European communities; there is stability of the social order in simpler communities. Emile Durkheim, founder of the French School of Sociology, made similar observations at the end of the nineteenth century. According to Durkheim, man in an ordered society knew what was expected of him, what his assignment was, and he was responsible for contributions; but in an industrial society he was no longer sure of himself. Even at the time Mayo wrote, things were changing, people were not adjusted. When change comes too rapidly people are unhappy. In the industrial society, it was argued, the family tie is weakened and there often is no group relation substituted for it. Mayo, writing in 1945, found two symptoms of social disruption in modern industrial society: (1) unhappiness, and (2) lack of cooperation between groups (Chapter V). To meet these he argued that every social group must secure for its individuals and groups: (1) satisfaction of material needs, and (2) cooperation throughout the organization.

Mayo wrote of the *established vs. the adaptive society*. In the established society people felt security in their common background, their communities, and their churches. (It is suggested that the student read on the Kula System of New Guinea Natives.)

Mayo defined *social skill* as being the capacity to receive communications from others, and to respond to the attitudes and ideas of others in such fashion as to promote congenial participation in a common task. *Technical skill,* he said, manifests itself as capacity to manipulate things in service of human purposes. William James pointed out in 1890 that every civilized language has two words for knowledge except English: *knowledge-of-acquaintance* (direct experience of fact and situation) and *knowledge about* (the product of reflective thinking or abstract thinking). Knowledge derived from experience is hard to transmit except by example, imitation, and trial and error; knowledge about is easily put into symbols, words, graphs, and maps. *Observation, skill, experiment,* and *logic* are the stages of advancement in science. The physical sciences, said Mayo, had been successful; the social sciences had not been (Chapter XIX — Henderson). While social scientists have a high standard of achievement intellectually, their knowledge-of-acquaintance of actual human situations is exceedingly low.

The so-called *rabble hypothesis* may be traced as follows:

1. Francois Quesnay in 1758 introduced two ideas that were new at that time into economic study: (a) that agriculture is superior to commerce and industry (this soon fell into disregard); and (b) that there is a natural and essential order of human societies. The last is the idea that man must learn to live according to nature and authorities must generally give up the idea of devising endless laws; they must let things alone. This was the *laissez faire* belief of the physiocrats, and of Adam Smith who wrote in 1776.

2. David Ricardo tried to use the relations which spontaneously arise among men living in a society to develop a science. He argued that: (a) natural society consists of a horde of unorganized individuals; (b) every individual acts in a manner to secure his self-preservation or self-interests; (c) every individual thinks logically to the best of his ability in the service of this aim. The last argument, says Mayo, is certainly a fallacy if interpreted that an individual thinks logically at all times.

3. The rabble hypothesis influenced thinking on law, government, and economics for many years; from the theory that there is a rabble of persons all acting without regard for others came the conviction of a need for a powerful state to impose authority on the rabble. Such economic theory led the general public, business leaders, and politicians to believe that mankind is an unorganized rabble upon which order must be imposed; such belief made its contribution to the creation of a Mussolini and a Hitler.

4. Jenks wrote that the success of the state meant the destruction of the clan. LePlay and Durkheim in the nineteenth century wrote of the satisfactions of small communities and warned about the future.

5. The social organization must secure for its members: (a) satisfactions of material needs, and (b) cooperation in social functions. The economic conception of a rabble of individuals competing for scarce goods, and a community of individuals ruled by a sovereign state discouraged study of social organizations.

Mayo used this theory in reporting on social studies made by the Harvard group and others. Two investigations are briefly reviewed here:

1. Investigations of a spinning department: these showed that a horde of solitaires can be transferred to a social group by someone interested in them. The president initiated rest periods. People lay down twice in the morning and twice in the afternoon, ten minutes each time. The rest periods helped, production went up, foot and psychological troubles were diminished. The efficiency experts had not consulted the workers; they had assumed a rabble hypothesis and individual self-interest which led nowhere. Consideration of worker attitudes and situations, however, led to surprising results.

2. In three plants (ABC) which made the same product, had the same labor market and the same location, absences at the beginning of World War II increased in Plants A and B and remained high. In C there was at first an increase, but then the absences in C fell. The answer: (a) for twenty years the foreman of Plant C had been instructed that a supervisor's duty has two parts: (1) technical competence; (2) capacity to handle human situations; (b) the foreman had assistants to help with technical matters and communications were good; (c) the foreman arranged for a day off in consultation, management took steps to see that individuals were contented with their work, and teamwork was encouraged. Mayo's conclusion was that the administration should disregard the rabble hypothesis and deal directly with the situation.

Robots of the Second Industrial Revolution — From the days of the first Industrial Revolution (last decades of the eighteenth century in England) to the present day there have been periods called the "Second Industrial Revolution." Some people have referred to all of the time since the Industrial Revolution as the "Mechanical Revolution" or "Mechanical Age." Certainly the last half of the twentieth century to date is worthy of the title "Second Industrial Revolution." [It has been called by some the "Triple Revolution" for new energy sources, new materials, and cybernation.] This is chiefly due to the digital computer, but there are many other factors contributing to the revolution that is taking place. The language of today is saturated with new words denoting the age of automation.

First, there is the word *robot* which was coined by Karel Capek in 1922. In his play *R.U.R.* (*Rossum's Universal Robots*) workers were replaced entirely by mechanical men. Despite the possibility that robots may go far in certain functions toward replacing man, they cannot compete with humans in certain functions. They cannot be transferred in most instances from one kind of work to another without retooling or reprogramming. The director of the mechanical translation group of the National Bureau of Standards said in 1960 that the more she and her group worked with electronic machines the more they felt in awe of the marvelous workings of the human mind, "the absolutely divine automatic machine" (ADAM).[3]

There are two categories of *computers:* the *analogue,* an electric computer some fifty years old, which is capable of measuring and comparing quantities in one operation but has no memory; (2) the *digital* ("electronic brain" or "mental giant" among the robots), capable of solving problems and counting precisely as well as sequentially, and it has a memory. Electronic computers are doing massive jobs in industry today despite the fact that they have been in use not much over a decade. In 1953 the first UNIVAC was sold for use in the Bureau of Census for statistical work. By 1961 the electronic computer had gone into educational, scientific, commercial, government, and military fields in great quantities. By 1964, the computer was expanding in all areas and was being of immeasurable benefit in the areas of chemistry, weather forecasting, missile design and operations, and protection from alien planes. It was estimated that in mid 1964 there were 18,000 of these machines already in use and some 9,000 were being installed or on order, making a total of 27,000 in use or being prepared for use.

In June of 1963 there were only three computers in use in the newspaper business; by June, 1964, there were sixteen already installed and about sixteen on order, or a total of thirty-two. In the newspaper business computers are being used for accounting information, billing, punching tape for typesetting advertisements; circulation and advertising makeup are also being considered as having computer application possibilities, and one installation already was using its computer to drive photocomposing machines both for display advertising and for straight matter.[4] One of the most widely publicized developments in the printing industry is the use of computers in newspaper composing rooms. Computers make electronic decisions on word-hyphenating and line-justifying — decisions normally performed by an operator at the keyboard of a typesetting machine. They may also be used to make editorial changes and corrections before the type is set.[5]

Computers are forcing men to think more clearly and precisely about what they are doing. Although they will probably never be able to substitute for good management, electronic computers enlarge brainpower just as many of the other machines and devices of automation are multiplying muscle power. They must be programmed minutely and that is why they force men to think. In 1964 sixty cents of each dollar spent for computer *hardware* was going for the central processor itself; the rest of the dollar was going for the input-output devices, files, and communications, known as "peripheral" equipment.

In another decade, however, according to the Diebold Group of management advisers, the peripheral equipment will take from seventy-five to eighty cents of the hardware dollar. The programming itself is known as *software* and is growing faster than the hardware industry; it is predicted that in seven years software volume will equal hardware volume.[6]

It took MIT's Lincoln Laboratories, working with IBM and Burroughs, seven years to develop SAGE (Semi-Automatic Ground Environment, designed to protect the United States against surprise air attack) to the point that the first of its sixteen centers could be completed in 1958. To write its original programs alone required 1,800 man-years' work. The system cost taxpayers $1.6 billion, but it is not only defending the country, it is teaching valuable business lessons as well. SAGE permitted the existence of SABRE which is the foundation of American Airlines' integrated control system. The Air Force uses over 400 of the some 800 or more computers operated by the Defense Department. The Air Force Logistics Command was helped by computers to reduce its head count in 1956 from 212,000 to 146,000.[7]

Dun and Bradstreet took its first step in 1963 to develop a universal coding system when its D-U-N-S (Data Universal Numbering System) assigned random identification numbers to 340,000 U. S. manufacturing establishments. The program will eventually identify all business establishments reported by Dun and Bradstreet. The numbers will permit access to a master file of manufacturers on whom information will be constantly kept up-to-date by over 2,000 field men. The value of this is that current material on all industrial markets in the United States is today readily available in one master file in a machine-readable format. Other benefits might include through additional coding criteria "rapid retrieval of information for sales forecasting, direct-mail campaigns, account analysis for acquisition efforts, and market research programs." The program might also include a basis for exchanging data among various businesses.[8]

For the individual firm *remote data collecting* (RDC) tells management at once how many people are at work on a given job, the tools and materials they are using, and the location and progress of all work being done. RDC consists of: *input stations* scattered throughout a plant, a *network of cables* or two-wire telephone lines connecting input stations to a central location near a computer, and a *receiver* or collector that transforms the data received to punched cards or paper tape to be fed directly into a computer or put into readable form on a teletype printer.

At Lockheed's Missiles and Space Company division in Sunnyvale, California, 10,000 messages ranging from simple to complex are fed daily into 206 remote input units wired directly to two RCA 304 computers. Lockheed has invested over $3 million in system development; the company expects to eliminate $2.8 million annually in direct labor costs. At the Sanborn Company in Waltham, Massachusetts, ten stations are used to record four basic types of information: *attendance, direct labor, non-productive labor* (labor not assigned to a job), and *parts movement*. The company estimates that its system saves twenty-eight man-hours of work a day in the direct-labor recording job alone, which is enough to pay the monthly rental cost of the equipment. Approximately fifteen per cent of the production at Corning Glass Works is on special orders that must be rushed through the plant; remote data collection permits a manager to know where each order is at all times and which machines are not operating at full capacity; no computer is needed to steer orders to areas where they may be rushed out.

RDC has changed much of the information flow in production from a costly paperwork process to a quickly available tool. One executive has listed three general ways in which RDC can improve profitability:

1. It will reduce in-process inventories by as much as 20 per cent.
2. A company that turns over its inventory five times a year can increase turnover to six times through RDC, reducing capital needs by more than 10 per cent.
3. In reporting labor costs on jobs, a remote collection system with ten stations will replace from three to five clerks.[9]

Not only is the computer changing *record-keeping* and *production,* it is changing *marketing* as well. Electronic department stores are predicted for the future. Computers will select delivery routes and be used in many other ways. The use of EDP equipment to keep track of inventory, shipping schedules, and production have enabled General Foods to reduce the heavy inventory that it must of necessity carry because of its great product mix; for instance, Jell-O inventories alone have been reduced thirty per cent. Within recent years the new distribution centers replete with electronic and other materials-handling devices have replaced or reduced the usage of old storage-center warehouses of the past. The Borden Company had reduced the 136 warehouses it had in 1960 to nine distribution centers in 1963 and expected eventually to have some sixteen to eighteen such centers. New bulk-loading vehicles have often been substituted for warehousing. Foreseen for the future are a number of giant distribution centers where many types of products can be packaged, bottled, drummed, and distributed to consumers with the record-keeping being done by EDP equipment.[10] Also foreseen for the future is EDP for retailers doing between $100,000 and $20,000,000 annual business.[11] In the giant organizations computers already do automatic ordering, leaving salesmen free to sell more complex equipment. This has given rise to a new type of middleman who may carry up to 90,000 items to be shipped out as the orders come in on computers.[12]

The more computers are used, the more uses man discovers they have. An MIT professor has invented a device that enables the user to communicate to a computer by messages written on pieces of paper. STRESS (Structural Engineering System Solver), being developed at the University of Illinois, has a vocabulary of some one hundred engineering words and can carry out orders from instructions using these words. *Sketchpad* is an electronic computer used in drawing blueprints. Drawings may be changed without redrawing, and freehand work is automatically transformed into neat lines; engineers use this device to draw designs while conversing with those for whom the designs are being made. A drawing may be moved, reduced, or enlarged up to 2,000 times, duplicated, and rotated.[13]

Computers have designed control systems and performed in five minutes the 70 million calculations to make a complete analysis of a single blood sample. A type of computer is used to digest the information obtained from an EEG (electro encephalogram) and report on the brain's workings in mathematical terms. [Taking 15 minutes and 225 million calculations, or 700 man years' work with a desk calculator, the computer gives a spectral analysis of a ten-second brain-wave record.] [14] Psychology laboratories are using computers in doing research on human reactions.[15] Computers are even being used by match-making agencies to help persons select their mates. They have also been used to direct traffic.[16] An electronic device is used to make the piloting of a submarine "as simple as driving an automobile." The Lykes Brothers Steamship Company led the way in automatization of shipping by mechanizing engine rooms on twelve cargo freighters in 1964. The NMU (National Maritime Union) already foresaw the problems to be raised by mechanized fleets.[17]

Robot-run training programs are being used to teach employees in many areas from basic photography to salesmanship (Mark II Auto-Tutor).[18] The Crowder teaching machine, marketed by U. S. Industries, permits a student to study parallel branches of information at the same time. This machine provides for multiple choice answers and has been felt by some to be best used for supplementing classroom courses and textbooks. The machine, originated by Harvard psychologist B. F. Skinner, rewards students who respond with correct answers; it does not permit students to make errors. It was felt that the program that uses this type of machine would replace textbooks and downgrade the teacher's role. Known as the step-by-step or linear method, such programming is considered by some to be adequate for teaching in mechanical areas; the multiple choice or branching method appears to be better for decision-making training. The teaching machine itself is not nearly as important as the program it employs. Further, the machines are not capable of determining whether or not the student has learned.[19]

Electronic systems operate pipe lines hundreds of miles away enabling them to carry many different products drawn from storage plants located along their routes.

It has, however, been the premium industry places upon four types of information that has done the most to usher in the new era of machine-centered management. These four types of data are: *accounting summaries, operations research* (OR), *technical reports,* and *machine produced indexes.* During a given week at Aluminum Company of America, over a million separate figures from more than one hundred locations are summarized into concise statements of divisional earnings shown in comparison with earnings of the year before and with budgeted amounts. Computers make this possible. They also aid companies like Monsanto Chemical Company to calculate the best configuration for chemical processes, raw material mixes, and market locations before beginning a pilot project. Data centers are becoming the central files and technical libraries for their companies, capable of searching great areas of technical literature in an instant. The breaking down of human actions, including subjective decisions, into step-by-step computer logic is shifting the balance of power from divisions where it has been for at least a decade back to corporate staff. Purchasing, warehousing, transportation, and billing supervisors are having their planning roles removed from them.

Information retrieval (IR) is one of the big problems of information management today. Accounting and OR simulations can be run in the accounting center, but for smooth operation IR is best handled in a separate facility so that engineers constantly asking for information do not interrupt data processing. Preferably the IR center should be fed information at night and should be free during the day for running searches for the stored data. The accounting center could then go ahead without interruption on its computational work.[20]

Three of the most significant innovations in IR methods are: (1) utilizing of electronic circuits able to use the type of insight human librarians do in interpreting word meanings; (2) improvements in microfilming that permit the reduction of printed matter to 1/150th of its original size; (3) development of bubble emulsion photo-paper on which microfilm images may be transmitted back to hard copy almost instantaneously. New IR techniques permit scanning titles rapidly [as many as 900,000 pages of documents in fifteen seconds] stopping on the frame matching the question, and reproducing a hard copy of the document in less than a second.[21]

The steps that must be taken to prepare for electronic IR are: (1) a records-retention schedule must be developed to clearly show what will be placed in the IR system from the past, the present, and the future; (2) everything to be placed in the system must be indexed; (3) abstracting certain documents kept in the information pool to enable executives to scan summaries to select the specific ones desired in order to eliminate the receiving of hundreds of documents on one subject; (4) analyzing how and why current files are maintained (the filing system should reflect corporate-wide philosophy); (5) designing a system for writing reference requests for data in the file (a request can be phrased in only one way and in clear terms, the machines cannot tolerate ambiguity); (6) if documentation to be filed is graphic, preparation must be made for necessary changes in original drawing standards to permit photographic reduction and reproduction, i.e., lettering may have to be done in ink; (7) form a standing IR committee to familiarize staff members with IR systems and machines. Files in some technical areas may be reduced or completely eliminated by relying on information services.[22]

OR has been defined as the "application of scientific methods to business decision-making." The Operations Research Society of America has over 3,000 members, a third of whom are working full time on OR; the Institute of Management Sciences has about the same number of members and is also made up of people engaged in OR. Over a third of the 500 largest corporations in the United States use OR; OR is greatly facilitated by computer use. One technique of OR is linear programming which is a technique of calculating least cost combinations or highest income combinations of alternative courses of action. Two OR developed scheduling systems (CPM and PERT) were defined in Chapter X. The OR approach to problem-solving generally involves eight steps: (1) defining the real problem; (2) collecting information on factors that may affect the results; (3) analyzing the data; (4) establishing a realistic criterion for measuring results; (5) developing a "model" (probably but not necessarily, mathematical) to represent the systems being studied; (6) testing the model on sample problems; (7) developing working tools, based on the model, to achieve the desired results; (8) integrating the new methods into company operations. In Bayesian statistical analysis a manager's best guesses are used as data in dealing with future uncertainties such as areas of marketing that otherwise defy analysis because of lack of standard data. A big problem in OR is that companies do not have the data that must be used if the mathematical formulas OR methods evolve are to work.[23]

Cybernetics, a term derived from the Greek word meaning steersman, is used to encompass all of the means of control and communication being used today, but chiefly those of automation and computers. Norbert Wiener, a pioneer in computers who originated the word cybernetics, has warned that computers could get out of man's control.[24] Although many others have denounced this idea, in 1962 Donald N. Michael in "Cybernation: The Silent Conquest," a 48-page pamphlet, warned that robot-minded computers were taking over man's world. He believed economic pressures and foreign competition would push the United States to such great reliance on cybernation that the threat was frightening. He predicted that by 1982 most of the routine tasks of both the blue-collar and the white-collar workers would have been replaced by cybernation.[25]

The term *automation* is used to include computer technology, transfer devices, and automated controls. Automation has been used in industry to some extent for many years. In the automatic handling of materials for processing and manufacturing finished goods, the machines completed their operations in a continuous flow or sequence as laid out by men, and men often operated the machines as well as the systems. Electronics permits the production lines to go forward but with a difference: there are automatic feedback control systems that enable the machines to make many adjustments needed in timing and other factors. Many consider the concept of *feedback* to be one of the most important concepts in the world today because everything that individuals, groups, and machines do in the process of adjusting to one another is governed by this concept. A common mechanical example of feedback at work is to be found in the thermostat which is used to control temperature level.[26]

Because automobile marketing men have become "model happy," production lines must be versatile enough to switch within a short time from one model to another or even to turn out different models simultaneously. This has brought on the necessity for adaptable equipment. Chrysler has provided for using giant cranes to shift the massive dies needed to crunch sheets of steel into auto-body shapes in order that an assembly line may be changed in fewer than six hours. The automobile industry has employed countless innovations to replace the work of human hands. In the decade from 1954 to 1964 this has resulted in a decline in automobile employment of 100,000 persons.[27]

There has long been automatic vending of merchandise, but today several billion dollars worth of merchandise from bulk confections to prepared foods is sold through the vending industry. Industrial firms are converting from cafeterias and catering services to complete vending of foods for employees.[28] To meet the needs of the vending machine companies and the demands of consumers for processed foods, technology has brought about revolutionary changes in packaging which is a $20 billion business in the United States. At least twenty different plastics are being used to house, protect, display, and transport countless consumer and industrial products. Paper, glass, and metal are still used, but competition has brought changes such as reducing the thickness of the tin-plated lining in steel cans to cope with the threat of aluminum. One of the most intriguing of the innovations in packaging is the use of ultrasonic vibration to seal certain plastics which cannot be sealed by any other method; ultrasonic sealing creates a natural molecular bond between the two surfaces.[29]

The major thrust forward in the power upheaval is being made by these new sources of power: (1) *sound energy,* which is produced by *ultrasonic* frequencies of 20,000 or more cycles a second; (2) *electron beam energy,* which comes from a finely focused stream of electrons that travel very rapidly to concentrate energy in a minute space; (3) *light energy,* created by the *laser beam*; (4) *nuclear energy,* which uses *radioactive isotopes*; (5) the *fuel cell.*

Ultrasonic energy has been used for many purposes from the shaking of dirt and oil from anything suspended in a tank of liquid, to slicing or drilling hard and brittle materials through lowering the vibrating tool to within a few thousandths of an inch of the part to be cut and then flooding the area between the tool and the part with a liquid containing minute bits of abrasive materials; a hole or groove the exact shape of the vibrating tool is cut. Sound energy is also used in welding, and it has been used to connect different materials that could not be connected with hot welding. When a precise magnet aims a mass of high-velocity electrons at a piece of metal, the energy of the *electron* beam is enough to melt the hardest materials or splatter them in fine mist. The electron beam has also been applied to welding and has been used to seal stainless steel cans containing activated uranium and other reactor fuels. EB techniques are generally carried on in a high vacuum, but a workable nonvacuum unit has been successful. *Lasers* have as yet done little practical work, but the potentialities of laser power are great; some have estimated that the laser will revolutionize metal processing techniques in the areas of drilling, welding, and machining by 1970. New properties are being added to detergents by radiation with *radioactive isotopes*.

Using irradiation to kill germs may also revolutionize food processing; fresh meat exposed to isotope energy may be left on a shelf for months without refrigeration. Plastic pipe treated with radiation is made stronger. The *fuel cell* is a radically new source of energy to be used in the two-man Gemini capsule. This tiny source of electric power, slightly larger than an electric typewriter, transforms tiny jets of pure oxygen and hydrogen gas into electricity that will power many of the communications and life support systems in the satellite. Applications in industry for the fuel cell will probably be in fork-lift trucks, golf carts, and messenger carts that are powered by conventional batteries or small gasoline engines. United Aircraft's Pratt and Whitney division has built a 500-watt unit for running a gas compressor station in Stanton, Kentucky.[30]

Changes in Management [31] — Currently the most visible change taking place in management due to the onslaught of the computers is in the area of middle management, particularly lower middle management. Many supervisory jobs are done away with because of the fact that automation is eliminating manpower directly; in addition, many of the functions are being eliminated and others are being created. The routine type of bookkeeper is among those whose services are no longer demanded. Further, because of the fact that top management has vast data at its command on which to base decisions it no longer needs the reports and advice of middle level people, particularly the middle-level staff people who have accumulated data and kept records. Credit management, warehouse management, and sales have been consolidated. One firm was able to reduce the number of management positions in several divisions by thirty per cent. The controller, on the other hand, has become a power behind the throne in companies where computers are widely used. The controller who has in the past dealt chiefly with accounting information and budgeting and who is suddenly in charge of data processing may also find his department having to schedule production projects, solve engineering and distribution problems, direct communication systems, run company libraries, and engage in inventory management, OR, and IR. During the past forty years many of the top managerial jobs were filled by persons with legal and financial background. One reason for this was that these people had a broad overview of the firm and were able to understand its place in the economy. In the future the systems and computer managers will probably occupy the favored position of knowing about the business. Accountants as a whole will be challenged by EDP to increase their own professional competence and creativity; many engineers are going into accounting because of their knowledge of computers and systems.

Because management's power to make accurate decisions on the basis of information almost instantly received has been greatly multiplied, it is predicted that management will become once again more centralized. Computer people say that there will be "centralized decentralization." Power that was delegated so short a time ago to others, often to division managers, is being called back. Making decentralization work has not always been easy, chiefly because of the fact that information was not quickly available to the co-ordinating heads of the large decentralized organizations. The computer has changed this. Companies such as General Motors [voted by *Dun's Review* Presidents' Panel in 1963 to be a best-managed company because of its organization] are computerizing world-wide communication systems. GM's communication network is designed to be used for ordering automobiles and parts, controlling inventories and production, and keeping the headquarters offices up to date on current happenings everywhere. The company will remain decentralized; the divisions themselves are, however, building up integrated data systems and tending toward more centralization. Standard Oil of New Jersey [also one of Dun's best-managed, for long-term record], another decentralized company, is preparing a Uniform Reporting System which by 1966 should transmit information for decision making to the company's top coordinators. United States Steel, often used as an example of too much decentralization, closed some twenty-five sales offices, coordinated sales research, created five area sales vice-presidents, and increased the responsibilities of operating and sales middle managers. Management in companies where automation has mastered certain phases of operations and information gathering has been left more time for such work as long-range planning, policy making, selecting staff members, deciding on new products and capital investments, financing, and public and labor relations.

Some people believe that the developments in the use of the computer will tend to humanize rather than dehumanize business. One company president has said that people upgrade their own performance because the constant monitoring of machines makes them feel they are a part of team effort since their performance must be judged without bias. Management still wants (and perhaps more than ever) people with innovative abilities. They are not looking for the conformers who give up the first time somebody says, "You can't do this," or "It won't work!" Information is still reported most widely by the written report and companies prize highly the technical specialists who write and edit reports; these people have generally had long experience in editing technical manuals.

Unemployment — Data have often been used to indicate that automation has not in the long run decreased employment. From 1939 through 1953 the population in the United States increased twenty-two per cent; the number of jobs increased by thirty-five per cent during this period.[32] There are those who look grimly upon the unemployment problems to be raised by computer applications, however, despite the fact that national employment has not yet felt the impact of automation. They say that this is due to several factors among which two stand out: (1) the increased jobs in computer manufacturing and in new installations have offset those persons displaced by computer applications; (2) since much of the initial cost is charged off to current expenses, the rate at which productivity is improving has been hidden. They further argue that automation will bring about unemployment to higher and higher degrees because: (1) the impact of the computers will arrive at a time when the labor force because of population growth is rising rapidly; (2) automation and cybernation will keep the number of blue-collar jobs at a standstill and many routine white-collar jobs will be eliminated; (3) computers not only make present machines more productive, they stimulate industry to continue buying newer and more efficient machines, further eliminating routine jobs.[33]

Unemployment comes from many different things such as over producing, over pricing, decreased demand for goods and services, cheap imports, and because some people simply are unemployable. Even a sudden scare (as with botulism in a can of tunafish) may throw people out of work. When people talk about automation changing or disrupting jobs, they are probably thinking of changes caused by a lot of things such as mechanization, instrumentation, electronics, computers, and labor-saving devices of all kinds. Inventiveness and creativeness are the greatest provokers of change. So, when we think of these things disrupting jobs and putting people out of work, we must also consider that it has been invention and creativeness plus better tools and venture capital that have put people to work through the years. Cellophane, for instance, was discovered in France. About 1925 the process was brought to this country and a small plant employing approximately 200 people began to manufacture the product in Buffalo, New York. The price was $2.50 a pound and the product was a luxury item. In twenty years twenty-one price cuts were made bringing the cost down to fifty cents a pound. New markets were opened. Thousands of persons were employed in a number of large plants in several different concerns just to make cellophane. Millions of hoola-hoops, it may be recalled, furnished considerable employment for a time.[34]

By 1970 computer programming will probably be employing 500,000 persons. The disemployment effects of the machine may be gauged by the net return on capital invested in it. The big question in the past has not been job displacement but what would provide a lift to the per capita growth rate. *Fortune* writer Gilbert Burck has said that the computer "will doubtless go down in history not as a scourge that blew unemployment through the roof, but as the technological triumph that enabled the American economy to maintain and gradually increase the secular growth rate on which its greatness depends." [35] When the computer enables a firm to produce products at a steadily decreasing real price, the demand for the products increases and more jobs are created in the area of distribution. Computers are evidently contributing to increasing employment due to at least four factors: (1) their manufacture and operation require people; (2) their contribution to the turning out of innumerable products many of which never existed before they came on the horizon thus creating a demand that did not exist before; (3) reduced costs of production brought on by the use of these products generally result in bringing down prices; (4) people spend the money they have saved because of reduced prices to buy more products that put other people to work.

In some fields of work, however, arguments, data, and the over-all picture do not salve the feelings of the man who is left without employment because he has been replaced with a machine. John I. Snyder, Jr., president and chairman of U. S. Industries, manufacturer of *TransfeRobot,* has often said that the United States economy has been losing jobs at the rate of 40,000 a week through automation [Bureau of Labor Statistics]. TransfeRobot, for instance, replaces people on the basis of one for one on jobs from assembling to welding. They can work fast, long hours, at low maintenance cost and purchase price. An automated press line built by Mr. Snyder's company for a Japanese automobile company is operated by two people; it replaced forty people.[36]

Although a number of companies are turning out robots capable of working endlessly, tirelessly, dipping hands into molten metal or diving a thousand feet beneath the sea, the most active robot is TransfeRobot which is being used by manufacturers of many types of products from clocks and typewriters to razors and electric motors. This robot makes us feel that we have come a thousand years from the days when F. W. Taylor experimented to get men to raise the average number of tons of pig iron carried per day from around twelve tons per man to forty-seven tons per man. It can make many motions of varying lengths within an over-all reach of twelve to eighteen inches, depending on the arm that has been installed. It can be programmed by a shop foreman to do up to fifteen complete cycles of its mechanical claw. Hughes Aircraft Company produces a diving mechanical worker known as *Mobot* which not only swims but sees, hears, turns lock screws, operates valves, grips pipes or hoses, and wields tools. The Pullman robot *Unimate* can be instructed to assemble parts, load lathes, operate welding guns, tend die casting machines, feed presses, spray paint, load conveyors, and do many other factory tasks. Although it must be taught each needed motion one at a time, it can learn up to 200 sequential commands, can pick up an egg without breaking it or grip a steel block with 300-pound force, and has a life expectancy of five years. *Fleximan* is a portable automatic hand (*pedipulator*) which can be programmed in a short time to perform as many as sixteen different operations at any combination of eight locations. GE is producing a robot with 12-foot legs that can march across rough terrain at thirty-five miles an hour; its probable name, "CAM" (cybernetic anthropomorphous machine, or machine like man).[37]

Innovations such as TransfeRobot have led some companies to completely automatize their assembly lines, as, for instance, a candy company replaced fifty-five girls on a packing line by fifty of these robots, while twelve girls were retained for filling hoppers and doing other specialized tasks. The machines were capable of packing 10,000 pounds of candy, 77 pieces to the box, in one day. There is always the possibility in converting to costly automation, however, that the product it was designed to help produce or the duty it was designed to perform may not be needed, desirable, or usable for a long enough period to absorb the costs of automating.[38] People who are being displaced because of automation in any form cannot find much comfort in the fact that their companies may have made errors of judgment in some cases in turning to mechanical and mental robots. Assembly people and many others whose work is of a routine nature must be retrained or face unemployment. This is particularly true of workers in the newspaper business where thousands may lose their jobs within the next few years. The effects of automation may thus be vast and far-reaching despite the over-all employment picture. Many untrainable people will be without opportunity to do the routine types of jobs that they formerly did; there will be the further problem of overeducated people forced to do certain routine tasks in connection with the machines of automation; they may need their education for some small part of their work and be unchallenged by the major routine part of it.

A survey of electronic digital computer installations in twenty large companies made by the Bureau of Labor Statistics found that 2,800 employees had been directly affected by the installations; about half of them had been moved from former assignments; a third were reassigned to other positions, and a sixth left employment by retirement, taking leaves of absence, or simply quitting.[39]

From the employee relations viewpoint also automation has had drastic effects on industry. Most of the large strikes in recent years have been due to job security and the question of carrying extra people. Railroad, oil, and newspaper workers as well as longshoremen have all been bothered by the problem of job security. When workers have forced firms to carry extra people in spite of price and competition the very lives of these firms have sometimes been threatened.

Blue-Collar Workers vs. White-Collar Workers — In September, 1963, it was estimated that there were some 30 million white-collar workers. This represented an increase of 48 per cent from 1947 to 1963. There were 29 million blue-collar workers, representing a decrease of 9 per cent during the same period.[40] Sixty years ago the number of white-collar jobs of all types was less than the number of blue-collar jobs. It has been predicted that white-collar jobs are likely to exceed blue-collar jobs by 36 per cent by 1970. [Nevertheless, it should be noted that while white-collar jobs increased at an average rate of 2.8 per cent a year between 1950 and 1960, in 1963 the rate of increase was less than 1 per cent.] [41] Professional and technical employment, the category requiring the most education, is growing rapidly. In 1950 there were a little under 5 million people in this group; in 1960, it grew to 7.5 million and is expected to reach 10.7 million by 1970, a doubling in a 20-year period. With such a sophisticated technology as exists today there will not be many jobs left for those who cannot read, write, or perform numerical manipulation.[42] One of the biggest changes brought by automation is the white-collar job that involves no decision on the part of the worker, and today he is so often isolated from those who do make decisions that it is practically impossible for him to feel "close to management." [43]

On the other hand, because many blue-collar workers have been upgraded through special training, and because the surroundings of the blue-collar workers have been made much more attractive in many cases, a revival of individual initiative among factory workers has been detected. To show a type of change taking place in the role of the blue-collar worker, the following story is related: Janitorial services in a certain factory had to be extremely efficient due to the fact that delicate radio tubes required dust-free surroundings. The cleaners were working at only half of potential effectiveness. The name of the janitorial job was changed from "custodian" to "environmental control." A manual was prepared to show exactly how cleaning was to be done and what it meant to the quality of the company's product. New cleaning equipment was developed for the workers. A saving of $100,000 a year in labor and materials was the result.[44]

The new jobs that have been and will be created will demand people with a higher degree of certain specific skills. Several hundred thousand programmers will be needed over the decade from 1963 to 1973. A National Office Management Association Seminar concluded that it was impossible to forecast the nature of office jobs for ten, fifteen or even five years in the future. Industrial progress is too fast for problems of the future to be specifically predicted. A Bureau of Labor Statistics study showed that despite the introduction of many labor-saving devices in banks, the number of employees in banks had increased from 1953-1963 about three times as fast as the employment in all nonagricultural industries combined. It is estimated, also, that approximately 400,000 new jobs will be created in banks in the years from 1963 to 1975. Without electronic data processing (EDP) the rise from 1960 to 1975 would have been according to estimates 100 per cent above the 610,000 employed in banking firms in 1960; with EDP the estimate is that there will be a sixty-four per cent increase in employment in banks in this period.

In the four-year period 1960-1963, manufacturing employment increased very little; during the same period manufacturing output rose eighteen per cent. Other employment during those same years, however, brought total employment up by some 3,200,000. In 1963 when increased productivity had the effect of reducing employment by about two million, non-farm wage and salary employment increased by over 1,500,000; thus in 1963 alone the economy in effect created a total of over 3,500,000 jobs, most of which were in private enterprise.[45]

By 1970 it is estimated that there will be over 87 million workers in this country. This estimate includes 26 million young workers coming into the labor force during the 1960's [of whom 7.5 million will have failed to earn a high-school diploma] and 3 million women returning to work, and it takes into account 15.5 million who will withdraw from the labor force. The rate of growth for employment of women workers is nearly twice that of men. Women today are employed in all occupations. In the federal government alone, women employees are reported in more than 400 white-collar and 500 blue-collar occupations. Many women work because of economic necessity. Almost four out of every ten women in the work force in March, 1962, were single, widowed, or divorced. Many women work to raise the standard of living of their families and the educational levels of their children. They have been freed from housekeeping by automation and have entered the work force during this century in droves.[46]

Measures To Help Meet the Problems Raised by Technological Changes — The changes that are taking place due to technological progress make it necessary that planning be done far in advance of changes so that measures can be taken to minimize the adverse effects on employees. W. H. Ferry, vice-president of the Fund for the Republic, believes that economic theories that were adequate for the first Industrial Revolution are not adequate for this one. Due to the complexity of the scientific-industrial state, more and more national planning is becoming necessary.[47] Employee satisfactions of a different type may need to be substituted for those that will be lost in the change. In some cases it will be necessary to change worker attitudes; in many cases it will be necessary to train them for the change.

Mortimer J. Adler, director, Institute for Philosophical Research, has been quoted as having said that "the new electronic revolution seems to fulfill the age-long dream of a time when all menial and routine tasks would be done by machinery." But even the ancients did not anticipate the problems of disemployment and labor-management disagreements that would be brought about by automation.[48]

Business itself has taken responsibility in many instances for the changes being brought about in the employment situation. The DuPont Company had a rayon plant employing some 2,000 people that had been in operation for thirty years. This was completely shut down, and a new dacron plant was built on the same site. Rayon employees were used to man the new plant. Retraining was done, and all but ten per cent of the employees continued to work for the company. These included the oldest employees; they were pensioned.[49] General Electric spends an estimated half a million dollars a year on over 100,000 courses from first-aid to remedial mathematics. One out of every eight of the company's employees is annually engaged in some kind of job-related training or education. It is anticipated that both the number being trained at a given time and the expenditure for training will increase.[50]

John I. Snyder, Jr., co-chairman of the American Foundation on Automation and Employment, has suggested the shorter work week as a temporary solution to the problem of unemployment; another manner in which the cost of automation may be shared by all is in increased governmental payments to individuals; another is to reduce prices to consumers. By reducing prices to consumers, jobs are not necessarily created but the consumers may continue to purchase consumer products at the same rate as before, provided prices are low enough. Mr. Snyder believes that labor, management, and government must get together for over-all economic planning; government, he feels, should not be delegated the power to do such planning alone.[51]

Robert Theobald, British-born economist and author, now a consultant in the United States, has suggested a form of guaranteed income. He suggested that the idea of compensation and the idea of work must be separated, that every person has a right to a minimum income for his lifetime. This concept is different from that of the *g.a.w.* in that there is not the concept of work involved at all. Jobless pay and social security already approach this. Nevertheless, the moral and ethical question as to whether a man should receive benefits he has not earned arises. In *The Affluent Society,* Galbraith suggested an unemployment compensation system that would fluctuate with the economic conditions, i.e., it would increase in a period of recession or depression and decline during a period of prosperity.[52]

Some corporations are accepting the social responsibility for persons who are being displaced by automation through contributing to funds for these workers. It is conceded, however, that the retraining and education of these people by both government and industry will in the long run contribute much more toward the "war on poverty" than will minimum donations of funds, leaving the persons who receive them to shift for themselves once the funds are gone. The editors of a volume called *Adjusting to Technological Change* suggest that state governments should take more interest in retraining programs and that the United States Employment Service might become an interstate exchange enabling workers to find job opportunities and move to where the jobs are available.[53] Another recent volume, *Jobs, Men, and Machines,* also supports the thesis that the private sector of the economy as much as the public sector of our society has an obligation for helping to solve the problems created by automation. The individual worker is concerned with his own individual job security as well he might be when it is considered that jobs are being eliminated at the rate of over two million in 1964.[54] It must not be forgotten, however, that other jobs are taking their places. IBM alone had an instructional staff of 1,800 that provided over ten million hours of instruction in 1963 to train customer employees in thirty-nine cities for new activities.[55]

The *Area Redevelopment Act* of 1961 created the ARA (Area Redevelopment Administration) which is charged with stimulating employment expansion in economically distressed areas through loans, grants, technical guidance, and occupational training. The *Manpower Development and Training Act* of 1962 (MDTA), jointly administered by the Department of Labor and the Department of Health, Education and Welfare, authorizes the secretary of HEW to institute on-the-job training programs for unemployed and underemployed persons. Training costs for the programs are financed by appropriations to the Labor Department. Most of the training under MDTA has been done in educational institutions to meet the local needs for adequately trained workers. Before training is given there must be expectation that employment requiring the newly acquired skill will be obtained. It is anticipated that the *Vocational Education Act* of 1963 will permit substantially increased vocational education and MDTA programs. Appropriation for 1964 was $60 million; this was almost doubled for 1965 and 1966; for 1967 and succeeding years, $225 million. After 1964, however, states must match the new Federal funds on a 50-50 basis.[56]

There have been many other suggestions for meeting the problems of unemployment due to automation: longer vacations, earlier retirement, public building projects [the student is referred to "Measures and Policies that Might Be Recommended Under (a) Classical Theory, and (b) Keynesian Theory," Chapter XXV] although construction does not offer as much opportunity for unskilled workers as it once did, and eliminating some people from "moonlighting," or working at second jobs.

Management is faced with restrictive work practices and jurisdictional conflicts on the part of labor unions. It feels, however, that it cannot continue to tolerate union restrictions on transfers, unrealistic manning, bogus, and a myriad of other artificial barriers to the exercise of flexibility that is needed to operate efficiently and competitively. Management believes that supervisors are in a position to "preach" the necessity of not *just adapting* to change but of *embracing* it. Union leaders must also realize that union philosophy and union laws must change with the changing times.[57]

Benefits of Automation — Automation, mechanization, and the experience of 170 years in organizing, have enabled the United States to bring the cost of food per hour of work to the lowest point in history. Only twenty per cent of family income after taxes is spent for food in the United States; in Russia the family spends fifty-six per cent of its income for food; in Sweden, twenty-seven per cent; in Italy, thirty-eight per cent; in Peru, forty per cent; in Nigeria, seventy per cent.[58]

The eighty cents out of every dollar left for "other things" in the United States can go for expenditures during those longer week-ends, longer vacations, and other leisure hours, thus creating more jobs for the people who make the things purchased. A Bureau of Labor Statistics study of fringe benefits in labor contracts showed that the average full-time worker in 1960 had 155 more hours of paid leisure than a worker had in 1940.[59] Executives often have a great deal more additional leisure time than do the workers who have written bargains for it into their contracts. They often take long lunch periods and leave for the week-end by three p.m. on Fridays; and the people who run the biggest organization in this country (Congress) often take off on Thursday afternoon and don't get back until Tuesday morning.[60] In justice, however, it must be said that many executives work much longer hours than the hourly workers.

A lengthy study entitled *Of Time, Work, and Leisure,* commissioned and published by the Twentieth Century Fund, contends that there really is no leisure, or at least only negligible amounts of it. The men of leisure even back in the days of the Greeks, it contends, devoted themselves to the state. More recent examples of such men are Sir Winston Churchill, the Roosevelts, and John F. Kennedy. Leisure is defined in this work as "freedom from the necessity of labor," and "free time" is distinguished from "leisure." In free time people may work very hard improving their houses or in "frantic interludes of family recreation." Leisure belongs to those who love ideas. They touch everything with "the play of thought." The man of leisure is therefore really always working at studying and thinking.[61] Leisure time or free time? For most people the benefit of having it is matched only by the problem of what to do with it, and for most the problem is probably solved by benefiting others who may have less than the man with the free time, unless, of course, he is poverty stricken or unemployed.

The Executive of Tomorrow — The *Dun's Review* Presidents' Panel members have said that top management people are going to need more than ever to have a well rounded education and extraordinarily good health. They will still need a great deal of ability in dealing with people. Top executives put experience, technical skill, and know-how after personal qualities, leaving the conclusion that if technical people are to be promoted up the chain of command they need more than their special skills.[62] The qualities and characteristics of middle and subordinate level management, such as specialization, conformity, and ability to give attention to details are often handicaps at the executive level. It is estimated that fewer than one person in 10,000 has the attributes and qualities desirable in a chief executive in adequate combination. A person being developed for a top executive place must be permitted to work at job assignments that are relatively unstructured.[63]

According to Richard W. Wallen there are three types of personalities that management may find in any organization: (1) the "modest helper," (2) the "strong achiever," and (3) the "detached critic." The modest helper rejects his aggressive capacities and embraces modesty; he finds satisfaction in helping others. The strong achiever rejects his tender impulses and embraces the tough ones. The detached critic is more complex. He views all associations coolly and logically and refuses to display either tender or tough emotions. All of these types can function in executive capacities; all could fail miserably if they happen to be functioning in wrong jobs. Management is increasingly a group operation; the value of the group is that it brings diverse personalities together.[64]

Too much agreement within a group may indicate that one person is dominating; competitiveness if not allowed to become destructive conflict is stimulating and leads to accomplishing goals that might never have been aimed at in the first place if the challenge of keeping up with or passing someone else had not been there. This does not mean that the type of headstrong determination that tramples on others on one's way to the top is desirable or is to be encouraged. The successful leader uses both conflict and compromise profitably and has the discriminatory ability to know when to use which.[65]

Approximately 20,000 executive jobs open up every month in the United States. Some ten to fifteen per cent of these places are filled from outside the given company's own employees. The Association of Executive Recruiting Consultants has pointed out that competition is the decisive factor in practically every segment of business, and companies want the man who can put together the knowledges of the engineer, the new-product idea man, and the financial wizard. *Theoretically a firm should get the best qualified man for the job whether he is from inside or outside of the firm.* In small companies in particular the generalist often must be a specialist also in some given area such as production or marketing since it may not be possible to pay the salaries of several vice presidents. In smaller companies, too, according to one executive recruiter, because of increasing banker control over smaller companies, there is a tendency for directors to appoint executives and reduce their authority in running the company. One area of opening for managers is in international operations. The heaviest demand for financial executives is in banks, insurance companies, and credit operations of retail firms. Engineers are the most sought for executive specialists; running a close second are research and development scientists. Electronics and aerospace industries are leaders in the hunt for management talent, some 37.5 per cent of the 1,300 executive jobs advertised on the open market in one month of 1963 were in these industries. While quizzical eyes were once raised at three job changes on a man's record, today he may have had as many as six changes without arousing distrust.[66]

Another change in recent years has been a tendency for many corporations to use what is known as "the dis-organization" man in middle management ranks to "needle, upset, and innovate." [The dis-organization man is one who flouts traditional management philosophy and substitutes his own brand of individualism.] At the right time and place he has also succeeded in the top executive's post. One dis-organization man, Harold Geneen, has spent half of his time traveling, and he has done his own sifting for information in preference to letting communication experts do this. He has increased company earnings (ITT) tremendously.[67]

Fortune conducted interviews over a period of four months with men in the employ of big corporations. About 150 large companies were also asked to cooperate in a supporting questionnaire sent to several thousand young executives who ranged in age from the early thirties to the middle forties. Culturally the young executives were found to be narrow men with a kind of narrowness that might handicap them later in their progress to higher goals.

A brief picture of the young executives is sketched from the *Fortune* report: They had desired to obtain a thorough education; over eighty-five per cent were graduated from college, one in three of these with honors. Over forty per cent of the college graduates took higher degrees. Eighty per cent of the college graduates worked to pay a part of their expenses of going to college; a third of them attended night school. These young executives make up the best educated group of persons ever to attain positions of importance in business. Most of them spent some time studying useful disciplines such as accounting, engineering, or economics. As a group they exhibit the characteristic drive of leaders; such drive is built of many factors and for each is the result of his own background. Their business organization contributed to their motivation by offering rewards to spur them on. They live in houses with an average value of $37,000 each; have an average of 2.8 children each; are away from home on the average of five days a month. They are unrecognized by the American public, but they prefer recognition by the president and the company. Their guiding philosophy is pragmatism; they measure their business significance by their effectiveness in the world outside themselves. They are interested in solving problems through plans that work. They do not have a grasp of good literature or knowledge of music. They are little interested in cultural or political freedom and may feel a lack of their background in these areas in the future; but it may be said of them that they are not cogs in a machine.[68]

From these young executives will come many of the top executives of the future; most top executives attempt to follow policies that will enable them to find, develop, and promote competent men.[69] Somewhere in the ranks are the men who must guide the giant and automated firms of tomorrow. These men because of the pressures brought upon them may have to retire earlier than did their predecessors. The acquiring of broad interests during the period when one is chiefly dedicated to work helps to prepare one for retirement. Interest in the arts and humanities, and understanding of man and his motives are important to happiness. Each partner in marriage lives in two worlds: the wife in a woman's world, the man in a man's world, and together they live in the world of family, friends, and community. When a man retires he must continue to be a part of the active world to the extent that he can feel a sense of accomplishment. For this there must be planning or the man, finding himself in a woman's world, will be greatly handicapped in adjusting, and both husband and wife will find increasing strain on their relationship. Hobbies and physical exercise may help, but they cannot substitute for the mental stimulation a person has received from work. Taking part in community work, political affairs, consulting services, or some type of retirement job will help. Executives who retire early sometimes go into part-time teaching; some even return to college to take courses they always had some interest in but did not previously have time to pursue.[70]

Some Conclusions — Today's plants are turning out only eighty per cent of the goods they could turn out; productivity increases have hidden the rising cost of marketing products. Manufacturing costs account for some forty-one per cent of the ultimate consumer cost; the remaining fifty-nine per cent is accounted for by nonmanufacturing costs of which physical distribution is the largest for most products. The profitability of most well-managed companies depends on their bringing out a constant stream of new products. Each of these new products returns a high profit margin to begin with and then when competition comes in their profits drop down.[71] Because they realize the value of bringing new products on the market, companies are allowing much leeway for individual workers to experiment on their own. The Minnesota Mining & Manufacturing Company [a *Dun's Review* Presidents' Panel best-managed company for success in inventing and marketing of new products] not only allows workers fifteen per cent of their working hours to do anything they would like to do, but the company's formal research and development program has built-in control elements that enable cross fertilization of technological, scientific, and creative ideas.[72]

That the marketing ability of industry is not today able to match its production know-how is evidenced by facts as follows: the copper industry in 1964 was operating at only eighty-five per cent of capacity, paper at eighty-five per cent, and the automobile industry can quickly change from 5.8 million cars a year to 7 million. Industrial goods makers furnish the best examples of the ability of production to consistently exceed marketing. As of 1964 over half of the industrial companies of the nation who had marketing research had started their marketing research programs during the previous five-year period. One of the uses of marketing research in industry has been what is called "market minus." It uses an inductive method of acquiring growth through going from the researching of a market to the purchase of other firms that are in a given market found to be a growing one. The "company plus" technique, considered a deductive method, consists of buying another firm and then working it forward into the market. Since even well-managed companies have difficulties in a declining market, the "market minus" approach is more often being used. Research done by Singer found that there were three areas of potential growth for that company. Each of these was thoroughly examined, and data-processing was finally selected as the area which offered Singer the greatest growth potential. Xerox has assembled economists and sociologists to do long-range searching for industrial markets.[73]

John R. Bunting offers as a solution to the problem created by the fact that scarcity has been overcome, at least in the United States (*The Affluent Society* by Galbraith), what he has called "reasonable featherbedding." There is no longer the need to cry "greater, ever greater productivity." Bunting's solution rests on the view that there will not be enough spending to consume all that we are capable of producing unless we create jobs for the unemployed. He does not wish to make a case for either scarcity or abundance, but is of the opinion that the economic system of the United States is threatened more by abundance than scarcity. The situation as Bunting sees it today is this:

> . . . as a result of moves motivated by self-interest, labor finds itself receiving high wage rates and generous fringe benefits; but the result is that jobs in industry are not growing. Businessmen have rushed the introduction of labor-saving machinery, and machines do not strike, effect production slowdowns or demand seniority rights.[74]

Bunting asks both business and labor to resist being dominated by self-interest, and he asks government to realize that "the really vital economic problems are still solved in the market place." Much of the government's fiscal and monetary juggling he believes to be redundant, or at least that it could be eliminated if the market were more competitive. His "reasonable featherbedding" is not actually featherbedding in its "pejorative sense." It is the creating of socially and industrially useful jobs where need as it has traditionally been thought of does not exist.

Henry Ford thought of business and industry as being first of all for public service. His own company's policy enabled a lot of people to buy and enjoy automobiles and gave a lot of men employment at good wages; he believed in reasonable profit, but the lowering of the price of his car and the giving of benefits to users and laborers resulted in benefits to his company. R. L. Bruckberger, a French scholar and priest, said that when Henry Ford adopted the eight-hour, $5-day he undermined the system that had previously existed and cut off a potential Marxist revolution and that what Ford did that day accomplished far more for the emancipation of workers than did the Russian October revolution of 1917. According to Ford's philosophy, when power, accuracy, economy, continuity, system, speed, and repetition are used to make complicated commodities, the door to plenty is thrown open; low prices and an improved standard of living are the results.[75]

ACKNOWLEDGMENTS AND REFERENCES

1 —————, "A $5-million Search for Answers," *Business Week,* July 4, 1964, p. 84ff.
2 Mayo, Elton, *The Social Problems of an Industrial Civilization,* Division of Research, Graduate School of Business Administration, Harvard University, Boston, 1945.
3 —————, "The March of the Robots," *Dun's Review,* January, 1963, p. 40ff.
—————, "Machines Are This Smart," *Newsweek,* October 24, 1960, p. 85ff.
4 Anderson, P. L., "Computer Developments," *Westprint Convention Daily,* June 9, 1964, p. 3ff. (A speech delivered at the ANPA Research Institute Production Management Conference, The Biltmore Hotel, Los Angeles, California, June 8, 1964.)
5 —————, "Special Computer for Printers," *Business Week,* March 7, 1964, p. 102ff.
6 Burck, Gilbert, "The Boundless Age of the Computer," *Fortune,* Vol. LXIX, No. 3, March, 1964, p. 101ff.
7 Burck, Gilbert, " 'On Line' in Real Time!," *Fortune,* Vol. LXIX, No. 4, p. 141ff. Burck, "The Boundless Age of the Computer," *op. cit.*
8 Topjian, H. Joseph, "The Numbers Game," *Dun's Review,* September, 1963, p. 114ff.
—————, "Pinpointing America: Analysis of Industrial Markets," *Dun's Review,* August, 1964, p. 43ff.
9 Klein, Herbert J., "Production's New Brew: Instant Data," *Dun's Review,* October, 1963, p. 38ff.
10 —————, "The New Nerve Centers of Distribution," *Dun's Review,* June, 1963, p. S104ff.
11 —————, "EDP Tells Main Street," *Business Week,* August 8, 1964, p. 66.
12 —————, "The Changing Anatomy of Industrial Distribution," *Dun's Review,* January, 1964, p. 37ff.
13 Pfeiffer, John, "Machines that Man Can Talk With," *Fortune,* Vol. LXIX, No. 5, May, 1964, p. 153ff.
14 —————, "Research—Electronics Weds Psychiatry," *Business Week,* September 5, 1959, p. 54ff.
—————, "Spotlight on Business," *Newsweek,* October 21, 1963, p. 92ff.
15 —————, "Computer Takes Over Laboratory for Air Force Psychologists," *Business Week,* November 18, 1961, p. 113ff.
16 —————, "Transportation—Computer To Direct Traffic," *Business Week,* February 3, 1962, p. 50ff.

17 ——————, "Labor—When Machines Replace Seamen," *Business Week,* January 25, 1964, p. 100ff.
——————, "Transportation—Piping All Hands to the Push-buttons," *Business Week,* January 25, 1964, p. 92ff.
——————, "Production Briefs," *Business Week,* April 18, 1964, p. 88.
18 ——————, "Management—Robot-run Training Programs," *Business Week,* August 26, 1961, p. 85ff.
19 Weiner, Jack B., "Programmed Learning: Return to Reality," *Dun's Review,* May, 1964, p. 46ff.
20 Nicholson, Scott, "The Bright Young Men of Information," *Dun's Review,* September, 1963, p. 96ff.
21 ——————, "There's Money in Memory," *Dun's Review,* September, 1963, p. 110ff.
22 Steere, Ralph E., Jr., "Preparing for IR," *Dun's Review,* September, 1963, p. 107ff.
23 ——————, "The ABC's of Operations Research," *Dun's Review,* September, 1963, p. 104ff.
24 Burck, Gilbert, "The Boundless Age of the Computer," *op. cit.*
25 ——————, "Life and Leisure," *Newsweek,* February 12, 1962.
26 Burck, Gilbert, *op. cit.*
27 Klein, Herbert E., "Detroit: Proving Ground for New Technology," *Dun's Review,* April, 1964, p. 49ff.
28 Felder, Robert H., "Survey of Vending Machine Firms in Houston, Texas," a master's thesis, Sam Houston State Teachers College, Huntsville, Texas, May, 1963.
29 Weiner, Jack B., "Technology Powers Ahead," *Dun's Review,* November, 1963, p. 155ff.
30 Klein, Herbert E., "New Power on the Production Line," *Dun's Review,* February, 1964, p. 43ff.
——————, "New Spark to Fuel Cells," *Dun's Review,* October, 1963, p. 47ff.
31 Golding, Jordan L., "The Nonauditing Aspects of EDP Installations," *The Journal of Accountancy,* July, 1964, pp. 43-46.
Burck, Gilbert, "Management Will Never Be the Same Again," *Fortune,* Vol. LXX, No. 2, August, 1964, p. 124ff.
Burck, "The Boundless Age of the Computer," *op. cit.*
Nicholson, Scott, "The Crisis in Controls," *Dun's Review,* July, 1963, p. 38ff.
——————, "New Tool, New World," *Business Week,* February 29, 1964, pp. 70-90.
Guzzardi, Walter, Jr., "Man and Corporation," *Fortune,* Vol. LXX, No. 1, July, 1964, p. 146ff.
——————, "The Ten Best-Managed Companies," *Dun's Review,* January, 1963, p. 32ff.
32 Hepner, Harry W., *Psychology Applied to Life and Work,* Prentice-Hall, Inc., Englewood Cliffs, New Jersey, 1957, p. 513.
33 Burck, Gilbert, "Management Will Never Be the Same Again," *op. cit.*
34 Campbell, D. B., "Automation, Unemployment and Industry," *Proceedings,* 25th Conference, Texas Personnel and Management Association, October 24-25, 1963, pp. 28-39.
35 Burck, Gilbert, "The Boundless Age of the Computer," *op. cit.*
36 Brooks, Thomas R., "Does Automation Require a New Economy?," *Dun's Review,* February, 1964, p. 51ff.
37 ——————, "The March of the Robots," *Dun's Review,* January, 1963, p. 40ff.
38 Klein, Herbert E., "The Cultural Lag in Manufacturing," *Dun's Review,* August, 1963, p. 37ff.
39 Brooks, Thomas R., "New Fit to the White Collar," *Dun's Review,* September, 1963, p. 98ff.

40 *Ibid.*

41 Burck, "Management Will Never Be the Same Again," *op. cit.*

42 —————, *American Women,* "Report of the President's Commission on the Status of Women, 1963," U. S. Government Printing Office, Washington, D. C., 1963.

43 Brooks, *op. cit.*

44 Brooks, Thomas R., "The Blue Collar Elite," *Dun's Review,* March, 1964, p. 121ff.

45 Burck, "The Boundless Age of the Computer," *op. cit.*

46 —————, *American Women, op. cit.*

47 Burck, *op. cit.*

48 Perry, John H., Jr., "Recent Trend in Newspaper Automation," *Westprint Convention Daily,* June 11, 1964, p. 2ff. (A speech delivered June 10, 1964, at the ANPA Research Institute, Biltmore Hotel, Los Angeles, California.)

49 Campbell, *op. cit.*

50 Brooks, "The Blue Collar Elite," *op. cit.*

51 Brooks, "Does Automation Require a New Economy?," *op. cit.*

52 *Ibid.*

53 *Adjusting to Technological Change,* edited by Gerald G. Somers, Edward L. Cushman, and Nat Weinberg, Harper & Row, New York, 1964.

54 *Jobs, Men, and Machines,* edited by Charles Markham, Frederick A. Praeger, New York and London, 1964.

55 —————, "Management—Meeting the Minds that Train Industry," *Business Week,* June 20, 1964, p. 56ff.

56 —————, "What's Being Done About Unemployment in Printing," *Printing Production,* 1276 West Third St., Cleveland 13, Ohio, Vol. 94, No. 10, July, 1964, p. 32ff.

57 Patrone, Miles, "New Technology and Its Impact On Labor Relations," *Westprint Convention Daily,* June 9, 1964, p. 8ff. (A speech delivered June 8, 1964, at the ANPA Research Institute, Biltmore Hotel, Los Angeles, California.)

58 Strohm, John, "Why Our Food Is a Bargain," *The Reader's Digest,* September, 1962, pp. 245-248.

59 —————, "In Labor," *Business Week,* March 31, 1962, p. 83.

60 —————, "Life and Leisure," *Newsweek,* July 16, 1962, p. 76.

61 DeGrazia, Sebastian, *Of Time, Work, and Leisure,* Twentieth Century Fund, New York, 1962.

62 —————, "The Changing American Executive," *Dun's Review,* January, 1964, p. 38ff.

   —————, "Who Do You Promote," *Dun's Review,* May, 1964, p. 50ff.

   Klein, Herbert, "Can Industry Harness the Elusive Engineer?," *Dun's Review,* May, 1964, p. 48ff.

63 McMurry, Robert N., "How to Pick a President," *Dun's Review,* October, 1963, p. 57ff.

64 Wallen, Richard W., "The 3 Types of Executive Personality," *Dun's Review,* February, 1963, p. 54ff.

65 Odiorne, George S., "Conflict: The Vital Corporate Ingredient," *Dun's Review,* March, 1964, p. 51ff.

66 Buckley, Noel, "The Most Wanted Men in Industry," *Dun's Review,* February, 1964, p. 49ff.

67 Weiner, Jack B., "The Dis-Organization Man," *Dun's Review,* April, 1964, p. 32ff.

68 Guzzardi, Walter, Jr., "The Young Executives," *Fortune,* Vol. LXIX, No. 6, June, 1964, p. 97ff.

69 —————, "A Hard Look at Middle Management," *Dun's Review,* March, 1964, p. 49ff.

70 Chapman, Gilbert W., "When Executives Retire," *Dun's Review,* October, 1963, p. 63ff.

71 —————, "The New Realities of Plant Investment," *Dun's Review*, March, 1963, p. 92ff.

72 Brooks, Thomas R., "3M's Formula for New Products," *Dun's Review*, August, 1963, p. 32ff.

73 Morse, Leon, "Can Industrial Marketing Match Production?," *Dun's Review*, February, 1964, p. 41ff.

74 Bunting, John R., "The Disturbing Economics of Affluence," *Dun's Review*, April, 1964, p. 40ff.

75 Bruckberger, R. L., *Image of America,* translated by C. G. Paulding and Virgilia Peterson, Viking Press, New York, 1959.

SECTION V — DISTRIBUTION

CHAPTER XXI

MARKETING AND MARKETING RESEARCH

Trends in Some of the Sociological and Other Factors Affecting Marketing — Marketing is affected by numerous factors. Only a few of these are commented upon here, however, since the student of business usually gets intensive training in the functions and factors of marketing. Of the organic functions of industry (marketing, production, and possibly finance) marketing is probably the area where psychology is most used. As *productivity* increases, marketing functions must be stepped up comparably. For instance, productivity from 1847 to 1947 increased at an annual rate of approximately two per cent; from 1947 to 1954 the increase generally was about three per cent annually. From 1954 for seven years productivity increases ran at about two and one half per cent annually. Since 1961 the annual increases have been three and one half per cent on the average. Currently there are great opportunities for those engaged in the many occupations connected with getting merchandise from the manufacturer to the consumer.

Population shifts have brought about shifts in the demands for certain types of products as well as in the emphasis of advertising and selling. Rural dwellers have moved to urban and suburban areas; while twenty-five per cent of the population was rural in 1930, by 1960 this figure had been reduced to about ten per cent. The population shifts have caused some areas to be highly overcrowded, as, for instance, the Pacific Coast area. Some of the less crowded areas have also grown. In the short period 1955-1960 the population of Nevada grew by almost one-third. The Southwest has grown rapidly also. Industrial and business firms have responded to population shifts with corresponding changes in products and appeals used in selling them.

From 1954 to 1964 the population of the United States has grown from approximately 161,000,000 to over 192,000,000; by the year 2,000 it is expected to be around 350,000,000. Not only do those with goods and services to sell watch the *population increase,* they watch the *percentage of change in different age groups.* Increasing youthfulness of the population, better education, higher income, keener desire for quality, and the increasing relative spending power of minority groups, including Negroes, are factors influencing marketing strategy today.

Some of the changes from 1955 to 1965 in age groups will show the extent to which data of this type may be helpful in planning:

Age Group	Percentage Change
10-14	+43½ %
15-19	+54 %
20-24	+25 %
25-41	− 1.2%
42-65	+17 %
Over 65	+25 %

The *composition of the work* force is also important to those who sell. Approximately a third of the work force is made up of women; women influence a large part of consumer spending. Family size has increased since the 1930's. There is a lower death rate of infants and longer life expectancy. Factors such as these could change the picture for people of the United States in the years ahead. For some years we have been able to say that with only six per cent of the world's population we consumed over fifty per cent of the world's goods and services. Will this picture change?

Work time and income changes during the last thirty years have influenced marketing. The shorter work week together with longer vacations and earlier retirement (with income!) have brought about a vast market for leisure-time activities and do-it-yourself products. The per capita personal income from 1953 to 1963 increased almost forty per cent. A larger percentage of the highest income families have moved to *suburbia* where they have tended to set styles and influence changes in the market. People spend more percentage-wise for food than they once did and much of the increase has gone for diet-type foods, dairy products and meat, fresh fruits, and prepared foods.

Some of the Trends in the Competitive Tools of Marketing — In the area of *product research and development* many changes are taking place. In addition to the many products for *leisure-time*, there are products for the young and the old; there are products to eliminate labor in the home as well as in business and industry. Automation has taken over. Home products include the pre-processed, prepared, canned, packaged, and frozen. These consumer products have been made more attractive with plastics, foils, and open-view materials being used in packaging. Large print is used on packages for TV viewers. To find the products that will sell and the package colors, designs, and styles that will appeal to consumers, product and psychological research are employed. In some areas package-development departments help to formulate and carry out policies relating to packages; sometimes special committees for packaging are used. Packaging has become, in fact, a concern of top-level management. A headline for a Celanese advertisement proclaims "Today the shopper takes the salesman home," thus emphasizing the importance of the package and the creative materials from which it is made.

Generally the getting of a new product on the market involves passing through six stages. [See Chapter II.] Through following these six steps companies assure the elimination of non-profitable products in the early stages. If the product fails in the commercialization stage, such failure can probably be traced to failure in the earlier stages.[1] Procter & Gamble's Gleem and Crest were tested in local markets, as was advertising copy on each, for nearly a year before the products were put into national distribution with "advertising outlays that by themselves wiped out any gross profit for the first year." Gleem's appropriation for first-year advertising by blitzkrieg was around $15,000,000.[2] P & G's new product Head and Shoulders (advertised for dandruff) was researched for approximately thirteen years before it was put on the market.

Today there is more standardization in packages, cans, bottles and other containers used in consumer marketing; there is, paradoxically, more variety, also. Fashion continues to be important; it is both high and informal. The Ivy League fashion is counterbalanced with the Beatnik. When someone refers to *"the market"* for a given product, he means a given group of buyers. There might, in fact, be numerous "markets" for a given product. Market research is concerned with finding the characteristics of a given "market or markets" for a given product or products. The "markets" for milk in a metropolitan area might be: route consumers, dealers (grocery stores and others selling milk in bottles and containers, and drug stores and drive-ins dispensing milk in various forms), industrial consumers (broken into a variety such as those using automation to dispense to employees, those using milk in other products such as cheese, ice cream, and so forth), institutional consumers (such as schools, hospitals, and so forth). Research is done to find out about each type of market served by a firm. The ultimate consumer is studied to determine numbers of factors: income, age, family size, education, needs and wants, where he buys, what he buys, when he buys, how much he buys.

Where the consumer buys or would like to buy may affect the *channel* through which the manufacturer markets. Today there is a trend toward direct marketing and more branch stores; the firm with something to sell tries to get closer to the consumer. Perishable and high-value items may be more likely to be sold directly. Necessities may be marketed indirectly. There is a trend away from certain types of wholesaling.

Pricing generally is competitive today; but there is also some follow-the-leader pricing. Consumers may elect to pay a higher price with trading stamps than without, although in some cases they may pay the same with or without the stamps. Certain types of items are sold either through budget accounts or installment pricing. Many people buy when they probably shouldn't because they don't have to pay immediately. From the psychological viewpoint this may be "good" in that they may work harder to succeed in order to pay the debts they have incurred. In other cases it may be "bad" because they may become careless and feel they do not have to pay the debts, thus developing dishonesty and losing the sense of responsibility.

To business and industry, price is a competitive tool and a number of competitive patterns have been distinguished: (1) *perfect collusion,* wherein is established a sales quota that is mutually satisfactory to the sellers, and when there are sufficient differences production is transferred to the most efficient companies; (2) *effective collusion,* where companies share the market in a predetermined manner and have the same prices; (3) *limited collusion,* where there is some agreement on price, but there is no arrangement for sharing the market [in recent years the collusion of the electrical companies is an example of this and it is illegal as are other forms of collusion]; (4) *price leadership,* in which one company is the recognized leader in price setting, and the others change up or down as the leader changes; (5) *chaotic competition,* in which, for a variety of reasons, companies act independently in pricing their own products.[3] The last-named pattern should perhaps be called "free competition," but some writers have used "chaotic."

Theoretically, the price which contributes the most to profit is the best; to find this price may require a trial-and-error method since competition, changing markets, and changing buying habits will always enter into the picture. Analysis through accounting and statistical methods is used to find the price level at which marginal revenue is equal to marginal cost.

Another method of determining price is to use the sales forecast to estimate the units that will sell. From this estimate unit costs are computed and a mark-up percentage is added as profit. In some cases new products are priced with the idea of "skimming" the market (getting the most profitable customers), or "penetrating" the market (setting a lower price to get as many customers as possible).

Pricing is usually done by line men at the top level. Those who sell are instructed in pricing policies, but they themselves have very little to do with the formulation of these policies.

Advertising in the United States is "big business." Advertising expenditures rose from \$2 billion in 1946 to \$10 billion in 1956 and by 1964 were running at over \$13 billion. In fact, it was said that to promote five words alone advertisers in this country spent in 1963 an estimated billion dollars each. The words: *white, power, mild, refreshing, relief.*[4]

Newspapers continue to receive approximately a third of the money expended for advertising; direct mail, television, and magazines (all types) receive approximately fifteen per cent each, although it is estimated that DM continues to receive a little more than TV and magazines and TV a little more than the magazines. Radio receives around six to seven per cent; with the advent of transistors and with so many automobile radios, expenditures for radio advertising which had been trending downward, started upward in 1956. Another factor in the continuing strength of radio is that its audience pattern is the reverse of that of television. It is highest during commuting hours in the early morning and late afternoon, with housework hours in between commuting hours rating high also. Radio audience rating is low during the prime evening hours of TV. Another factor in the continuing wide use of radio is the fact that in the local areas it is often a substitute for a community newspaper.

Outdoor advertising, transportation advertising, and countless forms of miscellaneous advertising devices are used. Advertising and marketing research are widely used by large advertisers to determine appeals and media to use in their campaigns.

Most major advertisers attempt to establish some relationship between anticipated sales in dollars or units and the advertising appropriations. It would be ideal if advertisers could set their appropriations so that the profit from sales produced by advertising would just equal the last dollar spent on advertising. Conditions change so rapidly, however, that if elasticity of demand could be determined as of a given time it would probably soon change.[5]

Companies in general formerly followed the policy of keeping stockholders uninformed as to the total amounts spent for advertising. More recently they are following the policy of full disclosure as to advertising costs. The newer policy of disclosure has probably come about because of the feeling that the stockholders recognize the advantages of advertising in influencing the capital market. Campbell Soup in 1954 found a ready market for 1,300,000 shares because of the familiarity of the public with the "Campbell Soup Kids." Ford Motor Company's half a billion dollars worth of stock was quickly snatched up when Ford first placed its stock on the open market.[6]

A study made in 1954 by the NICB showed that company relations with advertising agencies are always subject to shifts. Some companies use a single agency; some use more than one. Some get results that are favorable by switching agencies.[7] Advertising agencies have much to do with the policies of their clients relative to advertising. They plan, create, and place advertisements in media; they do market research for advertising and marketing campaigns; they handle public relations with consumers, employees, dealers, and stockholders; they merchandise packaging and product design, trademarks, names, labels, and package enclosures; their services may go so far as to include "selling aids, and recruiting, selecting, training, and stimulating salesmen." Agencies even find themselves being owned by the clients.[8] Although numerous persons, committees, executives, and agencies influence advertising, the appropriation decisions are usually made by top management.[9]

In the modern world of supermarkets, large department stores, and pre-selling, it is very important that advertising and selling work hand-in-hand. Point-of-sale displays and window displays are important. The sale which has been made through carefully planned advertising campaigns and the use of national and local media must not be lost because of neglect at the point where the sale is consummated.

In the area of *personal selling,* there is more careful selection of salesmen today, more college recruiting, more use of the weighted application blanks, and more sales training. In some instances sales training is under the person in charge of advertising, and dealers are often being trained by mail. Job evaluation is being used to a greater extent to determine pay for salesmen, and the salary plus commission basis of pay is being used (see Chapter XV). Policies relating to sales promotion of all types must be closely coordinated. These types include the nonpersonal consisting of advertising in all of its forms, displays, and services, and the personal, which is the personal salesmanship itself.

The *location* of a business may determine its success or failure. Some manufacturers today are locating plants over the country to cut down on transportation from the factory to the consumer; others find a central location in order to cut expenses by doing all of the manufacturing at one point. Retailers today must decide between remaining in the downtown areas or moving to the shopping centers. Through carefully analyzing the market potential at a proposed location for a retail outlet it can be determined in advance whether or not this should be a profitable location (see Chapter XX). Each section of the country has its own peculiar preferences for products and services. Consumer preferences also become increasingly individualized as disposable income increases; and by 1970 it is estimated that consumers will have $180 billion more than they had in 1961. Realizing this, companies are employing advertising agencies that specialize in the regional approach. Not only is the national market a constantly changing thing, in some cases for some products it is a non-existent thing. For others it is becoming increasingly regionalistic, even the regional market is constantly changing. Approximately forty million families move to new homes annually.[10]

Trends in Some of the Uncontrollable Areas — In the area of *marketing law* today there is more federal and state control of business and industry. The courts have been employed to maintain restrictions on monopoly and price fixing. Sales policies are affected by a number of acts, as: the Food, Drug, and Cosmetic Act controlling labeling and purity of these products and enforced by the Food and Drug Administration; McGuire Act, which reinstated the provisions of the Miller-Tydings Act permitting resale price maintenance and also enabling manufacturers to establish one resale price by signing a contract with only one dealer in a state, providing the state is a "fair-trade" state; the Robinson-Patman Act, which requires granting the same discounts and allowance to all buyers at a given level, with certain exceptions; the Lanham Act, which regulates the use of trademarks; the Wheeler-Lea Act, which amended the Federal Trade Commission Act of 1914, prohibits false advertising, and is administered by the Federal Trade Commission. Many other laws affect marketing. In addition to the laws themselves, numerous government bureaus and agencies take part in influencing company policies, and especially sales policies (see Chapter XXIV). There has been some legal attack upon the use of trading stamps at the consumer marketing level.

Competition is especially strong in some lines, namely hard lines, items that may be sold through discount houses, and automobiles. Discount houses have increased in numbers. There is a higher integration of retailers, and manufacturers own more outlets.

There is more long-term forecasting of *demand* for products. Individual firms within an industry determine their current share of the market and attempt to maintain that share or increase it. There is constant attempt to get a larger share of export markets as well as of domestic ones. While demand was at a low ebb in 1956, it was still high compared to certain former years. At mid 1964 demand for products continued high in the United States and the upswing in business was the longest on record for so-called normal, peacetime years. Economists had for a century believed that the United States could not combine price stability with economic growth for any sustained period of time. Business cycle data collected by the National Bureau of Economic Research for years from 1854 to the present indicate twenty-seven periods of business expansion. Prior to the expansion period 1961-1964, upswings have resulted in rising costs. Costs have declined somewhat during the 1961-1964 period; demand has kept output growing and prices have remained relatively stable; interest rates (ordinarily higher during an expansion period) remained from 1961-1964 at about the same level; the money supply during this period grew smoothly. Consumers during the period were optimistic (a psychological factor of great importance in keeping output, income, and employment up — Chapter XXV).[11] The increased study of consumer behavior, harder advertising and selling during periods of anticipated recession, knowledge of the types of governmental action that can be taken to forestall economic crises, and the taking of such action may all have had a part in creating the 1961-1964 period of economic prosperity.

In the area of determining of *costs* for the individual firms, there is today much more use of accounting and statistical methods. An individual firm has little or no control over certain costs that must be incurred, but it has much control over its own management of inventories and certain other costs. Decisions are more likely to be based upon factual data than upon guesswork or what has been done in the past.

The *structure of distribution* continues to undergo changes. Some of these have occurred in the following areas: supermarkets; self-service; one-stop shopping; automation; scrambled merchandising; discount houses; drive-ins; manufacturers' outlets; lake, beach, and many other types of tourist-trade and vacation facilities; communication facilities. In many instances the major part of the job from the factory to the consumer is being done by manufacturers.

Marketing continues to be influenced by many factors other than those mentioned thus far in this chapter. Only a few can be referred to: *transportation* (in this area rails have declined in importance for some types of products and airlines have gained; pipelines using automation have increased greatly); *storage* (locker plants for consumers and home freezers have cut down on retail sales, especially in meats; frozen foods have changed patterns in storage); *imports* (in some areas, as automobiles, inroads have been made on domestic firms); *exports* (consumer durables); *communication; research* (product, consumer and advertising, space, operations).

Quantitative Market Research — All of the factors discussed thus far in this chapter affect marketing. Some are, to some extent at least, controllable for the individual firm; some are not. Expenditures for advertising, media selected, appeals used, and consumer and product research are controllable. Because of the extent of the use of psychology in consumer and advertising research, the rest of this chapter will be devoted to quantitative marketing research; a full chapter is devoted to qualitative research.

What Is Market Research? — Marketing research is the use of scientific methods to obtain information about consumer and market behavior. Because this definition covers so much, hundreds of items might be listed as contributing to or being a part of market research. In the generation that has passed since management first began to investigate the problems of distribution of goods, product variety has multiplied many times; containers have been improved in physical appearance and are better. Many facts have been accumulated relative to customers, institutions, sales, inventories, margins, expenses, and so forth. Westinghouse's president stated in 1955 that forty cents of each dollar allotted to research by his company went for fundamental research, i.e., search for knowledge in the physical sciences not having to do specifically with the company. Search for new knowledge related to the business gets fifty cents of each research dollar. Applied research gets the last ten cents and this is used to do practical research relating to specific products.[12]

Some of the categories in market research readily identifiable are: (1) collection of facts; (2) analysis and interpretation of facts; (3) surveys of policies, practices, and techniques; (4) development of research techniques; (5) description of institutional structures and structural changes; (6) measurement of market and market potential (many practitioners think of this, narrowly, as market research); (7) development and application of administrative tools and techniques; (8) analysis of management functions and policies.[13]

Marketing research may be *primary* or *secondary*. Secondary research is done by using published data such as that contained in censuses and other government material and in publications of trade associations. It may also be done by using a company's records of sales and other consumer statistical data on accounts receivable, territorial sales, commodity sales, and sales control records. Sales analysis and control, distribution cost analysis and product research are as much a part of market research as are consumer and advertising research, and records are all important in these areas of research. Reports of salesmen may give valuable information that can be tabulated and classified as marketing research. Primary research is done chiefly through questionnaires that are mailed, used in personal interview, or telephoned. It may be done through observation and experimentation. The quantitative data of market research is useful as a basis of forecasting future sales and expenses of making the sales, as well as of forecasting results from advertising expenditures for an entire year or a specified campaign.

What Is Quantitative Research? — Dr. Burleigh B. Gardner has said that the words *"quantitative, statistical,* and *market research,"* are used to indicate the gathering and analyzing of facts about a market, such as: How many? Where? Who? How much? For what? The terms *"social science, motivational, qualitative,* and *psychological research"* are used to indicate the gathering of data about the characteristics of the market such as what are the people like as to social class, personality, attitudes, behavior, and so forth, and what reasons, needs or motives lie behind their actions, reactions, and opinions.[14] *Market research* may be viewed as an all-encompassing term embracing both *quantitative* and *qualitative* research.

Quantitative research generally involves a large number of interviews, from several hundred to as many as five thousand. The interviewees (or those sent questionnaires) are rather carefully selected according to an accepted sampling technique in order that the interviewers (who generally are not highly trained) may obtain data according to specific directions. If the questionnaire is not carefully studied and tested by a pilot study and revised accordingly, the results may be heavily weighted by the attitudes and ideas of those who constructed the form. The questions are simply stated for ease of understanding as the interviewers are instructed not to interpret or add to what is printed on the form. In most cases answers may be by checking blanks for "yes" or "no" answers or for multiple-choice answers. A simple "why" may be asked but no attempt is made to probe for real motives or to discover the reasons for seeming inconsistencies. College students are often employed by research firms to do this type of marketing survey. Student Marketing Institute, Inc., 235 East 42nd St., New York 17, has for many years used teachers of marketing and their students for making such surveys and to distribute various types of samples of products to students on college campuses. Instructions to the students making surveys often read: *"Ask every question exactly as worded."*

An example of quantitative data is the *area market potential.* Areas of high potential may be sold by direct representatives; agents may be used in areas of small potential. Marketing information that has been classified to the Standard Industrial Classification may be used in locating a firm's market potential. The need and demand for a product may be determined by a survey before the product is placed on the market.[15] Marketing management understands such surveys and the need for them; large parts of market-research texts are devoted to this type of research.

Advertisements have been tested by obtaining *opinion ratings* from representative consumers. In some instances the *consumer jury* is used to get presumably unbiased opinions from those the advertisements are supposed to influence. Only two advertisements may be presented and rated, or, a number may be presented and rated in order of effectiveness. One approach is to present several advertisements while the interviewer memorizes the fact that a certain one was looked at first, or a particular one held the viewer's attention the longest. Flaps may be used to cover the copy. These are raised by the interviewee and the observer notes which flap is raised first, and how much time is spent in reading copy.

In 1960 the Institute for Advertising Research (IAR) split off from its parent company, Social Research, Inc., both of Chicago, in order to pretest the effectiveness of advertising. The first step was to find basic market data for a given product, as for detergents. After finding that women do most of the buying, it was found that the buyers could be broken down into social classes. A sample was then selected to reflect these classes proportionately from among the women in the metropolitan area of Chicago. The interviewees are questioned first as to their judgment of the brand and then as to whether or not they think the advertisement will sell.[16]

Lazarsfeld and Stanton developed the "Program Analyzer" for determining interest in radio advertising. Studio guests pressed buttons to indicate unfavorable and favorable reactions to programs — unfavorable with the left hand, favorable with the right hand. Recorded programs could thus be evaluated before presentation to the general public. One firm takes complicated paraphernalia looking like a television set into homes in order to determine the effectiveness of television advertising.[17]

One value of the opinion method is that it checks the advertising before the big expenditures are made. The opinion method calls attention of the creative people to the things they may have overlooked in preparing the advertising.[18]

Once an advertisement has appeared, there are many methods of *concurrent* testing. The observation of readers is used. Observation of radio or television listening and/or viewing may be made by a member of a family group. Diaries of listening and/or viewing may be kept by listeners. The writer has filled in several such diaries for both the A. C. Nielsen Company and the American Research Bureau.

In the area of newspaper or magazine advertising the *split-run* test is sometimes used to determine which of two or more advertisements has the most pulling power. In using the split-run two versions of an advertisement for a given product may be placed in the same issue of a publication with one-half of the copies containing one of the advertisements and the other half containing the other and with the papers being alternated in such fashion that all classes of readers receive the two advertisements in equal numbers. Coupons in the advertisements are keyed (different box numbers) and it can be determined which advertisement produced the most inquiries and in advertising in other publications this version may be used. This is a scientific approach, but it has the limitation of not fitting easily into a campaign. Further, the advertisement that appeals most in one section of the country may not be the one that would appeal most in another section; thus, more than one split-run may have to be made.

Mechanical methods of measuring radio and television audiences are used; telephone calls may be made to the home and inquiry made if automatic recording devices (such as the *audimeter*) have not been attached to home sets. One of the audience rating firms was highly criticized when it was found that its data for rating included automatic recordings of programs tuned in daily in one residence where only a dog listened while its owner was away at work.

The American Research Bureau has used what it calls the *Arbitron system* for rating television programs, in which television sets in certain homes are connected by telephone to a central computing office where information is computed to give instant program ratings.[19]

Effectiveness of an advertisement may be tested by *memory tests*. These tests attempt to determine whether a person has seen or heard an advertisement and remembered it. The programs considered to have high prestige and those which are easy to remember are often reported despite the fact that the interviewees may not have heard or seen them. Recognition tests are used; these, too, are subject to error. If an advertisement appeals to the interviewee, he may say he has seen it even if he has not. A refinement of the memory test is the "play back" where the interviewee is asked to recall the advertisement, i.e., play it back (Gallup Impact Technique, Chapter XXII).

In order to check on advertising readership, the firm of Seymour Smith Associates has used a *tachistoscope*. This was first used to test aircraft recognition by flashing a plane's silhouette for a fraction of a second. Advertising of a given company along with that of its competitors may be flashed before the reader. He doesn't have enough time to study the advertising in order to fake familiarity with the object advertised. Previous readership of the advertisement may then be tested through questioning.[20] In this connection, *psychogalvanometers* have been used to determine the truthfulness of those answering questions about readership of advertisements as well as to determine emotional reactions to the advertisements and different parts of them.

Various measures based on inquiries and sales are used. The Audit Bureau of Circulation breaks down circulation on the basis of incentives provided for readers such as club subscriptions, premiums, discounts, and commissions. Newsstand sales are separated from subscriptions. These distinctions give an indication of readership.[21]

An example of *performance testing* is that of three groups of persons in a 6,000-member panel. The control group did not receive advertising; a second group received general recipes by direct mail; and a third group received a new-cookie advertisement. A month after the final mailing, all 6,000 persons were sent questionnaires. Results showed that use of the product had increased sixty-seven per cent in the families that received the cookie advertisements. Performance studies can, of course, show definite results which are what advertisers wish to have in order to show that they did spend their money wisely.[22]

Not only does quantitative marketing research obtain data on area potentials and on the effectiveness of advertising both before and after it has appeared, much research is done to determine the products that consumers are buying and on those they would like to be able to buy provided the products were available. General Foods Corporation, for example, finds out what new foods people want and then tells its laboratories to develop them.[23] The head of General Electric's marketing research stated in 1962 that for the marketing man in the future the real job would be "to help his company decide its true relationship to the consumer and how it can make any product or perform any service the customer may want and it has the competence to supply." [24]

Consumer panels selected according to income, family size, and other factors in proportion to the composition of the population with regard to these factors, are used to determine the products being consumed and their brand preferences. Researchers sometimes go into the homes and take inventories of what they find on pantry shelves.

National Family Opinion, Inc., of Toledo uses the *mail panel* technique. It has used as many as 25,000 families at a time and at the same time maintained a reserve of an additional 50,000 families. This firm once used nine-page questionnaires to find the types of pots and pans women use. Each woman received a pair of calipers with her instructions in order that measurements might be uniformly made. Some eighty-one per cent of the women replied. This firm has guaranteed eighty per cent response on product testing and eighty-five per cent response on shopping or living habits.[25]

Schoenfeld has pointed out that much data is gathered by the Department of Agriculture on what people eat and wear. In 1955 it published a 200-page volume, *Food Consumption of Urban Families in the*

United States. Its surveys do not answer all the questions. For instance, potato consumption in Minneapolis and St. Paul was found to be twice as much as in San Francisco. In San Francisco more tomatoes were eaten per person. Why is not answered. Consumer preference studies reveal that women prefer apples in loose piles. Those who want them sacked want larger sacks except in Philadelphia or Chicago where they want sacks under five pounds.[26] Data of this type can be obtained by counting and it does indicate consumer preference, but it does not answer "why?" Such data can, however, suggest motivation studies.

Sampling and Questionnaires — Questions and questionnaires used in marketing research should be *short* and aimed at getting only important information. Questions should be *clear* and should not suggest answers. Free-style answers should be provided for, as: "Do you prefer a brand we have not named? If so, what brand?" There should be provision for "Don't Know" answers in order that tabulation may be accurately made and checked and to determine definitely that the questions have been asked. Identification of the interviewer's product should be left until last in order to insure unbiased answers to questions; in some instances it is believed that it is best not to reveal the client's name or brand at all. Attempt should be made to find out what is disliked as well as what is liked about a product.

One writer has suggested that to cure the language problem in preparing of surveys the people who write survey questions should be sent "into the tenements, the potato fields, the dockside; for two weeks a year, every year." He felt that it was only by such actual experience in interviewing that a consumer research analyst could learn "the difference in 'speech,' language and 'reading' language. Only as an interviewer will he understand the blight of wordiness as he sees the people he is questioning squirm as he drones on and on. . . ." [27]

The size of the sample may be determined by using any one of various statistical approaches. The percentage of accuracy desired is a determining factor. One formula for finding sample size is:

$$N = \frac{4PQ}{S.E.^2}$$

In this formula N is equal to the size of the sample. P and Q together total 100 and indicate the total percentage of answers, or 100 per cent. S. E. is the sampling error to be permitted. To illustrate: in finding how many students own lighters and how many do not it may be found that 47 per cent do own lighters and 53 per cent do not. If the sampling error is to be permitted to be as much as 6.66 per cent then the number of interviews would be determined by substituting in the equation:

$$N = \frac{4 \ (47 \times 53)}{6.66^2} = 225$$

It is obvious that for certain other questions the percentages would change and that the closer the percentages are together and the smaller the percentage of allowable error, the larger the sample would have to be.

Restricted random sampling is that which is stratified although there is chance selection of the respondents. Restricted random sampling is illustrated by the following: from 225 students two-thirds may be men and one-third women to match the proportion of the men and women students in the student body; a certain number may be drawn from each class to conform to registration by classes; the sample may also conform to age groups; it might conform to academic-grade groups. *Unrestricted* random sampling draws from an unstratified universe. Since the purpose of this volume is not to develop skills but to give general information relative to the psychological uses of data obtained by them, the many approaches to selecting research samples are not discussed here. Suffice it to say that data obtained from market research is only as good as the questionnaire and the sample enable it to be.

The sample method must fit the particular problem being studied. The technique of matched samples must always be defective because it is not possible to match two samples on all factors. Matched samples cannot be random either because they are not alike on factors which have not been controlled. It is very difficult to match groups; matching of individuals within groups gives more accurate results. The more factors that are matched, however, the more difficult it becomes even to find representative individuals.[28]

Who Does Market Research? — Research done by Dr. Paul D. Converse showed that *academic men* did more basic research studies in marketing than private business, government, foundations and associations put together in the years 1944, 1952, and 1954. In 1949 the academic men did more such research than any one of the other groups and almost as much as all put together. Poles were taken in the years named by nominations of publications in terms of contributions to the theory or science of marketing.[29]

A survey of 168 companies released in 1953 by the American Management Association showed that at that time most *large companies* had *research departments.* Most companies that replied had over $5 million annual sales. They typically spent ten cents for each $100 of sales on market research. The weakest area was reported to be computation of sales potential. Following this were: sampling, interviewing, tabulation, and advertising research, especially the measuring of effectiveness of advertising.[30]

A NICB survey of 150 companies with 101 responses indicated that the *sales department* is the most important source of information for marketing research studies in fifty-seven per cent of the responding companies. Half of the companies responding had from one to three market analysts.[31]

Corning Glass Works is an example of a large company that has its own Market Research Opinion Center set up right in its Glass Center built in 1948 at Corning, New York. The many visitors to this center are asked to comment on consumer items that Corning helps to develop for other companies as well as on its own consumer products. Corning also has a consumer panel where it may put new products into from one to 500 homes within a fifty-mile radius of its plant for testing purposes.[32]

Advertising agencies do much marketing research for their clients. There are over 3,500 advertising agencies in the United States. With their wide knowledge of the factors of distribution and sales as well as of advertising media, agencies are well qualified to develop advertising campaigns and handle the complete advertising programs for their clients. The world's largest single advertising agency is J. Walter Thompson Company. The world's largest complex of advertising agencies is the Interpublic Group of Companies. This company's McCann-Erickson affiliate, H. K. McCann Co., mbH, is the largest agency operating in Germany, the most fertile advertising area on the European continent. In 1964 it was estimated that advertising expenditures in Europe were running around $6 billion. Both the European style of advertising and the European media differ from those in the United States. Television is, for instance, banned as a medium in a number of European countries. The agencies do three things:

First — they study the product or service.
Second — they analyze the present and potential market.
Third — acting on this study, analysis and knowledge, they formulate a definite plan.[33]

The agencies do three main kinds of research:

1. *Internal Research* — as within the client's own business, using client questionnaires, preparing agency data books on all aspects of the client's business, etc.

2. *General Research* — using government departments, libraries, trade associations and other sources of information.

3. *Field Research* — by mail or personal visits to consumers, salesmen, retailers, wholesalers, and others.[34]

The advertising agencies of the United States have branches all over the world today and are in position to feel the pulse of the population of practically any market for products produced in this country,[35] including Africa's millions.[36] Thousands of studies are conducted each year by hundreds of proficiently staffed organizations throughout the free-world market.[37]

The advertising agencies and *rating services* are believed to do most of the consumer opinion surveys and motivation research. Among the marketing research and rating services are the following: A. C. Nielsen Company (media rating and other types of marketing research); American Research Bureau (widely uses diary-type questionnaires on television and radio and does other types of research as well); Gallup and Robinson (readership surveys, impact technique, activation — see next chapter); Alfred Politz Research, Inc. (family-interest surveys); Daniel Starch (many types of human relations and marketing research studies, including readership studies); Psychological Corporation (many types of research, including marketing and social research); the National Research Bureau, Inc. (markets for consumer products; research is often of the secondary type, i.e., through culling information from published data and classifying same); Social Research, Inc. (many types of research, including marketing).

Starch began to study radio audiences in 1928 and magazine readership in 1931. He continues to use a technique used at that time: consumers are shown a magazine and as the interviewer turns through it he is asked which advertisements he noticed and/or read and whether or not he could identify the advertiser. Claude Hopkins (*My Life in Advertising*) even before this did a kind of advertising research when he observed consumers and sometimes interviewed them. He had a sense for knowing what would appeal to the masses. George Gallup began testing newspaper advertisements with reading and noting techniques in the late 1920's, and by the 1940's the Gallup & Robinson Impact Service utilized the recall of ideas transmitted by advertising to rate penetration of the message. Readership had to be proved by playback techniques. Later Gallup & Robinson's Television Impact Service used recall on the day following a program. Politz and Dichter have also engaged in measuring audiences. Despite these many services and those of the advertising agencies, most of the money spent for measuring services goes to those services that originated with Crosley, Hooper, and Nielsen in the 1930's.[38]

It was estimated that there were some 300 companies specializing in various forms of marketing research in 1964. The number of firms with their own marketing departments runs into the thousands.[39]

Many *media* have their own marketing research departments. These media are prepared to aid their clients in planning advertising campaigns and expenditures. The *Milwaukee Journal,* for instance, in 1964 in cooperation with the city's four television stations offered to advertisers through its Milwaukee Advertising Laboratory two closely matched samples of homes. An advertiser can vary the type and amount of advertising received by these homes and then measure the change in product purchases.[40]

A great deal of information may be obtained from the advertising and marketing magazines themselves: *Printers' Ink, Advertising Age, Journal of Marketing, Sales Management, Practical Psychology, Harvard Business Review, Editor and Publisher, Advertising Agency Magazine, Public Opinion Quarterly,* and others. *Executive Guide to Marketing 1964,* issued by *Printers' Ink* contains seven reports on national markets. These concern the whole market and the major segments of it including: youth, men, women, Negro, farm, and religious markets. The marketing blueprints provided by this publication and *Sales Management's Survey of Buying Power* are invaluable aids to those who have something to sell.

Many outside persons and firms as well as many persons, committees, and executives within a given firm may have a say in advertising. Appropriation decisions are, however, usually made by top management and top management may have final approval on an advertising theme, campaign, or program. Even the union may become involved in some instances. It may be said, also, that in spite of the mechanical devices that can aid manufacturers, retailers, and all businessmen in making their decisions relative to how much to spend where for advertising and what themes and appeals to use, a leading roll in still played by instinct, intuition, and good sound common sense.[41]

Conclusions — Those who sell goods or services should be well aware of the sociological and other factors that affect marketing such as productivity, population trends and shifts, composition of the work force, changes in income and work time, and changes in tastes and fashions. The controllable competitive tools of marketing such as product research and development, marketing channels, pricing, and personal selling are controllable only to the extent that management may make decisions on these factors in the light of scientifically obtained information. Uncontrollable factors such as legal action, competition, demand, cost, and public opinion must be determined and action guided in the light of such information as may be attainable. The factors themselves generally cannot be changed, at least not in the short run, but action can be amended or altered because of them.

Market research of many types must be done in order to forecast sales and costs, prepare budgets, and determine advertising campaigns. Quantitative data can give some idea of the possibility of the effectiveness of advertising before it is done. The actual effectiveness of spending large sums may be determined concurrently with the appearance of advertising or after it has been done.

Management believes in planning for the future and it wants a systematic approach for doing this. Advertising commitments must be made in some cases for a full year or more ahead. The most insistent demand of advertisers is, however, for measurement of the results of advertising,[42] which is largely done by quantitative research. If the "why" of the quantitative data is desired, then qualitative research is warranted.

One expert has said that research is "of greatest value when used continuously and as insurance on adequate returns of advertising expenditures." No formula can, however, be expected to cover all the angles such as the competition's advertising and selling activities, the past years of advertising a firm's own goods, and the activities of distributors.[43]

According to Daniel Yankelovich, marketing and communications researcher for such firms as General Electric, General Mills, and Dow Chemical, the sciences and professions of psychology, sociology, economics, and mathematics will contribute their insights and methods to marketing research in the future. "Skillful marketing research professionals will blend these into a theory and science of marketing of power and sensitivity.[44] Perhaps the most rewarding of all the research activities done by business can be found in the research that is initiated by business itself to improve the goods and services desired and needed by society. Such groups as General Electric's Behavioral Research Service are not out to find out how to inveigle the unsuspecting consumer to buy a product he does not want. Their aim is to find what society wants, a way of providing products and services that will satisfy those wants, and how best to let society know about these goods and services when they are available.

PROJECTS

1. Report on the current year's expenditures for advertising by media, indicating why certain media may have increased in popularity while others may have declined.

2. Write a short paper on "The Necessity for Consumer Research."

3. Write a short paper on "The Extent of Advertising Research in Foreign Countries."

ACKNOWLEDGMENTS AND REFERENCES

1 Randle, C. Wilson, "Putting New Product Ideas Through Their Paces," *The Management Review,* American Management Association, Inc., 1515 Broadway, Times Square, New York 36, N. Y., Vol. XLVI, No. 10, October, 1957, pp. 34-35.

2 Seligman, Daniel, "How Much for Advertising?," *Fortune,* Vol. LIV, No. 6, December, 1957, pp. 124-126, 224.

3 Howard, John A., *Marketing Management,* Richard D. Irwin, Inc., Homewood, Illinois, 1957, p. 48ff.

4 ——————, "Advertising," *Newsweek,* June 22, 1964, p. 71.

5 Frey, Albert Wesley, *How Many Dollars for Advertising,* The Ronald Press Co., New York, 1955, pp. 11-12, 31ff., 48, 82.

6 Knowles, William B., "9-Billion Advertising Race," *The Magazine of Wall Street and Business Analyst,* April 13, 1957.

7 Umemura, George M., *Keys to Efficient Selling and Lower Marketing Costs,* Studies in Business Policy, No. 71, NICB, 1954.

8 Glade, Frederick H., Jr., "Changes in the Scope of Advertising Agency Services and Compensation Problems," *Adaptive Behavior in Marketing,* edited by Robert D. Buzzell, Proceedings of the Winter Conference AMA, Cleveland, Ohio, December 27-28, pp. 75-87.

9 Howard, *op. cit.*

10 Weiner, Jack B., "Myth of the National Market," *Dun's Review,* p. 40ff.

11 ——————, "A Well-tempered Boom," *Business Week,* No. 1817, June 27, 1964, pp. 27-29.

12 Anshen, Melvin, "Fundamental and Applied Research in Marketing," *The Journal of Marketing,* Vol. XIX, No. 3, January, 1955, pp. 233-243.

13 *Ibid.*

14 Gardner, Burleigh B., "How the Social Sciences Are Used in Advertising," *Printers' Ink,* December 11, 1953, p. 50ff.

15 Kidder, Nathaniel, and Hummel, Francis E., *Sales Management,* Vol. 75, No. 2, July 15, 1955, pp. 57-67.

16 ——————, "Trying Ads Out on the Road," *Business Week,* May 7, 1960, pp. 123-127.

17 *Ibid.*

18 Lucas, Darrell Blaine, and Britt, Steuart Henderson, *Advertising Psychology and Research,* McGraw-Hill Book Company, Inc., New York, 1950, p. 101.

19 ——————, "New System of Instantaneous TV Ratings . . . ," *Business Week,* December 21, 1957, p. 45.

20 ——————, "Advertising Saves Sales Calls," *Business Week,* December 5, 1959, pp. 69-70.

21 Lucas and Britt, *op. cit.,* pp. 476-598.

22 Gerhold, Paul, "How to Take the Guesswork Out of Research," *Printers' Ink,* April 20, 1956, p. 40ff.

23 ——————, "New Ways to Size up how Consumers Behave," *Business Week,* July 22, 1961, p. 68.

24 ——————, "The Marketing Pattern," *Business Week,* July 14, 1962, p. 60.

25 ——————, "Woman to Woman Does It," *Business Week,* October 29, 1960, p. 45ff.

26 Schoenfeld, Jerome, "Washington Has Answers for You," *Sales Management,* Vol. 74, No. 8, April 15, 1955, pp. 92-95.

27 Katz, Samuel, "An Interviewer Tells How to Avoid Getting Wrong Answers from Research," *Printers' Ink,* Vol. 262, No. 2, January 10, 1958, pp. 73-74.

28 ——————, *Wood Chips of Information and Intelligence on Marketing Research,* Vol. I, A. J. Wood & Co., December, 1954, through April, 1956.

29 Converse, Paul D., "Who Does Basic Marketing Research?," *The Journal of Marketing,* Vol. XIX, No. 4, April, 1955, pp. 254-257.

30 ——————, "Market Research," *Business Week,* No. 1252, August 29, 1953, p. 163.

31 ——————, " 'Board' Meeting Hears Seven Tips for Better Selling," *Industrial Marketing,* Vol. 42, No. 11, November, 1957, p. 156ff.

32 ——————, "Corning Finds A Namesake — and New Profits," *Business Week,* July 16, 1960, pp. 136-142.

33 Gamble, Frederick R., "What Advertising Agencies Are — What They Do and How They Do It," American Association of Advertising Agencies, 420 Lexington Ave., New York, 1960, p. 8.

34 *Ibid.,* p. 9.

35 ——————, "Madison Avenue Circles the Globe," *Business Week,* July 1, 1961, pp. 34-37.

36 ——————, "The White Huckster," *Business Week,* April 23, 1962, pp. 86-89.

37 ——————, "Sizing Up Overseas Markets," *Printers' Ink,* Vol. 287, No. 10, June 5, 1964, p. 35ff.

38 Siegle, Henry J., "How Hard Does Advertising Work," *Printers' Ink,* Vol. 283, No. 11, June 14, 1963, pp. 353-354.

39 ——————, "Scouting the Trail for Marketers," *Business Week,* April 18, 1964, pp. 90-116.

40 ——————, "New Way of Testing Efficacy of Ads Draws Interest to Milwaukee Newspaper," *Business Week,* June 27, 1964, p. 98.

——————, "Isolating Media for Better Testing," *Printers' Ink,* Vol. 288, No. 3, July 17, 1964, pp. 42-43.

41 Hatch, Clarence, Jr., "The Changing Demands on the Advertising Agency," *Marketing's Role in Scientific Management,* edited by Robert Clewett, AMA, 27 East Monroe St., Chicago 3, Illinois, 1957, pp. 103-107.

42 Schachte, Henry M., "What Your Clients Want From Research," *Advertising Agency Magazine,* July 6, 1956, p. 38.

43 ——————, "Market Research Aids Chase Advertising Program," Burrough's Clearing House, Vol. 41, No. 4, January, 1957, pp. 26-27.

44 Yankelovich, Daniel, "More Who than How — Market Research — The Future," *Printers' Ink, Advertising Today, Yesterday, Tomorrow,* Vol. 283, No. 11, June 14, 1963, pp. 321-328.

CHAPTER XXII

USES OF PSYCHOLOGY IN ADVERTISING
AND MOTIVATION RESEARCH

Early Uses of Psychology in Advertising — Over fifty years ago Walter Dill Scott dedicated his volume *The Psychology of Advertising* to "That increasing number of American Businessmen who successfully apply science where their predecessors were confined to custom." In this early volume Scott asked:

> What is there in the modern newspaper that appeals to the better classes of society, and what motives should be appealed to in inducing them to begin a subscription? The problems here raised are clearly psychological and subject to the questionnaire method, which was employed in investigating them.[1]

Scott made a study in which 4,000 of Chicago's most outstanding business and professional men were questioned to determine what papers they read and why, how much time they spend in reading them and what induced subscriptions to them. The motives for beginning a paper subscription were found to be seven, but sixty-five per cent of the expressed motives could be classified as "To keep informed concerning current events," and ten per cent subscribed because of the ethical tone (including accuracy) of the paper subscribed to. Premiums and cartoons induced four per cent each; special articles, three per cent; reputation of the paper, one per cent; and best delivery service, one per cent.[2]

Scott stated four principles of improving one's own memory: repetition, intensity, association, ingenuity. For use in advertising, Scott thought association the most important.[3] He wrote at length on instincts, suggestion, will, habit, and reported on studies that showed the value of size in the advertisement. Two investigations he reported showed "the value of an advertisement increases as the size of the advertisement increases, and the increase of value is greater than the increase in the amount of space filled."[4]

Tons of volumes and articles have been written on the subject of advertising and the use of psychology in advertising since Scott first wrote on these subjects back in a day when newspapers had few competitors for the advertising dollar. Current articles relative to newspaper advertising indicate that for newspaper advertising to survive competition many new techniques are being developed: more color; more comics and supplements; volume discounts and market research services; suburban editions.[5]

Human Motivation — The Riddle of Consumer Behavior — It has been said by many writers that in order to influence any person it is necessary to appeal to his basic needs and wants. Basic needs and drives were briefly discussed in Chapter II in connection with motivation as a factor in study. Certainly these are also factors that influence consumer choice. The National Cash Register Company's vice-president in charge of sales, John M. Wilson, wrote in 1953 that the "big four" buying motives are: *gain, pride, fear,* and *imitation.* People, said he, are not aware of their needs and, therefore, *needs cannot be developed into wants without a knowledge of motives that drive people to favorable action.*[6]

A great deal of money has been spent in the United States to determine *why* consumers behave as they do. It was concluded in 1958, however, by a group of sixty outstanding advertising and marketing research experts that we still lack "basic theory and fact to explain buying behavior." *Life* magazine began a consumer survey in 1956 on which by April, 1958, it had spent some $2.5 million. The chief finding of this study was that consumer demands change and producers keep "hammering at change to keep goods moving." The sixty panelists asked many questions; they answered few.[7] Yet those who have something to sell feel compelled to continue to attempt to find the answers and to continue to effect the changes suggested by their findings.

Many theories have been advanced and each "expert" not only advances his own theories but develops his own techniques for finding the answers. Rosser Reeves, chairman of Ted Bates & Co., contended in *Reality in Advertising* that the consumer's brain is similar to a "small box with still smaller compartments for storing information on specific product categories. . . ." If a compartment is filled to overflowing with an advertisement for *your* product, there is not room for the products of others. He calls this the "Unique Selling Proposition" which must be "simple, forceful, and something the competition either cannot or does not offer." [8] Reeves has been particularly successful in using his formula; someone else might be less successful. Perhaps, too, it is simply that at a given time some persons are destined to be successful with their approaches to advertising and selling. Albert D. Lasker, about whom John Gunther wrote in *Taken at the Flood,* was particularly successful in his day with beauty contests, soap operas, radio commercials, and slogans that sold women on smoking and everybody on orange juice and Kleenex.[9] It is quite possible that the product and the idea create motives in men.

Objections to Discovering Human Motives and Appealing to Them in Advertising, and Other Criticisms of MR — Some objections have been raised to motivation research (MR) on moral grounds. Quantitative researchers have questioned its validity. Businessmen have also raised their eyebrows at qualitative information for they have been used to quantitative data such as audience sizes and dollar expenditures for their own companies and competitive companies.[10]

Several writers have criticized Vance Packard for the position he took relative to MR in *The Hidden Persuaders.* Packard raised the question of ethics, holding to the position that depth interviews go too far in probing into minds. Many persons, including Carroll J. Swan, a *Printers' Ink* editor, have taken the other side of the question. Swan asked, "Isn't a man's mind as private as he cares to make it?" He would agree that MR might be used to bring about mass persuasion, but he would ask, "Hasn't advertising always been designed to persuade?" The fear that MR would be used to bring about evil manipulation of the public Swan felt to be totally unfounded.[11]

Simon O. Lesser, research associate, Institute for Motivational Research, found Packard's criticisms highly unrealistic. The findings of MR, for instance, permit drawing of different and even opposite conclusions, and they must be evaluated along with many other elements and weighed and integrated with them. Further, the findings of MR are frequently rejected by the "patients." Just as in psychoanalysis the patients reject the remedies, so do businesses resist the findings of MR. Lesser proposed that Packard based his book on the *tabula rasa* conception of the mind (Locke's belief that the mind begins as a clean slate on which experiences are written from which came the behaviorist psychology). Also, Packard assumed that emotional reasons for doing anything are bad reasons; but MR is only trying to find the real satisfactions that people seek. MR merely urges sellers of goods to talk to consumers in terms of consumer needs and interests. In addition, with regard to writing an advertisement, Lesser stated that "Aristotle would agree, rhetoric can be looked upon as a branch of psychology."[12] Textbook author and market researcher Alderson has also referred to Packard's criticisms:

. . . If it is smart to regard the consumer as a dupe who can be exploited by playing on unconscious or instinctive impulses, then why not adopt that approach in relations between the advertising agency and its clients or between the motivation research organization on the one hand and manufacturers and advertising agencies on the other? [13]

Packard has, of course, played his part on the stage of the modern United States scene. He has criticized the social climbers and others in *The Status Seekers*; he has criticized practically everybody concerned with business and industry in *The Waste Makers*. Anybody not covered in these volumes and *The Hidden Persuaders*, he has taken care of in his *Pyramid Climbers*.

Vance Packard is not the only critic of MR, however. Robert J. Williams stated in an article in *The Journal of Marketing* that all the "why" questions of MR must be recast in the form of "how and what" questions. Thus the explanations of MR become identical to those offered by experimental-statistical approaches.[14]

Alfred Politz has pointed out that motivation research is not "the all" but only a part of the process of finding out the why of consumer behavior. The advertiser does want to know "with what frequency a particular psychological phenomenon exists in the consumer field." Research starts with counting the number of cases in which the phenomenon exists. This is the method of testing the hypothesis. The hunch or hypothesis may be provided by MR and the MR may be referred to in this case as "pilot test or study." Politz, along with many others, feels that too much reliance has been placed upon the "depth-interview concept." One may go to the very depths of the human mind, but if there is nothing there nothing will be found. Techniques used in the past to find what people intend to do have found them responding to one thing and doing another although they had no intention to deceive. Advertising, friends, salesmen, and other things entered into the picture to change their minds. Projective techniques might have produced better results; but even in the clinic where they were developed projective techniques have been recognized to have low validity. They do, however, provide ideas, hunches, and hypotheses. Quantitative devices, counting, measuring, determining frequencies then become useful.[15] We might conclude that Mr. Politz would probably agree that MR is better than guessing.

Perhaps the most scathing criticism of MR was that in a 1955 article written by N. D. Rothwell. She stated that clinical psychologists faced with patients unable to tell their thoughts or how they felt developed projective techniques. MR borrowed the techniques and claimed it could uncover reasons for customer reactions. Quoting authorities to substantiate her claims, Mrs. Rothwell said that the trained clinician could spend many hours with a patient and administer batteries of tests as checks. Needs and desires under such conditions may be revealed, but the very fantasies a patient builds up may be furnishing satisfaction for his desires. If MR reveals desires and drives, there is still no proof that these will be transformed into action. The personality "underground" responds differently to different interviews, voices, and environments. Results, therefore, are distorted. She charged that data collected by MR cannot be properly interpreted because there are no norms with which to compare (as Sherwood Dodge had stated a year before she wrote). She also charged that the depth and open-end, non-directive, long narrative interview in MR resulted only in finding out *why people say they buy* and not *why they buy*.[16]

W. D. Wells of Rutgers University and Benton and Bowles, Inc., answered Mrs. Rothwell's criticisms of motivation research by saying that none of the authors she quoted as having criticized MR concluded that projective methods are in general invalid and that none of their experimental results could be applied "intact to marketing studies." Further, the crimes she pinned on MR are defects of research in general, not just MR. He did agree that qualitative data are subject to misrepresentation. Mrs. Rothwell responded to his article with a rejoinder that held firmly to her original viewpoint. She recommended study of discrepancies between verbal responses and actual buying behavior, use of laboratories and clinics for basic research on motivation, and the use of sociometric techniques in market research.[17]

Most authorities agree that both quantitative and qualitative research are needed, that they must in fact work hand-in-hand. Dr. Ernest Dichter, President of the Institute for Motivational Research, Inc., has said that in "today's changing, dynamic, incalculable world it is MR which shows the way because it is able to outline, define, and often to solve, the fundamental problems of specific marketing, selling and advertising campaigns."[18]

Why MR? and What Is MR? — Determining the number of people who have seen an advertisement does not prove they were influenced to buy the product or even that they were qualified buyers of the product. It was estimated that some $4 billion a year was being spent on product research in 1955 and that one-half of one per cent of this amount would give a sizeable sum for uncovering vital information about consumer motives.[19] The people themselves may not be able to say "why" they buy certain items. MR developed to attempt to supply the "why?"

Speaking at a meeting of the American Marketing Association, Deryl

Case, Consultant in Consumer Marketing Research in the New York Office of General Electric's Marketing Services, said that "There is no established definition of motivation research. It means different things to different people." The broad definition he thought would include any type of research "designed to explain human behavior, regardless of the methods used." Some persons, however, would limit the definition to include only the types of research that apply social sciences to marketing studies.[20]

George Horsley Smith, who did a book on the subject of MR, published under the auspices of the Advertising Research Foundation, has said that ". . . motivation research focuses on what happens inside the person between the time a stimulus is applied and a response is made." [21] The stimulus might be any number of things from an advertisement to a store display or a television program. The question is what happens inside the person from the time the stimulus is given until the time he reacts by accepting or rejecting the product advertised. Actually, what has happened to the individual prior to the stimulus must be considered to be important, too. *What has happened prior to a stimulus may be as much or more responsible for what takes place within the individual after the stimulus as is the stimulus itself.*

One *Fortune* magazine writer has said that when the businessmen and advertisers became convinced that the apparent reasons consumers buy are evidently not the real reasons, they began to pay attention to MR, a part of which was "straight out of Freud." [22] MR has drawn on all the fields of psychology and several other social sciences for its methods of investigation and interpretation (Chapter I).

Pierre Martineau, Director of Research and Marketing, *Chicago Tribune,* has said:

> . . . Any advertising will obviously be more effective if it can tap the underlying emotion and attitudinal concepts which are important in specific areas, as well as utilize the practical advantages of the product or service. This is an objective of motivation research — to probe for and to evaluate these underlying forces, and thereby to supply directional help to the creative people.[23]

Martineau also asked how quantitative information could reveal "emotion, intuition, imagination, creativity, mood, personality structure." [24] He has emphasized the profound motivational differences between the lower-class and the middle-class and/or upper-class groups. A large problem area of advertising is the problem of communicating with the "mass man." [25]

Smith has said that doing motivational research involves: (1) thinking in terms of a set of psychological variables and (2) using the appropriate research tools to study these variables. The "inside-the-person" variables are related in a causal way to responses that are: (1) assumptions, beliefs, presuppositions; (2) frames of reference, attitudes; (3) sensations, feelings, images; ((4) motives; (5) identification and empathy. "Why?" research should focus on "the whole battery of inner conditions that play a dynamic part in a person's buying, responding favorably or unfavorably to some communication." [26]

Communication and the Creative Person — In an article entitled "Is Anybody Listening?" it was pointed out that advertising spends vast sums in attempting to find out about its audience, and yet its conception of life seems to be based "less on life than on the conception of it that previous advertising has erected." The advertisements recreate the scene of Main Street, "shady lawns, barbecue dinners in the back yard, mansarded roofs, the town firehouse, church suppers . . . But," asks the article, "do most Americans live on Main Street?" This is a problem of communication.[27] Martineau has said that two powerful sets of symbols must be used in communicating in advertising: rational claims for products require supplementary non-rational communication. The set of symbols that gains access to the emotions and intuition must be equally as strong as that set which sways "the consumer's economic logic." [28]

In doing motivation research there are problems of communication due to *various levels of awareness* of individuals. Even at the first level of awareness it may be difficult to collect and interpret accurate data through mere stating of preference. It is here that the special techniques of MR are helpful. At the second level are the motives that come about because people desire to impress others with something bigger and better. Prejudices and early memories also influence the second-level awareness. Trained persons can spot rationalizations. Repressed desires and deep unconscious motives of the third level of awareness are most difficult to penetrate, but recognition of these is useful in advertising. It is the task of MR to seek psychological variables in consumer behavior at all levels.[29]

The creative people of advertising use the results of company, product, competitor, market, and motivation research when creating the campaign or the individual advertisement. The outcome is the expenditure of billions of dollars in the various advertising media. The only type of advertising that does not cost is "word-of-mouth advertising." Some companies have experimented with the use of this kind of advertising.[30] The hypothesis that ideas do flow from radio, television, and print through opinion leaders to the less active persons and sections has been tested in studies that seem to verify the belief that "word-of-mouth" or "two-step flow of communication" does exist. These studies also indicate that there are sources of social pressure and social support and that the inter-personal associations of each of these are related to decision-making, each in a somewhat different manner.[31] The influence of the group is implied in the use of the term "reference group" to explain why it is that people with average incomes of, for instance, $85 a week will in one part of a city respond to an advertisement, whereas in another part of the city the same income group will not respond to the same advertisement. Their "reference groups" are different.[32]

Techniques and Methods of MR — It is generally conceded that it is in the problem-defining phase of research that the techniques of MR are of most value, and the beginning point of MR is usually the *exploratory interview*. This interview should precede the developing of a complete research plan. It should aim to find out what the reactions to certain questions will be and whether or not these questions must be followed up with others in order to elicit responses. The interviewees give the cues that provide the basis for the eventual questioning and research technique that will be used.[33]

Some of the techniques used to find the reasons for behavior of a given group or segment of it are: *word-association tests, sentence-completion tests, role playing, picture frustration* and *thematic apperception tests, Rorschach ink blots* and other tests of personality, the so-called *depth interviewing,* and *group interviewing.* These techniques are referred to as being "projective" since the respondent's motives are projected in his responses without his awareness of how much he is revealing.

In *word-association* tests the interviewee is read words, one at a time, and requested to immediately say the first word he thinks of upon hearing each of the words read to him. Through using this type of questioning researchers concluded in one survey that a major buying motive for toothpaste is to prevent offensive breath since to the word "toothpaste" the responses included "breath, mouth-odor, or halitosis," as often as "brush teeth," or "clean teeth." Responses of 1,000 persons to the word "doctor" brought 213 replies of "physician," 149 of "medicine," 104 of "sickness," and so forth. The *pleasant* associations which included such words as "better, kind, life, relief, smart, wise, and well" totaled 102. The *probably pleasant* responses, totaling eight, brought the pleasant total to 120. The responses classified as *definitely unpleasant* totaled 32, with 9 additional being classified as probably unpleasant.[34] Generally when response is being made without the use of a list, if the response to a word takes longer than three seconds the contention is that comparative emotional involvement exists and a substitute is being made for a first reaction believed by the respondent to be non-acceptable.

The application and interpretation of *sentence-completion tests* is much the same as with word-association tests. The technique has been used to study attitudes and reasons for special tensions. It has been used in employment testing and to discover consumer attitudes toward products.

In *role playing* people "guess" and put themselves in the place of other people. Smith defines four general tests used in the role-playing approach: *guess-and-imagine, personification, play technique, and errors of perception and recall.* In one *guess-and-imagine test,* young women were requested to write personality sketches of "a girl 'who goes into a store and buys X brand deodorant, and another girl who buys B brand.' " In one test respondents were asked to tell which of five brands a housewife would choose from a supermarket shelf when each brand was associated with an outstanding TV and/or radio figure. From the list of five personalities the interviewees selected Arthur Godfrey; projective results were backed up by free interview material. In using the guess-and-imagine approach much depends on careful wording of the items, but when used correctly this type of test can discover deeper motives. *Personification* was used in research on tea resulting in a finding that most people think tea to be feminine. A campaign emphasizing masculine appeals to tea drinkers ensued. The *play-technique* was used by C. W. Garber in interviewing prospects for garden tractors. Interviewing kits were used and props of small garden plot, rake, hoe, shovel, and two garden tractors. The interviewees used the play area to prepare seed beds. As they used the tractor and implements, the interviewer noted the comments and reactions. A disadvantage of this technique is that the interviews are too long; in the case of the garden tractor, an hour. *Errors of perception and recall tests* are constructed with the knowledge that what people believe or regard as fact usually correlates highly with their *opinions on a given issue.* Persons who are favorable to certain attitudes remember more of material presented relative to these attitudes than they do of material relative to attitudes they view unfavorably. Thus attitudes may be discovered by what people recall. What people see and where they locate it in space is "partly a function of . . . past experiences, purposes, assumptions, and preferences." People usually estimate time intervals as being long when they are bored. If they are asked to estimate the length of time taken for an excerpt from a TV show a clue is given as to their response to the show itself.[35]

Martin Zober of Drake University described two projective techniques for getting "why" answers: *picture frustration* (PF) and *thematic apperception test* (TAT). Rosenzweig's PF test consists of twenty-four cartoons representing different situations. There are two figures in each cartoon. The figures are rendered neutral by omission of facial characteristics. One of the figures says something; the other does not. The frustrated person, the one who says nothing, has a speech balloon left open. The interviewee is asked to fill in the blank. His own biases, presumably, are projected into each situation. Henry A. Murray and associates of Harvard developed the TAT, a test which consists of twenty cards with pictures selected from magazine illustrations, painting, and art sources. The respondent tells a story around each picture. He tells the events that lead to the situation or the outcome. He also describes thoughts, feelings, or personalities of the characters. Before designing a PF or TAT test, depth interviews or at least "exploratory interviews" should be conducted to "get the feel of the problem." The tests should be "tested" as they are being developed.[36]

The *Rorschach ink blots* have been widely used in personality testing (Chapter XIII). Rorschach's ink-blot test consists of ten cards on which are printed bisymmetrical blots. The interviewee is asked to tell what the blot is, what he sees in it, or what it makes him think about. Examiners look for several things, as: whether or not the respondent reacts to the whole blot, only a small part, or the white spaces; the combinations of determinants the respondent uses; the content of responses. The test has been useful in studying single individuals and groups. It is not so readily adaptable in solving business problems as TAT, but it has value in that it can be used to assess "the less variable aspects" of personality.[37]

Properly trained persons can aid in finding solutions to marketing problems through the use of *depth interviewing*. For some people the term "depth interviewing" means a tool that may be employed for numbers of purposes and little if any "depth" may be involved. For others it means going a little more deeply into the interviewee's personality than a fixed-answer questionnaire would go. For still others it means the using of an open-end questionnaire and non-directive probing with topical guides rather than fixed questions. Viennese psychologist Ernest Dichter has been a pioneer in the developing of depth-interview techniques. Only a trained psychologist should attempt to use the technique. Some writers have thought that the depth interview should be at least an hour long. One has defined it, however, as being "a three-hour detailed case study of the steps and reasons involved in a consumer's behavior." [38] Certainly the interviewer must use probing questions if he is to "unearth" the hidden motives and attitudes of respondents. Dr. Dichter himself said when the use of the technique was very new in advertising: "Depth psychology teaches us that unconscious reasons are usually more basic and powerful than the conscious ones. Obviously, a direct question runs no chance of success in uncovering unconscious motivations." [39] Because of the nature of the objective of depth interviewing it should be pointed out that researchers cannot be assured that even although proper techniques are used they will discover the "right" answers or that having discovered "right answers" they will recognize them as such.

If *group interviewing* is used, the groups should be small enough for discussions and have some degree of homogeneity. It has been contended that many people are more truly themselves in a group situation where they often give voice to feelings they may not have known they had. Persons who might be reluctant to talk about certain things in their own living rooms with family and friends sometimes lose their inhibitions and speak frankly in the group situation. Smith and others have written at length on depth and group interviewing if the student desires to delve more deeply into the subject. [40]

Closely associated with motivation research is the technique developed by George Gallup and known as *activation*. In 1928 Gallup became interested in finding out what kind of editorial and advertising material was of interest to readers. The answer was "that which the readers took the trouble to read." Research in readership grew greatly from 1930 to 1950 and had measurable influence on advertising. The basic limitation of this type of research, however, is that a person may read and testify that he has read but not recall the sales message or even the name of the sponsor. From 1945 to 1948 the "impact" technique was developed in which respondents were required to "play back" the advertising messages. This gave the registration of the sales message both quantitatively and qualitatively. Something was still lacking, for although ideas register that does not mean they sell goods. It became necessary to find a technique that would link the advertising stimulus with the sale. For a period of two years Gallup obtained what was called activation testimony; in no case during this time did he find that such testimony was contradicted by sales evidence. Getting the testimony is merely a matter of structuring the interview so as to obtain information from the respondent as to whether or not he made a purchase as a result of seeing the product advertised on TV or elsewhere. In the early stages activation research related solely to TV; more recently it has been used to get data on all major media. The six steps used in activation are. (1) start with the sale; find the purchaser at the supermarket or place of purchase and check on what has been purchased; (2) have respondents tell what they have bought as a result of advertising in what media; in this, concentration is on new products and products the respondent is returning to after using other products; the measure of the selling power of an advertisement is found in the attraction of new users and "switchers"; (3) the buyer is questioned about the program or the advertisement which caused him to buy in order to validate the testimony; attempt is made to determine whether or not the buyer can differentiate between the media that may have caused the sale; (4) the successful and unsuccessful campaigns are analyzed to find which techniques sold and which did not; the successful formula is: find what sells and do more of it and what does not sell and do less of that, or find out: "what to say; how to say it; where to say it; how often to say it; how long to say it"; (5) principles brought to light by activation research are applied to a specific product; the analysis of TV and print advertising by the impact method can be used to supplement the activation information; (6) there is continued flow of data in activation indexes; this is used to determine whether changes in campaigns based on the previous steps in the stages of research bring increased sales. Comparison of rate of sales achieved by a new campaign with sales made under the old campaign shows gains in advertising dollar efficiency. Activation begins and ends with the sale; the keys to activation are behavior situations and skillful inquiry.[41]

Perhaps the main problem in advertising has been brought about because of the excellence of today's products. One advertising authority has said that there is greatest creative challenge to advertising and marketing people in developing variety in product design, packages, advertising, and in many other features that lend variety to *brand image.* For every brand this means three objectives: (1) the normal sales objective; (2) the image objective; and (3) the market objective.[42] Charles E. Swensen, Research Manager of *The Saturday Evening Post,* reported on the basis of numerous studies that the printed "image of a brand or product can change the consumer's image of an ideal product." [43]

Subliminal Advertising — Subliminal advertising has been called "the little ad that isn't there." [44] It consists of momentarily flashing suggestions to viewers during the showing of a film. James M. Vicary reported on the effects of flashing the phrases "Eat Popcorn" and "Drink Coca Cola" at 0.003 of a second on a movie screen during the showing of a film. Reportedly the sales of Coca Cola increased eighteen per cent and the sales of popcorn increased fifty-seven per cent, despite the fact that the audience was unaware of the fact that it was being influenced.[45] Advertising of this type is almost a form of hypnotism, suggesting as it does a motor reaction on the part of someone who is totally unaware of the fact that he has been practically duped into action. Such attempts to control or motivate behavior are considered by many to be immoral and have brought on the criticisms of the Vance Packards and others. The FCC has not granted a patent for the use of such advertising on television and radio. The *limen* is defined as being the threshold of awareness, a stimulus intensity that is perceived half of the time, thus the use of the term *subliminal*.

What Makes Women Buy? — Women, composing approximately a third of the United States labor force, do or greatly influence much of consumer buying. A study of the Survey Research Center, University of Michigan, showed that women handle the money and pay the bills in thirty-eight per cent of the families; in thirty per cent, the husband does these things; in thirty-one per cent the two together do them.[46] Data of the National Consumers Finance Association (1963) show that women spend eighty-five per cent of family incomes as family purchasing agents; they own seventy-four per cent of titles to the nation's suburban homes as well as sixty-five per cent of private wealth and savings accounts.[47] One article entitled "What Makes Her Buy?" reported that MR's most promising use is probably in the finding of hypotheses that more conventional studies might attempt to prove.[48] Having overlooked the woman's personal satisfactions and relationships with other people, some things advertising could do according to Pierre Martineau are:

1. Make her feel better about her routine of duties.
2. Arouse feelings of pleasure in keeping house.
3. Give her more sense of achievement in getting things done.
4. Generate feelings of self-esteem and worthwhileness.
5. Alleviate her feelings of solitude in cleaning.
6. Recognize her feelings about her effort and her accomplishment.
7. Imply that the products are for real housewives with real feelings who have many other activities and goals besides cleaning.[49]

Table I indicates the increases in numbers and percentage-wise of men and women in different age groups during the period from 1960 to 1980. Those with something to sell to people in one of these age groups, knowing their own possibilities for a given share of the market in a given product, could project sales for the future. At the same time, MR and other marketing research might give clues that would enable one firm to obtain more than its projected share of the market at a given time.

TABLE XXII-1[50]

INCREASES IN WOMEN AND MEN FROM 1960–1980
(Figures in thousands)

Age Group in Years	WOMEN 1960	WOMEN 1970	WOMEN 1980	Per Cent Change '60–'80	MEN 1960	MEN 1970	MEN 1980	Per Cent Change '60–'80
15-19	6,631	9,316	10,942	+65.0	6,793	9,595	11,370	+67.4
20-24	5,570	8,471	10,164	+82.5	5,567	8,623	10,343	+85.8
25-29	5,525	6,846	9,505	+72.0	5,435	6,835	9,582	+76.3
30-34	6,076	5,738	8,646	+42.3	5,899	5,629	8,656	+46.7
35-39	6,402	5,635	6,949	+ 8.5	6,140	5,496	6,884	+12.1
40-44	5,948	6,094	5,768	− 3.0	5,733	5,893	5,626	− 1.9
45-49	5,541	6,337	5,600	+ 1.1	5,384	5,998	5,395	+ 0.2
50-54	4,897	5,785	5,962	+21.7	4,758	5,421	5,613	+18.0
55-59	4,322	5,282	6,079	+40.7	4,143	4,869	5,478	+32.2
60-64	3,744	4,533	5,402	+44.3	3,418	4,040	4,672	+36.7
65 & over	9,122	11,392	14,134	+54.9	7,536	8,643	10,324	+37.0

While the data do show that women do much buying, advertisers in the future must not be content to attempt to sell to men through women. Men depend less upon "whim" in buying; they look for quality. Irving Gilman of Dichter's has said that the American male of today is more mature than he was a decade ago and can be appealed to more through humor and sophistication. Males consume huge quantities of toiletries, gifts, and clothing, most of which are quality or luxury items.[51]

Some Advertising Principles — In the area of *media selection* alone much research must be done by the average advertiser. For industrial firms doing direct selling to a limited number of industrial consumers, some form of direct or trade advertising should probably be used. In selling most types of consumer goods, various forms of mass media should be employed. Experience and research are called upon to determine the percentage of the advertising dollar that should go to each type of medium. Computers are sometimes used to examine dozens of factors pertaining to thousands of advertisements and present the data in condensed form so that it can be of service in making decisions relative to media selection.[52]

With regard to *advertising expenditures,* a study by Vernon Van Diver of the advertising behavior of approximately 10,000 industrial companies in 800 business publications over a period of seven years resulted in the following methods of predicting future results:

Sales increases follow advertising increases, but not necessarily (in fact rarely) in the first year; they decline after advertising is cut back and with increasing momentum. Advertising held at the same level is no guarantee of increased or even equal sales because to retain a share of industry sales, a company must increase its advertising as much as the over-all industry average. To increase its share of the market it must increase its advertising faster than the industry norm over a period of four years or more.[53]

Mr. Van Diver has also used the same observations to predict consumer behavior.

The *writing of copy* depends not only upon research data relative to a company, its product and its competitors but also upon the creative ability of the writer. The advertisement is usually made up of four elements: *headline, copy, illustration,* and *signature.* A *slogan* is often worked into the advertisement since it is through the slogan that many products are quickly and easily identified. *Color* also plays a part in much advertising. It is generally conceded, however, that while the headline, illustration, and color may be the attention-getting factors, it is the copy that creates desire and makes the sale.

Copy should generally be *brief, clear, apt, interesting, personal,* and *convincing.*[54] Studies have shown that copy that is informative, i.e., contains merchandising facts, gets the best results. Advertisements that contain people in them are more likely to be read than those with broad generalizations or mere statements of fact about products.[55]

Changes are constantly taking place in the use of color in the printed media. Certain types of products are much more realistically and effectively advertised in color. The slick magazines and more recently color TV have had a monopoly in this area. Daily newspapers are today using *color-i* to get the very best in color reproductions. Color-i is a full-page newspaper insert; it may be used in magazines also, however. It is preprinted in colorgravure conveying the true-to-life colors of the products themselves; delivered in rolls to newspapers or magazines it has only to be run through the presses in order to print the back with news items, other advertising, or editorials. This has variously been called *preprint, hi-fi,* and, more recently, the latest refinement of this process has been called *Specta-Color.*[56]

It has long been said that the *"stoppers"* in advertising are: women, babies, children, and animals. One study of many readership reports that covered thousands of advertisements indicated that the pictures that interested men the most were those of men and those that interested women the most were those of women.[57] The *illustration* is the most noteworthy part of the advertisement in attracting attention. In 1898 E. St. Elmo Lewis used AIDA as the word containing the initial letters of the key words in the steps in selling: *attention, interest, desire,* and *action.* These have since been used in textbooks concerning the writing of sales letters, advertising, and salesmanship. The element of *conviction* was later inserted between the desire-creation and action-getting elements.

A statistical analysis of readership figures for 2,500 advertisements in *The Saturday Evening Post* made by Harold J. Rudolph concluded that the picture depicting what might happen to the reader should he not use the product advertised was the most effective attention-getter. Other types of pictures in order of their effectiveness as stoppers were: testimonial of user, product in use, irrelevant, product, results of use. However, the picture that proved to be a good stopper did not always prove effective in inducing reading of the copy. The greatest loss of readers occurred in the case of illustrations of products or packages and of the product in use. Irrelevant illustrations had the lowest reader loss of any type of illustration indicating that such illustrations arouse the reader's curiosity and entice him into reading.[58]

Layout as an attention-getting device may be effective. The white spaces in the advertisement are usually designed to lead the reader's eyes to follow down the page to the product being advertised and the signature of the firm that is selling the product. This is called *structural motion.* Some have called it *gaze motion,* but others have defined gaze motion as being the use of something alive (person, animal), or once alive, gazing at the product being advertised. The conventional layout has the illustration, headline, copy, and signature in this order. There are many other ways to lay out an advertisement: forward S; backward S; forward C; backward C; forward Z; backward Z. There are various artistic approaches to breaking up the parts of the page.

The *trademark* is conceded to be important in advertising. Opinion Research Corporation made a study in 1960 of trademarks and what they tell consumers about a company. The study attempted to find the images created in the following areas: achievement, action, product and customer, personality, and esthetic. Among the many findings: modern or abstract designs indicated a scientific, research-minded, and modern company; masculine symbols indicated strength, power, and male customers. Most of the findings confirmed long-standing beliefs; some findings were surprising, however, as: bright colors suggested low prices; symbols pointing to the right were almost unanimously preferred to those pointing to the left.[59]

The areas of advertising that lend themselves to research are vast and the purpose here can be no more than merely to indicate a few of these.

Conclusions — A pamphlet issued some years ago by N. W. Ayer & Son, *The Written Word,* says: "Few sonnets ever written — and we assume that the sonnet is one of the most finished forms of the literary art — have been prepared with the thought and anxiety (we grant the poet the divine afflatus) that go into the creation of an effective and compelling advertisement." By now the student must realize that a great deal of time and study go into the preparation for the launching of an advertising campaign or even the writing of a single advertisement. Research of many types precedes the selection of the advertising theme for a given campaign. In the process of the writing, designing, and testing of the many advertisements that will go into a campaign, both the theme and the campaign as planned may be somewhat altered.

Eventually the advertisements are prepared, the media are selected, and the billions of dollars are spent to put the advertising before the consuming public. The advertiser is not then satisfied merely to know of the success or failure of the advertising; he wants to know why. He would like to try again that which made the advertising successful (despite the fact that it might not work next time); he would like to avoid that which brought about failure (likewise, it might not fail next time, but he usually feels he must place his gambling odds on the winning appeals and techniques). The problems in advertising generally remain: what to say? where to say it? and how much to spend for saying it?

Creative people in advertising cannot, however, be restrained by the "scientific" formulas, electronic data, and mathematical evaluations. The formulas have arisen and been replaced by others. The creative person may come up with an idea counter to all that research has revealed and it may work splendidly. Certainly in business and in advertising where the rewards are for innovation creativity can neither be overlooked nor held down by tales conceived by electronic brains. (The creative process was briefly discussed in Chapter II; but creativity is an elusive thing, sometimes apparently totally without formula.)

A study of members of the Sales Promotion Executive Association has revealed that promotion executives are generally responsible for advertising in some form or other and that they perform the following functions in the order named: sales meetings, advertising, direct mail, sales bulletins, writing copy, merchandising planning, public relations, printing production, contests, point of purchase, sales training, audiovisual aids, market research, sales manuals, and catalogues.[60] This listing indicates the many items that come under sales promotion, of which advertising is but part of the over-all picture. What is learned about advertising through research is usually applicable in the other areas as well.

PROJECTS

1. Read on current research pertaining to any area of advertising research; write a two-page summary commentary.

2. Read an article relative to the latest developments in MR or one summarizing an MR study. Be prepared to report on this orally in class.

ACKNOWLEDGMENTS AND REFERENCES

1 Scott, Walter Dill, *The Psychology of Advertising,* Small, Maynard & Company, Boston, 1908, p. 227.
2 *Ibid.,* p. 228ff.
3 *Ibid.,* p. 8ff.
4 *Ibid.,* p. 177.
5 —————, "Big Newspapers Hit by Move from Cities to Suburbs," *Business Week,* May 27, 1961, p. 103ff.
6 Wilson, John M., *Open the Mind and Close the Sale,* McGraw-Hill Book Co., Inc., New York, 1953, p. 200.
7 —————, "The Riddle of Consumer Behavior," *Business Week,* March 29, 1958, p. 95.
8 —————, "Hit 'em Again," *Newsweek,* April 17, 1961, p. 84ff.
9 —————, "Advertising: Non-Organization Man," *Newsweek,* September 5, 1960, p. 61ff.
10 Bogart, Leo, "How to Get More Out of Market Research," *Harvard Business Review,* Vol. 34, No. 1, January-February, 1956, p. 81.
11 Swan, Carroll J., "Are Motivationists Machiavellis?," *Printers' Ink,* Vol. 259, No. 5, May 3, 1957, pp. 56-57.
12 Lesser, Simon O., "Motivation Research and the Art of Business Writing," *The ABWA Bulletin,* Vol. XXII, No. 5, February, 1958, pp. 22-26.
13 Alderson, Wroe, "Major Issues in Motivation Research," *Marketing's Role in Scientific Management,* edited by Robert L. Clewett, American Marketing Association, 1957, pp. 271-281.
14 Williams, Robert J., "Is It True What They Say About Motivation Research?," *The Journal of Marketing,* Vol. XXII, No. 2, October, 1957, pp. 125-133.
15 Politz, Alfred, "Motivation Research Pitfalls," *Advertising Agency Magazine,* May 13, 1955, p. 41.
16 Rothwell, N. D., "Motivational Research Revisited," *The Journal of Marketing,* Vol. XX, No. 2, October, 1955, pp. 150-154.
   Dodge, Sherwood, "Research Has Come of Age in the Marketing Community," *Advertising Agency and Advertising and Selling,* May 3, 1954, p. 64ff.
17 Wells, William D., "Is Motivation Research Really an Instrument of the Devil?," *The Journal of Marketing,* Vol. XXI, No. 2, October, 1956, pp. 196-198.
18 Dichter, Ernest, "The Case for Motivational Research," *Advertising Agency Magazine,* March 2, 1956, p. 43.
19 Duvall, J. A., "Research . . . What Can It Do for Industrial Advertising?," *Industrial Marketing,* Vol. 40, No. 12, December, 1955, p. 104ff.

20 Case, Deryl, "The Place of Motivation Research in Marketing Research," *Marketing's Role in Scientific Management*, edited by Robert L. Clewett, American Marketing Association, 1957, p. 282-3ff.

21 Smith, George Horsley, *Motivation Research in Advertising and Marketing*, McGraw-Hill Book Co., Inc., New York, 1954, pp. 3-4.

22 Stryker, Perrin, "Motivation Research," *Fortune*, Vol. LIII, No. 6, June, 1956, p. 144ff.

23 Martineau, Pierre, *Motivation in Advertising*, McGraw-Hill Book Co., Inc., New York, 1957, p. 200.

24 *Ibid.*, p. 8.

25 *Ibid.*, p. 9.

26 Smith, *op. cit.*, p. 5ff.

27 ——————, "Is Anybody Listening?," *Fortune*, Vol. XLII, No. 3, September, 1950, p. 77ff.

28 Martineau, *op. cit.*, p. 144.

29 Smith, *op. cit.*, pp. 18-24.

30 Whyte, William H., Jr., "The Web of Word of Mouth," *Fortune*, Vol. L, No. 5, November, 1954, p. 140ff.

31 Katz, Elihu, "The Two-Step Flow of Communication: An Up-To-Date Report on an Hypothesis," *Public Opinion Quarterly*, Spring, 1957, pp. 61-78.

32 Carlson, Robert O., "How Can the Social Sciences Meet the Needs of Advertisers," *Printers' Ink*, October 30, 1953, p. 44ff.

33 Crisp, Richard D., *Marketing Research*, McGraw-Hill Book Co., Inc., New York, 1957, p. 662.

34 Smith, *op. cit.*, pp. 80-86.

35 Alevizos, John P., *Marketing Research*, Prentice-Hall, Inc., Englewood Cliffs, New Jersey, 1959, pp. 387-388.
    Smith, *op. cit.*, pp. 102-113.

36 Zober, Martin, "Some Projective Techniques Applied to Marketing Research," *The Journal of Marketing*, Vol. XX, No. 3, January, 1956, pp. 262-268.

37 Smith, *op. cit.*, pp. 148-165.

38 Hepner, H. W., *Psychology Applied to Life and Work*, Third Edition, Prentice-Hall, Inc., Englewood Cliffs, New Jersey, 1957, p. 550.

39 Dichter, Ernest, "Depth Interviewing," a talk given at Market Research Council, October 15, 1943.

40 Smith, *op. cit.*, pp. 36-43, 58-71.

41 Gallup, George, "Which Ad Sells Best," *Printers' Ink*, Vol. 259, No. 10, June 7, 1957, p. 38ff.

42 ——————, "Research Can Back Up Creativity," *Advertising Agency Magazine*, December 21, 1956, p. 9.

43 Swanson, Charles E., "Branded and Company Images Changed by Advertising," *Marketing's Role in Scientific Management*, edited by Robert L. Clewett, American Marketing Association, 1957, pp. 302-317.

44 Brooks, J., *Consumer Reports*, Vol. XXIII, No. 1, 1958, pp. 7-10.

45 Results obtained by James M. Vicary and reported in a memorandum from Subliminal Projection Co., Inc., to the Federal Communication Commission, January 13, 1958.
    Wilhelm, R., "Are Subliminal Commercials Bad?," *Michigan Business Review*, January, 1958, p. 26.

46 Burck, Gilbert, "What Makes Women Buy?," *Fortune*, Vol. LIV, No. 2, August, 1956, p. 93ff.

47 ——————, "U. S. Market — Women," *Executives' Guide to Marketing, 1964*, Vol. 284, No. 9, August 30, 1963, p. 38.

48 ——————, "What Makes Her Buy?," *Printers' Ink*, October 18, 1957, pp. 35-40.

49 Martineau, *op. cit.*, pp. 91-92.

50 —————————, *Current Population Reports — Series P-25*, No. 251. Projections assume fertility continues to 1975-80 at 1955-57 level.

51 —————————, "U. S. Market — Men," *Executives' Guide to Marketing, 1964*, Vol. 284, No. 9, August 30, 1963, pp. 29-32.

52 Siegle, Henry J., "How Hard Does Advertising Work?," *Printers' Ink*, Vol. 283, No. 11, June 14, 1963, pp. 353-354.

53 *Ibid.*, p. 354.

54 Dirksen, Charles J., and Kroeger, Arthur, *Advertising Principles and Problems*, Richard D. Irwin, Inc., Homewood, Illinois, 1960, pp. 82-89.

55 Hepner, *op. cit.*, pp. 566-569.

56 McClure, J. Warren, "To Them, All Business Is Local — The Newspapers," *Printers' Ink*, June 14, 1963, Vol. 283, No. 11.
—————————, "Hi-Fi Color Perks Up Instant Sanka," *Printers' Ink*, Vol. 275, No. 2, April 14, 1961, p. 54ff.

57 Wiseman, Mark, "Illustrations: 1," *Advertising and Selling*, February, 1947, pp. 74-76.

58 Rudolph, Harold J., *Attention and Interest Factors in Advertising*, Printers' Ink Business Bookshelf, Funk and Wagnalls Co., in association with Printers' Ink Publishing Co., Inc., New York, 1947, p. 68ff.

59 —————————, "Marketing, How to Test Your Trademark," *Business Week*, November 5, 1960, pp. 104-110.

60 Harnett, Joel, "The Means Are Many, the Goal but One," *Printers' Ink, Advertising Today, Yesterday, Tomorrow*, Vol. 283, No. 11, June 14, 1963, pp. 358-362.

CHAPTER XXIII

THE PSYCHOLOGY OF SELLING

What Is Sales Management? — Sales management is a part of the larger area of marketing management. Selling is a line function considered "organic" along with production. To the economist marketing is even considered a part of production since production is the creation of utilities. Generally, however, we think of production as creating *form utility* and of the marketing function as creating *time* and *place utilities* (i.e., having the goods at the time and place needed through storage and transportation), and *ownership utility* (i.e., putting goods into the hands of industrial and ultimate consumers who have need of them).

The line of authority in selling may extend from the board of directors and the president through a vice-president of marketing, a general sales manager, an assistant sales manager, a regional sales manager, a branch or field manager, down to the salesman. In large concerns line management is aided by staff people (see staff functions, Chapter X). In marketing the staff organization may include persons whose specialties are in: research, advertising, sales training, recruiting, control (including records, reports analyses, performance evaluation, systems), legal, labeling, packaging, brands, trademarks, and product development.

What Is Sales Promotion? — Since this is not a course in sales management, attention will be given in this chapter only to the personal selling phase of sales promotion. Advertising, the other phase of sales promotion, has been considered. Some phases of sales training were discussed in Chapter XIV.

Marketing and advertising research, advertising, personal selling, selection of salesmen, and sales training are inseparably linked together and at some level must be co-ordinated. Advertising men may help with writing training material, with visual aids and group sales meetings. Sales training helps to co-ordinate sales efforts with advertising. Salesmen themselves may assist in developing advertising themes, in getting information on competitors and competitive advertising, and in obtaining reactions from customers. The product research and consumer research phases of marketing research may often be done in separate departments, but they must work closely and the results of each must be communicated to salesmen and sales trainees. Since so much selling today is done through carefully planned advertising campaigns it is extremely important that selling and advertising work together and that the sale not be lost because of neglect at the place where it should be consummated. Point-of-sale and window displays are very important as are all other types of dealer aids and training. Policies relating to sales promotion of every kind must, in fact, be closely co-ordinated.

Sales Training — Methods of recruiting and selecting sales trainees were discussed in Chapters XI-XII; some of the courses given sales trainees and the methods and devices used in training them were discussed in Chapter XIV. Additional phases of sales training are reviewed here.

Textbooks and teachers' manuals for college salesmanship courses carry the talk said to be the first standardized sales talk or canvass. Entitled "How I Sell a National Cash Register," it was prepared by Joseph H. Crane under date of July, 1887.[1] Sales training began at the NCR Company with that sales talk. There are three goals in training this company's salesmen: (1) teaching need for the product, (2) giving knowledge of the product, and (3) training in skills necessary to sell the product.[2] In selecting salesmen many companies are anxious even today to obtain the young man who has had NCR training.

The proceeds of a volume entitled *Open the Mind and Close the Sale,* written by John M. Wilson, NCR vice president of sales, go to the National Sales Executives, Inc. One of Wilson's booklets gives the "10 Commandments of Selling": (1) organize your mind for selling, (2) appeal to the prospect's interest; (3) uncover the need, (4) ask questions and listen, (5) demonstrate specific benefits, (6) anticipate objections, (7) be persuasive in presenting benefits, (8) put a premium on your time, (9) call, call, call, . . . creatively, (10) be enthusiastic about products you sell as well as their value to the prospects.[3]

Westinghouse Electric Corporation also began its sales-training program in the nineteenth century. Westinghouse publishes a handbook for use in its graduate-student training course; this contains information about the training program, the company, and positions for which students are trained.[4]

The year 1906 can be definitely named as the year when insurance selling became better and the year when a pure food and drug bill was finally passed (see next chapter). Fitting of life insurance to the needs of the prospect came about the time of World War I. Insurance companies began in this period to develop training programs. The colleges became interested in life insurance as a field of study. The Million Dollar Round Table and the American College of Life Underwriters were established. With shortages of manpower during World War II there was added need to emphasize selection and training of life underwriters.[5]

In June, 1916, work on testing in the selection of salesmen was begun by psychologists on the staff of the Bureau of Salesmanship Research. One battery of selection tests, first used in insurance but also used in other fields, is included in the Steward Personnel Appraisal System. This is made up of four tests (mental ability, personality, interest, traits). It includes also: a personal inventory of background factors which is really an application blank; a four-page folder containing hundreds of items in twelve categories, called "guide to appraisal decision"; a twelve-page manual containing instructions for the candidate to use in the completing of the tests and blanks; and a thirty-two-page manual designed to aid employers of sales people to make the best use of the completed tests and blanks.[6]

By 1949 the National Sales Executive Federation, with a membership of 12,000 salesmen, had set up forty-six sales-training clinics. These offered a source of sales training for some of the smaller companies which felt they could not afford it.[7] The period of rapid growth in sales-training programs has been since World War II. A survey made in 1957 revealed that fifty-two of eighty firms (eight did not answer) had had their training programs fifteen years or less.[8]

The pioneer work of Taylor and Gilbreath in time and motion studies in industrial plants (Chapter X) has led to the present-day wide acceptance in manufacturing of such studies. The breaking of a sales job into parts and studying of those parts intensively and individually is, however, a complicated task. Salesmen are sometimes asked to study their own jobs and report on all the activities in which they engage. Such studies are usually incomplete and lacking in proficiency. They can furnish data on time breakdowns. Supervisors can gather time and motion data when they travel with salesmen, but the job of obtaining full and complete time and motion studies of salesmen is one that requires the full time of an investigator or investigators for long enough to obtain complete reports on an adequate number of salesmen to have a large enough sample that data are representative.

One of the most complete time and motion studies of salesmen was made of wholesale drug salesmen and reported on by James H. Davis, Ohio State University. Data on time spent by the ten most efficient and ten least efficient country salesmen were compared. Among the interesting facts unearthed by the study was that the efficient group spent

73.6 per cent of its call time in activities considered essential. The least efficient group spent only 50.7 per cent of its time in essential activities.[9] McKesson & Robbins, Inc., whose salesmen were used in the study just referred to, was one of ten out of eighty-eight firms (eleven per cent) that indicated that they did make time and motion studies of salesmen and used them in sales training.[10]

Time and motion studies furnish supervisors with data that can be used in setting up standards for salesmen in general, although territories differ, distances covered are not the same, and every selling job must be viewed on somewhat of an individual basis. It is not necessary that time and motion studies be made, but some sort of job analysis must be done in order that job specifications and/or job descriptions may be written. A job specification is usually broken into two parts: characteristics and demands of the job and requirements in the man to fill the job.

Sales managers in most companies have been salesmen. Three-fifths of 256 companies included in a NICB study made in 1948 said that their new executives came from the ranks of employees. Of 251 companies, 159 said they did not have organized training programs for training sales executives; 92 companies said they had organized programs.[11] It must be considered that many more have such training programs today since most firms do sales training and since most managers come up through the selling route. Eighty-six of eighty-eight firms reported in 1957 that their sales managers and supervisors have come mainly from their selling forces.[12]

Practically all of the firms that give formal course training to sales trainees give them a course in "salesmanship" (Chapter XIV). Salesmanship has been referred to as being "a communication art, the art of persuasion, ability to establish rapport, people ability, and applied psychology." Some writers have spoken of salesmanship as "a science," and some have called it "a profession." All of these things may be said to apply to some degree to salesmanship. The 1898 formula of Lewis (AIDA) has found its way into every textbook on salesmanship and, in general, the basic elements of selling are usually considered to be: (1) finding a customer; (2) learning about the customer; (3) getting to see the customer and getting him interested in your product; (4) creating desire for the product through demonstration and/or presentation of facts; (5) convincing the customer that your product will improve his position and that it is not only all that you have claimed for it but it is at least as good as if not better than its leading competitive products; (6) successfully getting the customer's name on the dotted line or getting verbal agreement to buy, and (7) making a proper departure to keep the goodwill of the purchaser and later providing whatever follow-up is necessary for the type of product you have sold, i.e., service, telephone call, personal call, mailed literature, or even a mailed questionnaire to determine satisfaction with the purchase. You will note that these steps follow the *attention, interest, desire, conviction, action* pattern.

In teaching the steps in making a sale, practically all companies use one or more of the following methods: (1) organized sales talk, (2) sales canvass, or (3) informal sales talk which roughly follows the AIDA outline. The sales canvass is often referred to as the "standardized sales talk." The organized talk permits more leeway than the canvass; it is not memorized verbatim, but an outline is used. The informal talk permits wide variation within the fixed general outline.[13]

It has been said that the person who is going to sell successfully should know: himself and his abilities, his customers (or prospective customers), his product, the markets for his product, his company and its policies, his company's competitors, something about human nature and the motives of people in general, something about selling and the psychology of selling, and how to make reports. Through resident sales schools, field instruction, and correspondence courses salesmen are being trained in all of these areas (Chapter XIV).

Programmed learning is being used extensively in teaching salesmanship to company trainees in such companies as IBM, NCR, Schering Corporation, the Squibb division of Olin Mathieson, Minneapolis-Honeywell, and other companies are rapidly turning to programmed learning.[14]

The remainder of this chapter attempts to briefly outline the steps in selling although it is to be realized by the reader that the application of these steps will vary widely with the product being sold as does the period of sales training vary from a day to as much as two years or more. In selling to industrial buyers technical knowledge and know-how are often much more important than knowledge of the techniques of selling. In fact, many persons would probably take part in making a single sale of electronic data processing equipment; some of these people might be considered "super salesmen" but all of them would possess some degree of technical knowledge about the product.

Finding the Customer — A salesman may be sent forth with a specific list of firms to be approached, but in practically all situations the salesman is expected to keep alert for new prospects. The types of prospecting usually detailed in textbooks on salesmanship include: endless chain (being referred by one customer to another); center of influence (an influential person refers the salesman to prospects); observation (the salesman listens, looks, reads); junior salesmen or "spotters" (these people find the prospects through personal calls or observation and report to the senior salesmen); canvassing (sometimes called "cold-turkey" canvass since the salesman simply knocks on doors or calls at purchasing offices); direct mail and telephone (letters asking for cards to be returned requesting the salesman to call or invitations to demonstrations or showrooms, or telephone calls requesting permission to demonstrate or call); directories; newspapers; and trade magazines.[15]

Finding Out About the Prospective Customer — The salesman must decide whether or not the prospect is the person authorized to buy (whether it be a firm or a family he is selling), whether or not there is need, want, or desire for the product, and whether or not the prospect has the money or the credit to buy. Credit agencies are used to determine credit rating. From other customers, fellow salesmen, company records, and other sources the salesman must find out anything that will be helpful in making the sale. It is necessary not only to know a prospect's name but a great deal more such as personality, hobbies, organizations affiliated with, educational background, and so forth. It is quite possible that one advertising man sold himself to a president of the United States because he had learned so much about him through the president's former secretary who became the advertising man's wife! Knowledge is power wherever it is possessed.

Sheldon's differentiation of the three familiar types of temperament (*endomorph, mesomorph, ectomorph*) has some use in sizing up a prospective customer (Chapter IX). Since most persons are mixtures of the three distinct types, the general idea of the *morphs* is only mildly helpful to a salesman in trying to determine the motives of prospects.[16]

Getting To See the Customer — The salesman may simply call at the place of business of the prospect and announce his name, firm, and purpose. He may supplement this by presentation of his business card. He may telephone for an appointment; he may write ahead for an appointment, or his firm may write for him; he may carry a letter of introduction with him. The salesman who uses the straight-forward approach generally wins the goodwill of the receptionist or secretary chiefly responsible for getting him "in" to see the boss. It is usually not so difficult for a salesman to get to see the prospect; the difficulty is to get his attention and hold his interest until a presentation or demonstration can be made to show the benefits of the product to the prospect or to his firm.

The salesman may tell a good *anecdote* or joke to begin with; the story will work more effectively if it is directly connected with the salesman's proposition. He may use a *problem* or a *question* to start the interview; again there should be a tie-in with the product being sold. A *salient* fact about the product or even a *startling* one may be used as an opener. A *news story* or a *narrative* may be used; the name of a *mutual acquaintance* may be mentioned; something to *arouse curiosity* may be said or done. A *hypothetical statement* may start the prospect to thinking, as, for instance: "If someone could show you how to make a thousand extra dollars, you would listen wouldn't you? Well, I am going to show you something that will save you a thousand dollars!" The salesman may open his portfolio, pull out a model, set up an exhibit, or give a demonstration; but he has to have a certain sensitivity as to what is right to say and do in order to be allowed to get through a presentation and attempt a close. In the case of some types of selling, of course, the attention and interest phase of selling may go on for days or even weeks before the salesman is ready to present the type of program or proposition desired or needed by the prospect. He may, because of his prior tactfulness, be asked to present his plan for solving the prospect's problem. He must be alert enough to have a better plan than his competitor's salesman.

In getting and holding the attention of the prospect, a salesman should use the *talking points about his product* that he feels will *appeal to* and *motivate* this particular buyer. Motivation research may reveal the reasons that people in general and classes of people in particular buy a product; motivation research cannot tell a salesman why a certain person will or will not buy his product. The clues given by MR may aid him in evaluating his prospect; it is up to the salesman to do a little "digging" of his own if he is to unearth his client's motives.

In general people are motivated by: *pleasure; comfort; pride; ego-striving; economy of time and money; desire for wealth; imitation and emulation of others, and the opposite of this, desire to lead rather than follow; love of family, friends, and the opposite sex; love of adventure and desire for new experiences; curiosity; the urge to create; love of beauty; love of justice and right; patriotism; fear and caution; desire for immortality* (and some people are motivated by the same word with the *t* omitted!); *power; fame; need to establish roots, to belong; self-betterment; social approval; security; and basic motives and drives for food, clothing, and shelter.* In selling to a dealer, a businessman, or an industrialist, however, a salesman may find that the basic motives in buying are very practical, as: *turnover of merchandise; margin of profit; availability of parts and service; advertising aids and/or cooperative advertising (manufacturer assists the dealer in paying for advertising); quality and reputation of the product; reputation of the salesman's firm; discounts; other special inducements.* Nevertheless, every buyer is "human" although the business buyer is more inclined to be motivated by the practical and profitable, as a person he is likely to be appealed to as the father who wants to buy ponies for his children or take his family to Europe, or as the childless widower out to attain fame as a novelist! It is up to the salesman if he can do so to find the "gimmick" that makes a prospect tick; there is no formula that will work on the prospect who turns out to be clever enough to find the "gimmick" that makes the salesman tick!

Talking points must appeal to buying motives. In selling an automobile to someone motivated by economy, the talking point might be: "This little automobile will get thirty miles to the gallon." In selling to someone motivated by both comfort and economy the talking point might be: "This is the most comfortable little automobile on the market." In selling a laundryman who is motivated by profit, the talking point might be: "This machine will turn out twice the work of your present machine! You'll have to put it in! It will save you enough in six months to take care of the sunk cost in the old machine; after that, this machine will double your profit."

Creating Desire through the Demonstration and/or Presentation —Showmanship and *appeals to the senses* are important in selling some types of products; the senses of *sight, smell, taste,* and *touch* are appealed to if the salesman serves his prospects a meal cooked in the pots and pans he is selling. It is showmanship to have a "party" and present gifts to those people who buy the most of the product being sold, or who draw the lucky number or get the "door" prize. If a piano is being sold, the prospect *hears* it played, or even better he plays it. There are many ways of dramatizing a sale: through all types of *films, pictures, charts,* and *tables;* through letting the prospect actually *use* or *test* the product; through *models, samples, portfolios;* through *demonstrating* the many uses of a given product, or simply how to use a given product, as a sewing machine. There is dramatization through *visualizing* what the product will do for the customer, the pleasure it will give, the time it will save and what can be done with that "saved" time.

Comparison may be used to enable the prospect to see what the product will do for him and to help him better visualize its qualities. Figures of speech are helpful in comparison. Some of the more common figures of speech are: *metaphor, simile, hyperbole, personification,* and *analogy.* Useful also in selling, direct mail, and advertising are *alliteration* and *onomatopoeia.* Even *rhyming* and *rhythm* are employed especially in advertising and direct mail.

Figures of speech have ever been of aid to literary writers in attaining picturesqueness and clarity. Gene Fowler who wrote the delightful *Goodnight, Sweet Prince,* a story of John Barrymore's life, left a volume,

Skyline, that was published posthumously. In *Skyline* he described outstanding people of his day. He used hyperboles (gross exaggerations),
metaphors, similes, onomatopoeia, alliteration, and other figures of
speech and colorful languge. Babe Ruth's stomach didn't just rumble;
it rumbled like Mount Stromboli! Gertrude Stein was not just a friend
of left-bank artists; she was a "Left Bank Sappho singing through an
eggbeater." Brisbane, the great editor, didn't just pass one by; he
"plunged past us like Diogenes playing Holy Cross." [17]

The hyperbole is probably one figure of speech that should be used
sparingly by salesmen. An old Nash advertisement, however, contained
the following figures of speech, hyperboles and all:

If you see someone *buzzing* along — onomatopoeia
. . . when a car *goes ghosting* — alliteration and personification
"I haven't stopped in for gas for weeks" — hyperbole (probably!)
. . . it's *quiet as a mouse* — simile
You can *park it on a dime,* and *U-turn it on a nickel* — hyperbole
. . . that doesn't *rattle* or *squeak* — onomatopoeia
. . . soft coil springs *cushioning the wheels,*
　　you can't raise a bump even on a winter-*rutted road.* — metaphor
　　(implied — i.e., springs are cushions) and alliteration

If a salesman says, "This engine purrs like a kitten," he has used personification, onomatopoeia, and simile. The analogy is an extended
metaphor. In selling a farmer on building a shed for his combines,
tractors, and other expensive equipment, the contractor might look out
at the farmer's children playing nearby and say: "You wouldn't think
of requiring them to live out in the open to endure the rain and sun,
the cold and the heat. Of course, they are precious to you, your children, and you provide them with suitable shelter. But this equipment
is precious, too, in dollars and cents. You can add many years of life
to that combine if it is properly housed. In the long run this building I
propose will actually cost only a fraction of what it will save in longer
life for your equipment." The salesman should be able to follow this up
with actual figures or approximations.

The salesman may win the *belief* and *confidence* of his customer by
his *manner,* by his attitude toward his own company and product as well
as his attitude toward competitive products. It is usually best not to
"knock" a competitive product. A salesman should not, however, ignore
the existence of competitors' products especially if they have been mentioned, and he should not appear ill at ease when they are referred to
by the customer. He should know them well enough to know any strong
points to emphasize about his own product in comparing it with them.

Other ways of winning the prospect's belief in the product are: by offering a *guarantee;* by giving *test results,* testing the product, or letting the prospect test it; using *testimonials* of others who have used the product; by submitting a *list of satisfied users;* by giving a *sample;* by letting the prospect keep the product for a period of time, i.e., *free trial.* Perhaps nothing will win conviction, however, if the *reputation* of the firm is not good, or if the salesman is lacking in *information* about the product or the firm.

Answering Questions and/or Objections — The experienced salesman usually welcomes questions and even objections. These give him an opportunity to dispel whatever is in the mind of the buyer that is keeping him from buying. It is when a prospect says nothing but will not buy that the salesman becomes frustrated. He feels that if he could only find out "Why?" he could complete the sale. In some cases the salesman anticipates objections and answers them before they are raised. In most cases he answers immediately as the questions are raised. In other cases he may choose to ignore the questions altogether, as, for instance, if they are petty objections merely raised in the attempt to delay action. If the questions or objections pertain to price, they may be ignored at the time they are raised since the salesman may feel that he can answer such objections better after he has convinced the prospect that the product being sold will do more for him than any other similar product.

Some of the ways of meeting objections are: *boomerang,* i.e., turn the objection into a reason for buying; *direct denial; indirect denial* or *"yes-but"; compensation* or *"offset"; question;* and *pass-up* or *ignore.*[18]

In some instances one answer may encompass several of these techniques, as, for instance, a prospect who is himself a traveling salesman may object to buying an automobile: "This car is beautiful and I would like to own it, but it is too heavy. I had in mind a lighter, less expensive car." The salesman might reply, "Yes, the car is heavier than the one you have been driving and it does cost more, but that is the very reason you should buy it. You *need* a heavier, safer car. You are on the highway so much. It is like paying insurance; you don't need it if everything goes along all right; but you do want it, don't you, just in case something goes wrong? This car does cost more, but it is safer." This has some of the elements of the "yes-but," the "compensation," the "question," and the "boomerang" techniques. To the objection the salesman might have said: "No, it is not too heavy, and it doesn't cost too much for your income." From this direct denial (which is less tactful than the indirect denial) he might have gone on to use other arguments.

Closing the Sale — Swift & Company's booklet, *Six Ways to Ask for the Order,* names ways of closing a sale: (1) assume assent; (2) suppose; (3) dramatize; (4) command; (5) "No" means "Yes," and (6) isolate the objection.[19] Swift's products lend themselves to the standardized sales talk. The Scott and Fetzer Company, direct seller of vacuum cleaners, expects its salesmen to memorize a lengthy sequence designed to build up to a strong climax and close.[20] The Thomas A. Edison Industries requires that the voice-writing story be memorized. It also suggests aids for memorizing.[21] The Victor Adding Machine Company uses graphic illustrations of the steps in making a sale and cautions salesmen that because they must meet quotas they must draw from the only source available to them of constant quality: the canvass.[22] These firms illustrate processors or manufacturers of products that lend themselves to selling by use of standardized sales talks. It must be kept in mind that a sales engineer or any salesman who creates ideas for adapting products to company needs and at the same time sells could scarcely use a standardized talk. Nevertheless, he might employ some of the techniques of the standardized canvass.

Insurance is another area where the canvass can be used profitably. Abbot P. Smith has told the story of Harry to illustrate how a below-average salesman "established a record far above average" by following the company's prepared talk. Harry not only barged across the room to sit in the big chair so that prospects would sit across from him on the sofa, every word he spoke was from the canvass; he asked the questions the book said to ask; he gave the answers the book said to give; he closed the way the book said to close.[23]

Hegarty has given six ways to "topple the prospect who is almost but still not quite a buyer." Briefly here they are: (1) use a question that assumes the customer has bought; (2) one that shows what he will lose by not buying now; (3) one that leads into a summation; (4) one that offers reassurance; (5) one that brings out the point you've been holding as a reserve clincher; (6) a question that asks him to buy. If the original question that leads into each of these steps is skillfully worked out, the procedure is supposed to work.[24]

Each salesman would have to prepare his own questions for his particular product. If he is selling neckties in a retail store, he might say: "Do you want the blue one or the green one?" If the customer says, "I am just looking," the salesman might say, "These neckties just came in yesterday and they have been selling like hotcakes." The customer might reply, "They have!" The salesman could say, "Yes, this new weave sells itself and the colors are so subtle. These ties were featured in last month's *Playboy* (to the young man) or *Esquire* (or wherever they have been featured!)." The clincher might be the name of some well-known person who has just bought several of the ties. Finally, the salesman asks, "Why don't you take two or three of these ties; they will give you a lift." Or he might simply say, "How many do you want?"

Some additional ways to close are: *continued affirmation*, that is, getting "yes" answers to questions throughout the interview on the assumption that being in a "yes" frame of mind the prospect will say yes when he is asked to buy; *erecting barriers*, as when a salesman gets a prospect to say that he will buy if he can find a product that meets his specifications (the salesman gets the specifications and shows that his product meets them); *closing on a minor point*, as when the Cadillac salesman says that this brake is not only self-adjusting it cannot be released by anyone unless the engine is running and the brake has been pulled from "park" to "drive" and the customer who has heard about cars getting loose on inclines because children tampered with the brakes buys this one to be safe; *SRO* or *standing room only* technique which lets the customer know that if he doesn't buy or sign up now the product may be gone by tomorrow (to the ultimate consumer), or some other dealer may sign up to handle the product (to the dealer); using *emotion* such as fear, affection, or pride; offering *special inducements* such as "buy one and get another for a penny," or "buy now and pay later."

Following Up on the Sale — The sale itself is completed when the buyer says that he will buy; what is done in the next few minutes is, however, very important. The contract and the pen should be ready, and the salesman should be at ease in asking for the signature. If no written contract is needed, the manner of the salesman in completing the details of delivery should be appreciative but not so much so that the customer feels that he is doing the salesman a favor. A good salesman in a subtle manner makes the customer feel that a favor has been done for him. Appliance and automobile *dealer service* are extremely important in keeping customers sold; good service makes it easy for the salesman to sell the next time. Other ways of keeping the customer aware of the firm and its products are: publications for customers; letters and telephone calls to customers; occasional personal calls by the salesman although he may expect to sell nothing.

Conclusions — Persuasion is an art and selling requires persuasion. There are, of course, limits to persuasion if it is misapplied. Many people, however, like to be persuaded; they may not want to buy unless they are persuaded. To the extent that people want and expect to be sold, then salesmen are not to be condemned for applying the techniques that they believe will work in getting a particular prospect to buy.

Dr. Ernest Dichter has analyzed the many consumers who experience "serious inhibitions when faced with the problem of buying a product they have never used." These people may actually desire to possess the product and may have the money to buy, but they resist buying because they are novices. They quite often want to be sold, or, in effect, educated in how to use the product and overcome their self-consciousness. The problem of the novice is that others know what and how to do and what is expected; the novice does not. He is fearful that others are watching him. Dichter says that this *distortion* leads to *fears* that *threaten* his *self-image*. If the novice is not "reasonably well adjusted" he may conclude that he will fail in the new experience. The ways he may react are: (1) by *passive resistance,* that is, he just doesn't get around to "buying" or participating in the new experience; (2) *approach and retreat,* which leads to looking but finding excuses for not buying; (3) *exaggerated emotional resistance,* which leads the novice to over-react (by blushing, becoming angry, or firmly refusing to be swayed) to pressure to do, enter into, buy, use, or enjoy the thing that he wants; (4) *rationalization,* which leads to the concocting of "rational" reasons for not doing the thing he wants to do or buying the product he has coveted; (5) *destructive activity,* in which the novice (particularly if he is a child) may actually destroy another's property or break up the games of others.

Dr. Dichter gives ten ways (long used by parents and teachers but little used in selling) to teach the novice to buy: (1) make the novice welcome by dispelling his feeling of being an "outsider"; (2) make him feel that he was the very person for whom the product was created; (3) eliminate semantic problems by using language the prospect understands, i.e., forget the jargon of the specialized products and fields; (4) enable the prospect to visualize himself in the situation or using the product; (5) emphasize the pleasures of discovery; (6) lead the novice to experience by a step at a time; (7) indicate the rewards to be gained at once; (8) give permission to make mistakes; (9) don't emphasize the differences between the novice and the expert; (10) be patient and understanding.[25]

The salesman who teaches the old-maid schoolteacher how to drive an automobile may be aiding a novice to attain something she has always wanted but feared to buy because she thought people would see the mistakes she made when she drove for the first time. Salesmen have done their part to educate consumers as to the use of products and to help them overcome their anxieties at experiencing the "new" situation or possessing and using the new product.

PROJECTS

1. Find an advertisement for each of the following products and briefly indicate the main buying motives appealed to in each instance: (a) an item of clothing; (b) a drink; (c) a food product; (d) an automobile; (e) a household or garden tool of some type.

2. What appeals would you use in selling shoes to the following persons: (a) a woman teacher, unmarried; (b) a male teacher with a family; (c) a medical doctor; (d) a small-town department store owner; (e) a child ten years of age accompanied by her mother.

3. Give the talking points you would use in selling a suit to a man if his main motivation seemed to be (a) economy; (b) love of beauty; (c) desire for power and/or fame; (d) social approval; (e) love of adventure and new experiences.

4. Write a sales canvass (using the selling steps discussed in this chapter) suitable for use in selling any hard-line consumer product with which you are most familiar.

ACKNOWLEDGMENTS AND REFERENCES

1 Russell, Frederic A., and Beach, Frank Herman, *Teachers' Manual and Key to Student Workbook for Textbook of Salesmanship,* McGraw-Hill Book Company, Inc., New York, 1955, pp. 19-21.

2 —————, *Training Solutions of Company Problems,* Studies in Personnel Policy, No. 18, National Industrial Conference Board, Inc., 247 Park Avenue, New York 17, N. Y., 1940.

3 Wilson, John M., "10 Commandments of Selling," *Salesmanship as an Art,* The National Cash Register Company, Dayton, Ohio, 1957, pp. 55-56.

4 —————, *Handbook for Graduate Students,* Educational Department, Westinghouse Electric Corporation, Mansfield, Ohio, pp. 1-44.

5 —————, *Basic Reading Material,* Salesmanship, Volume II, The Mutual Benefit Life Insurance Company, 300 Broadway, Newark 4, New Jersey, no date, pp. 1-5.

6 Halsey, George D., *Selecting and Inducting Employees,* Harper & Brothers, New York, 1951, pp. 174-176.

7 —————, "What's the Matter with American Salesmanship?," *Fortune,* Vol. XL, No. 2, September, 1949, p. 67ff.

8 Adams, Loyce, "A Study of Sales-training Programs in Eighty-eight Firms," a dissertation, The University of Texas, Austin, 1959 (University Microfilms, Inc., 313 N. First St., Ann Arbor, Michigan), p. 48ff.

9 Phelps, D. M. *Sales Management,* Richard D. Irwin, Inc., Homewood, Illinois, 1953, pp. 758-769.

10 Adams, *op. cit.,* p. 53.

11 Fitzgerald, Thomas A., *Sales Organization and Compensation of Executives,* Studies in Personnel Policy, No. 28, National Industrial Conference Board, Inc., New York, 1948, pp. 18-34.

12 Adams, *op. cit.,* p. 64.

13 *Ibid.,* pp. 160-162.
14 Morse, Leon, "How To Create a Salesman," *Dun's Review,* December, 1963, p. 46ff.
15 Greif, Edwin Charles, *Modern Salesmanship Principles and Problems,* Prentice-Hall, Inc., Englewood Cliffs, New Jersey, 1958, pp. 186-198.
    Russell, Frederic A., Beach, Frank H., Buskirk, Richard H., *Textbook of Salesmanship,* Seventh Edition, McGraw-Hill Book Co., Inc., New York, 1963, pp. 152-176.
16 Sheldon, William H., *The Varieties of Human Physique,* Harper & Row, Publishers, Inc., New York, 1940, and *The Varieties of Temperament,* same publisher, 1942.
17 Fowler, Gene, *Skyline,* Viking Press, New York, 1961
18 Many textbooks on salesmanship have used these.
19 ——————, *Six Ways to Ask for the Order,* Swift & Company, Union Stock Yards, Chicago 9, Illinois.
20 ——————, *How to Sell Kirby,* The Scott and Fetzer Co., 1920 W. 114th Corner Franklin Blvd., Cleveland 2, Ohio, 1954, pp. 1-105.
21 ——————, *Voicewriter Sales Training,* Thomas A. Edison Industries, West Orange, New Jersey, no date.
22 ——————, *Salesmen's Basic Training Guide,* Victor Adding Machine Company, 3900 North Rockwell Street, Chicago 18, Illinois, 1953, Chart No. 7.
23 Smith, Abbot P., "How to Close on the First Call," *Salesmanship,* edited by Steven J. Shaw and Joseph W. Thompson, Henry Holt and Co., Inc., 383 Madison Avenue, New York 17, N. Y., 1960, pp. 406-409.
24 Hegarty, Ed. J., "How Good Are Your Clinchers?," *Salesmanship, ibid.,* pp. 414-419.
25 Dichter, Ernest, "Ten Ways of Teaching the Novice to Buy Your Product," *Salesmanship, ibid.,* pp. 153-157.

SECTION VI — PSYCHOLOGICAL INFLUENCES IN ECONOMICS

CHAPTER XXIV

CONSUMER MOVEMENTS

The year 1906 marks a turning point in the United States for consumers. The "crusade of the muckrakers" had had its beginning; Upton Sinclair's *The Jungle,* which attacked the meat industry, had recently been published. Florence Kelley and Jane Addams had crusaded for the downtrodden, for labor, and for consumers. Dr. Harvey W. Wiley, Chief of the Bureau of Chemistry, had made scientific reports on food adulteration. The Federal Food and Drug Act of 1906 was passed. This paved the way for legislation passed in the years from 1906 to the present time. Millions of pages have been written about consumers, consumer education, consumer leagues, consumer legislation, and consumer standards. The attitudes of those with something to sell changed with the changing tide, and business began programs to educate both consumers and employees. The generally high quality of consumer goods in the United States, the many services that go with those goods, and the generally higher type of salesmanship that exists in this country are not the results of sudden upheavals. They are the outcome of gradual development, movements, federal action, and changing objectives on the part of business.[1]

Early Social and Consumer Movements — The movement for laws to protect consumers had its beginning in the United States around 1880. Dr. Harvey W. Wiley, pioneer agitator for a food and drug law, proved that many of the preservatives used in the 1870's and 1880's were poison, or at least enough so to be dangerous. Harmful drugs were also being put on the market. Florence Kelley probably had as much share in early consumer movements as anyone. While studying in Zurich, Switzerland, she had translated *The Conditions of the Working Classes in England in 1844* by Frederick Engels. When her marriage ended she returned to the United States, resumed her maiden name, kept custody of her three children, and began a life of public work. In 1889 she read a paper on child labor before the chiefs and commissioners of labor statistics at their seventh annual convention. She published an article in 1890 based on the 1880 census report showing that a million children under fifteen years of age were working. It is significant, also, that in 1889 Hull House was founded in Chicago by Jane Addams; in New York Vida Scudder and others were at the same time setting up the College Settlement. These were the first social settlements in the United States.

To Hull House and to the home of Henry Demarest Lloyd, Florence Kelley brought her children in 1891. Lloyd was at the time engaged in writing *Wealth Against Commonwealth,* a study of oil, steel, and coal monopolies and their control of the railroads. So many things of social significance were happening in this period. The Haymarket riot of May 1, 1886, which resulted in the hanging of three persons (one committed suicide and three were imprisoned but later pardoned by Governor John P. Altgeld who had been pressed to give the pardon by the Hull House group, Lloyd, and others), was but one of many incidents that reflect the unrest of the latter part of the nineteenth century. The railroad strike of 1894 was another.[2]

Florence Kelley guided Illinois legislators to pass its first factory law in 1893: sanitary conditions were regulated; fourteen was fixed as the age at which children might be employed; an eight-hour statute was passed, the eight hours applying to women and children in factories. Governor Altgeld appointed Mrs. Kelley head of the Factory Inspection Department. When the eight-hour day provision was declared invalid by the Supreme Court of Illinois in 1895 on the basis that it interfered with the workers' "freedom of contract," Mrs. Kelley was highly critical, and in 1897 she was replaced as factory inspector. She remained at Hull House, however, speaking often, writing much. Her thirteen years of residing in settlement houses provided many of the stories related in *Some Ethical Gains Through Legislation.* Some of the stories, too, came out of service beginning in 1899 as Secretary of the National Consumers' League. The volume related stories of goods produced under the worst of conditions: nuts cracked at seven cents a pound by a tubercular father of a small boy who had lost both hands from cancer; stories of adulterated "imported" Italian olive oils and other foods; a consumptive woman propped among pillows making wedding cake boxes, moistening the edges by licking to make the gum hold; smallpox in the home of a tailor; typhoid germs in milk bottles; cream thickened by cornstarch, poisoning the diabetic trying to follow his fat diet; glucose for sugar; acetic acid for vinegar; paper in the shoe soles; smallpox, measles, scarlet fever, sore eyes, skin diseases in the newly purchased garments.[3]

Mrs. Kelley pointed out that enlightened ethical consumers were setting standards which must eventually bring changes in production and distribution. The masses of purchasers, however, being ignorant and uninformed, constituted the most formidable barrier to realizing change. These people would have to be educated. Physicians, philanthropists, public authorities, manufacturers, the Consumers' League, and chiefly the trade unions, Mrs. Kelley cited as sources of effort on behalf of consumers and their enlightenment. The press and the advertising merchants were cited as not contributing to the education of consumers; their efforts were meant to "persuade, incite, entice, and induce" purchases. Laws that existed had been brought about by producers protecting their own interests. Even the federal bureau's laboratories for investigation of imported articles operated not for protection of consumers but in the interest of producers. It was left to local boards of health, state chemists, and food and dairy commissions to furnish whatever protection they could.[4]

Early attempts at getting legislation brought about only the ineffectual methods that existed by 1905 for dealing with tenement manufacture. Nor had there been any success with getting a law to protect consumers. The first pure food and drug bill was introduced in 1889; it passed the Senate but not the House. Before the passage of the 1906 Pure Food and Drug Act, *140 such bills had been introduced.* A study of the literature of the period seems to reveal three outstanding factors that led at last to the passage of the 1906 act: (1) the fight on "big business," i.e., monopoly controls; (2) the crusade of the "muckrakers"; and (3) the consumers' movement led by various organizations, principal one of which was probably the Consumers' League.

MONOPOLY CONTROLS — The economic system which grew up following the railroads of the middle part of the nineteenth century brought about the trusts; big labor was also developing, but it was some laps behind. Stuart Chase has said that business, labor, and agriculture have all had their pressure groups. Strangely enough, or perhaps not so strangely, the consumer pressure group, the National Consumers' League, actually concerned itself chiefly with labor legislation.[5] While the League did have its origin in work for legislation to protect department store employees, it did become a force in getting consumer legislation passed. Likewise it may be said that although the Sherman Antitrust Act (1890) is usually thought of as regulating "big business" and not as being a law relating to consumers, actually the enforcement of the intent of the law (breaking up of monopolies) often does result in direct effect on consumers.[6]

During the 1880's mergers had formed at so rapid a rate that people had begun to fear that the small competitors would be driven out of business. The Sherman Act provided that agreements made "in restraint of trade" were illegal and declared monopolies illegal. Since it was believed that a good deal of monopolization could exist without breaking the law, the act was not strongly enforced.[7] The fact that the law was passed, however, indicated a change in thinking relative to government interference in business. From the time of the publication of Adam Smith's *The Wealth of Nations* (1776) and the days of the Physiocrats, business had operated under the *laissez-faire* doctrine. In justice to Adam Smith, who has been repeatedly quoted as the father of *laissez faire,* it must be said that although he advocated freedom of trade he never "fancied that the interests of the producer and the consumer were identical." [8] He couldn't help but notice that "whenever merchants get together they try to combine, to form a monopoly." [9] The Sherman Act marked a middle-class reform movement supported in politics "by the careers of Bryan, Roosevelt and the earlier Wilson." [10]

THE CRUSADE OF THE MUCKRAKERS — Following Dr. Wiley's scientific reports, the cudgel was taken up by *Ladies' Home Journal* and *Collier's Weekly* which campaigned against the patent medicine frauds. *McClure's Magazine* also published muckraking articles. The General Federation of Women's Clubs organized a committee in 1904 to get the public interested in getting a food and drug bill passed.[11] Coincidentally with the writing of Florence Kelley, other outstanding works appeared. In the *Appeal to Reason,* socialist weekly published in Girard, Kansas, Upton Sinclair's *The Jungle* appeared in 1905. This story of Packingtown's working-class life had been intended to hit "the public's heart." Instead it hit the public "in the stomach." *The Jungle* marked the climax of the muckraker era. Lincoln Steffens had written of municipal corruption; Tom Lawson of the sensations of Wall Street; Ray Stannard Baker (David Grayson) had written of the Beef Trust finance; Ida M. Tarbell had written about Standard Oil (mother of trusts). David Graham Phillips, Robert Herrick, Frank Norris and others had written about social problems. Jack London and fellow "social revolutionists" had been listened to by large numbers of people. Professor Thorstein Veblen had written *The Theory of the Leisure Class.* At a time when bullets were finding their mark in labor disputes, *The Jungle's* attack on the meat industry was enough to stir up notice. "Big Business," in return, attacked the free magazines that were carrying the muckraker stories, and the magazines asked their writers to discontinue searching into industrial conditions. "The Uncle Tom's Cabin of wage slavery," as Jack London called *The Jungle,* was a best seller in the United States, England, and the British colonies. Its appearance no doubt helped to bring about legislation. Nevertheless, the law as finally passed had had "its teeth drawn first." [12] *The Jungle's* author on the occasion of a visit to Chicago enjoyed sitting next to Jane Addams at dinner and delivering speeches similar to those found toward the end of his book.[13]

The writings of the muckrakers continued despite the protests of business on past the period 1880-1906. Accounts of their works and effects on the society of the United States can be found in Lincoln Steffens' autobiography (1931), and in *Literary History of the United States,* edited by Spiller, Thorp, Johnson, and Canby (1948). Upton Sinclair himself attacked the churches, distortion of journalism by pressure of advertisers, American universities, and the public schools. According to Fischer, much credit may go to movements that arose with the Muckrakers for the fact that by 1940 almost all of the Socialist platform of 1904 "had been enacted into law — by Republicans and Democrats." [14]

THE CONSUMERS' LEAGUE AND ORGANIZATIONS FOR CONSUMER LEGISLATION — The Consumers' League had its beginning in 1891 and during its first five years worked for legislation to protect department store employees; women in factories had a ten-hour law, but department store workers often worked much more than the ten-hour day. The first head of the Consumers' League was Josephine Shaw Lowell, widow of Charles Russell Lowell. Under her leadership the Consumers' League aspired to have goods marked with labels that guaranteed they had been produced "under good working conditions." In May, 1899, Mrs. Kelley became general secretary of the organization; in the year 1903 alone she addressed 111 meetings in fifteen states — and in a day when there were no airplanes or automobiles! It was an ordinary event for her to travel in the dead of winter to New England to address girls who were studying economics or sociology. Today the National Consumers' League label on white goods may seem, said Josephine Goldmark, "naive and negligible." In 1900 it was far ahead of its time. Today the FLSA and the collective bargaining of unions eliminate the work in tenement homes. Three provisos were required for qualifying for the label: prohibition of tenement homework and the work of children under sixteen, and the factory itself had to observe state laws. Although seventy firms in a ten-year period used the Consumers' League label, Mrs. Kelley was not satisfied; the label did not guarantee fair wages.[15]

The Period, 1907-1938 — During the years following the passage of the 1906 Pure Food and Drugs Act, many agencies at one time or another had responsibility for enforcing it: Bureau of Chemistry, 1907-1927; Food, Drug, and Insecticide Administration, 1928-1929; Food and Drug Administration, Department of Agriculture, 1930-1940. In 1940 the Food and Drug Administration was transferred from the

Department of Agriculture to the Federal Security Agency, and with the advent of the Department of Health, Education, and Welfare the FDA was under that department. Only six persons made reports during the period 1907-1949, beginning with Dr. Wiley who served until 1911.[16] There were numbers of attempts to pass a new law or to pass amendments, and five amendments to the law were passed. It is not the purpose here, however, to trace the many and varied legal and court processes so much as it is to indicate the climate of thinking of the people that led to the passage of other consumer legislation. There were many difficulties in enforcing the law. Because of these difficulties the people who had administered the act helped to prepare a bill introduced June 6, 1933. By this time forty-two states had their own laws; from June 12, 1933, through August 12, 1935, various forms of the Copeland bill and other similar bills, totaling over twenty, were introduced. A lobby against the Copeland bill was led by the Walgreen interests; drug, magazine, legal, and other organizations, however, lined up behind the law.[17] Nevertheless, the national legislature ran into the problem of jurisdictional jealousies in trying to enact a new law; the primary feud was between the FDA and the FTC. Politically the FTC seemed to have at the time more influence than the FDA.[18]

In 1938 the Federal Food, Drug, and Cosmetic Act was passed. It prohibited adulteration and misbranding of products in interstate and foreign commerce and was to be administered by the FDA. A complementary part of this act was the 1938 amendment of the Federal Trade Commission Act of 1914. Known as the Wheeler-Lea Act, it prohibited false advertising and was to be administered by the FTC. The laws thus overlap in application but are divided in administration. Supplementary acts include statutes regulating meat, butter, tea, and milk imports, filled milk and cheese, adulterated and renovated butter, oleomargarine, apples, pears, containers for fruits and vegetables, and agricultural products. Drug statutes include narcotics and human animal biological drugs.[19] There have been other amendments pertaining to food additives (1958) and drugs. In fact, since the FDA was placed under the Health, Education, and Welfare Department (created in 1954) there has been tremendous growth of government sponsored medical research and additional consumer legislation.[20]

Charles Wesley Dunn in *Printers' Ink* explained that under the Wheeler-Lea Act: (1) the Commission no longer need prove that the practice it is challenging is unfair to competitors; the act reached to unfair consumer practices as well as unfair trade practices; violation of cease and desist orders became subject to civil penalties and the court could "issue *pedente lite* writs against a method, act or practice subject to a cease and desist order before it for review, if deemed necessary to prevent injury to the public or competitors"; (2) strengthened the law as to advertisement of foods, drugs, devices, and cosmetics; provided that a commissioner should continue to serve at the expiration of his term of office until his successor qualified; extended the definition of a corporation to include the "Massachusetts trust"; redefined documentary evidence to include "books of account and financial and corporate records," which the commission was empowered in section nine to examine.[21]

INFLUENCES THAT HELPED TO BRING PASSAGE OF THE 1938 ACTS — The groups that lobbied for the consumer bills of 1938 did not spring up overnight. Sixteen national women's organizations were working on this legislation before it was passed. Most of these organizations continue today to work for consumer protection. Labor unions also carried the banner.[22] Consumers' Research was founded in 1929 and its circulation by 1935 for its *Consumers' Research Bulletin* was 55,000. In 1935 Arthur Kallet, secretary of the organization, sided with the workers in a strike. The strike was lost and ten of the losers, supported by CR subscribers, under Kallet's leadership established the rival agency, Consumers' Union.[23] These agencies had their part in the renewed consumer awakening that began with appearance of *Your Money's Worth in 1927* and other volumes that followed.

Consumers about this time were wondering about the various agencies that issued seals of approval; who appraised the appraisers? Mary Catherine Phillips in *Skin Deep* criticized the *Good Housekeeping* seal of approval. She remarked that it was seemingly unscientific in view of the facts; other magazines, too, received criticism. When *Good Housekeeping* came out favorably for the Tugwell revision of the food and drug act, a storm of protest developed from businessmen. GH said it had intended all along to print both sides of the question. Advertising man Ernest Elmo Calkins' story attacking the bill was published in GH, presumably to placate business.[24]

Through all of the years from 1906 to 1938, however, there were many influences at work. Florence Kelley and the people whose lives she had touched had a part in so many of these. Mrs. Kelley's work to eliminate the "tenement industries," abandon unfair labor practices, child labor, and discrimination against women workers, for all types of social legislation was all a part of the state-by-state groundwork laid during the first quarter of a century for the social legislation that would come during the 1930's. It is all an inseparable part of the lives of the people during this period. John R. Commons, Robert A. Woods, Louis D. Brandeis, Josephine Goldmark, Julia Lathrop (another resident of Hull House who became administrator of the 1916 Child Labor Law which was declared unconstitutional in the case of *Hammer vs. Dagenhart* in 1918), and a host of others played their part in the crusade.

Right after the United States entered World War I, Sidney Hillman came to Mrs. Kelley for help. The tenement workers were again edging into the clothing industry. This time the United States Government was a party to the crime; Army uniforms were being made in homes. It just so happened that the Secretary of War at the time was a past president of the National Consumers' League, Newton D. Baker. Through Mrs. Kelley, Hillman told his story to Baker. The committee Baker appointed reported that the facts were substantiated; the three members were then made a new board to see that there were labor standards even for Army clothing. Mrs. Kelley devoted six months of her time as a member of the board.[25]

When Mrs. Kelley's life and work were done (1932), many were the testimonials to her. Newton Baker in 1937 wrote:

> My acquaintance with Florence Kelley for forty years was intimate and close. . . . From that acquaintance and from a rather constant and wide association with great women in America during my generation, I do not have any hesitation in saying that Mrs. Kelley was intellectually the greatest woman I have known.[26]

The legislation of the 1930's came from the development of the preceding thirty-five years and the work of many. Not all of the movements and factors can be discussed here, but two additional groups of factors are briefly reviewed.

OTHER FEDERAL LAWS — *The Clayton Act,* amending the Sherman Antitrust Act, was passed in 1914. It declared that labor is not "a commodity in trade." It provided that nonstock, nonprofit agricultural associations were not to be prohibited under the antitrust laws. It blocked mergers formed when one company acquired the stock of another. [A 1950 amendment empowered the FTC to block mergers brought about by one company buying the assets of another company.] Its other provisions had less effect on consumers. The amendment to the Clayton Act, the *Robinson-Patman Act* of 1936, dealt for the most part with price and other discriminations as among business buyers. The *Federal Trade Commission Act* of 1914 set up the FTC to supplement the work of the Justice Department in enforcing laws relative to restraint of trade. Its original purpose was to protect manufacturers, but from the first some of its actions resulted in benefits to consumers. A *meat inspection law* passed in 1907 provided that inspectors inspect all meat sold in interstate commerce. The *Capper-Volstead Act* of 1922 legalized market operations of the agricultural associations provided no member had more than one vote and the dividends were no more than eight per cent per annum. Monopolistic control to enhance prices unduly was prohibited. The *Public Utility Act* was passed in 1935.

The *Miller-Tydings Act,* 1937, replaced in 1952 by the *McGuire Act,* was another Sherman Antitrust amendment. (See Chapter XXI.) The principal *labor laws* and their implications were discussed briefly in Chapter XVI. Changes in attitude of the federal government toward labor came during the depression which began in 1929. Consumers, too, were more aware of the problems of the economic system. Producers were given aid by the *National Industrial Recovery Act* and the *Agricultural Adjustment Administration.* The *Consumers' Advisory Board* was established in 1933. The Consumers' counsel of the AAA was established in 1933 and continued to function through a bimonthly publication, *Consumers' Guide.* The FLSA (1938) saw realization of the dreams of those who had fought through the years of tenement-sweating, consumer labeling, and child labor legislation. Government had left *laissez faire* behind.

THE "GUINEA-PIG" WRITERS AND THE FIVE-YEAR DRIVE FOR CONSUMER LEGISLATION — After Stuart Chase and Arthur Kallet's *Your Money's Worth* and other volumes came out the general shift was from the "salesmanship" to the "buymanship" point of view. Buyers became concerned with the problem of how and where the article bought was produced, but, said Roger W. Babson, they needed "Power No Less Than Knowledge." [27]

Horace Kallen in *The Decline and Rise of the Consumer* (1936) said that consumers had protected themselves through: (1) the church in the days of the guilds and before; (2) government legislation; (3) pressure groups. The first pressure-group effort was indirect and began in England in 1890, spreading to the United States the following year with the National Consumers' League. Early consumer organizations reflected the concern of some of the more privileged consumers over those not so privileged and over the wage-earning producers. [28]

The era of the "guinea-pig" writers got its name from the work of Arthur Kallet and F. J. Schlink, *100,000,000 Guinea Pigs,* published in 1933. Thus the real beginning of the period of "guinea-pig" writers came the same year that the five-year drive for consumer legislation was started. Schlink and Kallet had the first-hand information of Consumers' Research. Their work was a dramatic plea for consumers, the hundred million Americans who were acting as "test animals in a gigantic experiment with poisons, conducted by the food, drug, and cosmetic manufacturers." They suggested that at least 2,000 pages would be required to give a fair picture of all that had happened since passage of the 1906 Food and Drug Act. Dr. Wiley's 400-page *History of a Crime Against the Food Law* had rapidly sketched the period 1906-1929 and the decline in control had gone far since 1929. A big fault of the law was that the administrators had to proceed against goods instead of processors or manufacturers. An inspector couldn't stop a process even if rat poison were being added "before his very eyes." Without right of entry into plants what could be done? Some suggestions were made for group action and for individual consumers there was a chapter headed, "Your Responsibilities." [29]

Mary Catherine Phillips and F. J. Schlink published *Discovering Consumers* which proclaimed that the consumer needed a new deal in products that wouldn't be poisonous and in standards of grade and quality. The Bureau of Standards was charged with working "exclusively for the National Government and for business" although the customers paid the bill. Because business and farmers could organize, consumers were denied food free from poisons and protection from drugs that were worthless and adulterated. [30]

Phillips in *Skin Deep* used hundreds of cases to back up her plea for revision of the food and drug act with provision for proper cosmetic protection. Among them was the story of a young society matron of Dayton, Ohio, who became blind and whose face was disfigured for life from using Lash-Lure which contained a dangerous aniline dye. [31] Walter B. Pitkin's *Let's Get What We Want!* (1935) protested for housing programs, medical service, consumer labeling and grading, and other consumer needs including a Board of Consumer Inquiry to protect the American woman who was "an economic imbecile." [32]

Ruth deForest Lamb's *American Chamber of Horrors* (1936) reviewed the attempts at food and drug legislation in the years preceding its publication. The bitter attack of the book is revealed in some of its chapter titles: "Blood Money, The Death-Dealers, Medicine Swindles, Country Style, It's a Racket!, Let the Housewife Beware!, and How Much Poison is Poisonous?" [33]

The American Consumer Market (*Business Week*, 1932) largely a study of consumption expenditures, mentioned the development of technical literature to help consumers increase their efficiency in spending. Since it was one of the first such studies, it shows that thought was being turned toward the consumer on more fronts than one. [34]

George E. Sokolsky concludes his chapter on "Consumer Protections" in *The American Way of Life* with the statement that "Consumer protection is a social obligation of the government and of business. But business has a greater stake in the consumer not being 'gypped' than any other group." He classified consumer protection groups as follows:

1. Business organizations for self-policing.
2. Media protections.
3. Professional associations.
4. Government agencies.
5. Consumer associations.[35]

Among some of the specific groups he cited for service to consumers were the American Medical Association, the American Dental Association, and bureaus of the broadcasting companies.[36]

The period of the "guinea-pig" literature, it must be remembered, was a period of depression. In early 1933 some thirteen to fifteen million persons were unemployed. A hundred million man-years of work are estimated to have been lost in the 1930's.[37] Perhaps, as many of the writers of the period have said or implied, it was the years of depression that gave rise to the social legislation of the 1930's. Without the depression there may not have been legislation despite the long efforts of so many groups.

Toward the end of the drive for consumer legislation so many forces had been brought to bear on the problem that the annual report of the FTC for the fiscal year 1936-1937 showed that even that group was thinking of enlarging its own powers through proposed consumer legislation. Its annual report recommended amendment to the Federal Trade Commission Act to make "unfair or deceptive acts and practices" as well as "unfair methods of competition" unlawful. It also recommended making unlawful the acquiring by one corporation of the assets of another when the intent would be the same as acquiring the stock of another corporation with the result of restraining trade.[38] As reported earlier in this chapter, two acts were passed in 1938, one to be administered by the FDA and the other by the FTC. Charles Wesley Dunn's 1,370-page volume on the new Federal, Food, Drug, and Cosmetic Act of June 25, 1938, gives first the act as passed, and then the legislative record of the preceding bills that failed to pass. In it may be found first-hand drama! The years that have followed have shown him to be right when he said that the fight had not ended.[39]

The Period 1939 to the Present — Instead of being a period of agitation for passage of consumer laws, this period may be said to be characterized by several things: (1) consumer education; (2) consumer standards; (3) consumer research on the part of both business and consumer organizations; (4) consumer co-operatives; (5) enforcement of consumer laws. Each of these is a vast area in itself but can be gone into only briefly here.

CONSUMER EDUCATION — The consumer movement led to including of consumer courses in the public school curriculum, to adult courses in consumership, and these various courses in turn strengthened the "consumer movement." Professor Howard Wilson, Harvard School of Education, said in 1939: "Consumer education is neither an ephemeral fad nor a panacea for the ills of mankind, but it is an important phase of the realistic education for living which is the task of democracy's schools." [40]

CONSUMER STANDARDS — There are many standards for agricultural products (agencies under the Agricultural Adjustment Administration). There are many standards for manufactured goods also. The National Bureau of Standards of the United States Department of Commerce and the American Standards Association have helped in establishing standards and controlling weights and measures of products. The NBS is not a regulatory agent, but its purpose is to cooperate with industry and consumers. Over six hundred organizations participate in the work of the ASA. Some of the bases for standards are: quality, quantity, size, color, service, price. Standardization has helped to reduce the cost of marketing.[41]

Many federal agencies in the course of administering laws help to set standards for consumer goods and services. The *Health Education and Welfare Department* with a budget of over $8 billion (1965) administers a complex of six agencies. Since the work of this department concerns the welfare of citizens, each of the six agencies directly or indirectly affects people as consumers. The largest of the agencies is *Social Security*. In 1964 20,000,000 persons received Social Security payments; a million more families received aid for dependent children; 7,000,000 received relief payments through the agency known since 1963 as the *Welfare Administration*. The Public Health Service (including the National Institutes of Health: child health, medical sciences, mental health, neurology, allergy, heart, cancer, dentistry, arthritis) under the direction of the Surgeon General in January, 1964, made a report relative to research on tobacco usage and declared cigarettes to be a major health hazard. Scientists of the PHS have been credited during the decade 1955-1964 with advances in cancer, open heart surgery, influenza vaccines, and "partial cracking of the mysterious genetic code." The *Food and Drug Administration* has faced many crises from cranberries and lipstick to thalidomide since it became a part of HEW. It has responsibility not only for the safety of drugs but for literally thousands of other products. The *Office of Education* and the *Vocational Rehabilitation Administration* are the other two agencies under HEW.[42]

Six other regulatory agencies have influences upon consumer standards: The *Federal Trade Commission's* basic job is that of preventing unfair competition, but it also prevents monopolistic mergers and investigates deceptive advertising and faulty labeling. The *Federal Communication Commission* regulates the broadcasting industry. The *Federal Power Commission,* which regulates utilities, has been accused of siding with the oil and gas companies and supporting industry mergers opposed by the Justice Department. The *Civil Aeronautics Board* investigates airline accidents, regulates routes, rates, and safety, although the Federal Aviation Administration promulgates the safety rules themselves. The *Interstate Commerce Commission* regulates the railroads, truckers, barge lines, and gasoline- and oil-pipeline firms with a view to keeping competitive balance as well as looking out for the public interest through setting rates, granting franchises, and passing on mergers. The *Securities and Exchange Commission* attempts to see that the true facts are presented by those who sell securities and when it discovers that full disclosure has not been made or deception has existed, it withholds a stock from the market or brings legal action if it is already on the market.[43]

Additional agencies that help protect consumers: *Federal Deposit Insurance Corporation,* which guarantees bank deposits up to $10,000; *Post Office Department,* which protects against fraud by mail; *Treasury Department,* which administers labeling and advertising of distilled spirits; and there are others.

CONSUMER RESEARCH — Research done by Consumers' Research and Consumers' Union has primarily been done for their subscribers. It has been said that the subscribers' lists of both of these organizations are weighted with intellectuals. The information provided the subscribers concerns evaluation of products and the best buys for the prices charged.[44] The research center at the University of Michigan does much social and consumer research which it makes public through published bulletins.[45] Perhaps the best research being done today in the interest of consumers is that done by business itself. This includes particularly the research done to determine what people want and the product research that enables business to give them what they want. Business would not spend billions to advertise unwanted, unsafe, or fraudulent products.

CONSUMER CO-OPERATIVES — Consumer co-operatives had their beginning in England in 1845; a tailor in Boston instigated the first consumers' co-operative one year later in the United States. In some parts of the United States the consumer co-operative associations are important, but they have never done a great amount of business in this country. The following statement from the report of the second conference held by the Institute for Consumer Education shows why consumer co-operatives could not be left out in considering consumer movements:

> The cooperative movement does and must continue to participate with the rest of the consumer movement in advocating research in consumer problems, scientific mass purchasing, standards, grades, labeling and legislation favorable to the consumer.[46]

ENFORCEMENT OF CONSUMER LAWS — World War II brought numerous special agencies not only for handling of the war emergency itself but for controlling production and distribution of consumer goods. Among these were: The Office of Production Management, later a part of the office for Emergency Management and still later replaced by the War Production Board within the Office for Emergency Management; the Office of Civilian Defense; Office of Price Administration and Civilian Supply, which became the Office of Price Administration. There were all sorts of co-ordinators. The umpire was the Office of Economic Stabilization. These many agencies developed so soon after the passage of the laws of the 1930's calling for many new agencies or increased activities on the part of those already created, that government services formed a complicated pattern. In addition to the numerous acts and agencies already mentioned in this chapter, a new act to be administered by the FTC went into effect in 1951: The Federal Wool Products Labeling Act.[47] The war-time economy was anything but *laissez faire* and much of the planning done for war was carried over into peace.

The FTC has handled thousands of cases since 1939. In 1940 alone it examined 300,741 advertisements and quoted 24,106 of them as containing representations that appeared to be false or misleading.[48] It is almost like reading a novel to pursue the many interesting cases the FTC and FDA have concerned themselves with and to read the criticisms of the two agencies. The majority of the FTC's work is on behalf of industry, but indirectly there is the consumer to be thought of. A report made in June, 1955, by a committee of citizens which had spent five months studying the FDA made 110 recommendations, among them the increasing of FDA coverage because of changed customer habits and technological developments; the confusion or lack of clarity between the FDA and FTC responsibilities concerning labeling and advertising was criticized.[49] Since the 1955 report the FDA has received increased appropriations and certain of its activities have been greatly beneficial to the citizens of the United States. One of the most striking examples was the keeping of thaliomide (a sleeping pill that when taken by expectant mothers caused the birth of infants with phocomelia, a deformity resulting in flipper-like arms and malformed legs) off the market in this country; the product was sold in Europe and resulted in the birth of thousands of deformed babies.[50] Among the many actions taken in 1964 by the FDA was an order to review all drugs put on the market since 1938 to see if they met requirements of the 1962 prescription drug law.[51]

Conclusions — Whatever the trends may be or whatever the fights of the past have been, the legislative, judicial, and administrative bodies have struggled and continue to struggle to make, enforce, administer, and interpret the laws of the United States, including those specific economic laws affecting the consumer which have, together with the movements contributing to their enactment, enforcement, and administration, been the basis of this chapter.

That the years since 1938 have been years of informing the public, not years of crusading for protective laws, is reflected in M. C. Phillips' *More than Skin Deep* (1948) which informed rather than pled for action as did her *Skin Deep* of the "guinea-pig" era.[52] The 1949 publication of reports of the Federal Food, Drug, and Cosmetic Law, 1907-1949 (1,446 pages) credits the food, drug, and cosmetic industries for having given consumers better products that year than in any previous year.[53]

The United States has risen above the position that existed with respect to consumer protection during the last part of the nineteenth century and the first part of the twentieth. Paul Mazur writing in 1953 said, "Consumers' goods and not capital goods, consumption and not production, are the controlling forces of the American economy." [54] The problem is to keep "free" competition with all of the desirable elements it possesses while at the same time eliminating unfairness and dishonesty not only in competition among individual business firms but in all consumer transactions with business firms. Government, with its many social institutions, regulates in both of these areas. The individual business firm and the individual person operate within the confines of the legal restrictions of man-made social institutions, particularly those of the municipal, state, and federal governments.

Elton Mayo in *The Social Problems of an Industrial Civilization* quotes John Neville Figgis as saying:

> . . . In the real world, the isolated individual does not exist; he begins always as a member of something and . . . his personality can develop only in society, and in some way or other he always

embodies some social institution. I do not mean to deny the distinctness of individual life, but this distinction can function only inside a society.[55]

Although The Civil Rights Act of 1964 has not been mentioned previously in this chapter, its implications for business and citizens of the United States are far reaching. It marks the culmination of the fight of one specific group of consumers for rights not only as consumers but as citizens of the country in which they live.[56]

Two chapters in Stuart Chase's *For This We Fought,* which was published just at the close of World War II, are headed: "What the Veterans Want," and "What the People Want." In the second of these two chapters he cites William A. Lydgate, *What America Thinks,* as having quoted:

. . . chapter and verse to show where the people are often way ahead of Congress, ahead of the President, and several light years ahead of the editorials in most newspapers. Again and again, the people leave the leaders of the people buried in a cloud of dust.[57]

Chase mentions at the same time Carl Sandburg who said "the people were mostly right." But, after all, as he pointed out, Sandburg was a poet.[58] Shall we go further and say that poets are dreamers? This chapter covering consumer movements in relation to federal action has attempted to show that the dreamers who could fight for their dreams (and often die before they saw them realized) came first; the enactment, administration, enforcement, and interpretation of the consumer protective laws came second. It is the problem of legislative bodies not to legislate so harshly that private enterprise is destroyed; it is the problem of administrators, agencies, and groups to observe caution and attempt to maintain a balance between justice toward the individuals of society on the one hand and the business institutions on the other, and to be just as between business institutions themselves.

PROJECTS

1. Write a report on the activities of the FTC during the last five years.
2. Write a report on the activities of the FDA during the last five years.
3. Justify the inclusion of a chapter on "Consumer Movements" in a business and/or managerial psychology textbook.

ACKNOWLEDGMENTS AND REFERENCES

1 Adams, Loyce, "A Study of Sales-training Programs in Eighty-eight Firms," a dissertation, The University of Texas, Austin, 1959 (University Microfilms, Inc., 313 N. First St., Ann Arbor, Michigan), pp. 45-46. Much of the material in this chapter is adapted from "Consumer Movements in Relation to Federal Action in the Interest of Consumers, 1880-1959," unpublished paper, The University of Texas, pp. 1-101; the paper was based on 113 references many of which are repeated here.

2 Goldmark, Josephine, *Impatient Crusader,* University of Illinois Press, Urbana, 1953, pp. v, 9, 17-21, 27-29.
Addams, Jane, Twenty Years at Hull House, The Macmillan Co., New York, 1910, pp. 213-218.
Powderly, T. V., *Thirty Years of Labor, 1859 to 1889,* Excelsior Publishing House, Columbus, Ohio, 1889, pp. 543-548.

3 Goldmark, *op .cit.,* pp. 31-35, pp. 40-47; Addams, *op. cit.,* pp. 201-204.
Kelley, Florence, *Some Ethical Gains Through Legislation,* The Macmillan Co., London, 1905, pp. vii-viii, 211-225.

4 *Ibid.,* pp. 212, 217ff, 221-223.

5 Chase, Stuart, *Democracy Under Pressure,* The Twentieth Century Fund, New York, 1945, pp. 11-16.

6 Gordon, Leland J., *Economics for Consumers,* Second Edition, American Book Co., New York, 1944, pp. 620-621.

7 Fairchild, Fred Rogers, Buck, Norman Sydney, and Slesinger, Ruben Emanuel, *Principles of Economics,* The Macmillan Co., New York, 1954, pp. 703-705.

8 Powers, Richard H., "Adam Smith: Practical Realist," *The Southwestern Social Science Quarterly,* Vol. 37, No. 3, December 1956, pp. 227-238.

9 Brinton, Crane, *Ideas & Men,* Prentice-Hall, Inc., Englewood Cliffs, New Jersey, 1950, p. 429.

10 Dell, Floyd, *Upton Sinclair,* George H. Doran Co., New York, 1927, p. 109.

11 Sorenson, Helen, *The Consumer Movement,* Harper & Brothers, Publishers, New York, 1941, pp. 6-7.

12 Dell, *op. cit.,* pp. 104-110.

13 Sinclair, Upton, *The Jungle,* Harper & Brothers, Publishers, New York, 1905, (copyright, 1951, with introduction by John Fischer), p. xi.

14 *Ibid.,* pp. xv-xvi.

15 Goldmark, *op. cit.,* pp. 51-64.

16 —————, *Federal Food, Drug, and Cosmetic Law, Administrative Reports 1907-1949,* with an introduction by Paul B. Dunbar, Commerce Clearing House, Inc., New York 18, 1951.

17 Gordon, *op. cit.,* pp. 604-606, 608-620.
Lamb, Ruth deForest, *American Chamber of Horrors,* Grosset & Dunlap, Publishers, New York, 1936, pp. 329-332.
Chase, Stuart, *Democracy Under Pressure, op. cit.,* pp. 41-43.

18 Printers' Ink Bureau, Washington, D. C., "Official Family Feud," *Printers' Ink,* Vol. 178, No. 2, January 14, 1937, p. 20ff.

19 Dunn, Charles Wesley, "The Food and Drug Law in the United States," *Chemistry & Industry,* No. 34, September 1, 1956, pp. 878-888.
—————, "House Passes Bill Widening Powers of Federal Trade Commission," *The Commercial & Financial Chronicle,* Vol. 146, No. 3788, January 29, 1938, pp. 681-682.

20 —————, "Food Additives Under the Gun," *Business Week,* October 24, 1959, pp. 113-116.
—————, "That Pesky Food Additives Law," *Business Week,* April 4, 1964, pp. 54-58.

21 Dunn, Charles Wesley, "Amended Federal Trade Act Gives Commission Vast Powers Over Business," *Printers' Ink,* Vol. 182, No. 10, March 10, 1938, p. 26ff.
22 Sorenson, *op. cit.,* pp. 13, 59-109.
23 Beem, Eugene R., and Ewing, John S., "Business Appraises Consumer Testing Agencies," *Harvard Business Review,* Vol. 32, No. 2, March-April, 1954, pp. 113-126.
24 Phillips, M. C., *Skin Deep,* The Vanguard Press, New York, 1934, pp. 183-96.
25 Addams, Jane, *My Friend, Julia Lathrop,* The Macmillan Co., New York, 1935, pp. 119-121, pp. 127-131.
26 Goldmark, *op. cit.,* p. 207.
27 Babson, Roger W., and Stone, C. N., *Consumer Protection,* Harper & Brothers, Publishers, New York, 1938, pp. 58-65.
28 Kallen, Horace M., *The Decline and Rise of the Consumer,* D. Appleton-Century Co., New York, 1936, pp. 137-141.
29 Kallet, Arthur, and Schlink, F. J., *100,000,000 Guinea Pigs,* Grosset & Dunlap, Publishers, New York, 1933, pp. 196, 266-296ff.
30 Phillips, Mary Catherine, and Schlink, F. J., *Discovering Consumers,* The John Day Co., New York, pp. 16-24.
31 Phillips, M. C., *Skin Deep, op. cit.,* p. 10.
32 Pitkin, Walter B., *Let's Get What We Want!,* Simon & Schuster, New York, 1935, pp. x-xi.
33 Lamb, *op. cit.,*
34 ——————, *The American Consumer Market — A Study by The Business Week,* 330 West 42d St., New York, 1932, pp. 3-39.
35 Sokolsky, George E., *The American Way of Life,* Farrar & Rinehart, Inc., New York, 1938, pp. 150, 167ff.
36 *Ibid.,* pp. 159-165.
37 Chase, Stuart, *Where's the Money Coming From?. .* The Twentieth Century Fund, New York, 1943, p. 144.
38 ——————, "Annual Report of FTC," *The Commercial & Financial Chronicle,* Vol. 145, No. 3777, November 13, 1937, p. 3136.
39 Dunn, Charles Wesley, *Federal Food, Drug, and Cosmetic Act,* G. E. Stechert & Co., New York, 1938.
40 Sorenson, *op. cit.,* p. 23.
41 Phillips, Charles F., and Duncan, Delbert J., *Marketing Principles and Methods,* Third Edition, Richard D. Irwin, Inc., Homewood, Illinois, 1956; Dameron, Kenneth (editor), *Consumer Problems in Wartime,* McGraw-Hill Book Co., Inc., New York, 1944, pp. 276-277.
42 ——————, "Government . . . ," *Business Week,* April 4, 1964, pp. 54-58.
43 ——————, "The Alphabet Agencies Carry a Big Stick —," *Newsweek,* January 2, 1961, pp. 56-60.
44 Beem, *op. cit.,* pp. 113-126.
45 Katona, George, and Mueller, Eva, *Consumer Attitudes and Demand, 1950-1952,* Survey Research Center Institute for Social Research, University of Michigan, 1953.
46 Sorenson, *op. cit.,* pp. 152-153.
47 Dameron, Kenneth, *Consumer Problems in Wartime,* McGraw-Hill Book Co., New York, 1944, pp. 286, 295-297.
48 ——————, "Big Year for FTC," *Printers' Ink,* Vol. 194, No. 2, January 10, 1941, p. 23ff.
49 ——————, "Citizens Committee Urges Expansion for Food and Drug Agency," *Printers' Ink,* Vol. 252, No. 2, July 15, 1955, p. 73.
——————, "FDA: Weak and Ailing," *Chemical and Engineering News,* Vol. 33, No. 29, July 18, 1955, p. 3,000ff.

—————————, "Classic Complaint," *Chemical Week*, Vol. 77, No. 3, July 16, 1955, p. 14.

50 —————————, "Drug Scare Spurs Review of Safeguards," *Business Week*, August 4, 1962, pp. 70-71.

51 —————————, "FDA Gets Tough," *Business Week*, No. 1818, July 4, 1964, p. 19.

52 Phillips, M. C., *More Than Skin Deep*, Richard R. Smith, New York, 1948.

53 —————————, *Federal Food, Drug, and Cosmetic Law, Administrative Reports 1907-1949, op. cit.*, p. xvi.

54 Mazur, Paul, *The Standards We Raise*, Harper & Brothers, Publishers, New York, 1953, pp. 82, 138-139.

55 Mayo, Elton, *The Social Problems of an Industrial Civilization*, Division of Research, Graduate School of Business Administration, Harvard University, Boston, 1945, pp. 45-46.

56 —————————, " '. . . Shall Now Also Be Equal . . . ,' " *Business Week*, No. 1819, July 13, 1964, pp. 17-18.

57 Chase, Stuart, *For This We Fought*, The Twentieth Century Fund, New York, 1946, p. 36ff.

Lydgate, William A., *What America Thinks*, Crowell Publishing Co., New York, 1944.

58 Chase, *op. cit.*, p. 36ff.

CHAPTER XXV

THE KEYNESIAN ECONOMIC THEORY, ECONOMIC MATURITY, WORLD RESOURCES, AND NEW FRONTIERS

With each recession or onslaught of a depression, the business magazines begin to carry articles emphasizing the importance of salesmanship. In such times the part of the salesman in moving goods is doubly recognized. It is their task to keep consumers spending despite the fears which cause people to hold on to their savings and even attempt to save more. Since the deep depression of the 1930's and the publication in 1936 of John Maynard Keynes' *General Theory,* the necessity of keeping consumption and investment high in order to maintain output, income, and employment has been constantly reemphasized.[1] It takes good salesmanship to move consumption goods, or to convince investors that because consumption goods will continue to move their investments will not be lost. Salesmanship has played a big role also in bringing about high standards of living in the United States.[2] An impassioned sales manager was quoted in *Fortune* as having said:

. . . 'Whether we have apple vendors at every street corner or continue to have the jobs that are needed for the country's prosperity . . . will be decided by the salesmen of America. Unless salesmen in the years ahead succeed in their efforts to sell the products of the looms, of the rolling mills, of the forges, of the presses, of the farms and mines and factories, that vision of modern America which we hold so closely to our hearts will remain a mythical hope based on wishful thinking.'[3]

According to Keynesian economic theory there may be a great deal of truth in what the sales manager said. When people save instead of spending in order to put others to work, total national income is decreased. With decrease in income, there are further decreases in consumption and further drops in income. Although people wish to save more they cannot as a fact do so as a group for the group income falls by the amount saved if that sum is not invested. It might be said that if the theorists are correct the success of a capitalist economy does indeed depend upon consumers spending all their income, as it was assumed by the classical economists that they did. There is a burden then on advertising and selling to keep consumers spending.

Keynes' Underinvestment Theory vs. Malthus' Underconsumption Theory — Keynes' fundamental law is that *as income increases, consumption will increase but not by as much as the increase in income.* He says that the two factors that determine the level of consumption expenditures are:

1. *The level of real income* (what money will buy).
2. *The propensity to consume*, which depends on two factors:
   a. *Average propensity to consume* which is indicated by the slope and position of the curve $\frac{C}{Y}$ where "C" stands for consumption and "Y" stands for income.
   b. *Marginal propensity to consume*, from which he derived the investment multiplier, K; $\frac{dC}{dY} = 1 - \frac{1}{K}$ where "dC" is the added expenditure for consumption out of an increase in income at the margin or "dY."

If the marginal propensity to consume is two-thirds, that is, if the propensity is to spend two out of every three dollars of income at the margin, this means that the propensity to save is one-third and the multiplier, called "K," is "3." The multiplier is the reciprocal of the marginal propensity to save (MPS). This may be charted as follows when $1 at the margin is paid out to workers. They in turn pay out two-thirds of this to others who likewise spend two-thirds of what they receive, until the first dollar has put to work a total of $3 worth of wage earners.

$1.00
.67
.45
.30
.20
.13
.09
.06
.04
.03
.02
.01

Given any level of income, under Keynesian theory, consumption would depend on the consumption function (propensity to consume). The position and slope of the curve that illustrates the consumption function are determined by:

1. *Objective factors:*
   a. Three of which probably have little effect in shifting the function: change in the wage unit, change in accounting practice with respect to depreciation, etc., and change in interest rate.
   b. Windfall gains or losses.
   c. Changes in fiscal policy such as war measures and peacetime tax cuts or raises.
   d. Changes in expectations of relation between present and future levels of income — as the shift caused by expectations at the beginning of the Korean war.

2. *Subjective factors:* reduced to motives for saving:
   a. Individuals save because of foresight, avarice, calculation, enterprise, precaution, improvement, pride, independence.
   b. Businesses withhold for financial reasons, prudence, improvement, liquidity, and enterprise.[4]

Keynes reasoned that the objective factors cause shifts in the consumption function, although in the short run some of those are fairly stable; subjective factors he believed to be generally stable. If income rises, consumption rises as per schedule; the function does not necessarily shift, and, in the short run (the cyclical situation), the consumption function is probably rather stable. Thus consumption expenditures change only as income changes. *That leaves the conclusion that variations in the level of income depend on variations in the level of investment. An increase in investment brings an increase in income that is a multiple of itself, depending on the marginal propensity to consume.*

For underconsumptionists the level of consumption expenditure was the determinant of income, and the level of income changed only as consumption changed. Keynes' theory, therefore, is an *underinvestment* rather than an *underconsumption* theory.

The gap between the sum of consumption and investment and the value of output (income, employment) may be illustrated as on page 481.

Malthus had put forth a theory similar to Keynes' theory, but his was a theory of underconsumption. He maintained that if savers would save no more than the unproductive spenders are spending no difficulty

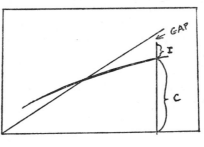

Consumption
and
Investment

Value of Output
C + I = Y

would arise as there would always be effective demand. Malthus agreed with Smith and Ricardo that capital accumulation is a necessary condition to the progress of wealth but not a sufficient one. He agreed that saving is necessary to capital accumulation. He maintained, however, that if too large a proportion of income is saved and invested there is expansion of productive capacity with at the same time a shrinking of demand for goods which must ultimately be sold to consumers. Accumulation of wealth, therefore, would result in underconsumption.

Say's law of the market underlies the classical theory of capital accumulation. On the basis of Say's law demand could never be deficient. Since goods create their own demand it would be impossible for capital to be accumulated so rapidly as to outrun the market. Ricardo admitted that there could be a general glut when funds for maintaining labor increased more rapidly than population. With wages high, profits low, and foregoing of consumption to save, consuming would be at a minimum. Malthus claimed that what Ricardo admitted would be true with consumption reduced to a minimum would be true if consumption were reduced at all. Ricardo relied on Say's law; Smith, too, held a similar theory, believing there would be no hoarding. Malthus criticized Say's law by attacking the four assumptions: (1) that goods exchange for goods without limit; (2) that human wants are insatiable; (3) that accumulation or increase in supply automatically increases demand; and (4) that no one withholds money or withholds goods. Malthus said that goods frequently exchange for labor or personal services and that goods must yield a profit for demand to be effective. He answered the second assumption by claiming that humans are indolent; beyond a point they would prefer more leisure to more goods. With regard to the third assumption, he said that the mere accumulation of wealth does not assure demand. Laborers cannot buy the entire output created by their efforts because they don't get all the output. There are profits. Further, the profits accumulated by capitalists reduce demand for consumer goods while increasing capacity to produce them. The fourth assumption he answered by saying that people do withhold money for precautionary motives, i.e., they save for emergencies. To the extent that money is saved, demand is withheld.

Malthus believed population increase would not increase production unless laborers are employed since they are not born with purchasing power. They cannot purchase the whole output of their work because there must be profits; prices will fail because demand is not increasing fast enough. Fertility of soil makes possible rapid increase of wealth, but it is not by itself sufficient. Technological progress might so greatly reduce price as to create a larger total demand with more total return to the capitalist (elastic demand). If there is not sufficient demand even though unit price is reduced, total revenue will not be greater (inelastic demand).

Increase in wealth then, according to Malthus, depends on two conditions: (1) *increase of productive capacity* (increased labor force, increased capital accumulation, fertility of soil, and technological improvements); (2) *effectual and unchecked demand for all that is produced*, with a union of the powers of production with the means of distribution. Some of the ways he suggested for increasing demand were: (1) *division of landed property*, which he rejected on political and social grounds but admitted would increase propensity to consume; (2) *extension of the markets*, external and internal, by providing goods that are desired and removing of restrictions on and improving of communication and transportation; (3) *a supply of unproductive consumers*, as government workers, servants, and landowners. He recommended public works and other governmental expenditures to increase consumption, and the employing of servants, private teachers, and others by the person of means in order that "total consumption" or "total expenditure" might be effected.[5]

Keynes' Full-Investment Economy vs. Hansen's Stagnant Economy — In present-day economy the reward for owning has not completely disappeared. Joseph A. Schumpeter, writing in the early part of the twentieth century, claimed that *profits are the result of successful innovation*. There was entrepreneurial profit only for the creator of new combinations, new products, new ways of transporting, new ways of storing. He believed ". . . profit as a special and independent value phenomenon is fundamentally connected with the role of leadership in the economic system."[6] He stated that "Without development there is no profit, without profit no development."[7]

Keynes' full-investment economy would be the point at which capital assets cease to be scarce and their rate of return is reduced to zero. Only at this point of full investment would over-investment have a mean-

ing. It would mean that additional investment would lower the marginal efficiency of capital (MEC) to a negative rate. [The MEC is the expectation of profit yield from a capital investment during its life, or as Keynes put it: the MEC is that rate of discount which would make the present value of the series of annuities given by the returns expected from the capital asset during its life just equal to the supply price. The SP is that price which would just induce a manufacturer newly to produce the capital asset. The determinants of investment are: the MEC and the rate of interest. The MEC is determined by the expectation of profit yields and the replacement cost of capital assets (SP); the rate of interest is determined by the quantity of money and the liquidity preference. Liquidity preference is the functional tendency which fixes the quantity of money the public will hold when the rate of interest is given; people hold money for transactions, precautionary motives, and speculative motives.] If the MEC is lowered to a negative rate there would be no incentive to invest; net investment would cease at the point of full investment. *At the point of full investment the redistribution of income would have automatically been taken care of because the reward for owning as such would have disappeared.* There would have to be 100 per cent consumption of net income; anything short of that would bring involuntary unemployment. Keynes thought at the time he wrote that a state of full investment, as he had defined it, had never occurred, not even momentarily.

To carry his reasoning further, if the MEC were zero, interest would have to be zero. It would be necessary to nationalize the banking system and banks could exist only with large service charges. Firms might realize profits due to *better management,* or to *windfall gains.* Some very small return would exist for *risk taking* for the economy as a whole. Profits for the system as a whole as a premium against loss even though small or nonexistent on the average might be substantial in a given enterprise.

Higgins says that Keynes' concept contains the "kernel of a doctrine of economic maturity." He says that it is likely that Keynes did conceive of an increasing gap between actual output and full employment output as the economy became more mature. An increasing gap seems implicit in his reasoning, unless the propensity to consume could be increased to a full 100 per cent of income.

Hansen's "stagnant" or "mature economy" is evidently an economy in which there is a *growing gap between potential output at full employment and actually realized output.* He evidently meant *laissez-faire* economy, and he offered governmental measures to fill the gap. He maintained that the marginal propensity to save had been constant, secularly (about seven per cent of cash income), and that the volume of savings had thus increased secularly. Offsets to savings are, therefore, necessary, and, since he thought that the automatic incentives to private investment have been weakened by (1) growing personal and corporate savings, (2) slowing of population growth, (3) disappearance of frontiers, and (4) capital savings nature of more recent technological improvements, there must be more government investment or expenditure. The stagnant economy about which Hansen wrote leaves room for potential expansion and further investment, with governmental measures as stimulants. Keynes' full investment economy in which there is no reward for owning would appear to be socialist.

Hansen, one of the leading interpreters of Keynes, wrote in the years of depression and after. He implied that economic stagnation could be averted for years to come by long-term government expenditures and other measures. Investment opportunities had been shrinking when he wrote and more investment was needed to maintain the level of income. The population growth had slowed at the time he wrote. Both of these trends have changed in the years since, but the application of theories advanced by Keynes, Hansen, and others, may have altered the first; without war in the 1940's and early 1950's, the second trend may not have been altered, i.e., the population explosion may never have had its beginning with "war babies."

By "capital saving inventions" Hansen probably meant the same or increasing results could be obtained with less capital per unit of output. In the 1930's business spent $60 billion on equipment, only $5 billion being net investment (the rest came from allowances), yet this gave the highly efficient WW II industrial machine. By "disappearance of frontiers" Higgins thought that Hansen probably meant the disappearance of areas in which there is increasing return to capital and labor with the existing techniques of production. Since Hansen wrote, the national income and GNP have continued to rise secularly. Savings absolutely have increased (people have saved a decreasing percentage of individual incomes, but there are more people in higher income groups). The population in 1964 had reached 192,000,000, considerably above the "stationary" 170,000,000 demographers had predicted for 1975. Further, the great change in the structure of the population (by 1960 there were 69 million under twenty years of age) has had much to do with the "boom" of the early 1960's. Technological improvements and outer space have extended the frontiers and have continued to absorb capital. Construction, one of the two most important constitutents of total investment must continue to provide for the increasing numbers of "new families" and this indicates the increased need for consumer durables. The increased need for construction materials and consumer durables might imply increased expenditures for the second big factor in investment, producers' durable equipment. Except for the savings function, factors in the economy generally point away from stagnation as viewed by Hansen.

The problem for the future, around 1980, may be lack of employment for the increased percentages of persons in the 20-29-year-old age group, those very people who as unproductive consumers provide stimulus to the economy in 1964. (See Table XXII-1.) There will be a greater likelihood of this possibility if there is too great a slackening of the birth rate between 1964 and 1980 since this would result in less increase percentage-wise in demand for products for the younger age groups.[8]

Distinction Between the Business Cycle, Classical Orthodox Theory of Economic Progress, and Stagnation — Business cycle theory has assumed that the economy is in equilibrium only at full employment and that economic fluctuations are about that full employment norm. It has treated depressions as temporary but recurring phenomena. Keynes held that the economy could be in equilibrium with involuntary unemployment and that labor is powerless to reduce the involuntary unemployment. It can revise money-wage bargains, but it cannot reduce unemployment through accepting lower money wages because this would only reduce prices proportionatcly and leave real wages, employment, and output unaffected. Keynes argues, based upon certain assumptions and logical reasoning, that although reduction in money wages might increase aggregate demand through reducing interest and increasing investment he would raise employment by increasing the quantity of money.

According to Dillard, one of Keynes' "translators," a depression may be defined as being ". . . a period in which the premium that must be paid for not-hoarding money exceeds the rate of return expected from building new capital assets of almost every type."[9] According to Keynes depressions result from instability of the MEC. When the capital goods industries increase their activity, bringing in larger profits and adding fuel to optimism, the expected rate of return is forced down below the interest rate. Investment ceases, and this leads to depression. The heart of Keynes' theory is his theory of employment. Dillard has stated it as follows:

. . . In a world in which the cconomic future is highly uncertain and in which money is an important form for storing wealth, the general level of employment depends upon the relation between the expected profits from investment in capital assets [MEC] and the interest premium which must be paid to induce wealth-holders to surrender control of their money. *If there is confidence in the future, real investment will occur and employment will be at a high level.* [Italics inserted.] [10]

Spiethoff and Schumpeter writing much earlier had agreed that the boom in the business cycle arises because more capital is put in new businesses bringing demand for raw materials, labor, equipment, and so forth. For Spiethoff, however, the boom is cut short and depression comes where there is overproduction of capital goods relative to capital and effective demand. For Schumpeter it is the appearance of the new enterprises, eliminating the old, that changes conditions and makes necessary a "special process of adaptation." He divided economic processes into three different classes: (1) the process of the circular flow, (2) those of development, and (3) "those which impede the latter's undisturbed course." [11]

His concept of the circular flow was that there is a stream of goods and a corresponding stream of money, the direction of which is opposite to that of the stream of goods, and the movements of which, upon the assumption that no increase of gold or any other one-sided change occurs, are only reflexes of the movement of goods. This "circular flow" concept lacks the Keynesian concept of the gap between demand for output (consumption plus investment) and the total production or output. Schumpeter apparently agreed with Say's law which classical economists all accepted. From Schumpeter's interpretation of the constant flow of goods there would not, however, at any single moment be "stocks" of goods piled up in preparation for production (as Adam Smith pictured). Instead stocks would always be flowing into the "reservoirs" he called income "in order there to be transformed into the satisfaction of wants." Nor would the holding of money stocks be necessary.[12]

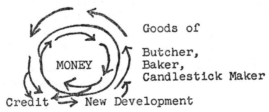

Business cycles would not develop, according to Schumpeter, if entrepreneurs appeared gradually and singly; but they *swarm* in all at once: (1) demanding new purchasing power; (2) producing new products, causing falling prices; (3) paying off debts because they can, and there are no other borrowers readily available. In the struggle toward the new equilibrium position, depression remains as long as no such equilibrium is approximately attained. Schumpeter suggests that these extensions and contractions of business may be the "correct type of reaction." At any rate, said he, ". . . both the rise and the fall of families and firms are much more characteristic of the capitalist economic system, of its culture and its results, than any of the things that can be observed in a society which is stationary in the sense that its processes reproduce themselves at a constant rate." [13]

The *classical theory of economic progress* held that the rate of profit tends to fall in the long run. All theories assume profit to be the motivating force in capitalist economic activity. Under classical theory, as population increases its forces resort to marginal land, and the population continues to increase to the limits of food supply. At the margin, output per laborer with a given technology diminishes; there is no rent and the laborer absorbs more as the margin is pushed down; there is less for the capitalist. The classicists believed there was a minimum below which profits could not fall; at this minimum, capital accumulation would cease. This rate would just induce maintenance of existing capital and induce no further accumulation. When capital accumulation ceased, demand for labor would become stationary. The population would continue increasing until wages fell to a minimum; population and net capital formation having ceased, the state would be at a stationary point but one in which the full employment equilibrium still held.

The *mature economy* of Hansen is not concerned with the cyclical fluctuations about a trend, but with the trend itself. It poses the possibility that the economy could settle down to a permanently depressed state. That theory has more in common with Marxian and underconsumptionist theory than with classical theory. Underconsumptionists, Keynes, and Hansen agree with Marx that it is forces generated within capitalism itself which create problems of under-employment depressions. For the classicists, however, the forces were outside the system: population and diminishing returns at the margin. The classical stationary state could go on forever. For Marx the economy would collapse. The stagnationists, however, think it is possible to avert or avoid economic stagnation by governmental measures. Marx's solution was total planning.

Measures and Policies that Might Be Recommended Under (a) Classical Theory, and (b) Keynesian Theory — Under *classical theory* equilibrium is that volume of employment at which the quantity demanded by employers is just equal to the quantity offered by laborers, demand being determined by marginal productivity of labor, and supply by marginal disutility of working. That is compatible with frictional and voluntary unemployment but not with involuntary unemployment. *Workers could increase employment by agreeing to accept lower wages. Because of Say's law, the classicists assumed this would not affect aggregate demand.* Thus classical economists could make the following suggestions for reducing unemployment: (1) *marginal disutility of work could be reduced;* the psychology of the workers could be changed, facilities could be improved, and the voluntary unemployment would be reduced; (2) *marginal productivity could be increased by new machinery and technology;* the employers could then afford to increase employment; (3) *frictional unemployment* could be reduced; the organization of the labor market could be improved and legal restrictions removed; (4) *consumption of non-wage earners could be shifted from wage goods to non-wage goods;* the wage goods would fall in price; workers could accept lower money wage; employers could employ more.

Keynes rejected the classical theory and Say's law on which it was based. For him the economy not only could be but often had been at equilibrium at less than full employment. In Keynesian theory, the level of employment is determined by the intersection of the aggregate demand schedule (based on proceeds which entrepreneurs think they would get for output of given amounts of employment) and the aggregate supply schedule (proceeds which would just induce employers to offer given amounts of employment), which admits of involuntary unemployment. This is effective demand. Labor can revise money-wage bargains, but it cannot reduce unemployment by accepting lower money wages. Prices would be reduced proportionately, leaving real wages, employment, and output unaffected.

The burden of keeping employment up then falls to aggregate demand, which is determined by: (1) *consumption,* which depends on real income and propensity to consume, and (2) *investment,* which in turn depends on the MEC and the interest rate. The MEC depends on the expectation of profit yields and replacement cost of capital assets (i.e., the supply price which is the price that would induce a manufacturer to newly produce an additional unit of such assets); the interest rate depends on the quantity of money and liquidity preference (reasons for preferring to hold money rather than spending it). Since Keynes assumed that consumption increases as income increases, but not by as much, and the consumption function (as argued above) is generally rather stable, variations in the level of income are dependent on variations in investment. The basis of policy measures for the government can, therefore, be found in the investment multiplier.

Measures to raise investment and maintain or raise consumption under *Keynesian theory* might include: (1) *Increased government expenditures;* if debt financed, such expenditures might increase prices but the effect on employment would be greater. With the rapid rate of population growth the demands for particular types of products will increase. Practically all age groups of boys nineteen or under, according to predictions, will increase from around fifty per cent to sixty-seven per cent from 1960 to 1980; practically all groups of girls will increase from around forty-eight per cent to sixty-five per cent during this period. Government expenditures, therefore, might be for such as the following: housing projects, slum clearance, public health, education, scholarships. (2) *Reduce income taxes* in order that small wage earners might retain more on the assumption that such wage earners spend everything for consumption. (3) *Eliminate excise and sales taxes to encourage consumption,* with the exception of taxes on items that might be considered harmful such as cigarettes and liquor. (4) *Reduce interest rates on government bonds,* except perhaps on E bonds which are widely held by the small wage earners. (5) *Keep rediscount rates low.* (6) *Encourage private business investment by permitting new companies to carry forward losses for some years.* (7) *Raise or lower basic income tax rates as economic conditions warrant.* Presumably the lowering of income taxes in 1964 prolonged the period of economic growth; what the results in the future may be are as yet unknown.

Business investment and government expenditures, minus revenues, are the autonomous variables; consumption depends on these, unless indeed the consumption function can be raised. If so, it would be through changing subjective reasons for saving and spending. Purchasing of life insurance, for instance, puts a larger burden on investment and as long as net insurance is increasing there is withdrawal from consumption demand. A prudent dividend policy in conjunction with an over-cautious depreciation policy on the part of corporations tends to lower the propensity to consume. In the short run, changes in consumption depend mainly on changes in income and not on changes in the propensity to consume.

The Strategic Discovery or Invention— it is the strategic discovery or invention that starts growth. The inventions of the United States have been: (1) those to overcome the handicaps of moving and communicating across great distances, and (2) those to overcome shortages of labor, particularly in the nineteenth century. One realizes this if he merely recalls some typical American inventions: the heavier-than-air craft of the Wright brothers (1903); Thomas Edison's harnessing of electricity, his motion picture camera, and others; the Westinghouse brake; Bell's telephone; the assembly line of Henry Ford; the atom bomb; and hundreds of other things. Europe, on the other hand, has been short of raw materials. [In some parts of Europe today there are labor shortages, but generally there have not been such shortages.] European inventions have been material-saving devices. Dr. Erich W. Zimmermann has said that Germany's progress in science, particularly chemistry, may be explained as being due to shortages. Germany made indigo from coal. During World War I when cut off from the nitrates of Chile (so necessary in making ammunition), Germany broke nitrogen from the air and through the use of coal and lignite recovered it. The Bessemer converter (England) may be regarded as a fuel-saving device. Buna rubber, named after butadiene, was also produced by Germany before World War II. Work had, in fact, begun on it during World War I when Germany was cut off from a supply of natural rubber.[14] The many *ersatz* goods produced by Germany during World War II further indicate the tendency of the Europeans to invent substitutes for those things with which nature did not provide them.

To briefly summarize the effect of the process of discovery and invention, one of Dr. Zimmermann's stories is used here. (1) Charles Goodyear in 1839 (Zimmermann says 1843 but there are other references that give 1839) discovered the vulcanizing process and made it possible to convert raw rubber into useful products thus giving impetus to the growth of a rubber industry. Natives were employed to go into the jungles of the Amazon basin to collect raw rubber. By 1850 annual shipments of rubber were around a thousand tons. Wild rubber production reached a peak in 1912 with some 70,000 tons of output, 42,000 of which came from Brazil. (2) In 1878 Henry A. Wickham removed seedlings by the thousands from the Amazon area. These were later transferred to Ceylon and the rubber plantation of that part of the world had its beginning. Plantation rubber output reached 400,000 tons in 1922 and approximately a million tons in 1939. Wild rubber had by this time almost gone out of use; during World War II the United States revived the wild rubber industry in order to have a source close at hand. (3) The third phase in the rubber saga is found in the story of synthetic rubber which had a great growth almost overnight in the United States to provide supply for the war machine of the 1940's. Both Germany and Russia had developed the synthetic rubber industry prior to World War II.[15] (4) All types of rubber are still used; but inventions of a multitude of synthetics have brought many substitutes.

The story of National Bagasse Products Corporation is but one of many more recent examples of how man's ingenuity and inventiveness may lead to rapid growth in a given area of industry, bringing growth also in other areas of activity from the production of raw material to the marketing and use of the finished product. The founder of this company, John R. Shattuck, had previously founded Cuban Bagasse Products, S.A., which went into full production in 1958, using a dry process to make structural board out of waste sugar cane fibers. The Cuban company was expropriated by the Cuban government in 1960 and National Bagasse Products Corporation was started in Louisiana. The highly automatic $2½ million plant produces fine-grained board called "Fibron" in a wide variety of thicknesses, useful for many products such as table tops, shelving, furniture.[16]

Many young people today want to have at the time they begin housekeeping all of the things their parents and others around them have: homes, automobiles, automatic kitchens, television, boats, and the many good things of life. They forget that their parents may have had to create, invent, perform, and make sacrifices in order to acquire these things. They are somewhat like the countries of the world that would overnight be possessors of industrial goods and wealth. They do not realize that it takes time to develop the type of culture that encourages inventiveness, produces managerial talent, and creates economic power. The peoples of the underdeveloped countries may have to live through the many years of educating parents, children, and grandchildren, of building schools and encouraging innovation, of building culture on top of culture. For it is the genius, the inventor, the innovator who enable the building of industrial empires, the earning of profit, the accumulation of wealth, and the putting to work of the unemployed.

Industry, according to *Dun's Review* Presidents' Panel, recognizes the need for stimulating the creative talent that is almost a universal human characteristic. People in firms that are progressive are stimulated to create, but very few companies can grow fast enough to keep staffs inspired in this manner. People must feel that their ideas are desired and they must be properly rewarded. Business has found that it cannot safely rely on educational institutions to develop capacity for innovation. Some of the presidents severely criticized the universities for training people to walk in ruts. Some have claimed that specialized technical training rarely "produces the men who turn out to be successful innovators." Liberal arts education, it is believed, is more likely to stimulate innovation.[17]

Birth-death Rate and Women Workers — Another one of Zimmermann's often lectured upon themes was that this nation which has only six per cent of the world's population consumes roughly about half of the world's goods. Reasons for this are: (1) its *culture,* and (2) its *women work* and add to the family income rather than spending all their time giving birth to babies that do not live to repay society in work. Further, death takes up the energies of all the people. This makes for a vicious circle in countries that have high birth and death rates. China, for instance, has been short in the factors of production excepting labor. So that nation has produced more sons to grow more rice in order to grow more sons to grow more rice. But the birth and death rates have been high, using up the energies of the people.

The *factors of production* include: *nature* (land and "resources"), *men* (labor and management), and *capital.* The United States has been better balanced than most countries in possession of these factors, especially when women supplement men in the labor force, for labor is the only factor in which the country has ever been short.

In April, 1963, there were nearly twenty-five million women workers, making up thirty-four per cent of all workers and thirty-seven per cent of women of working age in the United States. In March, 1940, only twenty-five per cent of all workers were women and this represented only twenty-eight per cent of the women of working age. In March, 1961, one-third of all married women were in the work force, accounting for about sixty of every one hundred women workers.[18]

In the early 1960's the birth and death rates of the United States per 1,000 population were running at about 24-10. This compares with about 32-17 birth and death rates per 1,000 in the early 1900's, and a rate of about 20-10 in the mid 1930's. In some countries the birth and death rates run as high as twice the current rates in the United States.[19] Some of the factors that have helped to bring on birth-control devices and drugs are: (1) a falling death rate in the earlier stages of the mechanical revolution, causing an almost explosive population increase, particularly in the white races, in the latter part of the nineteenth century; (2) people wanting a higher standard of living than they could have with large families; (3) the improvements of the technological and machine age enabled the use of automation so that it was no longer necessary to breed workers, as it is necessary to do in the vegetable (static) civilization; (4) World War II caused many of those who had been cautious about marrying and having children (due to the economic factor) to throw caution to the winds; marriages resulted in increased birth rate and population explosion; many young people marrying in the early sixties wished to postpone families until they could have more economic stability and the good things of life; young women as a result started taking birth-control pills before they were married; (5) mores of the people have changed to permit the use of birth control devices and drugs. Puerto Rico furnishes an example of the colonial demographic pattern. Its birth-death pattern was around 40-15 per 1,000 in the 1940's but by the late 1950's was around 32-7. The colonial pattern is usually determined by inability of the mother country to influence the population to cut down on births, but the improvements in medical aids cut down on death rates; thus the high-birth-low-death pattern. In Puerto Rico today, however, there are experiments with birth control pills; this has been in spite of the attitudes of the Catholic Church.

Birth control has been a major dispute dividing the Christian faiths. In the early years of Margaret Sanger's crusade, which began in 1912, many people opposed birth control in any form. It was so much opposed that doctors and scientists even feared to use the mails to send or receive birth control information. An old censorship law (1873) prohibited the sending of anything deemed by investigators to be obscene or indecent. This was used by those opposed to birth control to prosecute those who were using the mail to give contraceptive information. Margaret Sanger was herself indicted on nine counts in 1913 by the United States government. In view of the expanding world population (annual increase in the first half of the 1960's has been at 50 million) and the fact that low birth rates help to eliminate poverty (except, possibly, during the time the increased numbers are still under employment age as indicated above), opposition to birth control has greatly lessened, and many of the Catholic leaders and laymen have indicated willingness to alter their attitude. Canon Louis Janssens of the Catholic University of Louvain has presented arguments to the effect that the birth-control pills are not inherently evil, their use being similar to the use of the rhythm method sanctioned by the church. Dr. John Rock, distinguished Roman Catholic gynecologist, has argued that the oral contraceptive pills can be "considered morally acceptable because they imitate the body's own natural endocrine chemistry to prevent the female egg from maturing." Pope Paul at a meeting of twenty-seven cardinals at the Vatican proclaimed with regard to use of the birth-control pills on June 23, 1964, that ". . . up to now we do not have sufficient motive to consider out of date, and therefore not binding, the norms given by Pope Pius XII in this regard. Therefore they must be considered valid, at least until we feel obliged in conscience to change them." [20]

One of the world's authorities on population problems, Paul H. Landis, stated that bearing directly on the problem of need for a population policy are three sets of interrelated factors: "(1) international factors; (2) internal trends in numbers, quality, and composition of the population; (3) cultural compulsives in the national ethos." [21] As to the first of these points, Landis suggested that people who needed resources and had the populations to risk would be a threat to more favored nations unless some form of international organization achieved more equitable division of the world's raw materials (referred to by some writers as resources and by others as neutral stuffs or materials). The culture of one country could scarcely be distributed to another intact, and for many nations the culture of their people may be considered their greatest resource, as previously stated. On the second point Landis suggested that the nation could maintain a stationary population only by: (1) allowing immigrants to enter; (2) further reducing the death rate; or (3) an effective policy relative to increasing the birth rate; he thought the third alternative would be the one most likely to be chosen. He suggested the easing of the burden of marriage for those who wished to continue education at higher levels. Actually, the United States did this through the passing of the GI bill and more recent acts outlined in Chapter XX. Birth control information should be made available to all, according to Landis, in order that the differential in class birth rates might be eliminated. Greater provision should be made for public health; all children should be assured adequate food and clothing. Since cultural factors have so much to do with population growth and are themselves subject to sudden changes, predicting population developments for any time into the future is a hazardous thing for anyone to do. Nevertheless, ". . . population is the basic resource of all planning, and human welfare the ultimate objective." [22] While the biggest market ever is resulting in the 1960's from "war babies," writers are proclaiming that the rapid increase in world population, more threatening than war, is impoverishing the world and wiping out western-aid gains. Julian Huxley has called it "the gravest problem of our time, certainly more serious in the long perspective than war or peace." [23]

Business Leadership — The greatest assets of the United States are its people and their culture: the way the people themselves adjust, their abilities (including education and training), their inventions, their personalities, their mores, and their moral fibers. Opportunities are unlimited for those who know that education does not stop and who are capable of adapting to change and diverting change into profitable routes. The young man or young woman of today should seek more than specialization, although specialization may give the chance to begin, for the kinds of opportunities available tomorrow will require a broad background.

The chief executives of the leading corporations of the United States were surveyed by University of Michigan researchers in 1964 to provide information on the best preparation for leadership. Of those surveyed, twenty-six per cent had liberal arts training with majors in humanities or the social sciences; twenty-five per cent had some business school training; twenty per cent had legal background; nineteen per cent had training in the sciences or engineering.[24] The route up the ladder to top management for twenty-seven per cent of these people was through marketing and sales. Table I shows the routes followed by others.[25]

TABLE XXV-1[25]

ROUTE UP TO TOP GENERAL MANAGEMENT

ROUTE UP	PERCENTAGE OF RESPONDENTS					
		Major Field of Study				
	Total	*Business*	*Law*	*Liberal Arts*	*Science- Engi.*	*No Degree*
Marketing-sales	27	3	. .	11	3	11
Legal or special staff	21	5	12	3	2*	2*
General management	18	3	6	6	2*	. .
Production-engineering	12	. .	. .	2*	9	2*
Entrepreneurial	8	6	. .	. .	2*	. .
Finance	5	3	. .	. .	2*	. .
Research-scientific	3	. .	. .	2*	. .	2*
Personnel-industrial relations	2*	. .	2*	. .	. .	. .
Other	3	2*	. .	2*	. .	. .
Total	100	22	20	26	20	17

* Rounded from 1.5 per cent. Detail will not total 100 per cent because of rounding.

The executives thought that the special skills which would improve their present performance were: communication ability, eighteen per cent; public speaking ability, seventeen per cent; understanding and handling people, seventeen per cent; analytical abilities for decision making, fifteen per cent; general leadership abilities, five per cent; financial analysis, three per cent.[26]

Forty-seven per cent of the executives recommended business as a major field for graduate study; twenty-two per cent recommended business and legal graduate education; four per cent recommended business and engineering; four per cent recommended business and science.[27]

The student will note that eighty-two per cent of the respondents indicated *human relations,* eighty per cent indicated *psychology,* and sixty

TABLE XXV-2[28]

IMPORTANCE OF SELECTED SUBJECTS IN
PREPARATION FOR BUSINESS LEADERSHIP

	PERCENTAGE OF RESPONDENTS ANSWERING	
Subject	*"Very Important"*	*"Very Important"* *"Fairly Important"* *(combined)*
Business and government	76	84
Economics, principles of	71	88
English composition	65	82
Human relations	62	82
Management, principles of	62	80
Speech	61	85
Corporation finance	56	79
Accounting, principles of	55	81
Business report writing	48	72
Money and banking	45	81
Business policy	45	69
Political science	44	73
History	44	73
Managerial economics	44	71
Marketing	42	83
Managerial accounting	38	64
English literature	36	68
Industrial relations	36	75
Cost accounting	35	65
Psychology	33	80
Foreign trade	33	74
Philosophy	32	65
Economic history	30	77
Sales management	30	72
Personnel administration	30	66
Organization theory	29	73
Business law	29	64
Foreign language	27	60
Business cycles and forecasting	23	64
Production management	23	58
Statistical methods	23	56
Sociology	18	56
Business history	15	60
Advertising	11	46
Industrial engineering	6	43

per cent indicated *philosophy* as being very important or fairly important. The data do not show whether or not some individuals checked only one of these three areas. Since this is quite probable, it might be that one hundred per cent of the executives specified one or more of these three subjects. The executives generally preferred subjects that have a broad orientation, subjects that should or could be useful in any industry, rather than those for specific vocations or industries.[28]

The shortage of executive leadership is probably to be found not so much in lack of capable men but in the lack of training programs to develop executive leadership, at the college and university level as well as at the industrial level.

Frontiers of the Future Are Frontiers of the Mind — In an era when the demographers are saying that we may have to have ration cards for solitude in thirty-six years, i.e., we may need permits to take automobiles on the highways to seek the benefits of sea breezes and mountain air, we might well ask "What are the frontiers of the future?" When Hansen wrote of the "disappearance of frontiers" he probably did not refer to "geographic frontiers." In the last half of the twentieth century, however, all people of the world must be concerned with *liebensraum* just as the Germans were when they fought the second World War. It cannot be foreseen just what technology, automation, and the creative minds of the people will evolve during this most marvelous period in history to overcome the shortages of the gifts of nature, including land. In the free industrial nations of the world, however, creative selling and marketing will continue to be important. Discovery, invention, innovation, and the creative process will be all-important to growth and progress. The psychological climate of the masses of people will be able to make or break a nation's economic structure. As long as people are confident and spend, as long as consumption and investment remain high, as long as money and credit continue to flow in one stream while goods flow in the opposite direction, as long as there are persons and/or groups willing to take risk with credit and capital to chance the success of something new, so long will the free enterprise system and the democratic way of life offer freedom to create, freedom to speak, freedom to think and live in the frontiers of the mind, and all of the other freedoms so cherished by citizens of the United States and so often envied by many outside of its confines. In order that the freedoms we enjoy may operate for all, there are restrictions prohibiting any one group from infringing upon the freedoms of another. The success of the system depends upon the people, their adjustments, their consideration of others, their laws, their bureaucracies, and the honesty of their politicians, their bureaucrats, and their business leaders.

Ethics in Business — There is an increasing effort by large companies to improve the welfare of their employees; sound business practices are playing an increasingly dominant role in the modern enlightened businesses of our nation. Technology is after all only a means to an end. It is still felt by most people that the highest potential of each individual should be released. The deeper experiences of life are important. Bigness as such has been a problem recognized and condemned as far back as 1911 by Brandeis; Lilienthal in 1953 recognized it but praised it. Herd conformity has been said to be the essence, the sign, and the symbol of the ends and means agent that is the destroying element of our society. As the individual is coerced to conform he is made to serve an end outside his own knowing; he is forced to accept a stature less than that of a free human being.[29] Bunting said that ethical problems will come more nearly to being solved when business leadership is professional; ethics should be taught since the only reason for education is to *improve standards of living and conduct in society*. The struggle for good moral practice will continue as long as individuals believe that *a proper way of life* has its own rewards or until the goal of universal ethics has been achieved.[30]

Conclusions — This chapter was conceived not to take "sides" or "issue" with any certain economic theory or to evolve any "new" theory; its purpose has been to indicate that psychology is not only important in the area of economics, it is particularly so. Through conflicting theories run threads of similar hue; they imply the necessity for an optimistic outlook on the part of individuals and business firms in order that spending continue to entice innovation and risk taking. The cultural and mental climate of the people, their ability to adjust in crises, their economic and political systems, their technical and liberal education, their civic organizations, their scientific and social research are all inextricably interwoven. In a period of technological development and exploration of outer space, we must not forget the human relations and social science areas that have evolved through years of discovery and research. In the cross fertilization of fields such as economics, sociology, psychology, anthropology, geography, history, law, medicine, and various areas of science are the answers to the problems of mental health, adjustment, human relations, and incentives to create. Literature and art as well as the worthwhile innovations of business are the creative products that reflect the mental health, adjustment, and culture of the people.

Business and individuals must be geared for change in the years ahead. Just as "flexibility" and "stability" are necessary for a given business firm, they are also necessary for the economy as a whole. The economy must not only adjust to the social and economic instabilities in economy must not only adjust to the social and economic instabilities in the long run; it must recognize the short run values of optimism, risk-taking, and adjustment to sudden change.

For the individual man the words of Robert Oppenheimer who helped to bring about the atomic age may have an even deeper meaning in the future than they do today:

> We live with an expansion of knowledge overpoweringly beautiful, vast, ramified, quite unparalleled in the history of man. We live with a yearly enrichment of our understanding of nature and of man as part of nature, that doubles every decade . . . [but] we have so largely lost our ability to talk with one another . . . We hunger for nobility: the rare words and acts that harmonize simplicity and truth.

GENERAL REFERENCES

Ayres, C. E., *The Theory of Economic Progress,* The University of North Carolina Press, Chapel Hill, 1944.

Dillard, Dudley, *The Economics of John Maynard Keynes,* Prentice-Hall, Inc., New York, 1948.

Hansen, Alvin H., *A Guide to Keynes,* McGraw-Hill Book Co., Inc., New York, 1953.

Hansen, Alvin H., *Economic Policy and Full Employment,* McGraw-Hill Book Co., New York, 1947.

Hansen, Alvin H., *Fiscal Policy and Business Cycles,* W. W. Norton & Co., New York, 1941.

Harris, S. E., *The National Debt and the New Economics,* McGraw-Hill Book Co., New York, 1947.

Harris, S. E., "Post War Public Debt," *Post War Economic Problems,* edited by Seymour E. Harris, McGraw-Hill Book Co., New York, 1943.

Keynes, John Maynard, *The General Theory of Employment Interest and Money,* Harcourt, Brace & Co., New York, 1935.

McConnell, John W., *The Basic Teachings of the Great Economists,* The New Home Library, New York, 1943.

Malthus, T. R., *An Essay on Population,* Vols. I and II, E. P. Dutton & Co., Inc., New York, 1952 reprint.

Malthus, T. R., *Principles of Political Economy,* Augustus M. Kelley, Inc., New York 3, 1951.

Niesser, H., "General Overproduction: A Study of Say's Law of Markets," *Journal of Political Economy,* Vol. 42, 1934, pp. 433-465.

Roll, Eric, *A History of Economic Thought,* Third Edition, Prentice-Hall, Inc., Englewood Cliffs, N. J., 1956.

Schumpeter, J. A., "Capitalism in the Post War World," in *Post War Economic Problems,* edited by Seymour E. Harris, McGraw-Hill Book Co., New York, 1943.

Smith, Adam, *The Wealth of Nations,* The Modern Library, Random House, Inc., New York, 1937.

Stocking, George W., and Watkins, *Monopoly and Free Enterprise,* The Twentieth Century Fund, New York, 1951.

Zimmermann, Erich W., *World Resources and Industries,* Revised Edition, Harper & Brothers, Publishers, New York, 1951.

Writings of Benjamin Higgins, Alan Sweezy, John H. Williams, and D. B. Copland have also been read as have the writings of Ricardo, Senior, Mill, Chamberlin, West, and many others.

ACKNOWLEDGMENTS AND REFERENCES

1 Keynes, John Maynard, *The General Theory of Employment Interest and Money,* Harcourt, Brace & Co., New York, 1935.

2 Davis, James H., *Handbook of Sales Training,* Second Edition, Prentice-Hall, Inc., New York, 1954, p. v.

3 —————, "What's the Matter with American Salesmanship?," *Fortune,* Vol. XL, No. 3, September, 1949, p. 69.

4 Keynes, *op. cit.,* pp. 89-134.

5 Malthus, T. R., *Principles of Political Economy,* Augustus M. Kelley, Inc., New York, 1951.

6 Schumpeter, Joseph A., *The Theory of Economic Development,* translated from the German by Redvers Opie, Harvard University Press, Cambridge, Massachusetts, 1934, p. 147.

7 *Ibid.,* p. 154.

8 —————, "U. S. Market — Youth," *Executives' Guide to Marketing for 1964,* Printers' Ink, Vol. 284, No. 9, August 30, 1963, p. 27ff.

9 Dillard, Dudley, *The Economics of John Maynard Keynes,* Prentice-Hall, Inc., New York, 1948, p. 12.

10 *Ibid.,* p. 12, p. 41.

11 Schumpeter, *op. cit.,* pp. 215-218.

12 *Ibid.,* pp. 37-53.

13 *Ibid.,* p. 239ff.

14 Zimmermann, Erich W., *World Resources and Industries,* Revised Edition, Harper & Brothers, Publishers, New York, 1951, p. 34ff. and p. 392ff.

15 *Ibid.,* pp. 391-392.

16 —————, "Putting Waste To Work," *Business Week,* March 23, 1963, pp. 137-138.

17 —————, "Industry's Search for New Ideas," *Dun's Review,* September, 1963, p. 39ff.

18 —————, *American Women,* Report of the President's Commission on the Status of Women, Washington, D. C., 1963, p. 27ff.

19 *Ibid.,* p. 3.

20 —————, "Birth Control: The Pill and the Church," *Newsweek,* July 6, 1964, pp. 51-54.

21 Landis, Paul H., *Population Problems,* Second Edition prepared by Paul K. Hatt, American Book Co., New York, 1954, p. 511.

22 *Ibid.,* pp. 512-516.

23 —————, "Census Report — Biggest Market Ever Coming Up," *Business Week,* May 13, 1961, pp. 145-152.

—————, "How Many Babies Is Too Many?," *Newsweek,* July 23, 1962, pp. 27-34.

—————, "Built-in Recession Cure," *Life,* June 16, 1958, pp. 83-89.

24 Bond, Floyd A., Leabo, Dick A., and Swinyard, Alfred W., *Preparation for Business Leadership,* Bureau of Business Research, Graduate School of Business Administration, The University of Michigan, Ann Arbor, Michigan, 1964, pp. 5-7.

25 *Ibid.,* p. 9.

26 *Ibid.,* p. 13.

27 *Ibid.,* p. 21.

28 *Ibid.,* p. 38.

29 Childs, Marquis W., and Cater, Douglas, *Ethics in a Business Society,* Harper & Brothers, Publishers, 1954.

30 Bunting, James Whitney (editor), *Ethics for Modern Business Practice,* Prentice-Hall, Inc., Englewood Cliffs, New Jersey, 1953.

NAME INDEX*

A

Addams, 459f, 463
Adler, 8, 52
    Mortimer J., 391
Alderson, 4, 7, 8, 110, 426
Allport, 231f, 240
Anslinger, 39f
Altgeld, 461
Anthony, 353
Aristotle, 2, 24, 426
Aurner, 361
Ayer, 440

B

Babson, 467
Bacon, 41
Baker,
    Newton D., 466
    Ray Stannard, 462
Barnes, 155
Barrymore, 452
Bates, 425
Beers, 72
Bell, 232, 490
Benny, 44
Bentham, 78
Berrien, 86, 210
Binet, 223
Birren, 21
Black, 352
Bleuler, 3
Bonaparte, 78
Booz, 162
Brandeis, 465, 498
Brayfield, 351
Breck, 124
Brill,
    A. A., 3, 88, 93
    E. J., 9
    Henry, 115
Brisbane, 452
Bruckberger, 399
Bryan, 462
Bunting, 398

Burck, 387
Burgess, 58
Buros, 223
Byron, 55

C

Calkins, 465
Calvin, 78
Campbell, 112
Canby, 463
Capek, 375
Case, 429
Chase, 460, 467, 474
Chopin, 78
Churchill, 394
Coch, 350
Coffey, 133
Coleridge, 78
Commons, 465
Converse, 417
Copeland, 464
Cottrell, 58
Crane, 445
Crawford, 30
Crockett, 351
Crosley, 420
Crowder, 379

D

Dailey, 178, 221
Dasco, 62
Davis,
    J. H., 175, 446
    R. C., 133, 341
DeMartino, 27
Dewey, 139f, 145
Dichter, 419, 428, 433, 437, 456
Dickson, 124, 342
Dillard, 485
Dix, 72
Dodge, 428
Drucker, 152, 355
Dunn, 464, 469
Durkheim, 373f

Incomplete. Additional names are included in acknowledgments and references and company names are included with the subject index.

501

SUBJECT INDEX